Commodity Trading Advisors

John Wiley & Sons

Founded in 1807, John Wiley & Sons is the oldest independent publishing company in the United States. With offices in North America, Europe, Australia, and Asia, Wiley is globally committed to developing and marketing print and electronic products and services for our customers' professional and personal knowledge and understanding.

The Wiley Finance series contains books written specifically for finance and investment professionals, as well as sophisticated individual investors and their financial advisors. Book topics range from portfolio management to e-commerce, risk management, financial engineering, valuation, and financial instrument analysis, as well as much more.

For a list of available titles, visit our web site at www.WileyFinance.com.

Commodity Trading Advisors

Risk, Performance Analysis, and Selection

GREG N. GREGORIOU
VASSILIOS N. KARAVAS
FRANÇOIS-SERGE LHABITANT
FABRICE ROUAH

WILEY

John Wiley & Sons, Inc.

To my mother Evangelia, and in memory of my beloved father Nicholas—G.N.G.

To my parents Virginia and Nikos—V.K.

To the ones I love—F.S.L.

To my parents Jacqueline and Jean, and in loving memory of my grandfather David—F.R.

Published by John Wiley & Sons, Inc., Hoboken, New Jersey.
Published simultaneously in Canada.

For general information on our other products and services, or technical support, please contact our Customer Care Department within the United States at 800-762-2974, outside the United States at 317-572-3993 or fax 317-572-4002.

Wiley also publishes its books in a variety of electronic formats. Some content that appears in print may not be available in electronic books.

Mk For more information about Wiley products, visit our web site at www.wiley.com.

Library of Congress Cataloging-in-Publication Data

Commodity trading advisors : risk, performance analysis, and selection /
[edited by] Greg N. Gregoriou . . . [et al.].
p. cm.
ISBN 0-471-68194-6 (cloth)
1. Commodity trading advisors. I. Gregoriou, Greg N., 1956–
HG6046.5.C66 2004
332.64'4—dc22

2004007925

Printed in the United States of America

10 9 8 7 6 5 4 3 2 1

Contents

Preface ix

Acknowledgments xi

About the Editors xiii

About the Authors xv

Introduction xxiii

PART ONE
Performance 1

CHAPTER 1
Managed Futures and Hedge Funds: A Match Made in Heaven 5
Harry M. Kat

CHAPTER 2
Benchmarking the Performance of CTAs 18
Lionel Martellini and *Mathieu Vaissié*

CHAPTER 3
Performance of Managed Futures: Persistence and the Source of Returns 31
B. Wade Brorsen and *John P. Townsend*

CHAPTER 4
CTA Performance, Survivorship Bias, and Dissolution Frequencies 49
Daniel Capocci

CHAPTER 5
CTA Performance Evaluation with Data Envelopment Analysis 79
Gwenevere Darling, Kankana Mukherjee, and *Kathryn Wilkens*

CHAPTER 6
The Performance of CTAs in Changing Market Conditions 105
Georges Hübner and *Nicolas Papageorgiou*

CHAPTER 7
Simple and Cross-Efficiency of CTAs Using Data Envelopmennt Analysis 129
Fernando Diz, Greg N. Gregoriou, Fabrice Rouah, and *Stephen E. Satchell*

PART TWO
Risk and Managed Futures Investing 149

CHAPTER 8
The Effect of Large Hedge Fund and CTA Trading on Futures Market Volatility 151
Scott H. Irwin and *Bryce R. Holt*

CHAPTER 9
Measuring the Long Volatility Strategies of Managed Futures 183
Mark Anson and *Ho Ho*

CHAPTER 10
The Interdependence of Managed Futures Risk Measures 203
Bhaswar Gupta and *Manolis Chatiras*

CHAPTER 11
Managing Downside Risk in Return Distributions Using Hedge Funds, Managed Futures, and Commodity Indices 220
Mark Anson

PART THREE
Managed Futures Investing, Fees, and Regulation 233

CHAPTER 12
Managed Futures Investing 235
James Hedges IV

CHAPTER 13
The Effect of Management and Incentive Fees on the Performance of CTAs: A Note **248**
Fernando Diz

CHAPTER 14
Managed Futures Funds and Other Fiduciary Products: The Australian Regulatory Model **259**
Paul U. Ali

PART FOUR
Program Evaluation, Selection, and Returns **275**

CHAPTER 15
How to Design a Commodity Futures Trading Program **277**
Hilary Till and *Joseph Eagleeye*

CHAPTER 16
Choosing the Right CTA: A Contingent Claim Approach **294**
Zsolt Berenyi

CHAPTER 17
CTAs and Portfolio Diversification: A Study through Time **307**
Nicolas Laporte

CHAPTER 18
Random Walk Behavior of CTA Returns **326**
Greg N. Gregoriou and *Fabrice Rouah*

CHAPTER 19
CTA Strategies for Returns-Enhancing Diversification **336**
David Kuo Chuen Lee, Francis Koh, and *Kok Fai Phoon*

CHAPTER 20
Incorporating CTAs into the Asset Allocation Process: A Mean-Modified Value at Risk Framework **358**
Maher Kooli

CHAPTER 21
ARMA Modeling of CTA Returns **367**
Vassilios N. Karavas and *L. Joe Moffitt*

CHAPTER 22
Risk-Adjusted Returns of CTAs: Using the Modified Sharpe Ratio **377**
Robert Christopherson and *Greg N. Gregoriou*

CHAPTER 23
Time Diversification: The Case of Managed Futures **385**
François-Serge Lhabitant and *Andrew Green*

REFERENCES **399**

INDEX **417**

Preface

The idea for this book came about when we realized that a collection of managed futures articles dealing with quantitative and qualitative analyses of commodity trading advisors (CTAs) could be a useful and welcomed addition to existing books on the subject. The chapters that follow introduce readers to many of the issues related to managed futures that we believe are vital for proper selection and monitoring of CTAs. These issues include performance assessment, benchmarking, and risk management of managed futures investing, evaluation and design of managed futures programs, CTA management and incentive fees, and regulatory considerations.

All chapters in this book are written by leading academics and practitioners in the area of alternative investments. Although some chapters are technical in nature, we have asked the contributors of those chapters to emphasize the impact of their analytical results on managed futures investing, rather than to focus on technical topics.

We, therefore, believe this book can serve as a guide for institutional investors, pension funds managers, endowment funds, and high-net-worth individuals wanting to add CTAs to traditional stock and bond portfolios.

Acknowledgments

The editors would like to thank Richard E. Oberuc Sr. of Laporte Asset Allocation System (www.laportesoft.com) and Sol Waksman of the Barclay Trading Group, Ltd. (www.barclaygrp.com) for providing data and software. As well, we thank www.alternativesoft.com for their use of Extreme Metrics and HF Optimizer software. We thank Allison Adams at Institutional Investors Journals for allowing us to reproduce one of their articles (Chapter 18). We also thank Mr. Chris Bonnet at Peritus Group (www.peritus.ca) and everyone at Schneeweis Partners.

In addition, we would like to thank Bill Falloon, senior finance editor, and Liam Kuhn, editorial assistant, both at Wiley, for their enthusiastic support and constructive comments; this book could not have come at a better time. We also extend sincere and warmest thanks to Alexia Meyers, senior production editor at Wiley, for her wonderful assistance in editing and meticulously reviewing the manuscript.

About the Editors

Greg N. Gregoriou is Assistant Professor of Finance and faculty research coordinator in the School of Business and Economics at Plattsburgh State University of New York. He obtained his Ph.D. in Finance and his M.B.A. from the University of Quebec at Montreal and his B.A. in Economics from Concordia University, Montreal. Dr. Gregoriou is the hedge fund editor for the peer-reviewed journal *Derivatives Use, Trading and Regulation* based in the U.K and has authored over 35 articles on hedge funds and CTAs in various U.S. and U.K. peer-reviewed publications along with 20 professional publications in brokerage and pension fund magazines in Canada. He is also an Associate at Peritus Group, a Montreal-based consultancy.

Vassilios N. Karavas is currently Director of Research at Schneeweis Partners in Amherst, Massachusetts. His research focus is on alternative optimization techniques ranging from disequilibrium market models to hedge fund portfolio selection. Dr. Karavas holds a Ph.D. in Operations Research from the University of Massachusetts at Amherst, an M.Sc. and a Diploma in Industrial Engineering both from the Technical University of Crete, Chania, Greece. He is also a research associate of the Center for International Securities and Derivatives Market.

François-Serge Lhabitant is Head of Research at Kedge Capital, U.K., a Professor of Finance at Hautes Etudes Commerciales (HEC), University of Lausanne, Switzerland, and a Professor of Finance at the Edhec Business School, France. He was previously a Director at UBS/Global Asset Management in charge of quantitative analysis and a member of Senior Management at Union Bancaire Privée (UBP), Geneva, responsible for all quantitative research and risk analysis of UBP's alternative asset management group. Dr. Lhabitant received a Ph.D. in Finance, an M.Sc. in Banking and Finance, and a B.Sc. in Economics, all from the University of Lausanne, as well as a degree in Computer Engineering from the Swiss Federal Institute of Technology. He is the author of two Wiley books on hedge funds investing and emerging markets, and has published more than 300 articles in leading academic journals, edited books, and newspapers.

Fabrice Rouah is an Institut de Finance Mathématique de Montréal (IFM2) Scholar and a Ph.D. Candidate in Finance, McGill University, Montreal, Quebec. Mr. Rouah is a former Faculty Lecturer and Consulting Statistician in the Department of Mathematics and Statistics at McGill University. He holds an M.Sc. from McGill University and a B.Sc. in applied mathematics from Concordia University, Montreal, Quebec. Mr. Rouah specializes in the statistical and stochastic modeling of hedge funds and managed futures, and is a regular contributor to peer-reviewed academic publications on alternative investments. Mr. Rouah is also an Associate at Peritus Group.

About the Authors

Paul U. Ali is a Senior Lecturer in the Faculty of Law, University of Melbourne, and member of the University of Melbourne's Centre for Corporate Law and Securities Regulation. He is also a principal of Stellar Capital, a private investment firm in Sydney. Dr. Ali previously worked for several years as a finance lawyer in Sydney. He is also a coauthor of *Corporate Governance and Investment Fiduciaries* (Sydney: Lawbook Co., 2003), which examines the corporate governance aspects of managed investment products.

Mark Anson is the Chief Investment Officer for the California Public Employees' Retirement System (CalPERS). He has complete responsibility for all asset classes in which CalPERS invests, including domestic and international equity and fixed income, real estate, corporate governance, currency overlay, securities lending, venture capital, leveraged buyouts, and hedge funds. Dr. Anson earned his law degree from the Northwestern University School of Law in Chicago, his Ph.D. and Master's in Finance from the Columbia University Graduate School of Business in New York City, and his B.A. from St. Olaf College in Minnesota. Dr. Anson is a member of the New York and Illinois State Bar associations and has earned accounting and financial designations. He is the author of four books on financial markets and has published over 60 research articles on the topics of corporate governance, hedge funds, real estate, currency overlay, credit risk, private equity, risk management, and portfolio management. Dr. Anson is on the editorial boards of five financial journals and sits on Advisory Committees for the New York Stock Exchange, the International Association of Financial Engineers, AIMR's Task Force on Corporate Governance, the Center for Excellence in Accounting and Security Analysis at Columbia University, and the Alternative Investment Research Centre at the City University of London.

Zsolt Berenyi holds an M.Sc. in Economics from the University of Budapest and a Ph.D. in Finance from the University of Munich. His research focus includes the risk and performance evaluation of alternative investments, hedge funds, and leveraged and credit funds. After working years for

Deutsche Bank, Dr. Berenyi currently is working as a consultant in the area of asset management for various leading European financial institutions.

B. Wade Brorsen is a Regents Professor and Jean and Patsy Neustadt Chair in the Department of Agricultural Economics at Oklahoma State University.

Daniel Capocci is a Ph.D. student at the University of Liège in Belgium. His areas of research are hedge fund performance and performance persistence. He has published theoretical and empirical articles on hedge funds in several Belgian, English, French, Swiss, and Luxembourg journals and presented his work in various university-sponsored conferences. His main contribution is the development of a multifactor model to analyze hedge fund performance. Since September 2001, and independently of his academic research, he has worked for an international Luxembourg bank. Mr. Capocci received his Master's in Management Science from the University of Liège and his Master's in Finance from the Hautes Etudes Commerciales (HEC) Liège.

Manolis Chatiras holds an M.B.A. from the University of Massachusetts at Amherst with a concentration in finance. He received his B.S. (cum laude) in Business Administration from the University of Maine in Orono. He is currently a research associate at the Center for International Securities and Derivatives Markets at the University of Massachusetts, where he conducts research that focuses on the international diversification and risk management potential of hedge funds, managed futures, and CTAs.

Robert Christopherson is Associate Professor and Chair of Economics and Finance at the School of Business and Economics, State University of New York, (Plattsburgh). He received his Ph.D. in Economics from Wayne State University in 1990. Dr. Christopherson is a coeditor and contributing author of *The Virtuous Vice: Globalization*, published by Praeger in 2004, and has numerous articles, papers, and book reviews to his credit appearing in journals, books, and trade publications.

Gwenevere Darling holds a B.S. in Actuarial Mathematics and Management Engineering with a concentration in Quantitative Finance from Worcester Polytechnic Institute.

Fernando Diz is the Whitman Associate Professor of Finance at the Syracuse University Martin J. Whitman School of Management. He also has been Visiting Associate Professor of Finance at the Johnson Graduate School of Management, Cornell University, where he taught courses on derivatives and financial engineering. Professor Diz is also the Founder and President of M&E Financial Markets Research, LLC. He specializes in managed futures, money management, market volatility, and the use of derivative securities in investment and speculative portfolios as well as distress and value investing. His research has appeared in numerous peer-reviewed and industry publications. Professor Diz has presented his research at academic forums as well as industry forums such as the American Stock Exchange Derivatives Colloquium, the Managed Funds Association's Forum for Managed Futures, and the Chicago Board of Trade Research Seminars. Professor Diz received his doctorate from Cornell University.

Joseph Eagleeye is Cofounder and Portfolio Manager at Premia Capital Management, LLC, in Chicago. Premia Capital specializes in detecting pockets of predictability in derivatives markets by using statistical techniques. As a principal of the Quartile Group, Mr. Eagleeye also advises investment companies on hedging strategies, benchmark construction, index replication strategies, and risk management. He has been involved in the commodity markets since 1994. Prior to joining Premia, he developed programmed trading applications for Morgan Stanley's Equity Division and proprietary computer models for urban economics. From 1994 to 1998 he worked in the Derivative Strategies Group of Putnam Investments where he researched, back-tested, and implemented relative-value derivatives strategies. Mr. Eagleeye holds a degree in Applied Mathematics from Yale University and an M.B.A. from the University of California at Berkeley.

Andrew Green graduated in March 2004 with an MBA degree in Finance from Thunderbird, the American Graduate School of International Management. He is a former Research Assistant at the High Energy Particle Physics Lab of Colorado State University.

Bhaswar Gupta is a Ph.D. candidate in the Department of Finance at the University of Massachusetts and a Research Associate at the Center for International Securities and Derivatives Markets. He is currently working on his dissertation and is editorial assistant for the *Journal of Alternative Investments*. He is also a research associate with the Chartered Alternative Investment Analyst Association, a nonprofit educational association that focuses on alternative investment education and is the sponsoring organization for the Chartered Alternative Investment Analyst designation.

James Hedges IV is the Founder, President, and Chief Investment Officer of LJH Global Investments, LLC, in Naples, Florida, and San Francisco, California, and President of LJH Global Investments, Ltd., in London. LJH provides access to hedge fund managers who have been subjected to rigorous due diligence by hedge fund research analysts. The LJH organization also includes professionals in client development, sales force training, client service, and operations/reporting. In addition, LJH provides fund of hedge funds products for direct distribution to qualified investors.

Ho Ho, Quantitative Portfolio Manager in the Global Equity Unit for the California Public Employees' Retirement System (CalPERS), is responsible for research and development of internal active strategies for equity portfolios, hedge fund risk management, quantitative models for hedge fund risk attribution, manager monitoring, quantitative portfolio construction model development, and a team member of CalPERS' hedge fund program. He is also responsible for system and model validation of CalPERS' enterprise-wide risk management system. Prior to joining CalPERS, Mr. Ho was derivatives manager for Transamerica Life Insurance Company. He also worked for KPMG as manager of their Structure Finance Consulting Group. He holds an M.B.A. in Finance from the University of Chicago and a B.A. (Phi Beta Kappa) in Economics from the University of California, Irvine.

Bryce R. Holt began his education at Brigham Young University, where he earned his B.S. in Economics. As a part of his graduate studies at the School of Agricultural and Consumer Economics at the University of Illinois, he accepted an internship position at Kraft Foods and for four months performed fundamental analytical work in the coffee, sugar, and grain markets. After finishing his M.S. degree, he returned to Kraft Foods as a Commodity Analyst and was quickly promoted to Associate Risk Manager. In early 2001 he accepted a position as Corporate Purchasing and Price Risk Manager with ACH Food Companies, where he now has full supply chain and risk management responsibilities for commodity ingredients, energy, currency, and ACH's High Oleic Sunflower Oil program.

Georges Hübner holds a Ph.D. in Management from INSEAD. He is the Deloitte Professor of Financial Management at the University of Liège and also teaches finance at Maastricht University and EDHEC (Lille). He has taught at the executive and postgraduate levels in several countries in Europe, North America, Africa, and Asia. He has written two books on financial management and has authored several peer-reviewed research articles on hedge funds and derivatives. He was the recipient of the prestigious 2002 Iddo Sarnat Award for the best paper published in the *Journal of Banking and Finance* in 2001.

Scott H. Irwin earned his B.S. in Agricultural Business from Iowa State University and his M.S. in Agricultural Economics and Ph.D. from Purdue University. After completing his Ph.D. in 1985, Dr. Irwin joined the Department of Agricultural Economics and Rural Sociology at the Ohio State University. From 1993 to 1994 Dr. Irwin was a Visiting Scholar in the Office for Futures and Options Research at the University of Illinois. In 1996 he was named the first holder of the Francis B. McCormick Professor of Agricultural Marketing and Policy at the Ohio State University. In 1997 Dr. Irwin joined the Department of Agricultural and Consumer Economics at the University of Illinois. In 2003 Dr. Irwin was named the Laurence J. Norton Professor in Agricultural Marketing at the University of Illinois. He currently serves as the team leader for the farmdoc Project, is codirector of the AgMAS Project, and is an Associate in the Office for Futures and Options Research. His recent research focuses on the performance of farm market advisory services, investment performance, and market impact of managed futures, the value of public information in commodity markets, and the forecasting accuracy of corn and soybean futures prices. His work has been published in leading academic journals. In 2002 he received the Distinguished Group Extension Award from the American Agricultural Economics Association as part of the farmdoc team.

Harry M. Kat is Professor of Risk Management and Director of the Alternative Investment Research Centre at the Sir John Cass Business School City University, London. Before returning to academia, Professor Kat was Head of Equity Derivatives Europe at Bank of America in London, Head of Derivatives Structuring and Marketing at First Chicago in Tokyo, and Head of Derivatives Research at MeesPierson in Amsterdam. He holds MBA and Ph.D degrees in Economics and Econometrics from the Tinbergen Graduate School of Business at the University of Amsterdam and is a member of the editorial board of the *Journal of Derivatives* and the *Journal of Alternative Investments*. He has coauthored numerous articles in well-known international finance journals. His latest book, *Structured Equity Derivatives,* was published in July 2001 by John Wiley & Sons.

Francis Koh is Practice Associate Professor of Finance at the Singapore Management University. He is concurrently Director of the M.Sc. in Wealth Management Program. He holds a Ph.D. in Finance from the University of New South Wales and an M.B.A. from the University of British Columbia. Prior to joining Singapore Management University, Dr. Koh worked with a multibillion-dollar global investment company based in Singapore.

Maher Kooli is Assistant Professor of Finance at the School of Business and Management, University of Quebec, in Montreal. He also worked as a Senior Research Advisor at la Caisse de dépot et placement du Québec (CDP Capital).

Nicolas Laporte is a Member of the Investment Analysis and Advise Group at Citigroup Private Banking. He is involved in portfolio optimization and asset allocation. He was previously an Analyst with the Equity Research Group at Morgan Stanley Capital International. On the academic side, Nicolas Laporte received his M.Sc. in Banking and Finance from HEC Lausanne (Switzerland).

David Kuo Chuen Lee is Managing Director and Chief Investment Officer, Ferrell Asset Management. He holds a Ph.D. in Econometrics from the London School of Economics. He is also a guest lecturer specializing in alternative investments with the Centre for Financial Engineering and Faculty of Business Administration, National University of Singapore.

Lionel Martellini is a Professor of Finance at Edhec Graduate School of Business and the Scientific Director of Edhec Risk and Asset Management Research Center. A former member of the faculty at the Marshall School of Business, University of Southern California, he holds Master's degrees in Business Administration, Economics, and Statistics and Mathematics, and a Ph.D. in Finance from the Haas School of Business, University of California, Berkeley. Dr. Martellini is a member of the editorial board of the *Journal of Alternative Investments* and the *Journal of Bond Trading and Management*. He conducts active research in quantitative asset management and derivatives valuation, which has been published in leading academic and practitioner journals and has been featured in the *Financial Times* and the *Wall Street Journal*, and other financial newspapers. He is a regular speaker in seminars and conferences on these topics.

L. Joe Moffitt is a Professor in the Department of Resource Economics at the University of Massachusetts, Amherst. His research interests include the application of biology-based, quantitative-based methods to economics and econometrics. He holds a Ph.D. from the University of California, Berkeley.

Kankana Mukherjee is an Assistant Professor of Economics in the Department of Management at Worcester Polytechnic Institute. She received her Ph.D. from the University of Connecticut. Her principal research interest is in production analysis and issues relating to mergers, productivity, efficiency, as well as regional differences in competitiveness and productivity growth. Her published work has appeared in several peer-reviewed journals.

Nicolas Papageorgiou is an Assistant Professor in the Department of Finance at the Hautes études commerciales (HEC), University of Montreal, Canada. His main research interests and publications deal with fixed income securities, specifically the pricing of structured products and the analysis of fixed income arbitrage strategies used by hedge fund managers.

Dr. Papageorgiou has taught graduate-level courses in Canada and the U.K. and has presented at numerous academic and practitioner conferences in North America, Europe, and North Africa.

Kok Fai Phoon is Executive Director Designate, Ferrell Asset Management. He holds a Ph.D. in Finance from Northwestern University. Prior to joining Ferrell, he first worked with Yamaichi Research Institute, and subsequently at a multibillion-global investment company based in Singapore. He teaches courses on hedge funds, portfolio management and investment at the Centre for Financial Engineering, National University of Singapore, and the Singapore Management University.

Stephen E. Satchell is a Reader of financial econometrics at the University of Cambridge and specializes in financial econometrics and risk management. He is the editor of *Derivatives Use, Trading and Regulation* and the *Journal of Asset Management*, two leading peer-reviewed journals. He also acts as a consultant and academic advisor to a number of financial institutions.

Hilary Till is cofounder and Portfolio Manager at Premia Capital Management, LLC, in Chicago, which specializes in detecting pockets of predictability in derivatives markets by using statistical techniques. Ms. Till is also a Principal of Premia Risk Consultancy, Inc., which advises investment firms on derivatives strategies and risk management policy. Prior to Premia, Ms. Till was Chief of Derivatives Strategies at Boston-based Putnam Investments, where she was responsible for the management of all derivatives investments in domestic and international fixed income, tax-exempt fixed income, foreign exchange, and global asset allocation. Prior to Putnam Investments, Ms. Till was a Quantitative Equity Analyst at Harvard Management Company (HMC) in Boston, the investment management company for Harvard University's endowment. She holds a B.A. in Statistics from the University of Chicago and a M.Sc. in Statistics from the London School of Economics. Her articles on derivatives, risk management, and alternative investments have been published in several peer-reviewed academic journals.

John P. Townsend is currently Dean of Agriculture and Assistant Professor of Agribusiness at Oklahoma Panhandle State University in Goodwell, OK. Dr. Townsend teaches undergraduate courses in agribusiness, mathematics, and risk management and serves as Rodeo Club advisor in addition to his administrative duties. Dr. Townsend obtained his B.S. and M.S. in Agricultural Economics from New Mexico State University, and his Ph.D. in Agricultural Economics from Oklahoma State University.

Mathieu Vaissié is a Research Engineer at Edhec Risk and Asset Management Research Center, where he is in charge of the production of Edhec Alternative Indexes. Mr. Vaissié holds a Master's Degree in Business Administration from Edhec Graduate School of Business and is a Ph.D. candidate in Finance at the University Paris 9 Dauphine. He specializes in multifactor models and their use for benchmarking hedge fund returns.

Kathryn Wilkens is an Assistant Professor of Finance at Worcester Polytechnic Institute. She received her Ph.D. from the University of Massachusetts at Amherst. Her research analyzes asset allocation and portfolio performance issues and the bases of relative performance among alternative investment strategies. She is a research associate at the University of Massachusetts' Center for International Securities and Derivatives Markets and has published articles in several peer-reviewed journals. In collaboration with industry experts, she is also on the Chartered Alternative Investment Analyst curriculum committee.

Introduction

One of the key results of modern portfolio theory as developed by Nobel laureate Harry Markowitz in 1952 is that one can obtain a greater number of efficient portfolios by diversifying among various asset classes having negative to low correlation. The performance attributes of the various asset classes are independent among themselves and are not highly correlated. Commodity trading advisors (CTAs), which typically exhibit low and negative correlation with stock and bond markets, can help to provide downside protection during volatile and bear markets. CTAs trade managed futures using proprietary trading programs that buy and sell commodities and financial futures on options and futures markets around the world.

What makes CTAs special? They are different from hedge fund and long-only portfolio managers because they do not follow trends in stock or bond markets, but rather attempt to seize opportunities in a variety of commodity and financial futures markets. Many accredited investors today have understood the benefits of diversification by including CTAs in pension fund and institutional portfolios. The performance of CTAs can provide a better reward-to-risk ratio than equity mutual fund managers.

Recent academic studies have examined the benefits of adding CTAs to traditional stock and bond portfolios and have concluded that CTAs can reduce the standard deviation and increase the risk-adjusted returns of portfolios. Furthermore, in months where stocks markets have done poorly, CTAs have often returned positive numbers, offering a cushion in these down months.

Whether stock markets go up or down, CTAs can provide positive returns in both environments. Academic studies also have demonstrated that CTAs perform better than hedge funds in down markets. This is of paramount importance because over the last few years, volatility in stock markets has been very high and finding protection only with hedge funds may not yield an optimal investment portfolio.

PART One

Performance

Chapter 1 demonstrates how adding managed futures to a portfolio of stocks and bonds can reduce that portfolio's standard deviation more and more quickly than hedge funds can, and without the undesirable consequences that often accompany hedge fund allocations. Portfolios consisting of both hedge funds and managed futures are shown to exhibit even more desirable diversification properties.

Chapter 2 presents an original methodology for constructing a representative and pure commodity trading advisor (CTA) index that addresses some of the crucial issues investors can face during the allocation process. Using this index as a reference, the chapter also analyzes CTAs' return characteristics and the extent to which investors would be better off integrating CTAs in their global allocation.

Chapter 3 examines the many benefits to investing in CTAs. Past studies have found little evidence of performance persistence in the returns to CTAs. But these studies have used small data sets and methods with low statistical power. Larger data sets and a variety of statistical methods are used here to investigate whether some advisors or funds consistently outperform others. The analysis uses data from public funds, private funds, and CTAs and applies four distinct methods to evaluate performance persistence.

A small amount of performance persistence was found. It was stronger when a return/risk measure was used as the measure of performance. The persistence found was small relative to the noise in the data, and, therefore, precise methods and long time series had to be used to properly select funds or CTAs. Results also indicated that CTAs using long- or medium-run systems had higher returns than CTAs using short-term trading systems and that CTAs with higher historical returns tend to charge higher fees. Returns were negatively correlated with the most recent past returns, but were positive in the long run. Yet, when deciding whether to invest or withdraw funds, investors put more weight on the most recent returns.

Chapter 4 examines CTA performance, which has been analyzed by many academic and practioners. However, few studies attempt to determine whether there are significant differences in their performance over time. The study presented in this chapter investigates CTA performance using one of the biggest databases ever employed in performance analysis studies to determine if some funds consistently and significantly over- or underperform. The chapter also analyzes the survivorship bias present in CTAs as well as the dissolution frequencies of these funds.

Chapter 5 applies data envelopment analysis (DEA) to a performance evaluation framework for CTAs. The DEA methodology allows the authors to integrate several performance measures into one efficiency score by establishing a multidimensional efficient frontier. Two dimensions of the frontier are consistent with the standard Markowitz mean-variance framework. Additional risk and return dimensions include skewness and kurtosis. The chapter also illustrates a method of analyzing determinants of efficiency scores. Tobit regressions of efficiency scores on equity betas, beta-squared, fund size, length of manager track record, investment style (market focus), and strategy (discretionary versus systematic) are performed for CTA returns over two time frames representing different market environments. The authors find the efficiency scores to be negatively related to beta-squared in both time periods. Results also indicate that emerging CTAs (those with shorter manager track records) tend to have better DEA efficiency scores. This relationship is strongest during the period from 1998 to 2000, but not statistically significant during the period from 2000 to 2002. For both time periods, fund size is not related to efficiency scores.

Chapter 6 examines the performance of six CTA indices from 1990 to 2003, during which time four distinct market trends are identified as well as three extreme events. The authors show that traditional multifactor as well as multimoment asset pricing models do not adequately describe CTA returns. However, with a proper choice of risk factors, a significant proportion of CTA returns can be explained and the abnormal performance of each strategy can be assessed properly.

Chapter 7 applies the basic, cross-evaluation, and superefficiency DEA models to evaluate the performance of CTA classifications. With the ever-increasing number of CTAs, there is an urgency to provide money managers, pension funds, and high-net-worth individuals with a trustworthy appraisal method for ranking CTA efficiency. Data envelopment analysis can achieve this, with the important benefit that benchmarks are not required, thereby alleviating the problem of using traditional benchmarks to examine nonnormal returns.

CHAPTER 1

Managed Futures and Hedge Funds: A Match Made in Heaven

Harry M. Kat

In this chapter we study the possible role of managed futures in portfolios of stocks, bonds, and hedge funds. We find that allocating to managed futures allows investors to achieve a very substantial degree of overall risk reduction at, in terms of expected return, relatively limited costs. Apart from their lower expected return, managed futures appear to be more effective diversifiers than hedge funds. Adding managed futures to a portfolio of stocks and bonds will reduce that portfolio's standard deviation more and more quickly than hedge funds will, and without the undesirable side effects on skewness and kurtosis. Overall portfolio standard deviation can be reduced further by combining both hedge funds and managed futures with stocks and bonds. As long as at least 45 to 50 percent of the alternatives allocation is to managed futures, this will have no negative side effects on skewness and kurtosis.

INTRODUCTION

Hedge funds are often said to provide investors with the best of both worlds: an expected return similar to equity combined with a risk similar to bonds. When past returns are simply extrapolated and risk is defined as the standard deviation of the fund return, this is indeed true. Recent research, however, has shown that the risk and dependence characteristics of hedge funds are substantially more complex than those of stocks and bonds. Amin and Kat (2003), for example, show that although including hedge funds in a traditional investment portfolio may significantly improve that portfolio's mean-variance characteristics, it can also be expected to lead to significantly lower skewness. The additional negative skewness that arises when hedge funds are introduced in a portfolio of stocks and bonds forms a major risk, as one large negative return can destroy years of careful compounding. To hedge this risk, investors need to expand their horizon beyond stocks and bonds. Kat (2003) showed how stock index put options may be used to hedge against the unwanted skewness effect of hedge funds. Kat (2004) showed that put options on (baskets of) hedge funds may perform a similar task.

Of course, the list of possible remedies does not end here. Any asset or asset class that has suitable (co-)skewness characteristics can be used. One obvious candidate is managed futures. Managed futures programs are often trend-following in nature. In essence, what these programs do is somewhat similar to how option traders hedge a short call position. When the market moves up, they increase exposure, and vice versa. By moving out of the market when it comes down, managed futures programs avoid being pulled in. As a result, the (co-)skewness characteristics of managed futures programs can be expected to be more or less opposite to those of many hedge funds.

In this chapter we investigate how managed futures mix with stocks, bonds, and hedge funds and how they can be used to control the undesirable skewness effects that arise when hedge funds are added to portfolios of stocks and bonds. We find that managed futures combine extremely well with stocks, bonds, and hedge funds and that the combination allows investors to significantly improve the overall risk characteristics of their portfolio without, under the assumptions made, giving up much in terms of expected return.

MANAGED FUTURES

The asset class "managed futures" refers to professional money managers known as commodity trading advisors (CTAs) who manage assets using the global futures and options markets as their investment universe. Managed futures have been available for investment since 1948, when the first public futures fund started trading. The industry did not take off until the late 1970s. Since then the sector has seen a fair amount of growth with currently an estimated \$40 to \$45 billion under management.

There are three ways in which investors can get into managed futures.

1. Investors can buy shares in a public commodity (or futures) fund, in much the same way as they would invest in stock or bond mutual funds.
2. They can place funds privately with a commodity pool operator (CPO) who pools investors' money and employs one or more CTAs to manage the pooled funds.

3. Investors can retain one or more CTAs directly to manage their money on an individual basis or hire a manager of managers (MOM) to select CTAs for them.

The minimum investment required by funds, pools, and CTAs varies considerably, with the direct CTA route open only to investors who want to make a substantial investment. CTAs charge management and incentive fees comparable to those charged by hedge funds (i.e., 2 percent management fee plus 20 percent incentive fee). Like funds of hedge funds, funds and pools charge an additional fee on top of that.

Initially, CTAs were limited to trading commodity futures (which explains terms such as "public commodity fund," "CTA," and "CPO"). With the introduction of futures on currencies, interest rates, bonds, and stock indices in the 1980s, however, the trading spectrum widened substantially. Nowadays CTAs trade both commodity and financial futures. Many take a very technical, systematic approach to trading, but others opt for a more fundamental, discretionary approach. Some concentrate on particular futures markets, such as agricultural, currencies, or metals, but most diversify over different types of markets.

For our purposes, one of the most important features of managed futures is their trend-following nature. That CTA returns have a strong trend-following component can be shown by calculating the correlation between managed futures returns and the returns on a purely mechanical trend-following strategy. One such strategy underlies the Mount Lucas Management (MLM) index, which reflects the results of a purely mechanical, moving-average-based, trading strategy in 25 different commodity and financial futures markets. Estimates of the correlation between the MLM index and CTA returns are typically positive and highly significant.

DATA

We distinguish between four different asset classes: stocks, bonds, hedge funds, and managed futures. Stocks are represented by the Standard & Poor's (S&P) 500 index and bonds by the 10-year Salomon Brothers Government Bond index. Hedge fund return data were obtained from Tremont TASS, one of the largest hedge fund databases currently available. After eliminating funds with incomplete and ambiguous data as well as funds of funds, the database at our disposal as of May 2001 contained monthly net-of-fee returns on 1,195 live and 526 dead funds. To avoid survivorship bias, we created 455 seven-year monthly return series by, beginning with the 455 funds that were alive in June 1994, replacing every fund that closed down during the sample period by a fund randomly selected from the set of funds alive at the time of closure, following the same type of strategy and of similar age and size. Next we used random sampling to create 500 different equally weighted portfolios containing 20 hedge funds each. From the monthly returns on these portfolios we calculated the mean, standard deviation, skewness, and kurtosis and determined the median value of each of these statistics. Subsequently we selected the portfolio whose sample statistics came closest to the latter median values. We use this "median portfolio" to represent hedge funds.

Managed futures are represented by the Stark 300 index. This asset-weighted index is compiled using the top 300 trading programs from the Daniel B. Stark & Co. database.[1] The top 300 trading programs are determined quarterly based on assets under management. When a trading program closes down, the index does not get adjusted backward, which takes care of survivorship bias issues. All 300 of the CTAs in the index are classified by their trading approach and market category. Currently the index contains 248 systematic and 52 discretionary traders, which split up in 169 diversified, 111 financial only, 9 financial and metals, and 11 nonfinancial trading programs.

Throughout we use monthly return data over the period June 1994 to May 2001. For bonds, hedge funds, and managed futures we use the sample mean as our estimate of the expected future return. For stocks, however, we assume an expected return of 1 percent per month, as it would be unrealistic to assume an immediate repeat of the 1990s bull market. Under these assumptions, the basic return statistics for our four asset classes are shown in Table 1.1 The table shows that managed futures returns have a lower mean and a higher standard deviation than hedge fund returns. However, managed futures also exhibit positive instead of negative skewness and much lower kurtosis.[2] From the correlation matrix we see that the correlation of managed futures with stocks and hedge funds is very low. This means that, as long as there are no negative side effects, such as lower skewness or higher kurtosis, managed futures will make very good diversifiers. This is what we investigate in more detail next.

---

[1]Note that contrary to the Mount Lucas Management index, the Stark 300 is a true CTA index.

[2]Over the sample period the MLM index has a mean of 0.89 percent, a standard deviation of 1.63 percent, a skewness of –0.81 and a kurtosis of 3.42. The Stark 300 index has fundamentally different skewness and kurtosis properties than the MLM index.

TABLE 1.1 Basic Monthly Statistics S&P 500, Bonds, Hedge Funds, and Managed Futures

	S&P 500	Bonds	Hedge Funds	Managed Fut.
Mean	1.00	0.45	0.99	0.70
Standard deviation	4.39	1.77	2.44	2.89
Skewness	−0.82	0.58	−0.47	0.45
Excess kurtosis	1.05	1.45	2.67	0.21
	Correlations			
	S&P 500	Bonds	Hedge Fund	Managed Fut.
S&P 500	1			
Bonds	0.15	1		
HF	0.63	−0.05	1	
MF	−0.07	0.20	−0.14	1

STOCKS, BONDS, PLUS HEDGE FUNDS OR MANAGED FUTURES

Given the complexity of the relationship between hedge fund and equity returns, we study the impact of hedge funds and managed futures for two different types of investors. The first are what we refer to as 50/50 investors—investors who always invest an equal amount in stocks and bonds. When adding hedge funds and/or managed futures to their portfolio, 50/50 investors will reduce their stock and bond holdings by the same amount. This gives rise to portfolios consisting of 45 percent stocks, 45 percent bonds, and 10 percent hedge funds or 40 percent stocks, 40 percent bonds, and 20 percent managed futures. The second type of investors, what we call 33/66 investors, always divide the money invested in stocks and bonds in such a way that one-third is invested in stocks and two-thirds is invested in bonds.

The first step in our analysis is to see whether there are any significant differences in the way in which hedge funds and managed futures combine with stocks and bonds. We therefore form portfolios of stocks, bonds, and hedge funds, as well as portfolios of stocks, bonds, and managed futures. Table 1.2 shows the basic return statistics for 50/50 investors. Table 1.3 shows the same for 33/66 investors. From Table 1.2 we see that if the hedge fund allocation increases, both the standard deviation and the skewness of the portfolio return distribution drop substantially, while at the same time the return distribution's kurtosis increases. A similar picture emerges from

TABLE 1.2 Return Statistics 50/50 Portfolios of Stocks, Bonds, and Hedge Funds or Managed Futures

Hedge Funds					Managed Futures				
% HF	Mean	SD	Skewness	Kurtosis	% MF	Mean	SD	Skewness	Kurtosis
0	0.72	2.49	−0.33	−0.03	0	0.72	2.49	−0.33	−0.03
5	0.73	2.43	−0.40	0.02	5	0.71	2.37	−0.28	−0.18
10	0.74	2.38	−0.46	0.08	10	0.71	2.26	−0.21	−0.30
15	0.76	2.33	−0.53	0.17	15	0.71	2.16	−0.14	−0.39
20	0.77	2.29	−0.60	0.28	20	0.71	2.08	−0.06	−0.42
25	0.78	2.25	−0.66	0.42	25	0.71	2.00	0.02	−0.40
30	0.80	2.22	−0.72	0.58	30	0.71	1.95	0.10	−0.32
35	0.81	2.20	−0.78	0.77	35	0.71	1.91	0.18	−0.20
40	0.82	2.18	−0.82	0.97	40	0.71	1.89	0.24	−0.06
45	0.84	2.17	−0.85	1.19	45	0.71	1.89	0.30	0.08
50	0.85	2.16	−0.87	1.41	50	0.71	1.91	0.34	0.19

Table 1.3 for 33/66 investors, except that the drop in skewness is much more pronounced. With managed futures the picture is different. If the managed futures allocation increases, the standard deviation drops faster than with hedge funds. More remarkably, skewness rises instead of drops while kurtosis drops instead of rises. Although (under the assumptions made) hedge funds offer a somewhat higher expected return, from an overall risk perspective managed futures appear to be better diversifiers than hedge funds.

TABLE 1.3 Return Statistics 33/66 Portfolios of Stocks, Bonds, and Hedge Funds or Managed Futures

Hedge Funds					Managed Futures				
% HF	Mean	SD	Skewness	Kurtosis	% MF	Mean	SD	Skewness	Kurtosis
0	0.62	2.01	0.03	0.21	0	0.62	2.01	0.03	0.21
5	0.64	1.97	−0.05	0.13	5	0.62	1.93	0.09	0.17
10	0.66	1.93	−0.14	0.08	10	0.63	1.85	0.15	0.14
15	0.68	1.90	−0.24	0.04	15	0.63	1.79	0.22	0.15
20	0.69	1.87	−0.34	0.04	20	0.64	1.75	0.28	0.18
25	0.71	1.86	−0.43	0.09	25	0.64	1.71	0.34	0.24
30	0.73	1.85	−0.52	0.17	30	0.65	1.70	0.39	0.30
35	0.75	1.84	−0.60	0.31	35	0.65	1.70	0.42	0.36
40	0.77	1.85	−0.66	0.49	40	0.65	1.72	0.45	0.41
45	0.79	1.86	−0.71	0.70	45	0.66	1.76	0.47	0.43
50	0.80	1.89	−0.75	0.94	50	0.66	1.81	0.48	0.42

HEDGE FUNDS PLUS MANAGED FUTURES

The next step is to study how hedge funds and managed futures combine with each other. This is shown in Table 1.4. Adding managed futures to a hedge fund portfolio will put downward pressure on the portfolio's expected return as the expected return on managed futures is lower than that of hedge funds. From a risk perspective, however, the benefits of managed futures are again very substantial. From the table we see that adding managed futures to a portfolio of hedge funds will lead to a very significant drop in the portfolio return's standard deviation. With 40 percent invested in managed futures, the standard deviation falls from 2.44 percent to 1.74 percent. When 45 percent is invested in managed futures, skewness rises quickly—from −0.47 to 0.39, and kurtosis exhibits a strong drop—from 2.67 to −0.17. Giving up 10 to 15 basis points per month in expected return does not seem an unrealistic price to pay for such a substantial improvement in overall risk profile.

STOCKS, BONDS, HEDGE FUNDS, AND MANAGED FUTURES

The final step in our analysis is to bring all four asset classes together in one portfolio. We do so in two steps. First, we combine hedge funds and managed futures into what we will call the alternatives portfolio. Then we combine the alternatives portfolio with stocks and bonds. We vary the managed futures allocation in the alternatives portfolio as well as the alternatives allocation in the overall portfolio from 0 percent to 100 percent in 5 percent steps.

Without managed futures, increasing the alternatives allocation will significantly raise the expected return. When the managed futures alloca-

TABLE 1.4 Return Statistics Portfolios of Hedge Funds and Managed Futures

% MF	Mean	SD	Skewness	Kurtosis
0	0.99	2.44	−0.47	2.67
5	0.97	2.31	−0.37	2.31
10	0.96	2.18	−0.27	1.91
15	0.94	2.06	−0.15	1.46
20	0.93	1.96	−0.03	1.01
25	0.92	1.88	0.09	0.59
30	0.90	1.81	0.20	0.23
35	0.89	1.76	0.29	−0.01
40	0.87	1.74	0.36	−0.14
45	0.86	1.74	0.39	−0.17
50	0.85	1.76	0.39	−0.15

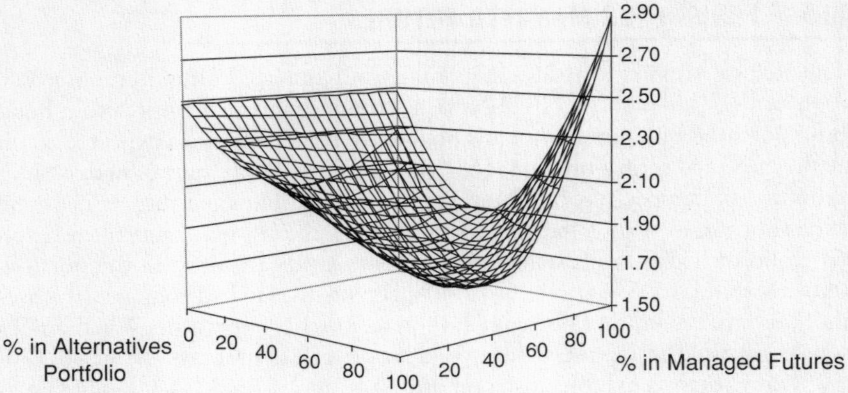

FIGURE 1.1 Standard Deviation 50/50 Portfolios of Stocks, Bonds, Hedge Funds, and Managed Futures

tion increases, however, the expected return will drop. This follows directly from the result that the expected return on hedge funds is 0.99 percent, but it is only 0.70 percent on managed futures (Table 1.1). On the risk front the picture is much more interesting. Figures 1.1 and 1.2 show that investing in alternatives can substantially reduce the overall portfolio return's standard deviation, for 50/50 as well as 33/66 investors. The drop, however, is heavily dependent on the percentage of managed futures in the alternatives portfolio. Surprisingly, for allocations to alternatives between 0 percent and 20 percent, the lowest standard deviations are obtained without hedge funds,

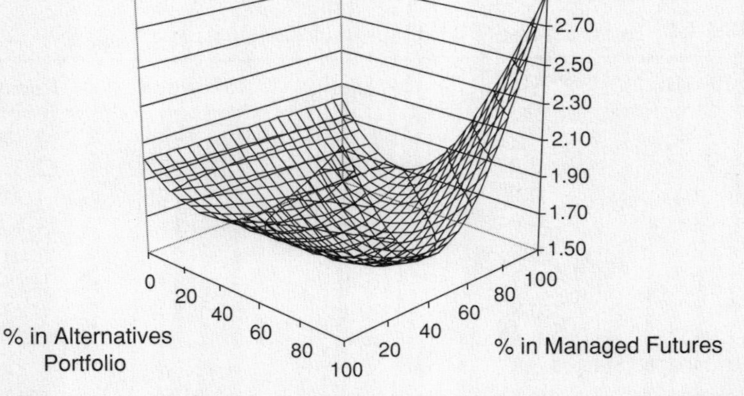

FIGURE 1.2 Standard Deviation 33/66 Portfolios of Stocks, Bonds, Hedge Funds, and Managed Futures

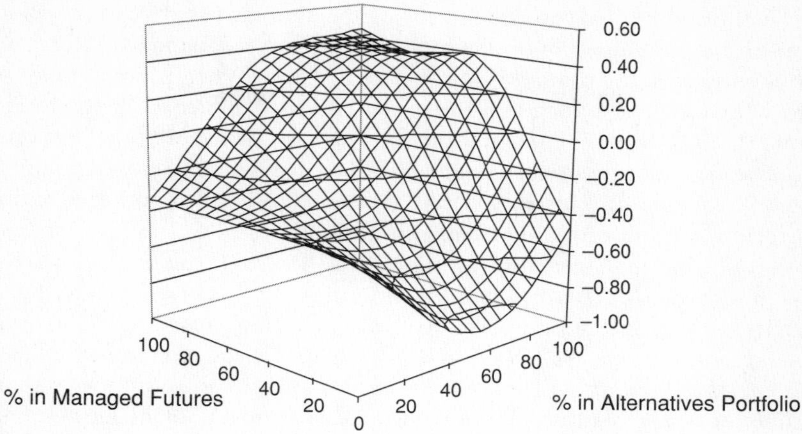

FIGURE 1.3 Skewness 50/50 Portfolios of Stocks, Bonds, Hedge Funds, and Managed Futures

that is, when 100 percent is invested in managed futures. For higher alternatives allocations, however, it pays also to include some hedge funds in the alternatives portfolio. This makes sense, because for the alternatives portfolio, the lowest standard deviation is found when 40 to 45 percent is invested in managed futures. We saw that before in Table 1.4.

Figures 1.3 and 1.4 show the impact of allocation on skewness, for 50/50 and 33/66 investors respectively. From these graphs we see once more

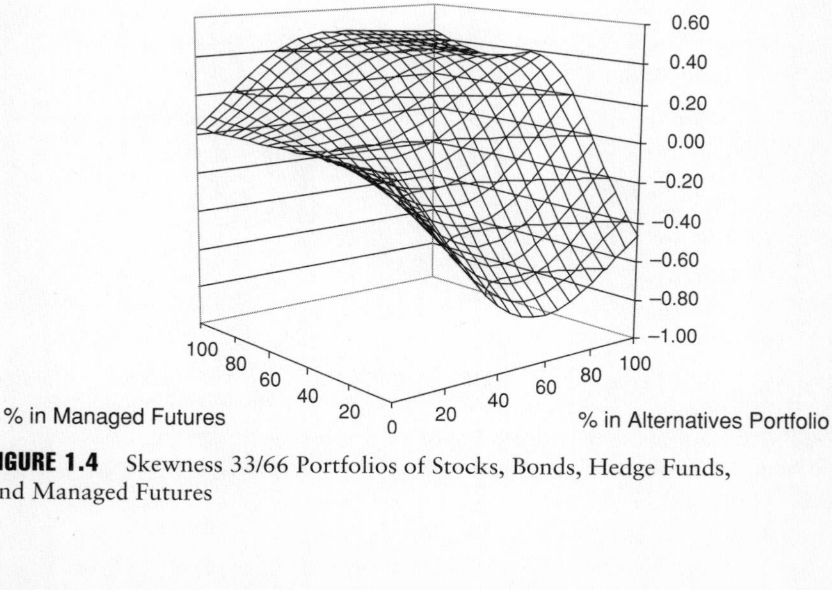

FIGURE 1.4 Skewness 33/66 Portfolios of Stocks, Bonds, Hedge Funds, and Managed Futures

that without managed futures, increasing the alternatives allocation will lead to a substantial reduction in skewness. The higher the managed futures allocation, however, the more this effect is neutralized. When more than 50 percent is invested in managed futures, the skewness effect of hedge funds is (more than) fully eliminated and the skewness of the overall portfolio return actually rises when alternatives are introduced. Finally, Figures 1.5 and 1.6 show the impact on kurtosis. With 0 percent allocated to managed futures, kurtosis rises substantially when the alternatives allocation is increased. With a sizable managed futures allocation, however, this is no longer the case, and kurtosis actually drops when more weight is given to alternatives.

To summarize, Figures 1.1 to 1.6 show that *investing in managed futures can improve the overall risk profile of a portfolio far beyond what can be achieved with hedge funds alone.* Making an allocation to managed futures not only neutralizes the unwanted side effects of hedge funds but also leads to further risk reduction. Assuming managed futures offer an acceptable expected return, all of this comes at quite a low price in terms of expected return forgone.

To make sure that these findings have general validity—that they are not simply due to the particular choice of index—we repeated the procedure with a number of other CTA indices, including various indices calculated by the Barclay Group. In all cases the results were very similar, which

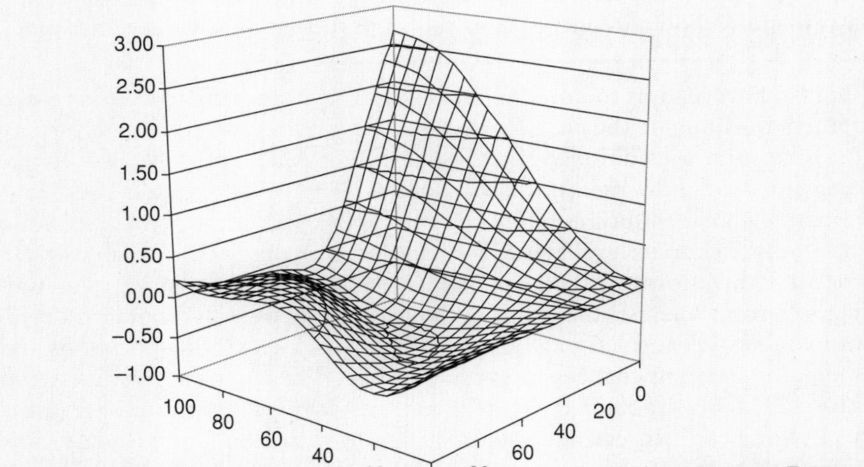

FIGURE 1.5 Kurtosis 50/50 Portfolios of Stocks, Bonds, Hedge Funds, and Managed Futures

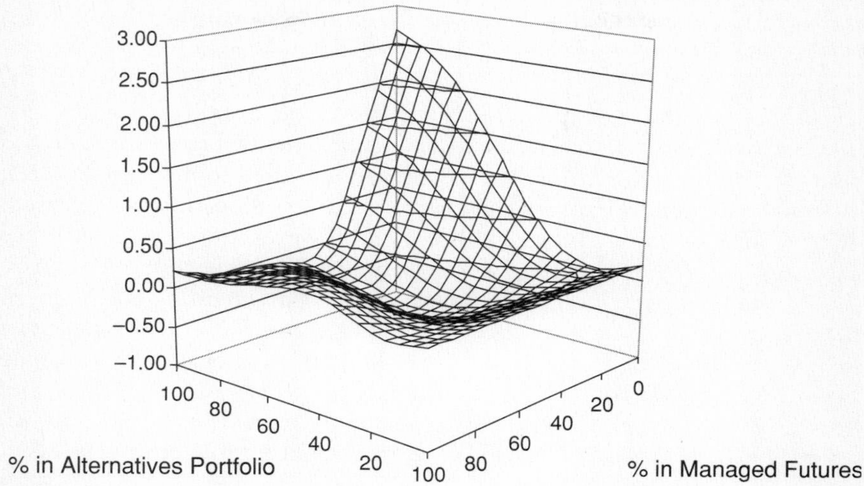

FIGURE 1.6 Kurtosis 33/66 Portfolios of Stocks, Bonds, Hedge Funds, and Managed Futures

suggests that our results are robust with respect to the choice of managed futures index.

SKEWNESS REDUCTION WITH MANAGED FUTURES

Our findings lead us to question what the exact costs are of using managed futures to eliminate the negative skewness that arises when hedge funds are introduced in a traditional portfolio of stocks and bonds. To answer this question we follow the same procedure as in Kat (2003). First, we determine the managed futures allocation required to bring the overall portfolio skewness back to its level before the addition of hedge funds, which is –0.33 for 50/50 investors and 0.03 for 33/66 investors. Next, we leverage (assuming 4 percent interest) the resulting portfolio to restore the standard deviation. Tables 1.5 and 1.6 show the resulting overall portfolio allocations and the accompanying changes in expected return (on a per annum basis) and kurtosis. From Table 1.6 we see that the optimal portfolios are quite straightforward. In essence, the bulk of the managed futures holdings is financed by borrowing, without changing much about the stock, bond, and hedge fund allocations. It is interesting to see that for smaller initial hedge fund allocations, the optimal hedge fund and managed futures allocation are more or less equal. This is true for 50/50 as well as 33/66 investors.

TABLE 1.5 Allocations and Change in Mean and Kurtosis 50/50 Portfolios of Stocks, Bonds, Hedge Funds, Managed Futures, and Cash with −0.33 Skewness and Standard Deviations as in Third Column of Table 1.2

Initial % HF	% Stocks	% Bonds	% HF	% MF	% Cash	Gain Mean per annum	Change Kurtosis
0	50.00	50.00	0.00	0.00	0.00	0.00	0.00
5	47.42	47.42	4.99	5.48	−5.30	0.66	−0.18
10	44.71	44.71	9.94	9.95	−9.30	1.15	−0.34
15	41.99	41.99	14.82	13.60	−12.40	1.53	−0.50
20	39.34	39.34	19.67	16.55	−14.90	1.83	−0.66
25	36.67	36.67	24.45	18.91	−16.70	2.05	−0.82
30	34.09	34.09	29.22	20.80	−18.20	2.23	−0.98
35	31.55	31.55	33.98	22.33	−19.40	2.37	−1.15
40	29.06	29.06	38.75	23.32	−20.20	2.46	−1.31
45	26.61	26.61	43.54	24.04	−20.80	2.53	−1.46
50	24.25	24.25	48.50	24.40	−21.40	2.60	−1.59

Looking at the change in expected return, we see that as a result of the addition of managed futures and the subsequent leverage, the expected return actually increases instead of drops. From the last column we also see that this rise in expected return is accompanied by a significant drop in kurtosis. This compares very favorably with the results in Kat (2003, 2004), where it is shown that the costs of skewness reduction through stock index or hedge fund puts can be quite significant.

TABLE 1.6 Allocations and Change in Mean and Kurtosis 33/66 Portfolios of Stocks, Bonds, Hedge Funds, Managed Futures, and Cash with 0.03 Skewness and Standard Deviations as in Third Column of Table 1.3

Initial % HF	% Stocks	% Bonds	% HF	% MF	% Cash	Gain Mean per annum	Change Kurtosis
0	33.33	66.67	0.00	0.00	0.00	0.00	0.00
5	32.08	64.16	5.07	6.70	−8.00	0.98	−0.07
10	30.54	61.07	10.18	12.71	−14.50	1.79	−0.15
15	28.83	57.66	15.26	17.96	−19.70	2.44	−0.22
20	26.99	53.99	20.25	22.37	−23.60	2.93	−0.31
25	25.11	50.22	25.11	26.06	−26.50	3.29	−0.42
30	23.21	46.41	29.84	29.04	−28.50	3.53	−0.56
35	21.32	42.63	34.44	31.41	−29.80	3.69	−0.73
40	19.47	38.94	38.94	33.15	−30.50	3.76	−0.93
45	17.65	35.29	43.31	34.35	−30.60	3.76	−1.15
50	15.85	31.71	47.56	35.18	−30.30	3.70	−1.38

Conclusion

In this chapter we have studied the possible role of managed futures in portfolios of stocks, bonds, and hedge funds. We have found that allocating to managed futures allows investors to achieve a very substantial degree of overall risk reduction at limited costs. Despite their lower expected return, managed futures appear to be more effective diversifiers than hedge funds. Adding managed futures to a portfolio of stocks and bonds will reduce that portfolio's standard deviation more effectively than hedge funds alone, and without the undesirable impact on skewness and kurtosis. This does not mean that hedge funds are superfluous. Overall portfolio standard deviation can be reduced further by combining both hedge funds and managed futures with stocks and bonds. As long as at least 45 to 50 percent of the alternatives allocation is allocated to managed futures, there will be no negative side effects on portfolio skewness and kurtosis. Assuming that hedge funds will continue to provide higher returns than managed futures, the inclusion of hedge funds also will boost the portfolio's expected return somewhat.

CHAPTER 2

Benchmarking the Performance of CTAs

Lionel Martellini and Mathieu Vaissié

The bursting of the Internet bubble in March 2000 plunged traditional market indices (stocks, bonds, etc.) into deep turmoil, leaving most institutional investors with the impression that portfolio diversification tends to fail at the exact moment that investors have a need for it, namely in periods when the markets drop significantly.[1] At the same time, most alternative investments (e.g., hedge funds, CTAs, real estate, etc.) posted attractive returns. They benefited from large capital inflows from high-net-worth individuals (HNWI) and institutional investors, who were both looking for investment vehicles that would improve the diversification of their portfolios. At the same time, many recent academic and practitioner studies have documented the benefits of investing in alternative investments in general, and hedge funds in particular (see Amenc, Martellini, and Vaissié 2003; Amin and Kat 2002, 2003b; Anjilvel Boudreau, Urias, and Peskin 2000; Brooks and Kat 2002; Cerrahoglu and Pancholi 2003; Daglioglu and Gupta 2003a; Schneeweis, Karavas, and Georgiev 2003).

Nevertheless, due to the "natural" (survivorship/selection) and "spurious" (backfilling/weighting scheme) biases that are present in hedge fund databases (see Fung and Hsieh 2000, 2002a), it remains challenging to come up with an accurate estimate of returns on hedge funds. The challenging nature of hedge fund return measurement has been exemplified by the heterogeneity in hedge fund index returns, which is now a well-documented problem (cf. Amenc and Martellini 2003; Vaissié 2004). As evidenced by Amenc and Martellini (2003), the correlation between indices representing

[1]Longin and Solnik (1995) provide evidence that the correlation between the stock markets in different countries converges toward 1 when there is a sharp drop in U.S. stock markets.

the same investment style may turn out to be as low as 0.43 for equity market neutral or 0.46 for equity long short. This fact may leave investors with a somewhat confused picture of the performance of alternative investment strategies. More surprisingly perhaps, index heterogeneity also may be of concern in the case of CTAs. Dealing with CTA index heterogeneity is discussed in the next sections. It is crucial for investors to pay particular attention to the selection of an appropriate index to benchmark their performance and to assess their exposure to risk factors. To respond to investors' expectations, in this chapter we present an original methodology to construct a pure and representative CTA index (also known as the Edhec CTA Global Index; hereafter referred to as the Edhec CTA Index). We then use the Edhec CTA Index to analyze CTA return characteristics and the extent to which investors would be better off integrating CTAs in their global allocation. Finally, we derive a five-factor model to identify the underlying risk factors driving CTA performance.

DEALING WITH CTA INDEX HETEROGENEITY

Because managed futures tend to trade more liquid assets than hedge funds and because they have to register with the Commodity Futures Trading Commission (CFTC), one would expect the different managed futures indices to exhibit negligible heterogeneity. This, however, is not the case. While the average correlation between the different indices available on the market[2] from January 1998 through September 2003 is 0.94, the difference between the monthly returns on two of these indices can be as high as 7.50 percent, the return difference between the S&P Index (+13.50 percent) and the Barclay CTA Index in December 2000. The corresponding average monthly difference amounts to 2.90 percent. This gives clear evidence that managed futures indices are not free from "natural" and/or "spurious" biases. As evidenced in Posthuma and Van der Sluis (2003), the backfilling bias is even higher for commodity trading advisers (CTAs) than for hedge funds (3.30 percent versus 2.23 percent). Liang (2003), perhaps surprisingly, drew the same conclusion with respect to survivorship bias, which turns out to be significantly higher in the case of CTAs (5.85 percent versus 2.32 percent).

Table 2.1 illustrates the consequences of the heterogeneity of index construction methodologies and fund selection in terms of risk factor expo-

[2]For example, CSFB/Tremont Managed Futures Index, the CISDM Trading Advisor Qualified Universe Index, the HF Net CTA/Managed Futures Average, the Barclay CTA Index, and the S&P Managed Futures Index.

TABLE 2.1 The Heterogeneity of CTA Indices' Risk Factor Exposure, September 1999 to September 2003

Risk Factors	CSFB	S&P	Barclay	HF Net	CISDM
Constant	4.52E–03	6.78E–03	2.93E–03	8.04E–03	4.27E–03
T-stats	1.1	1.1	1.0	2.5	1.5
S&P 500	–0.21			–0.09	
T-stats	–2.8			–1.3	
LEHMAN GLB. US TREASURY	0.89	1.49	0.67	0.76	0.71
T-stats	2.9	3.6	3.3	3.3	3.5
LEHMAN HIGH YIELD CORP		–0.39	–0.13	–0.21	–0.12
T-stats		–2.0	–1.4	–1.7	–1.3
US $ MAJOR CURRENCY	–0.69	–0.54	0.18	–0.46	–0.44
T-stats	–2.2	–1.2	1.7	–2.0	–2.1
US $ TO JAPANESE YEN	–0.54	–0.55	–0.20	–0.40	–0.39
T-stats	–2.8	–2.0	–1.9	–2.7	–2.9
Goldman Sachs Commodity Index	0.21	0.26	0.14	0.16	0.13
T-stats	3.3	2.7	3.0	3.2	2.8
Chg in VIX				–0.03	
T-stats				–1.4	

sures. To come up with a limited set of risk factors, we selected 16 factors known to be related to the strategies implemented by managed futures, namely stocks, bonds, interest rates, currency, and commodities factors. We then used stepwise regression with the backward entry procedure to avoid any multicollinearity problems and keep a sufficient number of degrees of freedom. While four factors are common to all indices (Lehman Global U.S. Treasury, U.S. dollar [USD] versus major currency, USD versus Japanese yen, and Goldman Sachs Commodity Index [GSCI], the corresponding exposures turn out to be very different. The S&P index yields a beta of 1.49 with the Lehman Global U.S. Treasury while the beta is 0.67 for the Barclay index. In the same vein, the CSFB index has a –0.69 beta with the USD versus major currency while the beta is 0.18 for the Barclay index. Only two indices (CSFB and HF Net) appear to exhibit significant exposure to the S&P 500 and only one (HF Net) to the evolution of the VIX (implied volatility on the S&P 500).

Since the choice of index may have a significant impact on the whole investment process (from strategic allocation through performance evaluation and attribution), investors should be aware of and tackle those differences in factor exposures. In what follows, we present an index construction methodology aimed at addressing this issue. Note that this methodology was first introduced in Amenc and Martellini (2003) and is now implemented to construct the Edhec Alternative Indices.[3]

Given that it is impossible to be objective on what is the best existing index, a natural idea consists of using some combination of competing indices (i.e., CTA indices available on the market) to extract any common information they might share. One straightforward method would involve computing an equally weighted portfolio of all competing indices. Because competing indices are based on different sets of CTAs, the resulting portfolio of indices would be more exhaustive than any of the competing indices it is extracted from. We push the logic one step further and suggest using factor analysis to generate a set of hedge fund indices that are the best possible one-dimensional summaries of information conveyed by competing indices for a given style, in the sense of the largest fraction of variance explained. Technically speaking, this amounts to using the first component of a Principal Component Analysis of competing indices. The Edhec CTA Index is thus able to capture a very large fraction of the information contained in the competing indices.

On one hand, the Edhec CTA Index generated as the first component in a factor analysis has a built-in element of optimality, since there is no other linear combination of competing indices that implies a lower information loss. On the other hand, since competing indices are affected differently by measurement biases, searching for the linear combination of competing indices that implies a maximization of the variance explained leads implicitly to a minimization of the bias. As a result, the Edhec CTA Index tends to be very stable over time and easily replicable.

CTA PERFORMANCE AT A GLANCE

Table 2.2 gives a comparative overview of the Edhec CTA Index, the S&P 500, and the Lehman Global Bond Index. Due to an average return that is slightly superior to the S&P 500 (0.73 percent versus 0.50 percent) and variance that is close to that of the Lehman Global Bond Index (0.84 percent versus 0.14 percent), the Edhec CTA Index obtains a Sharpe ratio that is significantly higher than stock and bond indices (0.72 versus 0.21 and –0.39, respectively). Its superiority in terms of risk-adjusted performance is even more marked when considering the Sortino ratio (11.01 versus 1.05

[3]Further details on the construction methodology of the Edhec Alternative Indices may be found at www.edhec-risk.com.

TABLE 2.2 Basic Statistical Properties of the Edhec CTA Global Index, January 1997 to September 2003

	Edhec CTA Global Index	S&P 500	Lehman Global Bond Index
Monthly Average Return	0.73%	0.50%	0.06%
Monthly Median Return	0.65%	0.76%	0.12%
Monthly Max. Return	6.91%	9.67%	2.15%
Monthly Min. Return	−5.43%	−14.58%	−3.94%
Maximum Uninterrupted Loss	−5.43%	−20.55%	−6.75%
Excess Kurtosis	−0.10	−0.28	1.44
Skewness	0.15	−0.43	−0.76
% of Winning Months	56.79%	55.56%	54.32%
Average Winning Return	2.52%	4.32%	0.83%
% of Losing Months	43.21%	44.44%	45.68%
Average Losing Return	−1.62%	−4.27%	−0.85%
Monthly Std Deviation Ann'd	9.17%	17.94%	3.75%
Monthly Variance Ann'd	0.84%	3.22%	0.14%
Monthly Semivariance Ann'd	0.39%	1.76%	0.08%
Monthly Downside Risk (MAR = Rf*)**	0.49%	1.85%	0.12%
VaR (99%)	−6.89%	−12.55%	−2.58%
Modified VaR (99%)	−6.52%	−13.49%	−3.31%
Sharpe Ratio	0.72	0.21	−0.39
Sortino Ratio (MAR = Rf*)	11.01	1.05	−8.11

*The risk-free rate is calculated as the 3-month LIBOR average over the period January 1997 to September 2003, namely 4.35 percent.

**This indicator is also referred to as the lower partial moment of order 2.

and −8.11) due to a limited downside risk (i.e., 0.49 percent versus 1.85 percent for the S&P 500). The Edhec CTA Index posts positive returns in about 57 percent of months, with an average gain of 2.52 percent versus an average loss of −1.62 percent in 43 percent of the cases. It is also worth noting that the Edhec index presents a smaller maximum uninterrupted loss than both the stock and bond indices.

Concerning extreme risks, the Edhec CTA Index is closer to the bond index than to the stock index with a modified value at risk (VaR) (also referred to as Cornish Fisher VaR[4]) of −6.52 percent as opposed to −13.49

[4]cf. Favre and Galeano (2002b) for more details on the Modified VaR and its application to hedge funds.

percent for the S&P 500 and –3.31 percent for the Lehman Global Bond Index. This is a very interesting property as low volatility strategies often present large exposures to extreme risks due to a transfer of the risk from second- to third- and fourth-order moments. Our analysis suggests that it is not the case with CTAs.

To account for the presence of extreme risks in the evaluation of risk-adjusted performance, we suggest computing the Omega ratio (cf. Keating and Shadwick 2002) of the CTA index:

$$\Omega(MAR) = \frac{\int_{MAR}^{b} [1 - F(x)]dx}{\int_{a}^{MAR} [F(x)]dx}$$

where $F(x)$ = cumulative distribution function,
MAR (minimum acceptable return) = gain/loss threshold,
$[a,b]$ = interval for which the distribution of asset returns is defined.

This performance measurement indicator has appealing properties because it does not require the distribution function of the underlying asset to be specified or any assumption to be made with respect to investors' preferences. It can thus account for the presence of fat tails in the case of non-normal distribution functions. Figure 2.1 compares the Omega ratios obtained by the Edhec index to those of the stock and bond indices. Again,

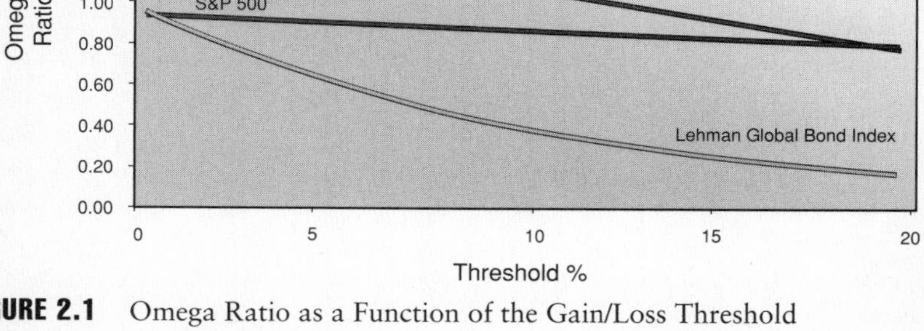

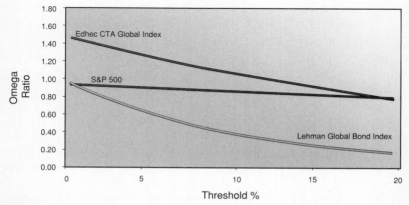

FIGURE 2.1 Omega Ratio as a Function of the Gain/Loss Threshold

up to an improbable loss threshold of roughly 18 percent per year, the Edhec index offers a better gain/loss ratio than both the S&P 500 and the Lehman Global Bond Index, which confirms the superiority of CTA risk-adjusted performance on a stand-alone basis.

MANAGED FUTURES IN THE ASSET ALLOCATION PROCESS: RETURN ENHANCERS, RISK REDUCERS, OR BOTH?

On a stand-alone basis, CTAs offer better risk-adjusted performance than traditional asset classes and thus may be used as return enhancers. However, investors expect alternative investments in general, and CTAs in particular, to be efficient in a portfolio context. To assess the extent to which CTAs may be used to improve investors' portfolio diversification, we will study the conditional correlation of the Edhec CTA Index with eight indices (S&P 500, S&P 500 Growth, S&P 500 Value, S&P Small Cap, Lehman Global Treasury/High Yield/Investment Grade/Global Bond Index) and a balanced portfolio made up of 50 percent stocks (i.e., S&P 500) and 50 percent bonds (i.e., Lehman Global Bond Index). We divide our sample (monthly returns from 09/99 through 09/03) into three subsamples (Low, Medium, High). The Low subsample corresponds to the most bearish months of the filtering index, and the High subsample to its most bullish months. We then computed the correlation of the Edhec CTA Index with the other indices for each of the three subsamples. As can be seen from Table 2.3, the Edhec CTA Index is systematically higher in the High subsample than in the Low subsample with both the stock and bond indices. The only exception is the correlation with the S&P Growth 500, which is slightly lower in market declines. A first striking feature is the propensity of the correlation with the Lehman Global Bond Index to remain stable through all market conditions. It is also worth noting that the Edhec CTA Index is systematically negatively correlated with stock indices during large down market trends. On top of that, as shown in the Table, correlations with stock and bond indices tend to be either "Good" or "Stable." No single correlation is significantly lower in the Low subsample than in the High subsample. This leads the CTA index to exhibit put option-like payoffs with respect to equity oriented indices (i.e., negative correlation during market declines, resulting in high positive returns, and low negative correlation during increasing markets, resulting in slightly negative returns) and straddlelike behavior with respect to most bond-oriented indices. In other words, CTAs may play the role of portfolio insurers. This interesting profile coupled with relatively low volatility suggests that CTAs are not only return enhancers but also risk reducers.

TABLE 2.3 Edhec CTA Global Index Conditional Correlations with Stock and Bond Indices, 1999 to 2003

	Correlation with Edhec CTA Global Index				
	Low	Med	High	High–Low	T-stats
S&P 500	–52.92%	0.53%	–24.79%	Good	(1.16)
S&P 500 Value	–49.55%	6.56%	–11.77%	Good	(0.96)
S&P Small Cap	–46.37%	13.03%	12.29%	Good	(1.26)
Lehman High Yield Index	–62.96%	29.75%	–17.31%	Good	(–0.19)
Balanced Portfolio (50% Stocks + 50% Bonds)	–45.04%	18.04%	11.90%	Good	(1.00)
S&P 500 Growth	–28.47%	6.61%	–29.54%	Stable	(1.95)*
Lehman Global Bond Index	23.59%	20.52%	25.60%	Stable	(–3.50)*
Lehman Global Treasury Index	26.31%	–7.71%	36.30%	Stable	(–4.40)*
Lehman Investment Grade Index	18.79%	–41.99%	39.83%	Stable	(–3.93)*

When the correlation differential between high and low subsamples is greater (lower) than 25 percent (–25 percent), the correlation of the Edhec index with the benchmark is regarded as a good (bad) correlation. When the correlation differential is between –25 percent and 25 percent, the correlation is regarded as Stable.
*Denotes significance at 5 percent level.

If CTAs offer good diversification potential while posting attractive risk-adjusted performance, this should be reflected with a translation of efficient frontiers to the top-left corner of the graph in Figure 2.2. Note that to take extreme risks into account, we defined the risk dimension as the modified VaR with 99 percent confidence level. Comparing the efficient frontier of stocks and bonds (S&P 500 + LGBI) and that of a balanced portfolio with CTAs (Balanced Portfolio + Edhec CTA Global), both represented by dashed lines in Figure 2.2, it is clear that CTAs can both reduce the risk and enhance the performance of the balanced portfolio. This fact should encourage investors to reconsider their strategic allocation to CTAs. However, to tap the diversification potential of CTAs in an optimal manner, investors need to have a better understanding of the extent to which CTAs differ from traditional asset classes. Such an understanding naturally implies better knowledge of the risk factors that drive their performance.

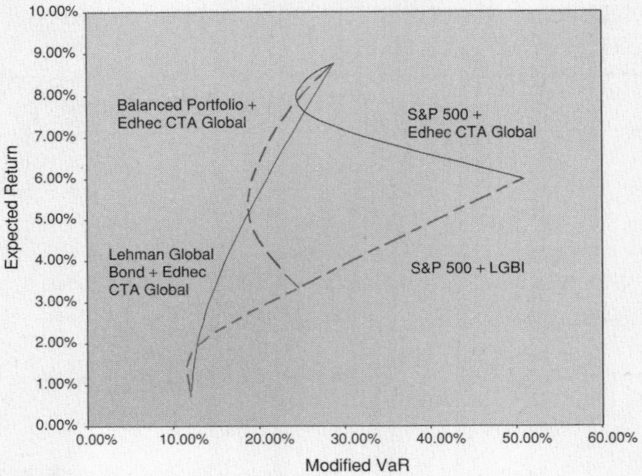

FIGURE 2.2 Efficient Frontiers, January 1997 to September 2003

OVERVIEW OF KEY PERFORMANCE DRIVERS OF CTAS

CTAs offer very attractive properties on a stand-alone basis as well as in a portfolio. To best allocate them, however, investors need to know which risk factors drive their performance. To do so, one may want to carry out a factor analysis with dozens of risk factors on a randomly selected CTA index. This would obviously lead to a high in-sample adjusted R^2, but the robustness of the results would certainly be low. Because the different CTA indices rely on different databases and are constructed according to diverse methodologies, it is highly probable that their returns are driven by different risk factor exposures (see Table 2.1). To circumvent the data snooping issue, we focused on the same 16 factors selected for the factor analysis presented in Table 2.1. We then applied stepwise regression with the backward entry procedure. To circumvent the index heterogeneity issue, we ran the analysis on the Edhec CTA Index. The advantage is twofold: First, the index is, by construction, more representative of the investment universe. Second, it is less prone to measurement biases such as survivorship, backfilling, or stale price bias. This second point is crucial because, as evidenced in Asness, Krail, and Liew (2001) and Okunev and White (2002), biases, and especially stale prices, may entail a significant downward bias with respect to risk factor exposure measurement. We should thus be able to identify purer risk factor exposures with the Edhec CTA Index.

As can be seen from Table 2.4, the Edhec CTA Index is exposed to five main factors: one stock market factor (S&P 500), one bond market factor

TABLE 2.4 Edhec CTA Index Risk Factors Exposure, September 1999 to September 2003

Risk Factors	Edhec	T-stats
Constant	4.54E-03	1.5
S&P 500	–0.11	–2.0
LEHMAN GLB. U.S. TREASURY	0.69	3.1
US $ MAJOR CURRENCY	–0.47	–2.0
US $ TO JAPANESE YEN	–0.41	–2.8
Goldman Sachs Commodity Index	0.17	3.5
Adj. R^2	0.42	

(Lehman Global Treasury), two currency factors (USD vs. major currency and USD vs. Japanese yen) and one commodity factor (Goldman Sachs Commodity Index [GSCI]). The most important factor turns out to be the GSCI, which stresses the still-prevalent exposure of CTAs to the commodity market. CTAs also appear to be strongly exposed to interest rates, with a long position on the Lehman U.S. Treasury Index. The other statistically significant factors are ones related to the foreign exchange market, with coefficients indicating that CTAs held long net positions on the USD over the analysis period (especially against the Japanese yen). Not surprisingly, the index return is negatively correlated with the S&P 500 return, which is consistent with the fact that CTAs post their best performance in large market declines.

To validate the influence of the aforementioned risk factors, we study the average performance of the Edhec CTA Index conditioned on the performance level of the risk factors. We again divide our sample into three subsamples corresponding to the most bearish (Low), stable (Medium), and most bullish (High) months for the five factors selected. The results are summarized in Table 2.5. The T-stats in the last column correspond to tests of the differences between Low/Med, Med/High, and Low/High subsample averages, respectively. Statistically significant differences at the 5 percent level are followed by an asterisk. Interestingly, the difference in mean returns is significant four out of five times between Low and Medium subsamples. In the same vein, it is worth noting that the average return obtained by the Edhec CTA Index in the Low subsample is particularly high in three out of four cases. This is especially true when considering the equity risk factor (i.e., S&P 500), which confirms the fact that CTAs are akin to portfolio insurance (i.e., long position on a put option on the S&P 500). Also, it is worth not-

TABLE 2.5 Edhec CTA Index Conditional Performance, September 1999 to September 2003

	Low	Med	High	T-stats
S&P 500	2.40%[a]	–0.86%	0.49%[b]	5.30* / –1.81* / 1.92*
LEHMAN GLB. U.S. TREASURY	–1.09%[c]	0.59%[b]	2.44%[a]	–1.79* / –2.34* / –3.97*
US $ MAJOR CURRENCY	1.78%[a]	–0.38%[c]	0.59%[b]	2.55* / –1.47 / 1.19
US $ TO JAPANESE YEN	1.39%[a]	–0.26%[c]	0.86%[a]	2.02* / –1.17 / 0.69
Goldman Sachs Commodity Index	0.02%[b]	0.34%[b]	1.59%[a]	–0.25 / –1.71 / –1.39

[a]Above average
[b]Below average but positive
[c]Below average and negative
*Significant at 5% level

ing that the Edhec CTA Index payoff resembles a long position on a put option on currency risk factors and a long position on a call option on the GSCI. We can thus conclude that the performance of the Edhec CTA Index is clearly affected by the evolution of the risk factors selected.

A word of caution is in order. Even if CTA managers generally continue to invest in the same markets and follow the same investment strategies, they may engage in various factor timing strategies to take advantage of macroeconomic trends. In other words, they tend to increase or decrease their exposure to specific markets according to their expectations, which may in turn lead to a change in factor exposures. To illustrate this phenomenon we ran regressions using two-year rolling windows starting from September 1999 through August 2001, each time with one nonoverlapping observation. We thus obtained betas from September 2001 through September 2003. Results are presented in Figure 2.3. It is interesting to note that the exposure to the Lehman Global U.S. Treasury Index, although evolving through time, remains high (around 1.00) during the whole period. This is in contrast with the beta with respect to the S&P 500 index, which remains relatively low (around 0) with a steady down trend until April 2003. The exposure to the GSCI is symmetrical to that of the S&P 500, showing an up trend from January 2003 though September 2003. In the same vein, over the period of analysis CTA managers progressively increased their bet on the rise of the USD against the yen while taking opposing bets on the USD versus

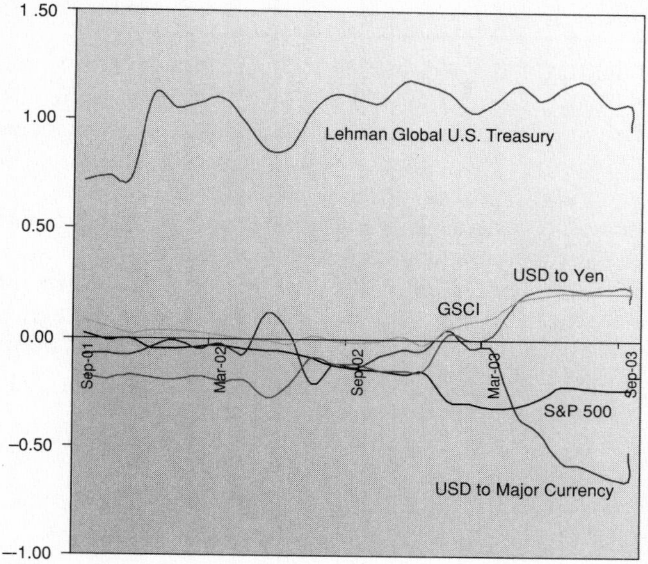

FIGURE 2.3 Edhec CTA Index Factor Exposure Evolution, September 1999 to September 2003
Source: Edhec Risk.

major currencies. Investors must obviously be aware of such time-varying effects when considering investment in CTAs.

Three conclusions may be drawn from this analysis.

1. The five risk factors selected can explain a significant part of the Edhec CTA Index variance.
2. The exposure of the Edhec CTA Index to these risk factors appears to be nonlinear.
3. Risk factor exposures evolve through time, suggesting that multifactor models such as the one we use may not be suited for performance measurement purposes.

As largely documented in the literature, it would be interesting to integrate conditional factor models (Gregoriou 2003b; Gupta, Cerrahoglu, and Daglioglu 2003; Kat and Miffre 2002; Kazemi and Schneeweis 2003) and/or models including nonlinear risk factors (see Agarwal and Naïk 2004; Fung and Hsieh 1997a, 2002b, 2003; Schneeweis, Spurgin, and Georgiev 2001) to better benchmark CTA performance.

CONCLUSION

Like hedge funds, CTAs are destined to play an important role in the diversification strategy of institutional investors. As evidenced in this chapter, they may be considered both risk reducers and return enhancers, due to their specific exposure to a variety of risk factors (e.g., stock markets, interest rates, commodity markets, foreign exchange markets, etc.). This chapter has presented an original method for constructing a representative and pure CTA index that addresses some of the crucial issues investors are facing in the allocation process. It also has analyzed CTA return characteristics and the extent to which investors would be better off integrating CTAs in their global allocation. Further research should now focus on identifying a conditional model with potentially nonlinear risk factors to replicate the Edhec CTA Global Index and measure CTA performance.

CHAPTER 3

Performance of Managed Futures: Persistence and the Source of Returns

B. Wade Brorsen and John P. Townsend

Managed futures investments are shown to exhibit a small amount of performance persistence. Thus, there do appear to be some differences in the skills of commodity trading advisors. The funds with the highest returns used long-term trading systems, charged higher fees, and had fewer dollars under management.

Returns were negatively correlated with the most recent past returns, but the sum of all correlations was positive. Consistent with work in behavioral finance, when deciding whether to invest or withdraw funds, investors put the most weight on the most recent returns. The results suggest that the source of futures fund returns is exploiting inefficiencies.

INTRODUCTION

There is little evidence from past research that the top performing managed futures funds can be predicted (Schwager 1996). Past literature has primarily used variations of the methods of Elton, Gruber, and Rentzler (EGR). Yet EGR's methods have little power to reject the null hypothesis of no predictability (Grossman 1987). Using methods with sufficient power to reject a false null hypothesis, this research seeks to determine whether performance persists for managed futures advisors. The data used are from public funds, private funds, and commodity trading advisors (CTAs). Regression analysis is used to determine whether all funds have the same mean returns. This is done after adjusting for changes in overall returns and differences in leverage. Monte Carlo methods are used to determine the power of EGR's

TABLE 3.1 Descriptive Statistics for the Public, Private, and Combined CTA Data Sets and Continuous Time Returns

Statistic	Public Funds	Private Funds	Combined CTAs
Observations	32,420	23,723	57,018
# Funds	577	435	1,071
Percentage returns			
Mean	0.31	0.62	1.28
SD	7.68	9.22	10.53
Minimum	–232.69	–224.81	–135.48
Maximum	229.73	188.93	239.79
Skewness	–2.08	–0.49	1.14
Kurtosis	133.91	40.70	24.34

methods. Then an out-of-sample test similar to that of EGR is used over longer time periods to achieve greater power. Because some performance persistence is found, we explain the sources of this performance persistence using regressions of (1) returns against CTA characteristics, (2) return risk against CTA characteristics, (3) returns against lagged returns, and (4) changes in investment against lagged returns.

DATA

LaPorte Asset Allocation provided the data, much of which originated from Managed Accounts Reports. The CTA data include information on CTAs no longer trading as well as CTAs who are still trading. The data include monthly returns from 1978 to 1994. Missing values were deleted by deleting observations where returns and net asset value were zero. This should help prevent deleting observations where returns were truly zero. The return data were converted to log changes,[1] so they can be interpreted as percentage changes in continuous time.

The mean returns presented in Table 3.1 show CTA returns are higher than those of public or private returns. This result is consistent with those

[1]The formula used was $r_{it} = \ln(1 + d_{it}/100) \times 100$, where, d_{it} is the discrete time return. The adjustment factor of 100 is used since the data are measured as percentages.

in previous literature. The conventional wisdom as to why CTAs have higher returns is that they incur lower costs. However, CTA returns may be higher because of selectivity or reporting biases. Selectivity bias is not a major concern here, because the comparison is among CTAs, not between CTAs and some other investment. Faff and Hallahan (2001) argue that survivorship bias is more likely to cause performance reversals than performance persistence. The data used show considerable kurtosis (see Table 3.1). However, this kurtosis may be caused by heteroskedasticity (returns of some funds are more variable than others).

REGRESSION TEST OF PERFORMANCE PERSISTENCE

To measure performance persistence, a model of the stochastic process that generates returns is required. The process considered is:

$$r_{it} = \alpha_i + \beta_i \bar{r}_t + \varepsilon_{it}, \qquad i = 1, \ldots, n \text{ and } t = 1, \ldots, T$$
$$\varepsilon_{it} \sim N(0, \sigma_i^2) \tag{3.1}$$

where r_{it} = return of fund (or CTA) i in month t
$\bar{r}_t$= average fund returns in month t
slope parameter β_i = differences in leverage.

The model allows each fund to have a different variance, which is consistent with past research. We also considered models that assumed that β_i is zero, with either fixed effects (dummy variables) for time or random effects instead. These changes to the model did not result in changes in the conclusions about performance persistence.

Only funds/CTAs with at least three observations are included. The model is estimated using feasible generalized least squares. The null hypothesis considered is that all funds have the same mean returns, provided that adjustments have been made for changes in overall returns and differences in leverage. This is equivalent to testing the null hypothesis H_0: $\alpha_i = \bar{\alpha}$ where $\bar{\alpha}$ is an unknown constant.

Analysis of variance (ANOVA) results in Table 3.2 consistently show that some funds and pools have different mean returns than others. This finding does contrast with previous research, but is not really surprising given that funds and pools have different costs. Funds and pools have different trading systems, and commodities traded vary widely. The test used in this study measures long-term performance persistence; in contrast, EGR measures short-term performance persistence.

TABLE 3.2 Weighted ANOVA Table: Returns Regression for Public Funds, Private Funds, and Combined CTA Data

Statistic	Public Funds	Private Funds	Combined CTAs
Sum of squared errors			
Ind. means	1,751	1,948	2,333
Group mean	28,335	10,882	22,751
Corrected total	62,221	36,375	82,408
R^2	0.48	0.35	0.31
Mean α	0.278	0.297	1.099
Variance of α	1.160	2.277	2.240
F-statistics			
α's	2.94	4.32	2.12
β's	47.44	24.10	20.61

Only about 2 to 4 percent of the variation in monthly returns across funds can be explained by differences in individual means. Because the predictable portion is small, precise methods are needed to find it. Without the correction for heteroskedasticity, the null hypothesis would not have been rejected with the public pool data. Even though the predictability is low, it is economically significant. The standard deviations in Table 3.2 are large, implying that 2 to 4 percent of the standard deviation is about 50% of the mean. Thus, even though there is considerable noise, there is still potential to use past returns to predict future returns.

As shown in Table 3.3, the null hypothesis that each fund has the same variance was rejected. This is consistent with previous research that shows some funds or CTAs have more variable returns than others. The rescaled residuals have no skewness, and the kurtosis is greatly reduced. The

TABLE 3.3 *F*-Statistics for the Test of Homoskedasticity Assumption and Jarque-Bera Test of Normality of Rescaled Residuals

Statistic	Public Funds	Private Funds	Combined CTAs
Homoskedasticity	1.41	4.32	5.15
Skewness	−0.17	−0.02	0.35
Relative kurtosis	3.84	3.05	2.72

rescaled residuals have a *t*-distribution so some kurtosis should remain even if the data were generated from a normal distribution. This demonstrates that most of the nonnormality shown in Table 3.1 is due to heteroskedasticity.

MONTE CARLO STUDY

In their method, EGR ranked funds by their mean return or modified Sharpe ratio in a first period, and then determined whether the funds that ranked high in the first period also ranked high in the second period. We use Monte Carlo simulation to determine the power and size of hypothesis tests with EGR's method when data follow the stochastic process given in equation 3.1. Data were generated by specifying values of α, β, and σ. The simulation used 1,000 replications and 120 simulated funds. The mean return over all funds, $\bar{r}_t$, is derived from the values of α and β as:

$$\bar{r}_t = \frac{\frac{\Sigma\alpha_i}{n} + \frac{\Sigma\varepsilon_{it}}{n}}{1 - \frac{\Sigma\beta_i}{n}}$$

where all sums are from $i = 1$ to n.

A constant value of α simulates no performance persistence. For the data sets generated with persistence present, α was generated randomly based on the mean and variance of β's in each of the three data sets. To simulate funds with the same leverage, the β's were set to a value of 0.5. The simulation of funds with differing leverage (which provided heteroskedasticity) used β's with values set to 0.5, 1.0, 1.5, and 2.0.

To match EGR's assumption of homoskedasticity, data sets were generated with the standard deviation set at 2. Heteroskedasticity was created by letting the values of σ be 5, 10, 15, and 20, with one-fourth of the observations using each value. This allowed us to compare the Spearman correlation coefficient calculated for data sets with and without homoskedasticity.

The funds were ranked in ascending order of returns for period one (first 12 months) and period two (last 12 months). From each 24-month period of generated returns, Spearman correlation coefficients were calculated for a fund's rank in both periods. For the distribution of Spearman correlation coefficients to be suitably approximated by a normal, at least 10 observations are needed. Because 120 pairs are used here, the normal approximation is used.

Mean returns also were calculated for each fund in period one and period two, and then ranked. The funds were divided into groups consisting of the top-third mean returns, middle-third mean returns, and bottom-third mean returns. Two additional subgroups were analyzed, the top three highest mean returns funds and the bottom three funds with the lowest mean returns. The means across all funds in the top-third group and bottom-third group also were calculated.

To determine if EGR's test has correct size, it is used with data where performance persistence does not exist (see Table 3.4). If the size is correct, the fail-to-reject probability should be 0.95. When heteroskedasticity is present (data generation methods 2 and 3), the probability of not rejecting is less than 0.95. The heteroskedasticity may be more extreme in actual data, so the problem with real data may be even worse than the excess Type I error found here.

Next, we determine the power of EGR's test by applying it to data where performance persistence really exists (see Table 3.5). The closer the fail-to-reject probability is to zero, the higher is the power. The Spearman correlation coefficients show some ability to detect persistence when large

TABLE 3.4 EGR Performance Persistence Results from Monte Carlo Generated Data Sets: No Persistence Present by Restricting $\alpha = 1$

	Data Generation Method		
Generated Data Subgroups	1[a]	2[b]	3[c]
Mean returns			
top 1/3	1.25	1.25	0.70
middle 1/3	1.25	1.25	0.72
bottom 1/3	1.25	1.22	0.68
top 3	1.25	1.15	0.61
bottom 3	1.26	1.19	0.68
p-values			
reject-positive *z*	0.021	0.041	0.041
reject-negative *z*	0.028	0.037	0.039
fail to reject	0.951	0.922	0.920
test of 2 means			
reject-positive	0.026	0.032	0.032
reject-negative	0.028	0.020	0.026
fail to reject	0.946	0.948	0.942

[a]Data generated using $\alpha = 1$, $\beta = .5$; $\sigma = 2$.
[b]Data generated using $\alpha = 1$, $\beta = .5$; $\sigma = 5, 10, 15, 20$.
[c]Data generated using $\alpha = 1$, $\beta = .5, 1, 1.5, 1$; $\sigma = 5, 10, 15, 20$.

TABLE 3.5 EGR Performance Persistence Results from Monte Carlo Generated Data Sets: Persistence Present by Allowing α to Vary

	Data Generation Method			
Generated Data Subgroups	1[a]	2[b]	3[c]	4[d]
Mean returns				
top 1/3	3.21	2.77	2.57	1.48
middle 1/3	1.87	2.09	1.85	1.30
bottom 1/3	0.80	1.41	1.15	1.14
top 3	4.93	3.47	3.26	1.68
bottom 3	−1.60	1.14	0.86	1.06
p-values				
reject-positive *z*	1.000	0.827	0.823	0.149
reject-negative *z*	0.000	0.000	0.000	0.003
fail to reject.000	0.000	0.173	0.177	0.848
test of 2 means				
reject-positive	1.00	0.268	0.258	0.043
reject-negative	0.000	0.000	0.000	0.012
fail to reject.000	0.000	0.732	0.742	0.945

[a]Data generated using $\alpha = N(1.099, 4.99)$; $\beta = .5, 1, 1.5, 2$; $\sigma = 2$.
[b]Data generated using $\alpha = N(1.099, 4.99)$; $\beta = .5$; $\sigma = 5, 10, 15, 20$.
[c]Data generated using $\alpha = N(1.099, 4.99)$; $\beta = .5, 1, 1.5, 2$; $\sigma = 5, 10, 15, 20$.
[d]Data generated using $\alpha = N(1.099, 1)$; $\beta = .5, 1, 1.5, 2$; $\sigma = 5, 10, 15, 20$.

differences are found in CTA data. But they show little ability to find persistence with the small differences in performance in the public fund data used by EGR. The test of two means has even less ability to detect persistence. Thus, the results clearly can explain EGR's findings of no performance persistence as being due to low power; Table 3.5 does show that EGR's method can find performance persistence that is strong enough.

HISTORICAL PERFORMANCE AS AN INDICATOR OF LATER RETURNS

Results based on methods similar to those of EGR are now provided. The previous Monte Carlo findings were based on a one-year selection period and a one-year performance period. Given the low power of EGR's method, we use longer periods here: a four-year selection period with a one-year performance period, and a three-year selection period with a three-year performance period. Equation (3.1) was estimated for the selection period and the performance period. Because the returns are monthly, funds having fewer than 60 or 72 monthly observations respectively were deleted to avoid having unequal numbers of observations.

The first five-year period evaluated was 1980 to 1984. The next five-year period was 1981 to 1985. Three methods are used to rank the funds: the α's (intercept), the mean return, and the ratio α/σ. For each parameter estimated from the regression, a Spearman rank-correlation coefficient was calculated between the performance measure in the selection period and the performance measure for the out-of-sample period. The null hypothesis is of no correlation between ranks, and the test statistic has a standard normal distribution under the null. Because of losing observations with missing values and use of the less efficient nonparametric method (ranking), this approach is expected to have less power than the direct regression test in (3.1).

Table 3.6 presents a summary of the annual results. Because of the overlap, the correlations from different time periods are not independent, so some care is needed in interpreting the results. All measures show some positive correlation, which indicates performance persistence. Small correlations are consistent with the regression results. Although there is performance persistence, it is difficult to find because of all the other random factors influencing returns.

The return/risk measure (α/σ) clearly shows the most performance persistence. This is consistent with McCarthy, Schneeweis, and Spurgin (1997), who found performance persistence in risk measures. The rankings based on mean returns and those based on α's are similar. Their correlations were similar in each year. Therefore, there does not appear to be as much gain as expected in adjusting for the overall level of returns.

The three-year selection period and three-year trading period show higher correlations than the four-year selection and one-year trading periods except for the early years of public funds. There were few funds in these early years and so their correlations may not be estimated very accurately. Rankings in the three-year performance period are also less variable than in the one-year performance period. The higher correlation with longer trading period suggests that performance persistence continues for a long time. This fact suggests that investors may want to be slow to change their allocations among managers.

The next question is: Why do the results differ from past research? Actually, EGR found similar performance persistence, but dismissed it as being small and statistically insignificant. Our larger sample leads to more powerful tests. McCarthy (1995) did find performance persistence, but his results

TABLE 3.6 Summary of Spearman Correlations between Selection and Performance Periods

Data Set Selection Criterion	Average Correlation	Years Positive (%)	Years Positive and Significant (%)
Four and one[a]			
CTA			
mean returns	0.118	83	25
α	0.114	83	25
α/σ	0.168	100	42
Public funds			
mean returns	0.084	75	33
α	0.088	75	33
α/σ	0.202	83	42
Private funds			
mean returns	0.068	58	17
α	0.047	58	0
α/σ	0.322	92	50
Three and Three[b]			
CTA			
mean returns	0.188	91	55
α	0.186	91	45
α/σ	0.253	100	64
Public funds			
Mean returns	−0.015	45	36
α	0.001	45	36
α/σ	0.149	55	36
Private funds			
Mean returns	0.212	91	36
α	0.221	91	36
α/σ	0.405	100	64

[a]Correlation between a four-year selection period and a one-year performance period. Averages are across the twelve one-year performance periods. The same statistic was used for the rankings in each period.
[b]Three-year selection period and three-year trading period.

are questionable because his sample size was small. McCarthy, Schneeweis, and Spurgin's (1997) sample size was likely too small to detect performance persistence in the mean. Irwin, Krukmeyer, and Zulauf (1992) placed funds into quintiles. Their approach is difficult to interpret and may have led to low power. Schwager (1996) found a similar correlation of 0.07 for mean returns. Schwager, however, found a negative correlation for his return/risk measure. He ranked funds based on return/risk when returns were positive, but ranked on returns only when returns were negative. This hybrid measure may have caused the negative correlation. Therefore, past literature is indeed consistent with a small amount of performance persistence. Performance persistence is found here because of the larger sample size and a slight improvement in methods. As shown in Table 3.6, several years yielded negative correlations, and many positive correlations were statistically insignificant. Therefore, results over short time periods will be erratic.

The performance persistence could be due to either differences in trading skills or differences in costs. There is no strong difference in performance persistence among CTAs, public funds, and private funds.

PERFORMANCE PERSISTENCE AND CTA CHARACTERISTICS

Because some performance persistence was found, we next try to explain why it exists. Monthly percentage returns were regressed against CTA characteristics. Only CTA data are used since little data on the characteristics of public and private funds were available.

Data and Regression Model

Table 3.7 presents the means of the CTA characteristics. The variables listed were included in the regression along with dummy variables. Dummy variables were defined for whether a long-term or medium-term trading system was used. The only variables allowed to change over time were dollars under management and time in existence.

The data as provided by LaPorte Asset Allocation had missing values recorded as zero. If commissions, administrative fees, and incentive fees were all listed as zero, the observations for that CTA were deleted. This eliminated most but not all of the missing values. If commissions were zero, the mean of the remaining observations was imputed.

A few times options or interbank percentages were entered only as a yes. In these cases, the mean of the other observations using options or interbank was imputed. When no value was included for non-U.S., options, or interbank, these variables were given a value of zero. Margins often were entered as a range. In these cases, the midpoint of the range was used. When only a maximum was listed, the maximum was used.

If the trading horizon was listed as both short and medium term, the observation was classed as short term. If both medium and long term or all

TABLE 3.7 Mean and Standard Deviation of CTA Characteristics

Variable	Units	Mean	SD
Commission	% of equity	5.7	4.7
Administrative fee	% of equity	2.5	1.5
Incentive fee	% of profits	19.9	4.5
Discretion	%	27.7	37.9
Non-U.S.	%	17.0	26.3
Options	%	5.3	15.7
Interbank	%	13.9	29.3
Margin	% of equity invested	21.8	10.9
Time in existence	months	55.0	45.4
First year		87.9	4.9
Dollars under management ($million)		34.8	131.6

Note: These statistics are calculated using the monthly data and were weighted by the number of returns in the data set.

three were listed, it was classed as medium term. Any observations with dollars under management equal zero were deleted.

Attempts were made to form variables from the verbal descriptions of the trading system, such as whether the phrase "trend following" was included. No significance was found. These variables are not included in the reported model because many descriptions were incomplete. Thus, the insignificance of the trading system could be due to the errors in the data. The remaining data still may contain errors. The most likely source of error would be treating a missing value as a zero. Also, the data are originally from a survey, and the survey itself could have had some errors. The presence of random errors in the data would cause the coefficients to be biased toward zero. Thus, one needs to be especially careful to not interpret an insignificant coefficient as being zero.

The fees charged are approximately half of what Irwin and Brorsen (1985) reported for public funds in the early 1980s. Thus, the industry appears to have become more competitive over time. The largest reduction of fees is in the commissions charged.

Cross-sectional heteroskedasticity was assumed. Random effects were included for time and for CTA. The conclusions were unchanged when fixed effects were used for time. Considering random effects for CTAs is important because many of the variables do not vary over time. Ignoring random effects could cause significance levels to be overstated.

Regression of Mean Returns on CTA Characteristics

Table 3.8 presents the regressions of monthly percentage returns against CTA characteristics. Short-term horizon traders had lower returns than the long-term and medium-term traders. The coefficient of 0.30 for medium-term traders means that monthly percentage returns are 0.30 higher for medium-term traders than for short-term traders. For comparison, CTA monthly returns averaged 1.28 percent. All three fee variables had positive coefficients. Two of them (administrative and incentive fee) were statistically significant. The fee variables represent the most recent fees. This means that CTAs with larger historical returns charge higher fees. It may also means that CTAs with superior ability are able to charge a higher price. A 20 percent incentive fee corresponds to monthly returns of 0.44 percentage points higher than a CTA with no incentive fee, so the coefficient estimates are large.

TABLE 3.8 Regressions of Monthly Returns versus Explanatory Variables

Variable	Coefficient	*t*-value
Intercept	13.900*	2.08
Long term	0.210*	1.84
Medium term	0.300**	3.20
Commission	0.014	1.31
Administrative fee	0.066**	2.04
Incentive fee	0.022*	1.95
Discretion	−0.001	−0.86
Non-U.S.	0.002	1.22
Options	−0.004	−1.73
Interbank	0.003	1.48
Margin	0.004	1.24
Time in existence	−0.016**	−2.45
First year	−0.145*	−1.91
Dollars under management	−0.00104**	−2.13
F-test for commodity		0.51
F-test for time		9.05**
F-test of homoskedasticity		8.71**

*significant at the 10 percent level
**significant at the 5 percent level

None of the coefficients for discretion, non-U.S., options, interbank, and margin were statistically significant. The set of dummy variables for commodities traded were also not statistically significant. However, the coefficients for options and interbank cannot be considered small since these variables range from zero to 100. Thus, the coefficient of –0.004 means that firms with all trading in options have monthly returns 0.4 percentage points lower than a CTA that did not trade options.

Both the time in existence and the year trading began had negative coefficients. The negative sign is at least partly due to selectivity bias. Some CTAs were added to the database after they began trading. CTAs with poor performance may not have provided data. This could cause CTAs to have higher returns in their first years of trading. A negative sign on the first-year variable suggests that the firms entering the database in more recent years have lower returns. Thus, selectivity bias may be less in more recent years.

CTA returns also may genuinely erode over time. If CTAs do not change their trading system over time, others may discover the same inefficiency through their own testing. Also, the way the CTA trades may be imitated if the CTA tells others about his or her system. CTAs are clearly concerned about this potential problem; most keep their system secret and have employees sign no-compete agreements.

The dollars under management have a negative coefficient. The coefficient implies that for each $1 million under management, returns are 0.00104 percentage points lower. This could be due to increased liquidity costs from larger trade sizes. Returns would go to zero when a CTA had $1 billion under management.

Following Goetzmann, Ingersoll, and Ross's (1997) arguments for hedge funds, managed futures exist because of inefficiencies in the market and because the CTA either faces capital constraints or is risk averse. By the very action of trading, the CTA is acting to remove these inefficiencies. Goetzmann, Ingersoll, and Ross (1997) argue that incentive fees exist partly to keep a manager from accepting too much investment. Dollars under management is a crude measure of excessive investment. Funds that trade more markets or more systems or trade less intensively presumably could handle more investment without decreasing returns.

Regression of the Absolute Value of Residuals on CTA Characteristics

We also estimated a model similar to the one in Table 3.8 to explain the differences in the level of risk of the CTA returns (see Table 3.9). The most important factor determining the level of risk of CTAs is the percentage

TABLE 3.9 Regressions of Absolute Value of Residuals versus CTA Characteristics

Variable	Coefficient	*t*-value
Long term	0.027	0.06
Medium term	0.083	0.24
Commission	0.117*	3.52
Administrative fee	−0.162	−1.37
Incentive fee	0.097*	2.29
Discretion	0.003	0.67
Non-U.S.	−0.013*	−2.39
Options	−0.011	−1.30
Interbank	−0.008	−1.02
Margin	0.092*	7.21
Time in existence	−0.029*	−10.45
First year	−0.260*	−5.34
Dollars under management	−0.001	−0.78
F-test for commodities traded	1.13	
F-test for time	7.74*	
F-test for homoskedasticity	11.96*	

Note: The absolute value of residuals is a measure of riskiness.
*significant at the 5 percent level.

devoted to margins. While diversified funds were the least risky, the difference was not statistically significant. More recent CTAs have lower risk have lowered their risk over time.

Commissions have a positive coefficient, but this may mean only that CTAs who trade larger positions generate more commissions. Incentive fees seem to encourage risk taking. Since the incentive fee is an implicit option (Richter and Brorsen 2000), the CTA should earn higher incentive fees by adopting a more risky strategy. CTAs with more funds in non-U.S. markets tend to have lower risk. Presumably the non-U.S. markets provide some additional diversification.

REGRESSIONS OF RETURNS AGAINST LAGGED RETURNS

To determine the weights to put on various lags, monthly returns were regressed against average returns over each of the last three years and the standard deviation of returns over the last three years combined. The model was estimated assuming cross-sectional heteroskedasticity and fixed effects

TABLE 3.10 Regressions of Monthly Managed Futures Returns against Lagged Returns and Lagged Standard Deviation

Regressor	CTAs	Public	Private
Average returns 1–12 months ago	−0.049* (−1.97)	−0.059 (−2.45)	−0.009 (−0.33)
Average returns 13–24 months ago	0.130* (5.93)	0.160* (7.02)	0.142* (5.46)
Average returns 25–26 months ago	0.069* (3.53)	0.074* (3.74)	0.027 (1.33)
Standard deviation last 3 years	0.056* (4.16)	−0.024 (−1.95)	−0.027 (−1.86)
F-test of time fixed effects	35.38*	83.60*	28.29*

*significant at the 5 percent level.

for time. Ordinary least squares and random effects for time yielded similar results. Random or fixed effects for CTAs are not included because a Monte Carlo study showed that such methods yielded tests with incorrect size.

As shown in Table 3.10 there are cycles in CTA and fund returns. CTAs tend to do well relative to other CTAs every other year. The sum of the three coefficients is positive, which confirms the previous results regarding a small amount of performance persistence. The negative coefficient on returns during the first lagged year supports Schwager's arguments that CTA/fund returns are negatively correlated in the short run.

More risk, as measured by historical standard deviation, leads to higher returns for CTAs. Since CTAs are profitable, CTAs with higher leverage should make higher returns and have more risk. In contrast, both public and private fund returns are negatively related to risk. Thus, risk may differ for reasons other than leverage.

DOES INVESTING IN LOSERS MAKE SENSE?

The regressions versus lagged returns in Table 3.10 offer some support for portfolio rebalancing and for Schwager's (1996) argument that investing with a manager after recent losses is a good idea. The theory behind the argument is that CTAs profit by exploiting inefficiencies and that returns are reduced when more money is devoted to a trading system. This idea is supported here by the results in Table 3.11. Further, the idea is consistent with arguments put forward by Goetzmann, Ingersoll, and Ross (1997).

TABLE 3.11 Regression of Monthly Returns and New Money against Various Functions of Lagged Returns

Variable	Monthly Returns	New Money[a]
1 month ago returns	0.001	0.155*
	(0.04)	(5.94)
1 month ago gains	0.026	−0.107
	(1.24)	(−2.83)
2 months ago returns	−0.083*	0.148*
	(−5.95)	(5.72)
2 months ago gains	0.064*	−0.082
	(3.14)	(−2.12)
3 months ago returns	−0.058*	0.087*
	(4.16)	(3.60)
3 months ago gains	−0.093*	0.001
	(4.55)	(0.03)
Average returns 4–12 months	−0.010	0.550*
	(−0.48)	(13.04)
Average returns 13–24 months	0.134*	0.198*
	(6.12)	(4.61)
Average returns 25–36 months	0.080	0.055
	(4.06)	(1.32)
36-month standard deviation	0.003	−1.3 E−4
	(0.22)	(−0.01)
F-test for time fixed effects	33.33*	2.09

[a]New money represents additions or withdrawals. More money was withdrawn than added so the mean was negative (−0.83 percent per month).
*significant at the 5 percent level.

We also tested whether money flows out as Schwager (1996) suggested. The new money in dollars under management (monthly percentage change in dollars minus percent returns) was regressed against lagged returns and lagged standard deviations. The term "new money" may be a misnomer, because money tends to be withdrawn rather than added. The lags for the most recent three months were separated, and a dummy variable was added for positive returns.

The results in Table 3.11 show that investment and disinvestment are a function of lagged returns. Only returns in the most recent two years were significantly related. The disinvestment due to negative returns is greater than the investment that occurs with positive returns for the most recent two months. This is an indication of some asymmetry. There is no asymmetry for lags greater than three months.

The flow of dollars does not match the changes in expected returns. People put most weight on the recent past and tend to over react to short-run losses. The movement of money out of funds may explain at least part of the short-run negative autocorrelations in returns. Thus, the results do offer some support for Schwager's (1996) hypothesis that money flows out.

PRACTICAL IMPLICATIONS

Some funds and CTAs have higher returns than others. Given the importance of the subject, we will try to address how to select the best funds. Recall, however, that the performance persistence is small and that in some years any method used will do worse than the average across all funds.

Because performance persistence is small relative to the noise in the data, it is important to use a lot of data. Unfortunately, the four-year and three-year selection periods used in this study may be too small. A regression approach would allow using all the data when some funds have two years of data and others eight. But data previous to when the CTA had made a major change in the trading system or a fund had switched advisors should not be used.

Because of the low predictability of performance, it would be difficult to select the single best fund or CTA. Therefore, it might be better to invest in a portfolio of CTAs. Picking CTAs based on returns in the most recent year may even be worse than a strategy of randomly picking a CTA.

CONCLUSION

This research finds a small amount of performance persistence in managed futures. Performance persistence could exist due to differences in either cost or in manager skill. Our results favor skill as the explanation, because returns were positively correlated with cost. A regression model was estimated including the average fund return as a regressor. The regression model indicated some statistically significant performance persistence. The performance persistence is small relative to the variation in the data (only 2 to 4 percent of the total variation), but large relative to the mean.

The regression method was expected to be the method with the highest power. Monte Carlo simulations showed that the methods used in past research often could not reject false null hypotheses and would reject true null hypotheses too often.

Out-of-sample tests confirmed the regression results. There is some performance persistence, but it is small relative to the noise in the data. A return/risk measure showed more persistence than either of the return measures. Although past data can be used to rank funds, precise methods and long time periods are needed to provide accurate rankings.

CTAs using short-term trading systems had lower returns than CTAs with longer trading horizons. CTAs with higher historical returns are now charging higher fees. CTA returns decreased over time and more recent funds have lower returns. At least part of this trend is likely survivorship bias. As dollars under management increased, CTA returns decreased. The finding of fund returns decreasing over time (and as dollars invested increase) suggests that funds exist to exploit inefficiencies.

The dynamics of returns showed small negative correlations for returns in the short run, especially for losses. The net effect over three years is positive, which is consistent with a small amount of performance persistence. The withdrawal of dollars from CTAs shows that investors weight the most recent returns more than would be justified by changes in expected returns.

Although several different methods of analysis were used, the results paint a consistent picture. To adequately select CTAs or funds based on past returns, several years of data are needed.

CHAPTER 4

CTA Performance, Survivorship Bias, and Dissolution Frequencies

Daniel Capocci

Using a database containing 1,892 funds (including 1,350 dissolved funds), we investigate CTA performance and performance persistence to determine if some CTAs consistently and significantly outperform their peers over various time periods. To test the persistence hypothesis, we use a methodology based on Carhart's (1997) decile classification. We examine performance across deciles and across CTA strategies to determine if some deciles are more exposed to certain strategies over time. We also analyze survivorship bias and its evolution over time. We conclude the study by analyzing the dissolution frequencies across deciles and their evolution over time.

INTRODUCTION AND LITERATURE REVIEW

Unlike hedge funds, which appeared in the first academic journal in 1997, commodity trading advisors (CTAs) have been studied for a longer time. Many studies were published in the late 1980s and in the early 1990s (see, e.g., Elton, Gruber, and Rentzler 1987, 1989, 1990; Edwards and Ma 1988). More recently, Billingsley and Chance (1996) and Edwards and Park (1996) showed that CTA funds can add diversification to stocks and bonds in a mean-variance framework. According to Schneeweis, Savanayana, and McCarthy (1991) and Schneeweis (1996), the benefits of CTAs are similar to those of hedge funds, in that they improve and can offer a superior risk-adjusted return trade-off to stock and bond indices while acting as diversifiers in investment portfolios.

Fung and Hsieh (1997b) showed that a constructed CTA style factor persistently has a positive return when the Standard & Poor's (S&P) has a negative return. According to Schneeweis, Spurgin, and Georgiev (2001), CTAs are known to short stock markets regularly. Fung and Hsieh (2001a) analyzed CTAs and concluded that their impact on portfolios is similar to that of a lookback call and a lookback put.[1] Gregoriou and Rouah (2003a) examined whether CTA percent changes in net asset values (NAVs) follow random walks. They found all classifications (except the diversified subindex) to behave as random walks. The effectiveness of CTAs in enhancing risk-return characteristics of portfolios could be compromised when pure random walk behavior is identified. Kat (2002) found that allocating to managed futures allows investors to achieve a very substantial degree of overall risk reduction at limited costs. Managed futures appear to be more effective diversifiers than hedge funds.

Regarding performance, Edwards and Caglayan (2001) concluded that during bear markets, CTAs provide greater downside protection than hedge funds and have higher returns along with an inverse correlation with stocks returns in bear markets. Schneeweis and Georgiev (2002) concluded that careful inclusion of CTA managers into investment portfolios can enhance their return characteristics, especially during severe bear markets. Schneeweis, Spurgin, and McCarthy (1996) observed that performance persistence was virtually inexistent between 1987 and 1995. There is little information on the long-term diligence of these funds (Edwards and Ma 1998; Irwin, Krukemeyer, and Zulauf 1992; Kazemi 1996). Schwager (1996) reviews the literature on CTA performance persistence and conducts his own analysis. He found little evidence that the top-performing funds can be predicted. According to Worthington (2001), between 1990 and 1998 the correlation of managed futures to the S&P 500 during its best 30 months was 0.33 and –0.25 during its worst 30 months. According to Georgiev (2001), one of the drawbacks of CTAs is that during bull markets, their performance is generally inferior to those of hedge funds.

Brorsen and Townsend (2002) show that a minimal amount of performance persistence is found in CTAs, and there could exist some advantages in selecting CTAs based on past performance when a long time series of data is available and accurate methods are used.

This chapter aims to detect performance persistence of CTAs. We want to determine if some CTAs consistently outperform their peers over time. In

---

[1]A lookback call is a normal call option, but the strike depends on the minimum stock price reached during the life of the option. A lookback put is a normal put option, but the strike depends on the maximum stock price reached during the life of the option.

the next section, we describe the database, reporting the descriptive statistics of the funds and analyzing the correlation between the various strategies reported. The following section focuses on survivorship bias. We analyze the presence of this bias over the whole period studied but also over different time periods, including a bull and a bear market period. Further, we report the methodology used to analyze CTA performance and performance persistence before reporting the results of the performance analysis in the next section. The next section reports the results of the persistence analysis and analyzes the exposure of the deciles constructed on previous year's performance to the individual strategies. Then we report the complete analysis of monthly and yearly dissolution frequencies.

DATABASE

In this section, we present our database and analyze the descriptive statistics of the data before reporting the correlation between the various strategies.

Descriptive Statistics

There are several CTA data providers. The providers most commonly used in academic studies are Managed Account Repots, TASS Management, and the Barclay Trading Group, Ltd. The latter represents one of the most (if not the most) comprehensive managed future databases.

For our analysis we use the Barclay Trading Group database, which contains 1,892 individual funds (including 1,350 dissolved funds) over the January 1985 to December 2002 period. The Barclay Trading Group classifies these funds in 7 categories that are subdivided in 17 strategies plus the no-strategy category. We grouped some strategies because they contain too few funds to give interesting results. As shown in Table 4.1, we obtained a total of 11 strategies. Note that we combined only those strategies that are in the same category.

To perform our performance analysis, we will use the whole database and the classifications reported in Table 4.1. This will allow us to determine whether results differ across strategies and whether funds in particular strategies significantly outperform others.

Previous studies often focused on fewer funds. For example, Schneeweis, Spurgin, and McCarthy (1996) studied 56 CTA funds from 1985 to 1991. Irwin, Zulauf, and Ward (1994) used a database containing 363 CTAs from 1979 to 1989. Other studies were larger. For example, Edwards and Park (1996) found 596 CTAs from 1983 to 1992 by supplementing the MAR/LaPorte CTA database with private sources. Diz (1996) and Fung and Hsieh (1997b) had 925 and 901 managed future programs from 1975 to

TABLE 4.1 Grouping of Barclay Trading Group Strategies

Grouped CTA Strategies	Barclay Trading Group Strategy
Technical Diversified	Technical Diversified
Technical Financial/Metals	Technical Financial/Metals
Technical Currency	Technical Currency
Other Technical	Technical Interest Rate Technical Energy Technical Agricultural
Fundamental	Fundamental Diversified Fundamental Interest Rate Fundamental Financial/Metals Fundamental Energy Fundamental Currency Fundamental Agricultural
Discretionary	Discretionary
Systematic	Systematic
Stock Index	Stock Index
Arbitrage	Arbitrage
Option Strategies	Option Strategies
No Category	No Category

Note: The left-hand side of the table reports the strategy classification used throughout the study; the right-hand side contains the original classification of the Barclay Trading Group.

1995, and from 1986 to 1996 respectively. They were both based on the Barclay Trading Group database.

Funds in the Barclay Trading Group database can be classified into more than one strategy. This can lead to a bias when we compare different strategies since they can contain the same funds. In order to deal with this issue, we report each fund in one strategy only.[2]

Before entering the body of the study, we analyze the composition of the database. Table 4.2 reports the descriptive statistics of the database. Funds are classified according to strategy. The last line reports the statistics for the whole database.

[2]Any fund that is reported in two strategies is classified into the one that contains the most funds.

TABLE 4.2 Descriptive Statistics

	CTA Strategies				January 1985–December 2002 (216 months)								
	No. of Funds	% of the Total	Living Funds	Dead Funds	Mean Return	t(mean) = 0	Std. Dev.	Median	Min	Max	Skewness	Kurtosis	Sharpe Ratio
Technical Diversified	264	14%	44	220	1.72	5.38	4.70	0.83	–6.9	31.6	3.02	14.68	0.28
Technical Financial/ Metals	86	5%	11	75	1.78	6.33	4.12	0.95	–5.2	29.8	2.95	14.11	0.33
Technical Currency	58	3%	18	40	1.58	6.49	3.58	1.07	–14.5	15.6	0.64	3.73	0.33
Other technical	8	0%	0	8	3.18	5.35	7.25	1.92	–18.7	47.5	2.00	9.58	0.38
Total technical	416	22%	73	343	1.75	6.33	4.06	0.72	–5.2	25.3	2.92	13.27	0.33
Fundamental	19	1%	2	17	1.83	3.55	7.60	1.17	–20.4	57.4	2.48	16.14	0.19
Discretionary	299	16%	67	232	2.03	9.93	3.01	1.31	–3.9	18.8	2.42	9.24	0.54
Systematic	897	47%	350	547	1.70	4.73	5.27	0.83	–8.3	26.4	1.86	6.35	0.24
Stock Index	52	3%	16	36	1.89	4.39	6.33	1.14	–18.4	38.4	2.05	10.46	0.23
Arbitrage	27	1%	2	25	1.25	5.76	3.19	1.07	–14.8	12.0	–0.36	4.28	0.26
Option strategy	9	0%	0	9	2.62	4.66	8.24	2.57	–23.3	36.5	0.53	2.51	0.27
No Category	180	9%	28	152	1.62	6.20	3.84	0.95	–4.9	28.5	3.14	15.07	0.31
Total	1,899	100%	611	1,288	1.75	6.51	3.95	0.98	–5.2	21.9	2.37	9.06	0.34

t(mean) = 0 reports the t-statistic for the hypothesis that the mean monthly returns equal zero. Std. Dev. = standard deviation; Min = minimum; Max = maximum. The Sharpe ratio is calculated with a 5 percent risk-free rate.

Note: The other technical strategy funds exist only for the August 1985–May 1995 period and for the October 1998–April 2001 period. Option strategy funds exist since September 1990.

Table 4.2 indicates that the systematic strategy is the most represented strategy (with 897 funds) followed by total technical funds (416 funds) and discretionary funds (299 funds). Other technical funds, option strategy funds, and fundamental funds count only 8, 9, and 19 funds respectively. The database contains 611 dissolved funds as a whole, 350 of which follow the systematic strategy. Note that all the other technical funds and option strategy funds are dissolved over the period studied. The median returns indicate the same patterns.

Regarding the statistics, the highest mean monthly return is achieved by the other technical funds (with 3.18 percent per month) followed by the option strategy funds and discretionary funds (with 2.62 percent and 2.03 percent per month). Many strategies offer a monthly return of between 1.6 percent and 1.9 percent per month. The lowest returns are those of the arbitrage funds (with 1.25 percent) followed by the technical currency funds (with a monthly return of 1.58 percent). All the monthly returns are significantly different from zero over the period studied.

The fundamental funds and the other technical funds are the more volatile funds with a standard deviation of 7.60 and 7.25 percent. Because there are few funds applying these strategies, there is no diversification effect, which can explain why the returns of these strategies are so volatile. The strategies that offer the most stable returns are the discretionary funds (with a standard deviation of 3.01 percent) and the arbitrage funds (with a standard deviation of 3.19 percent).

As one could expect, the strategies that are the most volatile also have the lowest minimum return and the highest maximum return. The monthly minimum returns can reach –20.4 percent for the fundamental strategy whereas the maximum of this strategy is 57.4 percent. The returns are usually positively skewed (the only exception is the arbitrage strategy) and their distributions tend to have fat tails, as evidenced by the large values for kurtosis.

When risk and returns are considered together through the Sharpe ratio,[3] the discretionary funds emerge with the highest Sharpe ratio (0.54) followed by other technical funds (with 0.38). Fundamental funds offer a Sharpe ratio of only 0.19.

Correlation Analysis

Table 4.3 reports the correlation coefficients between the various strategies for the January 1985 to December 2002 period. It indicates that the CTA

[3]The Sharpe ratio is the ratio of the excess return over the standard deviation. We use a risk-free rate of 5 percent for this calculation.

TABLE 4.3 Correlation between the CTA Strategies, January 1985 to December 2002

	Allcta	Arb	Discret	Funda	Option	Stock	System	Teccur	Tecdiv	Tecfin	Tecoth	Nocat
AllCTA	1.00	−0.18	0.41	0.25	0.12	0.26	0.98	0.68	0.93	0.73	0.14	0.81
Arb	−0.18	1.00	0.20	−0.02	0.08	0.05	−0.21	−0.18	−0.13	−0.05	0.24	−0.01
Discret	0.41	0.20	1.00	0.14	0.13	0.18	0.27	0.16	0.42	0.27	0.00	0.32
Funda	0.25	−0.02	0.14	1.00	0.01	0.08	0.22	0.17	0.22	0.20	−0.02	0.12
Option	0.12	0.08	0.13	0.01	1.00	0.62	0.12	−0.01	0.03	0.11	0.02	0.12
Stock	0.26	0.05	0.18	0.08	0.62	1.00	0.25	0.09	0.14	0.13	0.01	0.29
System	0.98	−0.21	0.27	0.22	0.12	0.25	1.00	0.70	0.89	0.71	0.18	0.79
Teccur	0.68	−0.18	0.16	0.17	−0.01	0.09	0.70	1.00	0.56	0.56	0.12	0.56
Tecdiv	0.93	−0.13	0.42	0.22	0.03	0.14	0.89	0.56	1.00	0.66	0.05	0.73
Tecfin	0.73	−0.05	0.27	0.20	0.11	0.13	0.71	0.56	0.66	1.00	0.10	0.50
Tecoth	0.14	0.24	0.00	−0.02	0.02	0.01	0.18	0.12	0.05	0.10	1.00	0.9
Nocat	0.81	−0.01	0.32	0.12	0.12	0.29	0.79	0.56	0.73	0.50	0.09	1.00

AllCTA = CTA Global Index; Arb = arbitrage; Discret = discretionary; Funda = fundamental; Stock = stock index; System = systematic funds; Teccur = technical currency; Tecdiv = technical diversified; Tecfin = technical financial/metals; Tecoth = other technical; Nocat = no category.

global index is almost exactly correlated with the systematic funds. This can be partly explained by the fact that this strategy contains the greatest number of funds. Forty-four coefficients out of sixty-six (66 percent of the coefficients) are under 0.5, indicating that most of the strategies are not correlated. The lowest coefficient is the one between arbitrage and systematic funds at –0.21. There are nine negative coefficients in total representing 14 percent of the coefficients.

SURVIVORSHIP BIAS

Performance figures are subject to various biases. One of the most important is the survivorship bias that appears when only surviving funds are taken into account in a performance analysis study. The common practice among suppliers of CTA databases is to provide data on investable funds that are currently in operation. When only living funds[4] are considered, the data suffer from survivorship bias because dissolved funds tend to have worse performance than surviving funds.

Survivorship bias has already been studied. Fung and Hsieh (1997b) precisely analyzed this bias and estimated it at 3.4 percent per year. They also concluded that survivorship bias had little impact on the investment styles of CTA funds. Returns of both surviving and dissolved CTA funds have low correlation to the standard asset classes.

Survivorship Bias over Various Time Periods

Here we analyze the presence of survivorship bias in CTAs returns over various long-term time periods. We first study the whole period covered before dividing it into subperiods.

Table 4.4 reports the survivorship bias obtained from our database. Survivorship bias is calculated as the performance difference between surviving funds and all funds. All returns are monthly and net of all fees. The first part of the table indicates a survivorship bias of 5.4 percent per year for the entire period. This figure is higher than the one obtained in previous studies. Table 4.4 shows the bias was higher during the 1990 to 1994 period (7.3 percent) and during the 1995 to 1999 period (6.2 percent) but lower during the 2000 to 2003 period (4.4 percent).

[4]By "living funds" we mean funds still in operation at the moment of the analysis.

TABLE 4.4 Survivorship Bias Analysis over Different Periods

Bias 1985–2003	0.5	per Month
	5.4	per Year
Bias 1985–1989	0.5	per Month
	5.5	per Year
Bias 1990–1994	0.6	per Month
	7.3	per Year
Bias 1995–1999	0.5	per Month
	6.2	per Year
Bias 2000–2003	0.4	per Month
	4.4	per Year

Our database contains 1,899 CTAs (611 survived funds and 1,288 dissolved funds as of December 2002).

Survivorship Bias over Time

Figure 4.1 reports the evolution of the survivorship bias calculated on a three-year rolling period starting January 1985 to December 1987 and ending January 2000 to December 2002. It allows us to analyze more precisely how the survivorship evolves over time.

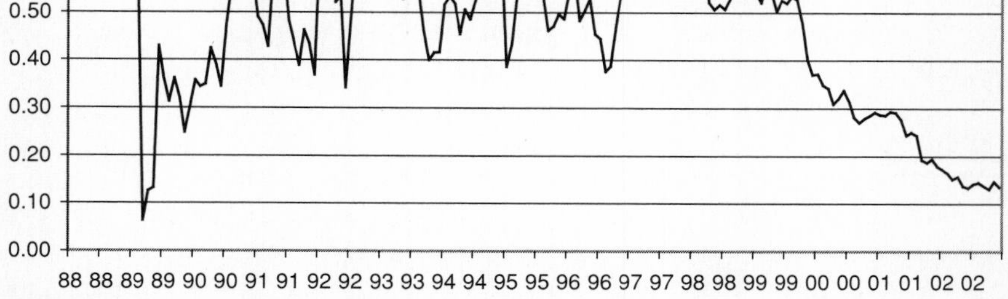

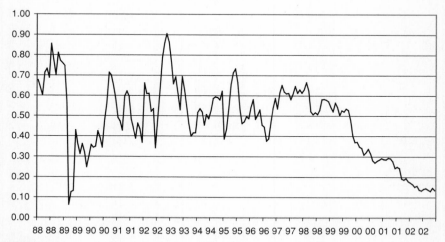

FIGURE 4.1 Evolution of the Survivorship Bias (3-year Rolling Period)
Our database contains 1,899 CTAs (611 survived funds and 1,288 dissolved funds as of December 2002). Numbers on the vertical axis are monthly percentages.

The figure indicates that the monthly bias ending January 1985 increases from around 0.7 percent at the beginning of the year to 0.85 percent after summer before reaching the bottom of 0.9 percent at the beginning of 1989. Afterward, it increases until January 1993 (0.9 percent) and then decreases to a mean around 0.55 percent for the periods ending between January 1994 and January 2000. Because the three-year periods end January 2000, the monthly survivorship bias decreases almost constantly to 0.12 percent in December 2002.

We analyze these results to determine how such variations are possible. On one hand, the sharp decrease in the January 1989 results (and the slow increase that follows) can be explained by the fact that the surviving funds underperformed the whole database in 1988 and 1989. The first underperformance was in December 1988 (1.87 percent for the surviving funds against 2.94 percent for the whole database). Moreover, this was the first major underperformance, which has been followed by others during the negative months in 1989 (e.g., –3.9 percent against –1.85 percent in March, –2.54 percent against –0.91 percent in April). On the other hand, the sharp increase in survivorship bias over the period ending November and December 1992 can be explained mainly by high overperformance in June, July, and August 1992 with an average of 3 percent monthly outperformance. To summarize, this figure identifies epochs during which surviving funds outperformed the whole database, and during which the difference between surviving funds and dissolved funds was less important.

We also analyze the survivorship bias calculated over the positive and negative months[5] for the whole database. Interestingly, Table 4.5 indicates that the mean survivorship bias is the same over the three periods studied at 0.48 percent. The standard deviation and the median of the survivorship are also almost equal. The only significant difference is in the minimum three-year rolling period, which is much higher for the negative months at 0.13 percent versus 0.06 percent for the whole period and the positive months. The maximum is also almost equal between 0.87 percent and 0.90 percent.

METHODOLOGY

The aim of this study is to determine if some CTAs consistently and persistently outperform their peers. To achieve this objective, we construct a CTA Global Index that contains all the funds present in our database and

[5]We take a month as a positive month if the whole database has a positive performance. We consider a month as negative if the whole database does not reach positive returns.

TABLE 4.5 Descriptive Statistics of the 3-Year Rolling-Period Survivorship Bias

	Mean	Std. Dev.	Median	Min	Max
Whole period	0.48	0.18	0.51	0.06	0.90
Positive months	0.48	0.18	0.51	0.06	0.90
Negative months	0.48	0.18	0.52	0.13	0.87

Std. dev. = standard deviation; Min = minimum; and Max = maximum of the 3-year rolling-period survivorship bias calculated over the whole period studied (January 1985–December 2002).

one index per CTA strategy. To test if some funds significantly outperform the indices, we use the following regression.

$$R_{pt} = \alpha_P + \beta_{p1} R_{It} + \varepsilon_{pt} \tag{4.1}$$
$$p = 1 \text{ to } 1{,}899 \text{ and } t = 1 \text{ to } 216$$

where R_{Pt} = return of CTA p at period t
R_{It} = return of the index considered at period t

We run this analysis for each fund compared to the whole CTA database index but also for each fund compared to its strategy index. Once we obtain results, we want to determine if momentum is present in CTA returns. Active CTA selection strategies could increase the expected return on a portfolio if CTA performance is really predictable. We define the hypothesis that a CTA with an above-average return in this period also will have an above-average return in the next period as the hypothesis of persistence in performance. Sirri and Tufano (1998) and Zheng (1999) stressed the importance of persistence analysis in mutual funds. They document large inflows of money into last year's best performers and withdrawals from last year's losers. Capocci and Hübner (2004) have stressed this for hedge funds. They find that newly invested money in these best-performing mutual funds is a predictor of future fund performance.

We apply the methodology of Carhart (1997) to our simple model. All funds are ranked based on their previous year's return. Every January we place all funds into 10 equally weighted portfolios, ranked from highest to lowest past returns. Portfolios 1 (High) and 10 (Low) are then further subdivided on the same measure. The portfolios are held until the following January and then rebalanced. This yields a time series of monthly returns on each decile portfolio from January 1985 to December 2002. Funds that disappear during the course of the year are included in the equal-weighted average until they disappear, then portfolio weights are readjusted appropriately.

Finally, in the last part of the study we want to determine empirically if some strategies are consistently better than others. To achieve this objective we use the next regression.

$$R_{Dt} = \alpha_P + \sum_{i=1}^{12} \beta_{P1} R_{It} + \varepsilon_{Pt} \tag{4.2}$$

$$P = 1 \text{ to } 10 \text{ and } t = 1 \text{ to } 216$$

where R_{Dt} = return of decile P at period t
R_{It} = return of the 12 indexes (CTA Global Index, technically currency, technically diversified, technically financial/metals, technically others, stock index, options, systematic, arbitrage, discretionary, fundamental, no category) at period t

We regress each decile against the CTA Global Index and each strategy index. Doing so, we determine if some deciles are exposed to some strategies, which indicates that that strategy is particularly present in the corresponding decile.

PERFORMANCE ANALYSIS

Here we apply the model just discussed to our database to determine if some strategies significantly outperform the CTA Global Index over different time periods. In the next section we investigate whether momentum exists in CTA performance.

Table 4.6 indicates some interesting results. First, we see that results are different across strategies, indicating that the classification in substrategies seems to be relevant. Second, the first column of the table reports the alpha of the different strategies once the performance of the CTA database considered as a whole is taken into account through the CTA Global Index. This is the performance not explained by the global CTA index. Seven out of the 11 strategies are significantly positive at the 5 or 1 percent significance level (technically financial/metals, technically currency, technically other, discretionary, stock index, arbitrage, and option strategies); two are not significantly different from zero (fundamental and no category); and two are significantly negative (technically diversified and systematic). These results indicate that all but two strategies produce returns significantly different from zero, which means that the individual strategies produce returns significantly different from their aggregation.[6]

[6]The CTA Global Index is composed of all the individual funds classified in the various strategies. It is the same funds classified differently.

TABLE 4.6 Relative Performance Analysis of Strategy Indices

	Alpha	CTA Index	R^2
Technically diversified	−0.28***	1.14***	0.92
Technically financial and metals	0.65**	0.64***	0.38
Technically currency	0.92***	0.38***	0.18
Technically other	2.56***	0.33**	0.04
Fundamental	0.52	0.56*	0.08
Discretionary	1.23***	0.39***	0.29
Systematic	−0.58***	1.30***	0.95
Stock	1.86***	−0.07	0.00
Arbitrage	1.01***	0.12*	0.02
Option	2.03***	0.53	0.03
No category	0.16	0.83***	0.74

This table reports the results of the regression from the strategy subindices to the whole database for the January 1985 to December 2002 period except for technically others (August 1985 to May 1995 and October 1998 to April 2001) and for option strategies (September 1990–December 2002).
t-stat are heteroskedasticity consistent.
***Significant at the 1 percent level.
**Significant at the 5 percent level.
*Significant at the 10 percent level.
Numbers in the table are monthly percentages.

The positive alphas range from a monthly percentage difference of 0.65 percent for technically financial/metals to 2.03 percent for option strategies; the negative alphas are −0.28 percent for technically diversified funds and −0.58 percent for systematic funds.

Third, most betas are significantly positive at the 1 percent significance level. For four strategies (fundamental, stock index, arbitrage, and option) the beta is either significant at the 10 percent level or not significant. These strategies all contain 52 funds or less, which means that they represent only a small part of the index. This fact partly explains their limited exposure to the CTA Global Index.

Finally, the R^2 column reports very different numbers. The R^2 ranges from 0.00 for stock funds to 0.95 for systematic funds. As we could have expected, the highest R^2 are obtained when the alphas are the lower and particularly low when the beta is not significant.

Table 4.7 reports the same results over different subperiods. We divide the analysis in three six-year periods (January 1985 to December 1990, Jan-

TABLE 4.7 Subperiod Performance Analysis of the Various CTA Strategies

Panel 1: Subperiod analysis

Jan 1985–Dec 1990	Alpha	CTA Index	R^2	Jan 1991–Dec 1996	Alpha	CTA Index	R^2
Tech divers.	−0.52**	1.20***	0.94	Tech divers.	−0.08	1.04***	0.89
Tech fin/met	1.55**	0.58***	0.30	Tech fin/met	0.44**	0.74***	0.62
Tech currency	1.73***	0.24**	0.08	Tech currency	0.30	0.85***	0.48
Tech other	3.82***	0.25*	0.03	Tech other	1.18	0.60	0.07
Fundamental	1.46	0.53	0.08	Fundamental	0.69	0.52**	0.07
Discretionary	2.53***	0.36***	0.26	Discretionary	0.93***	0.29***	0.22
Systematic	−1.25***	1.30***	0.96	Systematic	−0.50***	1.48***	0.97
Stock	3.66***	−0.28	0.03	Stock	0.54*	0.44**	0.17
Arbitrage	2.49***	0.15**	0.10	Arbitrage	0.54***	0.08	0.01
Option	NA	NA	NA	Option	1.29	0.79	0.04
No category	0.50*	0.90***	0.78	No category	0.04	0.62***	0.78

Panel 1 *(cont.)*: Subperiod analysis — Panel 2: Bull market analysis

Jan 1997–Dec 2002	Alpha	CTA Index	R^2	Jan 1998–Mar 2000	Alpha	CTA Index	R^2
Tech divers.	−0.09	0.92***	0.85	Tech divers.	−0.46**	1.11***	0.89
Tech fin/met	0.10	0.58***	0.44	Tech fin/met	0.56**	0.46***	0.43
Tech currency	0.49***	0.49***	0.33	Tech currency	0.86**	0.37**	0.17
Tech other	2.64*	−0.29	0.01	Tech other	NA	NA	NA
Fundamental	−0.35	0.47	0.03	Fundamental	0.72	0.07	0.00
Discretionary	0.62***	0.24***	0.13	Discretionary	0.81**	0.37**	0.15
Systematic	−0.26***	1.37***	0.98	Systematic	−0.37***	1.4***	0.98
Stock	1.21***	0.20	0.03	Stock	2.67***	−0.20	0.02

TABLE 4.7 *(continued)*

Jan 1997–Dec 2002	Alpha	CTA Index	R^2	Jan 1998–Mar 2002	Alpha	CTA Index	R^2
Arbitrage	0.73*	−0.75***	0.20	Arbitrage	0.51	−0.86***	0.27
Option	2.58***	0.25	0.01	Option	3.73***	−0.64	0.05
No category	0.34***	0.44***	0.39	No category	0.36**	0.23	0.19

Panel 2 *(cont.)*: Bear market analysis				Panel 3: 10-year analysis			
April 2000–Dec 2002	Alpha	CTA Index	R^2	Jan 1993–Dec 2002	Alpha	CTA Index	R^2
Tech divers.	0.08	0.84***	0.87	Tech divers.	−0.10	1.00***	0.85
Tech fin/met	0.15	0.49***	0.40	Tech fin/met	0.14	0.71***	0.51
Tech currency	0.22	0.51***	0.39	Tech currency	0.36***	0.58***	0.33
Tech other	3.43*	−0.50	0.04	Tech other	1.72*	−0.23	0.01
Fundamental	−1.81*	0.93*	0.11	Fundamental	0.62	0.34	0.02
Discretionary	0.56***	0.17**	0.11	Discretionary	0.70***	0.32***	0.20
Systematic	−0.21***	1.35***	0.98	Systematic	−0.33***	1.36***	0.97
Stock	0.42	0.24	0.05	Stock	0.99***	0.21*	0.03
Arbitrage	1.33**	−0.90**	0.24	Arbitrage	0.72***	−0.43**	0.09
Option	1.59**	0.26	0.02	Option	2.20***	0.18	0.00
No category	0.28	0.54***	0.45	No category	0.33***	0.48***	0.49

t-stat are heteroskedasticity consistent.

Tech. divers. = technical diversified; tech. fin/met = technical financial/metals; tech. cur = technical currency; tech. other = other technical; stock = stock index.

***Significant at the 1 percent level.

**Significant at the 5 percent level.

*Significant at the 10 percent level.

Numbers in the table are monthly percentages.

uary 1991 to December 1996, January 1997 to December 2002) in Panel 1 before isolating bull and bear market periods in the last subperiod in Panel 2. These periods are January 1998 to March 2000 for the bull market and April 2000 to December 2002 for the bear market. This last analysis is particularly interesting because we can determine how the strategies perform compared to their peers during a bull and a bear market. For information purposes we also include a 10-year analysis in Panel 3.

Results reported in Panel 1 indicate that few alphas change sign over the subperiods, and no alpha that was significantly positive or negative for the whole period becomes significantly negative or positive over the subperiods.

The first line indicates that technically diversified funds underperform the CTA Global Index over each subperiod, but this underperformance is significant only over the first and last subperiods. Panel 2 indicates that this strategy underperforms during the bull market and that it slightly outperforms (but not significantly) during the bear market. Over a 10-year period, this strategy slightly underperformed. The adjusted R^2 is high over each of the subperiods analyzed.

Panel 1 indicates that technically financial/metals, technically currency, technically other, stock funds, arbitrage, option, and no category funds outperform over some subperiods and are in line with the CTA Global Index over other. Discretionary and systematic funds always outperform their peers. Fundamental funds never significantly add to the performance of the CTA Global Index.

Panel 2 is interesting because it indicates when specific strategies perform better than their peers. Technically financial/metals and technically currency, stock funds, and the no-category funds perform better than their peers during bull markets, while arbitrage funds perform better during bear markets. Technically diversified funds significantly underperform in bull markets without deviating significantly from their peers in bear markets. Discretionary, systematic, and option funds always perform better than their peers whereas systematic funds always perform worse. Finally, fundamental funds perform in line with the CTA Global Index.

Let us now compare the subperiods one by one instead of analyzing how a strategy performed over each subperiod. In Panel 1, we see that few alphas are significant over the January 1991 to December 1996 period. This indicates that most of the strategies are in line with the CTA Global Index. We see this pattern also in Panel 2, where most strategies out- or underperform significantly during the bull market while few do so during the bear market. Finally, over the 10-year period, many strategies significantly outperform the CTA Global Index. Astonishingly, technically diversified and technically financial/metals that respectively significantly under- and outperform during the whole January 1985 to December 2002 period do not significantly deviate from the index over the last 10 years.[7]

Regarding the exposure to the index, some strategies (technically diversified, technically financial/metals, technically currency, discretionary, systematic) are always significantly exposed whereas others (technically other and arbitrage funds) are exposed over some subperiods without always being exposed. Fundamental, stock, and options funds are never or almost never exposed to the index.

The adjusted R^2 does not change heavily over the subperiods analyzed. The biggest variations in this coefficient occur for technically financial/metals from 0.30 for the January 1985 to December 1990 period to 0.62 for the January 1991 to December 1996 period, for technically currency funds from 0.08 over the January 1985 to December 1990 period to 0.48 for the January 1991 to December 1996 period and for the no-category funds from 0.78 for the January 1991 to December 1996 period to 0.39 over the December 1997 to December 2002 period.

Individual Fund Results

In this subsection we determine if the results obtained for the whole database are confirmed for individual funds. We will not report the results obtained for all the funds, but we will summarize. The first step in this analysis is to apply a filter on the database. To be included in the database, each fund must have at least 24 months of data. We delete 385 funds to reach a total of 1,508 funds. Then we apply the model to each individual fund regressed over the CTA Global Index. Results are summarized in Table 4.8.

The table indicates that 13.7 percent of the funds significantly outperform the index at the 1 percent significance level over the period studied. Another 8.0 percent of the funds outperform at the 5 percent level. However, 11.7 percent of the funds significantly underperform at the 1 percent significance level, and 5.7 percent do so at the 5 percent significance level. The right side of Table 4.8 indicates that 49.9 percent of the funds are positively significantly exposed to the CTA Global Index at the 1 percent significance level. Another 10.3 percent of the funds are significantly positively exposed to the index at the 5 percent significance level. Few funds are significantly negatively exposed to the CTA Global Index. 1.0 percent

[7]Logically, however, they respectively under- and outperformed during the first subperiod reported in Panel 1.

TABLE 4.8 Summary of the Individual Results of the Performance Analysis, January 1985 to December 2002

	Positive Alphas			Positive CTA Global Index Exposition		
Significance level	1%	5%	10%	1%	5%	10%
Number of funds	207	120	88	753	156	88
Percentage	13.7%	8.0%	5.8%	49.9%	10.3%	5.8%
	Negative Alphas			**Negative CTA Global Index Exposition**		
Significance level	1%	5%	10%	1%	5%	10%
Number of funds	176	86	84	15	24	20
Percentage	11.7%	5.7%	5.6%	1.0%	1.6%	1.3%

t-stat are heteroskedasticity consistent.
Numbers in the table are monthly percentages.

are exposed at the 1 percent significance level and 1.6 percent are exposed at the 5 percent significance level.

These results are interesting because they indicate that, as a whole, 21.7 percent of the funds significantly outperform the CTA Global Index while 15.4 percent significantly underperform. Outperformance is one thing; persistence is another. It will be interesting to determine if this outperformance is persistent and predictable or not. It is not surprising that most funds are significantly exposed to the index. However, there are some funds that are significantly negatively exposed to the index.

Table 4.9 reports descriptive statistics on the estimated coefficients. The average alpha is 0.14 percent (median 0.107 percent) with a standard devi-

TABLE 4.9 Descriptive Statistics of the Individual Performance Estimation, January 1985 to December 2002

	Mean	Std. Dev.	Median	Min	Max
Alpha	0.14%	1.84	0.11%	−8.06%	22.09%
CTA Global Index	0.89%	1.07	0.69%	−6.24%	5.45%
R^2	0.18	0.21	0.09	−0.04	0.87

Min = minimum; Max = maximum.
Std. Dev. = standard deviation; t-stat are heteroskedasticity consistent.
Numbers in the table are monthly percentages.

ation of 1.84 percent. The average beta (in our case the beta is measured relative to our CTA Global Index) is 0.89. This means that the average CTA is not completely exposed to the market. This number can be compared to the beta of a portfolio with an equity index like the S&P 500. The only difference is the reference index.

The average R^2 is 0.18 percent with a standard deviation of 0.21 percent. These figures may seem to be low, but R^2 is always lower for individual funds than it is for indexes. The minimum and maximum are respectively –0.04 and 0.87 indicating that the index explains almost 90 percent of the fund's performance.

PERSISTENCE IN PERFORMANCE

Now we want to determine if there is persistence in CTA performance. To achieve this objective, we rank the funds in deciles D1 through D10 each year based on previous performance. Decile 1 contains the worst-performing funds, while decile 10 contains the best-performing funds. We also divide the two extreme deciles (D1 and D10) into three subdeciles.

Global Results

Table 4.10 reports the descriptive statistics of each decile. It shows some interesting features. The mean returns are more or less stable between decile D1 and D7. The only exception is D6, which is slightly higher. Then, between D8 and D10, the increase is more pronounced. The last three deciles offer a higher performance. The median returns show the same pattern with lower figures. The standard deviation indicates that top-performing decile funds have returns that are much more variable. This effect is more important in the subdeciles, where the monthly standard deviation can reach almost 20 percent. There is no significant difference around the minima except for subdeciles where the minima are lower (particularly from top-decile funds). The maximum increases with the performance of the funds. The monthly maximum returns can reach 140 percent for top-performing funds.

The kurtosis is large and the skewness is positive for all deciles. Moreover, they both increase with the performance. This means that good-performing funds have positively skewed performance distribution with fat tails. This is in accordance with the minimum and maximum results. Finally, the Sharpe ratios calculated with a 5 percent risk-free rate are small in magnitude. The highest ratios are those of poorly performing funds. This is explained by the fact that the standard deviation is higher among the well-performing funds.

TABLE 4.10 Decile Descriptive Statistics Based on Previous Year's Performance

	Mean Return	Std. Dev.	Median	Min	Max	Skewness	Kurtosis	Sharpe Ratio
D1	1.24	4.71	0.39	−8.37	30.38	1.69	7.07	0.17
D2	1.02	3.34	0.51	−5.70	20.67	1.74	6.39	0.25
D3	1.07	3.00	0.51	−4.34	15.21	1.66	4.79	0.27
D4	1.10	3.22	0.61	−6.97	19.86	1.97	7.84	0.25
D5	1.05	3.22	0.56	−6.07	24.42	2.59	14.65	0.26
D6	1.35	3.79	0.82	−7.11	19.91	1.86	6.11	0.22
D7	1.21	4.08	0.59	−7.14	27.55	2.37	12.14	0.20
D8	1.67	4.56	1.10	−6.16	35.00	2.81	15.72	0.18
D9	1.87	5.66	0.85	−7.93	46.75	3.97	25.34	0.14
D10	2.67	6.18	1.68	−6.63	45.38	3.56	20.28	0.13
D1a	1.30	5.49	1.08	−12.86	58.46	5.70	57.77	0.15
D1b	1.33	5.09	0.76	−11.09	28.83	1.82	6.83	0.16
D1c	1.96	5.99	1.18	−12.74	50.10	3.58	24.20	0.14
D10a	3.17	19.99	0.85	−46.29	140.91	2.45	13.69	0.04
D10b	1.90	14.77	0.87	−29.39	100.95	1.93	10.16	0.06
D10c	1.31	7.72	0.77	−24.47	34.74	0.56	3.04	0.11

Std. Dev. = standard deviation; Min = minimum; Max = maximum. The Sharpe ratio is calculated with a 5 percent risk-free rate.
Numbers in the table are monthly percentages.

Table 4.11 contains the results of the persistence analysis. The alpha indicates that all deciles but decile 10 underperform relatively to the index. Underperformance is significant only for D2, D4, D5, D6, D7, and D9. These results indicate that when the performance of the index is taken into account, most funds do not add value (they destroy value) over the January 1985 to December 2002 period. Interestingly, D10 (containing previous year's best-performing fund) has a positive but not significant alpha. All deciles are positively exposed to the CTA Global Index, although D1, D6, D8, and D9 are the only ones that are significantly exposed. The adjusted R^2 obtained is quite high for each decile. However, for subdeciles (especially those for D1), the R^2 is relatively low.[8]

[8]We have analyzed the data to understand this point, and we have concluded that many funds in the worst-performing decile are dissolved each year. This means that these subdeciles do not contain a lot of funds, which leads to less stable returns compared to whole deciles.

TABLE 4.11 CTA Persistence in Performance, January 1986 to December 2002

	Mean	Std. Dev.	Alpha	CTA Index	R^2_{adj}
D1	1.24	4.71	−0.33	0.97***	0.57
D2	1.02	3.34	−0.20**	0.76***	0.70
D3	1.07	3.00	−0.09	0.71***	0.77
D4	1.10	3.22	−0.19**	0.80***	0.84
D5	1.05	3.22	−0.25***	0.80***	0.85
D6	1.35	3.79	−0.18**	0.94***	0.84
D7	1.21	4.08	−0.47***	1.04***	0.89
D8	1.67	4.56	−0.19*	1.15***	0.87
D9	1.87	5.66	−0.40***	1.40***	0.84
D10	2.67	6.18	0.20	1.52***	0.82
D1a	1.30	5.49	1.82	0.82***	0.02
D1b	1.33	5.09	−0.09	1.23***	0.09
D1c	1.96	5.99	0.16	0.71***	0.11
D10a	3.17	19.99	−0.39	1.04***	0.49
D10b	1.90	14.77	−0.27	0.99***	0.51
D10c	1.31	7.72	0.07	1.17***	0.52

This table reports the performance analysis of the performance decile regressed against the CTA Global Index.
t-stat are heteroskedasticity consistent.
***Significant at the 1 percent level.
**Significant at the 5 percent level.
*Significant at the 10 percent level.
Numbers in the table are monthly percentages.

Subperiod Analysis

Table 4.12 contains the persistence analysis over various subperiods. We report a bull market period (January 1998 to March 2000), a bear market period (April 2000 to December 2002), and the 10-year period ending December 2002. This analysis aims at determining if the previous results remain stable over different market environments. The left-hand side of the table indicates that worst-performing funds significantly underperform their peers over the bull market period. D1 to D4 and D6 have significantly negative intercept over the January 1998 to March 2003 period. D9 and D10 have positive alphas. Moreover, the alpha of D10 is significantly positive. These interesting results indicate that the previous year's best-performing funds (around 10 percent of the whole database) significantly outperform their peers over the bull market period. The results of subdecile

TABLE 4.12 Persistence in Performance Subperiod Analysis

Jan 1998–	Bull Market Period			Apr 2000–	BearMarket Period			Jan 1993–	Ten-Year Period		
Mar 2000	Alpha	Index	R^2_{adj}	Dec 2002	Alpha	Index	R^2_{adj}	Dec 2002	Alpha	Index	R^2_{adj}
D1	−1.05**	0.91**	0.20	D1	−0.45	1.22***	0.55	D1	−0.47**	1.12***	0.47
D2	−0.40**	1.01***	0.78	D2	−0.08	0.83***	0.61	D2	−0.28***	0.97***	0.68
D3	−0.21**	0.83***	0.84	D3	−0.19*	0.83***	0.87	D3	−0.13*	0.85***	0.82
D4	−0.31**	0.98***	0.86	D4	−0.01	0.90***	0.91	D4	−0.05	0.81***	0.85
D5	0.00	0.91***	0.89	D5	−0.17**	0.87***	0.95	D5	−0.12***	0.79***	0.89
D6	−0.26***	1.05***	0.94	D6	0.08	1.03***	0.91	D6	−0.10*	0.90***	0.88
D7	−0.15	0.80***	0.87	D7	−0.15	1.07***	0.92	D7	−0.26***	0.98***	0.89
D8	−0.21**	1.18***	0.87	D8	−0.12	1.11***	0.91	D8	−0.15***	1.13***	0.89
D9	0.02	1.19***	0.84	D9	−0.09	1.22***	0.85	D9	−0.25***	1.29***	0.86
D10	0.79**	1.34***	0.64	D10	−0.06	1.07***	0.75	D10	0.38**	1.21***	0.71
D1a	−0.02	2.13*	−0.02	D1a	−0.28	2.27**	0.18	D1a	−0.21	0.99***	0.44
D1b	2.17	0.02	−0.04	D1b	−1.73	0.88**	0.00	D1b	0.04	0.44***	0.20
D1c	−0.78	0.94**	0.03	D1c	1.15	0.32	-0.03	D1c	0.74**	0.70***	0.18
D10b	0.41	0.64***	0.15	D10a	−0.13	1.04***	0.68	D10a	2.57	1.00	0.00
D10c	−0.61**	0.64***	0.35	D10b	−0.07	0.54***	0.44	D10b	0.67	1.21**	0.02
D10c	0.29	0.43***	0.01	D10c	0.50	0.74***	0.46	D10c	0.64	0.28	0.00

This table reports the persistence in performance analysis of the performance decile regressed against the CTA Global Index over the January 1993–December 2002 period.
t-stat are heteroskedasticity consistent.
***Significant at the 1 percent level.
**Significant at the 5 percent level.
*Significant at the 10 percent level.
Numbers in the table are monthly percentages.

analyses are less significant.[9] The table also indicates that each decile is significantly exposed to the CTA Global Index. The R^2 is particularly high, especially for the upper deciles, but is generally low for the subdeciles.

The central part of Table 4.12 reports the decile analysis over the April 2000 to December 2002 period. This period corresponds to a bear market since the technology bubble exploded in March 2000. It indicates that all the deciles but D6 have negative alphas. The only one significantly negative is D5. This result indicates that no group of funds offers persistent returns during the bear market that began in the first half of 2000. As expected, the top-performing subdecile (D10c) yields a positive (but not significant) alpha. Nevertheless, each decile is significantly positively exposed to the CTA Global Index.

The right-hand part of Table 4.12 reports the analysis for the 10-year period ending December 2002. In this last case, all deciles but D10 are negative, and most of them significantly destroy value (D1, D2, D5, D7, D8, and D9 have all significantly negative alphas). As in the bull period analyzed before, D10 has a significantly positive alpha. This indicates that the funds in this particular decile persistently create value compared to their peers. The exposure to the market is significantly positive for all deciles, and as in all the other cases, R^2 is high for each decile.

Strategies Analysis

Once these results are obtained, we regress the same data over the various strategies returns[10] to determine if some strategies are statistically more represented in some deciles. Results are reported in Table 4.13.

The first column contains the alphas. These increase monastically across D1 to D8. Alphas for D9 and D10 are negative. Few of them are significant. D2, D3, and D4 are weakly negatively significant, and D8 is significantly positive at the 10 percent significance level. Interestingly, subdeciles D10a

---

[9]Subdeciles sometimes contain few funds when many of the funds were dissolved in the year after their classification in the top- or worst-performing decile. As we noted in analyzing the survivorship bias, this bias is important in CTA data and we have to take this factor into account.

[10]We have analyzed the relationship between the various strategies in the correlation analysis. We do not find high correlation between the strategies. The only correlations that could lead to problems in estimation are the high coefficients between the CTA Global Index and some strategies. To deal with this issue, we ran two estimations, with and without the CTA Global Index. The results obtained are qualitatively the same. We report only the results without the index.

TABLE 4.13 Decile Performance Analysis, January 1986 to December 2002

	Alpha	Arb	Discret	Fund	Option	Stocks	System	Techcur	Techdiv	Techfin	Techoth	Nocat	R^2_{adj}
D1	−0.58	−0.10	0.85**	−0.02	0.08**	0.03	0.50**	0.02	−0.03	0.21	0.00	0.38	0.56
D2	−0.49*	0.00	−0.09	0.05	0.00	0.08	0.37	0.28***	0.38**	−0.02	0.05**	0.34	0.74
D3	−0.27**	0.03	0.03	0.03	0.00	0.07	0.58***	0.13**	0.10	0.08	−0.01	−0.01	0.84
D4	0.22*	−0.03	0.10***	0.00	0.00	−0.06*	0.71***	−0.03	−0.05	−0.04	0.00	−0.05	0.87
D5	0.17	−0.06**	0.11**	−0.01	0.03**	−0.03	0.49***	−0.03	0.13*	−0.07	0.02*	−0.02	0.83
D6	0.05	−0.04*	0.04	0.00	−0.03	0.07	0.56***	−0.03	0.16**	−0.14**	0.01	0.06	0.84
D7	0.00	0.03	0.10*	−0.01	−0.01	0.03	0.75***	0.00	−0.03	−0.12**	0.00	0.01	0.88
D8	0.21*	0.02	0.14**	0.00	−0.01	−0.02	0.80***	−0.13*	0.08	−0.03	0.00	−0.05	0.87
D9	−0.14	0.05	0.17*	0.01	0.01	0.01	0.66***	−0.06	0.16	0.16	0.00	−0.11	0.76
D10	−0.27	−0.02	0.31**	0.03	−0.01	0.29	0.16	0.06	0.17	0.26**	0.01	0.31**	0.59
D10a	−0.74*	0.05	0.21	0.11**	0.00	−0.03	0.56**	−0.08	0.21	−0.08	0.04	0.56*	0.34
D10b	−0.03	−0.02	−0.21	0.01	0.01	0.05	0.30*	−0.05	0.08	0.01	−0.05*	0.26	0.19
D10c	−1.01**	−0.05	−0.36**	−0.05	−0.08	0.07	−0.57	−0.02	0.95**	0.78***	−0.02	0.46	0.28
D1a	1.66	−1.64	1.41	0.05	−0.34	0.75	−3.69	0.01	0.09	1.89	−0.09	3.77*	−0.16
D1b	−2.17	−0.39	4.06	−0.49	−0.11	−0.23	−0.54	−0.01	0.17	1.06	−0.17	2.5*	0.11
D1c	0.95	−0.43	1.02**	0.00	−0.09	0.09	−0.03	0.25	−0.50	−0.22	0.09	0.88	−0.09

This table reports the persistence in performance analysis of the performance decile regressed against the CTA Global Index and the CTA substrategy indices.

t-stat are heteroskedasticity consistent.

***Significant at the 1 percent level.

**Significant at the 5 percent level.

*Significant at the 10 percent level.

Numbers in the table are monthly percentages. Arb = arbitrage; Discret = discretionary; Fund = fundamental; Option = option strategy; Techdiv. = technical diversified; Techfin = technical financial/metals; Techcur = technical currency; Techoth = other technical; System = systematic; Stock = stock index; Nocat = no category.

and D10c are significantly negative. All these figures are different from the ones obtained in the performance or performance persistence analysis.

The other columns report the exposition of each decile to the strategies defined earlier. We analyze the table horizontally, then vertically, but first we want to underline the fact that negative significant exposure of a decile to a strategy means that the decile negatively contributes to the creation of alpha. Decile D1 (the worst-performing funds) is significantly positively exposed to discretionary and systematic funds and significantly negatively exposed to option funds. The mean return for decile D1 is 1.24 percent (see Table 4.11). Once we take the strategy performance into account, the alpha is –0.58 (See Table 4.13). The difference between these two numbers comes mainly from the exposure to fundamental and systematic funds.[11] D2 is significantly positively exposed to technical currency, technical diversified, and technically other funds. Interestingly, this decile is not significantly exposed to systematic funds. D3 is significantly positively exposed to systematic funds and to technical currency funds. D4 is positively exposed to discretionary funds and to systematic funds. D5 is significantly negatively exposed to arbitrage funds and significantly positively exposed to discretionary, option strategies, and systematic funds.

D6 is significantly positively exposed to systematic funds and technically diversified funds and negatively exposed to technical financial/metal funds. D7 is significantly positively exposed to systematic funds and negatively exposed to technical financial/metals, whereas D8 is positively exposed to discretionary funds and systematic funds. In this particular case, the strategies reported cannot completely explain the alpha (since it is still weakly significantly positive). D9 is significantly positively exposed to discretionary funds and systematic funds. Finally D10 is significantly positively exposed to discretionary funds, technical financial/metals, and to the no category. Note that it is the only decile exposed to the no-category strategy.

If we analyze the results in Table 4.13 by columns rather than by rows to detect the presence of certain strategies in particular deciles (top, middle, or bottom deciles), we find some interesting features. First of all, each strategy has at least one significant coefficient across the deciles (some of them have only weak coefficients). Interestingly, for most, significance appears only once out of the 10 deciles (arbitrage, fundamental, option, stocks, no category). Note, however, that most of these strategies contain only a few

[11]Recall that the systematic strategy is 0.98 correlated with the CTA Global Index (see Table 4.3). This means that the systematic strategy can be seen as the index in this particular case.

funds, which explains the nonsignificance of these factors for most of the deciles. Moreover, the funds of those strategies with very few funds are concentrated among one decile.

The evolution of certain coefficients is interesting. For the option strategy, for example, the coefficient is significantly negative for D1 and positive for D5. This indicates that this strategy impacts significantly inversely on some deciles. For technical currency funds, coefficients are significantly positive for D2 and D3. Then the coefficients decrease and the one of D8 is weakly negatively significant. This also indicates a pattern in the repartition of this particular strategy. The no category coefficient is high (but not significant) for D1 and D2 and then it decreases and becomes significantly positive for D10. The pattern of coefficient changes across deciles is perhaps a reflection of over- and under-representation of strategies within the deciles. The only exception is systematic funds that contain more than half of the observations. This strategy is presented across almost all deciles.

The R^2 reported in the last column indicates that the returns of the deciles are well explained by the model. Except for D1 and D10 they are all greater than 0.70 percent. The R^2 are lower in the subdeciles. This can be explained by the fact that the subdeciles contain fewer funds.

DISSOLUTION FREQUENCIES

Before concluding, we analyze the dissolution frequencies in our database, defined as the number of funds that stopped reporting to the database. This measure is similar to survivorship bias, the difference being that we analyze it per decile each year based on the previous year's performance. This analysis is interesting because it helps us determine if bad performance leads to a higher dissolution rate the following year and if good performance is a protection against dissolution.

Average Dissolution Frequencies

Capocci and Hübner (2004) have analyzed the dissolution frequencies in hedge funds. They found an average dissolution frequency of 15 percent for bad performing funds and 7 percent for good ones. They concluded that bad performers were more frequently dissolved but that good performance was not a protection against dissolution.

Figure 4.2 reports mean dissolution frequencies. The frequencies decrease monastically from 46.6 percent for the worst-performing funds to 11.6 percent for D6. They are at 12.1 percent for D7, 11 percent for D8, and 8.8 percent for D9. D9 has the lowest dissolution frequencies of all the

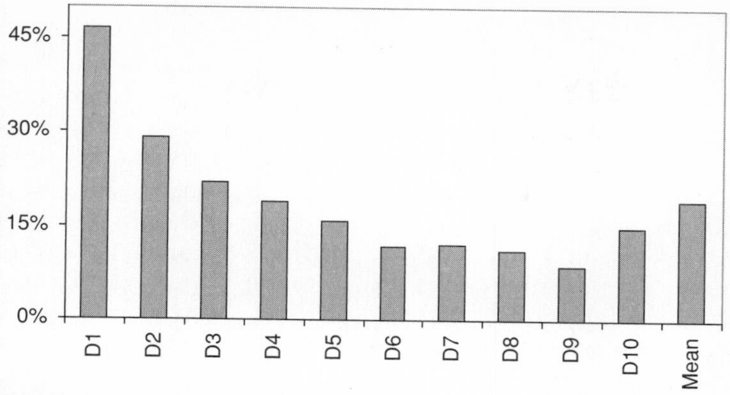

FIGURE 4.2 Average Dissolution Frequencies
CTA dissolution frequencies by year *t* as a function of year *t* – 1 decile. At the beginning of year *t*, all funds are placed into decile rankings on the basis of their returns in year *t* – 1. If a hedge fund ceases to report returns at any time before the end of year *t*, it is counted as dissolved.

deciles. Interestingly, D10 has a dissolution frequency of 14.9 percent. The average dissolution frequency is 19.2 percent.

These numbers indicate some interesting patterns. First, in absolute terms, the dissolution frequencies for CTA are impressively high. An examination of yearly rates per decile indicates that the maximum annual dissolution frequencies range from 21.9 percent for D8 (in 1998 and 1999) to 74.6 percent for D1 (in 2001). Second, poorly performing funds face impressively high dissolution frequencies. As indicated in the figure, the average dissolution frequency over the 1986 to 2002 period is more than 46 percent for previous year's worst-performing funds. This means that almost half of the poorly performing funds are dissolved the year following their bad performance. In recent years this trend is even stronger, with a maximum of dissolution of 74.6 percent in 2001. Third, the dissolution rate of D1 is much higher than that of the other deciles. The closest dissolution frequency is that of D2, at 23.9 percent. We can conclude that bad performance leads to dissolution. Finally, the dissolution rates diminish from D1 to D9 but increase for decile D10. This indicates that good performance is not a protection against dissolution. The dissolution frequency of D10 (best-performing funds) is higher than those obtained for D5 to D9. Capocci and Hübner (2004) found some qualitative results for hedge funds with lower values.

Yearly Dissolution Frequencies

Figure 4.3 reports the evolution over time of the yearly dissolution frequencies across deciles illustrated in Figure 4.2. Figure 4.3 indicates that the percentage of dissolved funds was close to zero in the first year studies. Then the dissolution frequencies increase across most deciles until 1993. In 1994 the dissolution rates increase for most deciles but decrease for both D1 and D2 (from 55.3 percent in 1993 to 47 percent in 1994 for D1 and from 44.6 percent in 1993 to 40 percent in 1994 for D2). Since then, depending on the year and on the decile considered, the dissolution frequencies increase or decrease.

Rates are particularly high in 1999 for the best- and worst-performing funds, with dissolution frequencies of respectively 39.5 percent (against 30.3 percent in 1998 and 29.6 percent in 2000) and 69.4 percent (against 61.4 percent in 1998 and 64.8 percent in 2000). Poorly performing funds face high dissolution frequencies in 1996 (72.9 percent), 1999 (69.4 percent), and 2001 (74.6 percent). Interestingly, D2 has a higher dissolution frequency at 60 percent in 1997, equal to the dissolution frequency of D1 for that year. Otherwise, in each particular year, D2 has dissolution frequencies always lower than D1, and D9 always has dissolution frequencies lower than D10.

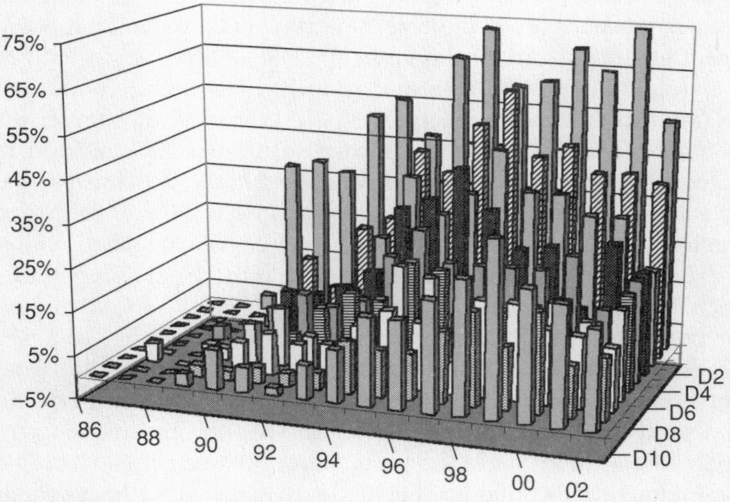

FIGURE 4.3 Evolution of the Yearly Dissolution Frequencies across Deciles between 1986 and 2002

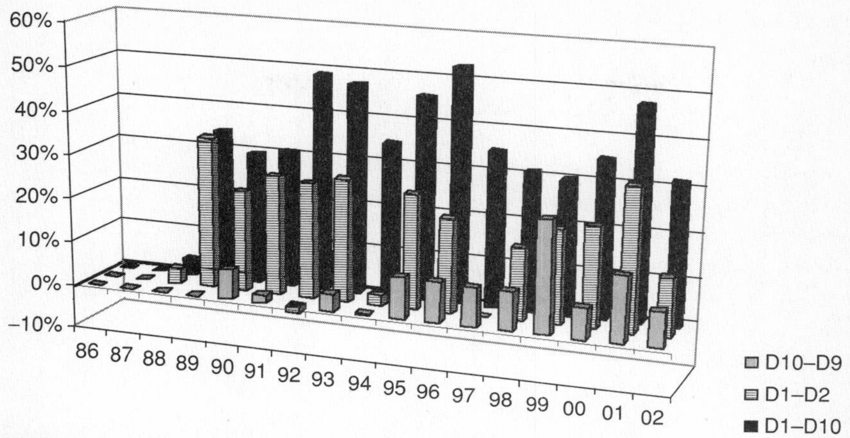

FIGURE 4.4 Spread between Dissolution Frequencies

Spread Analysis

Figure 4.4 reports the spreads between D1 and D2, D10 and D9, and D1 and D10. This figure is interesting because it shows how these spreads evolve over time. The front part of the figure (D10 minus D9) indicates that this spread is almost null (even negative at −1.3 percent in 1992) before 1995 and that it increases heavily in 1999, in the heart of the bull market. Spread D1 minus D2 is particularly low in 1994 and 1997. Spread D1 minus D10 is particularly high in 1993 (47.4 percent), 1996 (52.9 percent), and 2001 (47.8 percent).

This analysis of dissolution frequencies points to several interesting results. The dissolution frequencies are high for CTAs. Bad performance leads to dissolutions, and good performance is not a protection against it. The yearly dissolution frequencies increase heavily in the first year of analysis and then vary over time, but they are higher between 1999 and 2001 depending on the deciles considered.

CONCLUSION

In this study, we investigate CTA survivorship bias, performance, and performance persistence. After having made a literature review and analyzing the descriptive statistics, we have analyzed the correlation between the various CTA strategies. Our results indicate that most of the strategies defined are weakly correlated, indicating a need to separate the funds into investment strategies. The survivorship bias analysis indicates that our CTA database contains a bias of 5.4 percent per year over the whole January 1985 to

December 2002 period. The three-year rolling period survivorship analysis indicates that this bias varies significantly over time.

Our performance analysis has attempted to determine if some strategies outperform the CTA Global Index, which consists of all the funds in the database. Our results indicate that out of 11 strategies, 7 significantly outperform the index and 2 significantly underperform the index. Subperiod analysis indicates that over- or underperformance remains constant over time. Most strategies are significantly positively exposed to the CTA Global Index. Individual fund performance analysis indicates that 21.7 percent of the funds offer significantly positive alpha and 16.4 percent significantly underperform the index over the period studied at the 5 percent significance level.

To perform our persistence analysis, we apply the decile classification as suggested by Carhart (1997). Then we determine if certain deciles significantly out- or underperform the index over time. Our results indicate that most deciles significantly underperform the index over the whole period. Subperiod analysis indicates that the best-performing decile, D10, is the only one that significantly outperforms the CTA Global Index in most time periods. We also have analyzed the exposure of the deciles to the various strategy indices and have found that some deciles are more exposed to various strategies. Finally we have analyzed the dissolution frequencies in each decile over time. Our results indicate that the dissolution frequencies are particularly high for CTA, that bad performance leads to dissolution, and that good performance is not a protection against it.

Three results are particularly relevant for investors or fund of fund managers who want to allocate part of their portfolio to CTAs.

1. Some CTA strategies outperform the average over time. However, few funds offer persistence in performance. Most significantly underperform over time.
2. Over time, more than 20 percent of the individual funds significantly outperform their peers, but almost all funds classified in a decile on the basis of their previous year's performance underperform the CTA Global Index.
3. Dissolution is a real issue in CTA performance since dead funds significantly underperform existing ones, and dissolution frequencies can reach 60 percent in difficult months for poorly performing funds.

The next step in analyzing CTA performance is to apply our model and the decile analysis to individual strategies, to determine if there are differences in the results for individual strategies and to test the robustness of the results.

CHAPTER 5

CTA Performance Evaluation with Data Envelopment Analysis

Gwenevere Darling, Kankana Mukherjee, and Kathryn Wilkens

We apply data envelopment analysis to a performance evaluation framework for CTAs. The technique allows us to integrate several performance measures into one efficiency score by establishing a multidimensional efficient frontier. Two dimensions of the frontier are consistent with the standard Markowitz mean-variance framework, while additional risk and return dimensions include skewness and kurtosis. We also illustrate a method of analyzing determinants of efficiency scores. Tobit regressions of efficiency scores on equity betas, beta-squared, fund size, length of manager track record, investment style (market focus), and strategy (discretionary vs. systematic) are performed for CTA returns over two time frames representing different market environments. We find that the efficiency scores are negatively related to beta-squared in both time periods. Results also indicate that emerging CTAs (those with shorter manager track records) tend to have better efficiency scores as defined by the DEA model used in our study. This relationship is strongest during the period from 1998 to 2000, but not statistically significant during the period from 2000 to 2002. For both time periods, fund size is not related to efficiency scores.

INTRODUCTION

Industry performance reports for commodity trading advisors (CTAs) present multiple performance measures such as return, standard deviation, drawdowns, betas, and alphas. Investors and fund managers recognize the importance of considering a multitude of performance measures to analyze fund risk from various perspectives. It is particularly important for the growing alternative investment class of managed futures, which have different risk/return profiles from those of traditional mutual funds as well as those of many hedge fund strategies. For all asset classes, however, the academic literature has done little to offer a comprehensive framework that incorporates multiple risk measures in an integrated fashion (Arnott 2003). Too often, studies focus on single measure of risks, arguing for one relative to another.

"Managed futures" are a subset of hedge funds that uses futures contracts as one among several types of trading instruments (including swaps and interbank foreign exchange markets) and for which futures are a means, rather than an end, with which to implement their strategy. The name wrongly suggests that futures are the dog rather than the tail. Managed futures encompass the broad set of individual commodity trading advisors (CTAs). CTAs are also unfortunately named because, on balance, most of their trading is in the financial markets, not the commodity markets. Like any other class of alternative investments, managers are represented by a variety of styles and substyles. For example, there are systematic and discretionary CTAs, CTAs who exclusively try to capture trends, those who identify countertrend opportunities, and those who combine the two approaches.[1]

In this study we look at the performance of CTAs based on multiple criteria using data envelopment analysis (DEA). DEA establishes a multidimensional efficient frontier and assigns each CTA an efficiency score whereby 1 (or 100 percent) indicates perfect efficiency and scores lower than 1 represent relatively less efficient CTAs based on the performance criteria chosen.

The criteria we choose as bases for performance evaluation are monthly returns, kurtosis, minimum return, skewness, standard deviation of returns, and percentage of negative monthly returns. Although there are many other possibly appropriate criteria, those not included here are likely either to be redundant with variables included or to not make sense in an optimization framework. Criteria that make sense in this framework are those that are desirable to maximize or minimize across various market conditions. This aspect leads us to reject equity betas as a criterion in the DEA model, for example, because CTAs may desire a higher beta in up-market environments but negative betas in down-market periods.

In addition to applying the DEA methodology to evaluate CTA performance, we explore the relationship between the efficiency scores and fund size, investment style and strategy, length of the manager's track

[1]Another important dimension of styles is the time frame. There are long-term, short-term, and medium-term traders and those who combine time frames.

record, and measures of the covariance of CTA returns with equity market returns. We ask:

- Do emerging hedge fund managers[2] really do better than larger, established managers?
- Is there a relationship between efficiency scores and equity markets, and if so, does the market environment impact the relationship?
- Do strategies (systematic, discretionary, trend-based) or styles (diversified, financial, currency, etc.) matter in different market environments?

We analyze monthly CTA returns in two different market environments: over 24 months beginning in 1998, when equity market returns are predominantly positive, and over 24 months beginning in 2000, when they are more often negative. We find that emerging managers perform better than well-established managers in the sense that funds with shorter track records have a greater efficiency score. Fund size and manager tenure are weakly positively correlated. In contrast with the conventional wisdom, however, larger funds have better efficiency scores. These results provide some insight into capacity issues concerning optimal fund size. The fund size and manager tenure coefficients are, however, statistically significant only during the first (1998–2000) time period, indicating that capacity issues may be less important during flat equity markets.

For both time periods, squared equity beta is inversely related to the efficiency scores and the coefficient is highly significant. This result appears to be influenced by the risk-minimizing design of our DEA model. The style dummy variable (diversified versus nondiversified) was not a significant factor impacting efficiency scores. The systematic strategy variable was significant, but only during the second (2000–2002) down-market period. We consider these results as preliminary because several issues may be affecting their significance. Notably, when our sample size is broken down by investment style and strategy, the number of CTAs representing each group is very small. Nevertheless, we believe that the approach is a promising avenue for further research.

The next section of this chapter provides a background discussion on various risk measures and performance evaluation issues. The variables chosen as inputs to the DEA model and the regression model are then discussed in the context of prior research, and the data are described. The variable descrip-

---

[2]We consider managers with short track records to be emerging CTAs. This category is distinctly different from managers who invest in emerging markets.

tion is followed by an explanation of the DEA methodology and Tobit regressions used to explore determinants of the efficiency scores obtained from the DEA model. Results are presented and the final section concludes.

RISK MEASURES AND PERFORMANCE EVALUATION

A multitude of investment fund performance models and metrics exist in part because some measures are more appropriate for certain purposes than others. For example, the Sharpe ratio is arguably more appropriate when analyzing an entire portfolio, while the Treynor ratio is appropriate when evaluating a security or investment that is part of a larger portfolio.[3] The multitude of performance measures and approaches also suggests that more than one measure of risk may be needed to accurately assess performance. Conversely, some measures can be redundant. For example, Daglioglu and Gupta (2003b) find that returns of hedge fund portfolios constructed on the basis of some risk measures are often highly correlated, and sometimes perfectly correlated, with returns of portfolios constructed on the basis of others. Burghart, Duncan, and Liu (2003) illustrate that the theoretical distribution of drawdowns can be replicated with a high degree of accuracy given only a manager's average return, standard deviation of returns, and length of track record.

In this section we begin by briefly reviewing some of the traditional portfolio performance measures and analysis techniques. We review single parameter risk measures based on modern portfolio theory, we discuss expanded performance models that account for time-varying risk, discuss concerns over assuming mean-variance sufficiency, and consider multifactor models of style and performance attribution. This short review exposes a plethora of performance measures. The question of appropriateness and redundancy is revisited in the section that describes the data used in this study. The current section also discusses the seemingly paradoxical issue of using benchmarks to evaluate absolute return strategies[4] and concludes with a discussion of potential determinants of performance.

Alpha and Benchmarks

Traditional asset managers seek to outperform a benchmark, and their performance is measured relative to that benchmark in terms of an alpha.

---

[3]The Sharpe measure is appropriate when analyzing an entire portfolio, because the standard deviation, or total risk, is in the denominator whereas beta is the denominator of the Treynor measure, and beta measures the systematic risk that will contribute to the risk of a well-diversified portfolio.

[4]Absolute return strategies seek to make positive returns in all market conditions. In contrast, relative return strategies seek only to outperform a benchmark.

While CTAs follow absolute return strategies that seek to make positive returns in all market conditions, benchmarks now exist for CTAs and other hedge fund strategies. Before considering benchmarks for absolute return strategies, we first review the concepts in the context of traditional asset management. Jensen's (1968) alpha is generally a capital asset pricing model (CAPM)-based performance measure of an asset's average return in excess of that predicted by the CAPM, given its systematic risk (beta)[5] and the market (benchmark) return. Alphas also may be measured relative to additional sources of risk in multi-index models.

Whereas various single-index models are based on the CAPM and assume that security returns are a function of their co-movements[6] with the market portfolio, multi-index (or multifactor) models assume that returns are also a function of additional influences.[7] For example, Chen, Roll, and Ross (1986) develop a model where returns are a function of factors related to cash flows and discount rates such a gross national product and inflation. The purposes of multi-index models are varied and, in addition to performance attribution, include forming expectations about returns and identifying sources of returns.

Sharpe (1992) decomposes stock portfolio returns into several "style" factors (more narrowly defined asset classes such as growth and income stocks, value stocks, high-yield bonds) and shows that the portfolio's mix accounts for up to 98 percent of portfolio returns. Similarly, Brinson, Singer, and Beebower (1991) show that rather than selectivity or market timing abilities, it is the portfolio mix (allocation to stocks, bonds, and cash) that determines over 90 percent of portfolio returns. However, Brown and Goetzmann (1995) identify a tendency for fund returns to be correlated across managers, suggesting performance is due to common strategies that are not captured in style analysis.

Schneeweis and Spurgin (1998) use various published indexes (Goldman Sachs Commodity Index, the Standard & Poor's 500 stock index, the

[5]Within the Markowitz (1952) framework, total risk is quantified by the standard deviation of returns. Tobin (1958) extended the Markowitz efficient frontier by adding the risk-free asset, resulting in the capital market line (CML) and paving the way for the development of the capital asset pricing model, developed by Sharpe (1964), Lintner (1965), and Mossin (1966). The CAPM defines systematic risk, measured by beta (β), as the relevant portion of total risk since investors can diversify away the remaining portion.

[6]Usually CAPM-based performance models describe covariance with the market portfolio, however, as noted earlier, they can attempt to describe coskewness and cokurtosis as well.

[7]Arbitrage pricing theory (APT) establishes the conditions under which a multi-index model can be an equilibrium description (Ross, 1976).

Salomon Brothers government bond index, and U.S. dollar trade-weighted currency index, the MLM Index[8]) with absolute S&P 500 returns and intramonth S&P return volatility in a multifactor regression analysis to describe the sources of return to hedge funds, managed futures, and mutual funds. The index returns employed in the regression analysis are intended to be risk factors that explain the source of natural returns. The explanatory variable, absolute equity returns, captures the source of return that derives from the ability to go short or long. Returns from the use of options or intramonth timing strategies are proxies for the intramonth standard deviation. The MLM Index, an active index designed to mimic trend-following strategies, is used to capture returns from market inefficiencies in the form of temporary trends.

Seigel (2003) provides a comprehensive review of benchmarking and investment management. Despite the fact that CTAs and many hedge fund managers follow absolute return strategies, various CTA benchmarks now exist, as described by Seigel (2003).

Addressing Time-Varying Risk

Single-parameter risk measures are problematic if managers are changing fund betas over time, as they would if they were attempting to time the market. For example, when equity prices are rising, the manager might increase the fund's beta and vice versa. Although market risk can be measured if the portfolio weights are known, this information is generally not publicly available and other techniques must be employed.[9]

---

[8]Mount Lucas Management Index™ is based on a concept conceived in 1988 of an index methodology that involves changing (commodity) market sides long and short to measure economic return.

[9]Treynor and Mazuy (1966) added a quadratic term to the basic linear regression model to capture nonlinearities in beta resulting from market timing activities. Kon and Jen (1978, 1979) use a switching regression technique. Merton (1981) and Henriksson and Merton (1981) develop nonparametric and parametric option-based methods to test for directional market timing ability. The nonparametric approach requires knowledge of the managers' forecasts. The more commonly employed parametric approach involves adding an extra term to the usual linear regression model and is CAPM based. Ferson and Schadt (1996) note that fund betas may change in response to changes in betas of the underlying assets as well as from changing portfolio weights. They modify the classic CAPM performance evaluation techniques to account for time variation in risk premiums by using a conditional CAPM framework. This method removes the perverse negative performance often found in earlier tests and suggests that including information variables in performance analysis is important.

Mitev (1998) uses a maximum likelihood factor analysis technique to classify CTAs according to unobservable factors. Similarly, Fung and Hsieh (1997b) also use a factor-analytic approach to classify hedge funds. In both cases, the results identify general investment approaches or trading strategies (e.g., trend-following, spread strategies, or systems approaches) as sources of returns to these alternative investment classes. Factor analysis and multifactor regression analysis differ in their approach to identifying the factors (benchmarks) that serve as proxies for risk. In multifactor regression analysis, the factors are specified in advance. Factor analysis will identify funds that have common yet unobservable factors, although the factors can be inferred from the qualitative descriptions of the funds. While this may seem redundant, the clustering of funds is done independently of the qualitative descriptions in a formal data-driven process.

The data envelopment analysis methodology used in this chapter, and described in more detail in Wilkens and Zhu (2001, 2004), incorporates multiple criteria and "benchmarks" funds or other securities according to these criteria. This is distinctly different from multifactor analysis. Here benchmarks are not risk factors but rather are efficient securities as defined in *n* dimensions where each dimension represents risk and return criteria. Recently Gregoriou (2003) used the DEA method in the context of benchmarking hedge funds.

Skewness and Kurtosis: Questioning Mean-Variance Sufficiency

The standard CAPM framework assumes that investors are concerned with only the mean and variance of returns. Ang and Chau (1979) argue that skewness in returns distributions should be incorporated into the performance measurement process. Even if the returns of the risky assets within a portfolio are normally distributed, dynamic trading strategies may produce nonnormal distributions in portfolio returns. Both Prakash and Bear (1986) and Stephens and Proffitt (1991) also develop higher-moment performance measurements.

Fishburn (1977), Sortino and van der Meer (1991), Marmer and Ng (1993), Merriken (1994), Sortino and Price (1994), and others also have developed measures that take into account downside risk (or semivariance) rather than the standard deviation of returns. Although some differences exist among these measures, the Sortino ratio captures their essence. Whereas the Sharpe ratio is defined as excess return[10] divided by standard

[10]Return minus the risk-free rate.

deviation, the Sortino ratio is defined as return divided by downside deviation. Downside deviation (DD) measures the deviations below some minimal accepted return (MAR). Of course, when the MAR is the average return and returns are normally distributed, the Sharpe and Sortino ratios will measure the same thing. Martin and Spurgin (1998) illustrate that even if individual asset or fund returns are skewed, the skewness tends to be diversified away at the portfolio level. However, they also illustrate that managers may choose to follow strategies that produce skewed returns as a form of signaling their skill. Note that coskewness remains irrelevant if it can be diversified away, but skewness may have some signaling value. Additionally, the popularity of the related value at risk (VaR) measure[11] and the common practice of reporting drawdown[12] information for various alternative investments suggest that skewness may be important, whether in terms of investor utility or skill signaling.

Beta-Squared Coefficient The classic paper by Fama and MacBeth (1973), and several other early papers (e.g., Carroll and Wei 1988; Shanken 1992) empirically test a two-pass regression methodology for stock returns. Assuming a nonlinear relationship between stock returns, the tests include beta-squared in the second-pass regression. These tests find that the coefficient for beta-squared is negative and statistically significant, providing evidence of a nonlinearity in stock returns.

Schneeweis and Georgiev (2002, p. 7) provide evidence that CTAs have nonlinear returns with respect to the equity market: "When S&P 500 returns were ranked from low to high and divided into four thirty-three month sub-periods, managed futures offered the opportunity of obtaining positive returns in months in which the S&P 500 provided negative returns as well as in months in which the S&P 500 reported positive returns."

We include equity beta-squared in our Tobit regressions where the dependent variable is not the expected return of the CTA, but is rather the efficiency score obtained in the DEA models. Although the dependent variable is not the same as in the earlier stock studies, we might hypothesize that CTA efficiency scores are also negatively related to beta-squared.

---

[11]See Chung (1999) for a concise review of VaR methodologies.

[12]Drawdown information is generally reported as the maximum drawdown over a period and is defined as the return from a fund's net asset value peak to trough. The Calmar ratio is a similar measure that CTA investors are often interested in and is defined as the average annual return over the past three years divided by the absolute value of the maximum drawdown during that period.

We infer a direct correspondence between the efficiency score and expected return. The CTA returns observed by Schneeweis and Georgiev (2002), therefore, imply a positive coefficient. Finally, we note that the efficiency scores used in this study minimize variability. This leads to the hypothesis that the beta-squared coefficient is negatively correlated with the efficiency score, unless the enhanced return from high (absolute) betas is an offsetting factor.

Fund Size In his chapter "The Lure of the Small," Jaeger (2003) describes how small firms and small portfolios are desirable features of hedge funds. Small firms satisfy hedge fund managers' entrepreneurial spirit, and small portfolios are often necessary to enable hedge funds to implement their strategies, especially if they trade in markets that are sometimes illiquid. Gregoriou and Rouah (2002) find, however, that fund size does not matter to hedge fund performance. Being a subset class of hedge funds, CTAs are examined in this chapter to see if fund size or length of manager track record is related to the DEA efficiency scores.

Determinants of Performance Based on the discussion above, we choose as bases for performance evaluation in a DEA model monthly returns, kurtosis, minimum return, skewness, standard deviation of returns, and percentage of negative monthly returns. We then investigate the potential of fund size, length of track record, strategy, and style to impact performance scores of funds created by the DEA model.

DATA DESCRIPTION

Monthly CTA return data for 216 CTAs over two periods surrounding March 2000 are obtained from the Center for International Securities and Derivatives Markets (CISDM) Alternative Investment Database.[13] The first period is an up-market period for the equity market (March 31, 1998, to February 28, 2000) and the second period is a down market environment (April 30, 2000, to March 31, 2002). The daily high for the S&P 500 occurred in March 2000, as illustrated in Figure 5.1. The mean monthly return for the S&P 500 was 1.28 percent and –1.11 percent for the first and second periods, respectively.

[13]We selected funds from the database with the most complete information on investment styles and strategies.

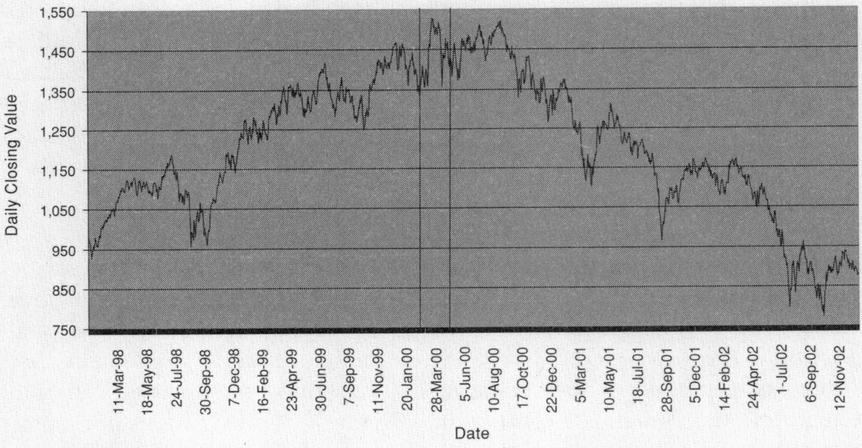

FIGURE 5.1 S&P 500 Daily Closing Values, from 1998 to 2002

Performance criteria used in the DEA model were calculated from the CTA returns for each of the two periods. The DEA approach to "estimating" the efficient frontier is a nonstatistical approach. As a result, all deviations from the efficient frontier are measured as inefficiency (i.e., there is no allowance for statistical noise). The efficiency measures obtained from this method are, therefore, very sensitive to the effect of outliers. Hence, for each performance criterion used in the DEA model, particular effort was made to detect any outliers. CTAs with outliers in one subperiod were deleted from both subperiods so as to have the same group of CTAs. Our final sample consisted of 157 CTAs that were used for analysis in the DEA model and the subsequent Tobit regression analysis. Table 5.1 provides descriptive statistics for the DEA model criteria over both periods and for the full and final sample.

Other information we use from the CISDM Alternative Investment Database includes the assets under management over time, the dates the funds were established, and information on the investment style[14]

[14]We follow the terminology established by Sharpe (1992) and call the market focus investment style.

TABLE 5.1 Descriptive Statistics for the DEA Model Criteria

Original Data		Standard Deviation	% Negative	Average Monthly Return	Skewness	Minimum Return	Kurtosis
All 216 CTAs for 1998–2000	Mean of CTAs	0.055	0.427	0.010	0.460	–0.091	1.637
	Standard Deviation	0.034	0.124	0.013	0.929	0.063	2.732
	Min	0.005	0.042	–0.024	–2.120	–0.530	–1.524
	Max	0.193	0.750	0.111	3.694	–0.006	16.370
All 216 CTAs for 2000–2002	Mean of CTAs	0.055	0.456	0.006	0.183	–0.103	1.223
	Standard Deviation	0.034	0.118	0.011	0.897	0.076	2.365
	Min	0.004	0.125	–0.032	–4.442	–0.483	–1.328
	Max	0.245	0.750	0.073	1.981	–0.003	20.812
157 CTAs for 1998–2000	Mean of CTAs	0.056	0.453	0.016	0.420	–0.093	1.040
	Standard Deviation	0.026	0.092	0.026	0.705	0.049	1.644
	Min	0.022	0.292	–0.018	–1.516	–0.247	–1.498
	Max	0.155	0.750	0.115	2.224	–0.012	6.249
157 CTAs for 2000–2002	Mean of CTAs	0.058	0.481	0.005	0.247	–0.109	0.635
	Standard Deviation	0.031	0.094	0.009	0.596	0.067	1.160
	Min	0.013	0.208	–0.032	–1.570	–0.385	–1.328
	Max	0.191	0.750	0.027	1.471	–0.018	4.748

TABLE 5.2 Number of CTAs, by Investment Style

Investment Style	# of CTAs	% of CTAs
Agriculture	6	4
Currency	20	13
Diversification	93	59
Financial	33	21
Stocks	5	3
Overall	157	100

(agriculture, currencies, diversified, financial, and stocks) and strategy (discretionary, systematic, and trend-based[15]) of the fund. The diversified investment style is most common, accounting for 59 percent of the CTAs in our final sample, as illustrated in Table 5.2. Comprising 66 percent of our final sample, the systematic investment strategy is the most common, as indicated in Table 5.3. Table 5.4 describes the distribution of the length of the managers' track record (maturity) in years, and Table 5.5 presents the distribution of the average funds under management for the two periods.

Table 5.6 presents correlation coefficients for the DEA model criteria. We see that in both periods, minimum return and standard deviation are highly (negatively) correlated, as one might expect. Kurtosis and skewness are also highly (positively) correlated, but only in the first period. We note that we are therefore potentially including redundant information in the model. That is, by maximizing the minimum return, we may not necessarily need to minimize correlated measures such as the standard deviation. Following Daglioglu and Gupta (2003b), however, we sort the portfolios by the various performance criteria and find that the returns to the sorted port-

[15]We follow Fung and Hsieh (1997a) and refer to the type of active management followed as the strategy, and we use the classification scheme available in the CISDM database.

TABLE 5.3 Number of CTAs, by Investment Strategy

Strategy	# of CTAs	% of CTAs
Discretionary	12	8
Systematic	103	66
Trend Based	42	27
Overall	157	100

folios are not as highly correlated as the variables themselves are. Table 5.7 presents these results.

After computing efficiency scores with the DEA methodology described in the following section, determinants of the scores are explored by regressing them against four additional variables: beta, beta-squared, average funds managed, and length of manager track record. Table 5.8 presents the summary statistics for these variables.

TABLE 5.4 Length of Managers' Track Record (Maturity) in Years

Length of Manager Track Record	# of CTAs	% of CTAs
<6	8	5
6 – <7	19	12
7 – <8	15	10
8 – <9	28	18
9 – <10	10	6
10 – <11	9	6
11 – <12	13	8
12 – <13	17	11
13 – <14	5	3
14 – <15	2	1
15 – <16	9	6
16+	22	14
Overall	157	100

TABLE 5.5 Distribution of the Average Funds under Management

1998–2000			2000–2002		
Average Fund Managed (000,000)	# of CTAs	% of CTAs	Average Fund Managed (millions)	# of CTAs	% of CTAs
<2.5	19	12	<2.5	23	15
2.5 – <5	14	9	2.5 – <5	17	11
5 – <10	13	8	5 – <10	17	11
10 – <20	25	16	10 – <20	15	10
20 – <30	8	5	20 – <30	17	11
30 – <40	14	9	30 – <40	11	7
40 – <50	6	4	40 – <50	9	6
50 – <100	27	17	50 – <100	14	9
100 – <150	7	4	100 – <150	8	5
150 – <200	2	1	150 – <200	5	3
200 – <400	14	9	200 – <400	15	10
400+	8	5	400+	6	4
Overall	157	100	Overall	157	100

TABLE 5.6 Correlation Coefficients for the DEA Model Criteria

1998–2000	Std. Dev.	Per Neg	Return	Skewness	Min Return	Kurtosis
Standard Deviation	1.000					
Percent Negative	0.320	1.000				
Return	0.354	−0.478	1.000			
Skewness	0.243	0.422	0.002	1.000		
Minimum Return	−0.838	−0.245	−0.133	0.124	1.000	
Kurtosis	0.210	0.181	−0.065	0.648	−0.088	1.000
2000–2002	**Std. Dev.**	**PerNeg**	**Return**	**Skewness**	**Min Return**	**Kurtosis**
Standard Deviation	1.000					
Percent Negative	0.217	1.000				
Return	0.271	−0.440	1.000			
Skewness	0.124	0.308	0.235	1.000		
Minimum Return	−0.846	−0.167	0.037	0.287	1.000	
Kurtosis	0.057	−0.133	−0.161	−0.417	−0.326	1.000

TABLE 5.7 Top and Bottom Correlation Matrix for the DEA Model Criteria, by Portfolio

1998–2000	Top Std. Dev.	Bottom Std. Dev.	Top PerNeg	Bottom PerNeg	Top COR	Bottom COR	Top Return	Bottom Return	Top Skew	Bottom Skew	Top MinRet	Bottom MinRet	Top Kurt	Bottom Kurt
Top Std. Dev.	1													
Bottom Std. Dev.	0.125	1												
Top PerNeg	–0.102	0.041	1											
Bottom PerNeg	–0.094	0.054	–0.085	1										
Top COR	–0.109	0.138	0.004	0.111	1									
Bottom COR	–0.027	0.082	0.015	–0.067	–0.075	1								
Top Return	0.147	–0.021	0.039	–0.042	–0.110	–0.003	1							
Bottom Return	0.041	–0.066	0.048	–0.122	–0.073	0.080	0.100	1						
Top Skew	0.185	0.008	–0.065	0.138	0.047	0.045	–0.076	–0.041	1					
Bottom Skew	–0.067	–0.087	–0.008	0.111	0.034	0.098	0.050	–0.029	0.025	1				
Top MinRet	0.023		–0.126	–0.206	0.089	–0.031	–0.002	–0.040	–0.089	0.050	1			
Bottom MinRet	–0.061	–0.025	0.038	0.035	0.016	0.122	0.064	–0.097	–0.099	0.099	0.164	1		
Top Kurt	–0.006	0.076	0.083	0.013	–0.154	0.168	–0.006	–0.050	0.042	–0.018	0.086	0.057	1	
Bottom Kurt	–0.006	0.276	0.059	0.040	–0.001	0.044	–0.010	0.025	0.066	–0.111	–0.178	–0.023	0.218	1

TABLE 5.7 *(continued)*

2000–2002	Top Std. Dev.	Bottom Std. Dev.	Top PerNeg	Bottom PerNeg	Top COR	Bottom COR	Top Return	Bottom Return	Top Skew	Bottom Skew	Top MinRet	Bottom MinRet	Top Kurt	Bottom Kurt
Top Std. Dev.	1													
Bottom Std. Dev.	−0.051	1												
Top PerNeg	−0.057	−0.009	1											
Bottom PerNeg	−0.076	0.158	−0.027	1										
Top COR	0.152	0.126	−0.061	−0.001	1									
Bottom COR	−0.137	0.038	0.044	−0.044	−0.142	1								
Top Return	−0.135	0.101	−0.078	−0.189	0.076	0.238	1							
Bottom Return	0.088	0.258	0.122	−0.082	0.089	−0.098	0.063	1						
Top Skew	−0.060	−0.163	−0.102	−0.138	0.146	−0.055	−0.052	0.070	1					
Bottom Skew	0.009	−0.002	−0.138	0.181	0.039	0.179	0.183		−0.028	1				
Top MinRet	0.052	−0.094	−0.201	0.106	−0.021	−0.014	−0.127	0.220	−0.012	−0.001	1			
Bottom MinRet	0.149	0.119	−0.041	−0.064	0.067	−0.037	−0.171	0.206	0.021	0.116	0.003	1		
Top Kurt	−0.112	0.131	−0.069	0.004	−0.009	0.071	0.032	0.076	−0.094	0.001	0.186	0.049	1	
Bottom Kurt	0.091	0.003	−0.139	0.114	0.146	0.088	0.003	−0.080	0.092	0.168	0.057	−0.035	−0.182	1

TABLE 5. 8 Summary Statistics for Variables Used in Regression Analysis

Variables	Mean	Std. Dev.	Min	Max
Beta	–0.068	0.205	–0.782	0.470
Beta Squared	0.046	0.096	0.000	0.612
Average Fund Managed	$90,659,049	$175,566,905	$86,542	$1,172,390,042
Length of Manager Track Record	11.055	4.362	5.667	22.167
Variables	**Mean**	**Std. Dev.**	**Min**	**Max**
Beta	–0.063	0.294	–0.870	0.868
Beta Squared	0.090	0.159	0.000	0.756
Average Fund Managed	$92,303,454	$222,082,600	$92,542	$2,078,385,875
Length of Manager Track Record	11.055	4.362	5.667	22.167

METHODOLOGY

Brief Background of Data Envelopment Analysis

Data envelopment analysis, a mathematical programming approach, was first developed by Charnes, Cooper, and Rhodes (1978) to measure the efficiency or performance of individual decision-making units (DMUs) in producing multiple outputs from multiple inputs. Unlike a parametric approach (like regression-based methods), which requires the researcher to make sometimes arbitrary assumptions about the functional relationship between inputs and outputs, the DEA approach does not require such assumptions. It allows us to create an efficient frontier based on the input-output combinations of the observed DMUs, without any apriori assumptions regarding the functional form of the relationship between them.

Consider an industry producing a vector of m outputs $y = (y_1, y_2, \ldots, y_m)$ from a vector of n inputs, $x = (x_1, x_2, \ldots, x_n)$. Let the vectors x_j and y_j represent, respectively, the input and output bundles of the j-th decision-making unit. Suppose that input-output data are observed for N DMUs. Then the technology set can be completely characterized by the production possibility set $T = \{(x, y) : y \text{ can be produced from } x\}$ based on a few regularity assumptions, which in case of variable returns to scale are:

1. All observed input-output combinations are feasible.
   $(x_j, y_j) \in T; (j = 1,2, \ldots N)$
2. T exhibits free disposability with respect to inputs.
   $(x_0, y_0) \in T$ and $x_1 \geq x_0 \Rightarrow (x_1, y_0) \in T$
3. T exhibits free disposability with respect to outputs.
   $(x_0, y_0) \in T$ and $y_1 \leq y_0 \Rightarrow (x_0, y_1) \in T$
4. T is convex.
   $(x_0, y_0) \in T$ and $(x_1, y_1) \in T$
   $\Rightarrow (\lambda x_0 + (1 - \lambda)x_1, \lambda y_0 + (1 - \lambda)y_1) \in T; 0 \leq \lambda \leq 1$

Within the DEA approach, efficiency[16] can be measured based on either of two orientations. The first yields an output-oriented measure of efficiency that describes the maximum proportional increase in outputs that can be achieved for the given level of inputs from the DMU. The second orientation yields an input-oriented measure for the maximum proportional reduction in inputs that can be achieved for the given level of outputs of the DMU.

Following Banker, Charnes, and Cooper (BCC) (1984) we can measure the output-oriented efficiency of the ith DMU by solving this linear programming problem:[17]

$$
\begin{aligned}
&\text{Max } \phi_i \\
&\text{Subject to} \\
&\sum_{j=1}^{N} \lambda_j y_{rj} \geq \phi_i y_{ri} \qquad r = 1, 2, \ldots, m \\
&\sum_{j=1}^{N} \lambda_j x_{sj} \leq x_{si} \qquad s = 1, 2, \ldots, n \\
&\sum_{j=1}^{N} \lambda_j = 1 \\
&\lambda_j \geq 0 \qquad j = 1, 2, \ldots, N
\end{aligned}
\tag{5.1}
$$

For an efficient DMU $\phi_i = 1$, whereas for an inefficient DMU $\phi_i > 1$.

On the other hand, an input-oriented measure of efficiency can be obtained for the ith DMU by solving the linear programming problem:

---

[16]The concept of efficiency used here is that of technical efficiency. It is used in the context of an expanded efficient frontier with n variables across n dimensions, rather than just the two familiar mean and variance dimensions.

[17]While the Charnes, Cooper, and Rhodes, (1978) model assumes constant returns to scale, the model proposed by Banker, Charnes, and Cooper (1984) allows for variable returns to scale.

$$
\begin{aligned}
&\text{Min } \theta_i \\
&\text{Subject to} \\
&\qquad \sum_{j=1}^{N} \lambda_j y_{rj} \geq y_{ri} \qquad r = 1, 2, \ldots, m \\
&\qquad \sum_{j=1}^{N} \lambda_j x_{sj} \leq \theta_i x_{si} \qquad s = 1, 2, \ldots, n \\
&\qquad \sum_{j=1}^{N} \lambda_j = 1 \\
&\qquad \lambda_j \geq 0 \qquad j = 1, 2, \ldots, N
\end{aligned}
\tag{5.2}
$$

In this case an efficient DMU will have $\theta_i = 1$, whereas an inefficient DMU will have $\theta_i < 1$.

One requirement of these two models is that the inputs and outputs must not be negative. However, the BCC output-oriented model (5.1) is invariant to input translations, and the BCC input-oriented model (5.2) is invariant to output translations (see Ali and Seiford 1990). By choosing the appropriate model, we are able to handle the case of negative outputs or negative inputs by translation.

Application of DEA to the Study of CTA Performance

In this study our objective is to obtain a multicriteria measure of efficiency for each individual CTA in our sample. Wilkens and Zhu (2001) provide a motivation for applying DEA to measure the efficiency of an individual CTA based on multicriteria. They also provide a detailed illustration of how DEA can be used for the evaluation of CTA efficiency. Following a similar approach, we measure the efficiency of each CTA by treating the standard deviation of returns and proportion of negative returns as "inputs" in the DEA model; we treat return (average monthly return), minimum return, skewness, and kurtosis "outputs" in the DEA model.[18]

Since many of our outputs were negative for several CTAs, we had to translate them to obtain positive values.[19] (Table 5.1 shows the summary

---

[18]Our model differs from that of Wilkens and Zhu (2001) because we use kurtosis as an additional "output" in our model.

[19]These translations were used to make each of our outputs positive: (1) return: We added 0.04 (i.e., 4 percent) to the return of each CTA; (2) minimum return: We added 1 to the minimum return of each CTA; (3) skewness: We added 5 to the skewness of each CTA; (4) kurtosis: We added 3 to our original measure of excess kurtosis for each CTA (thus obtaining measures of kurtosis rather than excess kurtosis).

statistics for the original data; Table 5.9 shows the summary statistics for our translated data.) As a result of this translation, we chose the input-oriented BCC model to measure the efficiency of each individual CTA since it is invariant to output translations.[20]

We follow Wilkens and Zhu (2001), but also add kurtosis to the model. Although extreme value theory generally views kurtosis as indicative of more risk, we take a more neutral approach by controlling for skewness, kurtosis, and return outputs while minimizing standard deviation and the percent of negative returns. One reason that we treat kurtosis as an output rather than as an input to the DEA model is the fact that our input-oriented DEA model only has limited ability to translate negative inputs. Another more compelling reason is that in our sample of CTA returns, the mean skewness is positive, indicating that extreme values are more often positive than negative.

Tobit Regressions: Explaining the Differences in Efficiency of CTAs

Once we measure the input-oriented efficiency scores for the individual CTAs in our sample, we address the question of what leads to the differences in efficiencies. We explore the potential for the size of the fund, the length of the fund's track record, its investment style, and investment strategy to explain the degree of efficiency in terms of the DEA criteria (maximizing monthly returns, minimum returns, skewness, and kurtosis and minimizing standard deviation of returns and percentage of negative monthly returns). However, we cannot carry out standard ordinary least squares (OLS) regression of efficiency scores ($\theta_i \leq 1$) on the explanatory variables because the efficiencies scores of a number of CTAs in our sample are clustered at the upper limit of 1. Because the dependent variable, which is the efficiency score, is censored, the appropriate model to use in this context is a Tobit regression model, which is a limited-dependent-variable model. (See Greene 2000.) In this study, therefore, we use Tobit regression models to explain the differences in efficiencies across CTAs.

RESULTS

Table 5.10 presents the frequency distribution for the efficiency scores of all 157 CTAs. Overall, the scores are higher during the first (up-market) time

[20]We recognize that standard deviation and percentage of negative returns are not really inputs that are used to produce the outputs (returns, minimum returns, skewness, and kurtosis). Nevertheless, we use the terms "inputs" and "outputs" here simply to convey clearly how each of these criteria is being used within the construct of the DEA model.

TABLE 5.9 Summary Statistics for Translated Data Values of the DEA Model Criteria

Original Inputs & Adjusted Outputs		Standard Deviation	Percent Negative	Average Monthly Return	Skewness	Minimum Return	Kurtosis
All 216 CTAs for 1998–2000	Mean of CTAs	0.055	0.427	0.050	5.460	0.909	4.637
	Standard Deviation	0.034	0.124	0.013	0.929	0.063	2.732
	Min	0.005	0.042	0.016	2.880	0.470	1.476
	Max	0.193	0.750	0.151	8.694	0.994	19.370
All 216 CTAs for 2000–2002	Mean of CTAs	0.055	0.456	0.046	5.183	0.897	4.223
	Standard Deviation	0.034	0.118	0.011	0.897	0.076	2.365
	Min	0.004	0.125	0.008	0.558	0.517	1.672
	Max	0.245	0.750	0.113	6.981	0.997	23.812
157 CTAs for 1998–2000	Mean of CTAs	0.056	0.453	0.048	5.420	0.907	4.040
	Standard Deviation	0.026	0.092	0.008	0.705	0.049	1.644
	Min	0.022	0.292	0.016	3.484	0.754	1.502
	Max	0.155	0.750	0.072	7.224	0.988	9.249
157 CTAs for 2000–2002	Mean of CTAs	0.058	0.481	0.045	5.247	0.891	3.635
	Standard Deviation	0.031	0.094	0.009	0.596	0.067	1.160
	Min	0.013	0.208	0.008	3.430	0.615	1.672
	Max	0.191	0.750	0.067	6.471	0.982	7.748

TABLE 5.10 Frequency Distribution for Efficiency Scores

Efficiency Range	1998–2000	2000–2002
<0.4	0	1
0.4 – <0.5	2	12
0.5 – <0.6	29	42
0.6 – <0.7	27	42
0.7 – <0.8	35	26
0.8 – <0.9	26	17
0.9 – <1	13	4
1	25	13
Overall	157	157
Mean	0.765	0.682
Standard Deviation	0.158	0.153
Min	0.412	0.384
Max	1	1

period with an average efficiency of 76.5 percent, in contrast to an average of 68.2 percent during the second (down-market) period.

Table 5.11 breaks the results down by investment style[21] (diversified versus nondiversified) and shows that the mean and the standard deviation of the two groups are very close. There is virtually no difference in the efficiency scores between the two investment style groups.

Table 5.12 breaks the results down by investment strategy (systematic, discretionary, and trend-following). There is weak evidence that the systematic strategy outperforms the other strategies on the basis of the performance criteria used in this study. In both periods, the systematic strategy has the highest mean efficiency score with a relatively low standard deviation.

Determinants of the efficiency scores (theta) are investigated using Tobit regressions with efficiency score as the dependent variable. The variables include beta, beta-squared, average funds under management, length of manager track record, and dummy variables for the investment styles and strategies. Table 5.13 presents a correlation matrix for all of these variables.

Tables 5.14 through 5.16 provide the results of three Tobit regressions and indicate that beta-squared is a significant factor inversely affecting the efficiency scores during both time periods. Beta and the length of the manager's track record (maturity) also inversely impact the efficiency scores, but

[21]Because there are so many diversified CTAs in the database, we group together all of the CTAs that are not labeled as diversified. This results in only two groups: diversified and nondiversified.

TABLE 5.11 Frequency Distribution of Efficiency Scores, by Investment Style

	Diversified		Nondiversified	
Efficiency Range	1998–2000	2000–2002	1998–2000	2000–2002
<0.4	0	1	0	0
0.4 – <0.5	1	10	1	2
0.5 – <0.6	23	20	6	22
0.6 – <0.7	16	25	11	17
0.7 – <0.8	21	18	14	8
0.8 – <0.9	11	10	15	7
0.9 – <1	10	2	3	2
1	11	7	14	6
Sum	93	93	64	64
Mean	0.745	0.679	0.793	0.687
Standard Deviation	0.156	0.155	0.157	0.151
Min	0.412	0.384	0.443	0.469
Max	1	1	1	1

TABLE 5.12 Frequency Distribution of Efficiency Scores, by Investment Strategy

	Discretionary		Systematic		Trend Based	
Efficiency Range	1998–2000	2000–2002	1998–2000	2000–2002	1998–2000	2000–2002
<0.4	0	1	0	0	0	0
0.4 – <0.5	1	1	1	6	0	5
0.5 – <0.6	3	5	18	26	8	11
0.6 – <0.7	2	1	14	28	11	13
0.7 – <0.8	0	1	26	18	9	7
0.8 – <0.9	3	0	15	14	8	3
0.9 – <1	0	0	10	3	3	1
1	3	3	19	8	3	2
Sum	12	12	103	103	42	42
Mean	0.755	0.671	0.778	0.695	0.736	0.655
Standard Deviation	0.204	0.222	0.157	0.148	0.145	0.143
Min	0.412	0.384	0.443	0.402	0.508	0.450
Max	1	1	1	1	1	1

TABLE 5.13 Correlation Matrix for Variables Used in the Regression Analysis

1998–2000	Theta	Beta	AveMg Funds	Maturity	Beta Squared
Theta	1				
Beta	−0.079	1			
AveMgFunds	−0.004	0.051	1		
Maturity	−0.186	−0.046	0.298	1	
Beta-Squared	−0.174	−0.524	−0.073	0.057	1
2000–2002	**Theta**	**Beta**	**AveMg Funds**	**Maturity**	**Beta Squared**
Theta	1				
Beta	0.028	1			
AveMgFunds	0.024	−0.104	1		
Maturity	−0.088	0.143	0.205	1	
Beta-Squared	−0.245	−0.144	−0.055	0.093	1

Note: Theta represents the efficiency score from the DEA analysis.

TABLE 5.14 Results of Tobit Regressions

Variables	1998–2000	2000–2002
Intercept	0.7446	0.6276
	(0.0544)	(0.0502)
Beta	−0.1651***	−0.0336
	(0.0595)	(0.0362)
AvFunds	0.0008	0.0005
	(0.0006)	(0.0004)
Maturity	−0.0060**	−0.0024
	(0.0025)	(0.0024)
I	0.0192	−0.0081
	(0.0222)	(0.0209)
S2	0.0421	0.0750*
	(0.0442)	(0.0433)
S3	0.0212	0.0460
	(0.0462)	(0.0464)
Beta-squared	−0.3477***	−0.1448**
	(0.1235)	(0.0649)

The figures in parentheses are the standard errors.
I, S2, and S3 are dummy variables for non-diversified investment style, systematic investment strategy, and trend-based investment strategy, respectively.
***The coefficient is significant at 1 percent.
**The coefficient is significant at 5 percent.
*The coefficient is significant at 10 percent.

TABLE 5.15 Results of Tobit Regressions

Variables	1998–2000	2000–2002
Intercept	0.7912	0.6916
	(0.0292)	(0.0280)
Beta	−0.1517***	−0.0305
	(0.0588)	(0.0346)
AvFunds	0.0010	0.0005
	(0.0006)	(0.0005)
Maturity	−0.0066***	−0.0026
	(0.0025)	(0.0024)
Beta-squared	−0.3515***	−0.1692***
	(0.1221)	(0.0626)

The figures in parentheses are the standard errors.
***The coefficient is significant at 1 percent.
**The coefficient is significant at 5 percent.
*The coefficient is significant at 10 percent.
Note that Average Funds is significant at the 10.08 percent level of significance during 1998 to 2000.

TABLE 5.16 Results of Tobit Regressions

Variables	1998–2000	2000–2002
Intercept	0.7727	0.6574
	(0.0348)	(0.0335)
Beta	−0.1619***	−0.0428
	(0.0595)	(0.0349)
AvFunds	0.0010*	0.0005
	(0.0006)	(0.0004)
Maturity	−0.0062**	−0.0021
	(0.0025)	(0.0024)
S2	0.0217	0.0393*
	(0.0224)	(0.0217)
Beta-squared	−0.3622***	−0.1531**
	(0.1221)	(0.0625)

The figures in parentheses are the standard errors.
*** The coefficient is significant at 1 percent.
** The coefficient is significant at 5 percent.
* The coefficient is significant at 10 percent.

these results are statistically significant during the first time period only. The coefficient for dummy variable for the systematic strategy is positive and statistically significant during the second time period.

CONCLUSION

We illustrate the use of the DEA methodology in an application for evaluating CTA performance, and we explore the relationship between such performance and fund size, length of the manager's track record, investment style and strategy, and measures of the covariance of CTA returns with equity market returns. Performance is quantified by efficiency scores where 1 (or 100 percent) indicates perfect efficiency and scores lower than 1 represent relatively less efficient CTAs based on the performance criteria chosen.

We find some evidence that emerging hedge fund managers outperform established managers. Specifically, the length of the managers' track record is negatively related to our DEA model efficiency scores, but the size of the fund is not related to efficiency scores.

We also find that beta-squared is a significant factor inversely affecting the efficiency scores during both strong and weak equity market environments. Beta also inversely impacts the efficiency scores, but the results for beta are statistically significant during the first time period only.

Our preliminary results indicate that strategies (systematic, discretionary, trend-based) and styles (diversified, financial, currency, etc.) do not affect efficiency scores calculated by the DEA methodology presented here. One exception is that the systematic strategy does well relative to the other strategies in a statistically significant sense during the second time period of flat and weak equity markets.

CHAPTER 6

The Performance of CTAs in Changing Market Conditions

Georges Hübner and Nicolas Papageorgiou

This chapter studies the performance of 6 CTA indices during the period 1990 to 2003. Four distinct phases of financial markets are isolated, as well as three extreme events. We show that traditional multifactor as well as multimoment asset pricing models do not adequately describe CTA returns for any of the subperiods. With a proper choice of risk factors, we can, however, explain a significant proportion of CTA returns and assess the abnormal performance of each strategy. Most indices display null or negative alphas, but they seem to exhibit positive market timing abilities. The currency index reports both types of positive performance during the first subperiod. Severe market crises do not seem to affect abnormal CTA returns, except the Asian crisis, which benefited investors in the discretionary index. The Russian crisis has a uniform, although insignificant, negative impact on CTA abnormal returns.

INTRODUCTION

Since the blossoming of an extensive literature on hedge funds, commodity trading advisors (CTAs) have profited from renewed interest among researchers. Following the initial studies by Brorsen and Irwin (1985) and Murphy (1986), Elton, Gruber, and Rentzler (1987) ascertained that commodity funds were not likely to provide a superior return to passively managed portfolios of stocks and bonds. As a result of these discouraging findings, for over a decade very little research was devoted to the analysis of CTAs.

Fung and Hsieh's paper (1997a) on the analysis of hedge fund performance rekindled academic interest in CTAs. In their paper the authors notice that the return distributions of certain hedge funds share some important characteristics with those of CTAs. Subsequently, Schneeweis and Spurgin (1997), Brown, Goetzmann, and Park (2001), and Edwards and Caglayan (2001) performed studies on a joint sample of CTA and hedge fund data. Fung and Hsieh (1997b) analyzed these two investment vehicles independently and discovered that CTA returns exhibit optionlike dynamics that may provide them with a peculiar role in portfolio management. Liang (2003) explicitly separated CTAs and hedge funds in his analysis and concluded that aside from the particular management rules that differentiate them from hedge funds, CTAs exhibit very low correlation with hedge funds strategies. Although they seem to underperform hedge funds and even funds-of-funds strategies in bullish markets, Edwards and Caglayan (2001) and Liang (2003) discovered that their creditable behavior in bearish market conditions indicates that CTAs could represent precious hedging instruments when markets are in a downtrend. This atypical behavior can be attributed at least in part to the nonnormality of the return structure of CTAs.

Although the particular return distributions of CTAs are now recognized, the measurement of their performance has yet to be adapted. By mimicry with the large stream of performance studies on mutual funds, virtually all studies on hedge funds have adopted the classical Sharpe ratio (1966) and Jensen's alpha (1968) as relevant performance measures. These questionable choices become all the more inaccurate when they are applied to CTAs [see Edwards and Liew (1999); Edwards and Caglayan (2001); Liang (2003)] because their underlying distributional properties, and, most of all, very low correlation with traditional risk factors do not support these measures. Edwards and Caglayan (2001) use catastrophic loss measures to assess the hedging properties of these funds, but this type of measure is applicable only to extremely risk-averse agents, which is not a framework that corresponds to real portfolio management constraints. The positive aspect of these measures is that they do not require prior knowledge of the underlying return-generating process, which eliminates most of the difficulties associated with the discovery of a proper pricing model for CTAs.

In this chapter we test a joint set of pricing models and performance measures that aim to better capture the distributional features of CTAs. The identification of risk premia and of the sensitivities of CTA returns to these factors will clear the way toward the use of less utility-based performance measures than the Sharpe ratio and to a more proper use of stochastic discount factor–based performance measures, such as Jensen's alpha, the Treynor ratio, or the Treynor and Mazuy (1966) measure of market timing ability.

The next section of this chapter examines the market trends and crises over the sample period and presents the descriptive statistics of the CTA index returns. An examination of the explanatory power of market factors as well as trading strategy factors in describing CTA returns follows. The next section looks at different performance measures on the CTAs.

DATA AND SAMPLE PERIOD

The data set that we use is the Barclay's Trading group CTA data for the period from January 1990 to November 2003. The data set is composed of end-of-month returns for the CTA index as well as for five subindices[1]: the Barclay Currency Traders Index, the Barclay Financial and Metal Traders Index, the Barclay Systematic Traders Index, the Barclay Diversified Traders Index, and the Barclay Discretionary Traders Index.

We divide the sample period into subperiods to investigate the behavior of the CTA indices under specific market conditions (see Table 6.1).

TABLE 6.1 Summary of Subperiods

Panel A: Bull and Bear Markets				
Market Trend	Start	Finish	Ann. Return	# Obs
Weak Bull	01:1990	12:1993	+10.0%	48
Moderate Bull	01:1994	09:1998	+19.0%	57
Strong Bull	09:1998	03:2000	+29.5%	18
Bear	03:2000	09:2002	−22.6%	30
Panel B: Financial Crises				
Extreme Event	Start	Finish	Magnitude	# Obs
Russian Crisis	10:1997	11:1997	−13.0%	2
Asian Crisis	08:1998	09:1998	−14.7%	2
Terrorist Crisis	09:2001	10:2001	−18.2%	2

For both panels, start and finish dates are identified as the end-of-month trading days surrounding the subperiod under study. In Panel A, annualized returns are computed using closing values of the S&P 500 index. In Panel B, the magnitude of the crisis is computed by taking the minimum and maximum values of the S&P 500 index during the event month.

[1]We do not include the Barclay Agricultural Traders Index in this study as the financial variables used for the return-generating model would not explain a significant proportion of the return variance.

The bull market that lasted from the early 1990s until the end of the dot-com bubble in March 2000 is broken down into three subperiods. We refer to the final 18 months prior to the market crash as "Strong Bull"; during this time the annualized return on the Standard & Poor's (S&P) 500 was 29.5 percent. We call the period from January 1990 to December 1993 "Weak Bull" and the period from January 1994 to September 1998 "Moderate Bull." Not only do the annualized returns nearly double from 10 percent to 19 percent over these two subperiods, the return distributions are considerably different over the two periods. The fourth and final subperiod that we investigate is the "Bear Market" that lasted from March 2000 to September 2002, during which time the annualized return on the S&P 500 was –22.6 percent.

Three significant market crises occur during our sample period, each of which caused a significant short-term drop in the market. Predictably, these three crises are the Russian default, the Asian currency crisis, and September 11 terrorist attacks. Interestingly, the magnitude and duration of these three shocks on the S&P 500 is very similar. Each event triggered a drop in the S&P 500 of about 15 percent, and the time required for the index to return to its preevent level was generally two to three months. The three crises occur in two different subperiods: "Moderate Bull" and "Bear."

Table 6.2 presents the descriptive statistics for the excess returns on the CTA indices for the entire period as well as for the four subperiods. Although each individual CTA index has certain intrinsic characteristics, certain general properties appear to be common to all the CTAs in our sample. More specifically, the Jarque-Bera tests over the entire sample period illustrate that all the CTA indices, with the sole exception of the diversified index, exhibit nonnormality in their excess returns. Another common trait is the very poor results during the "Strong Bull" period: all the CTA indices display negative excess returns for this period of very high returns in the stock markets. As a matter of fact, this is unanimously the worst subperiod in terms of performance for all the CTA indices. These results are in accordance with previous findings by Edwards and Caglayan (2001) and Liang (2003), who identified the poor performance of CTAs in bull markets. A further examination of the mean excess returns over the four subperiods reveals that for all the CTA indices, the highest excess returns are achieved in "Weak Bull," which includes the recession of the early 1990s, and "Bear," which followed the collapse of the dot-com bubble. This would seem to concur with the notion that CTAs possess valuable return characteristics during down markets.

The descriptive statistics for the excess returns of the CTA indices seem to indicate that there exist similar return dynamics across the different types of CTAs. The two subindices that exhibit marginally different return pat-

TABLE 6.2 Descriptive Statistics of Excess Returns

	Mean	Median	Max	Min	Std. Dev.	Skewness	Kurtosis	J-B
	0.24	−0.05	9.71	−6.13	2.67	0.38	3.36	4.98*
	0.31	−0.08	9.71	−6.13	3.15	0.46	3.40	1.99
CTA	0.28	0.04	5.95	−5.18	2.56	0.30	2.73	1.04
Index	−0.42	−0.81	2.24	−4.62	1.70	−0.41	3.22	0.55
	0.41	0.36	6.31	−4.66	2.53	0.28	3.00	0.40
	0.42	−0.04	14.17	−7.91	3.46	0.60	3.99	17.04**
	0.82	−0.21	14.17	−7.91	4.47	0.67	3.44	4.01
Systematic	0.37	0.31	7.11	−7.09	3.00	0.23	3.00	0.48
Traders Index	−0.56	−1.09	2.66	−5.03	2.01	−0.22	2.56	0.29
	0.56	0.48	7.06	−5.73	3.13	0.17	2.78	0.20
	0.30	0.05	6.72	−4.64	2.23	0.48	3.23	6.88*
Financial and	0.63	0.12	6.72	−3.84	2.04	0.80	3.67	5.96*
Metal Traders	0.18	0.15	5.88	−4.64	2.44	0.39	3.05	1.47
Index	−0.71	−1.04	1.51	−3.16	1.35	0.03	1.85	0.99
	0.53	0.22	5.89	−4.36	2.50	0.18	2.64	0.33

TABLE 6.2 *(continued)*

	Mean	Median	Max	Min	Std. Dev.	Skewness	Kurtosis	J-B
	0.46	0.06	11.71	–7.35	3.61	0.35	2.99	3.46
	0.73	0.17	11.71	–7.02	4.07	0.41	2.90	1.37
Diversified	0.46	0.07	9.76	–6.88	3.51	0.38	2.93	1.36
Traders Index	–0.52	–0.54	3.18	–5.77	2.43	–0.23	2.35	0.47
	0.64	0.53	7.97	–6.01	3.40	0.18	2.67	0.29
	–0.02	–0.05	7.85	–3.26	1.44	1.07	7.63	181**
	0.29	–0.03	7.85	–3.26	1.71	1.71	9.33	103**
Discretionary	–0.30	–0.48	3.92	–2.61	1.33	0.68	3.71	5.56*
Traders Index	–0.35	–0.03	1.80	–2.88	1.30	–0.48	2.55	0.84
	0.07	0.06	3.67	–3.07	1.42	0.23	3.17	0.31
	0.37	–0.35	14.37	–7.99	3.30	1.41	6.44	138**
	1.04	0.40	14.37	–7.99	5.22	0.79	2.97	4.96*
Currency	0.08	–0.44	6.99	–4.07	2.29	0.92	3.67	9.09**
Traders Index	–0.22	–0.55	2.76	–1.82	1.39	0.71	2.31	1.87
	0.12	–0.39	6.29	–2.41	2.09	1.44	4.42	12.95**

Excess returns are calculated as the difference between the returns on the CTA indices and the return on the 3-month treasury bill over the same period.

* The values are significant at the 10 percent level.

** The values are significant at the 5 percent level.

terns are the Discretionary Traders Index and the Currency Traders Index. These two indices display the highest skewness and kurtosis; the former is the only index to exhibit negative returns over the entire sample.

Table 6.3 examines the correlation coefficients between the different CTA indices as well as between the CTA indices and the first two return moments of the Russell 3000 (Russell squared). The results for the entire sample as well as the subsamples confirm our earlier findings. The correlation coefficient between the CTA index, the Financial and Metal Traders Index, the Systematic Traders Index, and the Diversified Traders Index are positive and close to 1 for all the different periods. The Currency Trader Index and the Discretionary Index have the lowest correlation coefficient with the other CTA indices. The coefficients are still positive between all the indices and for all the subperiods, but the correlation coefficient is much smaller. Over the entire period, all of the CTA indices have a small and negative correlation coefficient with the Russell 3000 index and a positive relation with the square of the Russell 3000 returns. These results are consistent during the four subperiods with the exception of the Currency and Discretionary indices, which have a positive relation with the Russell 3000 in certain subperiods. These correlations remain nonetheless small in magnitude.

EXPLAINING CTA RETURNS

Here we introduce three types of return-generating processes that may be helpful in understanding monthly CTA returns over the period. We first perform a classical multifactor analysis using risk premia similar to the Fama and French (1993) and Carhart (1997) models, with an additional factor related to stock dividend yields, in a similar spirit to Kunkel, Ehrhardt, and Kuhlemeyer (1999). We then use a simple specification aimed at capturing the exposure to skewness and kurtosis. Finally, we select several other factors that have been applied to performance studies of hedge funds and/or CTAs to identify the best linear asset-pricing model for each particular subperiod under study.

Multifactor Model

We start with the four-factor model proposed by Carhart (1997), but exclude the factor mimicking the value premium, namely the "High minus Low" (HML) book-to-market value of equity, that yields significant results for none of our regressions. This factor is replaced by an additional factor related to the risk premium associated with high-yield dividend-paying stocks. Although there is only limited and controversial evidence of the actual value added of this factor in the explanation of empirical returns, Kunkel et al. (1999) find that there is a significant empirical return compo-

TABLE 6.3 Correlations between Excess Returns on CTA Indices and Russell 3000

	CTA Index	Systematic	Fin. and Metal	Diversified	Discretionary	Currency	Russell	$Russell^2$
				Entire Period				
CTA Index	1							
Systematic	0.98	1						
Fin/Met	0.89	0.89	1					
Diversified	0.98	0.97	0.85	1				
Discretionary	0.57	0.50	0.47	0.56	1			
Currency	0.68	0.74	0.63	0.63	0.39	1		
Russell	−0.20	−0.19	−0.18	−0.23	−0.07	−0.10	1	
$Russell^2$	0.25	0.25	0.30	0.28	0.16	0.09	−0.34	1
				Weak Bull Market				
CTA Index	1							
Systematic	0.97	1						
Fin/Met	0.90	0.93	1					
Diversified	0.98	0.97	0.87	1				
Discretionary	0.64	0.53	0.52	0.65	1			
Currency	0.78	0.85	0.81	0.79	0.43	1		
Russell	−0.26	−0.20	−0.20	−0.26	−0.43	−0.22	1	
$Russell^2$	0.33	0.34	0.40	0.32	0.40	0.30	−0.10	1
				Average Bull Market				
CTA Index	1							
Systematic	0.99	1						
Fin/Met	0.90	0.91	1					

TABLE 6.3 *(continued)*

	CTA Index	Systematic	Fin. and Metal	Diversified	Discretionary	Currency	Russell	Russell^2
				Average Bull Market *(continued)*				
Diversified	0.97	0.96	0.84	1				
Discretionary	0.71	0.66	0.60	0.70	1			
Currency	0.68	0.68	0.63	0.53	0.43	1		
Russell	0.00	0.00	0.04	−0.07	0.12	0.09	1	
Russell^2	0.30	0.33	0.37	0.37	0.16	−0.02	−0.51	1
				Strong Bull Market				
CTA Index	1							
Systematic	0.98	1						
Fin/Met	0.85	0.83						
Diversified	0.98	0.98	0.78	1				
Discretionary	0.59	0.47	0.41	0.52	1			
Currency	0.38	0.36	0.38	0.26	0.30	1		
Russell	−0.22	−0.24	0.01	−0.26	−0.10	−0.10	1	
Russell^2	−0.11	−0.13	0.18	−0.15	0.01	−0.10	0.66	1
				Bear Market				
CTA Index	1							
Systematic	0.99	1						
Fin/Met	0.95	0.95						
Diversified	0.99	0.99	0.92	1				
Discretionary	0.33	0.26	0.29	0.30	1			
Currency	0.67	0.64	0.61	0.60	0.30	1		
Russell	−0.37	−0.35	−0.41	−0.36	0.19	−0.18	1	
Russell^2	0.19	0.19	0.18	0.24	−0.08	−0.02	−0.59	1

nent associated with high-yield dividend-paying stocks, which is explained in Martin and van Zijl (2003) by a tax differential argument. The equation for the market model is:

$$r_t = \alpha + \beta_1 Mkt_t + \beta_2 SMB_t + \beta_3 UMD_t + \beta_4 HDMZD_t + \varepsilon_t \qquad (6.1)$$

where r_t = CTA index return in excess of the 13-week T-Bill rate,
Mkt_t = excess return on the portfolio obtained by averaging the returns of the Fama and French (1993) size and book-to-market portfolios
SMB_t = the factor-mimicking portfolio for size ("*Small Minus Big*")
UMD_t = the factor-mimicking portfolio for the momentum effect ("*Up Minus Down*")
$HDMZD_t$ = difference between equally weighted monthly returns of the top 30 percent quantile stocks ranked by dividend yields and of the zero-dividend yield stocks *("High Dividend Minus Low Dividend").*

Factors are extracted from French's web site (http://mba.tuck.dartmouth.edu/pages/faculty/ken.french/data_library.html). Table 6.4 summarizes the results of this regression over the entire period and the four subperiods.

For all but one subperiod (Weak Bull), the adjusted R-squared coefficients are extremely low and often negative. The only statistically significant linear relationship is observed for the Weak Bull subperiod, while the model is unable to explain anything during the Strong Bull subperiod. The significance of the regressions is especially poor for the Discretionary and Currency strategies, whose different pattern of returns had already been observed through their correlation structure. During the period from 1990 to 1993, it appears that only the coefficient of the dividend factor is significantly positive for all indices except the Discretionary Index.[2]

These rather weak results confirm the inaccuracy of classical multifactor models for the assessment of required returns of commodity trading advisors. This is in contrast with pervasive evidence of the ability of the Carhart (1997) model to explain up to an average of 60 percent of the variance of hedge funds strategies (see Capocci, Corhay, and Hübner, 2003; Capocci and Hübner, 2004), providing further evidence of the completely different return dynamics of these financial instruments.

---

[2]Of course, the replacement of this risk premium, the only one that seems to have explanatory power, by the traditional HML factor would have yielded even lower adjusted R-squared.

TABLE 6.4 Regression Results Using Modified Fama-French Factors

		Entire Period	Weak Bull	Moderate Bull	Strong Bull	Bear
CTA Index	β_1	−0.061	−0.031	0.014	−0.090	−0.223
	β_2	0.001	0.373	−0.437**	0.062	0.011
	β_3	0.077*	0.217*	−0.119	−0.040	0.051
	β_4	0.064	0.658**	−0.175	−0.066	−0.082
	R^2_{adj}	0.047	0.324	0.051	—	0.044
Systematic	β_1	−0.063	0.058	0.014	−0.110	−0.280
	β_2	−0.003	0.583	−0.517**	0.062	0.019
	β_3	0.102**	0.222	−0.137	−0.020	0.060
	β_4	0.089	1.020**	−0.188	−0.060	−0.115*
	R^2_{adj}	0.043	0.286	0.057	—	0.046
Fin/Metal	β_1	−0.034	0.035	0.031	0.024	−0.270**
	β_2	0.009	0.171	−0.469	0.071	0.021
	β_3	0.043	0.101	−0.077**	−0.004	0.014
	β_4	0.070*	0.433**	−0.224	0.013	−0.087
	R^2_{adj}	0.033	0.308	0.087	—	0.065
Diversified	β_1	−0.120	−0.026	−0.045	−0.147	−0.331*
	β_2	−0.002	0.440	−0.599**	0.086	0.005
	β_3	0.098*	0.243	−0.242	−0.012	0.067
	β_4	0.062	0.853**	−0.236	−0.076	−0.143
	R^2_{adj}	0.050	0.314	0.057	—	0.059
Discretionary	β_1	−0.038	−0.153**	0.025	−0.034	−0.004
	β_2	−0.014	0.012	−0.170**	0.015	−0.041
	β_3	−0.031	0.056	−0.160*	0.036	−0.045
	β_4	−0.024	0.100	−0.191**	0.009	−0.040
	R^2_{adj}	—	0.172	0.111	—	—
Currency	β_1	0.021	−0.013	0.046	−0.015	−0.061
	β_2	−0.021	0.392	−0.176	0.003	0.084
	β_3	0.079	0.364	0.151	−0.070	0.006
	β_4	0.122**	0.915**	−0.071	−0.005	0.020
	R^2_{adj}	0.031	0.265	0.000	—	—

* The values are significant at the 10 percent level.
** The values are significant at the 5 percent level.

Multi-Moment Model

It is natural to suspect that the positive skewness and high kurtosis of CTA returns reported in Table 6.2 could render our index returns sensitive to a multimoment asset pricing specification. Such a framework also may capture a significant proportion of the optionlike dynamics of CTAs reported by Fung and Hsieh (1997b) and Liang (2003), because the nonlinear payoff structure of option contracts generates fat-tailed, asymmetric option return distributions.

We choose to adopt a simple specification for the characterization of a multimoment return-generating model, in a similar vein to the study of Fang and Lai (1997), who report significant prices of risk for systematic coskewness and cokurtosis of stock returns with the market portfolio. Their first-pass cubic regression resembles:

$$r_t = \alpha + \beta_1 r_{m,t} + \beta_2 r_{m,t}^2 + \beta_3 r_{m,t}^3 + \varepsilon_t \tag{6.2}$$

where $r_{m,t}$ = excess return on the market index

Unlike the prêt-à-porter specification proposed in equation 6.1, where the market factor chosen had to be neutral with respect to size considerations, the index chosen in equation 6.2 is the one whose influence on CTA returns is likely to be highest. In accordance with previous studies, we use the Russell 3000 index as a proxy for the market portfolio.

Table 6.5 summarizes the results of regression equation 6.2 over the entire period as well as the four subperiods.

The regressions still explain, on average, a very low proportion of the CTA returns variance. Yet four extremely interesting patterns can be noticed.

1. The multimoment regression seems to provide a slightly better fit than the multifactor model presented in equation 6.1, with the exception of the "Weak Bull" period, where the multifactor dominates for all but the Discretionary strategy.
2. The most significant regression coefficient appears to be β_2, which is the loading on the squared market return. It is positive for the global period as well as for the "Weak Bull" subperiod for most CTA indices.
3. The patterns of the Discretionary and Currency indices exhibit major differences with respect to the rest of CTA indices, which behave in very similar ways. For these indices, closely related to the behavior of financial markets, the coefficient of the Russell 3000 index is negative for the whole period, but only because it is significantly negative during the first

TABLE 6.5 Cubic Regression of CTA Indices on the Russell 3000 Index

		Entire Period	Weak Bull	Moderate Bull	Strong Bull	Bear
CTA Index	β_1	−0.115*	−0.522**	0.148	0.189	0.048
	β_2	0.021**	0.043**	0.022	0.081	−0.028
	β_3	0.001	0.005**	−0.0002	−0.017	−0.004
	R^2_{adj}	0.064	0.186	0.073	—	0.111
Systematic	β_1	−0.151	−0.629**	0.194	0.051	0.161
	β_2	0.026**	0.065**	0.027	0.122	−0.034
	β_3	0.000	0.007**	−0.000	−0.015	−0.006
	R^2_{adj}	0.053	0.156	0.098	—	0.118
Fin/Metal	β_1	−0.061	−0.317	0.175	0.167	0.005
	β_2	0.021*	0.035*	0.036	0.085	−0.031
	β_3	0.0003	0.004*	0.0002	−0.013	−0.004
	R^2_{adj}	0.082	0.231**	0.162	—	0.148
Diversified	β_1	−0.136	−0.584**	0.177	0.330	0.127
	β_2	0.026**	0.054**	0.028	0.131	−0.033
	β_3	0.0002	0.005	−0.001	−0.028	−0.006
	R^2_{adj}	0.081	0.150	0.109	0.065	0.121
Discretionary	β_1	−0.021	−0.093	0.067	0.053	0.105
	β_2	0.009*	0.022**	0.016	0.039	−0.002
	β_3	0.0003*	−0.001	0.0004	−0.006	−0.001
	R^2_{adj}	0.011	0.290	0.034	—	—
Currency	β_1	−0.193**	−0.755**	0.099	−0.055	−0.176
	β_2	0.026**	0.068**	−0.009	−0.015	−0.00
	β_3	0.002**	0.008*	−0.001	0.002	0.001
	R^2_{adj}	0.029	0.136	—	—	—

* The values are significant at the 10 percent level.
** The values are significant at the 5 percent level.

subperiod. From 1994 onward, it becomes positive, although not significant. Thus, this is not evidence of a systematic contrarian strategy. Notice that the coefficient for the Russell 3000 is typically greater (in absolute value) than the corresponding loading for the market return in Table 6.4, indicating that this index is more suitable as an explanatory variable for CTA indices than a proxy that gives more weight to large capitalization companies.

4. Neither the multifactor nor the multimoment specification has explanatory power for the most extreme movements, namely the "Strong Bull" and "Bear" market conditions.

These facts lead us to conclude that additional factors are essential to capture the dynamics of CTA returns and that a subperiod analysis is required since the returns seem to exhibit very little stationarity. Additionally, the Discretionary and Currency CTA indices need to be studied independently, as their return distributions are dissimilar to those of the other CTA indices.

Tailor-Made Specifications

The starting point of the analysis is driven mostly by empirical considerations. The traditional approaches discussed previously explain a fraction of the variations in CTA returns, but these factors need to be accompanied, and occasionally replaced, by alternative return-generating processes. It would be incorrect to assume that the strategies of CTA managers remain static over time; the managers adapt to changes in the financial and commodity markets as well as to specific market conditions that managed derivative portfolios such as CTAs are capable of exploiting. As a result, we would expect the pricing model to change with evolving market conditions.

Three families of factors can be used for the construction of empirically valid models. The first candidates are the ones we used in the previous subsections. Some of them, and especially the dividend factor for equation 6.1 and the squared market return for equation 6.2, should not necessarily be thrown out of the empirical model. We thus define variables SMB, HML, and HDMZD as in equation 6.1 and variables RUS, RUS2, and RUS3 corresponding to the Russell 3000 index to the power of 1, 2, and 3 respectively.

The second candidates are financial or commodity indices that have been used previously in the mutual or hedge funds performance measurement literature. Among the large set of potential candidates, we have selected: the return on the Goldman Sachs Commodity Index (GSCI), previously used by Capocci and Hübner (2004); the return on Moody's Commodity Index (MCOM); the U.S. Moody's Baa Corporate Bond Yield to proxy for the default risk premium (DEF) as well as the monthly change on this yield (ΔDEF); the U.S. 10-year/6-month Interest Rate Swap Rate to proxy for the maturity risk premium (MAT) as well as its monthly change (ΔMAT); and finally the monthly change in the U.S. dollar/Swiss franc exchange rate to proxy for the currency risk premium (FX). These data series were extracted from the JCFQuant database.

Finally, we use the option strategy factor proposed by Agarwal and Naik (2002) and Liang (2003) to capture the optionality component of CTA returns. We construct the series of returns on the one-month ATM call written on the Russell 3000 index (ATMC) for this purpose.

For each subperiod, we select the set of variables that provides the highest information content for the regressions. We use the same sets of variables for the Systematic, Finance/Metals, Diversified, and Global CTA indices, implying that the results do not strictly respect the minimization of the Akaike Information criterion. Table 6.6 presents the differentiated model results for these indices.

The results are consistent across the different indices, both in terms of sign and magnitude of the coefficients, but they vary considerably over the different subperiods. The results over the entire period show a marked increase in the adjusted *R*-squared when compared to the two previous model specifications. The explanatory power of the variables is, however, still relatively limited when we consider the entire period, with *R*-squared ranging from 12.2 percent for the CTA index up to only 19.4 percent for the Financial and Metals index. The square of the excess returns on the Russell 3000 (RUS2) and the change in the 10-year interest rate over the 6-month swap rate (ΔMAT) are significant for the four indices. Not surprisingly, these two factors are also important in explaining the CTA returns in the subperiods. ΔMAT is included as a factor in all the subperiods and is consistently significant. RUS2 helps explain the variations in returns during the "Weak Bull" and "Moderate Bull" periods. The two subperiods during which the tailor-made factor model best captures the return variations in the four indices are the "Weak Bull" and "Strong Bull" periods, which show adjusted *R*-squared of up to 40.4 percent. This leads us to conclude that given the appropriate risk factors, we are able to explain a considerable proportion of CTA returns in a linear setup. However, the results in Table 6.6 show that the factors having the best explanatory power change with market conditions.

As we noted earlier, the return characteristics of the Currency index and Discretionary index are considerably different from those of the other four indices, hence the factors that best capture their behavior are different. Tables 6.7 and 6.8 present the results for the tailor-made models for these two indices for the entire period as well as the four subperiods.

The Currency index proves to be the index for which the factors were least successful at explaining the excess returns (Table 6.7). For the entire period, the adjusted *R*-squared of the tailor-made model is 0.099. The results indicate that the returns on the currency index seem to exhibit an optionlike payoff distribution as the series of returns on the one-month ATM call writ-

TABLE 6.6 Tailor-Made Specification Results for CTA, Systematic, Financial and Metals, and Diversified Indices

	R^2_{adj}	Alpha	RUS	RUS2	RUS3	UMD	HDMZD	ΔMAT	ΔDEF
				Entire Period					
CTA Index	0.122	−0.094	−0.052	0.014**	—	0.048	0.045	−0.115**	—
Systematic	0.128	−0.030	−0.052	0.018**	—	0.062	0.063	−0.161**	—
Fin/Metal	0.194	−0.035	−0.029	0.015**	—	0.006	0.042	−0.147**	—
Diversified	0.133	−0.025	−0.099	0.021**	—	0.058	0.039	−0.154**	—
				Weak Bull					
CTA Index	0.326	−0.181	—	0.023	—	0.246*	0.382**	0.044	—
Systematic	0.293	0.095	—	0.037*	—	0.238	0.536**	−0.045	—
Fin/Metal	0.404	0.201	—	0.022**	—	0.068	0.258**	−0.115*	—
Diversified	0.325	0.164	—	0.028	—	0.297*	0.516*	0.089	—
				Moderate Bull					
CTA Index	0.150	−0.019	—	0.012*	—	—	—	−0.181**	—
Systematic	0.183	−0.014	—	0.021*	—	—	—	−0.228**	—
Fin/Metal	0.224	−0.172	—	0.019*	—	—	—	−0.196**	—
Diversified	0.187	−0.054	—	0.028**	—	—	—	−0.233*	—

TABLE 6.6 *(continued)*

	R^2_{adj}	Alpha	RUS	RUS2	RUS3	UMD	HDMZD	ΔMAT	ΔDEF
				Strong Bull					
CTA Index	0.335	−0.506	—	—	—	—	—	0.289*	0.522*
Systematic	0.371	−0.757	—	—	—	—	—	0.376**	0.591*
Fin/Metal	0.333	−1.011*	—	—	—	—	—	0.274**	−0.263
Diversified	0.358	−0.624	—	—	—	—	—	0.417*	0.781*
				Bear					
CTA Index	0.154	−0.141	—	—	−0.001	—	—	−0.153	—
Systematic	0.163	−0.140	—	—	−0.001	—	—	−0.202*	—
Fin/Metal	0.194	−0.054	—	—	−0.001	—	—	−0.180	—
Diversified	0.173	−0.139	—	—	−0.002	—	—	−0.199	—

* The values are significant at the 10 percent level.
** The values are significant at the 5 percent level.

TABLE 6.7 Tailor-Made Model Results for Currency Index

	R^2_{adj}	Alpha	ATMC	DEF	MAT	FX	UMD	HDMZD	RUS2
Entire Period	0.099	−3.188	−0.485**	2.364*	—	0.099	0.083*	0.122**	—
Weak Bull	0.332	0.372	−0.757*	—	—	—	0.409*	0.569**	0.030
Moderate Bull	—	—	—	—	—	—	—	—	—
Strong Bull	0.090	3.923	0.273	—	−3.172	—	—	—	—
Bear	—	—	—	—	—	—	—	—	—

ATMC = series of returns on the one-month ATM call written on the Russell 3000 index. *DEF* = U.S. Moody's Baa corporate bond yield. *MAT* = U.S. 10-year/6-month Interest Rate Swap Rate. FX = monthly change in the U.S. dollar/Swiss franc exchange rate. *UMD* (Up Minus Down) = average return on the two high prior return portfolios minus the average return on the two low prior return portfolios. *HDMZD* (High Dividend Minus Zero Dividend) = average return of the highest-dividend-paying stocks versus the stocks that do not dispense dividends. *RUS2* = square of the excess returns on the Russell 3000.

* The values are significant at the 10 percent level.
**The values are significant at the 5 percent level.

ten on the Russell 3000 index (ATMC) is a significant explanatory variable. Similar to the four previous indices, the "best-fit" regression is most successful at capturing the dynamics of the returns in the "Weak Bull" subperiod, with the adjusted *R*-squared equal to 0.332. For the "Moderate Bull" and "Bear" markets, no combination of risk factors manages to provide any insight into the return structure of the Currency index returns.

Table 6.8 presents the tailor-made regression results for the Discretionary index. Although the results are not impressive when we consider the entire period (adjusted *R*-squared of 0.097), the market factors are successful at explaining the Discretionary index returns for all the subperiods with the exception of "Strong Bull." The results during the "Bear" period are particularly impressive as the regression results report an adjusted *R*-squared of 0.47. The adjusted *R*-squared of the "Weak Bull" and "Moderate Bull" subperiods are comparable to those found for the previous indices; however, the factors that explain the variations in the returns are different across the indices. Overall we find that the factors that best explain the excess returns on the discretionary index are the currency risk premium (FX), the square of the excess returns on the Russell 3000 (RUS2), and the returns on the two commodity indices (GSCI and MCOM).

TABLE 6.8 Differentiated Model Results for Discretionary Index

	R^2_{adj}	Alpha	ATMC	FX	UMD	HDMZD	ΔMAT	GSCI	RUS2	RUS3	MCOM
Entire Period	0.097	−0.212*	—	—	—	—	—	0.091**	0.007**	—	—
Weak Bull	0.345	−0.025	—	—	0.117	0.089	0.092	—	0.018**	−0.002**	—
Moderate Bull	0.211	−0.184	—	−0.11**	−0.123	−0.096*	−0.091**	0.069	—	—	—
Strong Bull	—	—	—	—	—	—	—	—	—	—	—
Bear	0.472	−0.092	−0.202	0.166**	−0.052*	—	—	—	—	—	0.267**

ATMC = series of returns on the one-month ATM call written on the Russell 3000 index. FX = monthly change in the U.S. dollar/Swiss franc exchange rate. *UMD* (Up Minus Down) = average return on the two high prior return portfolios minus the average return on the two low prior return portfolios. *HDMZD* (High Dividend Minus Zero Dividend) = average return of the highest-dividend-paying stocks versus the stocks that do not dispense dividends. ΔMAT = change in the U.S. 10-year/6-month Interest Rate Swap Rate. GSCI = return on the Goldman Sachs Commodity Index. RUS2 = square of the excess returns on the Russell 3000. RUS3 = cube of the excess returns on the Russell 3000. MCOM = return on Moody's Commodity Index.

* The values are significant at the 10 percent level.

** The values are significant at the 5 percent level.

PERFORMANCE MEASUREMENT

Performance under Changing Market Conditions

Thanks to the effort put in the previous section to explain CTA expected returns over the subperiods, we can go beyond the use of the Sharpe ratio to characterize abnormal performance as extensively used in the CTA performance literature. This ratio is extremely useful for ranking purposes, but not to quantify the extent to which a given index has exceeded a benchmark return. Furthermore, the pervasive departure from normality of CTA returns casts doubt on the reliability of this performance measure, which uses variance as the measure of risk.

Here we apply four types of performance measures to each period:

1. The alpha of the regressions;
2. The Information Ratio (IR) (Grinold and Kahn 1992, 1995) defined as the ratio of alpha over the standard deviation of residuals;[3]
3. The Generalized Treynor Ratio (GTR), which extends the original Treynor ratio to a multi-index setup (Hübner 2003), defined as the ratio of the alpha over the total required return; and
4. The Treynor and Mazuy (1966) measure of market timing, which is simply the coefficient of the squared market return, proxied by RUS2 in our specification.

Although the alpha, the IR, and the GTR provide different portfolio rankings, the test for significance is essentially the same as it reduces to testing whether alpha = 0, which is typically performed using a Student *t*-test.

The analysis of Table 6.6 reveals unambiguous results on alphas. For all strategies, the regression results never allow us to reject the hypothesis of zero abnormal performance. The only noticeable exception is observed for the Finance/Metals strategy, which underperforms the market at the 10 percent significance level in the "Strong Bull" subperiod. Notice that all the alphas of the four strategies are negative during this bullish period, while the three substrategies display positive, yet relatively small in magnitude and insignificant, alphas during the "Weak Bull" period. This finding indicates that these types of CTA strategies tend to amplify market movement in the adverse direction. Not only are their required returns negatively correlated with market movement, but their abnormal performance is also contrarian. The Finance/Metals strategy seems to experience larger swings in both directions. The (insignificant) negative performance in the "Bear" market contra-

[3]Of course, the same caveat as for the Sharpe ratio applies to this measure as it implicitly uses the variance as a risk measure.

dicts this analysis, as the CTAs did not benefit from market conditions that should have favorably influenced their market contrarian strategies.

At the aggregate level, the magnitude of the (negative) alphas is rather low, but this has to be related to the low significance levels of the regressions resulting from the extreme heterogeneity of CTA behavior from one subperiod to another. Of course, these conclusions can be generalized to the IR and GTR performance measures, as none of the alphas is significant.

The analysis of Tables 6.7 and 6.8 is very different. The Currency index presented a negative (insignificant) alpha over the whole period, but mostly due to times in which we could not find any significant linear relationship with the factors ("Moderate Bull" and "Bear"). During the "Weak Bull" and "Strong Bull" periods, alphas were positive although not significantly different from zero. This is at least evidence that Currency CTAs, on average, did not follow the same amplifying strategies as the ones displayed in Table 6.6 but that they could extract some additional returns. The Discretionary index, on the other hand, exhibited negative abnormal performance over all subperiods, and the aggregate abnormal return over the entire period is even significantly negative (Table 6.8).

The Treynor and Mazuy (1966) measure of market timing ability, captured by the coefficient for RUS2, is much more informative. As a reminder, this coefficient is meant to account for the loading of the skewness-related risk premium: The greater this value, the more likely it is that the portfolio returns will have a positive (right) asymmetry, thus putting more weight to the more positive returns. When considered in the context of performance measurement, RUS2 captures the manager's market timing abilities, as it gives an asymmetric weight to positive and negative deviation from the mean market excess return. This interpretation is valid provided the expected market excess return is positive. For example, with a mean return of 1 percent and a coefficient of 1, a deviation of +1 percent with respect to this value will provide a positive return of $1 \times (1\% + 1\%)^2 = 4\%$, while a deviation of −1 percent will provide a return of $1 \times (1\% - 1\%)^2 = 0\%$. Thus, a positive coefficient signals positive market timing when markets are bullish and negative market timing ability otherwise.

For the CTA strategies reported in Table 6.6, market timing abilities are pervasive during the total period, mainly due to the "Weak Bull" and "Moderate Bull" periods. During the (much shorter) "Strong Bull" and "Bear" periods, this effect completely fades away; it does not even intervene in the tailor-made regressions. Very noticeable is the same positive sign of the alpha and the market timing coefficients during the "Weak Bull" period, a finding that contrasts with many previous studies of abnormal performance of managed portfolios.[4]

---

[4]See Bello and Janjigian 1997 for a review.

Tables 6.7 and 6.8 display again very different results, as the Currency index does not provide any evidence of market timing abilities while the regression for the Differentiated index supports positive market timing abilities for the total period, mainly driven by the "Weak Bull" period.

To summarize, available evidence seems to indicate that CTAs could generate asset selection as well as market timing performance during the first part of the sample period, but this performance seems to have faded away. There is no indication of positive or negative alpha or Jensen-Mazuy coefficient during the "Strong Bull" and "Bear" periods, even though consistently, yet not significantly, negative alphas do not suggest any positive portfolio abnormal performance of CTA funds during this period.

Performance during Extreme Events

In the previous section we studied the performance of CTA indices under different market conditions. Now we seek to take the investigation one step further and examine the behavior of these funds when exposed to extreme market fluctuations. Earlier we identified three specific events that caused significant short-term shocks in the overall market during our sample period: the Russian debt crisis, the Asian currency crisis, and the September 2001 terrorist attacks in the United States. These three events caused a considerable drop in market indices (we use the S&P 500 as our benchmark), and it generally took two months for the markets to revert to their preevent levels. We therefore seek to investigate the performance of the different CTA indices during the two-month period comprising the event and the recovery.

To measure the abnormal performance of a CTA index, we calculate its standardized abnormal returns over T months as:

$$SAR_{i,T} = \frac{\sum_{t=1}^{T} AR_{i,t}}{s(AR_i)\sqrt{T}} \qquad T = 1,2 \tag{6.3}$$

$$\text{with} \quad AR_{i,t} = R_{i,t} - \alpha_i - \sum_{j=1}^{k} \beta_{i,j} F_{j,t}$$

where, for index i,

$AR_{i,t}$ = the abnormal return in month t
$R_{i,t}$ = the return in month t
α_i = unexplained return by asset-class factors
$\beta_{i,j}$ = factor loading on the jth asset-class factor
$F_{j,t}$ = value of the jth asset-class factor in month t
$s(AR_i)$ = standard deviation of abnormal returns over entire sample period

TABLE 6.9 Abnormal Performance during Extreme Events

	T	Russian Crisis	Asian Crisis	Terrorist Attack
CTA Index	1 month	−2.78	−0.01	−0.54
		(2.32)	(2.32)	(2.24)
	2 months	−2.01	0.38	1.45
		(3.28)	(3.28)	(3.17)
Systematic	1 month	−2.75	0.02	−0.12
		(2.66)	(2.66)	(2.76)
	2 months	−1.94	0.17	3.14
		(3.77)	(3.77)	(3.91)
Fin/Metal	1 month	−3.55*	−0.45	−0.28
		(2.11)	(2.11)	(2.16)
	2 months	−3.03	1.59	3.19
		(2.98)	(2.98)	(3.06)
Diversified	1 month	−3.27	0.34	0.32
		(3.10)	(3.10)	(2.98)
	2 months	−3.00	0.92	3.69
		(4.39)	(4.39)	(4.22)
Discretionary	1 month	−1.21	2.03*	0.57
		(1.13)	(1.13)	(0.96)
	2 months	−1.72	3.55**	0.53
		(1.59)	(1.59)	(1.36)

Table 6.9 presents the results for the measures of abnormal performance for the different CTA indices for one-month and two-month periods following the extreme events.

According to the results in Table 6.9, no abnormal performance for the CTA indices appears to exist, with the noticeable exceptions of the Financial/Metal index during the first month of the Russian crisis and the Discretionary index during the Asian crisis. For the latter index, the abnormal performance is significantly positive and robust during the entire Asian crisis. It sharply contrasts the very low abnormal returns achieved by all other indices under the same circumstances.

In general, the Russian crisis appears to have a negative effect on CTA abnormal performance. Although the individual coefficients are not significant, they are uniformly negative. On the other hand, the Asian crisis, and more surprisingly the terrorist attacks, yield very small *t*-values for all the CTA indices.

CONCLUSION

Throughout our analysis of the behavior of CTA indices during the 1990 to 2003 period, we have outlined that the splitting of the time window into at least four subperiods is beneficial to capture the sensitivity of CTA returns to broad sources of risk. With our tailor-made specifications, we can explain an average of 25 percent of the variance of returns, which is much greater than the accuracy obtained using the traditional multifactor or multi-moment analyses.

Thanks to this improvement over classical specifications, we can soundly assess the abnormal performance of CTA strategies during changing market conditions. Among the indices studied in this chapter, only the Currency CTA index seems to exhibit significant security selection as well as market timing abilities. Although it is usually not significant, the performance of CTA indices during the most extreme market fluctuation,—"Strong Bull" and "Bear" market conditions—is typically negative and does not suggest that these investment vehicles could benefit from either type of market condition.

No severe market crisis seems to have affected CTA performance with the noticeable exception of the Asian crisis, whose exploitation by the Discretionary CTA strategy caused significant abnormal returns for investors.

Overall, this study indicates that most of the variance of CTA returns remains unexplained by traditional risk factors, at least in a linear setup. There is, however, considerable evidence of positive market timing ability associated with these types of securities.

CHAPTER 7

Simple and Cross-Efficiency of CTAs Using Data Envelopment Analysis

Fernando Diz, Greg N. Gregoriou, Fabrice Rouah, and Stephen E. Satchell

We apply data envelopment analysis and use the basic and cross-efficiency models to evaluate the performance of CTA classifications. With the ever-increasing number of CTAs, there is an urgency to provide money managers, institutional investors, and high-net-worth individuals with a trustworthy appraisal method for ranking their efficiency. Data envelopment analysis can achieve this, eliminating the need for benchmarks, thereby alleviating the problem of using traditional benchmarks to examine nonnormal returns. This chapter studies CTAs and identifies the ones that have achieved superior performance or have an efficiency score of 100 in a risk/return setting.

INTRODUCTION

Research into the performance persistence of commodity trading advisors (CTAs) is sparse, so there is little information on the long-term diligence of these managers (see, e.g., Edwards and Ma 1988; Irwin, Krukemeyer, and Zulaf 1992; Irwin, Zulauf, and Ward 1994; Kazemi 1996). It is generally agreed that during bear markets, CTAs provide greater downside protection than hedge funds and have higher returns along with an inverse correlation to equities. The benefits of CTAs are similar to those of hedge funds, in that they improve and may offer a superior risk-adjusted return trade-off to stock and bond indices and can act as diversifiers in investment portfolios (Schneeweis, Savanayana, and McCarthy 1991; Schneeweis, 1996).

Investors who have chosen to include CTAs in their portfolios have allocated only a small portion of their assets. This can be attributed to the mediocre performance of CTAs during the early 1990s (Georgiev 2001). Others are unaware that during periods of increased stock market volatility, careful inclusion of CTA managers into investment portfolios can enhance their returns especially during severe bear markets (Schneeweis and Georgiev 2002). Moreover, extreme volatility in international financial markets of this past decade, such as that experienced during the Asian currency crisis of 1997 and the Russian ruble crisis of August 1998, did not significantly affect CTA performance. In fact, during these periods of high volatility, CTAs make most of their money and produce superior returns relative to traditional market indices.

Much recent debate has centered on how to measure and evaluate the performance of CTAs. Comparing CTAs to standard market indices could be erroneous since CTAs are viewed as an alternative asset class and possess different characteristics from traditional stock and bond portfolios. Unlike mutual funds, it is difficult to identify factors that drive CTA returns (Schneeweis, Spurgin, and Potter 1996). Fung and Hsieh (1997b) apply Sharpe's factor "style" analysis to CTAs and find that very little of the variability in CTA returns can be attributed to variability of financial asset classes (in marked contrast to what Sharpe (1992) finds for mutual funds). They attribute the low R-squared values to the dynamic strategies of CTAs. Investors and analysts placing too much faith in these models are therefore at risk of being misled by biased alphas (Schneeweis, Spurgin, and McCarthy 1996). The underlying question of which benchmarks would be appropriate for each CTA strategy continues to be a controversial one.

How performance is measured also can be the reason for divergent results. Excess returns can display performance persistence when in fact it is nonexistent. A recent study by Kat and Menexe (2002) suggests that the predictability in returns is low.

The nonnormal returns that CTAs often display make it difficult to apply linear factor models that use traditional market indices since these do not offer a sufficient measure of CTA risk exposure. Fung and Hsieh (1997b) argue that the explanatory power of these models is weak and propose an extension of Sharpe's model to CTAs whereby specific CTA "styles" are defined. The traditional Sharpe ratio usually overestimates and miscalculates nonnormal performance, because this well-known risk-adjusted measure does not consider negative skewness and excess kurtosis (Brooks and Kat 2001).

Using CTA indices to examine performance persistence also can introduce biases. CTA indices are rebalanced and cannot properly reproduce the same composition during an entire examination period; consequently persistence could be wrongly estimated.

Regardless of the capability of existing and frequently used models to explain CTA returns, the dynamic trading strategies and skewed returns remain critical issues in the CTA performance literature, and further investigation is warranted.

We use simple and cross-efficiency DEA models to handle the problems encountered when using multifactor models to predict CTA returns. DEA allows us to appraise and rank CTAs in a risk-return framework without using indices. The efficient frontier is generated from the most efficient CTAs, and DEA calculates the efficiency of each CTA relative to the efficient frontier, thereby producing an efficiency score according to the input and output variables used. The selection of variables is discussed in the methodology and data section. DEA is a nonparametric technique that measures the relative efficiency of decision-making units (DMUs) on the basis of observed data and then presents an efficiency score as a single number between 0 and 100.[1] The main benefit of DEA is that it identifies the best-performing CTA and determines the relative efficiencies of a set of similar CTAs (peers). DEA, also called frontier analysis, was originally developed by Charnes, Cooper, and Rhodes (CCR) (1978). It was later adapted by Banker, Charnes, and Cooper (BCC) (1984), who expanded the Farrell (1957) technical measure of efficiency from a single-input, single-output process to a multiple-input, multiple-output process. The CCR and BCC models are the simple (or basic) DEA models and were developed originally for nonprofit organizations. Later we discuss an alternative DEA model: cross-efficiency.

The power of DEA is in its ability to deal with several inputs and outputs while not requiring a precise relation between input and output variables. DEA produces an efficiency score which takes into account multiple inputs and outputs, and uses the CTAs themselves as the benchmark. Using an alternative performance measure like DEA is beneficial because it enables investors to potentially pinpoint the reasons behind a CTA's poor performance. Once the weaknesses are recognized, the CTA can attempt to reach a perfect efficiency score by comparing itself to CTAs that have achieved an efficiency score of 100. Furthermore, numerous DEA software programs, such as the DEA solver in Zhu (2003), and Banxia's Frontier

[1]An efficiency score of 100 refers to an efficient fund (or best-performing fund that lies on the frontier); a score of less than 100 signifies the fund is inefficient.

Analyst, provide an improvement summary that can pinpoint the weaknesses from the CTA's inputs and outputs.

For institutional investors considering using CTAs as downside protection in bear markets, it is critical that a performance measure provide not only a precise appraisal of the CTA's performance, but also an idea of the quality of its management with respect to certain criteria (variables such as inputs and outputs). Using DEA could present investors with a useful tool for ranking CTAs, not by historical returns, but by peer group appraisal.

In the next section we discuss the different DEA methodologies. Then we describe the data, discuss the empirical results, and summarize our conclusions.

METHODOLOGY

In its most rudimentary form, DEA calculates an efficiency score that describes the relative efficiency of a CTA when compared to other CTAs in the sample. The first step in DEA is to obtain an efficient frontier from the inputs and outputs identified by Pareto optimality.[2] DEA then calculates the efficiency score of each DMU relative to the efficiency frontier. In this chapter, the DMUs are CTAs.

The efficiency frontier consists of the "best-performing" CTAs—the most efficient at transforming the inputs into outputs (Charnes, Cooper, and Rhodes, 1981). Any CTA not on the frontier would have an efficiency score less than 100 and would be labeled inefficient. For example, a CTA with an efficiency score of 80 is only 80 percent as efficient as the top-performing CTA. A best-performance frontier charts the maximum or minimum level of output (input) produced for any assumed level of input (output), where outputs represent the degree to which the CTA's goal has been achieved.

How the inputs and outputs are used in the efficiency analysis are essential because they establish the grounds on which the efficiency of the fund is calculated. The most extensively used DEA technique to measure efficiency takes the weighted sum of outputs and divides it by the weighted sum of inputs (Golany and Roll, 1994). In its simplest form, DEA calculates weights from a linear program that maximizes relative efficiency with a set

[2]Pareto optimality means the best that can be attained without putting any group at a disadvantage. In other words, a group of funds becomes better off if an individual fund becomes better off and none becomes worse off.

of minimal weight constraints.[3] Charnes, Cooper, and Rhodes (1978) proposed reducing the multiple-input, multiple-output model to a ratio with a single virtual input and a single virtual output.

Simple Efficiency

The main distinction between the two simple DEA models is that the BCC model uses varying returns to scale to examine the relative efficiency of CTAs, while the CCR model uses constant returns to scale.[4] To obtain robust results, a proper working sample ought to be on the order of three times the number of CTAs as the number of input and output variables (Charnes, Cooper, and Rhodes, 1981). In addition, DEA uses a comparative measure of relative performance framework.

We adapt the notation from Adler, Friedman, and Stern (2002) for the simple and cross-efficiency models. By comparing n CTAs with s outputs, denoted by y_{rk} in equation 7.1, where $r = 1, \ldots, s$, and m inputs denoted by x_{ik}, $i = 1, \ldots, m$, the efficiency measure for fund k is:

$$h_k = Max \frac{\sum_{r=1}^{s} u_r y_{rk}}{\sum_{i=1}^{m} v_i x_{ik}} \qquad (7.1)$$

where the weights u_r and v_i are positive. An additional set of constraints requires that the same weights, when applied to all CTAs, not allow any CTA with an efficiency score greater than 100 percent and is displayed in this set of constraints:

$$\frac{\sum_{r=1}^{s} u_r y_{rj}}{\sum_{i=1}^{m} v_i x_{ij}} \leq 1 \text{ for } j = 1, \ldots, n.$$

[3]Linear programming is the optimization of a multivariable objective function, subject to constraints.

[4]The BCC model permits a greater number of potential optimal solutions. With the BCC model, the number of funds with an efficiency score of 100 will, on average, be higher than with the CCR model. Choosing between these models requires insight into what the process will involve. For example, if the increase in inputs does not provide the same increase in outputs, then the variable returns to scale model should be used.

The efficiency score falls between 0 and 100, with CTA k regarded as efficient on receiving an efficiency score of 100. Therefore, each CTA selects weights to maximize its own efficiency.

$$h_k = Max \sum_{r=1}^{s} u_r y_{rk} + c_k$$

subject to the constraints:

$$\sum_{i=1}^{m} v_i x_{ij} - \sum_{r=1}^{s} u_r y_{rj} - c_k \geq 0 \text{ for } j = 1, \ldots n, \qquad (7.2)$$

$$\sum_{i=1}^{m} v_i x_{ik} = 1,$$

$$u_r \geq 0 \text{ for } r = 1, \ldots, s,$$

$$v_i \geq 0 \text{ for } i = 1, \ldots, m.$$

An extra constant variable, denoted by c_k, is added in the BCC model to allow variable returns to scale between inputs and outputs. For a CTA to be BCC technically efficient; its only requirement is to be efficient; for a CTA to be efficient in the CCR model, it must be both scale and technically efficient (Bowlin 1998).

A CTA is considered scale efficient if the level of its operation is optimal. If the scale efficiency is reduced or increased, the efficiency will weaken. A scale-efficient CTA will function at most favorable returns to scale. In essence, the distance on a production frontier between the constant returns to scale and the variable returns to scale frontier establishes the component labeled scale efficiency. A CTA is considered technically efficient if it is able to maximize each of its outputs per unit of input, thus signifying the efficiency of the conversion process of the variables. In this chapter technical efficiency is calculated using the BCC model.

In a production frontier, constant returns to scale implies that any increase in the inputs of a CTA will result in a proportional increase in its outputs. In other words, a linear relationship would be present between inputs and outputs. If a CTA were to increase its inputs by 5 percent, thereby producing a similar increase in outputs, the CTA would be operating at constant returns to scale. Consequently, irrespective of what scale the CTA operates at, its efficiency will stay the same.

If an increase in the inputs of a CTA does not induce a proportional transformation in its outputs, however, then the CTA will display variable returns to scale, which implies that as the CTA alters its level of day-to-day operations, its efficiency can increase or decrease. Therefore, since CTAs vary their leverage at different times to magnify returns, we employ the BCC model (varying returns to scale).

Cross-Efficiency

The cross-evaluation, or cross-efficiency, model was first seen in Sexton, Silkman, and Hogan (1986) and later in Oral, Ketani, and Lang (1991), Doyle and Green (1994), and Thanassoulis, Boussofiane, and Dyson (1995). It establishes the ranking procedure and computes the efficiency score of each CTA n times using optimal weights measured by the linear programs.

A cross-evaluation matrix is a square matrix of dimension equal to the number of CTAs in the analysis. The efficiency of CTA j is computed with the optimal weights for CTA k. The higher the values in column k, the more likely that CTA k is efficient using superior operating techniques. Therefore, calculating the mean of each column will provide the peer appraisal score of each CTA. The cross-efficiency method is superior to the simple efficiency method because the former uses internally generated weights as opposed to forcing predetermined weights.

The cross-evaluation model used here is represented by equation 7.3:

$$h_{kj} = \frac{\sum_{r=1}^{s} u_{rk} y_{rj}}{\sum_{i=1}^{m} v_{ik} x_{ij}}, \qquad k = 1, \ldots, n, \; j = 1, \ldots, n, \tag{7.3}$$

where h_{kj} = score of CTA j cross-evaluated by the weight of CTA k.

In the cross-evaluation matrix, all CTAs are bounded by $0 \le h_{kj} \le 1$, and the CTAs in the diagonal, h_{kk}, represent the simple DEA efficiency score, so that $h_{kk} = 1$ for efficient CTAs and $h_{kk} < 1$ for inefficient CTAs. Equation 7.3 shows that the problem of trying to distinguish the relative efficiency scores of all CTAs is generated n times.

The DEA method renders an ex-post evaluation of a CTA's efficiency and specifies the precise input-output relation. The relation must be realized without a level of efficiency greater than 100 when the coefficients are adapted to the CTAs in our sample. Efficiency scores, as they are relative to the other CTAs in the sample, are by no means absolute.

Papers on DEA have been published in many sectors, and the use of such analysis often has resulted in technical and efficiency improvements. DEA also has been used recently to evaluate the performance of mutual funds and determine the most efficient funds (see, e.g., McMullen and Strong 1997; Bowlin 1998; Morey and Morey 1999; Sedzro and Sardano 2000; Basso and Funari 2001). Barr, Seiford, and Siems (1994), however, suggest that using a single input/output ratio to assess management quality is impractical; instead they propose a multidimensional approach.

However, the CCR model is one of the first DEA models based on efficiency. It allows a set of optimal weights to be calculated for each input and output to maximize a CTA's efficiency score. If these weights were applied to any other fund in our database, the efficiency score would not exceed 100. The CCR score aggregates technical and scale efficiency. Despite the many modified DEA models in existence, the CCR model is the most broadly known and used. Basically, the BCC and CCR models offer two ways of considering the same problem.

As we noted earlier, cross-evaluation DEA is superior to either simple DEA method because efficiency is still measured relative to the CTA with the highest efficiency score, but having more than one combination of weights of a fund that maximizes its own efficiency adds an extra dimension of flexibility. The main idea of DEA is that it is flexible and can branch out to other CTAs to evaluate their individual performance. CTAs with high average efficiency from a cross-efficiency matrix can be considered as good examples for inefficient CTAs to work toward and improve their methods.

We adopt and expand the methodology of Sedzro and Sardano (2000), who investigated mutual funds, and apply it to CTA classifications. Since CTAs exhibit nonnormal distribution of returns and display fat tails, we use variables different from those used for mutual funds (Fung and Hsieh 1997a). In previous studies skewness was shown to have an influence on monthly average returns in stock markets (see Sengupta 1989).

The inputs and outputs must correspond to the activities of CTAs for the analysis to make sense. We use six variables in a risk-return framework, three for inputs and three for outputs, because a larger number might clutter the analysis. Three times the number of inputs and outputs will result in having sufficient observations (degrees of freedom) to get a good evaluation. Having a greater number of variables could result in an overlap of measuring inputs and outputs, thereby producing some problems in interpreting the results. If too many variables are used, the analysis could result in many CTAs being rated efficient.

Modern portfolio theory measures the total risk of a portfolio by using the variance of the returns. But this method does not separate upside risk, which investors seek, from the downside returns they want to avoid. Variance is not usually a good method for measuring risk, but semivariance is generally accepted and frequently used because it measures downside risk. Returns above the mean can hardly be regarded as risky, but variance below the mean provides more information during extreme market events. This is important for investors who worry more about underperformance than overperformance (Markowitz 1991).[5] Because CTAs can obtain positive returns in flat or down markets, they induce negative skewness in portfolio return. Adding CTAs to a traditional stock and bond portfolio to obtain higher risk-adjusted returns and lower volatility will therefore result in a trade-off between negative skewness and diversification of the portfolio (Diz 1999).

The mean and standard deviations of CTA returns can be misleading; examining higher moments such as skewness is recommended (Fung and Hsieh 1997a). The introduction of skewness in inputs and outputs might present some signaling assessment of each CTA classification because skewness does not penalize CTA by the upside potential returns. Although CTAs attempt to maximize returns and minimize risk, this comes at a trade-off; adding CTAs to traditional investment portfolios will likely result in high kurtosis and increased negative skewness, which are the drawbacks of this alternative asset class.

DATA

We use CTA data from the Barclay Trading Group/Burlington Hall Asset Management and examine five CTA classifications during the periods from 1998 to 2002 and 2000 to 2002. The subtype CTA classifications include Diversified, Financials, Currency, Stocks, and Arbitrage. We choose these time periods because we wish to determine whether the extreme market event of August 1998 had any impact on each of the classifications. The database provider warned us that using a longer time frame, for example, a 7- or 10-year examination period, would have resulted in significantly fewer CTAs. Our data set consists of monthly net returns, for which both management and performance fees are subtracted by the CTAs and forwarded to Barclay. We do not examine defunct CTAs.

The data were aggregated into separate DEA runs for the three-year and five-year periods for each classification. Both examination periods contain the same CTAs in each classification, which enables us to compare CTA rankings and efficiency scores across periods. The inputs are (1) lower mean monthly semiskewness, (2) lower mean monthly semivariance, and (3) mean monthly lower return. The outputs are (1) upper mean monthly semiskewness, (2) upper mean monthly semivariance, and (3) mean monthly upper return. The value of outputs is the value added of each CTA.

---

[5]Extreme market events include the Asian currency crisis of 1997 and the Russian ruble crisis of 1998.

EMPIRICAL RESULTS

An efficiency score of 100 signifies that a CTA is efficient and that no other CTA has produced better outputs with the inputs used. It does not imply that all CTAs with a score of 100 provide the same return during the examination period, merely that the return is at the maximum of the incurred risk. The efficiency score is not absolute. A CTA with an efficiency score of 100 returning 20 percent is considered more risky than a CTA with a score of 100 returning 15 percent. Note that the results obtained from DEA do not guarantee future efficiency; nonetheless, DEA is a very valuable selection and screening tool for institutional investors. Every CTA with an efficiency score of 100 can be considered to be as one of the best.

Simple efficiency is perhaps not quite enough to assess the performance appraisal of CTAs, though, because cross-efficiency goes beyond self-appraisal to peer appraisal (Vassiloglou and Giokas 1990; Sedzro and Sardano 2000). CTAs with an efficiency score of 100 in the simple model drop in value when the average cross-efficiency measure is used. However, the cross-efficiency scores signify the peer appraisal of each CTA, thus revealing a CTA's all-around performance in all areas.

Table 7.1 displays the number of efficient and nonefficient CTAs for both examination periods. The results indicate that a greater majority of CTAs are nonefficient according to the inputs and outputs we use. The reason possibly can be attributed to the various extreme market events, such as the Russian ruble crisis of August 1998, which led to increased volatility in commodities markets. To assess the performance of CTAs properly, the time series of each CTA classification must be long enough to include at least one extreme negative market event, as is the case during the 1998 to 2002 period. Although we find a low number of efficient CTAs in each classification, we are comforted by an earlier study that found only 8.9 percent of mutual funds investigated to have efficiency scores of 100 (Sedzro and Sardano 2000).

Tables 7.2 through 7.6 present basic statistics and simple and cross-efficiency scores for the five CTA classifications. A high score means the CTA performs well relative to its peers, based on the inputs and outputs used.[6] Some CTAs are rated as efficient by the simple BCC model, but

[6]The Babe Ruth analogy is a classic example. Babe Ruth was a great home run hitter. In terms of simple efficiency (basic DEA model), he would have achieved a score of 100. However, if he were to be compared to other players on the team, he may not have been an all-around player, thus making his cross efficiency score low compared to a good all-around player.

TABLE 7.1 Number of Efficient and Nonefficient and Summary Statistics for CTAs, 1997–2001 and 1999–2001

Classification	Cross-section Mean	Cross-section Median	Cross-section STD	Cross-section Min	Cross-section Max	Efficient	Nonefficient	Total
				1997–2001				
Stocks	15.17%	6.30%	18.99%	−35.22%	55.49%	4	9	13
Currency	9.21%	4.15%	14.56%	−48.33%	48.45%	3	37	40
Financials	10.62%	3.90%	16.57%	−37.07%	33.60%	8	36	44
Diversified	0.95%	5.71%	7.60%	−75.30%	80.29%	5	45	50
Arbitrage	14.54%	1.01%	12.91%	−7.45%	16.89%	3	0	3
Total	—	—	—	—	—	23	127	150
				1999–2001				
Stocks	12.17%	7.08%	17.50%	−35.22%	55.49%	5	8	13
Currency	5.73%	0.60%	13.01%	−48.33%	29.41%	3	36	39
Financials	8.53%	2.52%	16.32%	−37.07%	31.41%	10	35	45
Diversified	8.41%	2.83%	20.08%	−68.35%	36.61%	7	43	50
Arbitrage	14.49%	8.68%	8.47%	−5.63%	7.14%	3	0	3
Total	—	—	—	—	—	28	122	150

TABLE 7.2 Basic Statistics and Simple and Cross-Efficiency Scores for Stocks, 1997–2001 and 1999–2001

	1997–2001					
Stocks	Compounded Return	Average Annualized Return	Annualized Standard Deviation	Annualized Sharpe Ratio	5-Year Simple Efficiency Score BCC Model	5-Year Cross-Efficiency Score BCC Model
Allied Irish Capital Mgmt. Ltd.	26.28	4.78	4.68	0.11	100	54.90
Analytic Investment Mgmt.	94.99	14.00	10.91	0.89	100	54.55
Michael N. Trading Co. Ltd.	843.86	46.82	15.13	2.81	100	77.10
Minogue Investment Co.	25.47	15.13	47.87	0.23	100	12.57

	1999–2001					
Stocks	Compounded Return	Average Annualized Return	Annualized Standard Deviation	Annualized Sharpe Ratio	3-Year Simple Efficiency Score BCC Model	3-Year Cross-Efficiency Score BCC Model
Allied Irish Capital Mgmt. Ltd.	9.34	3.06	4.07	–1.00	100	14.41
Analytic Investment Mgmt.	28.29	8.87	10.58	0.44	100	20.66
Arcanu Investment Mgmt.	32.24	10.26	12.86	0.47	100	25.77
Michael N. Trading Co. Ltd	181.01	36.25	16.86	1.90	100	43.64
Trading Solutions	99.83	26.40	25.90	0.86	100	17.03

TABLE 7.3 Basic Statistics and Simple and Cross-Efficiency Scores for Currency, 1997–2001 and 1999–2001

	1997–2001					
Currency	Compounded Return	Average Annualized Return	Annualized Standard Deviation	Annualized Sharpe Ratio	5-Year Simple Efficiency Score BCC Model	5-Year Cross-Efficiency Score BCC Model
Hathersage Capital Mgmt. LLC	177.86	21.54	15.08	1.23	100	9.83
KMJ Capital Mgmt. Inc.	119.93	16.87	14.77	0.85	100	11.96
OSV Partners Inc.	110.37	15.16	6.41	1.70	100	8.41

	1999–2001					
Currency	Compounded Return	Average Annualized Return	Annualized Standard Deviation	Annualized Sharpe Ratio	3-Year Simple Efficiency Score BCC Model	3-Year Cross-Efficiency Score BCC Model
DKR Capital Inc.	31.57	9.33	5.67	0.90	100	17.62
KMJ Capital Mgmt. Inc.	72.52	19.02	12.31	1.20	100	19.88
OSV Partners Inc.	26.75	7.95	2.10	1.76	100	17.95

TABLE 7.4 Basic Statistics and Simple and Cross-Efficiency Scores for Financials, 1997–2001 and 1999–2001

	1997–2001					
Financials	Compounded Return	Average Annualized Return	Annualized Standard Deviation	Annualized Sharpe Ratio	5-Year Simple Efficiency Score BCC Model	5-Year Cross-Efficiency Score BCC Model
Appelton Capital Mgmt.	40.90	7.26	8.83	0.34	100	50.09
Carat Capital LLC	312.11	32.94	30.34	0.72	100	56.66
City Fund Mgmt. Ltd.	53.07	8.73	6.27	0.72	100	48.47
Eckhardt Trading Company	120.07	17.35	17.93	0.73	100	55.93
IIU Asset Strategies	49.99	0.70	2.30	0.53	100	63.96
Marathon Capital Growth Partners LLC	82.32	14.30	15.28	0.65	100	48.59
Moore Capital Mgmt. Inc.	121.16	16.77	12.88	0.97	100	53.11
Vega Asset Mgmt. (USA) LLC	53.32	8.70	4.96	0.90	100	52.39

TABLE 7.4 *(continued)*

Financials	Compounded Return	Average Annualized Return	Annualized Standard Deviation	Annualized Sharpe Ratio	3-Year Simple Efficiency Score BCC Model	3-Year Cross-Efficiency Score BCC Model
Carat Capital LLC	21.71	6.84	7.42	0.35	100	37.41
City Fund Mgmt. Ltd.	30.15	8.96	5.50	0.86	100	23.19
Eckhardt Trading Company	29.60	9.57	13.92	0.38	100	67.51
IIU Asset Strategies	22.17	7.00	7.99	0.34	100	52.11
International Trading Advisors BVBA	–11.04	–3.33	10.66	–1.00	100	36.01
Invesco Inc.	28.65	9.56	15.36	0.35	100	51.31
IXORCAP	4.97	1.78	5.74	–1.00	100	54.17
Marathon Capital Growth Partners LLC	45.73	13.87	16.10	0.60	100	49.57
Parthian Securities, S.A.	158.61	46.82	49.65	0.87	100	53.41
Vega Asset Mgmt. (USA) LLC	28.07	8.31	2.59	1.56	100	26.25

TABLE 7.5 Basic Statistics and Simple and Cross-Efficiency Scores for Diversified, 1997–2001 and 1999–2001

Diversified	Compounded Return	Average Annualized Return	Annualized Standard Deviation	Annualized Sharpe Ratio	5-Year Simple Efficiency Score BCC Model	5-Year Cross-Efficiency Score BCC Model
1997–2001						
AIS Futures Mgmt. LLC	–1.87	1.86	21.44	–1.00	100	53.14
Beach Capital Mgmt. Ltd.	157.23	19.90	13.34	1.17	100	64.51
Fort Orange Capital Mgmt. Inc.	53.93	12.08	26.84	0.29	100	44.97
Friedberg Commodity Mgmt. Inc.	–21.58	2.74	40.76	–1.00	100	37.57
Marathon Capital Growth Partners LLC	22.82	5.43	16.42	0.07	100	34.5
1999–2001						
AIS Futures Mgmt. LLC	44.10	14.17	20.10	0.49	100	54.61
Beach Capital Mgmt. Ltd.	64.42	17.64	14.18	0.94	100	66.91
Brandywine Asset Mgmt. Inc	–43.02	–17.40	15.67	–1.00	100	49.58
Fort Orange Capital Mgmt. Inc.	–28.19	–7.64	26.63	–1.00	100	59.08
Friedberg Commodity Mgmt. Inc.	–44.04	–12.01	37.61	–1.00	100	34.91
Marathon Capital Growth Partners LLC	–0.64	0.67	16.25	–1.00	100	45.15
Mississippi River Investments Inc.	58.88	17.00	17.65	0.72	100	47.75

TABLE 7.6 Basic Statistics and Simple and Cross-Efficiency Scores for Arbitrage 1997–2001 and 1999–2001

	1997–2001					
Arbitrage	Compounded Return	Average Annualized Return	Annualized Standard Deviation	Annualized Sharpe Ratio	5-Year Simple Efficiency Score BCC Model	5-Year Cross-Efficiency Score BCC Model
BAREP Asset Mgmt.	49.47	8.59	10.34	0.42	100	67.05
DKR Capital Inc.	74.42	14.21	6.82	1.46	100	65.87
TWR Mgmt. Corp.	98.12	14.54	12.91	0.79	100	88.03

	1999–2001					
Arbitrage	Compounded Return	Average Annualized Return	Annualized Standard Deviation	Annualized Sharpe Ratio	3-Year Simple Efficiency Score BCC Model	3-Year Cross-Efficiency Score BCC Model
BAREP Asset Mgmt.	9.81	3.67	10.57	-1.00	100	—
DKR Capital Inc.	67.26	17.48	6.71	1.97	100	79.34
TWR Mgmt. Corp.	38.86	11.50	10.23	0.71	100	41.96

TABLE 7.7 Champion CTAs 1997–2001 and 1999–2001

	1997–2001	
CTA	**Reference Set**	**Classification**
Michael N. Trading Co. Ltd.	12	Stocks
KMJ Capital Mgmt. Inc.	29	Currency
Marathon Capital Growth Partners LLC	28	Financials
AIS Futures Mgmt. LLC	30	Diversified
N/A	N/A*	Arbitrage
	1999–2001	
CTA	**Reference Set**	**Classification**
Trading Solutions	6	Stocks
KMJ Capital Mgmt. Inc.	18	Currency
Marathon Capital Growth Partners LLC	24	Financials
AIS Futures Mgmt. LLC	31	Diversified
N/A	N/A*	Arbitrage

*N/A = the sample set is too small.

when using the cross efficiency model their scores are among the lowest. The tables suggest that CTAs are more efficient in the shorter three-year period. This is due to the absence of extreme market events during this time frame. In Table 7.7 we identify the "champion" CTAs in each classification (except Arbitrage) by the number of times an efficient fund has been part of an inefficient CTA's reference set, derived by simple DEA. As the frequency of a CTA appearing in a reference set increases, the likelihood of the fund being a good performer increases. The efficient CTA appearing in the most reference sets can be considered the overall "champion." Inefficient funds can learn from that CTA's superior management and investment practices.

CONCLUSION

Data envelopment analysis is a novel method that pension funds, endowment funds, institutional investors, and high-net-worth individuals can use to select efficient CTAs. We believe DEA is an excellent complement to other risk-adjusted measures because it can present a more complete picture of hedge fund performance appraisal. DEA can provide reliable results even when using nonnormal returns.

As DEA becomes accepted and used by more academics, money managers, and institutional investors, CTAs with high cross-efficiency scores will become desirable. Future research could examine the efficiency of CTA indices from other database vendors, for example.

PART Two

Risk and Managed Futures Investing

Chapter 8 uses a unique data set from the Commodity Futures Trading Commission to investigate the impact of trading by large hedge funds and commodity trading advisors (CTAs) in 13 futures markets. Regression results show there is a small but positive relationship between the trading volume of large hedge funds and CTAs and market volatility. Further results suggest that trading by large hedge funds and CTAs is likely based on private fundamental information.

Chapter 9 examines the dynamic nature of commodity trading programs that tend to mimic a long put option strategy. Using a two-step regression procedure, the authors document the asymmetric return stream associated with CTAs and then provide a method for calculating value at risk. The authors also examine a passive trend-following commodity index and find it to have a similar put optionlike return distribution. The authors also demonstrate how commodity trading programs can be combined with other hedge fund strategies to produce a return stream that has significantly lower value at risk parameters.

Chapter 10 examines the relationships between various risk measures for CTAs. The relationships are extremely important in asset allocation. If two measures (e.g., beta and Sharpe ratio) produce identical rankings for a sample of funds, then the informational content of the two measures are similar. However, if the two measures produce rankings that are not identical, then the informational content of each measure as well as asset allocation decisions may be unique. Interdependence of risk measures has been examined previously for equities and recently for hedge funds. In this chapter the authors analyze 24 risk measures for a sample of 200 CTAs over the period January 1998 to July 2003.

Chapter 11 provides a simple method for measuring the downside protection offered by managed futures. Managed futures are generally considered to help reduce the downside exposure of stocks and bonds. The chapter also measures the downside protection provided by hedge funds and passive commodity futures indices. In each case, considerable downside protection is offered by each of these three alternative asset classes.

CHAPTER 8

The Effect of Large Hedge Fund and CTA Trading on Futures Market Volatility

Scott H. Irwin and Bryce R. Holt

This study uses a unique data set from the CFTC to investigate the impact of trading by large hedge funds and CTAs in 13 futures markets. Regression results show there is a small but positive relationship between the trading volume of large hedge funds and CTAs and market volatility. However, a positive relationship between hedge fund and CTA trading volume and market volatility is consistent with either a private information or noise trader hypothesis. Three additional tests are conducted to distinguish between the private information hypothesis and the noise trader hypothesis. The first test consists of identifying the noise component exhibited in return variances over different holding periods. The variance ratio tests provide little support for the noise trader hypothesis. The second test examines whether positive feedback trading characterized large hedge fund and CTA trading behavior. These results suggest that trading decisions by large hedge funds and CTAs are influenced only in small part by past price changes. The third test consists of estimating the profits and losses associated with the positions of large hedge funds and CTAs. This test is based on the argument that speculative trading can be destabilizing only if speculators buy when prices are high and sell when prices are low, which, in turn, implies that destabilizing specula-

The authors thank Ron Hobson, and John Mielke of the Commodity Futures Trading Commission for their assistance in obtaining the hedge fund and CTA data and answering many questions. This chapter is dedicated to the memory of Blake Imel of the CFTC, who first suggested that we analyze the hedge fund and CTA data and provided invaluable encouragement. We appreciate the helpful comments provided by Wei Shi.

tors lose money. Across all 13 markets, the profit for large hedge funds and CTAs is estimated to be just under $400 million. This fact suggests that trading decisions are likely based on valuable private information. Overall, the evidence presented in this study indicates that trading by large hedge funds and CTAs is based on private fundamental information.

INTRODUCTION

In recent years, hedge funds and commodity trading advisors (CTAs) have drawn considerable attention from regulators, investors, academics, and the general public.[1] Much of the attention has focused on the concern that hedge funds and CTAs exert a disproportionate and destabilizing influence on financial markets, which can lead to increased price volatility and, in some cases, financial crises (e.g., Eichengreen and Mathieson 1998). Hedge fund trading has been blamed for many financial distresses, including the 1992 European Exchange Rate Mechanism crisis, the 1994 Mexican peso crisis, the 1997 Asian financial crisis, and the 2000 bust in U.S. technology stock prices. A spectacular example of concerns about hedge funds can be found in the collapse and subsequent financial bailout of Long-Term Capital Management (e.g., Edwards 1999). The concerns about hedge fund and CTA trading extend beyond financial markets to other speculative markets, such as commodity futures markets. These concerns were nicely summarized in a meeting between farmers and executives of the Chicago Board of Trade, where farmers expressed the view that "the funds—managed commodity investment groups with significant financial and technological resources—may exert undue collective influence on market direction without regard to real world supply-demand or other economic factors" (Ross 1999, p. 3).

Previous empirical studies related to the market behavior and impact of hedge funds and CTAs can be divided into three groups. The first set of studies focuses on the issue of "herding," which can be defined as a group of traders taking similar positions simultaneously or following one another (Kodres 1994). This type of trading behavior can be destabilizing if it is not based on information about market fundamentals, but instead is based on a common "noise factor" (De Long, Schleifer, Summers, and Waldman 1990). Kodres and Pritsker (1996) and Kodres (1994) investigate herding behavior on a daily basis for large futures market traders, including hedge funds and CTAs, in 11 financial futures markets. Weiner (2002) analyzes

[1]See Eichengreen and Mathieson (1998) for a thorough overview of the hedge fund industry. A similar overview of the CTA industry can be found in Chance (1994).

herding behavior for commodity pool operators using daily data for the heating oil futures market. Findings are consistent across the studies. Herding behavior within the various categories of traders is positive and statistically significant in some futures markets, but typically explains less than 10 percent of the variation in position changes.

The second set of studies focuses on whether futures market participants rely on positive feedback trading strategies, where buying takes place after price increases and selling takes place after price decreases. If this trading is large enough, it can lead to excessively volatile prices. Kodres (1994) examines daily data on large accounts in the Standard & Poor's (S&P) 500 futures market and finds that a significant minority employ positive feedback strategies more frequently than can be explained by chance. Dale and Zryen (1996) analyze weekly position reports and find evidence of positive feedback trading for noncommercial futures traders in crude oil, gasoline, heating oil, and treasury bond futures markets. Irwin and Yoshimaru (1999) examine daily data on commodity pool trading and report significant evidence of positive feedback trading in over half of the 36 markets studied, suggesting that commodity pools use similar positive feedback trading systems to guide trading decisions.

The third set of studies directly analyzes the relationship between price movements and large trader positions. Brorsen and Irwin (1987) estimate the quarterly open interest of futures funds and do not find a significant relationship between futures fund trading and price volatility. Brown, Goetzmann, and Park (1998) estimate monthly hedge fund positions in Asian currency markets during 1997 and find no evidence that hedge fund positions are related to falling currency values. Irwin and Yoshimaru (1999) analyze daily commodity pool positions and do not find a significant relationship with futures price volatility for the broad spectrum of markets studied. Fung and Hsieh (2000a) estimate monthly hedge fund exposures during a number of major market events and argue there is little evidence that hedge fund trading during these events causes prices to deviate from economic fundamentals.

Overall, the available empirical evidence provides limited support for concerns about the market impact of hedge fund and CTA trading. There is evidence of positive feedback trading, but this is offset by the lack of evidence with respect to herding and increased price volatility. Caution should be used, however, in reaching firm conclusions due to the limited nature of evidence on the direct market impact of hedge funds and CTAs. With one exception, previous studies estimate market positions using low-frequency (quarterly or monthly) data. Fung and Hsieh (2000a, p. 3) argue that this is due to the difficulty of obtaining data on hedge fund and CTA trading activities:

A major difficulty with this kind of study is the fact that hedge fund positions are virtually impossible to obtain. Except for very large positions in certain futures contracts, foreign currencies, US Treasuries and public equities, hedge funds are not obliged to and generally do not report positions to regulators. Most funds do not regularly provide detailed exposure estimates to their own investors, except through annual reports and in a highly aggregated format. It is therefore nearly impossible to directly measure the impact of hedge funds in any given market.

Ederington and Lee (2002) report that hedge fund and CTA positions turn over relatively quickly on a daily basis. This fact suggests that higher-frequency data are needed to accurately estimate the market impact of hedge fund and CTA trading.

A unique data set is available that allows measurement of hedge fund and CTA positions on a daily basis in a broad cross-section of U.S. futures markets. Specifically, the Commodity Futures Trading Commission (CFTC) conducted a special project to gather comprehensive data on the trading activities of large hedge funds and CTAs in 13 futures markets between April 4 and October 6, 1994. The purpose of this study is to use the CFTC data to investigate the market impact of futures trading by large hedge funds and CTAs. This is the first study to directly estimate the impact of hedge fund and CTA trading in any market.

The first part of the chapter analyzes the relationship between hedge fund and CTA trading and market volatility. Drawing on the specifications of Bessembinder and Seguin (1993) and Chang, Pinegar, and Schacter (1997), regression models of market volatility are expressed as a function of: (a) trading volume and open interest for large hedge funds and CTAs, (b) trading volume and open interest for the rest of the market, and (c) day-of-the-week effects. The second part of the chapter analyzes whether the relationship between large hedge fund and CTA trading and market volatility is harmful to economic welfare. Three tests are used to distinguish between alternative hypotheses. The first test relies on a series of variance ratios to determine whether there are significant departures from randomness in futures returns over the sample period. The second test determines whether positive feedback trading is a general characteristic of hedge fund and CTA trading. The third test examines the profitability of hedge fund and CTA trading during the sample period.

DATA

To obtain the data used in this chapter, the CFTC applied a special collection process through which market surveillance specialists identified those accounts known to be trading for large hedge funds and CTAs (J. Mielke, personal communications, 1998). Once identified in the CFTC's large trader reporting database, the accounts were tracked and positions compiled.[2] Through this procedure, a data set was compiled over April 4 through October 6, 1994, consisting of the reportable open interest positions for these accounts across 13 different markets. A total of 130 business days are included in the six-month sample period. The U.S. futures markets surveyed are coffee, copper, corn, cotton, deutsche mark, eurodollar, gold, live hogs, natural gas, crude oil, soybeans, Standard and Poor's (S&P 500), and treasury bonds. For simplicity, large hedge fund and CTA accounts will be referred to as managed money accounts (MMAs) in the remainder of this chapter.

As received from the CFTC, data for a given futures market are aggregated across all traders for each trading day. These figures represent the total long and short open interest (across all contract months) of MMAs for each day. Then the difference between open interest (for both long and short positions) on day t and day $t - 1$ is computed to determine the minimum trading volume for day t. The computed trading volumes represent minimum trading volumes (long, short, net, and gross) and serve only as an approximation to actual daily trading volume, because intraday trading is not accounted for in the computation. In summary, the CFTC data consist of the aggregate (across contract months and traders) reportable open interest positions (both long and short), as well as the implied long, short, net, and gross trading volume attributable to MMAs.

Due to the aggregated nature of this data set, it is assumed that trading by MMAs is placed in the nearby futures contract. This is consistent with Ederington and Lee's (2002) finding that nearly all commodity pool (which includes hedge funds) and CTA trading in the heating oil futures market is in near-term contracts, and permits the use of nearby price series in the analysis. Five markets (corn, soybeans, cotton, copper, and gold), however, do not exactly follow the conventional nearby definition. In each of these markets there is a contract month, which even in its nearby state does not have the most trading volume and open interest. For example, the September corn and soybean contracts are only lightly traded through their existence. Liquidity in these markets shifts in late June from the July contract to the new crop contract (November for soybeans and December for corn).

---

[2]Ederington and Lee (2002) provide a detailed explanation of the line-of-business classification procedures used internally by the CFTC as a part of the large trader position reporting system.

Therefore, to follow the liquidity of these markets, a price series is developed that always reflects the most liquid contract. For most markets except the five listed above, it is equivalent to a nearby price series that rolls forward at the end of the calendar month previous to contract expiration.

Descriptive Analysis of Trading Behavior

The 13 markets included in this data set range from the more liquid financial contracts to some of the less liquid agricultural markets. Table 8.1 reports descriptive statistics on general market conditions between April 4 and October 6, 1994, including the average daily trading volume and open interest (for

TABLE 8.1 Average Levels of Volume, Open Interest, and Volatility for 13 Futures Markets, April 4, 1994–October 6, 1994 and January 4, 1988–December 31, 1997

	Daily Average					
	April 4, 1994–October 6, 1994			January 4, 1988–December 31, 1997		
	Contracts			Contracts		
Futures Market	Volume	Open Interest	Volatility %	Volume	Open Interest	Volatility %
Coffee	8,081	24,330	2.60	5,072	19,718	1.69
Copper	8,013	32,585	1.03	5,938	22,515	1.15
Corn	23,984	121,230	0.90	26,849	127,378	0.84
Cotton	5,170	26,094	0.92	4,328	21,796	0.88
Crude oil	50,897	96,306	1.43	40,640	80,689	1.33
Deutsche mark	42,895	92,186	0.47	33,130	71,328	0.46
Eurodollar	145,505	446,932	0.05	82,709	329,268	0.05
Gold	28,810	82,344	0.49	27,094	69,878	0.52
Live hogs	2,639	11,933	1.01	3,411	12,545	0.95
Natural gas	9,880	22,409	1.69	8,002	19,614	1.77
S&P 500	65,700	190,626	0.52	54,198	150,675	0.68
Soybeans	26,922	68,876	0.89	25,976	60,649	0.88
Treasury bonds	392,204	363,407	0.61	294,987	307,308	0.49

Note: Parkinson's (1980) extreme-value estimator is used to estimate the daily volatility of futures returns.

TABLE 8.2 Composition of Large Managed Money Account Trading Volume across 13 Futures Markets, April 4, 1994–October 6, 1994

	Percentage of Total Managed Money Account Trading Volume	
Futures Market	**Gross Volume %**	**Net Volume %**
Coffee	1.6	1.7
Copper	2.9	3.0
Corn	5.4	5.7
Cotton	2.3	2.6
Crude oil	4.0	8.4
Deutsche mark	8.2	7.3
Eurodollar	6.0	22.9
Gold	25.7	8.0
Live hogs	7.4	0.9
Natural gas	0.9	4.5
S&P 500	5.5	7.1
Soybeans	6.8	6.1
Treasury bonds	23.2	21.8

Note: Managed money accounts are defined as large hedge funds and CTAs. Gross volume equals long plus short volume. Net volume in this case equals the absolute value of long minus short volume. Percentages may not add to 100 due to rounding.

the modified nearby series) and the average daily volatility of futures returns.[3] To provide a basis for comparison, the table also reports descriptive statistics for the previous 10 years (January 4, 1988, to December 31, 1997). Comparison of these statistics suggests market conditions for the six-month period being studied is representative of longer-term conditions.

To reach conclusions regarding the effects of MMA trading, it is important first to understand which markets are traded. Any potential effects from their trading may be dependent on whether trading is concentrated in the more liquid financial futures or the less liquid commodity markets. The results shown in Table 8.2 are computed by dividing the gross (long plus short) or net (absolute value of long minus short) MMA trading volume for each day in each futures market by the total MMA trading volume across all

[3]Daily volatility is estimated by Parkinson's (1980) extreme-value (high-low) volatility estimator. Further details are provided here in the section entitled "Volume and Price Volatility Relationship."

futures markets for each day. More specifically, averages of the daily percentages across the six-month sample period are presented. Consistent with the findings in Irwin and Yoshimaru (1999), the results show that MMA trading volume is largely concentrated in the most liquid financial futures markets.

The two most liquid markets (eurodollar and treasury bonds) account for approximately 49 percent of MMA gross trading volume and 45 percent of MMA net trading volume. Only about 14 percent of MMA gross volume and 8 percent of MMA net volume is found in the four least liquid markets (live hogs, cotton, copper, and coffee, based on volume over the six months). The concentration of MMA trading volume in the most liquid futures markets suggests that hedge fund operators and CTAs are well aware of the size of their own trading volume and seek to minimize trade execution costs associated with large orders in less liquid markets.

Although, according to contract volume figures, MMAs concentrate trading in more active markets, it is also important to analyze their trading volume relative to the size of each market. The percentages shown in Table 8.3 are the average of the daily MMA gross or net (absolute value) trading volume divided by the nearby contract volume. The results show that MMA

TABLE 8.3 Trading Volume of Large Managed Money Accounts as a Percentage of Total Trading Volume in 13 Futures Markets, April 4, 1994–October 6, 1994

	Gross Volume of Managed Money Accounts		Net Volume of Managed Money Accounts	
Futures Market	Average%	Maximum%	Average%	Maximum%
Coffee	6.9	26.7	5.9	26.7
Copper	11.1	39.8	9.3	34.6
Corn	7.0	23.0	6.0	23.0
Cotton	12.9	39.4	11.1	39.4
Crude oil	5.4	19.5	4.4	16.3
Deutsche mark	5.3	20.1	4.8	20.1
Eurodollar	7.2	28.5	5.3	23.6
Gold	8.6	24.7	7.3	24.7
Live hogs	11.6	47.8	9.4	47.8
Natural gas	14.0	54.4	12.2	53.6
S&P 500	3.7	14.9	3.2	12.0
Soybeans	6.7	21.6	6.0	21.6
Treasury bonds	2.4	10.3	1.8	7.5

Note: Managed money accounts are defined as large hedge funds and CTAs. Gross volume equals long plus short volume. Net volume in this case equals the absolute value of long minus short volume.

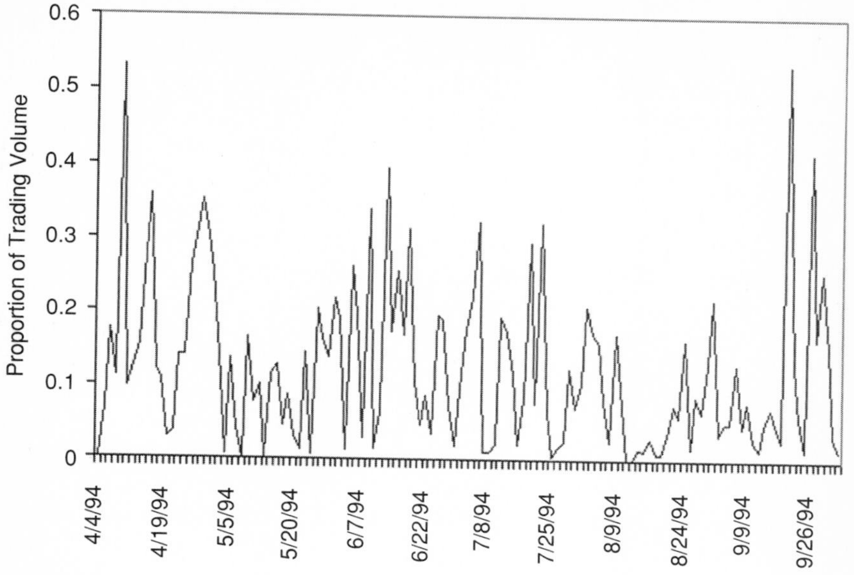

FIGURE 8.1 Large Managed Money Account Net Trading Volume as a Proportion of Total Nearby Trading Volume, Natural Gas Futures Market, April 4, 1994–October 6, 1994.

trading ranges from about 2 to 14 percent of total market volume, whether measured on a gross or a net basis. MMA gross trading volume averages 7.9 percent of market volume across all 13 markets, while MMA net trading volume averages 6.7 percent.[4] These statistics clearly show that MMAs are important participants in most of the 13 futures markets during the sample period. Furthermore, the one-day maxima are quite large, ranging from about 10 to 54 percent for gross volume and 7 to 54 percent for net volume.

Figure 8.1 provides a graphical representation of the "spiky" nature of MMA trading for the natural gas market. To summarize, although MMAs tend to focus trading in terms of numbers of contracts in the most liquid markets, their trading still may represent a large proportion of total market volume, especially for less liquid futures markets.

---

[4]The averages reported in Table 8.3 are roughly consistent with results found in Ederington and Lee (2002) for heating oil futures. Over the June 1993–March 1997 period, they report that the daily trading volume of commodity pools (which include hedge funds) and commodity trading advisors averages 11.3 percent.

To better understand the timing of trading by MMAs relative to trading by the rest of the market, simple correlation coefficients are computed between the contemporaneous trading volume of MMAs and the rest of the market. As reported in Table 8.4, estimated correlation coefficients are all positive and range from about 0.01 to 0.70. The average correlation across all markets is 0.39 and 0.38 on a gross and net basis, respectively. Statistically significant correlations (at the 5 percent level) are observed in 10 markets for gross volume of MMAs and 10 markets for net volume. The overwhelmingly positive relationships suggest that MMAs generally trade when others are trading. This result is the opposite of the negative relationships that Kodres (1994) found between position changes of hedge funds and other types of large traders. It is uncertain whether the positive relationships indicate the potential for stabilizing or destabilizing prices. On one hand, the positive relationships indicate MMAs tend to trade in more liquid market conditions, all else being equal. On the other hand, the positive relationships also may indicate that other traders follow the "leadership" of MMAs, which could destabilize prices through a herd effect (Kodres, 1994).

TABLE 8.4 Correlation between Large Managed Money Account Trading and All Other Market Trading Volume in 13 Futures Markets, April 4, 1994–October 6, 1994

	Correlation Coefficient	
Futures Market	Gross Trading Volume of Managed Money Accounts	Net Trading Volume of Managed Money Accounts
Coffee	0.35*	0.33*
Copper	0.53*	0.50*
Corn	0.61*	0.58*
Cotton	0.66*	0.64*
Crude oil	0.16	0.21*
Deutsche mark	0.42*	0.44*
Eurodollar	0.44*	0.34
Gold	0.66*	0.67*
Live hogs	0.05	0.01
Natural gas	0.07	0.06
S&P 500	0.28*	0.25*
Soybeans	0.52*	0.56*
Treasury bonds	0.30*	0.31*

Note: Managed money accounts are defined as large hedge funds and CTAs. Gross volume equals long plus short volume. Net volume in this case equals the absolute value of long minus short volume.
*Statistically significant at the 5 percent level.

Overall, the picture of MMA trading behavior that emerges is mixed. MMAs tend to focus trading in terms of numbers of contracts in the most liquid futures markets. However, MMA trading can represent a large proportion of total market volume, especially on certain days and in less liquid futures markets. Consequently, direct tests are needed to better understand the market impact of MMA trading. The next section investigates the relationship between the trading volume of MMAs and price volatility in futures markets.

Volume and Price Volatility Relationship

Karpoff (1987) provides an extensive and widely cited survey of the methodology and results of studies focusing on the relationship between volume and volatility. The chief difference between model specifications, up to the date of Karpoff's survey and since then, is the procedure used to accommodate persistence in volume and volatility. Due to the lack of a commonly accepted model specification for the relationship between volume and volatility, three basic specifications are used in the analysis for this study.

1. Following Chang, Pinegar, and Schachter (1997), the volume and volatility relationship is modeled without including past volatility.
2. Following Irwin and Yoshimaru (1999), volatility lags are included as independent variables to account for the time series persistence of volatility.
3. Following Bessembinder and Seguin (1993), the persistence in volume and volatility is modeled through specification of an iterative process.[5]

Since estimation results for the different model specifications are quite similar, only results for a modified version of Chang, Pinegar, and Schachter's specification are reported here.[6]

Chang, Pinegar, and Schachter (1997) regress futures price volatility on volume associated with large speculators (as provided by the CFTC large trader reports) and all other market volume. Including two additional sets

[5]Another approach would be to use a model with a mean equation and a volatility equation that has both volume and GARCH (generalized autoregressive conditional heteroskedasticity) terms. This approach is not used due to the limited time series of observations available for each market. Monte Carlo simulation results generated recently by Hwang and Pereira (2003) indicate that at least 500 observations are needed to efficiently estimate models with GARCH effects, substantially more than the number of daily observations available in this study (130).

[6]The full set of regression results can be found in Holt (1999).

of independent variables expands this basic specification. Daily effects on volatility are well documented, implying that a set of daily dummy variables should be included. In addition, the estimated specification includes the open interest for each market. As outlined by Bessembinder and Seguin (1993), open interest serves as a proxy for market depth, which is anticipated to have a negative relationship to volatility. This relationship implies that changes in volume have a smaller effect on volatility in a more liquid market (represented by higher open interest). Therefore, the regression model specification for a given futures market is

$$\sigma_t = \beta_1 + \beta_2 MMATV_t + \beta_3 MMAOI_t + \beta_4 AOTV_t + \beta_5 AOOI_t + \beta_6 Mon_t + \beta_7 Tue_t + \beta_8 Wed_t + \beta_9 Thu_t + \varepsilon_t \tag{8.1}$$

where σ_t = daily volatility (standard deviation) of futures returns
$MMATV_t$ = absolute value of net MMA trading volume
$MMAOI_t$ = absolute value of net MMA open interest
$AOTV_t$ = other market trading volume
$AOOI_t$ = other open interest
Mon_t, Tue_t, Wed_t, and Thu_t = dummy variables that represent day-of-the-week effects
ε_t = a standard normal error term.

Following Chang, Pinegar, and Schachter (1997) and Irwin and Yoshimaru (1999), the extreme-value estimator developed by Parkinson (1980) is used to estimate daily volatility of futures returns. For a given commodity, Parkinson's estimator can be expressed as

$$\hat{\sigma}_t = 0.601 \ln(H_t / L_t) \tag{8.2}$$

where H_t = trading day's high price
L_t = the day's low.

Wiggins (1991) reports that extreme-value estimators are more efficient than close-to-close estimators in many applications. Previous empirical results suggest that a positive relationship is expected between volume and volatility. They also suggest a negative relationship between volatility and open interest, as shown by Bessembinder and Seguin (1993) for example. However, open interest within any six-month period may not vary enough to efficiently estimate its impact on volatility. For the same reason, it is possible that daily dummy variables will not exhibit the U-shape documented in previous volatility studies.

Table 8.5 reports the estimated coefficients, corresponding *t*-statistics, and adjusted R^2 for each market. Due to the relative insignificance of the day-of-the-week variables, only the *F*-statistic for testing the joint significance of the dummy variables is reported. As shown by this *F*-statistic, significant daily

TABLE 8.5 Volatility Regression Results for 13 Futures Markets, April 4, 1994–October 6, 1994

Futures Market	Intercept	MMA Net Volume	Rest of Nearby Volume	MMA Net Open Interest	Rest of Nearby Open Interest	*F*-Statistic for Daily Effects	Adj. R^2
Coffee	3440.1*	−0.1200	0.4590*	−0.1444*	−0.1831*	1.31	0.51
	(6.39)	(−0.73)	(11.19)	(−4.85)	(−6.31)		
Copper	522.6*	0.0973*	0.1091*	−0.0018	−0.0214*	1.12	0.61
	(3.98)	(3.22)	(9.67)	(−0.37)	(−4.53)		
Corn	916.5*	0.0411*	0.0253*	−0.0147*	−0.0046*	1.15	0.49
	(3.17)	(2.30)	(6.41)	(−3.53)	(−1.98)		
Cotton	331.7	0.0379	0.1279*	0.0070	−0.0009	0.97	0.41
	(1.57)	(0.98)	(6.77)	(0.71)	(−0.14)		
Crude oil	739.4*	0.0539*	0.0357*	−0.0189*	−0.0094*	1.85	0.44
	(2.69)	(2.24)	(9.05)	(−4.22)	(−3.38)		
Deutsche mark	184.5	0.0088	0.0121*	0.0019	−0.0019	4.06*	0.45
	(1.64)	(1.09)	(7.94)	(1.01)	(−1.57)		
Eurodollar	35.7	0.0010*	0.0004*	−0.0002*	−0.0001	0.38	0.69
	(1.60)	(3.69)	(11.61)	(−3.88)	(−0.24)		
Gold	74.7	0.0234*	0.0154*	−0.0010	−0.0003	2.07	0.63
	(0.71)	(3.60)	(7.97)	(−0.77)	(−0.29)		
Live hogs	290.0	0.3929*	0.2272*	0.0081	−0.0306*	1.10	0.30
	(1.04)	(3.55)	(5.74)	(0.29)	(−3.05)		
Natural gas	120.6	0.1115*	0.1399*	0.0256*	0.0036	0.52	0.47
	(0.42)	(2.76)	(8.94)	(2.51)	(0.26)		
S&P 500	−657.7*	0.0268*	0.0099*	−0.0008	0.0035*	1.03	0.53
	(−3.61)	(3.34)	(10.19)	(−0.45)	(3.79)		
Soybeans	−121.2	0.0140	0.0423*	−0.0132	−0.0003	1.05	0.57
	(−0.44)	(0.71)	(9.94)	(−1.61)	(−0.09)		
Treasury bonds	83.8	0.0126*	0.0018*	−0.0006	−0.0006	2.16	0.69
	(0.78)	(4.75)	(12.96)	(−0.39)	(−1.93)		

MMA = managed money accounts, which are defined as large hedge funds and CTAs. The figures in parentheses are *t*-statistics. The *F*-statistic tests the null hypothesis that parameters for the day-of-the-week dummy variables jointly equal zero.
*Statistically significant at the 5 percent level.

effects are observed only for the deutsche mark futures market. The average adjusted R^2 across all 13 markets is 0.52, indicating a reasonable fit of the models, particularly in light of the relatively small sample size. The estimated coefficient for MMA trading volume is significantly positive at the 5 percent level in nine markets, with the remaining four markets having insignificant coefficients (coffee, cotton, deutsche mark, and soybeans). All of the estimated coefficients for the rest of market volume are significant and positive at the 5 percent level. Therefore, as expected, a positive relationship is exhibited between trading volume and price variability, regardless of the trader type (MMA or all other). Four of the estimated coefficients for MMA open interest are significantly negative (coffee, corn, crude oil, and eurodollar), while one is significantly positive (natural gas). For the rest of market open interest, coefficients are negative and significant in five markets (coffee, copper, corn, crude oil, and hogs) and significantly positive in one market (S&P 500). As mentioned previously, the mixed results for open interest are not surprising due to the relatively short time period studied.

Previous studies (e.g., Chang, Pinegar, and Schachter 1997) estimate volatility effects of different trader types by comparing the relative size of the parameter estimates associated with the traders. For example, estimates of β_2 and β_4 from regression equation 8.1 could be compared to determine the volatility effects of MMAs and all other traders. However, this comparison can be misleading if the means of the respective independent variables are not of similar magnitudes. A better approach is to compare volatility elasticities evaluated at the means of the independent variables.

Estimates for the volatility elasticity of volume and open interest are reported in Table 8.6. The volatility elasticity of MMA volume ranges from –0.02 to 0.14, with a cross-sectional average of 0.09. This implies, on average, that a 1 percent increase in MMA trading volume leads to about a one-tenth of 1 percent increase in futures price volatility. The volatility elasticity of all other volume ranges from 0.54 to 1.19, with an overall average of 0.86. This estimate means that a 1 percent increase in all other market volume (besides MMA volume) leads to slightly less than a 1 percent increase in futures price volatility. Therefore, on a percentage basis, increases in MMA trading volume lead to much smaller increases in volatility than do increases in all other market volume. Finally, it is interesting to note that open interest elasticities for MMAs average –0.10, indicating that MMA trading contributes positively to market depth and liquidity.

Explaining the Volume and Volatility Relationship

The results presented in the previous section provide strong evidence of a positive relationship between MMA trading volume and futures price

TABLE 8.6 Estimates of the Volatility Elasticity of Volume and Open Interest for 13 Futures Markets, April 4, 1994–October 6, 1994.

Futures Market	MMA Net Volume	Rest of Nearby Volume	MMA Net Open Interest	Rest of Nearby Open Interest
Coffee	−0.02	1.33	−0.43	−1.17
Copper	0.08	0.76	−0.02	−0.40
Corn	0.08	0.63	−0.22	−0.55
Cotton	0.03	0.60	0.06	−0.02
Crude oil	0.08	1.19	−0.26	−0.49
Deutsche mark	0.04	1.05	0.07	−0.31
Eurodollar	0.13	0.98	−0.59	−0.06
Gold	0.12	0.82	−0.04	−0.04
Live hogs	0.10	0.54	0.07	−0.11
Natural gas	0.08	0.69	0.15	0.03
S&P 500	0.11	1.22	−0.07	1.00
Soybeans	0.03	1.19	−0.12	−0.02
Treasury bonds	0.14	1.11	−0.01	−0.33

MMA = managed money accounts, which are defined as large hedge funds and CTAs.

volatility. However, on its own, this result is not sufficient to conclude that MMA trading is beneficial or harmful to economic welfare. A positive relationship between MMA trading volume and market volatility is consistent with either a private information hypothesis (e.g., Clark 1973), where the information-driven trading of MMAs tends to move prices closer to equilibrium values, or a noise trader hypothesis (e.g., De Long, Schleifer, Summers, and Waldman 1990), where MMA trading is based on "noise" such as trend-chasing or market sentiment and tends to move prices further from equilibrium values. Weiner (2002, p. 395) states the issue in succinct terms:

> *...the concern over whether these funds have a positive or negative effect on market functioning comes down to whether the funds can be characterized as "smart money"—undertaking extensive analysis on possible changes in future industry, macroeconomic, political, and so forth conditions and their likely consequences for prices—or "dumb money"—noise traders chasing trends or herding sheep, buying and selling because others are doing so.*

Following French and Roll (1986), three tests are used in this study in an attempt to distinguish between these two hypotheses.

Variance Ratio Tests Under market efficiency, price changes follow a random walk. Therefore, return variance for a long holding period is equal to the sum of the daily return variances. However, under the noise trader hypothesis, the cumulated daily return variances are expected to be greater than the long holding period variance. This assumes that, over a longer holding period, the market corrects errors associated with noise trading. The daily variances include the effects of noise trading, while the longer holding period variance presumably does not. Therefore, the presence of noise trading can be identified through an analysis of return variance ratios over different holding periods.

Variance ratios are computed following the methodology of Campbell, Lo, and MacKinlay (1997). The q-day variance ratio is

$$VR_q = \frac{\sigma_q^2}{\sigma_1^2 \cdot q} \tag{8.3}$$

where σ_q^2 = q-day holding period return variance
σ_1^2 = daily holding period return variance.

Note that overlapping q-period returns are used to estimate σ_q^2 and one-day returns are used to estimate σ_1^2. The use of overlapping returns increases the efficiency of the variance ratio estimator.[7] For a given commodity, the standardized test statistic to test the null hypothesis that the variance ratio equals 1 is

$$\psi_q = \sqrt{nq}(VR_q - 1)\left(\frac{2(2q-1)(q-1)}{3q}\right)^{-1/2} \tag{8.4}$$

where $nq + 1$ = number of original daily price observations.

Campbell, Lo, and MacKinlay (1997) show that ψ_q approximately follows a standard normal distribution in large samples. Variance ratios and associated test statistics are computed for six different holding periods: for q = 2, 3, 5, 10, 15, and 20 days.

[7]The formulas for the variance estimators are found on pp. 52–53 in Campbell, Lo, and MacKinlay (1997). One technical issue is how to handle the computation of futures returns when nearby futures price series roll from the "old" nearby contract to the "new" nearby contract. To resolve this issue, returns for the first active day of the "new" nearby contract are computed using the previous day's price for the "new" contract, rather than the previous day's price from the "old" contract.

An important statistical issue arises when interpreting the variance ratio test results. Specifically, what constitutes evidence against the null hypothesis? If variance ratios across holding periods are independent, then rejection of the null hypothesis of unity for one holding period is sufficient to reject the joint null hypothesis that variance ratios equal unity across all holding periods. Because of overlapping holding periods, it is unlikely that the independence assumption is valid. As a result, individual hypothesis tests likely have a higher probability of Type I error than the specified significance level.

To assess the joint significance of variance ratios correctly across holding periods, a joint test statistic is needed. The Bonferroni inequality provides a simple means for testing the joint null hypothesis that test statistics are not different from unity. The inequality provides an upper bound for rejection of the joint null hypothesis when the test statistics are correlated. Intuitively, the Bonferroni test simple scales up the p-value of the most significant test statistic to account for the dependency. Miller (1966) provides a full explanation of the Bonferroni inequality and resulting joint testing procedure.

To implement the Bonferroni joint test for a given commodity, we define the maximum standardized test statistic as

$$\psi^{\max} = \max_{q}\left\{\left|\psi_q\right|\right\} \tag{8.5}$$

where ψ_q = standardized test statistic for the q-day holding period.

The joint null hypothesis is rejected at the significance level α if $\psi^{\max}$ is greater than the critical value defined by

$$1 - \phi(\psi) = \frac{\alpha / c}{2} \tag{8.6}$$

where $\phi(\cdot)$ = standard normal cumulative distribution function
c = number of restrictions tested

Because variance ratios are estimated for six holding periods, a joint hypothesis test for a given futures market imposes six restrictions. As a result, the critical value for the Bonferroni joint test at the 5 percent level is 2.63.

Table 8.7 presents variance ratios and standardized test statistics for each of the 13 markets. In only 2 variance ratios out of 78 is the null hypothesis of unity rejected. The two significant ratios suggest the possibility of a short-run noise trading component in the gold market. The significant negative test statistics for the two-day and three-day holding periods indicate that two- and three-day holding period return variances are less than two and three times the estimated daily variance. This fact implies the daily return variances are larger due to the noise component. However, this noise component is traded away in the long run, as shown by the insignificant test statistics for the longer holding periods. The gold market also is the only market out of 13 where the Bonferroni joint test statistic is significant. This rejection rate (0.077) is only slightly greater than would be expected based on random chance and a 5 percent significance level. Overall, the variance ratio tests for this sample period do not support the noise trader hypothesis, but instead support the private information hypothesis for MMA trading.

Because the sample period considered in the previous tests is somewhat limited, a reasonable question is whether the results are sensitive to different time periods and longer sample periods. The first alternative sample period considered is the previous six-month period from October 1, 1993, through March 31, 1994. As shown in Table 8.8, only 6 of 78 variance ratios are significantly different from unity for this sample period. The Bonferroni joint test statistic is significant only for the eurodollar futures market, which again is only slightly greater than what would be expected based on random chance. The second alternative sample period considered is substantially longer and includes the previous six-and-one-quarter-year period from January 4, 1988, through March 31, 1994. As shown in Table 8.9, only 17 out of 78 variance ratios are significantly different from unity. However, the Bonferroni joint test statistic is significant for 4 of the 13 markets (cotton, crude oil, Eurodollar, and S&P 500), more than would be expected based on random chance.

The last finding indicates that variance ratio test results may be sensitive to the use of a relatively small sample size. Nonetheless, the variance ratio results for alternative sample periods do not provide convincing evidence that the conclusion reached on the basis of the original sample period is invalid. That is, variance ratio tests do not indicate substantial deviations from market efficiency that would be associated with noise trading on the part of MMAs. Instead, the results are more consistent with the hypothesis that MMAs base their trading on valuable private information.

Positive Feedback Trading Tests Buying after price increases and selling after price declines characterizes positive feedback trading. The existence of

TABLE 8.7 Variance Ratio Test Results for 13 Futures Markets, April 4, 1994–October 6, 1994

	Holding Period Lengths						
Futures Market	**2 Day**	**3 Day**	**5 Day**	**10 Day**	**15 Day**	**20 Day**	**Bonferroni Joint Test Statistic**
Coffee	1.08	1.12	1.19	1.25	1.49	1.53	1.21
	(0.86)	(0.95)	(1.00)	(0.84)	(1.32)	(1.21)	
Copper	0.92	0.91	0.92	0.96	0.97	1.00	0.86
	(−0.86)	(−0.69)	(−0.42)	(−0.15)	(−0.07)	(0.00)	
Corn	0.97	1.07	0.96	0.78	0.98	1.00	0.72
	(−0.30)	(0.56)	(−0.19)	(−0.72)	(−0.06)	(0.01)	
Cotton	1.08	1.06	1.10	0.99	0.98	0.86	0.91
	(0.91)	(0.45)	(0.52)	(−0.03)	(−0.06)	(−0.32)	
Crude oil	1.09	1.09	1.02	1.26	1.35	1.58	1.33
	(1.00)	(0.68)	(0.11)	(0.89)	(0.93)	(1.33)	
Deutsche mark	1.02	1.04	1.09	1.01	0.78	0.73	0.61
	(0.17)	(0.30)	(0.49)	(0.04)	(−0.60)	(−0.61)	
Eurodollar	1.12	1.19	1.16	0.78	0.74	0.71	1.43
	(1.39)	(1.43)	(0.81)	(−0.75)	(−0.69)	(−0.67)	
Gold	0.71*	0.72*	0.70	0.75	0.65	0.61	3.25*
	(−3.25)	(−2.16)	(−1.58)	(−0.86)	(−0.94)	(−0.90)	
Live hogs	1.03	0.97	0.90	0.84	0.74	0.51	1.11
	0.35)	(−0.21)	(−0.54)	(−0.54)	(−0.69)	(−1.11)	
Natural gas	0.97	1.06	1.24	1.24	1.18	1.19	1.24
	(−0.29)	(0.44)	(1.24)	(0.81)	(0.49)	(0.43)	
Soybeans	1.03	1.09	0.96	0.82	0.99	0.98	0.69
	(0.31)	(0.69)	(−0.23)	(−0.59)	(−0.02)	(−0.03)	
S&P 500	0.84	0.93	0.86	0.74	0.75	0.73	1.86
	(−1.86)	(−0.52)	(−0.71)	(−0.87)	(−0.66)	(−0.61)	
Treasury bonds	0.88	0.86	0.77	0.52	0.49	0.48	1.63
	(−1.35)	(−1.06)	(−1.18)	(−1.63)	(−1.37)	(−1.19)	

The figures in parentheses are *Z*–statistics.
*Statistically significant at the 5 percent level.

TABLE 8.8 Variance Ratio Test Results for 13 Futures Markets, October 1, 1993–March 31, 1994

Futures Market	Holding Period Lengths						Bonferroni Joint Test Statistic
	2 Day	3 Day	5 Day	10 Day	15 Day	20 Day	
Coffee	0.78*	0.74	0.62	0.46	0.44	0.39	2.46
	(−2.46)	(−1.95)	(−1.94)	(−1.79)	(−1.49)	(−1.39)	
Copper	0.95	0.98	1.01	1.00	1.02	0.95	0.57
	(−0.57)	(−0.14)	(−0.05)	(−0.01)	(−0.04)	(−0.12)	
Corn	1.03	0.97	0.92	1.05	1.31	1.74	1.68
	(0.39)	(−0.25)	(−0.41)	(0.16)	(0.83)	(1.68)	
Cotton	1.07	1.09	1.14	1.45	1.65	1.94*	2.13
	(0.76)	(0.67)	(0.71)	(1.49)	(1.72)	(2.13)	
Crude oil	0.99	1.03	1.03	1.11	1.21	1.39	0.88
	(−0.11)	(0.20)	(0.17)	(0.36)	(0.56)	(0.88	
Deutsche mark	0.97	1.03	1.03	0.87	0.93	0.95	0.43
	(−0.38)	(0.20)	(0.14)	(−0.43)	(−0.18)	(−0.12)	
Eurodollar	1.22*	1.25	1.43*	1.85*	2.41*	3.02*	4.58*
	(2.51)	(1.91)	(2.21)	(2.83)	(3.74)	(4.58)	
Gold	0.98	0.95	0.88	0.74	0.73	0.70	0.87
	(−0.22)	(−0.35)	(−0.60)	(−0.87)	(−0.72)	(−0.68)	
Live hogs	1.08	1.10	1.08	1.11	1.19	1.47	1.07
	(0.86)	(0.76)	(0.42)	(0.38)	(0.51)	(1.07)	
Natural gas	1.04	1.12	1.13	1.28	1.38	1.67	1.51
	(0.40)	(0.90)	(0.67)	(0.92)	(1.01)	(1.51)	
Soybeans	1.06	1.00	0.95	1.03	1.02	1.03	0.66
	(0.66)	(0.02)	(−0.27)	(0.11)	(0.05)	(0.08)	
S&P 500	0.93	0.96	1.02	0.87	0.76	0.71	0.82
	(−0.82)	(−0.28)	(0.11)	(−0.43)	(−0.63)	(−0.65)	
Treasury bonds	1.04	1.02	1.10	1.09	1.24	1.44	0.99
	(0.47)	(0.15)	(0.50)	(0.30)	(0.64)	(0.99)	

The figures in parentheses are Z-statistics.
*Statistically significant at the 5 percent level.

TABLE 8.9 Variance Ratio Test Results for 13 Futures Markets, January 4, 1988–March 31, 1994

Futures Market	Holding Period Lengths						
	2 Day	3 Day	5 Day	10 Day	15 Day	20 Day	Bonferroni Joint Test Statistic
Coffee	0.97 (−1.35)	0.96 (−1.07)	0.99 (−0.23)	0.97 (−0.34)	0.98 (−0.15)	1.01 (0.10)	1.35
Copper	1.03 (1.22)	1.02 (0.50)	1.00 (0.01)	1.02 (0.27)	1.00 (0.03)	0.98 (−0.15)	1.22
Corn	1.02 (−0.66)	0.97 (−0.87)	0.91 (−1.71)	0.86 (−1.66)	0.88 (−1.13)	0.89 (−0.87)	1.71
Cotton	1.10* (3.86)	1.11* (3.06)	1.12* (2.19)	1.18* (2.07)	1.27* (2.50)	1.34* (2.70)	3.86*
Crude oil	1.02 (0.97)	1.01 (0.39)	0.91 (−1.62)	0.76* (−2.78)	0.77* (−2.12)	0.81 (−1.53)	2.78*
Deutsche mark	1.03 (1.22)	1.01 (0.29)	0.98 (−0.41)	0.96 (−0.44)	1.00 (0.00)	1.03 (0.22)	1.22
Eurodollar	1.07* (2.96)	1.06 (1.64)	1.04 (0.64)	1.10 (1.22)	1.13 (1.21)	1.20 (1.58)	2.96*
Gold	0.97 (−1.18)	0.95 (−1.43)	0.91 (−1.63)	0.90 (−1.13)	0.92 (−0.78)	0.91 (−0.70)	1.63
Live hogs	1.03 (1.10)	0.99 (−0.14)	0.97 (−0.51)	0.98 (−0.26)	0.95 (−0.43)	0.94 (−0.49)	1.10
Natural gas	1.02 (0.76)	0.99 (−0.19)	1.01 (0.11)	1.11 (1.02)	1.24 (1.82)	1.37* (2.39)	2.39
Soybeans	1.06* (2.20)	1.04 (1.16)	1.04 (0.64)	1.01 (0.06)	1.00 (−0.01)	0.98 (−0.14)	2.20
S&P 500	0.94* (−2.21)	0.90* (−2.58)	0.84* (−2.90)	0.72* (−3.24)	0.70* (−2.81)	0.70* (−2.38)	3.24*
Treasury bonds	1.02 (0.92)	1.04 (1.10)	0.99 (−0.16)	0.93 (−0.88)	0.92 (−0.76)	0.93 (−53)	1.10

The figures in parentheses are Z-statistics.
*Statistically significant at the 5 percent level.

this type of trading may lead to decreases in market efficiency by creating excessive volatility. For instance, when new bullish fundamental information is received, and price increases to its new fundamental value through rational trading, positive feedback traders continue to buy, driving price past its rational value. Following Kodres (1994) and Irwin and Yoshimaru (1999), positive feedback trading is identified for a given market by estimating this regression model:

$$NETMMATV_t = \alpha_1 + \sum_{i=1}^{5} \beta_i \Delta p_{t-i} + \varepsilon_t \tag{8.7}$$

where $NETMMATV_t$ = net trading volume of MMAs (number of long contracts minus number of short contracts) on day t
Δp_{t-i} = continuously compounded futures return on day $t - i$
ε_t = standard normal error term.

Based on Irwin and Yoshimaru's results, five lagged price returns are included in the model for all markets. Note that $NETMMATV_t$ takes on positive values when MMAs are net buyers of contracts, negative values when MMAs are net sellers, and zero when no volume is recorded. Slope coefficients in equation 8.7 can be thought of as the sensitivities of MMA "demand" to past price movements. Positive slope coefficients are evidence of positive feedback trading by MMAs, whereas negative coefficients are evidence of negative feedback trading. The net feedback effect is given by the sum of slope coefficients for each regression. The significance of feedback trading is determined by testing whether the sum of the estimated slope coefficients (for lagged price returns) is greater than zero.

Table 8.10 provides estimation results for equation 8.7. The sum of slope coefficient estimates is positive in nine markets, close to zero in one market, and negative in three markets. Of the nine positive sums, t-statistics indicate six are significantly different from zero. Thus, statistically significant evidence of positive feedback trading among MMAs is found in about half of the markets studied. The average adjusted R^2 across all 13 markets is 0.09, ranging from a high of 0.35 (cotton) to a low of –0.02 (coffee). Overall, this provides some evidence of positive feedback trading on the part of MMAs. However, because positive feedback terms explain only 9 percent of the variation in MMA trading volume, it can be concluded that MMA trading decisions are influenced only in small part by past price changes. It is interesting to note the similarity of these results to Irwin and Yoshimaru's (1999) results for commodity pool trading volume. They

TABLE 8.10 Positive Feedback Regression Results for 13 Futures Markets, Large Managed Money Accounts, April 4, 1994–October 6, 1994.

Futures Market	Daily Price Change Lag $t-1$	$t-2$	$t-3$	$t-4$	$t-5$	Sum of Slopes	t-statistic	Adj. R^2
Coffee	−2.8	12.8	1.4	7.3	2.6	21.3	0.98	−0.02
	(−0.31)	(1.44)	(0.15)	(0.82)	(0.28)			
Copper	20.1	214.2*	38.9	141.1	−24.2	390.1*	2.23	0.05
	(0.27)	(2.84)	(0.52)	(1.87)	(−0.31)			
Corn	251.7*	190.5*	−8.4	−61.6	170.0*	542.2*	3.77	0.15
	(3.85)	(3.12)	(−0.14)	(−1.01)	(2.62)			
Cotton	628.7*	214.8*	230.7*	63.8	196.4*	1,334.4*	6.83	0.35
	(7.03)	(2.39)	(2.57)	(0.71)	(2.23)			
Crude oil	−381.8	712.4	−445.0	2,117.2*	−29.8	−144.2	−0.91	0.02
	(−0.44)	(0.82)	(−0.52)	(2.44)	(−0.03)			
Deutsche mark	−160.9	1,729.7*	468.3	553.2	77.4	2,667.6	1.76	0.01
	(−0.22)	(2.38)	(0.64)	(0.76)	(0.11)			
Eurodollar	−21,276.9	8,063.6	−6,149.2	−25,505.1	−15,490.5	−60,358.1*	−2.10	0.02
	(−1.52)	(0.58)	(−0.44)	(−1.83)	(−1.11)			

TABLE 8.10 *(continued)*

	Daily Price Change Lag							
Futures Market	$t-1$	$t-2$	$t-3$	$t-4$	$t-5$	Sum of Slopes	*t*-statistic	Adj. R^2
Gold	27.6 (0.17)	543.2* (3.24)	405.8* (2.41)	41.5 (0.25)	76.1 (0.47)	1,094.2*	2.74	0.07
Live hogs	183.2* (3.26)	139.2* (2.48)	64.0 (1.14)	83.7 (–1.50)	71.3 (1.27)	541.4*	4.01	0.11
Natural gas	–619.6 (–0.16)	16,136.4* (4.05)	11,659.5* (2.92)	–3,158.6 (–0.79)	–533.1 (–0.13)	23,484.6*	2.97	0.14
Soybeans	42.2 (1.92)	55.2* (2.66)	–1.6 (–0.08)	–0.2 (–0.01)	6.1 (0.28)	101.7	1.89	0.05
S&P 500	–135.8 (–1.48)	190.6* (2.08)	–62.7 (–0.65)	–192.2* (-2.03)	8.4 (0.09)	0.6	–0.98	0.04
Treasury bonds	–4,887.7* (–4.67)	669.0 (0.64)	68.4 (0.07)	–1,422.8 (–1.37)	–132.5 (–0.13)	–818.0	–1.55	0.14

Managed money accounts are defined as large hedge funds and CTAs.
The figures in parentheses are *t*-statistics to test the null hypothesis that a given slope parameter equals zero. The figures in the next to last column are *t*-statistics to test the null hypothesis that the sum of the slope parameters for a given market equals zero.
*Statistically significant at the 5 percent level.

found statistically significant evidence of positive feedback trading by commodity pools in half of the futures markets studied and an average adjusted R^2 across all markets of 0.12.

An additional frame of reference is provided through analysis of the positive feedback characteristics of the Commitment of Trader data as reported by the CFTC. The weekly reported open interest figures for each week of 1994 were used to compute noncommercial and commercial reporting traders' estimated minimum trading volume (using the same methodology as previously outlined for the MMA data set). Regression model 8.7 was then estimated using these weekly volume estimates and weekly price changes. Tables 8.11 and 8.12, respectively, present the results for the reporting noncommercial and commercial traders. The sum of slope coefficient estimates for noncommercial traders, presumably the group most closely related to MMAs, is positive for all 13 markets, and 6 are statistically significant. With an average adjusted R^2 of 0.27, past price changes explain more than three times the variation of trading volume for noncommercial traders as compared to MMAs.[8] These results indicate that noncommercial traders in general exhibited more positive feedback trading tendencies than MMAs. The sum of slope coefficient estimates for commercial traders, less obviously related to MMAs, is negative for 11 of the 13 markets, and 5 of the negative sums are statistically significant. Hence, negative feedback trading is generally observed for commercial firms. The explanatory power of the regressions for commercial firms is similar to that of noncommercial firms (average adjusted R^2 of 0.26).[9]

Profitability Tests According to Friedman (1953), in order for speculation to be destabilizing, speculators must buy when prices are above fundamental values and sell when prices are below fundamental values. This process

---

[8]Dale and Zyren (1996) report a similar level of explanatory power for positive feedback regressions applied to noncommercial positions in crude oil, gasoline, heating oil, and treasury bond futures.

[9]As Weiner (2002) points out, no conclusions should be drawn about price effects of noncommercial versus commercial trading based on the results in Tables 8.11 and 8.12. Since all futures markets are zero-sum games, correlations between noncommercial positions and past price movements necessarily imply just the opposite correlations between commercial positions and past price movements (assuming minimal trading volume on the part of nonreporting "small" traders). The results reported in Tables 8.11 and 8.12 are not sufficient to determine whether noncommercials ("speculators") move prices and commercials ("hedgers") follow, or vice versa. Results for both groups are reported only to provide a broader frame of reference for the hedge fund and CTA positive feedback regression results.

TABLE 8.11 Positive Feedback Regression Results for 13 Futures Markets, Noncommercial Traders, January 3, 1994–December 31, 1994

Futures Market	Weekly Price Change Lag					Sum of Slopes	*t*-statistic	Adj. R^2
	t – 1	*t* – 2	*t* – 3	*t* – 4	*t* – 5			
Coffee	30.4	4.8	–27.9	–1.9	1.5	6.9	0.16	–0.05
	(1.26)	(0.21)	(–1.16)	(–0.08)	(0.06)			
Copper	358.6*	218.4*	102.1	–230.8*	–173.1	275.3	1.12	0.34
	(3.38)	(2.06)	(0.98)	(–2.23)	(–1.67)			
Corn	3,957.6*	7.5	113.7	1,876.6	–701.3	5,254.2*	2.38	0.18
	(3.46)	(0.01)	(0.10)	(1.64)	(–0.61)			
Cotton	736.2*	686.9*	101.6	–20.2	–232.4	1,272.1*	3.64	0.40
	(4.49)	(4.01)	(0.62)	(–0.12)	(–1.37)			
Crude oil	11,002.2*	–1,612.3	–295.6	–759.4	1,121.7	9,456.5*	2.86	0.60
	(7.94)	(–1.15)	(–0.21)	(–0.55)	(0.77)			
Deutsche mark	8,500.7*	959.1	–900.5	–1,756.0	–844.3	5,959.0	1.71	0.49
	(6.61)	(0.75)	(–0.70)	(–1.37)	(–0.66)			
Eurodollar	15,759.6	–17,710.7	1,094.9	17,072.4	–5,494.9	10,721.4	0.23	–0.01
	(0.95)	(–1.09)	(0.06)	(1.03)	(–0.32)			

TABLE 8.11 *(continued)*

Futures Market	Weekly Price Change Lag $t-1$	$t-2$	$t-3$	$t-4$	$t-5$	Sum of Slopes	t-statistic	Adj. R^2
Gold	2,395.0*	861.2*	317.2	108.5	92.1	3,773.9*	6.65	0.74
	(11.05)	(3.97)	(1.52)	(0.52)	(0.45)			
Live hogs	65.5	297.5	136.4	52.0	101.3	652.8	1.90	0.00
	(−0.40)	(1.87)	(0.87)	(0.33)	(0.64)			
Natural gas	20,531.1*	7,204.2	2,533.5	99.0	2,197.5	32,565.3*	2.15	0.12
	(3.33)	(1.23)	(0.44)	(0.02)	(0.41)			
Soybeans	1,224.7*	593.5*	31.7	273.6	192.0	2,315.5*	4.38	0.45
	(5.68)	(2.88)	(0.16)	(1.33)	(0.89)			
S&P 500	325.6*	61.1	105.5	−111.1	−217.41*	381.1	0.55	0.19
	(3.07)	(0.56)	(0.95)	(−1.00)	(−2.06)			
Treasury bonds	3,292.3*	−940.6	−197.8	−403.9	1,620.7	3,370.8	−0.03	0.04
	(2.15)	(−0.59)	(−0.12)	(−0.25)	(1.06)			

Managed money accounts are defined as large hedge funds and CTAs.
The figures in parentheses are t-statistics to test the null hypothesis that a given slope parameter equals zero. The figures in the next-to-last column are t-statistics to test the null hypothesis that the sum of the slope parameters for a given market equals zero.
*Statistically significant at the 5 percent level.

TABLE 8.12 Positive Feedback Regression Results for 13 Futures Markets, Commercial Traders, January 1, 1994–December 31, 1994

	Weekly Price Change Lag							
Futures Market	$t-1$	$t-2$	$t-3$	$t-4$	$t-5$	Sum of Slopes	t-statistic	Adj. R^2
Coffee	–23.2	–20.5	29.8	4.0	7.5	–2.4	–0.07	–0.04
	(–0.90)	(–0.83)	(1.16)	(0.16)	(0.29)			
Copper	–397.8*	–163.6	–151.3	340.9*	187.8	–184.0	–0.56	0.27
	(–2.80)	(–1.15)	(–1.09)	(2.46)	(1.35)			
Corn	–5,531.6*	–330.1	109.3	–2,022.8	506.6	–7,268.6*	–2.92	0.26
	(–4.29)	(–0.26)	(0.08)	(–1.57)	(0.39)			
Cotton	–872.87*	–813.73*	–77.9	–23.9	277.1	175.3*	3.58	0.40
	(–4.41)	(–3.93)	(–0.39)	(–0.12)	(1.35)			
Crude oil	–17,143.6*	–939.6	1,739.0	2,338.5	935.3	–13,070.4*	–2.32	0.55
	(–7.27)	(–0.39)	(0.73)	(1.00)	(0.38)			
Deutsche mark	–12,334.1*	–1,510.3	415.2	1,821.7	1,260.6	–10,347.0*	–2.25	0.54
	(–7.26)	(–0.89)	(0.24)	(1.08)	(0.74)			
Eurodollar	–21,846.8	23,183.3	18,208.1	2,174.2	25,372.7	47,091.6	0.65	–0.03
	(–0.84)	(0.91)	(0.68)	(0.08)	(0.95)			

TABLE 8.12 *(continued)*

	Weekly Price Change Lag							
Futures Market	$t-1$	$t-2$	$t-3$	$t-4$	$t-5$	Sum of Slopes	t-statistic	Adj. R^2
Gold	−3,287.3*	−971.21*	−470.8	−189.8	83.3	−3,864.6*	−6.64	0.76
	(−11.81)	(−3.49)	(−1.76)	(−0.71)	(0.32)			
Live hogs	173.2	−125.5	−123.4	13.2	−155.3	−217.8	−0.95	0.04
	(−1.60)	(−1.18)	(−1.18)	(0.13)	(−1.47)			
Natural gas	−22,158.8*	−8,098.4	1,068.1	1,002.6	−2,214.4	−30,400.9	−1.82	0.12
	(−3.25)	(−1.25)	(0.17)	(0.16)	(−0.38)			
Soybeans	−1,360.1*	−625.50*	81.7	−553.50*	−169.8	−1,448.1*	−5.22	0.53
	(−6.62)	(−3.19)	(0.43)	(−2.82)	(−0.83)			
S&P 500	−115.5	−125.9	−235.0	29.6	110.3	−336.5	−0.94	0.00
	(−0.90)	(−0.95)	(−1.75)	(0.22)	(0.86)			
Treasury bonds	−2,370.3	726.3	1,025.1	−377.0	−1,338.8	−2,334.6	−0.47	−0.05
	(−1.31)	(0.38)	(0.54)	(−0.20)	(−0.74)			

Managed money accounts are defined as large hedge funds and CTAs.
The figures in parentheses are t-statistics to test the null hypothesis that a given slope parameter equals zero. The figures in the next-to-last column are t-statistics to test the null hypothesis that the sum of the slope parameters for a given market equals zero.
*Statistically significant at the 5 percent level.

creates excessive volatility by driving prices past their fundamental values. Rational speculators, however, recognize the deviation from fundamentals and take the opposite position, bringing prices back to a level reflecting the underlying fundamentals. Rational speculators, therefore, make a profit while destabilizing speculators lose money. The following analysis of MMA estimated profits is based on this theoretical argument.

The estimates of profits by MMAs during the period from April 4 through October 6, 1994, are based on the mark-to-market technique used by Hartzmark (1987) and Leuthold, Garcia, and Lu (1994). The price change (based on the close-to-close difference) on day t is multiplied by the net open interest position held by MMAs at the end of day $t - 1$. The daily profit/loss figures are then aggregated across all days within a market for each month to compute total monthly profit or loss for each market. Table 8.13 presents the profit/loss estimates for each month and market. Not surprisingly, results vary considerably through time and across markets. Total profits and losses by month range from a high of \$785.1 million (September) to a low of –\$539.2 million (August). Total profits and losses by market for the entire six-month period range from a high of \$430.7 million (coffee) to a low of –\$234.5 million (S&P 500).

Although the analysis is based on a relatively short time period, aggregating across all months and markets nonetheless provides additional statistical power. Under the assumption of independent price changes across the 13 markets (which is probably not true for some of the markets, such as corn and soybeans), this analysis is similar to using 78 months of data for one market (6 months multiplied by 13 markets). The average profit across all months and markets is \$30.6 million per month. The t-statistic to test the null hypothesis of zero profits per month is 2.45 and statistically significant at the 5 percent level. The aggregate total profit across all months and markets is \$397.6 million. While the statistical significance of average (or total) profits can be debated due to the lack of independence across some markets, the economic significance of the profits seems more apparent. A profit of almost \$400 million in six months is an economically nontrivial amount.

As noted, under the assumption of market efficiency, for speculative activity to be destabilizing, speculators must buy when prices are high and sell when prices are low. Trading in this manner should lead to trading losses as the market price returns to its underlying fundamental value. The profit estimates reported here suggest that MMA trading is not destabilizing, but instead is based on valuable private information. Of course, the economic significance of the profit results must be tempered to some degree by acknowledging the relatively brief time period over which the profits were earned. It is well known that the returns of MMAs vary widely over time (e.g., Schneeweis, Savanayana, and McCarthy 1991; Ackermann, McEnally, and Ravenscraft 1999). In addition, it is theoretically possible for noise traders to

TABLE 8.13 Estimated Gross Profits in Millions for Large Managed Money Accounts in 13 Futures Markets, April 4, 1994–October 6, 1994

Futures Market	April	May	June	July	August	September	Average Profit/ Loss	Total Profit/ Loss
Coffee	23.8	187.9	190.6	64.0	−22.3	−13.2	71.8	430.7
Copper	6.0	53.4	13.0	6.6	−1.6	−4.4	12.2	73.0
Corn	−0.6	−1.4	−22.8	10.8	−1.3	0.4	−2.5	−14.9
Cotton	12.3	−3.3	−39.2	−10.7	−1.6	−9.4	−8.6	−51.9
Crude oil	20.0	46.6	47.1	42.9	−64.6	−0.5	15.2	91.5
Deutsche mark	13.0	3.1	40.1	−3.1	−17.4	14.5	8.4	50.2
Eurodollar	54.0	127.5	40.1	−168.3	−17.5	231.6	44.6	267.4
Gold	−6.9	−29.2	−20.4	−0.6	−14.6	−10.2	−13.6	−81.7
Live hogs	4.9	11.5	5.9	−5.6	10.3	15.0	7.0	41.9
Natural gas	−10.3	16.0	−27.2	−1.5	63.4	22.8	10.5	63.2
S&P 500	−213.4	−79.9	251.0	−325.8	−388.1	521.7	−39.1	−234.5
Soybeans	−12.7	−17.7	−37.9	12.4	−3.1	14.6	−7.4	−44.3
Treasury bonds	−21.7	−40.3	−10.4	−42.1	−80.8	2.3	−32.2	−193.0
Average Profit/Loss	−10.1	21.1	33.1	−32.4	−41.5	60.4	—	30.6
Total Profit/Loss	−131.7	274.2	429.9	−420.8	−539.2	785.1	—	397.6

Managed money accounts are defined as large hedge funds and CTAs. Profits and losses for the first four business days of October are included in the monthly totals for September.

survive, and even profit, in the long run if they are numerous enough and the arbitrage capacity of rational traders is limited (e.g., De Long, Schleifer, Summers, and Waldman 1990).

CONCLUSION

The first part of the chapter analyzed the relationship between hedge fund and CTA trading and market volatility. Regression models of market volatility were specified as a function of: (a) trading volume and open interest for large hedge funds and CTAs; (b) trading volume and open interest for the rest of the market; and (c) day-of-the week effects. The regression results showed a small but positive relationship between the trading volume of large hedge funds and CTAs and market volatility. However, a positive relationship between hedge fund and CTA trading volume and market volatility is consistent with either a private information (e.g., Clark 1973) or noise trader hypothesis (e.g., DeLong, Schleifer, Summers, and Waldman 1990).

The second part of the chapter conducted tests to distinguish between the private information hypothesis and the noise trader hypothesis. The first test consisted of identifying the noise component exhibited in return variances over different holding periods. The efficient market hypothesis implies that a q day holding period return variance should be equal to q times the daily return variance. Only two of 78 estimated test statistics were significant during the six-month sample period, suggesting that a statistically identifiable noise component exists only in one market. Even in this market, however, the noise component was not significant for holding period returns greater than three days. Therefore, the variance ratio test results provide little support for the noise trader hypothesis during this six-month period.

The second test examined whether positive feedback trading characterizes large hedge fund and CTA trading behavior. Statistically significant evidence of positive feedback trading was found in about half of the markets studied. However, because positive feedback terms explained just 9 percent of the variation in large hedge fund and CTA trading volume, it can be concluded that their trading decisions are influenced only in small part by past price changes. Furthermore, additional tests showed that noncommercial traders as a group exhibit substantially more positive feedback trading effects than large hedge funds and CTAs.

The third test consisted of estimating the profits and losses associated with the positions of large hedge funds and CTAs. For speculative trading to be destabilizing, speculators must buy when prices are above fundamental values and sell when prices are below fundamental values. The implication of this hypothesis is that destabilizing speculators lose money and are driven from the market, having no negative effects on market efficiency. Across all 13 markets, profits for large hedge funds and CTAs were estimated to be just under \$400 million, a nontrivial amount. This fact suggests that the trading decisions of large hedge funds and CTAs are likely based on valuable private information.

Overall, the evidence presented in this study indicates that trading by large hedge funds and CTAs is most likely based on private fundamental information. Futures return variances exhibited a significant noise component in only one market. In addition, large hedge funds and CTAs generated nearly \$400 million in gross trading profits across the 13 markets. These findings imply that large hedge funds and CTAs likely enhance market efficiency by bringing valuable fundamental information to the market through their trading.

CHAPTER 9

Measuring the Long Volatility Strategies of Managed Futures

Mark Anson and Ho Ho

Certain hedge fund strategies create investment positions that resemble a long put option. Specifically, managed futures or commodity trading advisors have significant exposure to volatility events. This exposure is positively related to volatility much like a long option position. We identify and measure this long volatility exposure, which may not always be transparent from the trading positions of a commodity trading advisor. We also examine ways to apply these long volatility strategies to improve risk management.

INTRODUCTION

The managed futures industry has come full circle in its application over the last 15 years. In the early 1990s, global macro funds were the predominant form of the hedge fund industry. These funds were primarily managed futures funds run by commodity trading advisors (CTAs). As the 1990s progressed, other types of hedge fund strategies came to the forefront, such as relative value arbitrage, event driven, merger arbitrage, and equity long/short. As these strategies grew, managed futures became a smaller part of the hedge fund industry.

Now, however, managed futures have achieved a renewed interest because of their risk reducing properties relative to other hedge fund strategies. Specifically, most CTA strategies employ some form of trend-following strategy. These trend-following strategies pursue both up- and down-market movements in futures markets. These strategies also may be called momentum strategies because they follow the momentum of the market and then liquidate their positions (or reverse them) when they detect that the momentum is changing or about to change.

Whether we call managed futures trend-following or momentum strategies, they have one important characteristic: They capitalize on the volatility in the futures market. Trend-following strategies tend to be "long-volatility" strategies; that is, they profit during volatile markets. Long-volatility strategies can be useful risk management tools for other active trading strategies that tend to be short volatility.

We begin with a brief overview of the managed futures industry. We then measure the long-volatility exposure captured these strategies. Next we apply Monte Carlo simulation to estimate the value at risk for long-volatility strategies. Last, we demonstrate some practical risk management strategies that may be employed with managed futures.

BRIEF REVIEW OF THE MANAGED FUTURES INDUSTRY

Managed futures is often referred to as an absolute return strategy because their return expectations are not driven by broad market indices, such as the Standard & Poor's (S&P) 500, but instead by the specialized trading strategy of the commodity trading advisor. More specifically, their return expectations are an absolute level of return sufficient to compensate them for the risk associated with trading in the futures markets. This absolute level is established independently of the return on the stock market.

The managed futures industry is another skill-based style of investing similar to hedge fund managers. In fact, managed futures is considered a subset of the hedge fund world. Commodity trading advisors use their special knowledge and insight in buying and selling futures and forward contracts to extract a positive return. This skill and insight can be applied regardless of whether the stock or bond markets are rising or falling, providing the absolute return benefits described above.

Commodity trading advisors have one goal in mind: to capitalize on price trends in futures markets. Typically, CTAs look at various moving averages of commodity prices and attempt to determine whether the price will continue to trend up or down, and then trade accordingly. Some CTAs also use volatility models such GARCH (generalized auto-regressive conditional heteroskedasticity) to forecast both price trends and volatility changes.

Prior empirical studies have indicated that managed futures, or commodity trading advisors, have investment strategies that tend to be long volatility. Fung and Hsieh (1997a) found that trend-following styles have a return profile similar to a long option straddle position—a long volatility position. Fung and Hsieh (1997b) documented that commodity trading advisors apply predominantly trend-following strategies.

In our research we use three Barclay Commodity Trading Advisor indices to capture the trading dynamics of the CTA market: Commodity Trading Index, Diversified Commodity Trading Advisor Index, and Systematic Trading Index. These indices are an equally weighted average of a group of CTAs who identify themselves as belonging to one of the three strategies.

There are alternative ways to gain exposure to the futures markets without the use of a CTA. One way is a passive managed futures index, such as the Mount Lucas Management Index (MLMI).

The MLMI applies a mechanical trading rule for following the price trends in several futures markets. It uses a 12-month look-back window to calculate the moving average unit asset value for each futures market in which it invests. Once a month, on the day prior to the last trading day of the month, the algorithm examines the current unit asset value in each futures market compared to the average value for the prior 12-month period. If the current unit asset value is above the 12-month average, the MLMI purchases the futures contract. If the current unit asset value is below the 12-month moving average, the MLMI takes a short position in the futures contract.

The MLMI invests in and is equally weighted across 25 futures contracts in seven major commodity futures categories: grains, livestock, energy, metals, food and fiber, financials, and currencies. The purpose of its construction is to capture the pricing trend of each commodity futures contract without regard to its production value or trading volume in the market.

Our next step is to document the long volatility strategy of the managed futures industry.

DEMONSTRATION OF A LONG VOLATILITY STRATEGY

In this section we use the direction of the stock market to demonstrate the asymmetric payout associated with managed futures. That is, we expect that large downward movements in the stock market will result in large gains from managed futures. Conversely, we expect that large positive movements in the stock market will result in a constant return to managed futures. This type of return pattern is consistent with a long put option exposure. Therefore, this section plots the direction of the stock market versus the returns earned by managed futures. In the "Mimicking Portfolios" section we specifically incorporate a measure of volatility to determine its impact on these hedge fund strategies.

We start by producing a scatter plot of the excess return to the Barclay Commodity Trading Index returns versus the excess returns to the Standard

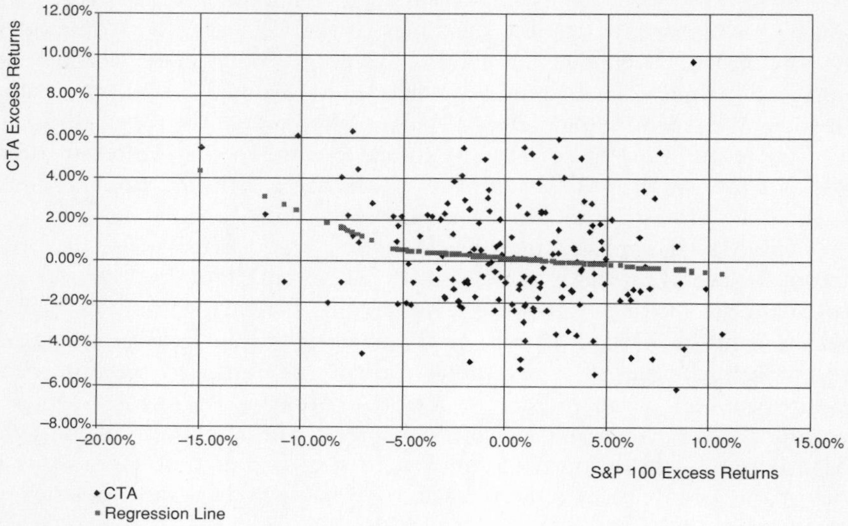

FIGURE 9.1 Barclay Commodity Trading Index

& Poor's (S&P) 100.[1] We use the S&P 100 because this is the underlying index for which the VIX volatility index is calculated. We use the VIX index in the next section. Figure 9.1 presents this scatter plot.

On the scatter plot in Figure 9.1, we overlay a regression line of the excess return to the Barclay Commodity Trading Index on the excess return to the S&P 100. Note that the fitted regression line is "kinked." The kink indicates that there are really two different relationships between the excess returns to the stock market and the excess returns to managed futures.

To the right of the kink, the relationship between the returns earned by the CTAs and the stock market appears orthogonal. That is, there is no apparent relationship between the returns to CTAs who pursue a diversified trading program and the returns to the stock market, when the returns to the stock market are positive.

When the stock market earns positive returns, the Commodity Trading Index earns a consistent return regardless of how positive the stock market

[1]Excess return is simply the total return minus the current risk-free rate.

performs. This part of the graphed line is flat, indicating a constant, consistent return to managed futures when the stock market earns positive returns. In this part of the graph, the excess return provided by the Commodity Trading Index is almost zero. That is, after taking into account the opportunity cost of capital (investing cash in treasury bills), the return to this style of managed futures is effectively zero, when there is no volatility event. This result highlights a point about the managed futures industry: It is a zero-sum game, similar to Newton's law of physics: For every action, there is an equal and opposite reaction.

However, to the left side of the kink, there is a distinct linear relationship between the returns to managed futures and the S&P 100. Declines in the stock market driven by volatility events result in large, positive returns for the Barclay Commodity Trading Index. In fact, the fitted regression line in Figure 9.1 mirrors the payoff function for a long put option.

Figures 9.2 through 9.4 demonstrate a similar "kinked" relationship for the Barclay Diversified Trading Index, Systematic Trading Index, and the MLMI. Each figure demonstrates a long put optionlike exposure. In the next section, we examine how this kinked relationship can be quantified.

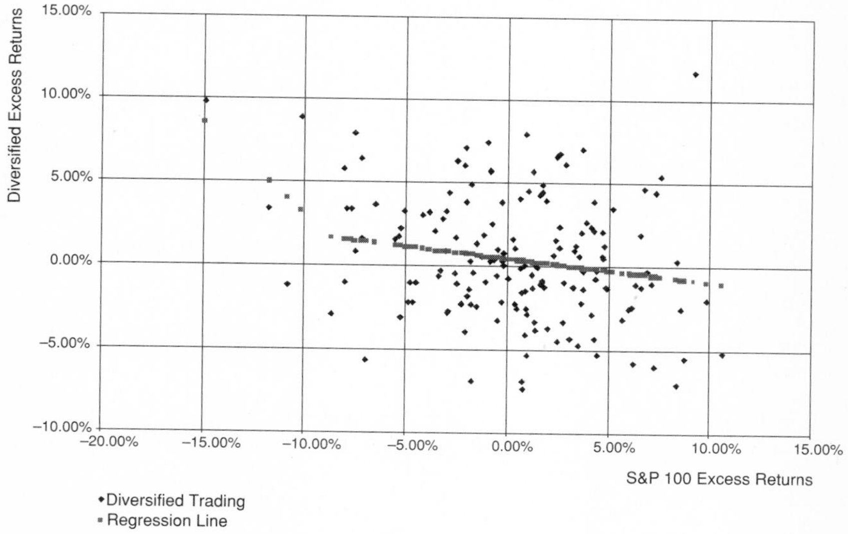

FIGURE 9.2 Barclay Diversified Trading Index

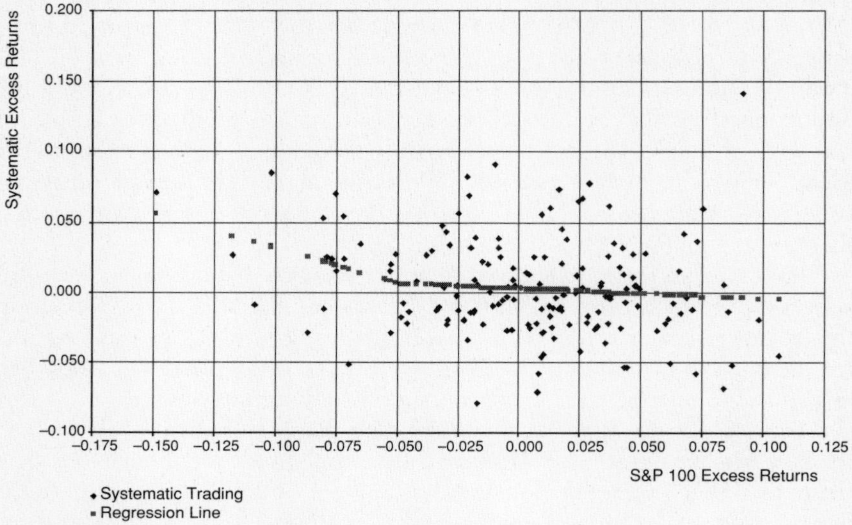

FIGURE 9.3 Barclay Systematic Trading Index

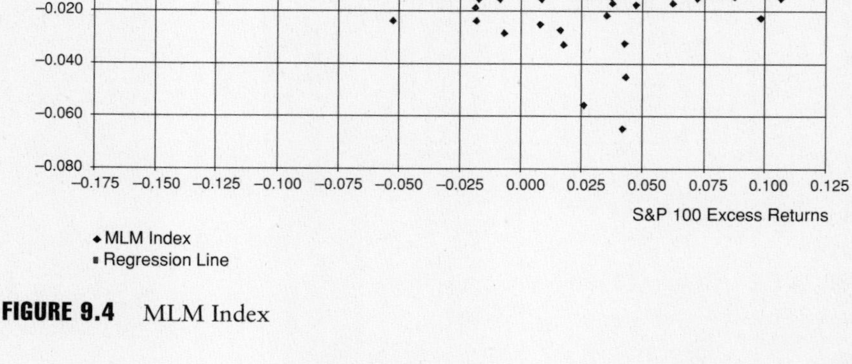

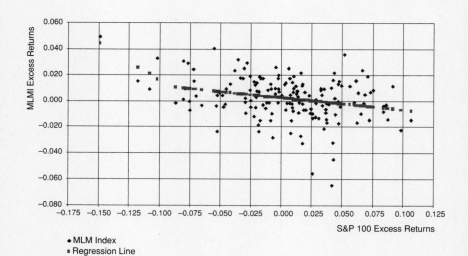

FIGURE 9.4 MLM Index

FITTING THE REGRESSION LINE

The previous discussion provides a general framework in which to describe empirically the long volatility exposure embedded within CTA trend-following strategies. To fit the kinked regression demonstrated in Figures 9.1 through 9.4, we use a piecewise linear capital asset pricing model (CAPM)–type model. The model can be described as:

$$R_{tf} - R_f = (1 - D)[\alpha_{\text{low}} + \beta_{\text{low}}(R_{OEX} - R_f)] + D[\alpha_{\text{high}} + \beta_{\text{high}}(R_{OEX} - R_f)] \qquad (9.1)$$

where

R_{tf} = return to the trend-following strategy
R_f = risk-free rate
R_{OEX} = return to the S&P 100
$\alpha_{\text{low}}, \beta_{\text{low}}$ = regression coefficients to the left-hand side of the kink
$\alpha_{\text{high}}, \beta_{\text{high}}$ = regression coefficients to the right-hand side of the kink
D = 1 if $R_{OEX} - R_f >$ the threshold
D = 0 if $R_{OEX} - R_f <$ or equal to the threshold.

In essence we plot two regression lines that have different alpha and beta coefficients depending on which side of the kink the market returns fall. The trick is to maintain continuity at the kink in the fitted regression line. To insure this, we impose this following condition:

$$\alpha_{\text{low}} + \beta_{\text{low}}(\text{Threshold}) = \alpha_{\text{high}} + \beta_{\text{high}}(\text{Threshold}) \qquad (9.2)$$

Our regression equation then becomes:

$$R_{tf} - R_f = (1 - D)[\alpha_{\text{low}} + \beta_{\text{low}}(R_{OEX} - R_f)] + D[\alpha_{\text{low}} + (\beta_{\text{low}} - \beta_{\text{high}})(\text{Threshold}) + \beta_{\text{high}}(R_{OEX} - R_f)] \qquad (9.3)$$

We express our regression equation in this fashion to demonstrate how the threshold value is explicitly incorporated into the solution. Table 9.1 presents the results for our fitted regression lines.

For the Barclay Commodity Trading Index, the threshold value (the kink) is –5.2 percent.[2] Several observations can be made from the regresion

---

[2]We found the threshold value through a recursive method that minimizes the residual sum of squares in equation 9.3.

TABLE 9.1 Two-Step Regression Coefficients

	Commodity Trading		Diversified Trading		Systematic Trading		MLM Index	
	Coefficient	*t*-statistic	Coefficient	*t*-statistic	Coefficient	*t*-statistic	Coefficient	*t*-statistic
Threshold	−0.0526		−0.0868		−0.0485		−0.0926	
Alpha_low	−0.0158	−1.2699	−0.0793	−1.7150	−0.0175	−1.2127	−0.0437	−1.7743
Beta_low	−0.3962	−2.1083	−1.1018	−2.1911	−0.4923	−2.1703	−0.5893	−2.3223
Alpha_high	0.0014		0.0043		0.0029		0.0022	
Beta_high	−0.0676	−1.1759	−0.1384	−2.0820	−0.0717	−0.9365	−0.0929	−3.2138
S.E.	0.0264		0.0353		0.0343		0.0155	
Regression								
R square	0.0555		0.0745		0.0520		0.1203	
Adj *R* square	0.0437		0.0629		0.0402		0.1094	

coefficients. First, the value of β_{low} is negative and significant at the 5 percent level, with a *t*-statistic of –2.11. This demonstrates that when the returns to the S&P 100 are negative, the commodity trading strategies earn positive excess returns. In particular, the value of β_{low} is –0.396, indicating that CTAs earn, on average, about a 0.4 percent excess return for every 1 percent decline in the S&P 100 below the threshold value.

This is similar to a put option being exercised by the CTA manager when the returns to the stock market are negative, but created synthetically as a consequence of the trend-following strategy. As long as stock market returns remain positive, CTAs earn a constant return equal to a cash (treasury bill) rate. However, when the stock market suffers a negative volatility event that drives market returns into negative territory, the synthetic put option is exercised, leading to large positive returns.

The coefficient for β_{high} is close to zero (–0.067). It is neither economically nor statistically significant.[3] Trend-following CTAs do not earn excess returns when the returns to the stock market are positive. When the returns to the S&P 100 are positive, there is no need to exercise the put option. In addition, α_{high} is also close to zero, indicating a lack of excess returns over this part of the graph. Managed futures earn a treasury bill rate of return when the returns to the stock market are positive. The lack of any excess return over this part of the graph can be considered the payment for the put option premium. That is, trend-following CTAs forgo excess returns when the returns to the stock market are positive in return for a long put option exposure to be exercised when the returns to the stock market are negative.

Similar results are presented in Table 9.1 for diversified trading managed futures, systematic trading, and the passive MLMI index. In each case, β_{low} is economically and statistically significant. In addition, β_{low} always has a negative sign, indicating positive returns to managed futures when the stock market earns negative returns. Also, α_{high} is close to zero for each category of managed futures. Once again, this indicates that managed futures do not generate any excess returns when the returns to the stock market are positive. All that is received is a cash return equal to treasury bills.

β_{high} is statistically significant in two categories: diversified trading and the MLMI. The sign of the β_{high} is negative, indicating a downward sloping curve. However, the coefficient is small and lacks economic significance. Still, this indicates that managed futures can be countercyclical when the stock market has positive returns.

---

[3]There is no *t*-statistic for α_{high} because this coefficient is a linear combination of the other regression coefficients (see equation 9.2).

MIMICKING PORTFOLIO

Here we specifically incorporate the long volatility exposure trend-following strategies to build mimicking portfolios of the strategies. The idea is that if we can build portfolios of securities that mimic the returns to CTAs, we can then simulate how trend-following strategies should perform under various market conditions.

We use three components to build the mimicking portfolios: long OEX (options ticker symbol for S&P 100) put options, long the S&P 100 index, and long the one-month risk-free treasury security. The long OEX put option is used to capture the synthetic long put option exposure. The long S&P 100 index is used to capture any residual market risk that exists when the market performs positively. Last, we use the risk-free rate to measure the option premium that must be paid by CTAs to the right-hand side of the threshold value (when the stock market performs positively). We use the coefficient estimates from equation 9.3 to construct the mimicking portfolio.

Long OEX Put Option

Strike = OEX index × (1 + Threshold + risk-free rate)
Volatility = VIX index
The number of options bought = $(\beta_{low} - \beta_{high})$

Short the S&P 100[4]

The number of S&P 100 to buy is = β_{high}

Long Risk-Free Security

The number of risk-free securities to buy = $1 - \beta_{low}$

Figures 9.5 through 9.8 present the results from our mimicking portfolios. Similar to Figure 9.1, Figure 9.5 contains the scatter plot of the excess returns earned by the Barclay Commodity Trading Index plotted against the excess returns of the S&P 100. In addition, it contains the return of our mimicking portfolio.

---

[4]Since the beta (high) is negative, a short amount of a negative number is equal to a long position in the stock market.

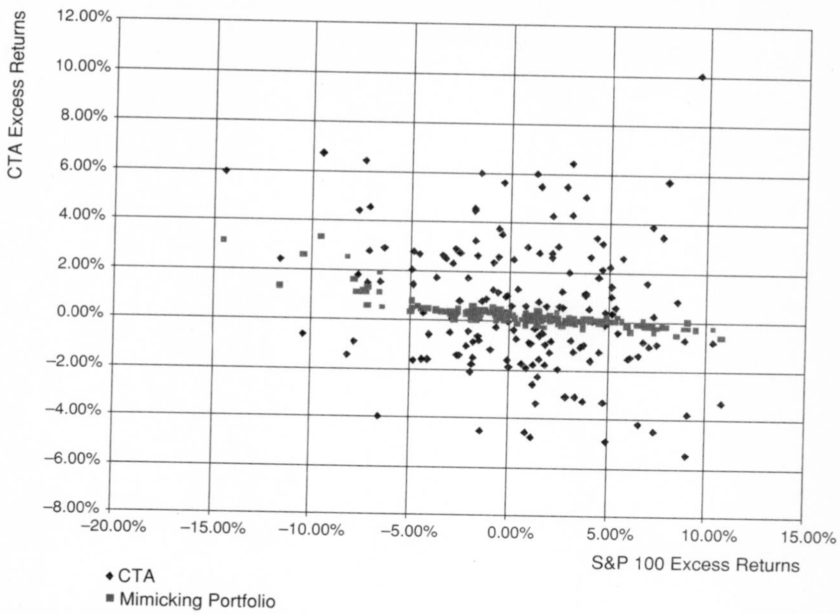

FIGURE 9.5 Mimicking Portfolio Returns for the Barclay Commodity Trading Index

Our mimicking portfolio performs relatively well and has the same characteristics of the fitted regression line in Figure 9.1. First, the mimicking portfolio has a distinct "kink" in its shape. Additionally, the slope of the mimicking portfolio is flat to the right-hand side of the kink and has a negative slope to the left-hand side of the kink. In sum, our mimicking portfolio captures the upside of a long put option exposure.

Figures 9.6 to 9.8 provide similar information for the other trend-following strategies. We can see in each case that to the right of the kink, there is a negative slope to our mimicking portfolio, just as there was for the fitted regression lines. Each mimicking portfolio demonstrates a long put option exposure.

In summary, we are able to build mimicking portfolios using traditional securities that mimic the return patterns of trend-following CTA strategies. Specifically, these mimicking portfolios capture both the long volatility exposure of a long put option as well as the premium payment when all performs well. Our next step is to provide some Value at Risk analysis.

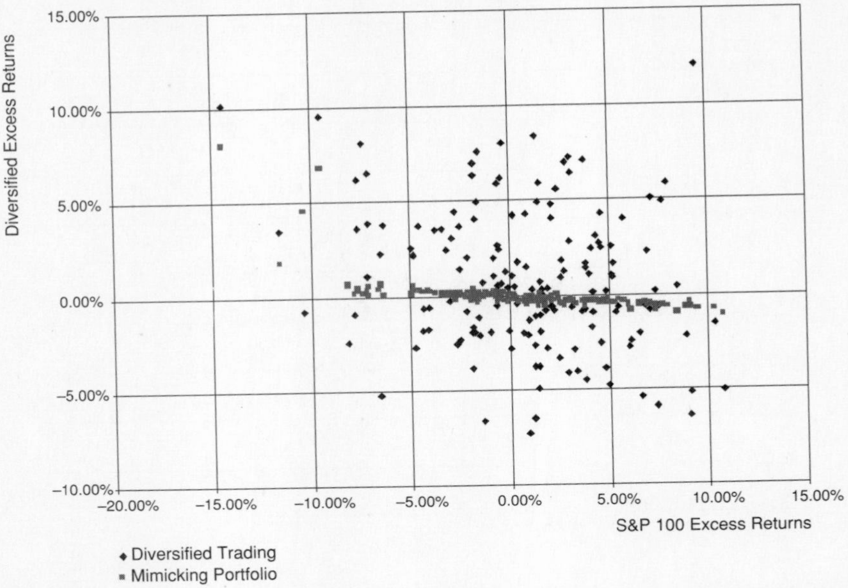

FIGURE 9.6 Mimicking Portfolio Returns for the Barclay Diversified Trading Index

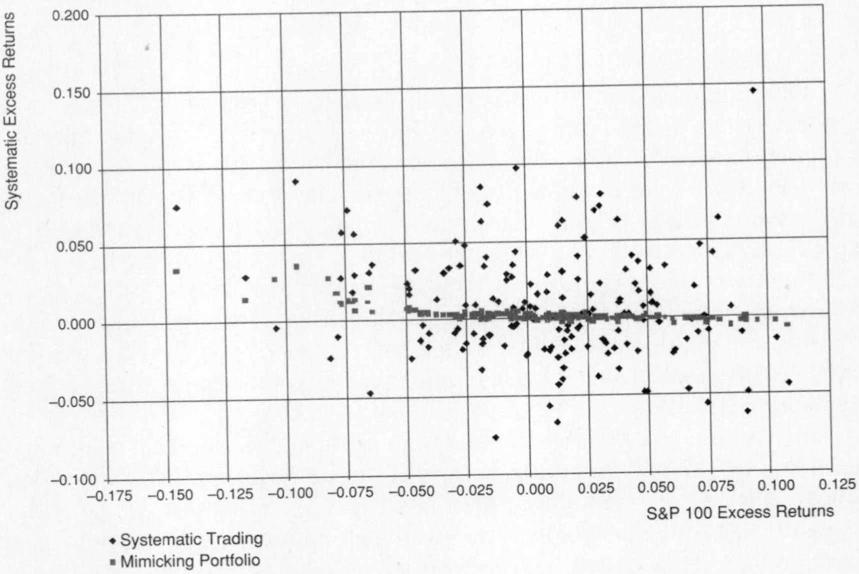

FIGURE 9.7 Mimicking Portfolio Returns for the Barclay Systematic Trading Index

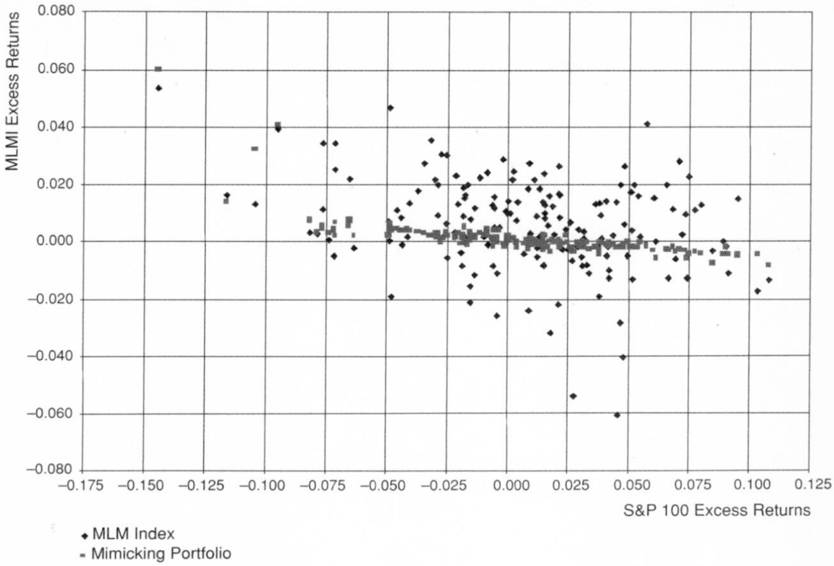

FIGURE 9.8 Mimicking Portfolio Returns for the MLM Index

VALUE AT RISK FOR MANAGED FUTURES

The main reason for building mimicking portfolios is to simulate the returns to trend-following strategies for developing risk estimates. Specifically, we can run Monte Carlo simulations with our mimicking portfolios and estimate value at risk (VaR). Armed with these data, we can estimate the probability of the risk of loss associated with long volatility strategies. This is important to help us understand the off-balance sheet risks associated with trend-following strategies.

In addition, we can use Monte Carlo simulations to graph the frequency distribution of returns. Doing so allows us to demonstrate pictorially the return patterns associated with long volatility strategies. A review of these return patterns can provide some sense of the downside risk of loss. Using the mimicking portfolios we run 10,000 simulations for the managed futures strategies. Table 9.2 presents the results.

For example, the one-month VaR for the Barclay Commodity Trading Index is –0.93 percent at a 1 percent confidence level and –0.69 percent at a 5 percent confidence level. This means that we can state with a 99 per-

TABLE 9.2 Monte Carlo Simulation of Value at Risk

	CTA	Diversified	Systematic	MLM
1 Month VaR @ 1% Confidence Level	–0.93%	–1.46%	–0.97%	–1.18%
1 Month VaR @ 5% Confidence Level	–0.69%	–1.14%	–0.74%	–0.89%
Maximum Loss	–1.31%	–1.99%	–1.35%	–1.64%
Number of Simulations	10,000	10,000	10,000	10,000

cent (95 percent) level of confidence that the maximum loss sustained by a diversified CTA manager will not exceed 0.93 percent (0.69 percent) in any given month. Table 9.2 also contains the VaR for the other trend-following strategies.

Figures 9.9 to 9.12 present the frequency distributions for the four trend-following strategies based on our Monte Carlo simulations. For example, for the Barclay Diversified CTA Index, the return distribution demonstrates a positive skewness of 2.64 and a large positive kurtosis of 11.35. The other strategies have similar distribution characteristics. In short,

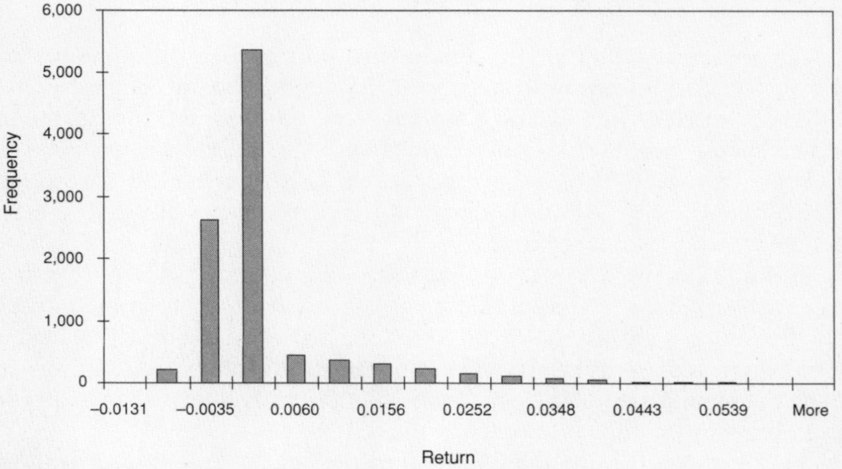

FIGURE 9.9 Simulated Commodity Trading Index Return Distribution

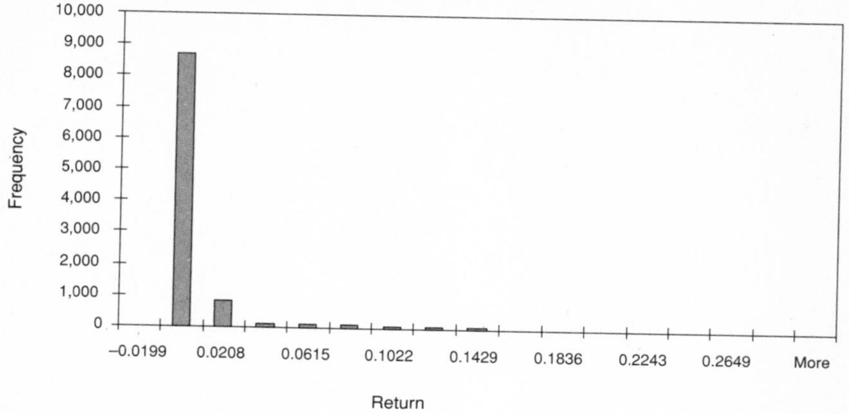

FIGURE 9.10 Simulated Diversified Trading Index Return Distribution

trend-following strategies tend to provide a large upside tail—the same risk exposure as a long put option.

The positive skew indicates that these return distributions tend to have more large positive returns than large negative returns. Additionally, the large value of kurtosis indicates that these return distributions have fat tails.

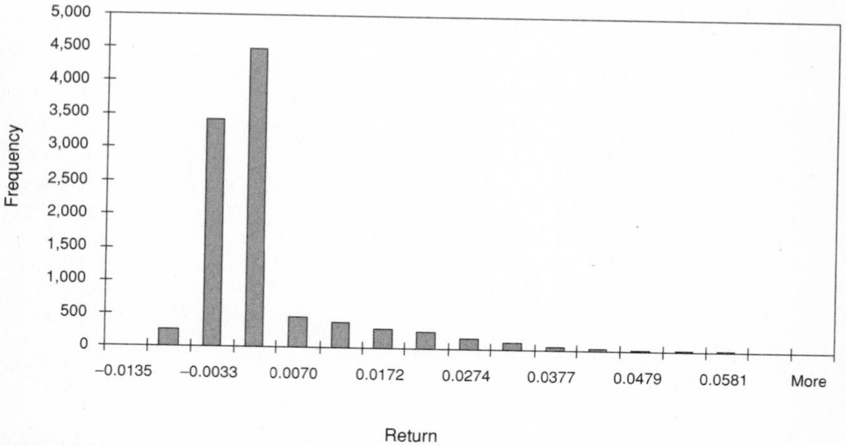

FIGURE 9.11 Simulated Systematic Trading Return Distribution

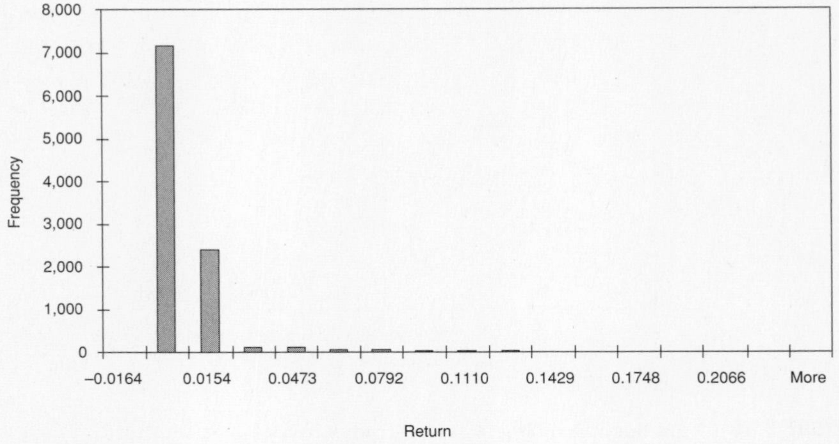

FIGURE 9.12 Simulated MLM Index Return Distribution

That is, the returns to managed futures are exposed to outlier events compared to a normal, bell-curve distribution. Together, a positive value of skew and a large value of kurtosis indicate that managed futures have significant exposure to large positive returns. This return profile is very similar to a long options position.

RISK MANAGEMENT USING LONG VOLATILITY STRATEGIES

At the beginning of this chapter we noted that managed futures can be used for risk management purposes with respect to other hedge fund strategies. Specifically, those hedge fund strategies that use short-volatility strategies will benefit from the diversification benefits of adding long-volatility strategies to a portfolio of hedge fund managers. Two hedge fund styles use short-volatility strategies: merger arbitrage and event driven.

Merger arbitrage managers take a bet that the merger will be completed. They analyze antitrust regulations, consider whether the bid by the acquiring company is hostile or friendly, and check on potential shareholder opposition to the merger. If the merger is completed, the merger arbitrage manager earns the spread that it previously locked in through its long and short stock positions. However, if the merger falls through, the merger arbitrage manager may incur a considerable loss that cannot be known in advance.

From this perspective, merger arbitrage hedge funds can be viewed as merger insurance agents. If the merger is completed successfully, the merger arbitrage manager will collect a known premium (the spread it previously locked in). However, if the merger fails to be completed, the merger arbitrage manager is responsible for the loss instead of the shareholders from whom the shares were purchased or sold. For example, Favre and Galeano (2002a) describe relative value hedge fund strategies as selling economic disaster insurance.

This asymmetric insurance contract payoff exactly describes that of a short put option exposure. The hedge fund manager sells the put option, collects the option premium, and increases total return. If the option expires unexercised (the merger is successfully completed), the hedge fund manager keeps the premium. However, if the option is exercised against the hedge fund manager (the merger deal collapses), the loss can be substantial.[5]

The dangers of selling options has been discussed previously. Lo (2001), Weisman (2002), and Anson (2002b) all demonstrate that hedge fund strategies that are short volatility will be falsely accorded superior performance based on a mean-variance analysis.

We proceed with the same analysis as for CTAs. Figure 9.13 presents the scatter plot of merger arbitrage versus the S&P 100 as well as the fitted regression line and the regression statistics. Notice that α_{low} and β_{low} are economically and statistically significant.

Figure 9.13 demonstrates a short put position—the mirror image of the managed futures strategies. This analysis is reinforced in Figure 9.14, where we present the frequency distribution for merger arbitrage returns. We note that merger arbitrage has a large negative skew of –2.76 and a large positive kurtosis of 11.54, indicating a fat downside tail. This profile of a distribution is consistent with a short put option position (short volatility) and the mirror image of the return distributions presented in Figures 9.9 to 9.12.

To prove that managed futures are an excellent diversifying agent for other hedge fund strategies, we construct a portfolio that is 50 percent managed futures and 50 percent merger arbitrage. Table 9.3 presents the Monte Carlo VaR for merger arbitrage alone and for the combined portfolio of merger arbitrage/managed futures. We note first that the VaR for merger arbitrage alone are significantly larger (in absolute value) than that for the combined portfolio. This is consistent with a short put option position—being on the hook for potential losses in a market downturn.

---

[5]See Anson and Ho (2003) for an examination of the nature of short volatility strategies.

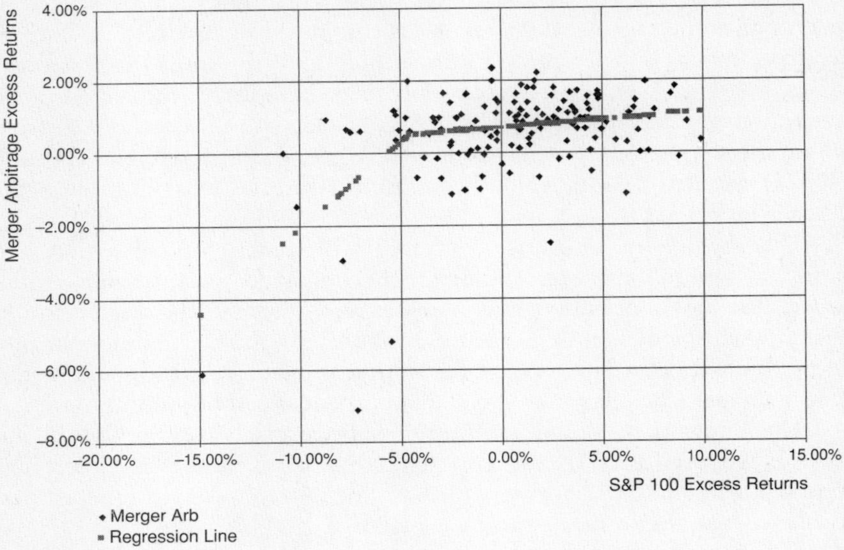

	Coefficient	*t*-statistic
Threshold	−0.0451	
α_{low}	0.0265	5.67
β_{low}	0.4769	6.10
α_{high}	0.0069	
β_{high}	0.0410	1.50
S.E. Regression	0.0112	
Adj. *R*-Squared	0.2692	

FIGURE 9.13 Merger Arbitrage

We also can see that the VaR at the 1 percent level and 5 percent for the combined portfolio as well as the maximum loss are approximately one-half of that for merger arbitrage alone. These results demonstrate the complementary behavior of managed futures with merger arbitrage. The combination of managed futures with merger arbitrage greatly reduces the risk of loss compared to merger arbitrage as a stand-alone investment. Our work supports that of Kat (2002) for blending managed futures with other hedge fund styles to minimize and manage volatility risk.

TABLE 9.3 Monte Carlo Value at Risk

	Merger Arbitrage	Merger Arbitrage and Managed Futures
1 Month VaR @ 1% Confidence Level	–6.04000%	–3.1500%
1 Month VaR @ 5% Confidence Level	–3.1400%	–1.7340%
Maximum Loss	–10.7400%	–5.5210%
Number of Simulations	10,000	10,000

Finally, in Figure 9.15, we present the distribution of returns associated with our combined portfolio managed futures and merger arbitrage. As can be seen, the negative skewness has been reduced dramatically from that presented in Figure 9.14. The distribution in Figure 9.15 demonstrates greater symmetry than that in Figure 9.14.

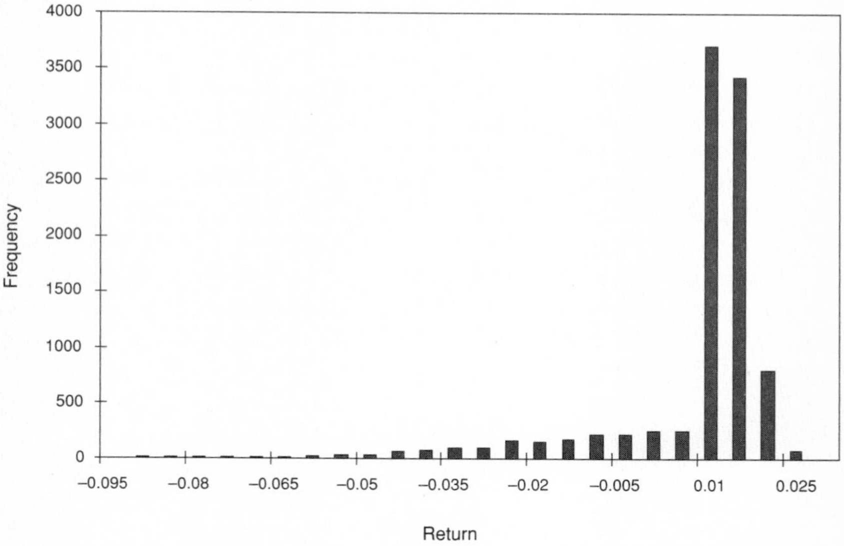

FIGURE 9.14 Distribution of Returns for Merger Arbitrage

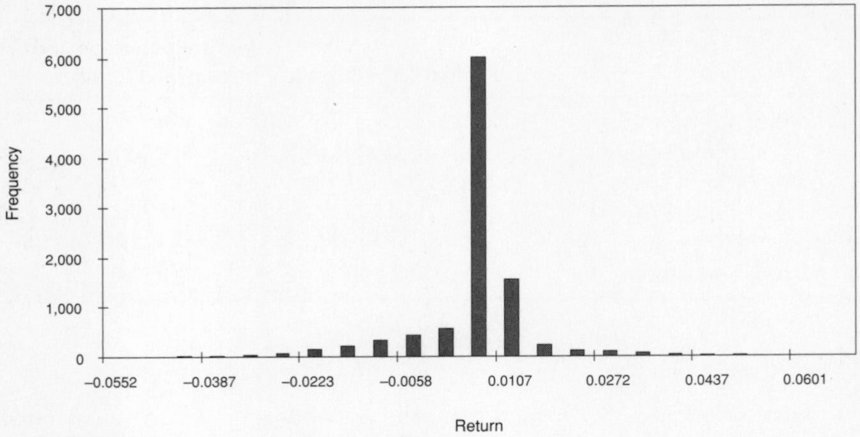

FIGURE 9.15 Combined Portfolio Return Distribution

CONCLUSION

In this chapter we demonstrate that managed futures or commodity trading advisors tend to be "long volatility" strategies. That is, the trend-following or momentum strategies of CTAs provide an economic exposure that is similar to a long put option. This synthetic put option exposure can be used to offset the short volatility exposure of other hedge fund strategies such as merger arbitrage and event driven.

When we formed our mimicking portfolios, we observed that the mean return to these portfolios was zero. This underlines the fact that the futures market is a zero-sum game. However, managed futures should not be considered in isolation; their risk-reducing properties vis-à-vis short-volatility strategies provides measurable portfolio benefits. In sum, while the glory days of global macro funds may be over, there is a new reason to seek the benefits of CTAs.

CHAPTER 10

The Interdependence of Managed Futures Risk Measures

Bhaswar Gupta and Manolis Chatiras

Practitioners today are faced with a wide choice of methods to measure return and risk in portfolios, either in absolute or relative terms. The Sharpe ratio, maximum drawdown, and semideviation are common examples. We classify 24 such measures into six groups and attempt to gauge how the measures interact, by using data on five different CTA strategies. For each measure, two groups of portfolios are created, containing CTAs with the lowest and highest values of the measure. We find evidence of high correlation between the measures in some of the CTA strategies, pointing to information overlaps and suggesting that some of these measures may be redundant.

INTRODUCTION AND REVIEW OF THE LITERATURE

The managed futures industry has grown from just under $1 billion in 1985 to more than $40 billion as of June 2003. This growth has led to closer scrutiny of the diversification properties as well as risk management of managed futures. The term "managed futures" represents an industry composed of professional money managers known as commodity trading advisors (CTAs) who manage client assets on a discretionary basis using global futures and options markets (CISDM 2002). The risks in managed futures are inherently more complex than traditional investments as they undergo rapid change over time. Hence a thorough understanding of the risks of the different market segments CTAs trade in is essential to effectively manage these risks. This chapter examines risk surrogates for certain CTA portfolios.

The risks in the different market segments have been explored in several articles. Tomek and Peterson (2001) have reviewed risk management practices in agricultural markets. Their review highlights gaps between concepts and implementation and notes that even though many well-developed models of price behavior exist, appropriate characterization and estimation of probability distributions of commodity prices remain elusive. Their conclusions discuss what academic research can and cannot accomplish in assisting producers with risk management decisions.

Risk surrogates also have been explored in several articles. Cooley, Roenfeldt, and Modani (1977), using returns of a sample of 943 firms having data for the period January 1966 to January 1974, calculate 11 risk measures to indicate the wide range of risk surrogates. Daglioglu and Gupta (2003b) study the interdependence of hedge fund risk measures. Using 330 hedge funds that had complete data for the period January 1996 to September 2002, they construct 48 portfolios (24 top 50 percent and 24 bottom 50 percent) based on 24 risk measures. The 330 funds belonged to seven strategies. Their results had several implications:

- Although certain risk measures are relevant for some strategies, they are not relevant for others.
- Certain risk measures for some strategies are perfectly correlated for both the top and bottom portfolios. This suggests that there is strong information overlap and the use of any one would suffice.
- For some strategies (e.g., equity hedge and fund of funds), the risk measures are not perfectly correlated.
- The occurrence of low correlations is much greater for the market-neutral strategy than for any other strategy.

Daglioglu and Gupta (2003b) note that these results point to an important conclusion: Risk measures should be chosen carefully for inclusion in performance reports so that redundancy is avoided.

Gordon (2003) also examines several risk measures, such as historical standard deviation, downside deviation, semideviation, and maximum drawdown. Using data from a large hedge fund of funds over the period December 1991 to December 2000, he analyzes out-of-sample performance to predict results in the nonoverlapping subsequent period of investment in each hedge fund. He finds that historical standard deviation tends to be somewhat helpful in predicting future risk. He also finds that correlation between preinvestment standard deviation, downside deviation, and maximum drawdown is significant. Gordon concludes that standard deviation appears to be a better predictor of future losses than downside risk measures such as historical downside deviation and maximum drawdown. Although this advantage is not statistically significant for some of the downside risk measures, he notes that standard deviation should probably be favored over all other downside risk measures because it is simple and well understood.

In this chapter we analyze the significance of the same 24 risk measures used in Daglioglu and Gupta (2003b) for certain CTA portfolios. The 24 measures are used as much in CTA performance reports as they are in hedge fund reports. Our results shed greater light on the implications of these measures for particular CTA strategies. They also provide a clearer understanding of the interdependence of these two measures for certain CTA portfolios. We provide empirical evidence on the redundancy of certain risk surrogates, to help investors determine the relevance and applicability of these risk measures when evaluating CTA portfolios.

In the next section we describe the methodology used for this study. Then we describe the data, present the empirical results, and conclude.

METHODOLOGY

We study the 24 risk measures that were analyzed in Daglioglu and Gupta (2003b) to ascertain the degree of informational overlap among them. We use correlation analysis in our study. We divide the degree of correlation into four groups:

1. (P) means *Perfectly Correlated,* correlation = 1.00.
2. (H) means *Highly Correlated,* 0.90 < correlation < 1.00.
3. (M) means *Moderately Correlated,* 0.65 < correlation < 0.90.
4. (L) means *Low Correlated,* correlation < 0.65.

The 24 risk measures are:

1. Average Monthly Gain
2. Average Monthly Loss
3. Standard Deviation
4. Gain Standard Deviation
5. Loss Standard Deviation
6. Semideviation
7. Skewness
8. Kurtosis
9. Coskewness
10. Sharpe ratio
11. Calmar ratio
12. Maximum Drawdown
13. Gain/Loss Ratio
14. Beta
15. Annualized Alpha
16. Treynor Ratio
17. Jensen Alpha
18. Information Ratio
19. Up Capture
20. Down Capture
21. Up Number Ratio
22. Down Number Ratio
23. Up Percentage Ratio
24. Down Percentage Ratio.

These measures can be classified into six groups:

1. Absolute return measures
2. Absolute risk measures
3. Absolute risk-adjusted return measures

4. Relative return measures
5. Relative risk measures
6. Relative risk-adjusted return measures

DATA

The data for this study came from the Center for International Securities and Derivatives Markets (CISDM) database. We selected a sample of 200 CTA managers who had complete return data for the period from January 1998 to July 2003. The CTAs covered five strategies:

1. Agriculture
2. Currencies
3. Diversified
4. Financials
5. Stocks

Using these monthly rates of return, we calculated the 24 risk measures for the overall period, January 1998 to July 2003. These risk measures are indicative of the wide range of risk surrogates suggested in the literature on CTA analysis and portfolio management.

We then ranked all of the CTAs by these 24 risk measures for the five different CTA strategies. Next, we took the first half and second half to construct bottom 50 percent and top 50 percent portfolios for these strategies. In other words, we created 48 portfolios (24 portfolios for bottom 50 percent, 24 portfolios for top 50 percent) for each CTA strategy. Tables 10.1, 10.3, 10.5, 10.7, and 10.9. present annualized returns, standard deviations, and Sharpe ratios of these portfolios and Tables 10.2, 10.4, 10.6, 10.8, and 10.10 present the correlations between the portfolios.

EMPIRICAL RESULTS

Agriculture

Table 10.1 presents summary statistics for the agriculture portfolios, and Table 10.2 presents the correlation matrix. The top 50 percent monthly standard deviation, top 50 percent gain standard deviation, top 50 percent loss standard deviation, and top 50 percent semideviation yield exactly the same results as do the bottom 50 percent portfolios for the four risk measures. Similarly the top 50 percent portfolio of the up percentage ratio yields the same results as the top 50 percent portfolio of the down percentage ratio, and the bottom 50 percent portfolio of the up percentage ratio yields the

TABLE 10.1 Summary Statistics for Agriculture Portfolios

Agriculture		Annualized Return	Standard Deviation	Sharpe Ratio
Top 50%	Average Monthly Gain	6.66%	9.82%	0.29
Bottom 50%	Average Monthly Gain	4.43%	7.25%	0.09
Top 50%	Average Monthly Loss	5.54%	7.04%	0.25
Bottom 50%	Average Monthly Loss	5.64%	12.96%	0.14
Top 50%	Compound (Geometric) Monthly ROR	7.56%	9.83%	0.38
Bottom 50%	Compound (Geometric) Monthly ROR	3.18%	8.20%	-0.07
Top 50%	Monthly Standard Deviation	5.28%	9.96%	0.15
Bottom 50%	Monthly Standard Deviation	6.23%	7.27%	0.33
Top 50%	Gain Standard Deviation	5.28%	9.96%	0.15
Bottom 50%	Gain Standard Deviation	6.23%	7.27%	0.33
Top 50%	Loss Standard Deviation	5.28%	9.96%	0.15
Bottom 50%	Loss Standard Deviation	6.23%	7.27%	0.33
Top 50%	Semi Deviation	5.28%	9.96%	0.15
Bottom 50%	Semi Deviation	6.23%	7.27%	0.33
Top 50%	Skewness	5.61%	9.54%	0.19
Bottom 50%	Skewness	5.59%	10.09%	0.18
Top 50%	Kurtosis	4.27%	8.30%	0.06
Bottom 50%	Kurtosis	7.34%	12.01%	0.29
Top 50%	Sharpe Ratio	7.56%	9.83%	0.38
Bottom 50%	Sharpe Ratio	3.18%	8.20%	-0.07
Top 50%	Calmar Ratio	6.94%	7.85%	0.40
Bottom 50%	Calmar Ratio	4.01%	10.38%	0.02
Top 50%	Maximum Drawdown	4.20%	6.97%	0.06
Bottom 50%	Maximum Drawdown	7.50%	12.71%	0.29
Top 50%	Gain/Loss Ratio	5.90%	7.29%	0.29
Bottom 50%	Gain/Loss Ratio	5.31%	11.48%	0.13
Top 50%	Beta	6.22%	8.37%	0.29
Bottom 50%	Beta	4.93%	10.09%	0.11
Top 50%	Annualized Alpha	7.56%	9.83%	0.38
Bottom 50%	Annualized Alpha	3.18%	8.20%	-0.07
Top 50%	Treynor Ratio	4.13%	8.40%	0.04
Bottom 50%	Treynor Ratio	7.80%	9.37%	0.43
Top 50%	Jensen Alpha	6.22%	8.37%	0.29
Bottom 50%	Jensen Alpha	4.93%	10.09%	0.11
Top 50%	Information Ratio	7.56%	9.83%	0.38
Bottom 50%	Information Ratio	3.18%	8.20%	-0.07
Top 50%	Up Capture	6.66%	9.82%	0.29
Bottom 50%	Up Capture	4.43%	7.25%	0.09
Top 50%	Down Capture	5.28%	9.96%	0.15
Bottom 50%	Down Capture	6.23%	7.27%	0.33
Top 50%	Up Number Ratio	5.20%	7.87%	0.18
Bottom 50%	Up Number Ratio	6.13%	12.08%	0.19
Top 50%	Down Number Ratio	4.68%	7.94%	0.11
Bottom 50%	Down Number Ratio	7.09%	9.54%	0.34
Top 50%	Up Percentage Ratio	6.41%	8.01%	0.33
Bottom 50%	Up Percentage Ratio	4.75%	9.77%	0.10
Top 50%	Down Percentage Ratio	6.41%	8.01%	0.33
Bottom 50%	Down Percentage Ratio	4.75%	9.77%	0.10

TABLE 10.2 Correlation Matrix for Agriculture Portfolios

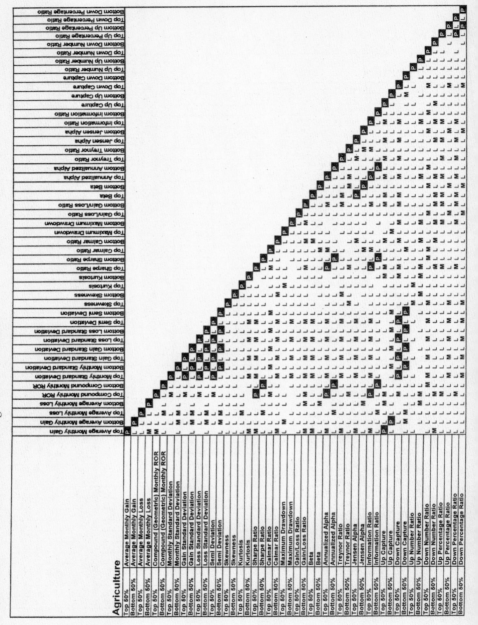

Agriculture		Top Average Monthly Gain	Bottom Average Monthly Gain	Top Average Monthly Loss	Bottom Average Monthly Loss	Top Compound Monthly ROR	Bottom Compound Monthly ROR	Top Monthly Standard Deviation	Bottom Monthly Standard Deviation	Top Gain Standard Deviation	Bottom Gain Standard Deviation	Top Loss Standard Deviation	Bottom Loss Standard Deviation	Top Semi Deviation	Bottom Semi Deviation	Top Skewness	Bottom Skewness	Top Kurtosis	Bottom Kurtosis	Top Sharpe Ratio	Bottom Sharpe Ratio	Top Calmar Ratio	Bottom Calmar Ratio	Top Maximum Drawdown	Bottom Maximum Drawdown	Top Gain/Loss Ratio	Bottom Gain/Loss Ratio	Top Beta	Bottom Beta	Top Annualized Alpha	Bottom Annualized Alpha	Top Treynor Ratio	Bottom Treynor Ratio	Top Jensen Alpha	Bottom Jensen Alpha	Top Information Ratio	Bottom Information Ratio	Top Up Capture	Bottom Up Capture	Top Down Capture	Bottom Down Capture	Top Up Number Ratio	Bottom Up Number Ratio	Top Down Number Ratio	Bottom Down Number Ratio	Top Up Percentage Ratio	Bottom Up Percentage Ratio	Top Down Percentage Ratio	Bottom Down Percentage Ratio
Top 50%	Average Monthly Gain	P																																															
Bottom 50%	Average Monthly Gain	L	P																																														
Top 50%	Average Monthly Loss	L	L	P																																													
Bottom 50%	Average Monthly Loss	M	L	L	P																																												
Top 50%	Compound (Geometric) Monthly ROR	M	L	L		P																																											
Bottom 50%	Compound (Geometric) Monthly ROR	L	L	M	L	L	P																																										
Top 50%	Monthly Standard Deviation		L	L		M	L	P																																									
Bottom 50%	Monthly Standard Deviation	L	M	M	L	L	L	L	P																																								
Top 50%	Gain Standard Deviation		L	L		M	L	P	L	P																																							
Bottom 50%	Gain Standard Deviation	L	M	M	L	L	L	L	P	L	P																																						
Top 50%	Loss Standard Deviation		L	L		M	L	P	L	P	L	P																																					
Bottom 50%	Loss Standard Deviation	L	M	M	L	L	L	L	P	L	P	L	P																																				
Top 50%	Semi Deviation		L	L		M	L	P	L	P	L	P	L	P																																			
Bottom 50%	Semi Deviation	L	M	M	L	L	L	L	P	L	P	L	P	L	P																																		
Top 50%	Skewness	L	L	L	L	L	L	L	L	L	L	L	L	L	L	P																																	
Bottom 50%	Skewness	L	L	L	L	L	L	L	L	L	L	L	L	L	L	L	P																																
Top 50%	Kurtosis	L	L	M	L	L		L	L	L	L	L	L	L	L	L	L	P																															
Bottom 50%	Kurtosis	M	L	L			L	M	L	M	L	M	L	M	L	L	L	L	P																														
Top 50%	Sharpe Ratio	M	L	L		P	L	M	L	M	L	M	L	M	L	L	L	L		P																													
Bottom 50%	Sharpe Ratio	L	L	M	L	L	P	L	L	L	L	L	L	L	L	L	L		L	L	P																												
Top 50%	Calmar Ratio	L	L	L	L	M	L	L	M	L	M	L	M	L	M		L	L	L	M	L	P																											
Bottom 50%	Calmar Ratio	M	L	L	L	L	L	M	L	M	L	M	L	M	L	L	M	L	L	L	L	L	P																										
Top 50%	Maximum Drawdown	L	M		L	L		L	L	L	L	L	L	L	L	L	L	M	L	L		L	L	P																									
Bottom 50%	Maximum Drawdown		L	L			L	M	L	M	L	M	L	M	L	L	L	L			L	L	L	L	P																								
Top 50%	Gain/Loss Ratio	L	L	L	L	L	L	L	L	L	L	L	L	L	L	L	L	L	L	L	L	L	L	L	L	P																							
Bottom 50%	Gain/Loss Ratio	M	L	L	M	M	L	M	L	M	L	M	L	M	L	L	L	L	L	M	L	L	M	L	M	L	P																						
Top 50%	Beta	M	L	L	L	L	L	M	L	M	L	M	L	M	L	L		L	L	L	L	L	M	L	L	L	L	P																					
Bottom 50%	Beta	L	L	L	M	L	L	L	L	L	L	L	L	L	L		L	L	L	L	L	M	L	L	L	L	L	L	P																				
Top 50%	Annualized Alpha	M	L	L		P	L	M	L	M	L	M	L	M	L	L	L	L		P	L	M	L	L		L	M	L	L	P																			
Bottom 50%	Annualized Alpha	L	L	M	L	L	P	L	L	L	L	L	L	L	L	L	L		L	L	P	L	L		L	L	L	L	L	L	P																		
Top 50%	Treynor Ratio	M	L	L	L	L	L	M	L	M	L	M	L	M	L	L	M	L	L	L	L	L		L	L	L	M	M	L	L	L	P																	
Bottom 50%	Treynor Ratio	L	L	L	L	M	L	L	L	L	L	L	L	L	L	M	L	L	L	M	L		L	L	L	L	L	L	M	M	L	L	P																
Top 50%	Jensen Alpha	M	L	L	L	L	L	M	L	M	L	M	L	M	L	L		L	L	L	L	L	M	L	L	L	L	P	L	L	L	M	L	P															
Bottom 50%	Jensen Alpha	L	L	L	M	L	L	L	L	L	L	L	L	L	L		L	L	L	L	L	M	L	L	L	L	L	L	P	L	L	L	M	L	P														
Top 50%	Information Ratio	M	L	L		P	L	M	L	M	L	M	L	M	L	L	L	L		P	L	M	L	L		L	M	L	L	P	L	L	M	L	L	P													
Bottom 50%	Information Ratio	L	L	M	L	L	P	L	L	L	L	L	L	L	L	L	L		L	L	P	L	L		L	L	L	L	L	L	P	L	L	L	L	L	P												
Top 50%	Up Capture	P	L	L	M	M	L		L		L		L		L	L	L	L	M	M	L	L	M	L		L	M	M	L	M	L	M	L	M	L	M	L	P											
Bottom 50%	Up Capture	L	P	L	L	L	L	L	M	L	M	L	M	L	M	L	L	L	L	L	L	L	L	M	L	L	L	L	L	L	L	L	L	L	L	L	L	L	P										
Top 50%	Down Capture		L	L		M	L	P	L	P	L	P	L	P	L	L	L	L	M	M	L	L	M	L	M	L	M	M	L	M	L	M	L	M	L	M	L		L	P									
Bottom 50%	Down Capture	L	M	M	L	L	L	L	P	L	P	L	P	L	P	L	L	L	L	L	L	M	L	L	L	L	L	L	L	L	L	L	L	L	L	L	L	L	M	L	P								
Top 50%	Up Number Ratio	L		L	L	L	L	L		L		L		L		M	L	M	L	L	L	L	L	L	L	L	L	L	L	L	L	L	L	L	L	L	L	L		L		P							
Bottom 50%	Up Number Ratio		L	L	M	M	L		L		L		L		L	L	M	L	M	M	L	L	M	L	M	L	L	L	L	M	L	L	L	L	L	M	L		L		L	L	P						
Top 50%	Down Number Ratio	L	L	L	L	L	M	M	L	M	L	M	L	M	L	M	L	L	L	L	M	M	L	L	L	M	L	L	M	L	M	L	L	L	M	L	M	L	L	M	L	L	L	P					
Bottom 50%	Down Number Ratio	M	L	L	L	M	L	L	L	L	L	L	L	L	L	L	L	L	L	M	L	L	M	L	M	L	M	M	L	M	L	L	L	M	L	M	L	M	L	L	L	L	L	L	P				
Top 50%	Up Percentage Ratio	L	L	L	L	M	L	L	L	L	L	L	L	L	L	L	L	L	L	M	L	L	L	L	M	L	M	M	L	M	L	M	L	M	L	M	L	L	L	L	L	L	L	L		P			
Bottom 50%	Up Percentage Ratio	L	L	L	L	L	L	M	L	M	L	M	L	M	L	M	L	L	L	L	L	L	L	L	L	M	L	L	M	L	L	L	L	L	M	L	L	L	L	M	L	L	L		L	L	P		
Top 50%	Down Percentage Ratio	L	L	L	L	M	L	L	L	L	L	L	L	L	L	L	L	L	L	M	L	L	L	L	M	L	M	M	L	M	L	M	L	M	L	M	L	L	L	L	L	L	L	L		P	L	P	
Bottom 50%	Down Percentage Ratio	L	L	L	L	L	L	M	L	M	L	M	L	M	L	M	L	L	L	L	L	L	L	L	L	M	L	L	M	L	L	L	L	L	M	L	L	L	L	M	L	L	L		L	L	P	L	P

same results as the bottom 50 percent portfolio of the down percentage ratio. The top 50 percent up capture portfolio yields exactly the same results as the top 50 percent average monthly gain portfolio, and the bottom 50 percent up capture portfolio yields exactly the same results as the bottom 50 percent average monthly gain portfolio. As expected, these portfolios are perfectly correlated with each other. There are also several high and moderate correlations and many low correlations. The low correlations can be explained by the characteristics of our sample. Seven funds have complete data over the period of our study. Three are trend followers and four are not. If the risk measures split the sample in a way that trend followers were in one sample and non-trend followers in the other for the top and bottom 50 percent portfolios, then one would expect low correlations among the portfolios. However, if the portfolios were split in such a way that they contain equal numbers of trend-following and non-trend-following funds, then one would expect moderate to high correlations.

We also examined the sectors traded by these trading advisors. All seven indicated that they traded grains; three said they traded meats; and three said they traded softs. One indicated that he traded currencies and interest rates, and another indicated that he traded energy and metals. Given the diverse characteristics of these portfolios, the low correlation between certain risk measures is a natural consequence.

Currencies

Twenty-seven currency CTAs had complete data for the period of our study. Table 10.3 presents the summary statistics for the currency portfolios; Table 10.4 presents the correlations among the portfolios. There were only two instances of perfect correlations, the top and bottom 50 percent monthly standard deviation portfolios with the top and bottom 50 percent average monthly gain portfolios, and the top and bottom 50 percent semideviation portfolios with the top and bottom 50 percent loss standard deviation portfolios. There were several instances of high, moderate, and low correlations. Of the 27 funds, three indicated that their trades had a short-term time horizon; four indicated that their trades had short-, medium-, and long-term horizons. Eight of the funds indicated that their trades had a medium-term horizon; four indicated that they had a long-term horizon. Two indicated that they traded intraday. Seven of the funds were classified as discretionary, 15 as systematic, 2 as trend-based, and 3 as trend-identifier.

There is considerable variety even within the strategies. For example, a certain fund that was classified as systematic and short term had a correlation of only 0.19 with another fund that was classified as systematic and medium term for the time period studied. Another pair where both were classified as systematic and medium term had a correlation of 0.25. Systematic funds can be either trend followers or contrarian; in this case one was a systematic trend follower and the other was a systematic non-trend

TABLE 10.3 Summary Statistics for Currency Portfolios

Currencies		Annualized Return	Standard Deviation	Sharpe Ratio
Top 50%	Average Monthly Gain	8.72%	12.19%	0.40
Bottom 50%	Average Monthly Gain	5.81%	3.08%	0.65
Top 50%	Average Monthly Loss	6.64%	3.57%	0.79
Bottom 50%	Average Monthly Loss	8.07%	12.27%	0.35
Top 50%	Compound (Geometric) Monthly ROR	11.68%	9.12%	0.86
Bottom 50%	Compound (Geometric) Monthly ROR	2.98%	6.16%	-0.13
Top 50%	Monthly Standard Deviation	8.72%	12.19%	0.40
Bottom 50%	Monthly Standard Deviation	5.81%	3.08%	0.65
Top 50%	Gain Standard Deviation	9.55%	11.71%	0.49
Bottom 50%	Gain Standard Deviation	5.00%	3.27%	0.37
Top 50%	Loss Standard Deviation	6.73%	11.39%	0.26
Bottom 50%	Loss Standard Deviation	8.02%	3.73%	1.13
Top 50%	Semi Deviation	6.73%	11.39%	0.26
Bottom 50%	Semi Deviation	8.02%	3.73%	1.13
Top 50%	Skewness	9.01%	9.77%	0.53
Bottom 50%	Skewness	5.67%	5.82%	0.32
Top 50%	Kurtosis	7.00%	7.69%	0.42
Bottom 50%	Kurtosis	7.84%	8.20%	0.49
Top 50%	Sharpe Ratio	10.92%	6.39%	1.11
Bottom 50%	Sharpe Ratio	3.71%	9.54%	-0.01
Top 50%	Calmar Ratio	10.17%	5.87%	1.08
Bottom 50%	Calmar Ratio	4.48%	9.87%	0.07
Top 50%	Maximum Drawdown	8.12%	4.19%	1.03
Bottom 50%	Maximum Drawdown	6.54%	11.49%	0.24
Top 50%	Gain/Loss Ratio	9.26%	8.70%	0.63
Bottom 50%	Gain/Loss Ratio	5.44%	6.94%	0.24
Top 50%	Beta	8.57%	4.68%	1.02
Bottom 50%	Beta	6.07%	11.20%	0.20
Top 50%	Annualized Alpha	11.68%	9.00%	0.88
Bottom 50%	Annualized Alpha	2.98%	6.28%	-0.13
Top 50%	Treynor Ratio	5.60%	7.61%	0.24
Bottom 50%	Treynor Ratio	9.44%	7.58%	0.74
Top 50%	Jensen Alpha	10.02%	5.63%	1.11
Bottom 50%	Jensen Alpha	4.59%	10.43%	0.08
Top 50%	Information Ratio	11.43%	7.63%	1.00
Bottom 50%	Information Ratio	3.24%	8.01%	-0.07
Top 50%	Up Capture	8.88%	11.80%	0.43
Bottom 50%	Up Capture	5.69%	3.25%	0.58
Top 50%	Down Capture	6.15%	11.54%	0.20
Bottom 50%	Down Capture	8.62%	3.92%	1.23
Top 50%	Up Number Ratio	8.25%	4.87%	0.91
Bottom 50%	Up Number Ratio	6.40%	11.27%	0.23
Top 50%	Down Number Ratio	5.58%	8.01%	0.22
Bottom 50%	Down Number Ratio	9.42%	7.67%	0.73
Top 50%	Up Percentage Ratio	9.97%	6.41%	0.96
Bottom 50%	Up Percentage Ratio	4.68%	9.50%	0.09
Top 50%	Down Percentage Ratio	9.07%	5.78%	0.91
Bottom 50%	Down Percentage Ratio	5.61%	9.96%	0.18

TABLE 10.4 Correlations for Currency Portfolios

Currencies		Top Average Monthly Gain	Bottom Average Monthly Gain	Top Average Monthly Loss	Bottom Average Monthly Loss	Top Compound Monthly ROR	Bottom Compound Monthly ROR	Top Monthly Standard Deviation	Bottom Monthly Standard Deviation	Top Gain Standard Deviation	Bottom Gain Standard Deviation	Top Loss Standard Deviation	Bottom Loss Standard Deviation	Top Semi Deviation	Bottom Semi Deviation	Top Skewness	Bottom Skewness	Top Kurtosis	Bottom Kurtosis	Top Sharpe Ratio	Bottom Sharpe Ratio	Top Calmar Ratio	Bottom Calmar Ratio	Top Maximum Drawdown	Bottom Maximum Drawdown	Top Gain/Loss Ratio	Bottom Gain/Loss Ratio	Top Beta	Bottom Beta	Top Annualized Alpha	Bottom Annualized Alpha	Top Treynor Ratio	Bottom Treynor Ratio	Top Jensen Alpha	Bottom Jensen Alpha	Top Information Ratio	Bottom Information Ratio	Top Up Capture	Bottom Up Capture	Top Down Capture	Bottom Down Capture	Top Up Number Ratio	Bottom Up Number Ratio	Top Down Number Ratio	Bottom Down Number Ratio	Top Up Percentage Ratio	Bottom Up Percentage Ratio	Top Down Percentage Ratio	Bottom Down Percentage Ratio
Top 50%	Average Monthly Gain	P																																															
Bottom 50%	Average Monthly Gain	L	P																																														
Top 50%	Average Monthly Loss	L	M	P																																													
Bottom 50%	Average Monthly Loss	H	L	L	P																																												
Top 50%	Compound (Geometric) Monthly ROR	H	L	M	H	P																																											
Bottom 50%	Compound (Geometric) Monthly ROR	H	L	L	H	M	P																																										
Top 50%	Monthly Standard Deviation	P	L	L	H	H	H	P																																									
Bottom 50%	Monthly Standard Deviation	L	P	M	L	L	L	L	P																																								
Top 50%	Gain Standard Deviation	H	L	M	H	H	H	H	L	P																																							
Bottom 50%	Gain Standard Deviation	M	M	M	M	M	L	M	M	L	P																																						
Top 50%	Loss Standard Deviation	H	L	L	H	H	H	H	L	H	M	P																																					
Bottom 50%	Loss Standard Deviation	M	M	H	L	M	L	M	M	M	M	L	P																																				
Top 50%	Semi Deviation	H	L	L	H	H	H	H	L	H	M	P	L	P																																			
Bottom 50%	Semi Deviation	M	M	H	L	M	L	M	M	M	M	L	P	L	P																																		
Top 50%	Skewness	H	L	M	H	H	M	H	L	H	L	H	M	H	M	P																																	
Bottom 50%	Skewness	M	L	L	M	M	H	M	L	M	M	M	L	M	L	L	P																																
Top 50%	Kurtosis	M	L	M	M	M	M	M	L	H	L	H	M	H	M	H	M	P																															
Bottom 50%	Kurtosis	H	L	L	H	H	M	H	L	M	M	H	L	H	L	M	M	L	P																														
Top 50%	Sharpe Ratio	M	M	M	M	H	L	M	M	M	M	M	M	M	M	M	M	M	M	P																													
Bottom 50%	Sharpe Ratio	H	L	L	H	M	H	H	L	H	L	H	L	H	L	H	M	H	M	L	P																												
Top 50%	Calmar Ratio	M	M	M	M	H	L	M	M	M	M	M	M	M	M	M	L	M	M	H	L	P																											
Bottom 50%	Calmar Ratio	H	L	L	H	M	H	H	L	H	L	H	L	H	L	H	M	H	M	L	H	L	P																										
Top 50%	Maximum Drawdown	M	M	H	M	M	L	M	M	M	M	M	H	M	H	M	L	M	M	M	L	H	L	P																									
Bottom 50%	Maximum Drawdown	H	L	L	H	H	H	H	L	H	M	H	L	H	L	H	M	H	M	M	H	M	H	L	P																								
Top 50%	Gain/Loss Ratio	H	L	M	H	H	M	H	L	H	L	H	M	H	M	H	L	M	H	M	M	M	M	M	H	P																							
Bottom 50%	Gain/Loss Ratio	M	L	L	H	M	M	M	L	M	M	H	L	H	L	M	H	M	M	M	M	M	M	L	H	L	P																						
Top 50%	Beta	M	M	M	M	M	L	M	M	M	M	M	M	M	M	M	L	M	M	M	L	M	M	H	M	M	M	P																					
Bottom 50%	Beta	H	L	L	H	H	H	H	L	H	M	H	L	H	L	H	M	M	H	M	H	M	H	M	H	H	M	L	P																				
Top 50%	Annualized Alpha	H	M	M	H	H	M	H	M	H	M	H	M	H	M	H	M	M	H	H	M	H	M	M	H	H	M	M	H	P																			
Bottom 50%	Annualized Alpha	H	L	L	H	M	H	H	L	H	L	H	L	H	L	M	H	M	M	L	H	L	H	L	H	M	M	L	H	M	P																		
Top 50%	Treynor Ratio	H	L	M	H	M	H	H	L	H	M	H	M	H	M	H	M	H	M	M	H	M	H	M	H	M	M	M	H	M	H	P																	
Bottom 50%	Treynor Ratio	H	L	M	H	H	M	H	L	H	M	H	M	H	M	H	M	M	H	H	M	H	M	M	H	H	M	M	H	H	M	M	P																
Top 50%	Jensen Alpha	M	M	M	M	H	L	M	M	M	M	M	M	M	M	M	L	M	M	H	L	H	L	M	M	M	M	H	L	H	L	M	M	P															
Bottom 50%	Jensen Alpha	H	L	L	H	M	H	H	L	H	L	H	L	H	L	H	M	M	M	L	H	M	H	L	H	H	M	L	H	M	H	H	H	L	P														
Top 50%	Information Ratio	H	M	M	M	H	M	H	M	H	M	M	M	M	M	H	M	M	H	H	M	H	M	H	M	H	M	M	M	H	M	M	H	H	M	P													
Bottom 50%	Information Ratio	H	L	L	H	M	H	H	L	H	L	H	L	H	L	M	M	H	M	L	H	L	H	L	H	M	M	L	H	M	H	H	M	L	H	L	P												
Top 50%	Up Capture	H	L	L	H	H	H	H	L	H	M	H	L	H	L	H	M	H	H	M	H	M	H	M	H	H	H	M	H	H	H	H	H	M	H	M	H	P											
Bottom 50%	Up Capture	L	H	H	L	M	L	L	H	L	M	L	H	L	H	M	L	L	L	M	L	M	L	H	L	M	L	M	L	M	L	L	M	M	L	M	L	L	P										
Top 50%	Down Capture	H	L	L	H	H	H	H	L	H	M	H	L	H	L	H	M	M	H	M	H	M	H	M	H	H	M	M	H	H	H	H	H	M	H	M	H	H	L	P									
Bottom 50%	Down Capture	L	M	H	L	M	L	L	M	L	L	L	H	L	H	M	L	M	L	M	L	M	L	H	L	L	L	M	L	M	L	L	M	H	L	M	L	L	M	L	P								
Top 50%	Up Number Ratio	M	M	M	M	M	L	M	M	L	H	M	M	M	M	L	M	L	M	H	L	H	L	M	M	L	M	M	L	M	L	L	M	H	L	H	L	M	M	L	M	P							
Bottom 50%	Up Number Ratio	H	L	L	H	H	H	H	L	H	L	H	L	H	L	H	M	H	M	M	H	M	H	M	H	H	M	M	H	H	H	H	M	L	H	M	H	H	L	H	L	L	P						
Top 50%	Down Number Ratio	H	L	L	H	M	H	H	L	H	L	H	L	H	L	M	M	H	M	L	H	M	H	M	H	M	M	M	H	M	H	H	M	M	H	M	H	H	L	H	L	L	H	P					
Bottom 50%	Down Number Ratio	H	L	M	M	H	M	H	L	M	M	M	M	M	M	H	M	M	H	H	M	H	M	M	M	M	M	M	H	H	M	M	H	M	M	H	M	M	M	M	M	M	M	L	P				
Top 50%	Up Percentage Ratio	M	M	M	M	H	L	M	M	M	M	M	M	M	M	M	M	L	M	H	L	H	M	M	M	M	M	M	M	H	L	M	H	H	M	H	L	M	M	M	M	H	M	L	H	P			
Bottom 50%	Up Percentage Ratio	H	L	L	H	M	H	H	L	H	L	H	L	H	L	H	M	H	M	L	H	L	H	M	H	H	M	L	H	M	H	H	M	L	H	M	H	H	L	H	L	L	H	H	M	L	P		
Top 50%	Down Percentage Ratio	M	L	M	M	H	L	M	L	M	M	M	M	M	M	H	L	M	M	H	M	H	M	M	M	M	M	M	M	H	L	M	H	M	M	H	L	M	M	M	M	M	M	L	H	H	L	P	
Bottom 50%	Down Percentage Ratio	H	L	L	H	M	H	H	L	H	L	H	L	H	L	M	M	M	M	M	H	M	H	M	H	H	M	M	H	M	H	H	M	M	H	M	H	H	L	H	L	L	H	H	M	M	H	L	P

follower. However, a pair where both funds were classified as systematic trend followers had a correlation of 0.47. As expected, the discretionary funds had low correlations. Given the diversity of the funds classified as currency, the correlation patterns of risk measures are along expected lines.

Diversified Portfolios

Table 10.5 presents the summary statistics for the diversified portfolios; Table 10.6 presents the correlations among the portfolios. For the period of our study, 107 diversified CTAs had complete data. One interesting result in the case of diversified CTAs is that no portfolios are perfectly correlated with each other. However, a majority of portfolios had high correlations, a few had moderate correlations, and none had low correlations. Of the 107 funds, 10 were classified as discretionary, 69 as systematic, 24 as trend based, and 4 as trend identifier. Clearly since more than half of the funds were systematic, these funds dominated the portfolios in all cases. Another reason why the portfolios exhibited high correlations is that many of the funds had high correlations before analysis. Although there were pairs—for example, two funds classified as long-term systematic with a correlation of 0.46—these did not impact the rankings enough to show that the risk measures are not interdependent. Another reason for these results is the markets diversified CTAs trade in. Diversified CTAs encompass agriculture, currencies, financials, and stocks. Because most diversified CTAs trade in a majority of these markets, their return patterns showed similar risk characteristics.

Financial Portfolios

Table 10.7 presents the summary statistics of the financial portfolios and Table 10.8 presents the correlations. In this case the portfolios were mostly highly or moderately correlated with only one perfectly correlated portfolio pair. The top 50 percent and bottom 50 percent information ratio portfolios were perfectly correlated with the top and bottom 50 percent Sharpe ratio portfolios. Thirty-nine CTAs had complete data for the period of our study. Of these 5 were discretionary, 21 were systematic, 10 were trend based, and 3 were trend identifiers. Clearly the systematic or trend-based funds dominated the portfolios. The return patterns of these portfolios suggest that they have similar risk characteristics.

TABLE 10.5 Summary Statistics for Diversified Portfolios

Diversified		Annualized Return	Standard Deviation	Sharpe Ratio
Top 50%	Average Monthly Gain	16.70%	18.92%	0.68
Bottom 50%	Average Monthly Gain	8.13%	7.12%	0.61
Top 50%	Average Monthly Loss	10.02%	8.54%	0.73
Bottom 50%	Average Monthly Loss	14.96%	17.79%	0.63
Top 50%	Compound (Geometric) Monthly ROR	19.79%	17.52%	0.91
Bottom 50%	Compound (Geometric) Monthly ROR	5.41%	8.76%	0.18
Top 50%	Monthly Standard Deviation	16.09%	18.23%	0.67
Bottom 50%	Monthly Standard Deviation	8.80%	7.84%	0.64
Top 50%	Gain Standard Deviation	16.14%	18.27%	0.68
Bottom 50%	Gain Standard Deviation	8.75%	7.79%	0.64
Top 50%	Loss Standard Deviation	14.71%	17.23%	0.63
Bottom 50%	Loss Standard Deviation	10.22%	8.98%	0.71
Top 50%	Semi Deviation	15.79%	18.19%	0.66
Bottom 50%	Semi Deviation	9.09%	7.90%	0.67
Top 50%	Skewness	14.29%	14.73%	0.71
Bottom 50%	Skewness	10.76%	11.80%	0.59
Top 50%	Kurtosis	13.32%	13.31%	0.72
Bottom 50%	Kurtosis	11.75%	13.24%	0.60
Top 50%	Sharpe Ratio	17.75%	13.83%	1.01
Bottom 50%	Sharpe Ratio	7.44%	12.75%	0.29
Top 50%	Calmar Ratio	16.94%	13.04%	1.01
Bottom 50%	Calmar Ratio	8.21%	13.49%	0.33
Top 50%	Maximum Drawdown	10.88%	9.50%	0.74
Bottom 50%	Maximum Drawdown	14.16%	16.75%	0.62
Top 50%	Gain/Loss Ratio	15.60%	14.27%	0.83
Bottom 50%	Gain/Loss Ratio	9.48%	12.28%	0.46
Top 50%	Beta	9.07%	7.02%	0.75
Bottom 50%	Beta	15.68%	19.98%	0.59
Top 50%	Annualized Alpha	19.60%	18.67%	0.85
Bottom 50%	Annualized Alpha	5.46%	7.63%	0.22
Top 50%	Treynor Ratio	8.86%	12.02%	0.42
Bottom 50%	Treynor Ratio	16.39%	14.53%	0.87
Top 50%	Jensen Alpha	13.61%	10.21%	0.96
Bottom 50%	Jensen Alpha	11.25%	17.01%	0.44
Top 50%	Information Ratio	18.55%	14.83%	0.99
Bottom 50%	Information Ratio	6.70%	11.58%	0.25
Top 50%	Up Capture	17.24%	18.84%	0.71
Bottom 50%	Up Capture	7.64%	7.19%	0.53
Top 50%	Down Capture	14.60%	17.90%	0.60
Bottom 50%	Down Capture	10.27%	8.18%	0.79
Top 50%	Up Number Ratio	16.09%	12.47%	0.99
Bottom 50%	Up Number Ratio	9.01%	14.10%	0.37
Top 50%	Down Number Ratio	11.29%	12.36%	0.61
Bottom 50%	Down Number Ratio	13.81%	14.22%	0.70
Top 50%	Up Percentage Ratio	16.97%	14.89%	0.89
Bottom 50%	Up Percentage Ratio	8.20%	11.15%	0.40
Top 50%	Down Percentage Ratio	13.42%	12.14%	0.79
Bottom 50%	Down Percentage Ratio	11.66%	14.21%	0.55

TABLE 10.6 Correlations for Diversified Portfolios

Diversified		Top Average Monthly Gain	Bottom Average Monthly Gain	Top Average Monthly Loss	Bottom Average Monthly Loss	Top Compound Monthly ROR	Bottom Compound Monthly ROR	Top Monthly Standard Deviation	Bottom Monthly Standard Deviation	Top Gain Standard Deviation	Bottom Gain Standard Deviation	Top Loss Standard Deviation	Bottom Loss Standard Deviation	Top Semi Deviation	Bottom Semi Deviation	Top Skewness	Bottom Skewness	Top Kurtosis	Bottom Kurtosis	Top Sharpe Ratio	Bottom Sharpe Ratio	Top Calmar Ratio	Bottom Calmar Ratio	Top Maximum Drawdown	Bottom Maximum Drawdown	Top Gain/Loss Ratio	Bottom Gain/Loss Ratio	Top Beta	Bottom Beta	Top Annualized Alpha	Bottom Annualized Alpha	Top Treynor Ratio	Bottom Treynor Ratio	Top Jensen Alpha	Bottom Jensen Alpha	Top Information Ratio	Bottom Information Ratio	Top Up Capture	Bottom Up Capture	Top Down Capture	Bottom Down Capture	Top Up Number Ratio	Bottom Up Number Ratio	Top Down Number Ratio	Bottom Down Number Ratio	Top Up Percentage Ratio	Bottom Up Percentage Ratio	Top Down Percentage Ratio	Bottom Down Percentage Ratio
Top 50%	Average Monthly Gain	P																																															
Bottom 50%	Average Monthly Gain	H	P																																														
Top 50%	Average Monthly Loss	H	H	P																																													
Bottom 50%	Average Monthly Loss	H	H	H	P																																												
Top 50%	Compound (Geometric) Monthly ROR	H	H	H	H	P																																											
Bottom 50%	Compound (Geometric) Monthly ROR	H	H	H	H	H	P																																										
Top 50%	Monthly Standard Deviation	H	H	H	H	H	H	P																																									
Bottom 50%	Monthly Standard Deviation	H	H	H	H	H	H	H	P																																								
Top 50%	Gain Standard Deviation	H	H	H	H	H	H	H	H	P																																							
Bottom 50%	Gain Standard Deviation	H	H	H	H	H	H	H	H	H	P																																						
Top 50%	Loss Standard Deviation	H	H	H	H	H	H	H	H	H	H	P																																					
Bottom 50%	Loss Standard Deviation	H	H	H	H	H	H	H	H	H	H	H	P																																				
Top 50%	Semi Deviation	H	H	H	H	H	H	H	H	H	H	H	H	P																																			
Bottom 50%	Semi Deviation	H	H	H	H	H	H	H	H	H	H	H	H	H	P																																		
Top 50%	Skewness	H	H	H	H	H	H	H	H	H	H	H	H	H	H	P																																	
Bottom 50%	Skewness	H	H	H	H	H	H	H	H	H	H	H	H	H	H	H	P																																
Top 50%	Kurtosis	H	H	H	H	H	H	H	H	H	H	H	H	H	H	H	H	P																															
Bottom 50%	Kurtosis	H	H	H	H	H	H	H	H	H	H	H	H	H	H	H	H	H	P																														
Top 50%	Sharpe Ratio	H	H	H	H	H	H	H	H	H	H	H	H	H	H	H	H	H	H	P																													
Bottom 50%	Sharpe Ratio	H	H	H	H	H	H	H	H	H	H	H	H	H	H	H	H	H	H	H	P																												
Top 50%	Calmar Ratio	H	H	H	H	H	H	H	H	H	H	H	H	H	H	H	H	H	H	H	H	P																											
Bottom 50%	Calmar Ratio	H	H	H	H	H	H	H	H	H	H	H	H	H	H	H	H	H	H	H	H	H	P																										
Top 50%	Maximum Drawdown	H	H	H	H	H	H	H	H	H	H	H	H	H	H	H	H	H	H	H	H	H	H	P																									
Bottom 50%	Maximum Drawdown	H	H	H	H	H	H	H	H	H	H	H	H	H	H	H	H	H	H	H	H	H	H	H	P																								
Top 50%	Gain/Loss Ratio	H	H	H	H	H	H	H	H	H	H	H	H	H	H	H	H	H	H	H	H	H	H	H	H	P																							
Bottom 50%	Gain/Loss Ratio	H	H	H	H	H	H	H	H	H	H	H	H	H	H	H	H	H	H	H	H	H	H	H	H	H	P																						
Top 50%	Beta	M	H	M	H	M	H	M	M	M	M	H	M	H	M	M	M	M	M	M	H	M	H	M	H	M	H	P																					
Bottom 50%	Beta	H	H	H	H	H	H	H	H	H	H	H	H	H	H	H	H	H	H	H	H	H	H	H	H	H	H	M	P																				
Top 50%	Annualized Alpha	H	H	H	H	H	H	H	H	H	H	H	H	H	H	H	H	H	H	H	H	H	H	H	H	H	H	M	H	P																			
Bottom 50%	Annualized Alpha	H	H	H	H	H	H	H	H	H	H	H	M	H	H	H	H	H	H	M	H	M	H	H	H	H	H	H	H	H	P																		
Top 50%	Treynor Ratio	H	H	H	H	H	H	H	H	H	H	H	H	H	H	H	H	H	H	H	H	H	H	H	H	H	H	M	H	H	H	P																	
Bottom 50%	Treynor Ratio	H	H	H	H	H	H	H	H	H	H	H	H	H	H	H	H	H	H	H	H	H	H	H	H	H	H	M	H	H	H	H	P																
Top 50%	Jensen Alpha	H	H	M	H	H	H	H	H	H	H	H	H	H	M	H	M	H	M	M	H	M	H	M	H	M	H	H	M	H	H	M	H	P															
Bottom 50%	Jensen Alpha	H	H	H	H	H	H	H	H	H	H	H	H	H	H	H	H	H	H	H	H	H	H	H	H	H	H	M	H	H	H	H	H	M	P														
Top 50%	Information Ratio	H	H	H	H	H	H	H	H	H	H	H	H	H	H	H	H	H	H	H	H	H	H	H	H	H	H	M	H	H	H	H	H	H	H	P													
Bottom 50%	Information Ratio	H	H	H	H	H	H	H	H	H	H	H	H	H	H	H	H	H	H	H	H	H	H	H	H	H	H	H	H	H	H	H	H	H	H	H	P												
Top 50%	Up Capture	H	H	H	H	H	H	H	H	H	H	H	H	H	H	H	H	H	H	H	H	H	H	H	H	H	H	M	H	H	H	H	H	H	H	H	H	P											
Bottom 50%	Up Capture	H	H	H	H	H	H	H	H	H	H	H	H	H	H	H	H	H	H	H	H	H	H	H	H	H	H	M	H	H	H	H	H	H	H	H	H	H	P										
Top 50%	Down Capture	H	H	H	H	H	H	H	H	H	H	H	H	H	H	H	H	H	H	H	H	H	H	H	H	H	H	H	H	H	H	H	H	H	H	H	H	H	H	P									
Bottom 50%	Down Capture	H	H	H	H	H	H	H	H	H	H	H	H	H	H	H	H	H	H	H	H	H	H	H	H	H	H	M	H	H	H	H	H	M	H	H	H	H	H	H	P								
Top 50%	Up Number Ratio	H	H	H	H	H	H	H	H	H	H	H	H	H	H	H	H	H	H	H	H	H	H	H	H	H	H	H	H	H	H	H	H	H	H	H	H	H	H	H	H	P							
Bottom 50%	Up Number Ratio	H	H	H	H	H	H	H	H	H	H	H	H	H	H	H	H	H	H	H	H	H	H	H	H	H	H	M	H	H	H	H	H	M	H	H	H	H	H	H	H	H	P						
Top 50%	Down Number Ratio	H	H	H	H	H	H	H	H	H	H	H	H	H	H	H	H	H	H	H	H	H	H	H	H	H	H	H	H	H	H	H	H	H	H	H	H	H	H	H	H	H	H	P					
Bottom 50%	Down Number Ratio	H	H	H	H	H	H	H	H	H	H	H	H	H	H	H	H	H	H	H	H	H	H	H	H	H	H	M	H	H	H	H	H	M	H	H	H	H	H	H	H	H	H	H	P				
Top 50%	Up Percentage Ratio	H	H	H	H	H	H	H	H	H	H	H	H	H	H	H	H	H	H	H	H	H	H	H	H	H	H	H	H	H	H	H	H	H	H	H	H	H	H	H	H	H	H	H	H	P			
Bottom 50%	Up Percentage Ratio	H	H	H	H	H	H	H	H	H	H	H	H	H	H	H	H	H	H	H	H	H	H	H	H	H	H	M	H	H	H	H	H	H	H	H	H	H	H	H	H	H	H	H	H	H	P		
Top 50%	Down Percentage Ratio	H	H	H	H	H	H	H	H	H	H	H	H	H	H	H	H	H	H	H	H	H	H	H	H	H	H	M	H	H	H	H	H	M	H	H	H	H	H	H	H	H	H	H	H	H	H	P	
Bottom 50%	Down Percentage Ratio	H	H	H	H	H	H	H	H	H	H	H	H	H	H	H	H	H	H	H	H	H	H	H	H	H	H	H	H	H	H	H	H	H	H	H	H	H	H	H	H	H	H	H	H	H	H	H	P

TABLE 10.7 Summary Statistics for Financial Portfolios

Financials		Annualized Return	Standard Deviation	Sharpe Ratio
Top 50%	Average Monthly Gain	12.80%	16.35%	0.55
Bottom 50%	Average Monthly Gain	9.06%	5.52%	0.95
Top 50%	Average Monthly Loss	9.60%	6.32%	0.92
Bottom 50%	Average Monthly Loss	12.49%	15.94%	0.55
Top 50%	Compound (Geometric) Monthly ROR	14.78%	15.19%	0.72
Bottom 50%	Compound (Geometric) Monthly ROR	7.19%	6.70%	0.51
Top 50%	Monthly Standard Deviation	12.16%	15.41%	0.54
Bottom 50%	Monthly Standard Deviation	9.83%	6.23%	0.97
Top 50%	Gain Standard Deviation	12.37%	15.86%	0.54
Bottom 50%	Gain Standard Deviation	9.57%	5.85%	0.99
Top 50%	Loss Standard Deviation	12.53%	14.46%	0.60
Bottom 50%	Loss Standard Deviation	9.54%	7.20%	0.80
Top 50%	Semi Deviation	12.20%	15.65%	0.54
Bottom 50%	Semi Deviation	9.75%	6.21%	0.96
Top 50%	Skewness	11.19%	11.47%	0.64
Bottom 50%	Skewness	11.06%	10.41%	0.70
Top 50%	Kurtosis	10.99%	9.24%	0.78
Bottom 50%	Kurtosis	11.23%	12.85%	0.58
Top 50%	Sharpe Ratio	13.21%	9.72%	0.97
Bottom 50%	Sharpe Ratio	8.94%	12.42%	0.41
Top 50%	Calmar Ratio	12.39%	8.39%	1.02
Bottom 50%	Calmar Ratio	9.72%	13.83%	0.43
Top 50%	Maximum Drawdown	10.52%	6.49%	1.04
Bottom 50%	Maximum Drawdown	11.54%	15.68%	0.49
Top 50%	Gain/Loss Ratio	11.90%	12.66%	0.64
Bottom 50%	Gain/Loss Ratio	10.26%	9.48%	0.68
Top 50%	Beta	8.64%	5.59%	0.87
Bottom 50%	Beta	13.35%	17.23%	0.55
Top 50%	Annualized Alpha	14.47%	15.88%	0.67
Bottom 50%	Annualized Alpha	7.42%	6.12%	0.59
Top 50%	Treynor Ratio	9.50%	10.46%	0.55
Bottom 50%	Treynor Ratio	12.84%	11.68%	0.77
Top 50%	Jensen Alpha	10.56%	7.06%	0.96
Bottom 50%	Jensen Alpha	11.45%	15.73%	0.49
Top 50%	Information Ratio	13.21%	9.72%	0.97
Bottom 50%	Information Ratio	8.94%	12.42%	0.41
Top 50%	Up Capture	13.58%	16.20%	0.60
Bottom 50%	Up Capture	8.27%	5.73%	0.78
Top 50%	Down Capture	11.79%	15.92%	0.50
Bottom 50%	Down Capture	10.14%	5.88%	1.08
Top 50%	Up Number Ratio	11.14%	8.34%	0.88
Bottom 50%	Up Number Ratio	11.01%	13.93%	0.52
Top 50%	Down Number Ratio	10.12%	12.21%	0.52
Bottom 50%	Down Number Ratio	12.14%	10.04%	0.83
Top 50%	Up Percentage Ratio	13.06%	12.60%	0.73
Bottom 50%	Up Percentage Ratio	9.10%	9.26%	0.57
Top 50%	Down Percentage Ratio	11.00%	7.96%	0.90
Bottom 50%	Down Percentage Ratio	11.11%	14.47%	0.51

TABLE 10.8 Correlations for Financial Portfolios

Financials		Top Average Monthly Gain	Bottom Average Monthly Gain	Top Average Monthly Loss	Bottom Average Monthly Loss	Top Compound Monthly ROR	Bottom Compound Monthly ROR	Top Monthly Standard Deviation	Bottom Monthly Standard Deviation	Top Gain Standard Deviation	Bottom Gain Standard Deviation	Top Loss Standard Deviation	Bottom Loss Standard Deviation	Top Semi Deviation	Bottom Semi Deviation	Top Skewness	Bottom Skewness	Top Kurtosis	Bottom Kurtosis	Top Sharpe Ratio	Bottom Sharpe Ratio	Top Calmar Ratio	Bottom Calmar Ratio	Top Maximum Drawdown	Bottom Maximum Drawdown	Top Gain/Loss Ratio	Bottom Gain/Loss Ratio	Top Beta	Bottom Beta	Top Annualized Alpha	Bottom Annualized Alpha	Top Treynor Ratio	Bottom Treynor Ratio	Top Jensen Alpha	Bottom Jensen Alpha	Top Information Ratio	Bottom Information Ratio	Top Up Capture	Bottom Up Capture	Top Down Capture	Bottom Down Capture	Top Up Number Ratio	Bottom Up Number Ratio	Top Down Number Ratio	Bottom Down Number Ratio	Top Up Percentage Ratio	Bottom Up Percentage Ratio	Top Down Percentage Ratio	Bottom Down Percentage Ratio
Top 50%	Average Monthly Gain	P																																															
Bottom 50%	Average Monthly Gain	M	P																																														
Top 50%	Average Monthly Loss	H	H	P																																													
Bottom 50%	Average Monthly Loss	H	M	M	P																																												
Top 50%	Compound (Geometric) Monthly ROR	H	M	H	H	P																																											
Bottom 50%	Compound (Geometric) Monthly ROR	H	H	H	H	M	P																																										
Top 50%	Monthly Standard Deviation	H	M	H	H	H	H	P																																									
Bottom 50%	Monthly Standard Deviation	H	H	H	H	H	H	H	P																																								
Top 50%	Gain Standard Deviation	H	M	H	H	H	H	H	H	P																																							
Bottom 50%	Gain Standard Deviation	H	H	H	H	H	H	H	H	H	P																																						
Top 50%	Loss Standard Deviation	H	M	H	H	H	H	H	H	H	H	P																																					
Bottom 50%	Loss Standard Deviation	H	H	H	H	H	H	H	H	H	H	H	P																																				
Top 50%	Semi Deviation	H	M	M	H	H	H	H	H	H	H	H	H	P																																			
Bottom 50%	Semi Deviation	H	H	H	M	H	M	M	H	H	H	M	H	M	P																																		
Top 50%	Skewness	H	M	H	H	H	H	H	H	H	H	H	H	H	H	P																																	
Bottom 50%	Skewness	H	H	H	H	H	H	H	H	H	H	H	H	H	M	H	P																																
Top 50%	Kurtosis	H	H	H	H	H	H	H	H	H	H	H	H	H	H	H	H	P																															
Bottom 50%	Kurtosis	H	M	H	H	H	H	H	H	H	H	H	H	H	H	H	H	H	P																														
Top 50%	Sharpe Ratio	H	M	H	H	H	M	H	H	H	H	H	H	H	H	H	H	H	H	P																													
Bottom 50%	Sharpe Ratio	H	M	M	H	H	H	H	H	H	M	H	H	H	M	H	H	H	H	H	P																												
Top 50%	Calmar Ratio	H	M	H	H	H	M	H	H	H	H	H	H	H	H	H	H	H	H	H	M	P																											
Bottom 50%	Calmar Ratio	H	M	H	H	H	H	H	H	H	M	H	H	H	M	H	H	H	H	H	H	M	P																										
Top 50%	Maximum Drawdown	H	H	H	H	H	H	H	H	H	H	H	H	H	H	H	H	H	H	H	H	H	H	P																									
Bottom 50%	Maximum Drawdown	H	M	H	H	H	H	H	H	H	H	H	H	H	M	H	H	H	H	H	H	H	H	H	P																								
Top 50%	Gain/Loss Ratio	H	M	H	H	H	M	H	H	H	M	H	H	H	H	H	H	H	H	H	H	H	H	H	H	P																							
Bottom 50%	Gain/Loss Ratio	H	H	H	H	H	H	H	H	H	H	H	H	H	M	H	H	H	H	H	H	H	H	H	H	M	P																						
Top 50%	Beta	M	H	H	M	M	H	M	H	M	H	M	H	M	H	M	M	H	M	M	M	M	M	H	M	M	M	P																					
Bottom 50%	Beta	H	M	M	H	H	M	H	H	H	M	H	H	H	M	H	H	H	H	H	H	H	H	H	H	H	H	M	P																				
Top 50%	Annualized Alpha	H	M	H	H	H	M	H	H	H	H	H	H	H	M	H	H	H	H	H	H	H	H	H	H	H	H	M	H	P																			
Bottom 50%	Annualized Alpha	M	H	H	M	M	H	M	H	M	H	M	H	M	H	H	M	H	M	H	M	H	M	H	M	M	H	H	M	M	P																		
Top 50%	Treynor Ratio	H	H	M	H	H	H	H	H	H	H	H	H	H	M	H	H	H	H	H	H	M	H	H	H	H	H	M	H	H	M	P																	
Bottom 50%	Treynor Ratio	H	M	H	H	H	M	H	H	H	H	H	H	H	H	H	H	H	H	H	H	H	H	H	H	H	H	M	H	H	M	M	P																
Top 50%	Jensen Alpha	M	M	H	M	M	M	M	H	M	H	M	H	M	H	H	M	H	M	H	M	H	M	H	M	M	H	H	M	M	H	M	H	P															
Bottom 50%	Jensen Alpha	H	M	M	H	H	H	H	H	H	M	H	H	H	M	H	H	H	H	H	H	H	H	H	H	H	H	M	H	H	M	H	H	M	P														
Top 50%	Information Ratio	H	M	H	H	H	M	H	H	H	H	H	H	H	H	H	H	H	H	P	H	H	H	H	H	H	H	M	H	H	H	H	H	H	H	P													
Bottom 50%	Information Ratio	H	M	M	H	H	H	H	H	H	M	H	H	H	M	H	H	H	H	H	P	M	H	H	H	H	H	M	H	H	M	H	H	M	H	H	P												
Top 50%	Up Capture	H	M	H	H	H	H	H	H	H	H	H	H	H	M	H	H	H	H	H	H	H	H	H	H	H	H	M	H	H	M	H	H	M	H	H	H	P											
Bottom 50%	Up Capture	M	H	H	M	M	H	M	H	M	H	M	H	M	H	H	M	H	M	H	M	H	M	H	M	M	M	H	M	M	H	M	M	M	M	H	M	M	P										
Top 50%	Down Capture	H	M	H	H	H	H	H	H	H	H	H	H	H	M	H	H	H	H	H	H	H	H	H	H	H	H	M	H	H	M	H	H	M	H	H	H	H	M	P									
Bottom 50%	Down Capture	M	H	H	M	H	H	M	H	M	H	M	H	M	H	H	H	H	M	H	M	H	M	H	M	H	H	H	M	M	H	M	H	H	M	H	M	M	H	M	P								
Top 50%	Up Number Ratio	H	H	H	H	H	H	H	H	H	H	H	H	H	H	H	H	H	H	H	H	H	H	H	H	H	H	M	H	H	M	H	H	M	H	H	H	H	H	H	H	P							
Bottom 50%	Up Number Ratio	H	M	H	H	H	H	H	H	H	M	H	H	H	H	H	H	H	H	H	H	H	H	H	H	H	H	M	H	H	M	H	H	M	H	H	H	H	M	H	M	M	P						
Top 50%	Down Number Ratio	H	M	H	H	H	H	H	H	H	M	H	H	H	H	H	H	H	H	H	H	H	H	H	H	H	M	M	H	H	M	H	H	M	H	H	H	H	H	H	H	H	H	P					
Bottom 50%	Down Number Ratio	H	M	M	H	H	H	H	H	H	H	H	H	H	M	H	H	H	H	H	H	H	H	H	H	M	H	M	H	H	M	H	H	H	H	H	H	H	M	H	M	H	H	M	P				
Top 50%	Up Percentage Ratio	H	M	H	H	H	M	H	H	H	H	H	H	H	H	H	H	H	H	H	H	H	H	H	H	H	H	M	H	H	M	H	H	M	H	H	H	H	M	H	H	H	H	H	H	P			
Bottom 50%	Up Percentage Ratio	H	H	H	H	H	H	H	H	H	H	H	H	H	M	H	H	H	H	H	H	H	H	H	H	H	H	M	H	H	M	H	H	M	H	H	H	H	H	H	H	H	H	H	H	H	P		
Top 50%	Down Percentage Ratio	H	M	H	H	H	M	H	H	H	H	H	H	H	H	H	H	H	H	H	H	H	H	H	H	M	H	M	H	H	H	M	H	H	M	H	H	H	M	H	H	H	H	M	H	H	M	P	
Bottom 50%	Down Percentage Ratio	H	M	H	H	H	H	H	H	H	H	H	H	H	M	H	H	H	H	H	H	H	H	H	H	H	H	M	H	H	M	H	H	M	H	H	H	H	M	H	M	H	H	H	H	H	H	M	P

TABLE 10.9 Summary Statistics for Stock Portfolios

Stocks		Annualized Return	Standard Deviation	Sharpe Ratio
Top 50%	Average Monthly Gain	25.55%	9.77%	2.23
Bottom 50%	Average Monthly Gain	6.41%	5.29%	0.49
Top 50%	Average Monthly Loss	10.56%	4.56%	1.48
Bottom 50%	Average Monthly Loss	22.88%	12.21%	1.56
Top 50%	Compound (Geometric) Monthly ROR	27.63%	9.22%	2.59
Bottom 50%	Compound (Geometric) Monthly ROR	4.28%	8.00%	0.06
Top 50%	Monthly Standard Deviation	24.62%	10.01%	2.08
Bottom 50%	Monthly Standard Deviation	7.38%	3.69%	0.97
Top 50%	Gain Standard Deviation	25.55%	9.77%	2.23
Bottom 50%	Gain Standard Deviation	6.41%	5.29%	0.49
Top 50%	Loss Standard Deviation	20.63%	10.12%	1.66
Bottom 50%	Loss Standard Deviation	11.43%	4.26%	1.79
Top 50%	Semi Deviation	22.60%	10.65%	1.77
Bottom 50%	Semi Deviation	9.33%	3.82%	1.45
Top 50%	Skewness	23.54%	9.02%	2.19
Bottom 50%	Skewness	8.42%	6.43%	0.72
Top 50%	Kurtosis	9.07%	6.98%	0.76
Bottom 50%	Kurtosis	24.98%	9.20%	2.30
Top 50%	Sharpe Ratio	27.24%	8.57%	2.74
Bottom 50%	Sharpe Ratio	4.70%	8.27%	0.11
Top 50%	Calmar Ratio	27.24%	8.57%	2.74
Bottom 50%	Calmar Ratio	4.70%	8.27%	0.11
Top 50%	Maximum Drawdown	12.89%	4.64%	1.96
Bottom 50%	Maximum Drawdown	20.10%	11.46%	1.42
Top 50%	Gain/Loss Ratio	18.74%	8.30%	1.80
Bottom 50%	Gain/Loss Ratio	13.50%	7.29%	1.33
Top 50%	Beta	20.26%	11.04%	1.49
Bottom 50%	Beta	11.56%	6.78%	1.14
Top 50%	Annualized Alpha	27.54%	8.58%	2.77
Bottom 50%	Annualized Alpha	4.40%	8.26%	0.07
Top 50%	Treynor Ratio	15.51%	9.87%	1.19
Bottom 50%	Treynor Ratio	16.96%	7.17%	1.83
Top 50%	Jensen Alpha	23.10%	10.89%	1.77
Bottom 50%	Jensen Alpha	8.66%	6.12%	0.79
Top 50%	Information Ratio	27.63%	9.22%	2.59
Bottom 50%	Information Ratio	4.28%	8.00%	0.06
Top 50%	Up Capture	24.62%	10.01%	2.08
Bottom 50%	Up Capture	7.38%	3.69%	0.97
Top 50%	Down Capture	19.12%	9.86%	1.55
Bottom 50%	Down Capture	13.07%	4.84%	1.92
Top 50%	Up Number Ratio	23.10%	10.89%	1.77
Bottom 50%	Up Number Ratio	8.66%	6.12%	0.79
Top 50%	Down Number Ratio	6.17%	6.89%	0.34
Bottom 50%	Down Number Ratio	28.77%	9.87%	2.53
Top 50%	Up Percentage Ratio	24.41%	9.30%	2.22
Bottom 50%	Up Percentage Ratio	7.42%	7.78%	0.47
Top 50%	Down Percentage Ratio	19.56%	8.68%	1.82
Bottom 50%	Down Percentage Ratio	12.38%	9.37%	0.92

TABLE 10.10 Correlations for Stock Portfolios

Stocks		Top Average Monthly Gain	Bottom Average Monthly Gain	Top Average Monthly Loss	Bottom Average Monthly Loss	Top Compound Monthly ROR	Bottom Compound Monthly ROR	Top Monthly Standard Deviation	Bottom Monthly Standard Deviation	Top Gain Standard Deviation	Bottom Gain Standard Deviation	Top Loss Standard Deviation	Bottom Loss Standard Deviation	Top Semi Deviation	Bottom Semi Deviation	Top Skewness	Bottom Skewness	Top Kurtosis	Bottom Kurtosis	Top Sharpe Ratio	Bottom Sharpe Ratio	Top Calmar Ratio	Bottom Calmar Ratio	Top Maximum Drawdown	Bottom Maximum Drawdown	Top Gain/Loss Ratio	Bottom Gain/Loss Ratio	Top Beta	Bottom Beta	Top Annualized Alpha	Bottom Annualized Alpha	Top Treynor Ratio	Bottom Treynor Ratio	Top Jensen Alpha	Bottom Jensen Alpha	Top Information Ratio	Bottom Information Ratio	Top Up Capture	Bottom Up Capture	Top Down Capture	Bottom Down Capture	Top Up Number Ratio	Bottom Up Number Ratio	Top Down Number Ratio	Bottom Down Number Ratio	Top Up Percentage Ratio	Bottom Up Percentage Ratio	Top Down Percentage Ratio	Bottom Down Percentage Ratio
Top 50%	Average Monthly Gain	P																																														
Bottom 50%	Average Monthly Gain	L	P																																													
Top 50%	Average Monthly Loss	L	L	P																																												
Bottom 50%	Average Monthly Loss	M	L	L	P																																											
Top 50%	Compound (Geometric) Monthly ROR	M	L	L	L	P																																										
Bottom 50%	Compound (Geometric) Monthly ROR	L	L	L	L	L	P																																									
Top 50%	Monthly Standard Deviation	H	L	L	H	L	L	P																																								
Bottom 50%	Monthly Standard Deviation	L	L	L	L	L	L	L	P																																							
Top 50%	Gain Standard Deviation	P	L	L	M	M	L	H	L	P																																						
Bottom 50%	Gain Standard Deviation	L	P	L	L	L	L	L	L	L	P																																					
Top 50%	Loss Standard Deviation	M	L	L	H	L	L	H	L	M	L	P																																				
Bottom 50%	Loss Standard Deviation	L	L	L	L	L	L	L	M	L	L	L	P																																			
Top 50%	Semi Deviation	M	L	L	H	L	L	H	L	M	L	H	L	P																																		
Bottom 50%	Semi Deviation	L	L	L	L	L	L	L	L	L	L	L	M	L	P																																	
Top 50%	Skewness	H	L	L	L	L	L	H	L	H	L	M	L	M	L	P																																
Bottom 50%	Skewness	L	M	L	L	L	L	L	L	L	M	L	L	L	L	L	P																															
Top 50%	Kurtosis	L	L	L	M	L	H	L	L	L	L	L	L	L	L	L	L	P																														
Bottom 50%	Kurtosis	L	L	L	L	H	L	M	L	L	L	L	L	M	L	L	L	L	P																													
Top 50%	Sharpe Ratio	M	L	L	L	H	L	L	L	M	L	L	L	L	L	M	L	L	H	P																												
Bottom 50%	Sharpe Ratio	L	L	L	M	L	H	L	L	L	L	L	L	L	L	L	L	H	L	L	P																											
Top 50%	Calmar Ratio	M	L	L	L	H	L	L	L	M	L	L	L	L	L	M	L	L	H	P	L	P																										
Bottom 50%	Calmar Ratio	L	L	L	M	L	H	L	L	L	L	L	L	L	L	L	L	H	L	L	P	L	P																									
Top 50%	Maximum Drawdown	L	L	L	L	L	L	L	L	L	L	L	H	L	H	L	L	L	L	L	L	L	L	P																								
Bottom 50%	Maximum Drawdown	M	L	L	H	L	L	H	L	M	L	H	L	H	L	M	L	L	L	L	L	L	L	L	P																							
Top 50%	Gain/Loss Ratio	H	L	L	L	L	L	M	L	H	L	M	L	M	L	H	L	L	L	L	L	L	L	L	M	P																						
Bottom 50%	Gain/Loss Ratio	L	M	L	M	L	L	L	L	L	M	L	L	L	L	L	H	L	L	L	L	L	L	L	L	L	P																					
Top 50%	Beta	L	M	L	H	L	L	M	L	L	M	M	L	M	L	L	L	L	L	L	L	L	L	L	M	L	M	P																				
Bottom 50%	Beta	L	L	L	L	L	L	L	L	L	L	L	L	L	L	L	L	L	L	L	L	L	L	L	L	L	L	L	P																			
Top 50%	Annualized Alpha	M	L	L	L	H	L	L	L	M	L	L	L	L	L	M	L	L	M	H	L	H	L	L	L	M	L	L	L	P																		
Bottom 50%	Annualized Alpha	L	L	L	M	L	M	L	L	L	L	L	L	L	L	L	L	M	L	L	H	L	H	L	L	L	L	M	L	L	P																	
Top 50%	Treynor Ratio	L	L	L	H	L	L	M	L	L	L	M	L	M	L	L	L	L	L	L	L	L	L	L	M	L	L	H	L	L	M	P																
Bottom 50%	Treynor Ratio	L	L	L	L	L	L	L	L	L	L	L	L	L	L	L	L	L	L	L	L	L	L	L	L	L	L	L	H	L	L	L	P															
Top 50%	Jensen Alpha	L	L	L	H	L	L	M	L	L	L	M	L	M	L	L	L	L	L	L	L	L	L	L	M	L	M	H	L	L	M	H	L	P														
Bottom 50%	Jensen Alpha	L	L	L	L	L	L	L	L	L	L	L	L	L	L	L	L	L	L	L	L	L	L	L	L	L	L	L	H	L	L	L	M	L	P													
Top 50%	Information Ratio	M	L	L	L	P	L	L	L	M	L	L	L	L	L	L	L	L	H	H	L	H	L	L	L	L	L	L	L	H	L	L	L	L	L	P												
Bottom 50%	Information Ratio	L	L	L	L	L	P	L	L	L	L	L	L	L	L	L	L	H	L	L	H	L	H	L	L	L	L	L	L	L	M	L	L	L	L	L	P											
Top 50%	Up Capture	H	L	L	H	L	L	P	L	H	L	H	L	H	L	H	L	L	M	L	L	L	L	L	H	M	L	M	L	L	L	M	L	M	L	L	L	P										
Bottom 50%	Up Capture	L	L	L	L	L	L	L	P	L	L	L	M	L	L	L	L	L	L	L	L	L	L	L	L	L	L	L	L	L	L	L	L	L	L	L	L	L	P									
Top 50%	Down Capture	H	L	L	H	L	L	H	L	H	L	H	L	H	L	M	L	L	M	L	L	L	L	L	H	M	L	M	L	L	L	M	L	M	L	L	L	H	L	P								
Bottom 50%	Down Capture	L	L	L	L	L	L	L	L	L	L	L	M	L	M	L	L	L	L	L	L	L	L	H	L	L	L	L	L	L	L	L	L	L	L	L	L	L	L	L	P							
Top 50%	Up Number Ratio	L	L	L	H	L	L	M	L	L	L	M	L	M	L	L	L	L	L	L	L	L	L	L	M	L	M	H	L	L	M	H	L	P	L	L	L	M	L	M	L	P						
Bottom 50%	Up Number Ratio	L	L	L	L	L	L	L	L	L	L	L	L	L	L	L	L	L	L	L	L	L	L	L	L	L	L	L	H	L	L	L	M	L	P	L	L	L	L	L	L	L	P					
Top 50%	Down Number Ratio	L	L	L	L	L	H	M	L	L	L	L	L	L	L	L	L	M	L	L	M	L	M	L	L	L	L	L	L	L	M	L	L	L	L	L	H	M	L	L	L	L	L	P				
Bottom 50%	Down Number Ratio	L	L	L	L	H	L	L	L	L	L	L	L	L	L	L	L	L	M	H	L	H	L	L	L	L	L	L	L	M	L	L	L	M	L	H	L	L	L	L	L	M	L	L	P			
Top 50%	Up Percentage Ratio	L	L	L	M	M	L	L	L	L	L	L	L	M	L	L	L	L	M	M	L	M	L	L	L	L	M	M	L	M	L	M	L	M	L	M	L	L	L	L	L	M	L	L	H	P		
Bottom 50%	Up Percentage Ratio	L	L	L	L	L	M	L	L	L	L	L	L	L	L	L	L	M	L	L	L	L	L	L	L	M	L	L	L	L	L	L	L	L	L	L	M	L	L	L	L	L	L	H	L	L	P	
Top 50%	Down Percentage Ratio	L	M	L	L	M	L	L	L	L	M	L	L	L	L	L	L	L	M	M	L	M	L	L	L	L	L	M	L	L	L	M	L	M	L	M	L	L	L	L	L	M	L	L	M	H	L	P
Bottom 50%	Down Percentage Ratio	M	L	L	L	L	L	L	L	M	L	L	L	L	L	L	L	M	L	L	L	L	L	L	L	L	L	L	L	L	L	L	L	L	L	L	L	L	L	L	L	L	L	M	L	L	H	L	P

Stock Portfolios

Table 10.9 presents the summary characteristics of the stock portfolios; Table 10.10 presents the correlations. Several portfolios were perfectly correlated. For example, the top and bottom 50 percent gain standard deviation portfolios were perfectly correlated with the top and bottom 50 percent average monthly gain portfolios, and the top and bottom 50 percent information ratio portfolios were perfectly correlated with the top and bottom 50 percent compounded monthly rate of return portfolios. There were several instances of weakly correlated portfolios. Of the 15 funds that were analyzed, 3 were discretionary, 9 were systematic, and 3 were trend-based. The return patterns of stock futures can vary depending on the stock index; that is one explanation of the weakly correlated portfolios.

Implications

One immediate application of the results of this analysis is in due diligence. Because the measures analyzed in this study are commonly used by investors to evaluate the performance of CTAs, perfect or high correlations can lead to redundancy. Our results are also important for performance reporting. Investors may want to examine correlations between ranked portfolios of these risk measures to avoid redundancy.

CONCLUSION

This research can be extended in many ways. For managed futures, we could further classify the CTAs as systematic trend following, systematic non-trend following, or discretionary. It would be interesting to attempt to identify similar correlation patterns for discretionary and systematic CTAs in the different market segments. We also could explore performance characteristics of these portfolios to verify whether the top portfolios always performed better than the bottom portfolios for the whole period. In addition, we could perform out-of-sample testing to see whether the rankings had any significance in other periods.

CHAPTER 11

Managing Downside Risk in Return Distributions Using Hedge Funds, Managed Futures, and Commodity Indices

Mark Anson

This chapter examines how alternative investments can provide downside return protection in a portfolio composed of U.S. stocks and bonds. Adding active, "skill-based" strategies such as hedge funds or managed futures to the portfolio leads to important improvements in downside returns, Sharpe ratio, and cumulative performance improvement, often without reducing upside expected returns. In some cases, the same benefits can be realized by adding passive commodity futures indices instead of skill-based strategies.

INTRODUCTION

Every investor is concerned with downside risk management. This is why diversification is a uniform portfolio tool. The better diversified an investment portfolio, presumably, the less the portfolio is exposed to months where the return is negative.

Yet it is an unfortunate fact of life that when things hit the fan, they tend to do it all at the same time. For example, a number of studies have examined the correlation of the U.S. domestic and international equity markets during periods of market stress or decline. The conclusion is that the equity markets around the world tend to be more highly correlated during periods of economic stress. (See Erb, Harvey, and Viskanta 1994;

Sinquefield 1996.) Therefore, international equity diversification may not provide the requisite diversification when a U.S. domestic investor needs it most—during periods of economic turmoil or decline.

The equity markets have become a single, global asset class for four reasons.

1. Policymakers from major industrial nations regularly attend economic summits where they attempt to synchronize fiscal and monetary policy. The Maastricht Treaty and the birth of "Euroland" is an example.
2. Corporations are expanding their operations and revenue streams beyond the site of their domestic incorporation.
3. The increased volume of international capital flows suggests economic shocks will be felt globally as opposed to locally.
4. Nations such as Japan have undergone a "big bang" episode where domestic investors have greater access to international investments. This provides for an even greater flow of capital across international boundaries. As a result, distinctions between international and domestic stocks are beginning to fade.

This diversification vacuum is one reason why "skill-based" investing has become so popular with investors. Hedge funds and managed futures and other skill-based strategies might be expected to provide greater diversification than international equity investing because the returns are dependent on the special skill of the manager rather than any broad macroeconomic events or trends. However, diversification need not rely solely on active skill-based strategies. Diversification benefits also can be achieved from the passive addition of a new asset class such as commodity futures.

This chapter examines the downside portion of the return distribution for a diversified portfolio of stocks and bonds. We then blend in hedge funds, managed futures, and commodity futures to see how the distribution changes when these alternative asset classes are added.

DESCRIBING DOWNSIDE RISK

The greatest concern for any investor is downside risk. If equity and bond markets are indeed becoming increasingly synchronized, international diversification may not offer the protection sought by investors. The ability to protect the value of an investment portfolio in hostile or turbulent markets is the key to the value of any macroeconomic diversification.

Within this framework, investment strategies and asset classes distinct from financial assets have the potential to diversify and protect an invest-

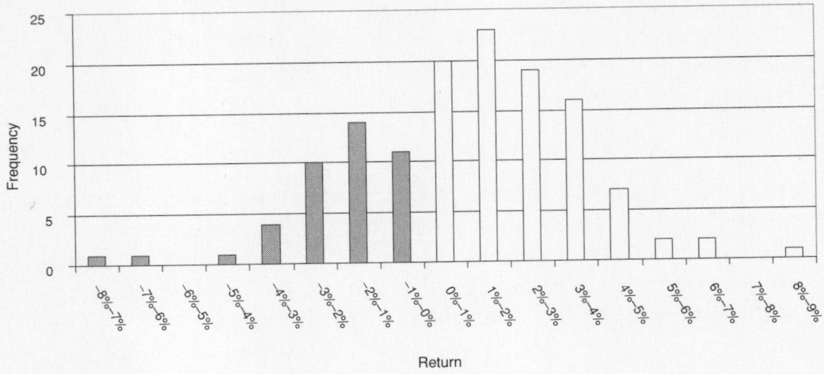

FIGURE 11.1 Frequency Distribution, Portfolio with 60/40 Stocks/Bonds

ment portfolio from hostile markets.[1] Hedge funds, managed futures, and commodity futures are a good choice for downside risk protection.

To demonstrate this downside risk protection, we start with a standard portfolio of stocks and bonds. We begin with a portfolio that is 60 percent the Standard & Poor's (S&P) 500 and 40 percent U.S. treasury bonds. In Figure 11.1 we provide a frequency distribution of the monthly returns to this portfolio over the time period 1990 to 2000.

Our concern is the shaded part of the return distribution, which shows both the size and the frequency with which the combined portfolio of 60 percent S&P 500 plus 40 percent U.S. treasury bonds earned a negative return in a particular month. It is this part of the return distribution that corresponds to downside risk and that investors attempt to avoid or limit. (See Strongin and Petsch 1996.)

We measure downside risk two ways: First we take the average return in the shaded part of the return distribution presented in the figure. Second we examine the number of months of negative returns associated with the distribution of returns for the stock/bond portfolio.

Table 11.1 shows that the average monthly return to a 60/40 stock/bond portfolio in the shaded part of the distribution is –2.07 percent. In other words, when the standard stock/bond portfolio earned a negative return in any given month, on average the magnitude of that return was –2.07 percent. These negative returns are exactly the downside

[1]We argue that hedge funds represent alternative investment strategies within existing asset classes rather than a distinct asset class.

TABLE 11.1 Downside Risk Exposure with Stocks and Bonds

Portfolio Composition	Expected Return	Standard Deviation	Sharpe Ratio	Average Downside
60/40 US Stocks/US Bonds	0.91%	2.60%	0.177	–2.07%
55/35/10 Stocks/Bonds/EAFE	0.86%	2.66%	0.155	–2.11%

Portfolio Composition	Number of Downside Months	Cumulative Downside Protection	Cumulative Return Potential	Cumulative Performance Improvement
60/40 US Stocks/US Bonds	42	N/A	N/A	N/A
55/35/10 Stocks/Bonds/EAFE	44	–5.90%	–6.60%	–12.50%

risk that investors want to reduce through diversification. In addition, the number of months of negative returns is 42 out of 132, a frequency of 31.8 percent.

To demonstrate the synchronization of the global equity markets, we blend in a 10 percent allocation to international stocks to our 60/40 U.S. stock/U.S. bond portfolio. The exact allocation is 55 percent S&P 500, 35 percent U.S. treasury bonds, and 10 percent EAFE.[2] We then calculate the return distribution for this new portfolio in the same manner by which we produced the return distribution for the 60/40 U.S. stock/U.S. bond portfolio.

Table 11.1 provides the statistics regarding the return distribution for the 55/35/10 U.S. stock/U.S. bond/international stock portfolio. Again, we concentrate on the downside portion of the distribution. The average monthly return to the downside portion of this distribution is –2.11 percent. That is, a 10 percent allocation to international stocks provided *an additional* monthly exposure to downside risk of –4 basis points, on average.

Therefore, over this time period, an allocation to international stocks did not diversify an investment portfolio comprised of domestic stocks and bonds. In fact, a 10 percent allocation to international stocks increased the exposure to downside risk. Also, the number of months with negative returns increased to 44 (a 33.3 percent frequency) for the 55/35/10 U.S. stock/U.S. bond/international stock portfolio from 42 months for our initial 60/40 U.S. stock/U.S. bond portfolio.

[2]Europe, Asia, and the Far East (EAFE) is an international stock index developed and maintained by Morgan Stanley Capital International.

Finally, the addition of international equities to the standard 60/40 stock and bond portfolio resulted in a decline of the expected monthly return down to 0.86 percent, a reduction in average monthly return of 5 basis points, with a commensurate decline in the associated Sharpe ratio. Unfortunately, this is an example where international equity diversification did not provide downside risk protection.

MANAGING DOWNSIDE RISK WITH HEDGE FUNDS

We have described and demonstrated the risk that investors attempt to avoid through diversification. The question we now address is whether hedge funds can help investors manage this risk. There has been some speculation as to whether hedge funds, in fact, can hedge an investment portfolio. (See Asness, Krail, and Liew 2001.)

We use data on hedge funds from Hedge Fund Research Inc. (HFRI), and include several categories of hedge funds in our portfolio mix to determine how each style changed the return distribution for the blended portfolio. We begin with funds of funds (FOF). Using the HFRI FOF index, we construct a portfolio of 55 percent U.S. stocks, 35 percent U.S. treasury bonds, and 10 percent FOF. We build the same frequency distribution as presented in the exhibit and focus on the downside portion of the return distribution.

For hedge FOF, we find that the average downside return was –1.90 percent. This indicates that, on average, the addition of hedge FOF to the standard stock/bond portfolio provided 27 basis points of downside risk protection. The number of downside months was the same at 42. Table 11.2 presents the results of the blended portfolios of 55 percent U.S. stocks, 35 percent U.S. treasury bonds, and 10 percent hedge funds, for each category of hedge fund.

We also consider what trade-off might be necessary to achieve this level of downside protection. It is possible some upside potential was sacrificed to provide the downside protection. In Table 11.1 we saw that the average monthly return to our initial U.S. stock/U.S. treasury bond portfolio was 0.91 percent. In Table 11.2 we see that the average monthly return when hedge fund of funds is added is 0.92 percent. Therefore, no upside return potential was sacrificed to achieve the downside risk protection. Last, the Sharpe ratio increased for the portfolio with hedge FOF.

We can calculate the cumulative performance improvement to the stock/bond/hedge fund of funds portfolio from downside risk protection and upside return enhancement by:

$$(-1.90\% \times 42 \text{ months}) - (-2.07 \times 42 \text{ months}) + [(0.92\% - 0.91\%) \times 132 \text{ months}] = 8.46\%$$

TABLE 11.2 Downside Risk Protection Using Hedge Funds

Portfolio Composition	Expected Return	Standard Deviation	Sharpe Ratio	Average Downside	Number of Downside Months	Cumulative Downside Protection	Cumulative Upside Potential	Cumulative Performance Improvement
60/40 US Stocks/ US Bonds	0.91%	2.60%	0.177	–2.07%	42	N/A	N/A	N/A
55/35/10 Stocks/ Bonds/FOF	0.92%	2.45%	0.191	–1.90%	42	7.14%	1.32%	8.46%
55/35/10 Stocks/ Bonds/Equity L/S	1.00%	2.54%	0.215	–2.03%	40	5.74%	13.88%	19.62%
55/35/10 Stocks/Bonds/ Convertible Arb	0.93%	2.42%	0.197	–1.88%	41	9.86%	3.57%	13.43%
55/35/10 Stocks/Bonds/ Market Neutral	0.92%	2.40%	0.195	–1.83%	42	10.08%	1.32%	11.40%
55/35/10 Stocks/Bonds/ Distressed Debt	0.95%	2.45%	0.204	–1.84%	43	8.25%	4.37%	12.62%
55/35/10 Stocks/Bonds/ Event Driven	0.95%	2.49%	0.201	–1.91%	42	6.72%	5.28%	12.00%
55/35/10 Stocks/Bonds/ Fixed Income Arb	0.90%	2.36%	0.189	–1.86%	41	10.68%	–1.32%	9.36%
55/35/10 Stocks/Bonds/ Global Macro	0.97%	2.51%	0.207	–2.04%	40	5.34%	9.86%	15.20%
55/35/10 Stocks/Bonds/ Market Timing	0.95%	2.50%	0.198	–2.03%	40	5.74%	7.18%	12.92%
55/35/10 Stocks/Bonds/ Merger Arbitrage	0.93%	2.43%	0.196	–1.90%	41	9.04%	3.57%	12.61%
55/35/10 Stocks/Bonds/ Short Selling	0.85%	2.02%	0.198	–1.63%	37	26.63%	–7.92%	18.71%

The cumulative performance improvement of 8.46 percent may be split into two parts, the cumulative return earned from downside risk protection (7.14 percent) and the amount earned from upside return potential (1.32 percent).

Table 11.2 presents several interesting results. In every case, the downside risk was reduced. The cumulative downside protection for each hedge fund strategy is positive. Average monthly downside risk ranged from –1.63 percent for short sellers to –2.04 percent for global macro hedge funds. It is not surprising that global macro hedge funds offered the least in downside protection because these funds tend to take significant market risk the same as stocks and bonds. (See Anson 2000.) Also, it is not surprising that short sellers offered the best downside risk protection because the very nature of this strategy is to profit in months when the stock and bond markets perform poorly.

In every case but two (short sellers and fixed income arbitrage), the average monthly return of the whole return distribution increased when hedge fund strategies were added to the initial stock/bond portfolio. More important, for every hedge fund strategy, the cumulative performance improvement is positive. Also, Sharpe ratios improved uniformly for all hedge fund strategies. Last, in only one strategy, distressed debt, did the number of downside months increase (by one, to 43), but the average downside return was much lower (–1.84 percent) compared to the stock/bond portfolio.

In conclusion, we found that hedge funds uniformly offered downside risk protection, and in many cases, this protection was considerable. Also, in only two cases did this downside risk protection come at the sacrifice of upside return potential (for short sellers and fixed income arbitrage), but the cumulative downside protection received was sufficient to offset the reduction of cumulative return potential. In every other instance, downside risk protection was achieved in combination with *increased* return potential.

Managing Downside Risk with Managed Futures

Managed futures refers to the active trading of futures contracts and forward contracts on physical commodities, financial assets, and currencies. The purpose of the managed futures industry is to enable investors to profit from changes in futures prices. This industry is another skill-based style of investing. Investment managers attempt to use their special knowledge and insight in buying and selling futures and forward contracts to extract a positive return. These futures managers tend to argue that their superior skill is the key ingredient to derive profitable returns from the futures markets.

Within this framework, an asset class distinct from financial assets has the potential to diversify and protect an investment portfolio from hostile markets. It is possible that skill-based strategies such as managed futures investing can provide the diversification that investors seek. Managed futures strategies might provide diversification for a stock and bond portfolio because the returns are dependent on the special skill of the commodity trading advisor (CTA) rather than any macroeconomic policy decisions made by central bankers or government regimes. (See, e.g., McCarthy, Schneeweis, and Spurgin 1996; Schneeweis, Spurgin, and Potter 1997; and Edwards and Park 1996.)

To analyze the impact of managed futures on the distribution of returns in a diversified portfolio, we use the Barclay CTA managed futures indices. There are four actively traded strategies: CTAs that actively trade in agricultural commodity futures, CTAs that actively trade in currency futures, CTAs that actively trade in financial and metal futures, and CTAs that actively trade in energy futures. If managed futures can provide downside protection, we would expect the average monthly downside return to be smaller than that observed for our initial stock/bond portfolio.

Once again, we build a blended portfolio of 55 percent U.S. stocks, 35 percent U.S. treasury bonds, and 10 percent CTA strategy. We then develop a frequency distribution of monthly returns over the period 1990 to 2000. In Table 11.3 we present the results from the return distribution generated by this CTA-blended portfolio for each CTA strategy. For example, for CTA agriculture, the average downside return is −1.81 percent. This is an improvement of 26 basis points over the average downside return observed with the stock/bond portfolio. The number of downside months with CTA agriculture managed futures added to the portfolio increased by one month to 43.

Unfortunately, some upside potential was sacrificed, as the expected monthly return of the investment portfolio declined from 0.91 percent to 0.88 percent when CTA agriculture managed futures are added. Still, even with the decrease in expected return for the portfolio, the reduction in downside risk would have added 5.15 percent of cumulative performance improvement to the portfolio over this time period:

$$[(-1.81\% \times 43 \text{ months}) - (-2.07\% \times 42 \text{ months})] \\ + [(0.88\% - 0.91\%) \times 132 \text{ months}] = 5.15\%$$

Table 11.3 indicates that the 5.15 percent of cumulative performance improvement can be split into 9.11 percent of cumulative downside protection and −3.96 percent of cumulative return potential. The table also presents results for the other CTA managed futures strategies. In every case,

TABLE 11.3 Downside Risk Protection Using Managed Futures

Portfolio Composition	Expected Return	Standard Deviation	Sharpe Ratio	Average Downside	Number of Downside Months	Cumulative Downside Protection	Cumulative Return Potential	Cumulative Performance Improvement
60/40 US Stocks/ US Bonds	0.91%	2.60%	0.177	–2.07%	42	N/A	N/A	N/A
55/35/10 Stocks/Bonds/ CTA Agriculture	0.88%	2.37%	0.182	–1.81%	43	9.11%	–3.96%	5.15%
55/35/10 Stocks/ Bonds/CTA Currency	0.90%	2.39%	0.190	–1.96%	39	10.50%	1.38%	11.88%
55/35/10 Stocks/Bonds/ CTA Financial & Metals	0.89%	2.39%	0.182	–1.95%	40	8.94%	–0.86%	8.08%
55/35/10 Stocks/Bonds/ CTA Energy[a]	0.92%	2.38%	0.197	–1.86%	31	6.24%	–10.80%	–4.56%

[a]The downside protection and cumulative performance improvement for CTA energy is adjusted to reflect data ending in 1998.

downside risk protection is observed. However, with respect to CTA energy managed futures, this downside risk protection came at the expense of significant upside return potential; the cumulative Performance Improvement is –4.56 percent.[3]

These results highlight the concept that managed futures products should not be analyzed on a stand-alone basis. The downside risk protection demonstrated by managed futures products is consistent with the research of Scheeweis, Spurgin, and Potter (1996). Their true value is best achieved in a portfolio context.

MANAGING DOWNSIDE RISK WITH COMMODITY FUTURES

Hedge funds and managed futures fall into the category of skill-based investing. That is, the returns derived from these strategies are dependent on the active skill of the individual hedge fund or managed futures manager. However, downside risk protection may be achieved without active management. To demonstrate, we blend passive commodity futures into the initial stock and bond portfolio.

A commodity futures index represents the total return that would be earned from holding only long positions in an unleveraged basket of commodity futures. Commodity futures indices are constructed to be unleveraged. The face value of the futures contracts are fully supported (collateralized) either by cash or by treasury bills. Futures contracts are purchased to provide economic exposure to commodities equal to the amount of cash dollars invested in the index. Therefore, every dollar of exposure to a commodity futures index represents one dollar of commodity price risk.

We consider four commodity futures indices: the Goldman Sachs Commodity Index (GSCI), the Dow-Jones/AIG Commodity Index (DJ-AIGCI), the Chase Physical Commodity Index (CPCI), and the Mount Lucas Management Index (MLMI).[4] The GSCI, DJ-AIGCI, and the CPCI are unleveraged indices of long-only positions on physical commodities. The MLMI

[3]Data for the CTA energy managed futures index is available only through 1998. Therefore, the data are not strictly comparable to the other managed futures indices, particularly with respect to the number of downside months. However, in Table 11.3, the cumulative downside protection, cumulative return potential, and the cumulative performance improvement have been adjusted to reflect the different time period examined for this trading strategy.

[4]More details regarding these indices can be found in Anson (2001).

differs from the other three indices in that it holds physical, financial, and currency futures; it may invest long or short; and it follows a 12-month trend-following rule.

It is the last difference, the 12-month moving-average rule, that is the most distinguishing feature of the MLMI. The 12-month moving average is designed to provide a mechanical rule to capturing price trends in the futures markets. In this respect, the MLMI represents a good benchmark by which to measure the returns associated with managed futures accounts because it reflects a naive rule for active trading.

We perform the same portfolio construction rule as described in the previous sections. We construct a portfolio that is 55 percent U.S. stocks, 35 percent U.S. treasury bonds, and 10 percent commodity futures index. We then observe the distribution of returns and measure the downside risk of the distribution. Table 11.4 presents the results.

Taking, for example, the MLMI, we observe that the average downside return is –1.88 percent, a considerable improvement over the initial stock/bond portfolio. We also observe that the stock/bond/MLMI portfolio experiences two less months of downside performance (40) than that for the stock/bond portfolio. Also, the expected return declines slightly to 0.90 percent per month. Therefore, the cumulative performance improvement is:

$$[(-1.88\% \times 40 \text{ months}) - (-2.07\% \times 42 \text{ months})] \\ + [(0.90\% - 0.91\%) \times 132 \text{ months}] = 10.42\%$$

The return amount of 10.42 percent may be split between cumulative downside protection of 11.74 percent, and cumulative return potential of –1.32 percent. Similar results are obtained for the other three indices. We note that while the DJ-AIGCI provided downside risk protection, this protection came at the sacrifice of significant upside return potential.[5] The cumulative performance improvement was –5.45 percent.

Last, we compare the MLMI to the CTA strategies presented above. We note that the cumulative performance improvement with respect to the MLMI exceeded that for every CTA strategy. Therefore, a simple trend-following strategy such as that presented in the MLMI may provide better downside protection and upside return potential than active managed futures strategies.

[5]The DJ-AIGCI was available only through 1991 and therefore is not strictly comparable to the other indices, particularly with respect to the number of downside months. In Table 11.3 we adjust the cumulative downside protection, the cumulative return potential, and the cumulative performance improvement for this shorter time period.

TABLE 11.4 Downside Risk Protection Using Passive Commodity Futures Indices

Portfolio Composition	Expected Return	Standard Deviation	Sharpe Ratio	Average Downside	Number of Downside Months	Cumulative Downside Protection	Cumulative Return Potential	Cumulative Performance Improvement
60/40 US Stocks/ US Bonds	0.91%	2.60%	0.177	−2.07%	42	N/A	N/A	N/A
55/35/10 Stocks/ Bonds/GSCI	0.90%	2.39%	0.187	−1.79%	43	9.97%	−1.32%	8.65%
55/35/10 Stocks/ Bonds/CPCI	0.91%	2.38%	0.192	−1.86%	41	10.68%	0.09%	10.68%
55/35/10 Stocks/ Bonds/MLMI	0.90%	2.33%	0.191	−1.88%	40	11.74%	−1.32%	10.42%
55/35/10 Stocks/ Bonds/DJ-AIGCI[a]	0.92%	2.30%	0.205	−1.81%	37	4.09%	−9.54%	−5.45%

[a]The downside protection and cumulative performance improvement for the DJ-AIGCI is adjusted to reflect data beginning in 1991.

CONCLUSION

We examined the downside return protection offered by international stocks, hedge funds, managed futures, and commodity futures. We found that hedge funds, managed futures, and commodity futures all offer downside protection to a traditional stock and bond portfolio. In most cases, this protection accumulated to several percentage points over the time period 1990 to 2000. We did not, however, find any downside risk protection offered by international stocks. International stocks were poor portfolio diversifiers during the observed period.

PART Three

Managed Futures Investing, Fees, and Regulation

Chapter 12 focuses on managed futures. As one of many different trading strategies in the alternative investment universe, managed futures investing involves speculative investments in gold, oil, and other commodities that change in value in accordance with price fluctuations. Managed futures improve portfolio performance because they typically have zero correlation to traditional markets. The chapter also addresses various styles of CTAs, classifying them as discretionary, trend followers, and systematic. However, these categories tend to overlap. As investors become increasingly educated about the universe of alternative investments and, in particular, managed futures, CTAs will continue to grow in popularity.

Chapter 13 empirically investigates the effect of incentive compensation contracts of commodity trading advisors on their performance. The analysis, an extension of Golec (1993), examines the effects of incentive compensation contracts on the risk and return of commodity trading advisors. The results of cross-sectional regression models shed light on how the management and incentive fees of CTAs are related both to the returns CTAs generate, and to the volatility in those returns.

Chapter 14 examines the Australian regulatory model for managed futures funds and other fiduciary investment products whose returns are derived from the trading of futures products. All fiduciary investment products are regulated in the same manner in Australia, under a combination of the managed investment scheme and financial product provisions of the Australian corporations legislation. This chapter considers the difficulties of applying this model to the diverse range of fiduciary futures products and discusses recent proposals to reform the regulation of individually managed futures accounts.

CHAPTER 12

Managed Futures Investing

James Hedges IV

Managed futures investing is increasing in popularity as investors look for ways to profit in a volatile environment. Managed futures involves speculative investments in gold, oil, and other commodities that change in value in accordance with price fluctuations and improves portfolio performance because they typically have zero correlation to traditional markets. The analysis investigates how commodity trading advisors use global futures and options markets as an investment medium.

INTRODUCTION

As global investors continue to seek ways to diversify their portfolios, an increasingly popular approach is managed futures investing, which constitutes one of the many different trading strategies in the alternative investment universe. Simply defined, managed futures investing involves speculative investments in gold, oil, and other commodities that change in value in accordance with price fluctuations. There is approximately $40 billion invested in managed futures today, a number that has expanded tremendously over the last 20 years. Managed futures had net inflows of $2.10 billion during the first quarter of 2003, reports Bloomberg (see Figure 12.1). This growth is largely attributable to demand from institutional investors such as pensions, endowments, and banks, but lower minimum investment levels are also attracting more high-net-worth investors than ever.

Managed futures had a banner year in 2002, with an approximate 20 percent surge in performance (see Figure 12.2). Part of the allure of managed futures are their ability to profit in a volatile environment. Indeed, today's economic conditions, war-related concerns, global instability, and regulatory environment set the stage for them to prosper.

A 25-year study recently conducted by Goldman Sachs (2003) concluded that a 10 percent allocation of a securities portfolio to managed

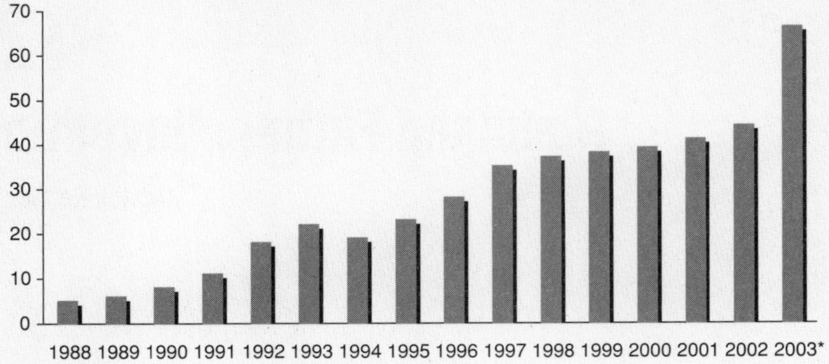

FIGURE 12.1 Growth of Managed Futures, 1988–2002
Source: Barclay Trading Group, Ltd. "Money Under Management in Managed Futures," www.barclaygrp.com.

*First quarter 2003.

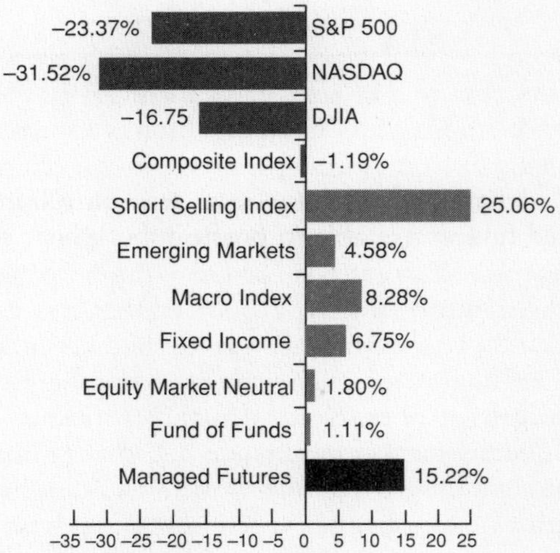

FIGURE 12.2 Performance Comparison 2002
Source: Equities: International Traders Research (ITR), an affiliate of Altegris Investments; Hedge Funds; Hedge Fund Research, Inc. © HFR, Inc. [15 January 2003], www.hfr.com; Managed Futures; ITR Premier 40 CTA Index.

Note: Stocks offer substantially greater liquidity and transparency than the alternative investment products noted and may be less costly to purchase.

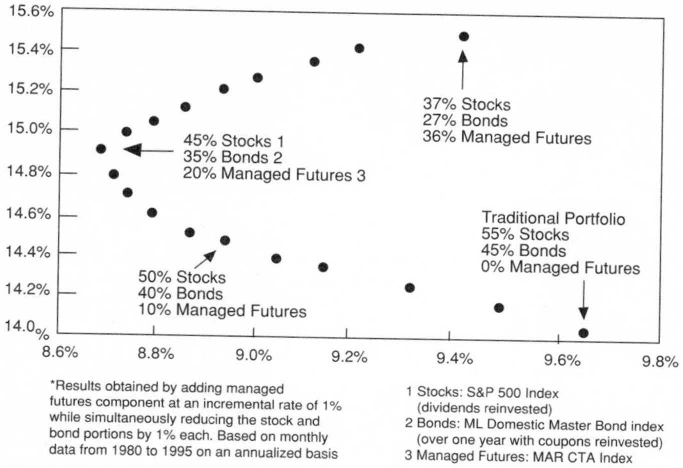

FIGURE 12.3 Impact of Incremental Additions of Managed Futures to the Traditional Portfolio
Source: www.marhedge.com.

futures (commodities) helps investors to vastly improve performance. A similar study conducted by the Chicago Board of Trade (2002) concurred, stating that "portfolios with as much as 20 percent of assets in managed futures yielded up to 50 percent more than a portfolio of stocks and bonds alone."

One feature of managed futures that enables them to improve portfolio performance is that they typically have zero correlation to traditional markets. Managed futures are able to profit in both bear and bull markets, and consistently demonstrate their ability to capitalize on price movements to the benefit of investors. However, it is important to realize that as a speculative investment strategy, managed futures investing is best pursued over the long term. The strategy's cyclical nature means that it should not be relied on as a short-term investment strategy. Indeed, most experts recommend a minimum three-year investment.

As is the case with any investment strategy, investors must evaluate both qualitative and quantitative factors before determining whether to allocate capital to managed futures. Such factors include, but are not limited to, investment time horizon, level of risk aversion, level of diversification of existing portfolio, and intended market exposures (see Figure 12.3).

Advantages of managed futures investing include: low to negative correlation to equities and other hedge funds; negative correlation to equities and hedge funds during periods of poor performance; diversified opportunities, in both markets and manager styles; substantial market liquidity;

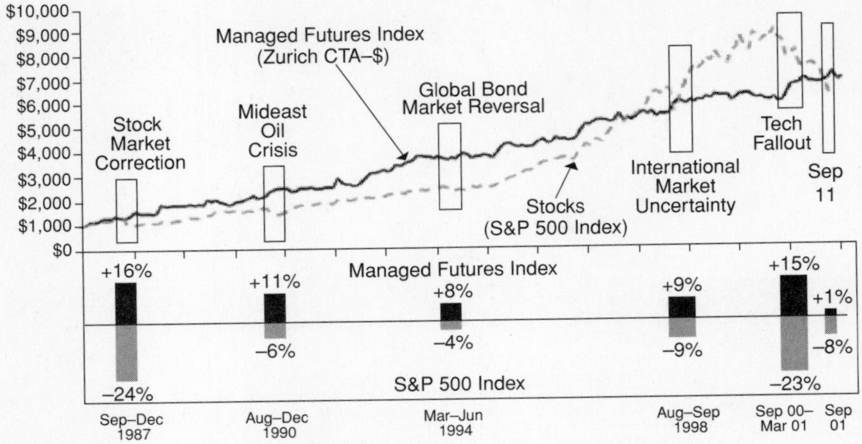

FIGURE 12.4 Low Correlation to Traditional Investments, January 1987–December 2001
Source: www.smithbarney.com.

transparency of positions and profits/losses; and multilayer level of regulatory oversight. The strategy's disadvantages may include a high degree of volatility, high fees, and the high level of advisor attention required (see Figure 12.4).

Commodity trading advisors (CTAs) who use global futures and options markets as an investment medium note that managed futures investing differs from hedge fund and mutual fund investing in a number of fundamental ways, including transparency, liquidity, regulatory oversight, and the use of exchanges. These underlying distinctions provide support for adding managed futures investments to a portfolio that includes both traditional and alternative investments.

Because futures contracts are, by definition, traded on organized exchanges across the globe, the bid and offer prices on specific contracts are publicly quoted. Consequently, investors can ascertain the current value and calculate the gain or loss on outstanding positions with relative ease. Additionally, open interest, which is the number of contracts that are currently outstanding on a particular asset, are quoted too. In contrast, hedge funds often engage in transactions involving esoteric over-the-counter (OTC) derivatives, whose market values may not be readily available. This can potentially inhibit managers' ability to monitor their positions effectively (see Figure 12.5).

Again, the exchange-based nature of futures contracts plays a significant role. Positions can be entered into and exited continuously, regardless

Financial Markets

Interest Rates	Currencies	Stock Indices
The Americas	Major	U.S.
Europe	Minor	Europe
Asia	Exotic	Asia

Commodity Markets

Agriculture	Metals	Energy
Grains	Precious	Crude Oil
Livestock	Base	Gasoline
Coffee, Sugar, Etc.		Heating Oil

FIGURE 12.5 Investment Opportunities of Managed Futures Programs

of size. This fact becomes critical when a CTA believes that a large position needs to be liquidated to avoid huge losses. A hedge fund may have significant positions in a particular type of instrument that it wishes to unload due to adverse market conditions, but the illiquidity of that particular market may inhibit it from doing so. Liquidity allows CTAs to reduce and/or eliminate significant positions during periods of sharp declines.

Mutual funds offer investors many of the same benefits as managed futures, such as diversification, daily liquidity, and professional management, yet they lack the potential to profit in bear markets (see Table 12.1).

TABLE 12.1 Mutual Funds versus Managed Futures

Mutual Funds	Managed Futures
Diversification	Diversification
Professional Management	Professional Management
Highly Regulated: SEC & States	Highly Regulated: CFTC & NFA
Liquidity: Daily	Liquidity: Daily
Potential Profit in Bull Markets: Yes	Potential Profit in Bull Markets: Yes
Potential Profit in Bear Markets: No	Potential Profit in Bear Markets: Yes

Source: www.usafutures.com

REGULATORY ISSUES

The Commodity Futures Trading Commission (CFTC) was created by Congress in 1974 as an independent agency with the mandate to regulate commodity futures and option markets in the United States. The agency protects market participants against manipulation, abusive trade practices, and fraud. Essentially, the CFTC is the Securities and Exchange Commission equivalent of the traditional securities markets. The commission performs three primary functions: (1) contract review, (2) market surveillance, and (3) regulation of futures professionals.

To ensure the financial and market integrity of U.S. futures markets, the CFTC reviews the terms and conditions of proposed futures and option contracts. Before an exchange is permitted to trade futures and options contracts in a specific commodity, it must demonstrate that the contract reflects the normal market flow and commercial trading practices in the actual commodity. The commission conducts daily market surveillance and can, in an emergency, order an exchange to take specific action or to restore order in any futures contract that is being traded.

CTAs must be registered with the CFTC, file detailed disclosure documents, and be members of the National Futures Association (NFA), a self-regulatory organization approved by the commission. The CFTC also seeks to protect customers by requiring registrants to disclose market risks and past performance information to prospective customers, by requiring that customer funds be kept in accounts separate from those maintained by the firm for its own use, and by requiring customer accounts to be adjusted to reflect the current market value at the close of trading each day (marked to market). In addition, the CFTC monitors registrant supervision systems, internal controls, and sales practice compliance programs. Last, all registrants are required to complete ethics training.

Additionally, the NFA serves to protect the public investor by maintaining the integrity of the marketplace. The association screens all firms and individuals wishing to conduct business with the investing public. It develops a wide range of investor protection rules and monitors all of its members for compliance. The NFA also provides investors with a fast, efficient method for settling disputes when they occur.

Member exchanges provide an additional layer of investor protection. Exchange rules cover trade clearance, trade orders and records, position and price limits, disciplinary actions, floor trading practices, and standards of business conduct. Although an exchange primarily operates autonomously, the CFTC must approve any rule additions or amendments. Exchanges also are regularly audited by the CFTC to verify that their compliance programs are operating effectively.

During 2002, the CFTC continued to pursue regulatory reform in accordance with the Commodity Futures Modernization Act, including a hard look at derivatives clearing organizations, rules governing margins for security futures, and dual trading by floor brokers. The agency also embarked on a massive review of energy trading in the wake of the 2001 Enron scandal and has been acknowledged publicly due only to widespread public interest. In addition, fraud related to unregistered commodity pool operators (CPOs) and CTAs, as well as Ponzi schemes, tops the CFTC's list of issues. A comprehensive risk management assessment is also an agency focus.

To further protect investors, the provisions of the 2001 U.S.A. Patriot Act now require certain registered CTAs to establish anti–money laundering provisions.

HEDGERS VERSUS SPECULATORS

Individuals or entities that transact in futures markets historically have been described as one of two types: *hedgers* or *speculators*. Hedgers use futures contracts to protect against price movements in an underlying asset that they either buy or sell in the ordinary course of business. For example, farmers who rely on one crop for all of their revenue cannot afford a sharp decline in the price of the crop before it is sold. Therefore, they would sell a futures contract that specifies the amount, grade, price, and date of delivery of the crop. This agreement effectively reduces the risk that the price of the crop will decline before it is harvested and sold. Speculators, however, have no intention of physical settlement of the underlying asset. Rather, they simply are seeking short-term gains from the expected fluctuation in futures prices. Most futures trading activity is, in fact, conducted by speculators, who use futures markets (as opposed to transacting directly in the commodity) because it allows them to take a significant position with reasonably low transaction costs and a high amount of leverage.

Managed futures investors attempt to profit from sharp price movements. However, the main distinction is that a speculator trades directly while the managed futures investor employs a CTA to trade on his or her behalf. Managed futures investors can take the form of private commodity pools, public commodity funds, and, most recently, hedge funds. Although hedge funds that engage in futures trading are considered to be managed futures investors, they differ from private pools and public funds in that futures are not the core of their strategy, but rather are a single component of a synthesis of instruments.

Managed futures portfolios can be structured either for a single investor or for a group of investors. Portfolios that cater to a single investor are known as individually managed accounts. Typically these accounts are structured for institutions and high-net-worth individuals. As mentioned, managed futures portfolios that are structured for a group of investors are referred to as either private commodity pools or public commodity funds. Public funds, often run by leading brokerage firms, are offered to retail clients and often carry lower investment minimums combined with higher fees. Private pools are the more popular structure for group investors and, like individually managed accounts, attract institutional and high-net-worth capital. Private pools in the United States tend to be structured as limited partnerships where the general partner is a CPO and serves as the sponsor/salesperson for the fund. In addition to selecting the CTA(s) to actively manage the portfolio, the CPO is responsible for monitoring their performance and determining compliance with the pool's policy statement.

CTAs typically rely on either *technical* or *fundamental* analysis, or a combination of both, for their trading decisions. Technical analysis is derived from the theory that a historical study of the markets themselves can reveal valuable information that can be used to predict future commodity prices. Such information includes actual daily, weekly, and monthly price fluctuations, volume variations, and changes in open interest. Technical traders often utilize charts and sophisticated computer models in their analyses.

In contrast, fundamental analysis relies on the study of external factors that affect the supply and demand of a particular commodity to predict future prices. Such factors include the nature of the economy, governmental policies, domestic and foreign political events, and the weather. Fundamental analysis is predicated on the notion that, over time, the price (actual value) of a futures contract must reflect the value of the underlying commodity (perceived value) and, further, that the value of the underlying commodity is based on these external variables. The fundamental trader profits from the convergence of perceived value and actual value.

Methodologies employed by CTAs fall into three general classifications: *discretionary, trend followers,* and *systematic*. However, as will be illustrated, these categories tend to overlap. Discretionary advisors, in their purest form, rely on fundamental research and analytics to determine trade executions. For example, a fundamental advisor may come to understand that severe weather conditions have reduced the estimate for the supply of wheat this season. Basic rules of supply and demand dictate that the price of wheat (and, hence, wheat futures) should rise in this circumstance. Whereas the systematic trader would wait until these fundamental data are reflected in the futures price before trading, the pure discretionary advisor immediately trades on this information.

Few advisors are purely discretionary; rather, almost all of them rely on systems to some extent. There is simply too much information that diversified advisors must digest in order to make sound trading decisions. For example, a discretionary advisor may use automated information to spot trends and judgment to determine position size. Another possibility is that after deciding to make a trade based on fundamental research, a discretionary advisor may analyze technical data to confirm opinions and determine entry and exit points. The main distinction between discretionary and systematic advisors is that discretionary advisors do not rely primarily on a computerized model to execute trades.

The main argument against discretionary advisors is that they incorporate emotion into their trades. Like other investment strategies, managed futures investing is only as successful as the discipline of the manager to adhere to its requirements in the face of market adversity. Given the extreme volatility often found in managed futures trading, discretionary traders may subject their decisions to behavioral biases. Another argument is that the heavy reliance on individual knowledge and focus creates a serious investment risk. The ability of the advisor to avoid ancillary distractions becomes paramount when the CTA uses discretionary tactics.

Systematic advisors lie at the opposite extreme. These advisors use sophisticated computerized models, often referred to as black boxes, that typically include neural nets or complex algorithms to dictate trading activity. Advisors differ in what factors they use as inputs into their models and how their models interpret given factors. Some systematic advisors design systems that analyze historical price relationships, probability measures, or statistical data to identify trading opportunities; however, the majority rely to some extent on trend following.

For a trade entry signal, systematic advisors rely on technical data such as price patterns, current price relative to historical price, price volatility, volume, and open interest. Profitable positions may be closed out based on one of these signals, if a trend reversal is identified, or the end of a trend is signaled based on an overbought/oversold situation. Some systematic advisors use a single system approach. However, others employ multiple systems that can operate either in tandem or in mutual exclusivity. An example of a multisystem approach operating in tandem is when one system generates a buy signal and the other system indicates a flat or sell signal. The result will be no trade because both systems are not in agreement. Systems that operate independently would each execute a trade based on the respective signal. The main advantage of a multisystem approach is diversification of signals.

Although systematic trading effectively removes the emotional element from trade execution, the use of a systematic methodology does not imply that there is a human disconnect. On the contrary, the systems typically are developed and monitored by humans with extensive trading experience. In addition, although specific market entry and exit points usually are determined by the system, human discretion often is included in decisions such as portfolio weightings, position size, entry into new markets, stop losses, margin/equity ratios, and selection of contract months.

The final classification of methodologies is trend following, which is a trading method that seeks to establish and maintain market positions based on the emergence of major price trends through an analysis of market price movement and other statistical analyses. This technique is consistent with the underlying concept of managed futures investing, according to which prices move from equilibrium to a transitory stage and back to equilibrium. Trend followers attempt to capture this divergence of prices through the detection of various signals. Although trend followers may either employ computerized systems or rely on human judgment to identify trends, they typically choose the former. As a result, trend followers often are classified in the general category of systematic advisors.

One common misconception about trend followers is that they attempt to time the market perfectly—that is, entering and exiting markets at the most favorable prices. On the contrary, trend followers are reactionary—they do not attempt to predict a trend; rather, they *respond* to an existing trend. Generally, they seek to close out losing positions quickly and hold profitable positions as long as the market trend is perceived to exist. Consequently, the number of losing contracts may vastly exceed the number of profitable contracts; however, the gains on the favorable positions are expected to more than offset the losses on losing contracts.

RISK MANAGEMENT

CTAs manage risk in three fundamental ways: (1) through diversification, (2) the use of stop losses, and (3) the use of leverage.

Diversification

As mentioned, CTAs can diversify in a number of ways, such as trading different markets or employing different strategies or systems. These systems often determine and limit the equity committed to each trade, each market, and each account. For example, the risk management system of one CTA attempts to limit risk exposure to any one commodity to 1 percent of the total portfolio and to any one commodity group to 3 percent of the total portfolio.

Stop Losses

Unprofitable positions often are closed out through the use of stop losses, where every position in a program has a price barrier associated with it that, if hit, will result in executing orders to close out the positions. Stop losses are designed to limit the downside risk on any given position. They can be based on price stops, time stops, volatility stops, and the like.

Leverage

The easiest way to think of leverage is as the ratio of face market value of all the investments in the portfolio to the equity in the account. One common misconception is that leverage is bad; an example of a good use of leverage is to lever markets with less movement to match volatilities across a portfolio. In other words, the manager is equalizing risk across the opportunities within that portfolio. The amount of leverage then will change over time based on ongoing research, program volatility, current market volatility, risk exposure, or manager discretion. For example, during periods of high volatility, managers often reduce the amount of leverage because the total number of contracts needed to satisfy the position has been reduced. Another example is that managers often decrease leverage during periods of declining profits to preserve capital and limit losses. There is no "standard" amount of leverage; however, in general, CTAs use leverage as a multiple of between three and six times capital.

TIMING CONSIDERATIONS

Regardless of the chosen methodology, managed futures investments can be short, medium (intermediate), or long term. Short-term trades typically last between three to five days, but can be as short as intraday or as long as one month. Intermediate trades, on average, last 12 weeks while long-term trades typically exceed 9 months.

Managers focusing on short-term trades try to capture rapid moves and are out of the market more than their intermediate and long-term counterparts. Because these managers base their activity on swift fluctuation in prices, their returns tend to be noncorrelated to long-term or general advisors or to each other. In addition, they are more sensitive to transaction costs and heavily rely on liquidity and high volatility for returns. Strong trending periods, which often exceed the short-term time frame, tend to hamper the returns of these advisors and favor those with a longer time horizon.

When analyzing potential alternative investment opportunities, it is important not only to review past performance returns and variability of returns, but also to carefully analyze the degree of correlation of a particular strategy with other types of traditional and alternative investments. Managed futures investments are low to negatively correlated with fixed income and equity asset classes, as well as other hedge fund strategies. This fact provides support for managed futures as a diversification vehicle. Further, recent research conducted by Schneeweis, Spurgin, and Potter (1996) provides evidence that managed futures offer downside protection as a result of their negative correlation with equities and other hedge funds when those investments experience poor performance.

Similar to equity portfolios, multimanaged CTA portfolios benefit from increased diversification. Investors seeking to gain from the benefits of managed futures can lower their portfolio risk by investing in a diversified portfolio of managed futures advisors. Of course, the number of managers to include in a particular portfolio depends on the current diversification of that portfolio (i.e., current allocation to stocks and bonds), as well as the percentage of capital that the investor is willing to commit to managed futures. For example, an investor seeking to commit 30 percent of a diversified portfolio to managed futures would want to employ more managers than an investor looking only for 5 percent exposure. These same investors then would want to analyze their current portfolio weightings of traditional and alternative investments before determining how many managers will be allocated capital. Given that there are different styles (i.e., discretionary and systematic) as well as diversified futures markets (i.e., commodities, financials, and currencies), diversification can be accomplished with relative ease. Note, however, that there tends to be a high degree of correlation between trend-following managers. Although these managers may be utilizing completely different techniques to make trading decisions, they are still essentially relying on a common source of value to make profits.

The evidence supporting managed futures and other alternative investment strategies should not be surprising. Investors who have historically been long only in equity and fixed income markets have experienced periods of positive performance and periods of negative performance. The ability to take long or short positions in futures markets creates the potential to profit whether markets are rising or falling. Due to the wide array of noncorrelated markets available for futures investing, there can be a bull market in one area and a bear market in another. For example, U.S. soybean prices may be rising while the Japanese yen is falling. Both of these occurrences offer the potential to gain.

Like any investment strategy, managed futures present some shortcomings. It is important to illuminate some of these weaknesses to ensure that investors can make educated decisions based on as much complete information as possible.

First, as a stand-alone investment, managed futures tend to be highly volatile, producing uneven cash flows to the investor. This is because annual returns are heavily generated by sharp, sudden movements in futures prices. Because the nature of this strategy is primarily based on such movements, returns undoubtedly will continue to be volatile. However, managed futures typically are not chosen as a stand-alone investment. Rather, they are selected as a single component of a diversified portfolio. Due to their historically low correlation with other alternative investments, their volatility actually can reduce the overall risk of the portfolio.

Investors also have voiced negative sentiment regarding the lack of advisor attention to the customized fit of managed futures into their portfolio. Due to the many different styles and markets of managed futures investing, clients certainly can benefit from specialized attention. In this light, consulting services can be truly beneficial to a client's portfolio. Consultants can offer their clients a careful explanation of CTA investment objectives, and comfort that careful due diligence of CTAs has been performed. As CTA performance varies greatly, these services can be of paramount importance.

CONCLUSION

Overall, investors are becoming increasingly educated about the universe of alternative investments and, in particular, managed futures. As more sophisticated investors become aware of the noncorrelated nature of managed futures to hedge funds and equities, asset growth into this category is expected to continue. Institutional participation will increase as a result of the increased use of insurance products and investable indices. Increased use of equity trading may become prevalent, as the performance of managed futures still lags the S&P 500. Overall, increased globalization should result in more opportunities for managed futures investors. To succeed, many advisors may have to make some important changes to their organization, such as increasing staff size, enhancing coordination, improving communication, and employing greater technology.

CHAPTER 13

The Effect of Management and Incentive Fees on the Performance of CTAs: A Note

Fernando Diz

This chapter examines the effect of management and incentive fees on the performance and volatility of CTA track records. Evidence of a structural change in incentive compensation is presented that points to a larger reliance on incentive fees as opposed to management fees. Management fees have no relationship to performance. No systematic performance or volatility penalty is suffered by investors by this type of compensation. Incentive fees are found to be positively related to both net of fees returns and volatility. An increase in the incentive fee parameter from 10 percent to 20 percent will increase performance by an average of 6.58 percent per year. The performance increase is net of the effects of leverage and other variables affecting performance. There is also a small tendency for CTAs with larger amounts of assets under management to have slightly better performance.

INTRODUCTION

This chapter empirically examines the effect of incentive compensation contracts of commodity trading advisors (CTAs) on their performance. The analysis is an extension of Golec (1993) and examines the effects of incentive compensation contracts on the risk and return of CTAs. The contribution of this chapter is twofold. In Golec, the sample used was too small to

---

Partial support for the completion of this study was provided by a grant from the Foundation for Managed Derivatives Research. The author wishes to thank the Foundation for its support, and Sol Waksman for his invaluable comments.

draw reliable inferences about the effect of incentive compensation on the risk and return of CTAs. Current events in the money management world associated with manager compensation abuses have heightened the importance of measuring the effects of compensation more accurately. A much larger database than the one used in Golec allows us to measure these effects with less error. The advantages of using a larger database are even more important in view of the structural changes in the composition of total compensation in managed futures, as documented by Diz and Shukla (2003). In addition, this study measures the effects of management and incentive fees on the risk and returns of CTAs more accurately by controlling for known effects that other very important variables have on these measures of performance (see Diz 2003).

CTA COMPENSATION STRUCTURE

CTA compensation contracts generally contain two types of fees: a management fee, k_m, which represents a fixed percentage of end-of-period assets under management, and an incentive fee, k_i, which represents a fixed percentage of investment gains over a year period.

The CTA total fee income for period t can be written as:

$$\Phi_t = k_m A_t + \begin{cases} k_i(A_t - A_{t-1}) & \text{if } R_{pt} > 0, \\ 0 & \text{if } R_{pt} \le 0, \end{cases}$$

or (13.1)

$$\Phi_t = kmA_t + k_i \max[0, A_t - A_{t-1}]$$

where A_{t-1} and A_t = dollar value of assets under management at the end of periods $t - 1$ and t respectively.

Defining R_{pt} as the CTA's portfolio rate of return for one period ($t - 1$ to t), we can redefine A_t as $A_{t-1}(1 + R_{pt})$. We can then rewrite the total compensation equation as:

$$\Phi_t = kmA_{t-1}(1 + R_{pt}) + k_i \max[0, A_{t-1}R_{pt}] \tag{13.2}$$

Equation 13.2 shows the dependence of CTA total compensation on the level of assets under management (A_{t-1}), the one period performance (R_{pt}), the management fee (k_m), and the incentive fee (k_i). Base compensation is a linear function of the level of assets under management. Incentive compensation is a nonlinear function of performance. Table 13.1 contains summary statistics for the variables included in equations 13.1 and 13.2. The median management and incentive fees for a sample of 974 CTAs over

TABLE 13.1 Summary Statistics for CTA Management and Incentive Fees, Assets Under Management[a] Variables, and Returns

Variable	Mean	Std. Dev.	Median	Q(1)	Q(3)	Min	Max
Management fee (%)	2.46	0.013	2.00	2.00	3.00	0.00	6.00
Incentive fee (%)	20.27	0.044	20.00	20.00	20.00	0.00	50.00
Assets (Millions$)	34.68	186.950	1.80	0.50	10.52	0.10	2,954.00
Monthly return[b](%)	0.99	0.013	0.94	0.38	1.50	–5.23	10.00

[a]Assets under management can and often do include notional assets
[b]Reported returns are net of management and incentive fees.

this study sample period (1974 to 1998) were 2 percent and 20 percent respectively.

Although the management and incentive fees presented in Table 13.1 appear high when compared to mutual funds (e.g., Golec 1993), average monthly returns appear higher than what one finds for mutual funds for the same time period. This is especially telling if one considers that CTA reported performance figures are net of all fees. To date, no study has accurately accounted for all fee-adjusted performance of mutual funds when comparing them to fee-adjusted performance in the managed futures industry. Further, it is a known fact that mutual fund fees have continued to increase and that this increase has not translated into higher returns for individual investors. It is generally acknowledged that higher fees in the mutual fund industry have reduced returns to investors (Trzcinka 1998). Management fees in the managed futures industry have followed a downward trend from an average high of 2.81 percent in 1982 to an average low of 1.85 percent in 2002. More of CTA compensation in 2002 came in the form of incentive fees (Diz and Shukla 2003). The results in Table 13.2 highlight the change in the total compensation structure for CTAs. Almost 50 percent of total CTA compensation came from management fees in 1982 while in 2002 only 35 percent of total CTA compensation came from these asset-based fees. Two-thirds of CTA compensation came from performance based fees in 2002. Golec's study used CTA data from 1982 to 1987. The structural change that is evident in the 1990s is a third reason for reviewing Golec's (1993) findings.

Because the purpose of this study is not to explore the theory of compensation contracting, we refer the reader to Golec (1993) for such a review.

TABLE 13.2 Evolution of Management, Incentive Fees, and Total Compensation in the Managed Futures Industry, 1982–2002

N	Year	Average Management Fee[a]	Average Incentive Fee[a]	MF as % of Fee Revenue	IF as % of Fee Revenue
49	1982	2.81	17.14	49	51
71	1983	2.72	17.36	48	52
105	1984	2.83	17.70	48	52
158	1985	2.82	17.46	49	51
202	1986	2.72	17.31	48	52
262	1987	2.73	17.46	48	52
309	1988	2.77	18.09	47	53
357	1989	2.79	19.17	46	54
417	1990	2.71	19.31	45	55
473	1991	2.69	19.68	45	55
562	1992	2.52	19.60	43	57
622	1993	2.40	19.78	42	58
626	1994	2.36	19.83	41	59
582	1995	2.14	20.03	39	61
582	1996	2.15	20.03	39	61
562	1997	2.12	19.99	38	62
536	1998	2.06	20.13	38	62
515	1999	1.98	20.10	37	63
487	2000	1.92	20.21	36	64
459	2001	1.90	20.31	35	65
96	2002	1.85	20.48	35	65

[a]Management and incentive fees are reported fees. Actual average fees are likely to be lower since these are subject to negotiation.
Source: Diz and Shukla (2003).

What is clear from equation 13.2 is that total CTA compensation is a function of performance (R_{pt}), the level of assets under management (A_t), and the management and incentive fee rates (k_m and k_i).

DATA

The data used in this chapter consist of individual CTA monthly returns provided by the Barclay Trading Group. The database contains records for 1,253 CTAs and includes both programs that were still listed as of February 1998 as well programs that were delisted anytime from 1975 to January 1998. Of the total 1,253 programs, 798 had been delisted by February 1998. Only 455 programs were listed as of February 1998. Of the 1,253 programs, only 989 (80 percent) reported margin to equity ratios.

Fifteen programs were eliminated from the sample for various reasons ranging from missing observations to duplication. This left us with a sample of 974 programs. Golec's sample includes only 80 CTAs. The time spanned by the two samples is also worth noting. Our sample spans a period of 24 years starting in 1975 and ending in 1998. Golec's sample spans only a five-year period from May 1982 to December 1986. Summary statistics were calculated for each CTA in the sample. Table 13.3 provides a summary of the averages for these statistics.

The average length of a CTA track record for the sample is about 5.5 years. The longest track record is 23 years and the shortest only 5 months. The average monthly rate of return for the combined CTAs was 1.31 percent and the annual standard deviation of returns for the cross section of CTAs was 26.24 percent. These results are consistent with Brorsen (1998) for his combined CTA sample. Golec's study reports a monthly average rate of return of 1.35 percent with an annual standard deviation of 11.56 percent. The sample used in this chapter is more similar in size, composition, and performance to Brorsen's.

The average management fee for the sample is 2.46 percent while the same average is 3.96 percent in Golec's sample. More strikingly, the median management fee for this study's is 2.00 percent while it is 4.00 percent in Golec's sample. The average incentive fee for the sample in this study is 20.27 percent while the same average is 16.33 percent in Golec's sample. The median incentive fee for this study's sample is 20.00 percent and only 15.00 percent in Golec's sample. Finally, the average assets under management in this study were $34.68 million compared to $5.01 million in

TABLE 13.3 Summary of CTA Average Attributes, February 1974–February 1998, 974 CTA Programs

Attribute	Mean	Std. Error	Min	Max
Months listed	65.14	45.91	5.00	278.00
Average monthly return (%)	1.31	1.34	–3.14	13.47
Margin to equity ratio (%)	19.40	10.58	1.03	100.00
Annual compounded rate of return (%)	12.75	15.14	–47.51	139.00
Annual standard deviation (%)	26.24	18.41	0.79	142.89
Maximum drawdown	–0.27	0.18	–0.99	0.10
Management fee (%)	2.46	1.31	0.00	6.00
Incentive fee (%)	20.27	4.45	0.00	50.00
Assets (Millions $)	34.68	186.95	0.10	2,954.00

Golec's sample. The median amount of assets under management for this sample was \$1.8 million versus \$1.5 million for Golec's sample.

It is clear from the data that the sample is our study is broader in coverage, size, composition, performance variability, and time span than Golec's. As such, it is perhaps more suitable to accurately measure the effects of compensation structure on CTA performance.

CTA COMPENSATION PARAMETERS AND PERFORMANCE

In this section we empirically explore the relationship between CTA returns and the standard deviation of returns to their compensation parameters by replicating Golec's (1993) analysis. We examined the issue by fitting two ordinary least squares (OLS) cross-sectional regressions on the means and standard deviations of returns of the CTAs on their fee parameters as follows:

$$AROR_j = \beta_0 + \beta_1 k_m + \beta_2 k_i + \beta_3 \ln(A_{t-1}) + e_j \tag{13.3}$$

$$\sigma_j = \alpha_0 + \alpha_1 k_m + \alpha_2 k_i + \alpha_3 \ln(A_{t-1}) + u_j \tag{13.4}$$

where $AROR_j$ = annual compounded rate of return for CTA_j
σ_j = annual standard deviation of CTA_j returns
e_j, u_j = error terms.

Because the distribution of assets under management is clearly skewed, we use the natural logarithm of assets under management as the "size" variable. Significance tests use White's (see Greene 2000) heteroskedasticity consistent standard errors. Table 13.4 presents OLS estimates of regression

TABLE 13.4 Estimation of the Relationship between Compensation Parameters and CTA Mean Annual Compounded Returns and Standard Deviation of Returns

		Independent Variables		
Dependent Variables	Intercept	k_m	k_i	$ln(A_{t-1})$
Mean Annual Returns	–0.255*	0.580	0.693*	0.016*
	(0.075)	(0.583)	(0.259)	(0.003)
Standard Deviation	0.229*	1.424*	0.654*	–0.009*
	(0.057)	(0.482)	(0.156)	(0.003)

*Significant at the 1 percent level under $H_0 = 0$.

coefficients from equations 13.3 and 13.4, along with white standard errors in parentheses.

The results in Table 13.4 show that cross-sectional variation in mean returns is not related to management fees. This result is in agreement with Golec (1993), and it is good news for investors as it suggests that there are no systematic abuses in management fees that penalize performance. The cross-sectional variation in mean returns also is shown to be positively associated with the incentive fee parameter. This is also in agreement with Golec's results, and it is also good news for investors because greater incentive fee parameters lead to greater CTA effort or ability that in turn leads to higher performance. If the incentive fee parameter k_i were to increase from 10 percent to 20 percent, performance should be expected to increase by 5.8 percent. The magnitude of the increase is roughly half of what was found in Golec and seems like a much more reasonable number. A 10 percent increase in Golec's study would have accounted for a 1 percent per month increase in performance or more than 12 percent per year, a very large number. It is important to highlight that the performance increase is net of all fees. Other things being equal, a CTA with higher incentive fees is likely to deliver larger performance after fees.

We find the amount of assets under management to have a positive effect on performance while Golec (1993) finds the opposite result. Our finding is likely to reflect a known fact in the industry that successful CTAs tend to capture the bulk of assets under management. The amount of assets under management tends to reflect performance. The newly created Barclay BTOP50 Index for managed futures is only a reflection of this known fact. The increase in performance associated with assets under management is not spectacular. An increase in assets under management from $100,000 to $3 billion is associated with a 16-basis-point increase in performance. Although the effect appears to be statistically different from zero, its economic importance is very small. A similar increase in assets under management is associated with a decrease in performance of 71 basis points in Golec. Figure 13.1 illustrates the annual increases/decreases in performance as a function of assets under management found in this study and in Golec (1993).[1]

The volatility of CTAs' track records appears to be positively associated with the incentive fee parameter (Table 13.4). The relationship supports the idea that CTAs who charge larger incentive fees take on larger risks. It also appears that risk taking pays off as viewed from the relationship between mean returns and the incentive fee parameter. The amount of assets under

[1]Golec's results were annualized to make them comparable to the results of this study.

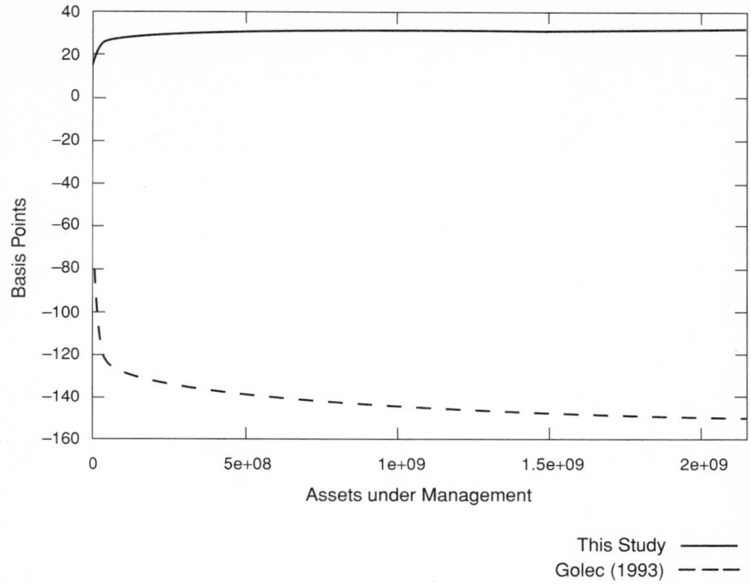

FIGURE 13.1 Effects of Assets under Management on Average Annual Returns

management appears to be negatively associated with the volatility of CTAs' track records. Although the effect is rather small, this result is consistent with Golec's findings. Golec's explanation of this empirical observation is appealing. Risk aversion is likely to rise with wealth, and this in turn may induce CTAs to reduce risk levels. Some indirect support for this explanation is found in Diz (2003), where the level of leverage of "surviving" CTAs (the larger ones) appears to be smaller.

One surprising finding is that management fees appear to be positively associated with the volatility of CTAs' track records. There is no clear explanation for this finding other than measurement error.

Because a substantial amount of relative total compensation is contingent on positive performance (incentive fee), common sense and theory suggest that all factors associated with performance have a potential impact on total compensation. For example, Diz (2003) shows that CTAs' level of leverage is related to performance. CTAs with larger margin to equity ratios tend to have larger returns and volatility. As other variables such as leverage are strongly associated with the performance of a cross section of CTAs, the exclusion of such variables in regression equations 13.2 and 13.3 may substantially alter the size, sign, and level of statistical significance of their coefficients. In an effort to reduce the omitted variable problem, we fit this augmented model to the data:

$$AROR_j = \beta_0 + \beta_1 k_m + \beta_2 k_i + \beta_3 \ln(A_{t-1}) + \beta_4 mdd + \beta_5 me + \\ + \beta_6 vr + \beta_7 surv + \beta_8 Diver + \beta_9 Syst + \beta_{10} Disc + e_j \tag{13.5}$$

$$\sigma_j = \alpha_0 + \alpha_1 k_m + \alpha_2 k_i + \alpha_3 \ln(A_{t-1}) + \alpha_4 mdd + \alpha_5 me + \\ + \alpha_6 vr + \alpha_7 surv + \alpha_8 Diver + \alpha_9 Syst + \alpha_{10} Disc + u_j \tag{13.6}$$

where:

k_m = management fee parameter in %
k_i = incentive fee variable in %
$\ln(A_{t-1})$ = natural log of the amount of assets under management in the previous month
mdd = maximum drawdown variable (drawdown is defined as the percentage size of an equity retracement)
me = margin to equity ratio
vr = ratio of "positive" to "negative" volatility
$surv$ = dummy variable that takes a value of 1 when the CTA is still in business and 0 when the CTA or program is no longer available
$Diver$ = dummy variable that takes a value of 1 when the CTA is diversified and 0 otherwise
$Syst$ = dummy variable that takes a value of 1 when the CTA is systematic in trading approach and 0 otherwise
$Discr$ = dummy variable that takes a value of 1 when the CTA is discretionary in trading and 0 otherwise
e_j, u_j = error terms

The results in Table 13.5 suggest that management fees are unrelated to both the level and volatility of CTA returns. The effect of the incentive fee parameter remains positive and statistically significantly different from zero under the augmented model specification. Moreover, the magnitude of the effect of the incentive fee parameter on the level of returns appears to be the same as in the previous model specification. The robustness of the incentive fee parameter to different model specifications lends credence to the conclusion that CTAs' incentive fee structure is strongly associated with their level of net returns. Under the augmented model, an increase in the incentive fee parameter from 10 percent to 20 percent will increase performance by an average of 6.58 percent annually.

Incentive fees continue to be associated with the overall volatility of CTA track records. Larger incentive fee parameters are associated with

TABLE 13.5 Estimation of the Relationship between Compensation Parameters and CTA Mean Annual Compounded Returns and Standard Deviation of Returns, Augmented Specification

	AROR		σ	
Performance Variable	Coefficient	S.E	Coefficient	S.E.
Constant	−0.275**	0.072	−0.076*	0.038
k_m	0.790	0.546	−0.183	0.283
k_i	0.658**	0.246	0.229*	0.102
$ln(A_{t-1})$	0.009**	0.003	−0.003	0.002
mdd	0.186**	0.036	−0.637**	0.029
me	0.300**	0.062	0.247**	0.042
vr	0.051**	0.007	0.060**	0.006
surv	0.078**	0.015	0.034**	0.007
Diver	0.000	0.011	0.008	0.006
Syst	−0.009	0.013	−0.001	0.007
Discr	0.004	0.019	0.009	0.011

*Significant at the 5 percent level for $H_0 = 0$.
**Significant at the 1 percent level for $H_0 = 0$.

larger levels of volatility, although this effect is reduced considerably in the augmented model. The amount of assets under management continues to be associated with the mean level of returns. The effect appears to be of the same order of magnitude in the augmented model. The level of assets under management is unrelated to the volatility of the CTA track record. This is in contrast with Golec (1993), who finds a negative and significant relationship between assets under management and volatility and casts doubts about the existence of any relationship between size and volatility once one accounts for other volatility variables.

CONCLUSION

This study examines the effect of incentive contracting on CTA performance and volatility. Evidence of structural changes in incentive compensation is presented that points to a larger reliance on incentive fees as opposed to management fees. Management fees are shown to have no relationship with performance. This is good news for investors, as the evidence seems to suggest that this type of compensation results in no systematic performance penalty to investors. Management fees are not associated with systematic variation in CTA return volatility, either. Both results are in agreement with previous research by Golec (1993).

Incentive fees are found to be positively related to both returns and the volatility of CTA returns. An increase in the incentive fee parameter from 10 percent to 20 percent will increase performance by an average of 6.58 percent per year. The performance increase is net of all fees and independent of the amount of leverage used by the CTA. The level of incentive fees may play a role in the selection of truly outstanding CTAs.

Finally, it is shown that CTA size measured by the level of assets under management is positively related with the level of returns. The effect is small and likely to be caused by money flowing to successful CTAs.

CHAPTER 14

Managed Futures Funds and Other Fiduciary Products: The Australian Regulatory Model

Paul U. Ali

This chapter investigates the Australian regulatory model for managed futures funds and other fiduciary investment products whose returns are derived from the trading of futures products. All fiduciary investment products are regulated in the same manner in Australia, under a combination of the managed investment scheme and financial product provisions of the Australian corporations legislation. The difficulties of applying this model to the diverse range of fiduciary futures products is discussed, and recent proposals to reform the regulation of individually managed futures accounts are examined.

INTRODUCTION

Hedge funds and other alternative fiduciary investment products (products where investors have provided funds to a professional fund manager to invest on their behalf) are coming under increasing regulatory scrutiny, especially in the United States. The U.S. Treasury Department has proposed a series of measures under the PATRIOT Act that will require the operators of onshore as well as offshore wholesale hedge funds, commodity pools, and private equity funds to provide the department with certain basic information about the fund manager, the investors in the fund, and the value of assets under management—measures that are likely to undermine the confidentiality now enjoyed by these funds (see Financial Crimes Enforcement Network 2002). In addition, the National Association of Securities Dealers (NASD) has expressed concern that its members may not be fulfilling their legal obligations to customers, particularly retail customers, when promoting hedge funds and funds of hedge funds to them (see NASD 2003). More recently, the Securities and Exchange Commission (SEC) has raised concerns about the increasing retailization of hedge funds, commodity pools, and private equity funds, the unregulated nature of these products and the potential for fund managers to defraud investors, and the market impact of hedge fund investment strategies such as short selling (SEC 2003).[1] The SEC's concerns are usefully summarized in Wider and Scanlan (2003).

In Australia, the Australian Prudential Regulation Authority (APRA), the prudential regulator of banks, insurance companies, and pension funds, recently has questioned the increasing allocation of funds by Australian pension funds to hedge funds and other alternative investments. APRA (2003) has explicitly stated that if it "is not satisfied that an investment in hedge funds is to the benefit of [pension] fund members, it will step in to protect their interests."

This chapter discusses the regulation, in Australia, of fiduciary investment products whose returns are derived from the trading of futures contracts. This is of interest for two broad reasons. First, hedge funds, managed futures, and other alternative fiduciary investment products are subject to the retail regime that governs conventional mutual funds. This provides a useful counterpoint to the debate in jurisdictions such as the United States[2] and the United Kingdom[3] as to whether the differential status of

---

[1]In contrast, the Commodity Futures Trading Commission has recently introduced rules that have the effect of placing the majority of U.S. hedge funds and offshore hedge funds that invest in U.S. commodity futures outside the scope of the registration and licensing provisions of the Commodity Exchange Act. These rules commenced operation on August 28, 2003, and are summarized in note 2.

[2]The Investment Company Act of 1940 regulates "investment companies," which are funds that are engaged primarily in the business of investing in or trading securities. However, funds that have fewer than 100 investors (section 3(c)(1)) and funds whose investors are "qualified purchasers" (e.g., persons with at least US $5 million of investment assets and fund managers whose assets under management are at least US $25 million) (sections 2(a)(51) and 3(c)(7)) are excluded from the definition of "investment company." U.S. hedge funds and offshore hedge funds offered to U.S. investors are deliberately structured to take advantage of one or both of these exceptions. The majority of hedge funds also fall outside the scope of the Commodity Exchange Act. That act regulates "commodity pools," which are funds that engage in U.S. commodity futures transactions (booking a single transaction will be sufficient to render a fund a commodity pool: CFTC Interpretative Letter 98-18). However, funds that do not engage predominantly in commodity futures transactions and whose investors are all "accredited investors" (as defined in Rule 501, Regulation D of the Securities Act) have been excluded by the CFTC from the definition

such investment products should be continued. Second, the Australian Securities and Investments Commission (ASIC) has recently signaled its intention to distinguish between individually managed accounts and managed funds for regulatory purposes (2003).

Fiduciary Futures Products in Australia

Fiduciary futures products—where a futures broker or investment manager seeks to generate a positive return on the funds entrusted to it by its clients, by utilizing those funds to trade futures contracts—come in two varieties in Australia: managed futures funds and individually managed futures accounts. Managed futures funds are structured along the same lines as mutual funds and hedge funds in Australia. The cash contributions of several investors are pooled by the fund manager for the purposes of investing in one or more of the classes of futures contracts (as well as options on futures contracts) listed on the Sydney Futures Exchange. Individually managed futures accounts fall into the broader class of investment products known variously as individually managed accounts (IMAs), managed discretionary accounts (MDAs), and managed portfolio services. IMAs are a custodial and administrative investment service, not intermediated investment vehicles as is the case with managed futures funds (Jorgensen 2003). An investor in an IMA deposits funds in a separate trading account with a futures broker and grants the futures broker broad discretion to invest those funds in futures contracts on the investor's behalf, without the need for the investor to grant prior approval to individual trades.

Of the two types of fiduciary futures products, IMAs are the more common in Australia. Retail investors can open an IMA with a futures broker with a minimum investment of A$100,000 (Doig 2003). Managed futures funds in Australia typically are structured as wholesale investment funds, open only to institutional and professional investors and requiring minimum investments of A$500,000. Nonetheless, the strong growth recently experi-

of "commodity pool": CFTC Rule 4.13(a)(3). In addition, the operators of funds that offer fund interests to only highly sophisticated investors (including "qualified purchasers") are exempt from registration as Commodity Pool Operators by the CFTC: CFTC Rule 4.13(a)(4).

[3]The Financial Services Authority, which regulates the U.K. financial services industry, has decided for the time being to leave hedge funds outside the regime governing retail collective investment schemes, although it has indicated that it may change its position depending on the level of demand for hedge fund participation by retail investors: see Financial Services Authority (2003).

enced by the Australian hedge fund sector is likely also to lead to increased interest among institutional investors in managed futures funds (Ali, Stapledon, and Gold 2003).

Investors also can obtain exposure to the underlying commodities of futures contracts by investing in commodity-linked securities. These are generally debt securities with embedded futures contracts or the over-the-counter commodity derivatives, where the value of the principal returned to investors on maturity of the securities is dependent on the price performance of the underlying commodity during the term of the securities (Anson 2002a). Commodity-linked products, however, remain relatively uncommon in Australia.

Australian Futures Market

Futures contracts and options on futures contracts are traded in Australia chiefly on the Sydney Futures Exchange (SFE).[4] According to the Sydney Futures Exchange Corporation (2002), the SFE is the tenth largest futures exchange in the world, by annual volume of futures contracts traded.[5] The SFE is the second-largest futures exchange in the Asia-Pacific region, ranking behind the Korea Stock Exchange and ahead of the Singapore Exchange, Osaka Securities Exchange, and the Korea Futures Exchange.

Trading on the SFE is dominated by financial futures contracts. According to the Sydney Futures Exchange Corporation (2003a) Australian interest rate futures contracts (comprising interbank rate, bank bill, interest rate swap, and treasury bond futures contracts) accounted for 89.4 percent and 88.7 percent of the total trading volume in the first half of 2003 and the whole of 2002 respectively, while the next most popular class of product, Australian equity futures contracts (comprising Australian equity index and single stock futures contracts), accounted for 10.4 percent and 11.1 percent in the same periods. Interestingly, single-stock futures contracts, which received regulatory approval in the United States under the Commodity Futures Modernization Act of 2000 but which have been available in Australia since 1994, have remained a peripheral product, with very low trad-

[4]Electricity, equity index, grain (barley, canola, sorghum, and wheat), and wool futures contracts are also traded (in relatively small volumes) on the Australian Stock Exchange.

[5]The nine futures exchanges that rank ahead of the SFE in terms of annual trading volume are (in descending order): Korea Stock Exchange; Eurex; Chicago Mercantile Exchange; Chicago Board of Trade; Euronext-LIFFE; Euronext-Paris; Brazilian Mercantile & Futures Exchange; Chicago Board Options Exchange; and Tel Aviv Stock Exchange.

ing volumes (Ali 2002). The other classes of product traded on the SFE are Australian dollar, cattle, electricity, and wool futures contracts.

Rationale for Investing in Fiduciary Futures Products

Investment in fiduciary futures products has been justified on two broad grounds. The first concerns the low correlation between the returns of commodity futures contracts and the returns of conventional investments such as shares and bonds. Thus, the inclusion in an investment portfolio of fiduciary futures products that have heavily invested in commodity futures contracts should create a more efficient return profile for that portfolio. The combination of the fiduciary futures product with long share or bond positions in the portfolio should generate a higher aggregate return for the portfolio for the same level of risk or reduce the investment risk of the portfolio without changing the level of return (Edwards and Park 1996; Edwards and Liew 1999).

Fiduciary futures products offer similar portfolio benefits to hedge funds. A recent study has concluded that fiduciary futures products will, in general, outperform hedge funds in bear market conditions while market-neutral, event-driven, and global macrohedge funds will outperform fiduciary futures products over all markets (Edwards and Caglayan 2001). The various hedge fund strategies are explained in Ali, Stapledon, and Gold (2003). A second study has concluded that while fiduciary futures products may have a lower expected return than hedge funds, they provide more effective portfolio diversification benefits than hedge funds (Kat 2002).

There is, however, one qualification: The correlation of the price performance of commodity futures contracts to the price performance of shares and bonds has been observed to be considerably unstable, a fact that may erode the claimed portfolio benefits of fiduciary futures products (Jensen, Johnson, and Mercer 2000).

The second benefit of fiduciary futures products is that they are considered to be a hedge against inflation, on the grounds that there is a positive correlation between the price performance of commodities and inflation. Again, this depends on the futures contracts in which the fiduciary futures product is invested. The putative hedge against inflation may not eventuate where the fiduciary futures product is significantly invested in financial futures contracts (Edwards and Park 1996).

Regulation of Fiduciary Futures Products in Australia

All fiduciary investment products, whether fiduciary futures products or hedge funds and whether offered to retail or institutional investors, are potentially subject to Chapter 5C of the Australian Corporations Act 2001, which regulates "managed investment schemes," and Chapter 7, which regulates "financial products."

Chapter 5C of the act is a "bottom-up" approach to the regulation of fiduciary investment products. A fiduciary investment product that is a managed investment scheme or financial product is subject to regulation by the act, and the onus is then on the operator of the scheme (typically, the fund manager) to explain in the disclosure documentation provided to investors the investment strategy of the scheme or product and the classes of assets in which the scheme or product invests. Accordingly, there is no need for the act to distinguish—and, indeed, the act does not do so—between managed futures products and other fiduciary investment products or between hedge funds and other fiduciary investment products.

FIDUCIARY FUTURES PRODUCTS AND MANAGED INVESTMENT SCHEMES

According to the Corporations Act 2001 (Cth), section 9, a fiduciary futures product (or other fiduciary investment product) is a "managed investment scheme" if it possesses three attributes:

1. Investors in the product contribute money or assets (e.g., securities) to acquire right to the financial benefits generated by the product.
2. The investors' contributions are pooled or used in a common enterprise by the operator of the product, to produce financial benefits for the investors.
3. Day-to-day control over the operation of the product (including the design and implementation of its investment strategy) is in the hands of a third party, not the investors.

Managed Futures Funds

Managed futures funds clearly satisfy these requirements. Investors in a managed futures fund invest by purchasing or subscribing for interests in the fund; the fund manager pools the consideration they provide for the acquisition of such interests and allocates it to futures contracts (or options over futures contracts). Moreover, the fund manager decides to invest in or close out futures contracts, not the investors, thus control over the operation of the fund is in the hands of a party other than the investors.

Only managed futures funds that have been structured as noncorporate "funds" can be "managed investment schemes." Section 9, paragraph (d) of the act expressly excludes from the definition of "managed investment scheme" corporate investment vehicles, for instance, where the investors have subscribed for securities in a corporation and the subscription proceeds have been invested by the corporation in futures contracts. The issue of units or other equity interests by the trustee of a trust to investors where the subscription proceeds are invested by the trustee in futures contracts will, on the other hand, constitute the trust a managed investment scheme.

The status of debt securities issued by the trustee of a managed futures trust remains uncertain. Section 9, paragraph (j) of the Corporations Act excludes "debentures" issued by a corporation (which includes corporate trustees) from the definition of "managed investment scheme." Debt securities that have been structured as bills of exchange or promissory notes (in the case of the latter, with a face value of at least A$50,000) are not debentures, and according to section 9, paragraphs (c)(iii) and (d), this fact should render the corporate trustee of a managed futures fund that issues such securities subject to Chapter 5C. Other debt securities issued by corporate trustees should fall outside the scope of Chapter 5C. However, the act also provides that debentures do not include debt securities where the issuer of the securities is not in the business of borrowing or lending money, and the investors have purchased the securities in the ordinary course of a business that involves lending money. It therefore can be argued that debt securities issued to professional investors by the trustee of a managed futures fund, irrespective of whether those securities are bills of exchange or promissory notes, are not debentures and thus potentially subject to Chapter 5C (Clayton 2003). (See Corporations Act 2001 (Cth), section 9, paragraph (a).)

Collateralized Synthetic Obligations

Regulation covers also securitization programs in Australia, including the emerging class of collateralized synthetic obligations (CSO). A CSO is very similar to a managed futures fund. The issuer in a CSO, like the manager of a managed futures fund, aims to generate profits by trading derivatives. Although the latter trades futures contracts, the former engages in the active trading of the class of over-the-counter derivatives known as credit derivatives. The different types of credit derivatives and their regulatory status are discussed by Ali (2000).

Credit default swaps are the most common type of credit derivative. In a credit default swap, one party (the protection seller) agrees with its counterparty (the protection buyer), in exchange for the payment of a premium or fee, to assume the credit risk on a portfolio of loans or bonds (reference obligations) made by the protection buyer to, or issued by, one or more third parties (reference entities). If a credit event (e.g., where a reference entity defaults on the reference obligations or becomes insolvent), the protection seller will be obligated to purchase the reference obligations for their face value from the protection buyer (in the case of a physically settled credit default swap) or make a payment to the protection buyer of the difference between the face value of the reference obligations and their then market value (in the case of a cash-settled credit default swap).

Thus, just as the manager of a managed futures fund seeks to service the principal and interest payments on any debt securities issued by it out of trading profits, the issuer of debt securities in a CSO seeks to service those securities out of the premiums received by the issuer from selling credit risk protection under credit derivatives and any profits realized from the trading of credit derivatives (Tavakoli 2003). Corporate trustee issuers in CSOs, in contrast to corporate issuers that are not trustees, are potentially subject to Chapter 5C of the Corporations Act.[6]

Individually Managed Futures Accounts

The status of individually managed accounts (IMAs) is less obvious. It seems clear that the attribute of pooling is absent since the futures broker or other operator of the IMA manages the investor's account as a discrete investment portfolio. Despite the separate management of investors' funds, there is a risk that an Australian court may nonetheless decide that an IMA involves "pooling" where the investments attributable to each account are held by the IMA operator or a custodian in a single omnibus account.[7] The existence of discrete investment portfolios and book-entry segregation of portfolio investments may not be sufficient to avoid the characterization of the portfolio manager's business as involving the pooling of investor contributions.

Having said that, ASIC has taken the view that IMAs are managed investment schemes on the basis that the operator of the IMA and the investor in the IMA are involved in a "common enterprise" (see ASIC 2003). This position is also supported by Horgan (2003).

This expansive view of "common enterprise" ignores the fact that it is the fund manager or account operator who is solely engaged in the enterprise and that the investors are merely passive participants. It is the operator of the IMA who makes the decision as to the selection of futures contracts for the investor's account, not the investor. The characterization of the relationship between an investor and a fund manager as a common enterprise appears to be predicated on the fact that both parties expect to derive a profit (positive

[6]It remains unclear whether the carve-outs for bills of exchange and certain promissory notes would apply to the limited recourse debt securities issued in CSOs (and other securitizations).

[7]See *ASIC v. Enterprise Solutions 2000 Pty Ltd* (2000), 33 ACSR 620 (where the court deemed pooling to have occurred, in relation to individual wagering accounts whose credit balances were held in a common bank account).

investment returns for the investor and fees for the manager) from the IMA. This interpretation not only renders otiose the requirement for pooling of investor contributions but also means that every financing relationship (i.e., shareholder-issuer, bondholder-issuer, lender-borrower, depositor-deposit holder, as in all these cases both parties expect to derive some profit from the relationship) is potentially a common enterprise and thus a managed investment scheme. (The impact of this categorization is lessened by the exemptions for corporations, debentures, and lender-lender/borrower transactions discussed in the context of managed futures funds.)

Registration of Fiduciary Futures Products

According to the Corporations Act 2001 (Cth), sections 601ED(1) and (2), managed futures funds and IMAs, as managed investment schemes, must be registered with ASIC under Chapter 5C unless the fund or IMA falls within one of the two categories:

1. A wholesale fund or account. A managed futures fund is a wholesale fund and an IMA is a wholesale account where the offer of interests in the fund or the offer of accounts does not require a product disclosure statement to be given to investors. Product disclosure statements are only required in respect of offers to retail clients;[8] or
2. A private fund or account. A managed futures fund is a private fund and an IMA is a private account where there are fewer than 20 investors in the fund or in a single IMA promoted by the operator (IMAs will invariably have fewer than 20 investors in a single account), and the fund or account was not promoted to the investors by a professional promoter.

The application of Chapter 5C to hedge funds and mutual funds is discussed further by Ali, Stapledon, and Gold (2003) and Baxt, Black, and Hanrahan (2003) respectively.

---

[8]An investor is a "retail client" unless: (a) the minimum subscription price for interests in the managed futures fund or the minimum amount required to open an IMA is A$500,000; (b) the investor has net assets of at least A$2.5 million or has a gross income of at least A$250,000 for each of the two financial years preceding the investment; or (c) is a professional investor (e.g., holders of an Australian financial services license, pension funds with net assets of at least A$10 million, banks, life insurance companies, general insurance companies): Corporations Act 2001 (Cth), sections 761G(1), (7)(a) and (7)(c); Corporations Regulations 2001 (Cth), regulations 7.1.18(2), 7.1.19(2), and 7.1.28.

According to section 601ED(5) of the act, failure to register a registrable managed futures fund or IMA will render the fund manager or operator of the account subject to criminal liability (punishable by a fine or imprisonment). In addition, the investors in the fund or account will be entitled to demand the return of the amounts invested by them, or apply to have the fund or account wound up (sections 601EE(1) and 601MB(1)).

The act provides a powerful economic incentive to register unregistrable managed futures funds and IMAs (Ali, Stapledon, and Gold, 2003): According to section 601FC(4), a registered managed investment scheme cannot invest in an unregistered scheme. Registration therefore expands the class of potential investors for unregistrable funds and accounts.

Registration imposes seven additional compliance obligations on the manager of the managed futures fund and the operator of the IMA:

1. The fund manager or operator (the responsible entity) must be a public company (section 601FA).
2. The responsible entity must hold an Australian financial services license from ASIC authorizing it to operate the fund or account (sections 601FA and 601FB(1)). The manager of an investment fund will typically be the responsible entity. Alternatively, where the fund has been structured as a trust and there is a segregation of the title-repository and investment roles, the trustee of the fund may be the responsible entity with the trustee delegating the selection of investments for the fund to the fund manager (Ali, Stapledon, and Gold 2003).
3. The responsible entity is subject to paramount statutory duties in favor of the investors in the fund or account (including duties of care, honesty, and loyalty) (Section 601FC(1) and (3)).
4. The responsible entity is deemed to hold the assets in the fund or account on trust for the investors in the fund or account (section 601FC(2)). The operation of this statutory obligation in the case of managed futures funds (and other investment funds) that have not been structured as trusts remains uncertain. Would this provision, in the case of a fund that has been structured as a limited partnership, for instance, render the general partner (the fund manager) the trustee of the partnership property for the limited partners (the investors)?
5. The legal instrument (e.g., the trust deed) governing the operation of the fund or account must contain certain stipulated covenants (sections 601GA and 601GB, see also ASIC 1998b).
6. The fund or account must have an independently audited compliance plan (Corporations Act 2001 (Cth), section 601HA(1); Corporations Regulations 2001 (Cth), reg. 5C.4.02; see also ASIC 1998a).

7. If fewer than half of the directors of the responsible entity are external directors, a separate compliance committee with a majority of external members must be established for the fund or account. (Corporations Act 2001 (Cth), sections 601JA(1) and 601JB(1); Corporations Regulations 2001 (Cth), reg. 5C.5.01).

Fiduciary Futures Products and Financial Products

The characterization of a fiduciary futures product as a "financial product" under Chapter 7 of the Corporations Act carries with it two important regulatory consequences. First, the manager of the managed futures fund or the operator of the IMA will be taken to be conducting a financial services business in Australia, for which it requires an Australian financial services license from ASIC (sections 911A(1) and 911D).

The responsible entity of a registered managed investment scheme also is required to hold this license by Chapter 5C of the act. A responsible entity of a registered managed investment scheme is taken to be carrying on a financial services business in Australia (sections 761A, 761C, and 766A(1)(d)). The operation of an unregistrable managed investment scheme also will constitute the carrying on of a financial services business in Australia where interests in the scheme are financial products. The issuer of interests in the scheme to investors and the party who is responsible for the obligations owed to the investors under the scheme (the fund manager or trustee of a managed futures fund or the operator of an IMA) will be taken to be "dealing" in a financial product and thus carrying on a financial services business (sections 761A, 761C, 761E(1)(b) and (4), and 766A(1)(b)).

Second, the offer of a financial product to "retail clients" requires those investors to be provided with a product disclosure statement at the point of sale, setting out such information as retail clients would reasonably require to make a decision on whether to acquire the financial product (sections 1011B, 1012B(3) and (4), 1013A(1), 1013C, and 1013D; see also ASIC 2001). A product disclosure statement is not required for wholesale managed futures funds and wholesale IMAs, as the investors in such products are not retail clients.[9] Nor is a product disclosure statement required for small-scale offers to retail clients.[10]

---

[9]See note 8.

[10]According to Corporations Act 2001 (Cth), section 1012E, a small-scale offer is one that does not result in more than 20 investors acquiring the financial product or more than A$2 million being raised from investors in a 12-month period.

Failure to comply with the above licensing and disclosure requirements will lead to imposition of criminal liability (punishable by a fine or imprisonment) (section 1311).[11] In addition, if a product disclosure statement is not provided or a defective product disclosure statement is provided, the investors in the fiduciary futures product will be entitled to recover any loss incurred by them that is attributable to the noncompliance with the act's disclosure requirements (section 1022B).

Interests in retail managed futures funds and IMAs are financial products (sections 762A(2) and 764A(1)(b)), as are interests in wholesale managed futures funds and IMAs (sections 762A(2) and 764A(1)(ba)).

Interests in private managed futures funds and IMAs, in contrast, are not financial products, and such funds and accounts therefore fall outside the scope of Chapter 7 (sections 762A(3) and 765(1)(s)).[12] If an IMA is not a managed investment scheme and thus falls outside the scope of Chapter 5C, it nonetheless may be regulated as a financial product since the "investment" head of the general definition of "financial product" does not require the pooling of investors' contributions or a common enterprise, in contrast to the definition of "managed investment scheme" (sections 762A(1), 763A(1)(a) and 763B).

Individually Managed Futures Accounts—Futures Exchange Requirements

The Sydney Futures Exchange (SFE) imposes four additional disclosure and trading requirements on certain IMAs (the term used in the SFE By-laws is "managed discretionary accounts") promoted by SFE members and that invest in SFE-traded futures contracts (By-laws G. 52 and 53; see also SFE 2003).

1. The operator must ensure that the IMA is suitable for the investor, having regard to the investor's other investments and the investor's personal and financial situation.

---

[11]The act provides for multiple criminal offenses for failing to provide a product disclosure statement or providing a defective product disclosure statement: sections 1021C-1021O. In addition, criminal liability may be incurred for making false or misleading statements in the product disclosure statement to induce persons to subscribe for or buy the financial product: section 1041E(3).

[12]This exception applies only if the IMA can be properly characterized as a managed investment scheme.

2. A disclosure document containing prescribed particulars must be provided to the investor before the operator can open an IMA for the investor or make trades for the IMA.
3. The operator must not engage in "churning"—that is, it must ensure that the trades in futures contracts booked for the IMA are not excessive in size or frequency.
4. The operator must not engage in leveraged trading for the IMA; that is, it cannot finance or arrange finance for the positions booked for the IMA.

It is, however, difficult to see what scope there is for the application of these requirements given the view taken by ASIC of IMAs. According to By-law G.1.1., paragraph (ii)(c), Sydney Futures Exchange Corporation (2003b) the SFE managed discretionary accounts By-laws do not apply to an IMA that is a managed investment scheme. (The SFE also, in By-law G.1.1., paragraphs (ii)(b) and (iii), expressly exempts IMAs that are registered managed investment schemes or unregistrable, wholesale managed investment schemes. These two exemptions would seem to be superfluous, given the unqualified exemption for managed investment schemes.) If ASIC's view is correct that an IMA is a managed investment scheme under the Corporations Act due to there being a common enterprise between the investor and the account operator, this means that the SFE MDA rules are redundant, a view that the SFE and its members do not appear to share.

Regulatory Reform—Individually Managed Futures Accounts

The Australian Securities and Investments Commission recently has released for public comment proposals to simplify the regulation of retail IMAs. In short, these proposals involve placing retail IMAs outside the scope of Chapter 5C of the Corporations Act and regulating them solely under Chapter 7.[13] The operators of retail IMAs must still hold an Australian financial services license authorizing them to deal in the IMAs, but the IMAs will no longer be required to be registered as managed investment schemes with ASIC (ASIC 2003b pp. 15, 18, 19). The operator of a retail

---

[13]These proposals mirror the changes to the regulatory status of Separately Managed Accounts (SMAs) and wrap accounts implemented by ASIC in 2000: see ASIC 2003b, pp. 33 and 50.

IMA also will be exempted from the requirement to provide a product disclosure statement to the investors but instead, will be subject to the less onerous disclosure requirements in relation to the provision of advice to investors about the IMA and the underlying investments of the IMA (ASIC 2003b, pp. 15 and 21–22).

Despite deeming retail IMAs not to be managed investment schemes, the operator of a retail IMA will, under ASIC's proposals, continue to be subject to the statutory duties of care, honesty, and loyalty that apply to the responsible entities of registered managed investment schemes (ASIC 2003b, p. 17). In addition, a retail IMA will, in common with registered managed investment schemes, generally be prohibited from investing in managed futures funds and wholesale IMAs that have not been registered under Part 5C (ASIC 2003b, p. 32).

The overriding rationale for these reforms seems to be the desire on the part of the regulator to lower the transaction costs associated with establishing retail IMAs (ASIC 2003b, p. 37). This commercial imperative aside, it is difficult to provide a coherent justification for the reforms. The reforms draw an artificial distinction between managed investment schemes (where the fund manager has the discretion to select investments for the scheme) and retail IMAs, which are deemed not to be managed investment schemes (even though it is the operator that has the discretion to select investments for the accounts). Also, the reforms create an incongruous situation where wholesale IMAs (they are managed investment schemes, albeit unregistrable ones) are subject to more onerous regulatory requirements than retail IMAs.

CONCLUSION

The regulation of managed futures funds and individually managed futures accounts in Australia is characterized by a "bottom-up" approach. These investment products are subject to the same regulatory regime—a combination of the managed investment and financial product chapters of the Australian Corporations Act—as all other fiduciary investment products in Australia, such as hedge funds and mutual funds.

This uniform regulation of fiduciary investment products is not, however, without shortcomings. The status of individually managed accounts in a regime designed for pooled investment products, such as managed futures funds, hedge funds, and mutual funds, is not free from doubt. It is also unclear what the regulatory status of a managed fund is, where the fund has been structured as a trust and the investors in the fund have acquired their exposure to the fund's investment portfolio via commercial paper, notes, or other capital market debt securities issued by the trustee. This is less of an issue for managed futures funds, hedge funds, and mutual funds, where the interests in the fund held by investors are predominantly equity instruments such as units or shares. It is, however, a major issue for Australian securitization programs, including collateralized synthetic obligations, an innovative investment product very similar to a managed futures fund. It is also a major issue for collateralized private equity obligations and collateralized fund of hedge fund obligations, which are securitizations of equity interests in private equity funds and hedge funds respectively (Ali, Stapledon, and Gold 2003).

Finally, the current proposals to streamline the regulation of retail individually managed accounts (including retail individually managed futures accounts) in Australia will, if implemented, result in the unusual spectacle of a retail investment product being subjected to less onerous regulation than its wholesale counterparts.

PART Four

Program Evaluation, Selection, and Returns

Chapter 15 discusses the issues involved in setting up a commodity futures trading program from start to finish. The chapter covers these areas that a new entrant into the futures markets must consider: trade discovery, trade construction, portfolio construction, risk management, leverage-level determination, and how the trading program will make a unique contribution to an investor's overall portfolio.

Chapter 16 analyzes the ex-post performance of CTA managed funds with a higher moment-based, contingent-claim replication method. The performance of each managed futures fund is compared to individually created benchmark assets having the same risk profile in terms of particular higher moments. Benchmark assets are constructed using the S&P 500, options, and the risk-free asset. Using these benchmark assets, the author estimates the efficiency gain or loss each CTA produces and analyzes the robustness of this kind of efficiency measurement with respect to the number of moments used.

Chapter 17 aims at providing an overview of the industry and to quantify its added value when included in portfolios (mean/variance optimization). Different statistics and asset allocations studies are displayed within a fixed or dynamic framework. A dynamic framework takes into account time evolutions. On the asset allocation side, it then implies working in a three-dimensional environment (mean/variance/time framework) and dealing with efficient surfaces rather than efficient frontiers.

Chapter 18 examines whether CTA percent changes in NAVs follow random walks. Monthly data from January 1994 to December 2000 are tested for nonstationarity and random walk with drift, using the Augmented Dickey-Fuller test. All classifications (except the diversified subindex) are found to behave as random walks, but many of the series show evidence of a positive drift parameter, an indication that trends could be present in the series. The effectiveness of CTAs in enhancing risk-return characteristics of portfolios could be compromised when pure random walk behavior is identified.

Chapter 19 examines the risk and performance characteristics of different strategies involving the trading of commodity futures, financial futures, and options on futures used by CTAs. The authors rank the returns of the S&P 500 and MSCI Global Indices from the worst to the best months, and partition the sample into 10 deciles. For each decile, they compute the relationship between the CTA indices and the equity indices, and compared their risk and return characteristics.

Chapter 20 analyzes the risk and return benefits of CTAs, as an alternative investment class. Then it shows, using a modified Value at Risk as a more precise measure of risk, how CTAs can be integrated into existing investment strategies and how we can determine the optimal proportion of assets to invest in such products. Overall, the results of the study show that an efficiently allocated portfolio consisting of CTA and traditional assets should provide a better reward/risk ratio than an investment in traditional assets only.

Chapter 21 uses time series processes to model the return series of the 10 largest CTAs from 1996 to 2003. Series are tested for stationarity, and an appropriate ARMA model is applied to each CTA. The authors conduct a similar analysis on the excess returns—relative to the CISDM CTA Index. Last, stability tests are performed—through a Chow test—to investigate possible structural changes in the parameters of the ARMA models.

Chapter 22 investigates the risk-adjusted returns of CTAs using the modified Sharpe ratio. Because of the nonnormal returns of this asset class, the traditional Sharpe ratio may not be appropriate. The CTAs are divided into three categories in terms of ending millions under management.

Chapter 23 examines one of the most important features of managed futures, their trend-following nature. This topic has been extensively exploited to justify the inclusion of managed futures in traditional portfolios, where they act as risk diversifiers during bear markets. However, managed futures still may be risky over short-term horizons. How long does one have to invest so that it is virtually certain a managed futures portfolio will do better than cash or bonds? To answer this question, the authors examined monthly holding periods of the CSFB Tremont Managed Futures Index. Their conclusion is that although managed futures are relatively safe in the long run from a capital preservation perspective, their shortfall risk remains and should not be neglected.

CHAPTER 15

How to Design a Commodity Futures Trading Program

Hilary Till and Joseph Eagleeye

We provide a step-by-step primer on how to design a commodity futures trading program. A prospective commodity manager not only must discover trading strategies that are expected to be generally profitable, but also must be careful regarding each strategy's correlation properties during different times of the year and during eventful periods. He or she also must ensure that the resulting product has a unique enough return stream that it can be expected to provide diversification benefits to an investor's overall portfolio.

INTRODUCTION

When designing a commodity futures trading program, a commodity manager needs to create an investment process that addresses these issues:

- Trade discovery
- Trade construction
- Portfolio construction
- Risk management
- Leverage level
- How the program will make a unique contribution to the investor's overall portfolio

This chapter covers each of these subjects in succession.

TRADE DISCOVERY

The first step is to discover a number of trades in which it is plausible that the investor has an "edge," or advantage. Although a number of futures trading strategies are well known and publicized, commodity managers continue to apply them. Three examples of such strategies follow.

Grain Example

In discussing consistently profitable grain futures trades, Cootner (1967) stated that the fact that they "persist in the face of such knowledge indicates that the risks involved in taking advantage of them outweigh the gain involved. This is further evidence that... [commercial participants do] not act on the basis of expected values; that... [these participants are] willing to pay premiums to avoid risk" (page 98). Cootner's article discussed detectable periods of concentrated hedging pressure by agricultural market participants that lead to "the existence of... predictable trends in future prices." It provided several empirical examples of this occurrence, including "the effect of occasional long hedging in the July wheat contract." Noting the tendency of the prices of futures contracts to "fall on average after the peak of net long hedging," Cootner stated that the July wheat contract should "decline relative to contract months later in the crop year which are less likely to be marked by long hedging." Table 15.1 summarizes Cootner's empirical study on a wheat futures spread. The spread on average declined by about 2.5 cents over the period. The significant issue for us is that this phenomenon, which is linked to hedging activity, was published in 1967. Does this price pressure effect still exist today? The short answer appears to be yes.

From 1979 to 2003, on average, this spread declined by 3.8 cents with a Z-statistic of –3.01. Figure 15.1 illustrates the yearly performance of this spread.

TABLE 15.1 Cootner's Empirical Study on the July versus December Wheat Futures Spread

1948 to 1966 Average of July Versus December Wheat Futures Price on the Indicated Dates	
January 31	–5.10 cents
February 28	–5.35 cents
March 31	–5.62 cents
April 30	–5.69 cents
May 31	–6.55 cents
June 30	–7.55 cents

Source: Paul Cootner, "Speculation and Hedging." *Food Research Institute Studies,* Supplement 7, (1967): 100.

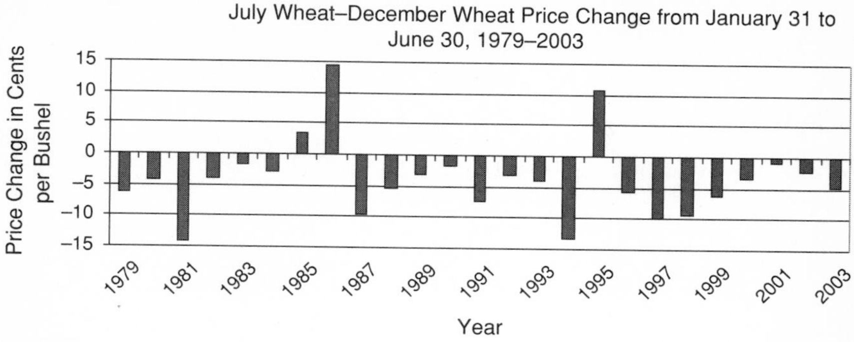

FIGURE 15.1 Cootner's Example Out of Sample
Source: Premia Capital Management, LLC.

This trade is obviously not riskless. To profit from this trade, a manager generally would short the spread, so it is the positive numbers in Figure 15.1 that would represent losses. Note from the figure the magnitude of potential losses that this trade has incurred over the past 25 years. That said, Cootner's original point that a profitable trade can persist in the face of knowledge of its existence seems to be borne out 36 years later.

Figure 15.2 summarizes the information in Figure 15.1 differently to emphasize the "tail risk" of a July to December wheat spread strategy. If a manager took a short position in this spread, the possible outcomes incorporate losses that are several times the size of the average profit. Again, in a short position, the manager wants the price change to be negative, so the historical losses on this trade are represented by the positive numbers in Figure 15.2. A manager might conclude that this trade can continue to exist

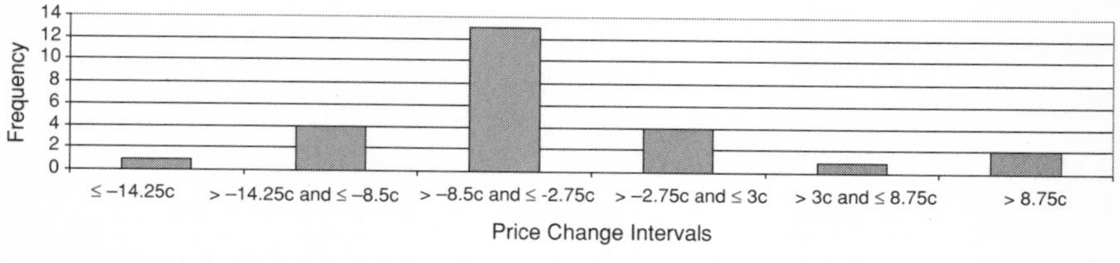

FIGURE 15.2 Histogram of the Frequency Distribution for the July Wheat–December Wheat Price Changes, 1979–2003
Source: Premia Capital Management, LLC.

because of the unpleasant tail risk that must be assumed when putting on this trade.

Petroleum Complex Example

Are there any persistent price tendencies that can be linked to structural aspects of the petroleum market? After examining the activity of commercial participants in the petroleum futures markets, it appears that their hedging activity is bunched up within certain time frames. These same time frames also seem to have detectable price trends, reflecting this commercial hedging pressure.

Like other commodities, the consumption and production of petroleum products are concentrated during certain times of the year, as illustrated in Figure 15.3. This is the underlying reason why commercial hedging pressure also is highly concentrated during certain times of the year.

The predictable price trends that result from concentrated hedge pressure may be thought of as a type of premium the commercial market participants are willing to pay. That commercial participants will engage in hedging during predictable time frames and thus will pay a premium to do so may be compared to individuals willing to pay higher hotel costs to visit popular locations during high season. They are paying for this timing convenience.

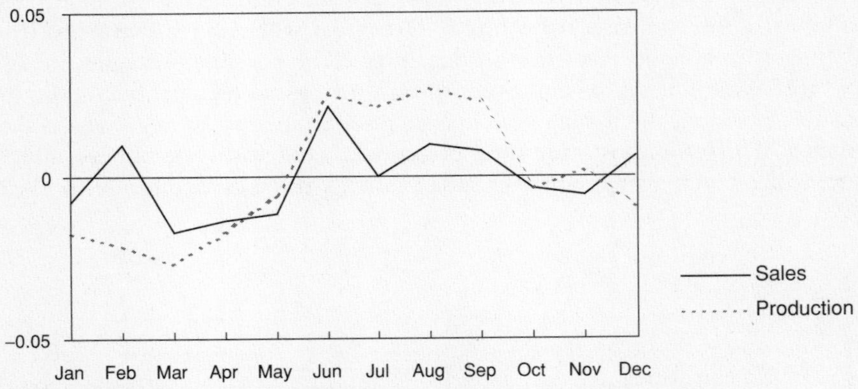

FIGURE 15.3 Petroleum Seasonal Sales and Production Patterns
Source: Jeffrey Miron, *The Economics of Seasonal Cycles* (Cambridge, MA: MIT Press, 1996), p. 118.

Note: The seasonal coefficient plotted for each month is the average percentage difference for that month from a logarithmic time trend.

Corn Example

Corn provides another example of a persistent price pressure effect. The futures prices of some commodity contracts, including corn, sometimes embed a fear premium due to upcoming, meaningful weather events. According to a Refco (2000) commentary: "The grain markets will always assume the worst when it comes to real or perceived threats to the food supply" (page 1). As a result, coming into the U.S. growing season, grain futures prices seem to systematically have a premium added into the fair value price of the contract. The fact that this premium can be easily washed out if no adverse weather occurs is well known by the trade. Notes a Salomon Smith Barney (2000) commentary: "The bottom line is: any threat of ridging this summer will spur concerns of yield penalties. That means the market is likely to keep some 'weather premium' built into the price of key markets. The higher the markets go near term, the more risk there will be to the downside if and when good rains fall" (page 1). By the end of July, the weather conditions that are critical for corn yield prospects will have already occurred. At that point, if weather conditions have not been adverse, the weather premium in corn futures prices will no longer be needed. According to the Pool Commodity Trading Service (1999): "In any weather market there remains the potential for a shift in weather forecasts to immediately shift trends, but it appears as though grains are headed for further losses before the end of the week. With 75% of the corn silking, the market can begin to get comfortable taking some weather premium out" (page 1). Again, this example shows that the commercial trade can be well aware of a commodity futures price reflecting a biased estimate of future valuation, and yet the effect still persisting.

TRADE CONSTRUCTION

Experience in commodity futures trading shows that a trader can have a correct commodity view, but how he or she constructs the trade to express the view can make a large difference in profitability.

Outright futures contracts, options, or spreads on futures contracts can be used to express a commodity view.

At times futures spreads are more analytically tractable than trading outright. Usually some economic boundary constraint links related commodities, which can (but not always) limit the risk in position taking. Also, a trader hedges out a lot of first-order, exogenous risk by trading spreads. For example, with a heating oil versus crude oil futures spread, each leg of the trade is equally affected by unpredictable OPEC shocks. Instead, what typically affects the spread is second-order risk factors, such as timing differences in inventory changes among the two commodities. It is sometimes easier to make predictions regarding these second-order risk factors than the first-order ones.

PORTFOLIO CONSTRUCTION

Once an investor has discovered a set of trading strategies that are expected to have positive returns over time, the next step is to combine the trades into a portfolio of diversified strategies. The goal is to combine strategies that are uncorrelated with each other to end up with a dampened-risk portfolio.

Diversification

Figure 15.4 illustrates a commodity futures portfolio from June 2000, which combined hedge-pressure trades with weather-fear-premium trades. The figure shows the effect of incrementally adding unrelated trades on portfolio volatility.

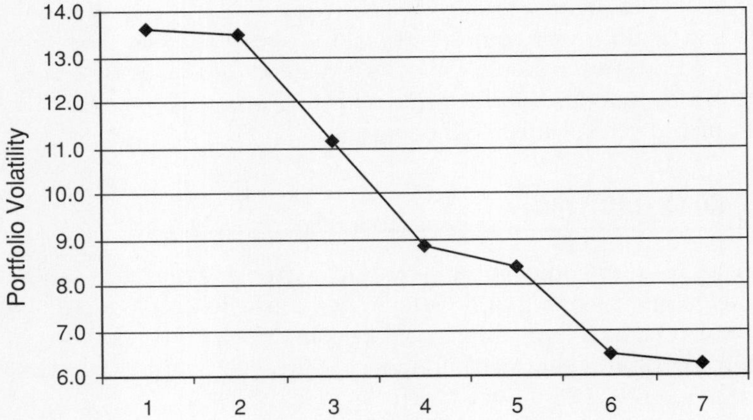

FIGURE 15.4 Annualized Portfolio Volatility versus Number of Commodity Investment Strategies, June 2000
Source: Hilary Till, "Passive Strategies in the Commodity Futures Markets," *Derivatives Quarterly* (2000), Exhibit 5.

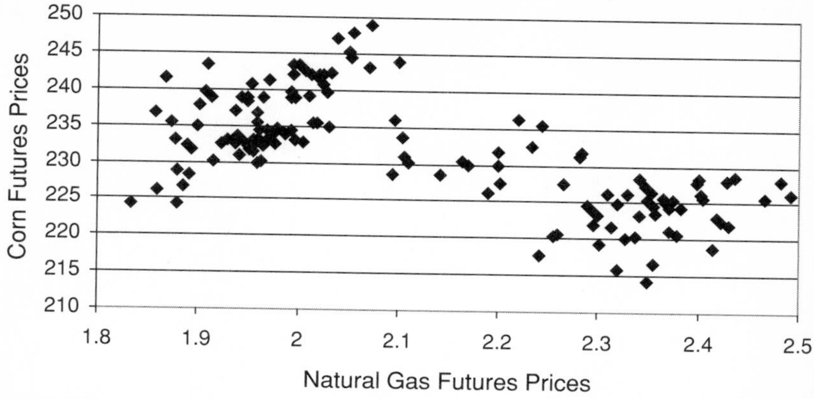

FIGURE 15.5 September Corn Futures Prices versus September Natural Gas Future Prices, November 30, 1998, to June 28, 1999
Source: Hilary Till, "Taking Full Advantage of the Statistical Properties of Commodity Investments," *Journal of Alternative Investments* (2001), Exhibit 3.
Note: Using a sampling period of every three days, the correlation of the percent change in corn prices versus the percent change in natural gas prices is 0.12.

Inadvertent Concentration Risk

A key concern for all types of leveraged investing is inadvertent concentration risk. In leveraged commodity futures investing, one must be careful with commodity correlation properties. Seemingly unrelated commodity markets can become temporarily highly correlated. This becomes problematic if a commodity manager is designing a portfolio so that only a certain amount of risk is allocated per strategy. The portfolio manager may be inadvertently doubling up on risk if two strategies are unexpectedly correlated.

Figures 15.5 and 15.6 provide examples from the summer of 1999 that show how seemingly unrelated markets can temporarily become quite related.

Normally natural gas and corn prices are unrelated, as shown in Figure 15.5. But during July, they can become highly correlated. During a three-week period in July 1999, the correlation between natural gas and corn price changes was 0.85, as illustrated in Figure 15.6.

Both the July corn and natural gas futures contracts are heavily dependent on the outcome of weather in the U.S. Midwest. And in July 1999, the

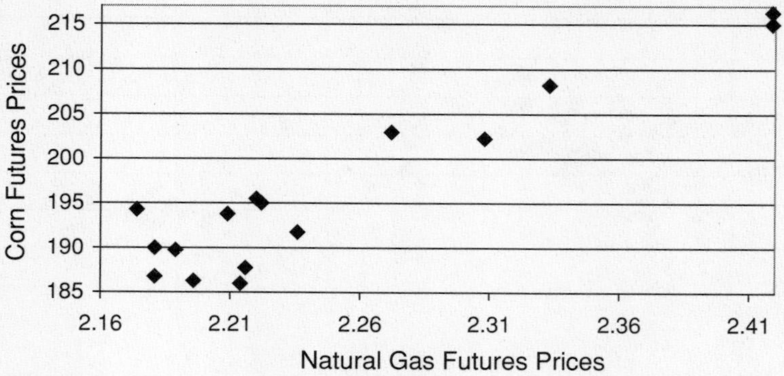

FIGURE 15.6 September Corn Futures Prices versus September Natural Gas Prices, June 29, 1999, to July 26, 1999
Source: Hilary Till, "Taking Full Advantage of the Statistical Properties of Commodity Investments," *Journal of Alternative Investments* (2000), Exhibit 4.

Using a sampling period of every three days, the correlation of the percent change in corn prices versus the percent change in natural gas prices is 0.85.

Midwest had blistering temperatures (which even led to some power outages). During that time, both corn and natural gas futures prices responded in nearly identical fashions to weather forecasts and realizations.

If a commodity portfolio manager had included both natural gas and corn futures trades in a portfolio during this time frame, then that investor would have inadvertently doubled up on risk.

In order to avoid inadvertent correlations, it is not enough to measure historical correlations. Using the data in Figure 15.5, an investor would have concluded that corn and natural gas price changes are only weakly related. An investor needs, however, to have an economic understanding of why a trade works in order to best be able to appreciate whether an additional trade will act as a portfolio diversifier. In that way, the investor will avoid doubling up on the risks that Figure 15.6 illustrates.

RISK MANAGEMENT

The fourth step in designing a commodity futures trading program is risk management, because the portfolio manager needs to ensure that during both normal and eventful times, the program's losses do not exceed a client's comfort level.

Risk Measures

On a per-strategy basis, it is useful to examine each strategy's:

- Value at risk based on recent volatilities and correlations
- Worst-case loss during normal times
- Worst-case loss during well-defined eventful periods
- Incremental contribution to portfolio value at risk
- Incremental contribution to worst-case portfolio event risk

The last two measures give an indication if the strategy is a risk reducer or risk enhancer. On a portfolio-wide basis, it is useful to examine the portfolio's:

- Value at risk based on recent volatilities and correlations
- Worst-case loss during normal times
- Worst-case loss during well-defined eventful periods

Each measure should be compared to some limit, which has been determined based on the design of the futures product. So, for example, if clients expect the program to lose no more than, say, 7 percent from peak-to-trough, then the three portfolio measures should be constrained to not exceed 7 percent. If the product should not perform too poorly during, say, financial shocks, then the worst-case loss during well-defined eventful periods should be constrained to a relatively small number. If that worst-case loss exceeds the limit, then the manager can devise macro-portfolio hedges accordingly, as will be discussed later.

For the purposes of extraordinary stress testing, we would recommend examining how a portfolio would have performed during the four eventful periods listed in Table 15.2.

TABLE 15.2 Meaningful Eventful Periods

October 1987 stock market crash
1990 Gulf War
Fall 1998 bond market debacle
Aftermath of 9/11/01 attacks

TABLE 15.3 Strategy-Level Risk Measures

Strategy	Value at Risk	Worst-Case Loss during Normal Times	Worst-Case Loss during Eventful Period
Deferred Reverse Soybean Crush Spread	2.78%	−1.09%	−1.42%
Long Deferred Natural Gas Outright	0.66%	−0.18%	−0.39%
Short Deferred Wheat Spread	0.56%	−0.80%	−0.19%
Long Deferred Gasoline Outright	2.16%	−0.94%	−0.95%
Long Deferred Gasoline vs. Heating Oil Spread	2.15%	−1.04%	−2.22%
Long Deferred Hog Spread	0.90%	−1.21%	−0.65%
Portfolio	3.01%	−2.05%	−2.90%

Source: Hilary Till, "Risk Management Lessons in Leveraged Commodity Futures Trading," *Commodities Now* (September 2002).

A commodity portfolio that would do poorly during these time frames may be unacceptable to clients who are investing in a nontraditional investment for diversification benefits. Therefore, in addition to examining a portfolio's risk based on recent fluctuations using value at risk measures, a manager also should examine how the portfolio would have performed during the eventful times listed in Table 15.2.

Tables 15.3 and 15.4 provide examples of the recommended risk measures for a particular commodity futures portfolio. Note, for example, the properties of the soybean crush spread. It is a portfolio event-risk reducer, but it also adds to the volatility of the portfolio. An incremental contribution to risk measure based solely on recent volatilities and correlations does not give complete enough information about whether a trade is a risk reducer or risk enhancer.

Macro-Portfolio Hedging

Understanding a portfolio's exposure to certain financial or economic shocks can help in designing macro-portfolio hedges that would limit exposure to these events. For example, a commodity portfolio from the summer

TABLE 15.4 Portfolio-Effect Risk Measures

Strategy	Incremental Contribution to Portfolio Value at Risk[a]	Incremental Contribution to Worst-Case Portfolio Event Risk[a]
Deferred Reverse Soybean Crush Spread	0.08%	−0.24%
Long Deferred Natural Gas Outright	0.17%	0.19%
Short Deferred Wheat Spread	0.04%	0.02%
Long Deferred Gasoline Outright	0.33%	0.81%
Long Deferred Gasoline vs. Heating Oil Spread	0.93%	2.04%
Long Deferred Hog Spread	0.07%	−0.19%

[a]A positive contribution means that the strategy adds to risk while a negative contribution means the strategy reduces risk.
Source: Hilary Till, "Risk Management Lessons in Leveraged Commodity Futures Trading," *Commodities Now* (September 2002).

of 2002 consisted of these positions: outright long wheat, a long gasoline calendar spread, and short outright silver. When carrying out an event-risk analysis on the portfolio, one finds that the worst-case scenario was a 9/11/01 scenario. This is because the portfolio was long economically sensitive commodities and short an instrument that does well during time of flights to quality. Normally, though, these positions are unrelated to each other. Given that the scenario that would most negatively impact the portfolio was a sharp shock to business confidence, one candidate for macroportfolio insurance was short-term gasoline puts to hedge against this scenario.

LEVERAGE LEVEL

Another consideration in designing a commodity futures program is how much leverage to use. Futures trading requires a relatively small amount of margin. Trade sizing is mainly a matter of how much risk one wants to assume. An investor is not very constrained by the amount of initial capital committed to trading.

What leverage level is chosen for a program is a product design issue. The manager needs to determine how the program will be marketed and what the client's expectations will be.

According to Barclay Managed Funds Report (2001), a number of top commodity trading advisors (CTAs) have had losses in excess of –40 percent, which have been acceptable to their clients since these investment programs sometimes produce 100+ percent annual returns. Investors know up front the sort of swings in profits and losses to expect from such managers.

Choosing the leverage level for a futures program is a crucial issue because it appears that the edge that successful futures traders are able to exploit is small. Only with leverage do their returns become attractive. Table 15.5 shows how the returns to futures programs, here labeled "managed futures," become competitive only after applying the most amount of leverage of any hedge fund strategy.

In Patel (2002), Bruce Cleland of Campbell and Company, a pioneer of futures investing, discusses how essential leverage is to his firm's success: "Campbell's long-term average rate of return compounded over 31 years is over 17.6 percent net [of fees]. No market-place is going to be so inefficient as to allow any kind of systematic strategy to prevail over that period of time, to

TABLE 15.5 Levered and Delevered Returns by Hedge Fund Strategy, 1997 to 2001

Style	Average Levered Return (%)[a]	Average Delevered Return (%)[a]
Short Biased	13.7	9.3
Global Macro	16.8	8.9
Emerging Markets	16.9	8.8
Event Driven	14.7	8.3
Merger Aritrage	14.7	7.0
Long/Short Equity	14.0	6.3
Fixed income	9.6	4.8
Convertible Arbitrage	10.6	4.2
Managed Futures	10.5	4.2
Distressed Securities	n/a	n/a

[a]Leverage analysis was done for funds with five-year historical leverage and performance data.

Source: Altvest, CSFB/Tremont, EACM, HFR, Institutional Investor (June 2002), and CMRA.

Leslie Rahl, "Hedge Fund Transparency: Unraveling the Complex and Controversial Debate," RiskInvest 2002, Boston, December 10, 2002, Slide 52.

that extent. 'Our true edge is actually only around 4 percent per year, but through leverage of between 4-1 and 5-1 you are able to get a much more attractive return,' Cleland says" (page 49). This quote from the president of Campbell is very instructive for neophyte futures traders who must determine how much leverage to use in delivering their clients an attractive set of returns.

UNIQUE CONTRIBUTION TO THE INVESTOR'S OVERALL PORTFOLIO

A final consideration in creating a futures trading program is to understand how the program will fit into an investor's overall portfolio. For investors to be interested in a new investment, that investment must have a unique return stream: one that is not already obtained through their other investments. More formally, the new investment must be a diversifier, either during normal times or eventful times.

It is up to investors to determine how a new investment should fit into their portfolios. A futures trading program may be evaluated on how well it diversifies an equity portfolio. Or it may be judged based on how well it diversifies a basket of veteran CTAs. Finally, a new futures trading program may be evaluated on how well it improves a fund of hedge fund's risk-adjusted returns. Examples of each kind of evaluation follow.

Equity Diversification Example

One potential commodity futures investment is based on the Goldman Sachs Commodity Index (GSCI). One way to evaluate its potential benefits for an international equity portfolio is to use a portfolio optimizer to create the portfolio's efficient frontier both with and without an investment in the GSCI. Figure 15.7 from Satyanarayan and Varangis (1994) illustrates this approach. The efficient frontier with commodity assets lies everywhere higher than the portfolio without commodity assets, implying that for the same levels of return (risk), the portfolio with commodity assets provides lesser (higher) risk (return). This would be regarded as attractive provided that the historical returns, volatilities, and correlations used in the optimizer are expected to be representative of future results.

CTA Diversification Example

A futures program that invests solely in commodities has a natural advantage in claiming diversification benefits for a portfolio of CTAs. As Table

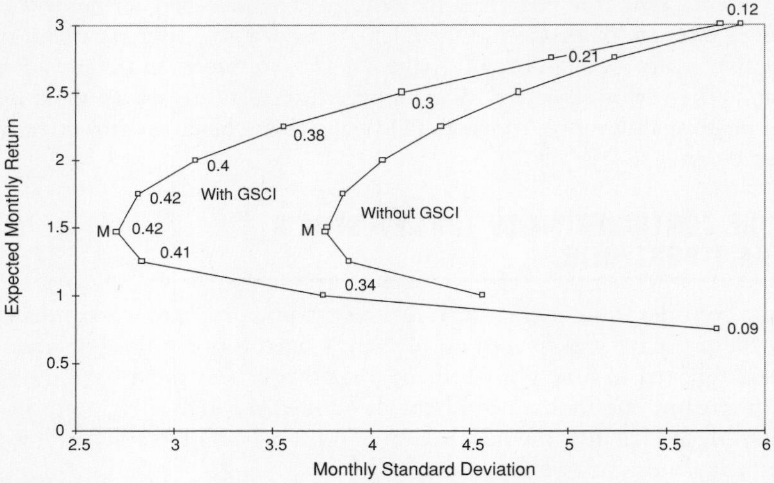

FIGURE 15.7 Optimal International Portfolios with and without Commodity Assets
Source: Sudhakar Satyanarayan and Panos Varangis, "An Efficient Frontier for International Portfolios with Commodity Assets," *Policy Research Working Paper 1266,* The World Bank, March 1994, p. 19.

Note: The numbers on the mean-standard deviation frontier refer to the percentage of the portfolio invested in commodity assets. M = minimum-risk portfolio.

15.6 illustrates, an index of managed futures returns is most strongly related to investment strategies focused on currencies, interest rates, and stocks. Commodities are in fourth place.

One way of demonstrating that a commodity investment strategy is of benefit to a diversified portfolio of CTAs is to calculate how the Sharpe ratio (excess return divided by standard deviation) would change once the new investment is added to the portfolio. Table 15.7 shows how the addition of a particular commodity manager to three diversified portfolios increases the Sharpe ratio of each portfolio. The three diversified portfolios are represented by CTA indices provided by Daniel B. Stark & Co.

Figure 15.8 illustrates another way of confirming that a futures trading program would be a diversifier for an existing investment in a basket of futures traders. Figure 15.8 shows that the Stark Diversified CTA index alone has a Sharpe ratio of about 0.72. If 60 percent is allocated to the Stark index and 40 percent to a specific advisor's program, the Sharpe ratio rises to 1.0 even though the specific advisor's program alone has a Sharpe ratio of below 1.0.

TABLE 15.6 Regression of Managed Futures Returns on Passive Indices and Economic Variables, 1996 to 2000

	Coefficient	Standard Error	*T*-Statistic
Intercept	0.00	0.00	0.01
S&P 500	0.00	0.07	0.05
Lehman US	0.29	0.39	0.76
Change in Credit Spread	0.00	0.01	0.30
Change in Term Spread	0.00	0.00	0.18
MFSB/Interest Rates	1.27	0.24	5.24
MFSB/Currency	1.37	0.25	5.48
MFSB/Physical Commodities	0.27	0.15	1.79
MFSB/Stock Indices	0.36	0.11	3.17
R-Squared	0.70		

Source: Center for International Securities and Derivatives Markets (CISDM), 2nd Annual Chicago Research Conference, May 22, 2002. Slide 48.

Note: The Managed Futures Securities Based (MFSB) Indices are designed to mimic the performance of CTAs who employ trend-following or countertrend strategies.

Fund of Hedge Fund Diversification Example

Similarly, if the futures program is expected to be a diversifier for a fund of hedge funds portfolio, whether the Sharpe ratio of the enhanced portfolio improves as well must be verified. This is illustrated in Table 15.8.

TABLE 15.7 Example of How the Sharpe Ratio of CTA Indices Changes with the Addition of a Particular Commodity Futures Program, September 1999 to March 2003

	Index Alone			With 10% GA[b] Component		
Index	CARR[a]	Vol %	Sharpe Ratio	CARR	Vol %	Sharpe Ratio
Stark Fund Index	6.80%	13.60%	0.50	7.80%	11.80%	0.66
Stark 300 CTA Index	8.70%	10.80%	0.80	9.40%	9.60%	0.98
Stark Diversified CTA	9.50%	11.60%	0.82	10.10%	10.30%	0.98

[a]Compounded annualized rate of return
[b]Global Advisors Discretionary Program, a futures trading program
Source: "The Case for Commodities," *Global Advisors* (June 2003).

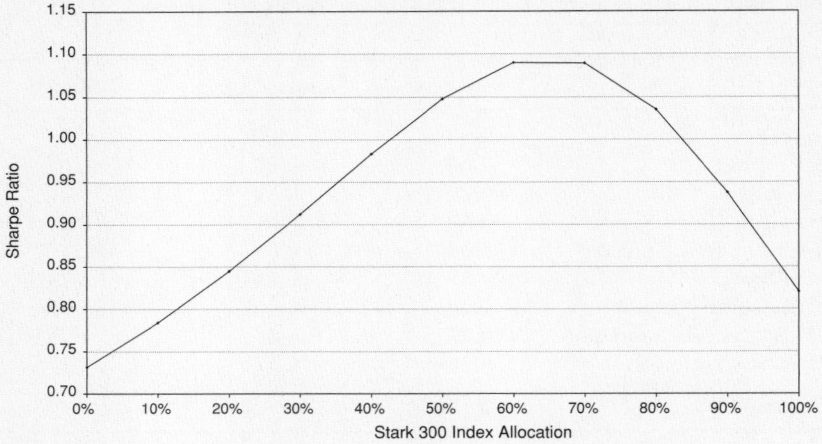

FIGURE 15.8 Efficient Portfolio GALP[a] + Stark Diversified CTA Index, September 1999 to March 2003
Source: "The Case for Commodities," *Global Advisors* (June 2003), Chart 1.
[a]Global Advisors LP.

Note: The vertical axis is the Sharpe ratio. The horizontal axis is the amount allocated to the Stark Index; the balance is allocated to the GALP trading program.

TABLE 15.8 Example of How the Sharpe Ratio of a Fund of Hedge Funds Changes with the Addition of a Particular Commodity Futures Program, September 1999 to March 2003

	Index Alone			With 10% GA[a] Component		
Index	CARR[b]	Vol%	Sharpe Ratio	CARR	Vol%	Sharpe Ratio
Model Fund of Funds Portfolio[c]	7.80%	5.00%	1.56	8.50%	5.00%	1.7

[a]Global Advisors Discretionary Program, a futures trading program
[b]Compounded annualized rate of return
[c]The model fund of funds portfolio comprises Edhec Business School indices in the following weights: 40 percent Long/Short Equity, 10 percent Convertible Arbitrage, 10 percent Global Macro, 10 percent Managed Futures, 5 percent Equity Market Neutral, 5 percent Fixed Income Arbitrage, 5 percent Distressed Securities, 5 percent Emerging Markets, 5 percent Merger Arbitrage, and 5 percent Event Driven.
Source: "The Case for Commodities," *Global Advisors* (June 2003).

CONCLUSION

This chapter has outlined the considerations involved in creating a commodity futures trading program. Commodity managers need to be aware that trading strategies can exhibit periods of high correlation, which can lead to doubling risk. We showed that adding commodity futures to a portfolio can potentially reduce overall portfolio risk. We also showed that futures programs must employ leverage in order for their returns to be competitive. To provide diversification benefits to investors, commodity managers must produce return streams that are sufficiently unrelated to those of other manager strategies as well as to traditional investments.

CHAPTER 16

Choosing the Right CTA: A Contingent Claim Approach

Zsolt Berenyi

Managed futures have enjoyed a significant increase as investments during the last one and a half decades, both on a stand-alone basis and as part of a well-diversified portfolio. Managed futures accounts, indeed, seem to offer investors significant advantages not accessible elsewhere. Yet ranking such investment opportunities either on an ex-ante or an ex-post basis is still difficult because the risk and return structure of managed futures accounts often differs from that of (more or less) common benchmarks, and the risk structure of such investments may be unstable since CTAs may change the risk exposure of the funds individually.

In this chapter we investigate the ex-post performance ranking of CTAs based on a contingent claim performance approach. In this approach, the performance of each managed futures fund is compared to individually created benchmark assets having the same risk profile in terms of particular higher moments. Benchmark assets are constructed ("replicated") using the S&P 500, options, and the risk-free asset. Using benchmark assets, we estimate the efficiency gain or loss each CTA produces and analyze the robustness of this kind of efficiency measurement with respect to the number of moments used.

INTRODUCTION

Commodity funds, which are managed by commodity trading advisors (CTAs), belong to the modern alternative investment class. Managed commodity funds (managed futures) are publicly offered investment vehicles that invest in futures and options of a wide range of financial assets as well as commodities and may employ a variety of leverage-creating techniques.

Managed futures accounts offer investors significant advantages not accessible elsewhere, due to their unconventional investment strategies. These forms of investment offer, in much the same way other modern alternative investment forms do, both diversification advantages and return profiles different from traditional investments.

From this background, research on alternative investments, predominantly on CTAs and hedge funds, has mushroomed. A particularly interesting field continues to be the performance evaluation of those alternative investments. Because they may offer highly nonnormal and optionlike return profiles, traditional performance measures used elsewhere suffer from serious disadvantages (i.e., they produce controversial results and, in particular, may be subject to gambling behavior). The performance of CTAs and hedge funds remains, however, a particularly important issue because, in spite of the somewhat controversial theoretical results on persistence in CTA performance (see, e.g., Schneeweiss 1996), investors evaluate investments, at least partially, based on past performance.

This chapter reviews the performance of a series of managed futures funds with a contingent claim–based efficiency measure, which is based on a moment-based performance evaluation methodology. First, we investigate the efficiency of CTAs as stand-alone investments based on the comparison to option-based strategies. The basis for the comparison is the risk profile of the given CTA asset, where risk is defined as some set of statistical moments. Then we compare the moment-based efficiency measures to find out whether using a more complete replication pays off in terms of monetary advantages and accuracy.

MOMENT-BASED EFFICIENCY MEASURE

Distributional Performance Evaluation

Assessing performance in case of opaque or continuously changing portfolios such as managed funds remains difficult because finding or creating a proper benchmark is still not an easy task. Here we propose a methodology in which the performance of CTA funds will be measured using synthetically created benchmarks. The main idea is to compare any investment portfolio (especially those with nonnormal return distributions like managed funds) to artificial, so-called replicating benchmarks possessing risk characteristics similar to the primary investment.

The idea that investors compare portfolios based on some statistical (or other) risk profile should not be very surprising. In the most fundamental consideration about investments, investors buy *risky time,* that is, a particular portfolio return profile provided by holding risky assets for a predefined period. Throughout this chapter, the distributional features of return streams will be called risk characteristics (valid for the particular holding period).

Return distributions certainly can be arbitrary, not just normal (as would be the usual assumption in case of equity investments). Going one step further, the particular portfolio payoff and return distribution are limited in their shape by the available investment opportunities. Performance measurement, consequently, denotes the evaluation of the particular risk characteristics of the individual payoff profiles.

The payoff distribution pricing model of Dybvig (1988a), provides a related perspective. Dybvig develops a pricing framework for assets with arbitrary return distributions. The basic idea of his work is that agents minimize the cost of any one-period return distribution, regardless of the factors that drive state probabilities. He calls the price of the minimum cost portfolio for any return distribution the distributional price (to distinguish it from the normal asset price). That is, economic agents compare return distributions resulting from any kind of investment opportunity directly.

This approach neglects the underlying structure of portfolios, considering it as irrelevant for performance comparison. However, because investors usually use cash returns from the noncash investments for consumption, we argue it is legitimate to do so. That is, it is of no relevance whether a portfolio contains common stocks or hedge funds, because *only the distribution of the investment returns for the holding period* is important for the performance assessment. This approach also may be justified by acknowledging factors like investment barriers and relative illiquidity.

Contingent Claim–Based Performance Evaluation

The possibility to create and transform arbitrary return distributions is an important property of options that has been known and used by practitioners for a long time (cf. Reback 1975). Reback (1975) states that derivative assets are able to alter the pattern of any portfolio return to create any desired shape of return distribution. Thus it is possible to create optioned portfolios mimicking other portfolios in risk characteristics by using options.

Because the return distribution of optioned portfolios can be shaped arbitrarily, they can be used as a common benchmark asset. Thus, the use of optioned markets as the reference point suggests extending the performance evaluation framework to multiple asset classes as well. Doing this facilitates the broadening of the classical one asset view to more asset classes competing with each other. In addition, also multimanager funds theoretically could be analyzed with optioned markets, if the underlying structure of the investments remains immaterial.

Indeed, the use of optioned benchmark portfolios for performance measurement purposes itself is not a novel idea. The work of Dybvig (1988a, b) also signifies implicitly that optioned portfolios can be compared to portfolios of other asset classes, regardless of the underlying asset. Glosten and Jagannathan (1994) propose the use of options to re-create contingent claims for mutual fund performance evaluation. Dynamic strategies, in much the same way as options, also can be used to create any particular payoff profile. Recently Amin and Kat (2001) have proposed a similar methodology to evaluate hedge fund returns in using path-independent dynamic strategies that have positive correlation with the underlying index. The novelty of this chapter in proposing optioned portfolios for benchmark purposes lies, however, in reducing the risk characteristics of the replicating portfolio to a handful of higher statistical moments.

EFFICIENCY GAIN/LOSS MEASURE

This section proposes using so-called replicating portfolios for benchmark purposes. Replicating portfolios are optioned portfolios designed to reproduce the risk characteristics of a given asset by combining a benchmark asset with options and the risk-free asset.

The expected return on a replicating portfolio for a given risk shape (of a particular asset) will be called the replicating return. The replicating return can be interpreted as the alternative return an investor may achieve if, holding the risk exposure (defined here in terms of return variance, skewness, and a number of higher moments) constant, she chooses to invest in the optioned market instead of investing in a given portfolio.

The efficiency gain/loss measure or excess replicating return is simply the difference between the expected return of the asset under investigation and that of its synthetic benchmark asset. The expected return of this replicating benchmark asset will be termed as the replicating return.[1]

This asset-specific replicating return embodies, at the same time, the minimum acceptable return on investments having the same risk structure, and serves thus as a natural benchmark. That is, investors always have the

[1]Certainly the replicating benchmark asset will have to be computed to achieve maximum expected return within the set of possible replicating assets with the same (moment-based) risk characteristics.

alternative of being paid the return of the replicating optioned portfolio. Consequently, this replicating return has to be exceeded by other investments exhibiting similar risk characteristics.

The efficiency gain/loss measure (the excess replicating return) takes the form

$$ERR_p = E(r_p) - RR(r_p) \tag{16.1}$$

where $E(r_p)$ = expected return on portfolio p
$RR(r_p)$ = expected replicating return

The excess replicating return can be directly interpreted as an efficiency gain, if it is positive, or an efficiency loss, if it is negative. If the replicating optioned return is higher than the expected return for an arbitrary CTA portfolio, this underlying asset offers an inferior performance (compared to the benchmark asset). That is, the comparable investment in form of an optioned portfolio offers a higher expected return for the same risk characteristics of returns. The fund's shareholder would do better with a different fund (of course, as stand-alone investment only). The excess replicating return provides a simple measure in assessing whether a portfolio outperformed others on an ex-post basis.

This measure is in a close relationship with the excess return measure proposed by Ang and Chau (1979), which is an alpha-like composite performance ratio. An important distinction is that, in the replicating case, individual portfolios do not have to possess the same systematic risk characteristics as the benchmark asset. It is sufficient if both share the same return distribution shapes.

Construction of Replicating Portfolios

As defined earlier, replicating portfolios are portfolios that have the same risk structure in terms of some statistical moments (of order three and higher) as the portfolio being assessed. The foundation for including replicating portfolios in the performance assessment is the assumption that portfolios can be created to "mimic" the risk structure of the underlying asset as benchmarks.

The present replicating framework will be termed partial, because only a reduced set of the return characteristics (the moments) is used for describing any return distributions, thereby reducing the return distribution's dimensionality.

It is very important to note that the term "replication" as we use it does not intend to create the same payoff profile in terms of identical probability distributions, nor does it intend to create portfolios having the same payoff in every possible state of nature.

For the construction of individual replicating portfolios, we used the Standard and Poor's (S&P) 500 index as underlying. Based on the assumption that returns from the index are independent and follow a lognormal distribution—a simplification that greatly facilitates the use of contingent claim–based performance evaluation but is not essential—we calculated prices for a specified number of Black-Scholes call options. Considering only call options ensures that asset returns are not linearly dependent. For the sake of simplicity, a holding period of one year is assumed.

In the next step, we used nonlinear programming for generating returns on replicating portfolios, with variance and (a predefined number of) higher statistical moments being set to that of the CTA under investigation.

This approach provides a relatively simple and robust means for calculating individual benchmark returns. This idea parallels the work of Amin and Kat (2001). They propose a point-by-point optimization algorithm with a 500-pins-setting, that is, they match 500 separate points of the return distribution, to calculate hedge fund efficiency gains/losses.

The optimization algorithm that produces replicating portfolio weights x_i, can be formulated:

$$\operatorname*{Max}_{xi} Z = \sum_i x_i E(r_i) \tag{16.2}$$

subject to

$$\begin{aligned} \sigma^2 &= \sigma_0^2 \text{ target variance} \\ s^3 &= s_0^3 \text{ target skewness} \end{aligned} \tag{16.3}$$

and the constraints on the portfolio weights

$$\sum_i x_i = 1$$

where $E(r_i)$ = expected return on asset i
σ_0^2 s_0^3 = target values for variance and skewness, respectively.

The constraints in equation 16.3 can be expanded to include moments of order higher than three.

MARKET DATA USED

For the testing, we used CTA data publicly available from TradeView (www.tradeview.com). The chosen data set contains 110 CTAs with a monthly return history of five years, from January 1998 to December 2002.

From the monthly returns, "semi ex-ante" annual discrete returns were generated with a bootstrap-like methodology i.e., drawing 12 samples with replacement from the set of monthly data, using 1,000 repetitions for each fund. This bootstrapping methodology is in the vein of the technique applied by Ederington (1995).

We used the Standard and Poor's monthly return series as underlying. As proxy for the risk-free rate, we took the one-month U.S. Dollar (USD) London Interbank Offered Rate (LIBOR).

RESULTS

Nonnormality of Returns

We test for nonnormality of returns with the Jarque and Bera (1987) test (see Greene 2000). Analyzing the samples, we find that the null hypothesis of normally distributed returns cannot be rejected at the 1 percent level for only 14 cases (11 percent of the observations) and at the 5 percent level for only 11 cases (8.7 percent). Clearly, the sample of CTA funds is highly nonnormal. This should underline the need for a performance measure that accounts for nonnormality of returns.

Portfolio Efficiency Rankings by the Excess Replicating Return

The excess replicating return (ERR) is, in much the same way as the Sharpe ratio, a composite—risk-adjusted—performance measure. It is risk adjusted because the ERR is calculated always to a given level of risk. Thus risk adjustment takes place indirectly by applying an additive, not multiplicative, rule.

The ERR, again, denotes the return differential between the expected return of a particular asset and its replicating counterpart. It is designed to assess the value added by the portfolio manager—that is, the efficiency gain or loss. Negative values would mean that the investor is better off buying the same risk structure through options instead of investing in the given asset/CTA and vice versa.

We investigated the efficiency of the CTA sample. Figures 16.1 and 16.2 summarize the main results of the analysis. The first diagram displays the excess replicating returns for the second moment case (variance only), sorted by magnitude. It is evident that, for the sample being investigated, CTAs provided a risk-adjusted performance that is—to a large extent—not accessible on the stock markets. That is, about 80 percent of the CTAs perform better than the replicating optioned portfolios based on the S&P 500.

Nonetheless, two factors have to be considered.

1. In the time period investigated, the S&P delivered an annual return of about 5.6 percent, which is barely higher that the estimated risk-free rate (4.2 percent).
2. For technical reasons, we have not accounted for possible survivorship bias, which may be expected to have a substantial impact on the overall performance.

Figure 16.2 displays the excess replicating returns for the nine-moment case, but in the same ranking order, as in Figure 16.1. It is noticeable that the basic performance characteristics of the CTAs are mirrored fairly well with the two-moment method; this suggests that a large part of the replicating return is attributable to the variance itself. Yet we certainly can also ascertain some significant discrepancies between the rankings of the two cases that should be subject to a closer look.

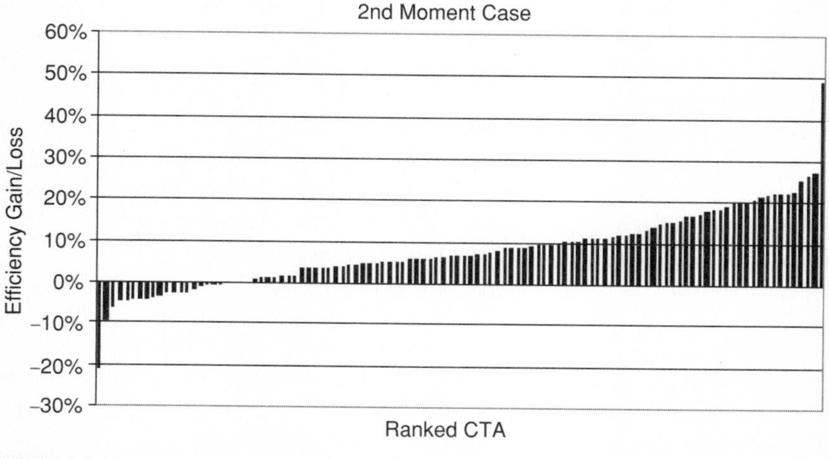

FIGURE 16.1 Efficiency Gain/Loss Measure (Variance Only) for the CTA Samples, Sorted

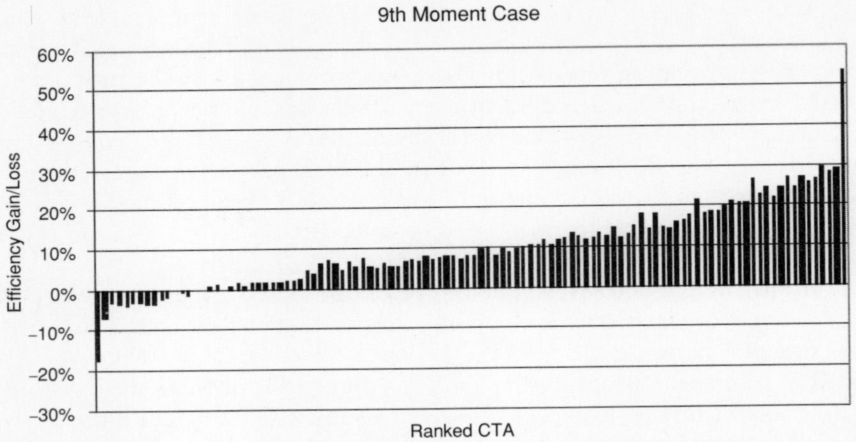

FIGURE 16.2 Efficiency Gain/Loss Measure for the CTA Samples, Sorted by Rankings of the Variance Only Case

Rank Correlation Statistics

Let us assume that the more complete description of the CTA return distributions (the use of more moments) enables a more robust and exact performance measurement. We would like to investigate the overall properties of the moment-based replicating measures and determine how the ranking result is affected by calculating replicating returns with a lower number of moments. Using the optimization algorithm, we obtained eight portfolios, M2 through M9, by specifying 2 through 9 moments in the constraints, respectively. We then replicated returns in each portfolio and obtained the Sharpe ratio and ERR measures of the replicated returns. Next, we calculated rank correlations (Spearman correlations) between the particular ERR measures and Sharpe ratio, which evaluates the closeness of the rankings produced by the different methods of performance evaluation. Table 16.1 sums up the results of the calculation. As can be seen, the moment-based measures lie within a limited range, that is, the rankings provided by them are very close to each other: The rank correlations are always higher than 0.99. It is also noticeable that the rank correlation between the Sharpe ratio and the moment-based measures is high but lower than the rank correlation between the moment-based measures themselves.

Then we repeated the analysis with a slightly different frame, drawing small samples repeatedly and comparing the percentage of identical decisions regarding the best possible CTA. Not surprisingly, when drawing sam-

TABLE 16.1 Simple Rank Correlation Between Particular Performance Measures

	Sharpe Ratio	ERR M2	ERR M3	ERR M4	ERR M5	ERR M6	ERR M7	ERR M8	ERR M9
Sharpe Ratio	1.0000								
ERR M2	0.7675	1.0000							
ERR M3	0.7669	0.9999	1.0000						
ERR M4	0.7696	0.9997	0.9998	1.0000					
ERR M5	0.7595	0.9981	0.9984	0.9985	1.0000				
ERR M6	0.7575	0.9974	0.9978	0.9979	0.9995	1.0000			
ERR M7	0.7497	0.9952	0.9956	0.9956	0.9964	0.9966	1.0000		
ERR M8	0.7439	0.9958	0.9961	0.9958	0.9959	0.9959	0.9956	1.0000	
ERR M9	0.7288	0.9935	0.9939	0.9935	0.9930	0.9928	0.9927	0.9958	1.0000

TABLE 16.2 Ratio of Identical Decisions (Sample Size 10, 1,000 Times) with Particular Performance Measures

	Sharpe Ratio	ERR M2	ERR M3	ERR M4	ERR M5	ERR M6	ERR M7	ERR M8	ERR M9
Sharpe Ratio	1								
ERR M2	0.353	1							
ERR M3	0.394	1.000	1						
ERR M4	0.409	0.998	1.000	1					
ERR M5	0.354	0.922	0.963	0.943	1				
ERR M6	0.362	0.941	0.948	0.949	0.994	1			
ERR M7	0.374	0.861	0.903	0.902	0.896	0.919	1		
ERR M8	0.336	0.92	0.917	0.937	0.903	0.949	0.937	1	
ERR M9	0.326	0.871	0.918	0.928	0.918	0.931	0.899	0.945	1

TABLE 16.3 Contribution of Higher Moments to the Replicating Returns

	Moment 3	Moment 4	Moment 5	Moment 6
Absolute contribution	–0.062%	–0.032%	–0.261%	–0.069%
Relative contribution	–1.540%	–0.730%	–5.974%	–1.348%

	Moment 7	Moment 8	Moment 9
Absolute contribution	–0.602%	–0.477%	–0.422%
Relative contribution	–15.530%	–11.985%	–13.001%

ples of 10 CTAs 1,000 times, it turns out that the moment-based replicating measures produce also very similar results, as it can be seen in Table 16.2.

How Many Moments?

Thus the different moment-based replicating measures produce very similar results. The most important question is: How many moments are sufficient to reproduce the results of the quasi-benchmark (i.e., the nine-moment case)?

To cast some light on this question, we calculated the absolute as well as the relative contributions of every higher moment to the replicating returns. That is, we tried to determine whether the absolute as well as the relative contribution (i.e., the absolute difference between two corresponding moment replicating returns divided by the level of the replicating return) diminishes as the number of moments increases.

As Table 16.3 shows, this is, unfortunately, not the case. Somewhat surprisingly, the moments 7, 8, and 9 have all an average relative contribution to the replicating return of over 10 percent. This fact indicates that considering the first few moments only may provide a good correlation in the ranking properties but not necessarily a good approximation in terms of absolute value of the replicating return.

Put differently, for such nonnormal cases, we found only weak evidence for supporting the use of only the variance in the calculation of replicating returns.

CONCLUSION

We investigated the ranking properties of the moment-based replicating efficiency measures on a sample of CTA managed funds.

Summing up, we found that (neglecting any possible survivorship bias) using these measures, the majority of the funds investigated had a performance superior to the S&P 500. We also found that the moment-based replicating measures of efficiency gain/loss produce results very close to each other in terms of rank correlation. In addition, the Sharpe ratio and the moment-based efficiency measures produce a higher rank correlation but a lower rate of identical decisions.

However, we also found that the higher moments have a high absolute and relative contribution to the replicating return. This fact implies that although the replicating measures may be very useful for ranking assets with nonnormally distributed returns, the magnitude of the replicating returns is not robust to the number of moments used in the replication. In particular, important contributions to replicating returns will be omitted if moments of low order only (like the variance) are used. Thus, further research is needed to evaluate the usefulness of approximations of the true replicating return based on two (or three) moments.

CHAPTER 17

CTAs and Portfolio Diversification: A Study through Time

Nicolas Laporte

The standard mean/variance framework and the concept of efficient frontiers are one way of assessing the portfolio added value of a hedge fund strategy such as CTAs. However, even if it provides interesting results, this framework is a two-dimensional one and it gives a static vision of the CTAs' industry. Changes in correlation or volatility over time are ignored. To provide a more dynamic approach, this chapter presents a three-dimensional framework with time as the third variable. It assesses the evolution of the CTAs' diversification abilities in a portfolio environment over the last decade.

INTRODUCTION

Commodity trading advisors (CTAs) are professional money managers. They manage the assets of their clients using derivative instruments (futures, forwards, and options) on commodities and money markets around the world. As an asset category in the alternative investment industry, they are classified as "managed futures." CTAs' strategies range from systematic models to discretionary approaches, the first one being the most common. CTAs are, most of the time, considered trend followers.

Even though CTAs have existed for a while, only a few studies have been published about them. The term "CTAs" appears regularly in publications but, most of the time, is far from being the main topic. Usually CTAs are mentioned because of their affiliation to the hedge fund industry. Looking at the practitioner side, the same conclusion can be made.

Although it is true that most of the financial players are familiar with CTAs (CTAs, in fact, have the reputation of being low/negatively correlated to any asset family, including hedge funds), most of the time, this interesting feature is all they know about them.

Based on these findings, it is interesting to propose a study focusing uniquely on the CTA industry with, as main objective, the definition of their added value in portfolio allocation. Different statistics and portfolio frameworks (with two or three dimensions) are then considered. Each brings new information and helps in understanding the managed futures universe. Note that the three-dimensional framework used with portfolio allocations is definitively the "pioneering" part of this study.

The chapter is organized in three parts. The first part compares CTAs with other assets. Two types of values are computed: plain statistics (static view of the CTA industry) and rolling statistics (dynamic approach, which takes into account time evolutions). The second part focuses on portfolio optimization and efficient frontiers. Its objective is to assess the CTAs' diversification capacity. As in the first part, CTAs are considered under a static and a dynamic perspective. The dynamic perspective considers time evolutions using a three-dimensional representation.

CTAs

CTAs' Quantitative Description

As for any financial asset, the CTAs' universe is assessable through indices compiled by several providers. In theory, these indices should match each other in terms of volatility and performance since they are constructed on the same original universe (they are supposed to proxy the same industry). In practice, it is rarely the case. Indices are constructed using different methodologies (each methodology defines rebalancing dates, index component selections, survivorship bias correction, etc.) and, even more important, different data sources. It generates, most of the time, significant patterns dissimilarity between them.

In the case of CTAs, there are two major index providers: CSFB/Tremont and Barclay Group. It is interesting to consider these two indices[1] (see Figure 17.1). Because they are traceable from December 1993, our historical

[1]Of course, the purpose of this comparison is not to run an index quality test. As mentioned, it is logical to find differences between indices since their methodologies and universe selection process are different.

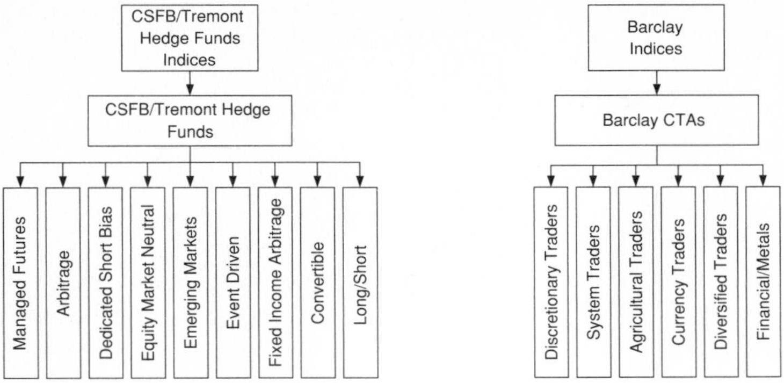

The CSFB/Tremont Hedge Fund Indices are asset weighted. CSFB/Tremont uses the TASS database. The CSFB/Tremont universe consists only of funds with a minimum of US $10 million under management and a current audited financial statement. Funds are separated into primary subcategories based on their investment style. Managed Futures proxies the CTAs' universe. Funds are not removed from the index until they are liquidated or fail to meet the financial reporting requirements. The index is calculated on a monthly basis. Funds are reselected quarterly.

The Barclay CTA Index is unweighted and rebalanced at the beginning of each year. To qualify for inclusion in the CTA Index, an advisor must have four years of prior performance history. The restrictions offset high turnover rates of trading advisors as well as artificially high short-term performance records.
The Barclay CTA Index also includes six separate subindices of managed futures programs, based on portfolio composition and trading style.
For a managed program to be included in any of these subindices, they must have at least 12 full months of prior performance history, with no extracted performance.

FIGURE 17.1 CSFB/Tremont CTA Index versus Barclay

index database goes from this date to December 2002, which corresponds to 109 monthly index levels. From this database, it is easy to extract some statistics. They are displayed in Figure 17.2 and provide a first step in the CTAs' performance assessment.

Clearly, the CTA index and the managed futures index present similar annualized returns (respectively 6.44 percent and 6.26 percent). However, their volatilities differ significantly: The annualized standard deviations are, respectively, 8.39 percent and 11.94 percent (40 percent superior to the Barclay volatility). CSFB/Tremont provides a riskier (or more volatile) view of the industry than Barclay Group.

In a risk/return framework, CTAs do not have an exceptional profile compared to other hedge fund investment strategies (e.g., global macro) or even some traditional equity groups (e.g., real estate investment trust [REIT] equities).

Actually, only two hedge funds families have lower returns than CTAs: the dedicated short bias and the emerging markets. Such a finding is not that surprising, and the origin of their poor results is related to their invest-

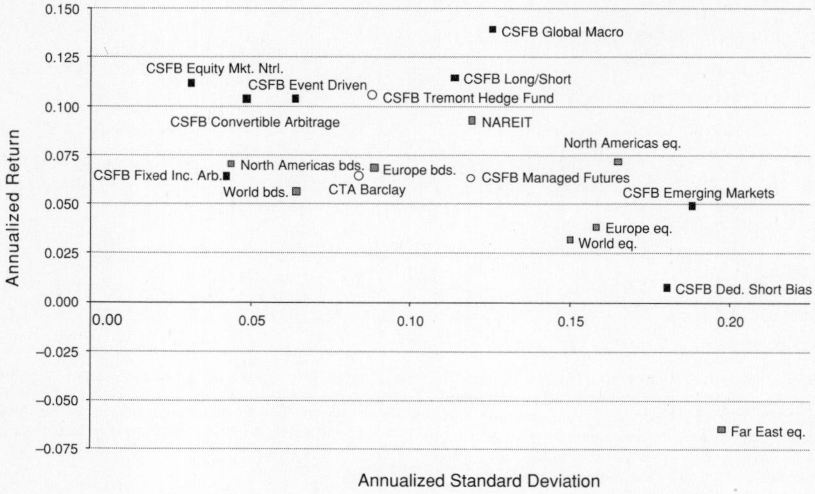

	Annualized returns	Annualized std. dev.	Min	Max
World bonds	0.0581	0.0628	−0.0354	0.0585
North Americas bonds	0.0703	0.0441	−0.0249	0.0384
Europe bonds	0.0682	0.0887	−0.0500	0.0849
World equities	0.0314	0.1503	−0.1445	0.0853
North Americas equities	0.0715	0.1652	−0.1548	0.0938
Europe equities	0.0384	0.1586	0.0037	0.0033
Far East equities	−0.0649	0.1980	−0.1295	0.1676
NAREIT	0.0926	0.1197	0.0075	0.0076
CSFB Tremont Hedge Fund	0.1054	0.0882	0.0096	0.0097
Convertible Arbitrage	0.1013	0.0488	0.0090	0.0090
Ded. Short Bias	0.0079	0.1805	−0.0010	−0.0009
Emerging Markets	0.0489	0.1885	0.0047	0.0042
Equity Mkt. Ntrl.	0.1095	0.0316	0.0092	0.0094
Event Driven	0.1038	0.0643	0.0087	0.0087
Fixed Inc. Arb.	0.0661	0.0416	0.0059	0.0060
Global Macro	0.1396	0.1260	0.0125	0.0127
Long/Short	0.1149	0.1139	0.0105	0.0105
Managed Futures	0.0626	0.1194	0.0045	0.0046
CTA Barclay	0.0644	0.0839	0.0055	0.0057

FIGURE 17.2 Statistics for CTA Performance Assessment
All calculations are based on monthly data from December 1993 to December 2002. Data sources are Morgan Stanley Capital International (equity and bond indices), NAREIT (REIT index), CSFB/Tremont (hedge fund indices, including the managed futures index), and Barclay Group (CTA index).

ment styles and their ensuing relation with the markets. Concerning the dedicated short bias, this strategy lost most of its interest during the strong telecom/information technology bull period. The emerging markets funds focus on hazardous businesses; because they invest in debt, equity, and trade claims of companies located in emerging countries, they deal with an important lack of transparency and have many uncertainties linked to economical, political, and social factors. (The Russian bond default is one extreme example.)

As with the two previous hedge funds strategies, the relative underperformance of CTAs is, in large part, explainable by the specificities of their business. Future managers focus on a few highly volatile and speculative markets, which reduces their physical investment opportunities. CTAs did not really take advantage of the increasing markets globalization (compared to some other hedge funds families). Moreover, most of them are trend followers, meaning that they go long or short with a lag compared to the markets. In the best cases, this lag reduces their benefits; in the worst cases, it generates heavy losses. It is true that managers significantly leverage their positions to increase their returns, but the use of leverage does not compensate for the lack of diversification and the important risk bearing.

Besides these negative issues, investors see in CTAs an interesting investment vehicle because they have been historically low/negatively correlated to the other financial assets. This characteristic is the logic consequence of their business (CTAs do not invest in standard assets but instead deal with futures, a product not frequently used by the other hedge fund managers), and it is clearly verified Figure 17.3. CTAs do provide a low correlation level with standard assets (stocks and bonds) and hedge fund strategies. Of course, because of the index methodologies differences, results differ from one index to the other. The values range from –0.207 to 0.376 for the CTA index and from –0.283 to 0.339 for the managed futures index. The difference in methodologies and data sources between the two indices is assessed by the managed futures/CTAs index correlation: The value is 0.805 (a relatively low result for two products proxying the same industry).

CTAs through Time

Even if findings are interesting and help in defining the CTAs' behavior relative to other assets, they give a static view of this investment strategy, so they are unable to detect any temporal change in return, volatility, or correlation. Time variations are simply ignored.

A dynamic approach that uses rolling windows is therefore warranted. This technique uses moving subsamples as inputs for the statistics' compu-

	CTA Barclay	Futures	CSFB Hedge Fund	Conv. Arb.	Ded. Short Bias	Emerging Markets	Equity Mkt. Ntrl.	Event Driven	Fixed Inc. Arb.	Global Macro	Long Short
CTA Barclay	1										
Managed Futures	0.805	1									
CSFB Tremont Hedge Fund	0.219	0.073	1								
Convertible Arbitrage	−0.100	−0.283	0.408	1							
Ded. Short Bias	0.213	0.295	−0.471	−0.224	1						
Emerging Markets	−0.120	−0.164	0.647	0.349	−0.568	1					
Equity Mkt. Ntrl.	0.218	0.158	0.335	0.324	−0.391	0.236	1				
Event Driven	−0.156	−0.269	0.657	0.598	−0.609	0.699	0.391	1			
Fixed Inc. Arb.	0.041	−0.120	0.453	0.546	−0.063	0.299	0.091	0.381	1		
Global Macro	0.376	0.239	0.861	0.300	−0.113	0.405	0.207	0.365	0.463	1	
Long/Short	−0.018	−0.093	0.781	0.267	−0.738	0.591	0.353	0.662	0.205	0.422	1

	Europe Bonds	North Americas Bonds	Europe Equity	North Americas Equity	Far East Equity	NAREIT Equity	CTA Barclay	Futures
Europe Bonds	1							
North Americas Bonds	0.394	1						
Europe Equity	0.054	−0.117	1					
North Americas Equity	−0.189	−0.037	0.781	1				
Far East Equity	0.014	−0.109	0.514	0.521	1			
NAREIT	0.035	0.005	0.286	0.292	0.089	1		
CTA Barclay	0.170	0.366	−0.207	−0.193	−0.094	−0.047	1	
Managed Futures	0.310	0.339	−0.197	−0.269	−0.035	−0.093	0.805	1

FIGURE 17.3 Correlation of CTAs with Standard Assets and Hedge Fund Strategies
All calculations are based on monthly data from December 1993 to December 2002. Data sources are Morgan Stanley Capital International (equity and bond indices), NAREIT (REIT index), CSFB/Tremont (hedge fund indices, including the Managed Futures index) and Barclay Group (CTA index).

tation. From the practical perspective, the choice of the subsample length (or rolling window) is the sensitive step. A large window limits the number of statistics and smooths results while increasing the econometric significance. A small one does exactly the opposite. With a database going from December 1993 to December 2002, a time period of 36 months is a good compromise. It allows the generation of 73 sets of statistics (starting in December 1996).

This time approach provides interesting results on the CTAs' standard deviation for two reasons (Figure 17.4). First, it highlights the strong instability of volatility through time, which was not assessable with the previous statistics (see Figure 17.2). Second, even if the range of values differs from one index to the other (from 0.067 to 0.092 for the CTA index and 0.099 to 0.131 for the managed futures index), the trend is similar, which is comforting (the two indices are a proxy of the same universe). Note that the managed futures standard deviation is more volatile than the CTA standard deviation. It confirms observations obtained with the previous statistics.

Another interesting application for the rolling statistics is on correlations. Based on a 36-month window, the correlation is estimated exactly as for the standard deviation. The main results are shown in Figures 17.5 and 17.6.

Figure 17.5 illustrates the evolution of the CTAs' correlation with several equity indices. Similar to the standard deviation, there is clearly instability through time, and the two indices have a similar trend. The correlation had a strong move-down in late summer 1998 and decreased since that period. In December 2002, CTAs are negatively related to the equity industry. For the CTAs' index, the values range from −0.59 (North Americas/

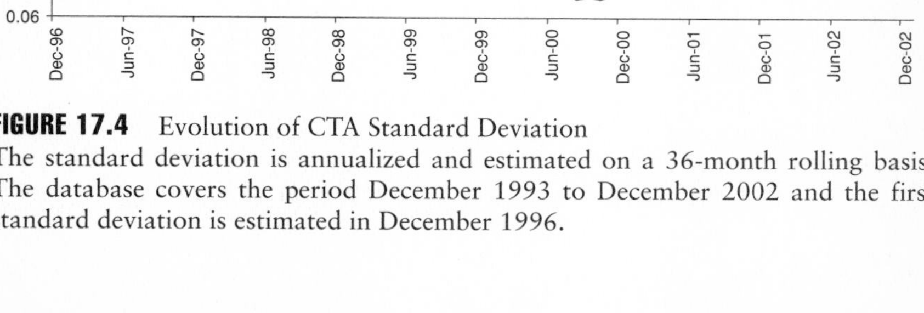

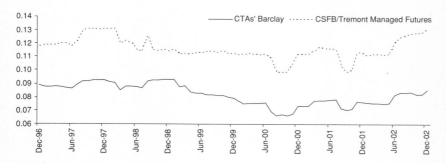

FIGURE 17.4 Evolution of CTA Standard Deviation
The standard deviation is annualized and estimated on a 36-month rolling basis. The database covers the period December 1993 to December 2002 and the first standard deviation is estimated in December 1996.

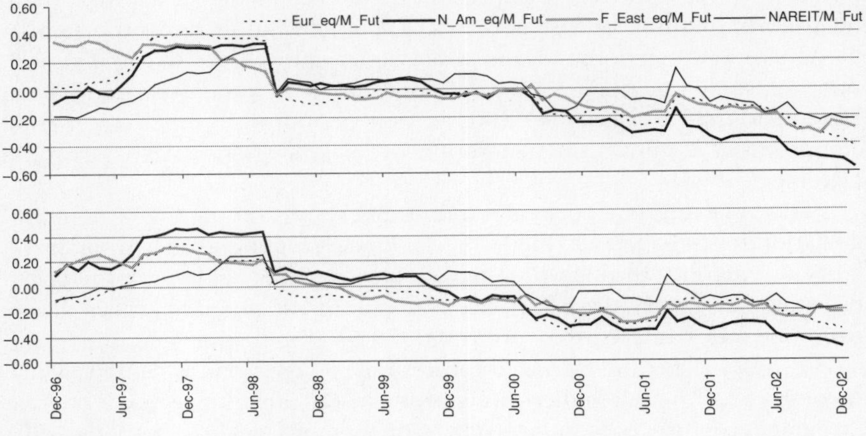

FIGURE 17.5 Evolution of CTA Correlation with Equity Indices
The correlation is estimated on a 36-month rolling basis. The database covers the period December 1993 to December 2002, and the first correlation is estimated in December 1996.

CTAs) to –0.21 (REIT/CTAs). This negative correlation implies that CTAs provide positive returns when equities do not, which is a nice feature.

More generally, when looking at the overall period covered by Figure 17.5, CTAs tend to be positively or neutrally correlated to markets in bullish periods while being negatively correlated in bearish markets.

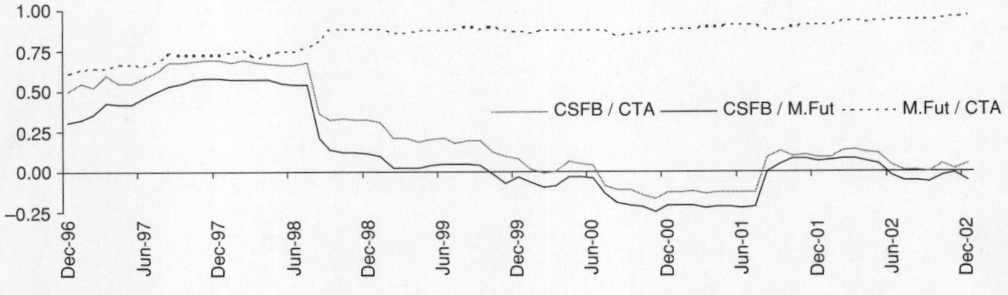

FIGURE 17.6 Correlation at the Two CTA Indices with Each Other and with the CTA/Tremont Hedge Fund Index
The correlation is estimated on a 36-month rolling basis. The database covers the period December 1993 to December 2002, and the first correlation is estimated in December 1996.

Figure 17.6 shows the correlation of the two CTAs indices with each other and the correlation with the Credit Suisse First Boston FBCS/Tremont Hedge Fund index. The two CTAs versus hedge funds profiles are identical, but the correlation through time (as for the standard deviation) fluctuates. With the progression of the years, the managed futures indices are less and less related to the hedge fund industry. In December 2002 (based on the last 36-month values), the correlation is around zero. With such results, CTAs also can be expected to be a source of diversification for hedge fund portfolios.

Note that the correlation between the two CTAs indices ranges from 0.6 at the beginning of 1997 to almost 1 in December 2002. This convergence is consistent with the previously observed common trends on standard deviation and correlation for the two indices. It reflects increasing similarities on the different index provider's universes. (The current data available for the index computations are definitively more transparent and accessible for any index provider than they were six or eight years ago.)

CTAs AND PORTFOLIO OPTIMIZATION

Our findings lend support to the claim that CTAs are without a doubt an extra source of diversification in portfolios. This claim is far from being new and is actually the main market players' belief about CTAs. However, because something everyone believes is not necessarily true, we now focus on verifying this assumption through a simple portfolio optimization framework. This framework is based on three steps:

1. Creation of different pools of assets, including pools without CTAs.
2. Construction of efficient frontiers with each of the pools.
3. Comparison of the efficient frontiers built with CTAs to those constructed without CTAs and determination if this hedge fund strategy adds value at the portfolio level or not in terms of risk/returns.

Recall that, in a risk/return framework, the efficient frontier represents all the risk/return combinations where the risk is minimized for a specific return (or the return is maximized for a specific risk). Each minima (or maxima) is reached thanks to an optimal asset allocation. The process of constructing efficient frontiers through an asset weight optimization is summarized in this definition:

> *For all possible target portfolio returns, find portfolio weights (i.e., asset allocation) such as the portfolio volatility is minimized and the following constraints are respected: no short sale, full investment, and weight limits if any.*

Clearly, the resulting efficient frontier depends on the returns, volatility, and correlations of the considered assets, but it also depends on the constraints (maximum and minimum weight limit, no short selling, and full investment) fixed by the portfolio manager.

Assets used in this chapter are indices only. There are advantages in considering indices for a portfolio optimization, because they cover market areas large enough to avoid an excessive number of elements in the pool and cover the most relevant asset classes. Of course, they must be selected in such a way they do not overlap each other. Practically, the chosen assets are either standard indices (equities and bonds) or alternative investment indices (hedge funds):

- Bonds indices: MSCI North Americas, MSCI Europe.
- Stock indices: MSCI North Americas, MSCI Europe, MSCI Far East, NAREIT index.
- Hedge funds indices: CSFB/Tremont and its nine subindices (Convertible Arbitrage, Dedicated Short Bias, Emerging Markets, Equity Market Neutral, Event Driven, Fixed Income Arbitrage, Global Macro, Long/Short, Managed Futures).
- Two CTAs indices are available. To avoid the multiplication of figures, only the managed futures index from CSFB/Tremont is considered for the portfolio optimizations.

Based on a database of 108 monthly returns (December 1993 to December 2002), four pools of indices are created (see Figure 17.7). The first one contains only traditional assets (stocks and bonds). The second corresponds to the first one plus CTAs. The third one has traditional assets and all the hedge funds strategies except CTAs. Finally, the last one is made of all traditional assets and hedge funds strategies including CTAs. Whether to consider or not consider CTAs in the pools should affect the generated efficient frontiers and highlight any diversification capacity of CTAs.

Concerning the portfolio optimizations, two frameworks are used: a classical two-dimensional risk-return framework and a three-dimensional one (a risk/return/time framework; the time being introduced with rolling statistics). The three-dimensional framework should capture time changes, which are rarely presented in portfolio allocation studies.

Portfolio Optimization and Constraints

Before being specific about CTAs, it is important to have a brief reminder of portfolio optimization and constraints. As mentioned, the efficient frontier's shape strongly depends on the weight threshold applied during the

								Hedge Funds Indices							
	Europe bonds	Europe equity	North American bonds	North American equity	Far East equity	REIT equity	**Managed Futures**	Convertible	Arbitrage	Dedicated Short Bias	Emerging Markets	Equity Market Neutral	Event Driven	Fixed Income Arbitrage	Long/Short
Pool of assets I	x	x	x	x	x	x									
Pool of assets II	x	x	x	x	x	x	**x**								
Pool of assets III	x	x	x	x	x	x		x	x	x	x	x	x	x	x
Pool of assets IV	x	x	x	x	x	x	**x**	x	x	x	x	x	x	x	x

FIGURE 17.7 Four Pools of Indices
Each pool is made of several assets: equity indices (MSCI), bond indices (MSCI), a REIT index (NAREIT), different hedge funds strategies (CSFB/Tremont), and a CTA index (Barclay Group).

portfolio optimization. The "best" efficient frontiers always are built when there are no weight limits (see Figures 17.8a and b.) However, unconstrained efficient frontiers do not represent real investment conditions. Most of the time, a "free" optimization allocates unrealistic weights to the assets. They also do not fit, most of the time, either the investor's legal requirements and/or the risk profile (see Figure 17.9).

CTAs' Portfolio Optimization, Full Data

This section determines whether the common belief about CTAs, that CTAs are an attractive investment vehicle and they bring diversification to portfolios, is true. We have seen that, from the statistical point of view, there is a high probability of CTAs adding value to portfolios. But, do they really add value for all types of portfolios, or only under a particular asset allocation environment? To answer to these questions, several efficient frontiers are generated with various baskets of assets and constraints.

Varying the asset to be included in portfolios and the constraints highlights several interesting features about CTAs. In a traditional asset universe (no hedge funds), CTAs do in fact add value to conservative

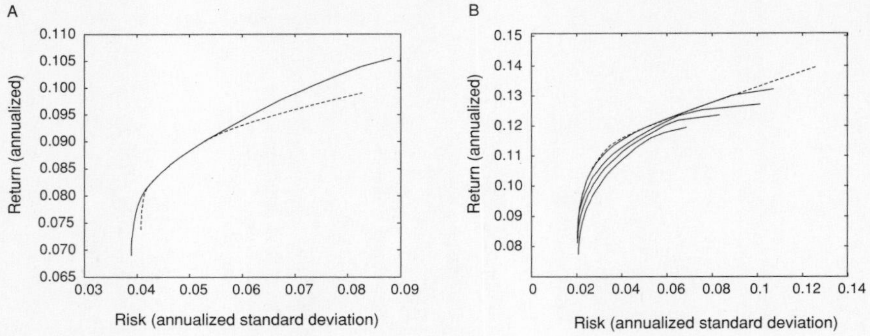

FIGURE 17.8 Efficient Frontiers and Asset Allocation Constraints
Two efficient frontiers are built on the pool of assets II (Figure A). The two optimizations assume a full investment and no short sale. The first efficient frontier (solid line) is generated without weight constraints and the second one (dashed line) with weight constraints (a maximum 50 percent allocation per asset). If the weight increases (the constraint is less strict), the efficient frontier tends to be similar to the unconstrained efficient frontier (Figure B, dashed line). Four efficient frontiers (solid lines) are built on the pool of assets IV (portfolio fully invested and no short sale).

portfolios (they significantly increase low-risk portfolio returns). But this return enhancement rapidly decreases and becomes null when considering higher risk portfolios (see Figures 17.10 and 17.11a). The return enhancement is verified in constrained and unconstrained environments. With a constant asset universe, the lower the weight threshold is, the more important is the CTAs' added value, which was expected (assets such as hedge funds are rapidly capped).

Finally, when considering a portfolio mixing traditional and alternative assets, CTAs also add value but only if the optimization process is constrained (see Figures 17.10 and 17.11b). The added value itself is much smaller than when constructing efficient frontiers with standard indices. CTAs apparently cannot compete with the other hedge funds strategies on a free asset allocation construction. Once again, this conclusion was expected. In fact, even if CTAs are low correlated with the hedge funds industry, their returns are not exceptionally impressive. And correlation is only one of the factors to be considered in a portfolio optimization. Weight constraints, returns, and volatility (standard deviation) definitely influence the definition of the optimal weight of an optimal portfolio.

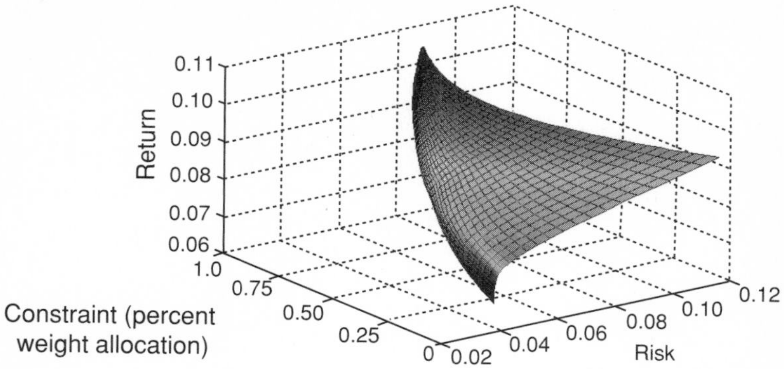

FIGURE 17.9 Consequence of Weight Constraints on the Efficient Surface
The efficient surface is built on the pool of assets II. Leverage is not allowed and the portfolio is fully invested. For each efficient frontier, the same asset is constrained (the North Americas index) with an increasing fixed weight in the portfolio. The range of weight goes from 0 percent (unconstrained portfolio) to 100 percent (portfolio made of a single asset). As a constraint increases, the efficient surface is reduced and tends to a single risk/return combination (100 percent allocation in a single asset).

As an example, let us focus on one portfolio optimization (Figures 17.11a and b). These assumptions are applied on the pool of assets IV (15 members): no constraints, full investment, and no short sell. The optimization includes assets having the best risk/return profiles. Hedge funds strategies like global macro or the REIT equities are immediately selected, which is not the case for CTAs. CTAs are not included in any efficient portfolio construction. The asset allocation is totally different when weight restrictions are applied: The best risk/return assets are rapidly capped, and the optimization process considers other assets such as CTAs.

Note that in the real world, portfolio allocations are weight-capped. No investor takes the risk to be fully invested in a single asset family (absence of diversification). Moreover, most of the time, investors have to deal with regulations that forbid excessive weights. As it has been demonstrated that, in a constrained universe, CTAs add diversification to portfolios (especially when the original portfolio is made of standard assets) this strategy is worth being considered. It confirms the results discussed earlier and also investors' belief about CTAs as a diversification vehicle.

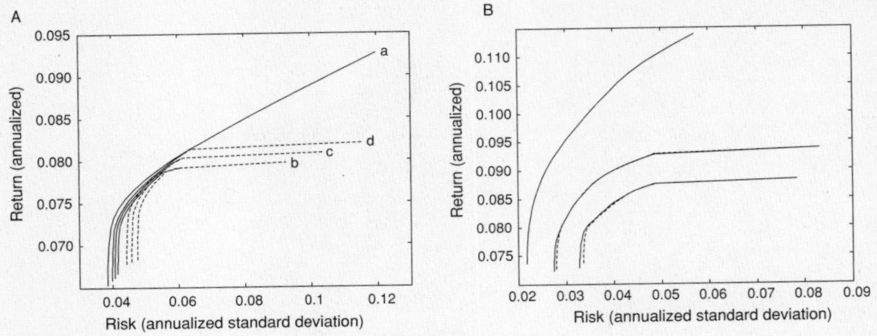

FIGURE 17.10 Comparative CTA Portfolio Optimization
In the first figure (A), four efficient frontiers are built with different weight thresholds (absence of constraints (line a), maximum weight per asset of 0.4 (lines b), 0.45 (lines c) and 0.5 (lines d)). The assets considered below to the pools I (standard assets, without CTAs (dashed lines)) and II (standard assets, with CTAs (solid lines)). The optimizations assume a full investment of the portfolio with no short sell. With a low cap level, the inclusion of CTAs significantly improve the performance of risk averse investors.
Similar results are obtained with the pool of assets III/IV (standard and alternative assets, without/with CTAs) for two of the three efficient frontiers (Figure B). The performance improvement is less significant than the one observed with the first figure. CTAs are not included in the unconstrained portfolio (single solid line).

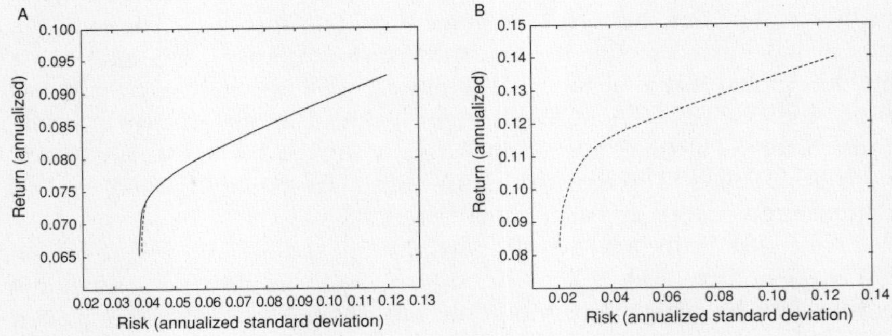

FIGURE 17.11 Comparative Unconstrained CTA Portfolio Optimization
In figure A, two unconstrained efficient frontiers are generated on the pools of assets I (without CTAs, dashed line) and II (with CTAs, solid line). Managed futures add diversification to low-risk portfolios. The inclusion of CTAs on a pool of assets including standard (equities and bonds) and alternative (hedge funds) vehicles is useless in an unconstrained environment (Figure B).

CTAs' Portfolio Optimization, Rolling Window

Because the previous efficient frontiers use the full database, the results give an interesting but static view of the CTAs' diversification ability. Furthermore, time is ignored. Over the period December 1993 to December 2002, many economical, financial, and even political events impacted the markets and influenced the CTAs' industry. Consequently, the inclusion of time as a parameter in an efficient frontier study should provide interesting results.

In practice, this time perspective is included in the efficient frontier construction simply by combining the portfolio optimization with the rolling windows technique. For each of the rolling windows (subsample of the historical database), an efficient frontier is computed. Each efficient frontier reflects the subsample allocation structure.

Because this approach considers three different variables, the clearest way to represent results is to construct a three-dimensional framework, the axes being the risk, the return, and the time. The resulting surface is generated based on a sequence of efficient frontiers, and it can be considered as a three-dimensional efficient surface. Practically, the surface is built in this way:

- Select a 36-month data range, starting in December 1993.
- Compute portfolio statistics for this range of data.
- Construct the efficient frontier.
- Move to the next month and start the same process again.
- Repeat the same procedure for each month until December 2002.

The efficient surface presented in Figure 17.12 is the result of the constrained portfolio optimization through time on pool of assets II. The surface is unstable; significant jumps in values and some brutal length reductions are observable. Nevertheless, this instability is logical. Because the input needed for each of the efficient frontiers (the rolling statistics) varied significantly through time, so does the resulting efficient surface. This instability implies that, every month, the available efficient portfolios are different. They evolve from one month to the next. Some risk/return combinations are not reachable anymore (combinations not accessible by any weight allocation[2]) or no longer efficient. New combinations also may emerge.

---

[2]The same portfolio construction rules are kept through time. The introduction of leverage, for example, would substantially modify the results.

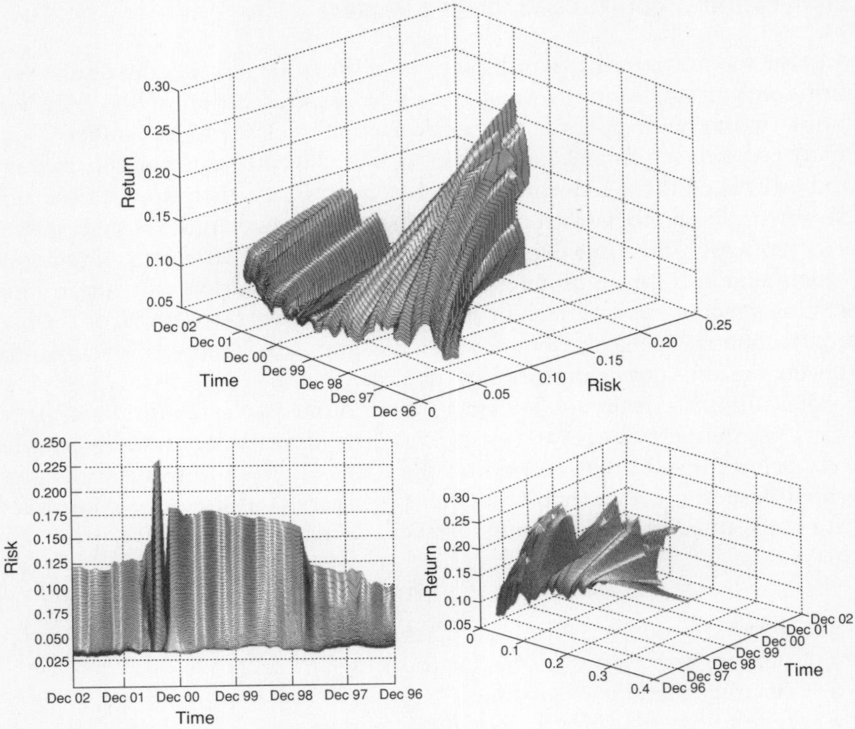

FIGURE 17.12 Efficient Surface
The efficient surface is built on the pool of assets II with a 30 percent weight constraints. The efficient surface is an interpolation derived from a sequence of efficient frontiers (generated on a monthly basis, starting December 1996). The surfaces highlight the instability of efficient portfolios through time.

For example, there were no high risk/return portfolios "available" in the years 1997 and 1998. High risk portfolios were attainable during the period 1999 to late 2001, but in December 2002, it was not possible to invest in such portfolios anymore (in other terms, in December 2002, there were no weight allocations that enabled the creation of a portfolio with a high risk/return profile).

Aside from the instability of the efficient frontier through time, it is interesting to note that the lowest risk level for a portfolio based on the pool of assets II remains relatively stable (but the returns fluctuate).

The concept of efficient surface and its visualization through a three-dimensional framework is meaningful. It illustrates the importance of time variations in portfolio construction. And it explicitly highlights the importance, for portfolio managers, of considering dynamic allocations.

But there is another way to look at the efficient surface and to extract information; it consists of comparing two efficient surfaces: one built on a pool of assets including CTAs and one built on a similar pool without CTAs. Such an approach determines periods where CTAs did add value to the portfolios, and at the same time it quantifies the extra returns. This comparison can be performed easily because the efficient frontiers are built on the same framework. Note that interpolation is used during the creation of the efficient surfaces. It is therefore important to choose a sufficiently fine partition (or grid) for the range of standard deviations.

Compared to Figure 17.12, the interpretation of the resulting surface is straightforward and much more explicit in Figure 17.13. When there is no added value in including CTAs in a portfolio, the surface (a "diversification surface") is flat. When it is penalizing to include CTAs (in terms of risk/return), the surface goes below zero.[3] When CTAs add value to the portfolio, the surface has a positive shape. The shape itself depends on how much the asset adds in terms of returns. With this representation, "abnormal" reliefs can be seen. They appear only if the efficient frontier including CTAs has a wider range of risk/return combinations than the one without CTAs or if it is the contrary (the efficient frontier without CTAs has a wider range of combinations than the one with CTAs). In these cases, peaks (respectively positive and negative) emerge on the diversification surface; the peaks' height are equal to the return provided by the considered portfolio.

The diversification surface presented in Figure 17.13 reflects the differences between the efficient portfolios generated with the pool of assets II (pool that includes CTAs) and the ones generated with the pool of assets I (no CTAs in this pool). The constraints are no short selling, full investment, and a weight threshold (30 percent maximum per asset).

From the diversification surface, one clearly sees that, except for the period October 1996 to March 1997, managed futures generated new low risk portfolios (peaks on the surface with a height equal to the new portfolio's return).

CTAs also occasionally bring diversification to medium-risk portfolios. It is significant during 1999 and then decreases a lot the first quarter of 2000. Therefore, Figure 17.13 confirms the previous observations on CTAs. They add value to portfolios, but this diversification ability is not constant over time and not verified for all efficient portfolios.

[3]This case was not observable because no minimum weight was imposed.

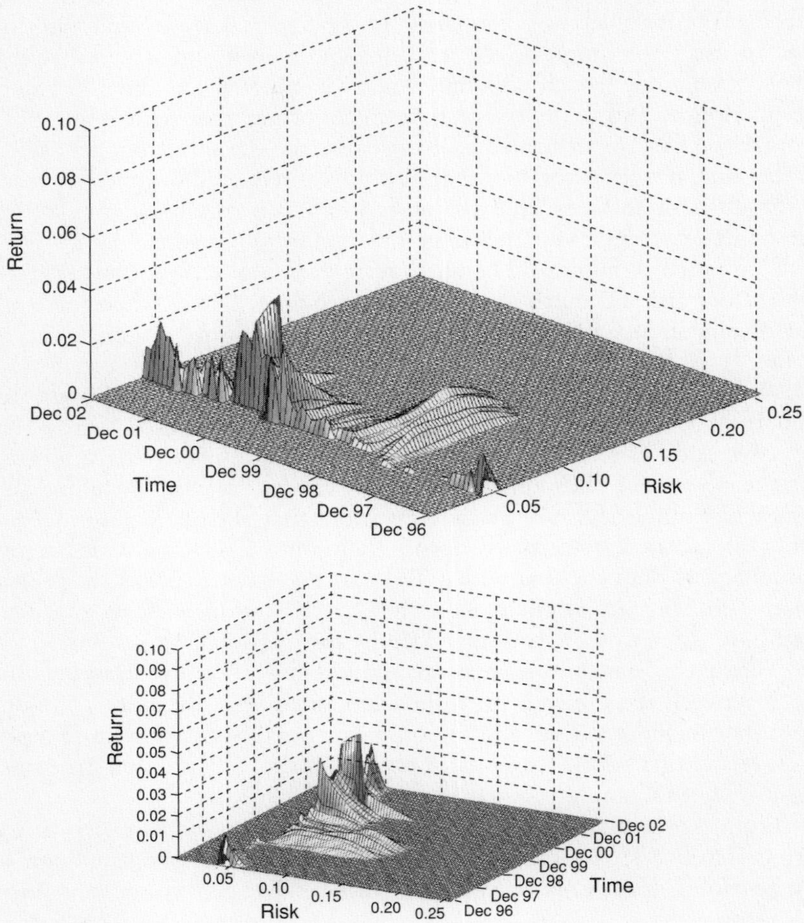

FIGURE 17.13 Diversification Surface
Diversification surface generated using two efficient surfaces; the first one has some exposure to CTAs while the second one does not invest in any CTAs. The shape of the surface highlights the CTAs' diversification capacity through time and for different risk levels; the higher the "relief," the more important the CTAs' added value for a portfolio.

CONCLUSION

This chapter confirms that CTAs add value to portfolios but only under certain conditions. Results demonstrated that CTAs bring diversification as long as the asset allocation environment is constrained. This diversification ability clearly increases the lower the weight threshold is (the stricter the constraints are) and if the included assets are only standard assets.

Aside from the demonstration of the CTAs' added value, the rolling window analyses illustrate the time variability of the efficient frontiers. This finding was expected because the input factors are themselves evolving through time, proving the necessity of using dynamic asset allocation. Moreover, the analyses also reveal that CTAs did not systematically improve portfolio returns over the period 1996 to 2002.

More generally, the three-dimensional graphs presented are one of the first attempts at using surfaces as a visualization and assessment tool for asset allocation. The frameworks prove interesting for decision making, understanding efficient portfolio constructions, and temporal dynamics. It is exciting to represent simultaneously the evolution of three variables. And with the growing information technology resources, this graphical representation should be used more frequently in the future.

CHAPTER 18

Random Walk Behavior of CTA Returns

Greg N. Gregoriou and Fabrice Rouah

This chapter examines whether CTA percent changes in NAVs follow random walks with drift. Monthly data from January 1994 to December 2000 are tested for nonstationarity and random walk with drift, using the Augmented Dickey-Fuller test. All classifications (except the diversified subindex) are found to behave like random walks, but many of the series show evidence of a positive drift parameter, an indication that trends could be present in the series. The effectiveness of CTAs in enhancing risk-return characteristics of portfolios could be compromised when pure random walk behavior is identified.

INTRODUCTION

This chapter investigates whether monthly percent changes in net asset values (NAVs) of commodity trading advisor (CTA) classifications follow random walks. Previous econometric studies of financial time series have employed unit root tests, such as the Augmented Dickey-Fuller test (ADF), to identify random walk behavior in stock prices and market indices, for example. The characteristics of CTAs are such that investment into this alternative investment class can enhance portfolio returns, but these characteristics are likely to be mitigated if pure random walk behavior is present because that would imply a lack of evidence of value added to the portfolio (differential manager skill).

Research into the performance persistence of CTAs is sparse, so there is little information on the long-term diligence of these managers (Edwards

This article previously appeared in *Journal of Alternative Investments,* No. 2, 2003. Reprinted by permission of the publisher.

and Ma 1988; Irwin, Krukemeyer, and Zulauf 1992; Irwin, Zulauf, and Ward 1994; Kazemi 1996). However, it is generally agreed that during bear markets, CTAs provide greater downside protection than hedge funds, and have higher returns along with an inverse correlation with stock returns in bear markets (Edwards and Caglayan 2001). The benefits of CTAs are similar to those of hedge funds, in that they improve and can offer a superior risk-adjusted return trade-off to stock and bond indices while acting as diversifiers in investment portfolios (Schneeweis, Savayana, and McCarthy 1991; Schneeweis 1996).

During the 1990 to 1998 period the correlation of managed futures to the Standard & Poor's (S&P) 500 during its best 30 months was 0.33 and −0.25 during its worst 30 months (Worthington 2001). The benefit of low correlation cannot be easily replicated through other investment alternatives. According to Schneeweis, Spurgin, and Georgiev (2001), CTAs are known to short stock markets regularly. One drawback, however, is that during bull markets their performance is generally inferior to those of hedge funds (Georgiev 2001).

Investors who choose to include CTAs in their portfolios usually allocate only a small portion of their assets (Georgiev 2001). Others are unaware that during increased periods of stock market volatility, careful inclusion of CTA managers into investment portfolios can enhance their return characteristics, especially during severe bear markets (Schneeweis and Georgiev 2002). Moreover, international financial markets in times of extreme volatility this past decade, such as the Asian currency crisis of 1997 and the Russian ruble crisis of August 1998, did not really affect CTAs. In fact, CTAs make their money and produce superior returns during such periods of high volatility. One must consider the possibility that CTA percent changes in NAVs follow random walks, for that would indicate that temporary shocks in the NAVs are persistent and not reverting to the mean level. Such behavior would likely affect the timing of CTA allocation in and out of investment portfolios.

Time series that are "mean reverting" are usually defined as second-order stationary, weak stationary, or simply stationary in the statistical literature. These are characterized by a constant mean and variance and by autocorrelations that depend only on the time lag. Nonstationarity (the violation at least one of these three conditions) can be ascertained by testing for the presence of a unit root, using so-called unit root tests such as the ADF test.

We use the ADF test because of its popularity as a unit root test and due to its simplicity, since Monte Carlo studies such as Haug (1993a, 1993b) discovered that it performs well. Some authors have suggested that unit root tests suffer from low power and that the test does not discriminate very well between mean reverting series and series that do not mean revert at all (Kennedy 1998). However, the robustness of the ADF test is increased when lags are used.

If a series is found to be nonstationary by the ADF test, it does not necessarily imply that it behaves like a random walk, because random walks are but one example of nonstationary time series. Fortunately, the ADF test also can be used to test specifically for random walks. No CTA strategy that relies solely on historical prices can be continuously profitable if markets are efficient and the random walk hypothesis holds true. In this case, future percent changes in NAVs would be entirely unrelated by the historical performance (Pindyck and Rubinfeld 1998).

Recent studies have shown that a minimal amount of performance persistence is found in CTAs and there could exist some advantages in selecting CTAs based on past performance when a long time series of data is available and accurate methods are used (Brorsen and Townsend 2002). Schneeweis, Spurgin, and McCarthy (1996) observe that performance persistence is virtually inexistent during the 1987 to 1995 time frame.

The next section of this chapter presents the data along with a brief discussion of the ADF test and random walks. Following that, we display the results of the analyses, while the final section summarizes and concludes the findings.

DATA AND METHODOLOGY

The data set consists of CTA subindices from the Zurich Capital Markets database/CTA database[1] provided LaPorte Asset Allocation System, covering monthly percent changes in NAVs from January 1994 to December 2000. The database separates CTAs into these classes: discretionary, trend follower, currency, diversified, financial, European, systematic, and stock index (see Table 18.1).

We use the NAVs in each CTA subindex. It is well documented in the mutual fund literature that daily data provide better estimates than monthly data, and help increase the power of tests (Busse and Bollen 2001; Kothari and Warner 2001). Unfortunately, CTA database vendors only provide monthly data.

[1]The Zurich indices during the investigation period do not suffer from survivorship bias.

TABLE 18.1 Zurich Advisor Qualified Universe Indices as of December 2000

Trading Style Subindex	Number of Advisors	Equity ($US Billions)	Definition of Investment Style
Discretionary	54	9.8	Use fundamental/ economic analysis to make trading decisions
Trend Follower	68	5.5	Focus only on trend-following strategies
Systematic	200	17.6	Use systematic, but not purely trend-following strategies
Market Subindex	**Number of Advisors**	**Equity ($US Billions)**	**Definition of Investment Style**
Diversified	193	17.8	Limit risk by holding a large number of positions
Currency	45	5.9	Specialize in currency trading
European	43	3.6	Specialize in European commodities markets
Financial	57	9.1	Currency, interest rate, stock index, and precious metals
Stock Index	17	0.2	Specialize in stock index futures and options

Source: T. Schneeweis, R. Spurgin, and G. Georgiev. "Benchmarking Commodity Trading Advisor Performance with a Passive Futures-Based Index." CISDM Working Paper, Isenberg School of Management, University of Massachusetts, Amherst, MA, 2001, p.14.

The ADF test (Dickey and Fuller 1981; Hamilton 1994) supposes that the monthly mean CTA return, Y_t, can be described by equation 18.1:

$$Y_t = Y_{t-1} = \alpha + \beta t + (\rho - 1)Y_{t-1} + \sum_{j=1}^{p} \lambda_j \Delta Y_{t-j} + \varepsilon_t \qquad (18.1)$$

where $\Delta Y_t = Y_t - Y_{t-1}$ are the first differences

the number of lags, p, chosen is sufficiently large so that the resulting error terms ε_t are serially independent.

This condition can be verified by examining the resulting Durbin-Watson statistic; a value near 2, indicating serial independence. The ADF test works by running a regression on model 18.1 and calculating a *t*-statistic (called the tau-statistic) to test whether the regression parameter $\rho - 1 = 0$ (or equivalently, $\rho = 1$). Failure to reject this test indicates the presence of a unit root and that nonstationarity cannot be rejected. In that case, one often performs the test using first differences: denote these as $W_t = Y_t = Y_{t-1}$, replace Y_t by W_t in equation 18.1, and repeat the analysis.

As explained by Pindyck and Rubinfeld (1998), to test for random walks, one must suppose that Y_t in equation 18.1 can be described without lagged first differences,

$$Y_t = Y_{t-1} = \alpha + \beta_t + (\rho - 1)Y_{t-1} + \varepsilon_t \tag{18.2}$$

and test whether $\beta = 0$ and $\rho = 1$ simultaneously. This determines whether Y_t instead follows a random walk with drift parameter α, sometimes referred to as a difference-stationary process (DSP) (Gujarati 1995)

$$Y_t = \alpha + Y_{t-1} + \varepsilon_t \tag{18.3}$$

One then runs the ADF test with $p = 1$, so that equation 18.1 becomes the "unrestricted" model

$$Y_t - Y_{t-1} = \alpha + \beta_t + (\rho - 1)Y_{t-1} + \lambda_1 \Delta Y_{t-1} + \varepsilon_t \tag{18.4}$$

while the "restricted" model ($\beta = 0$ and $\rho = 1$) is

$$Y_t - Y_{t-1} = \alpha + \lambda_1 \Delta Y_{t-1} + \varepsilon_t \tag{18.5}$$

The error sums of squares from models 18.4 and 18.5 are used to construct an *F*-statistic for the test of $(\alpha, \beta, \rho) = (\alpha, 0, 1)$. Large values of the *F*-statistic will lead to the rejection of this hypothesis and to the conclusion that the model with trend 18.4, rather than the random walk model with drift 18.5, is the model of choice. Failure to reject this hypothesis provides evidence toward random walk behavior. Under the null hypothesis (when the series are nonstationary), neither test statistic just described follows an *F*- or a *t*-distribution, even in large samples, so to assess significance, the statistics must be compared to critical values tabulated by MacKinnon (1991), who updated those from Dickey and Fuller (1981).

EMPIRICAL ANALYSIS

We used up to four lags in the eight CTA subindices but realized that in each case one lag was sufficient for the ε_t to be serially independent. Table 18.2 contains results of the ADF tests (equation 18.1 with $p = 1$), on the original series and on their first differences, along with values of the Durbin-Watson statistic. We find that none of the CTA subindices is stationary, as evidenced by the small values of the ADF statistics, ranging from –4.17 to –1.58, none of which is large enough (in absolute value) to reject the hypothesis of nonstationarity at the 1, 5, or 10 percent significance level. However, when first differences are employed, the ADF statistics are all large enough (in absolute value) to reject nonstationarity at the 1 percent level in all classes. Durbin-Watson statistics from the original and differenced series are all near 2, providing evidence of serial independence among the errors and vindicating our choice of $p = 1$ in equation 18.1.

Thus, it appears that further analyses of these data need only consider first differences to achieve stationarity and that these analyses would likely not be exposed to dangers associated with overdifferencing.

Results of the random walk test are found in Table 18.3, which presents parameter estimates for models 18.4 and 18.5 for the original series Y_t, along with corresponding standard errors in parentheses. The F-statistic for testing $(\alpha, \beta, \rho) = (\alpha, 0, 1)$ is presented in the last column. We find evidence

TABLE 18.2 ADF Test Statistics of Nonstationarity and Durbin-Watson Statistics of Serial Correlation (Equation 18.1 with $p = 1$), for Monthly CTA Mean Returns, (1994 to 2000)

	ADF Statistic (DW Statistic)	
CTA Trading Advisor Subindexes	**Original Series Y_t**	**First Differenced Series W_t**
Discretionary Advisor	–3.48 (1.98)	–6.44* (2.00)
Trend Follower	–2.76 (1.95)	–6.08* (1.94)
Financial Program	–2.62 (1.96)	–5.74* (1.94)
Diversified Advisor	–4.17 (1.94)	–6.82* (1.91)
Currency Program	–2.73 (1.96)	–7.79* (1.96)
European Advisor	–2.74 (1.87)	–6.48* (1.78)
Systematic	–2.69 (1.92)	–6.40* (1.90)
Stock Index	–1.58 (2.03)	–5.95* (2.07)

*Significance of ADF statistic at the 1 percent level, from MacKinnon (1991).

TABLE 18.3 Parameter Estimates from Dickey-Fuller Unit Root Tests of Monthly CTA Class Mean Returns, (1994 to 2000), on Original Series

Zurich CTA Trading Advisor Subindex		α	β	$\rho - 1$	λ_1	*F*-statistic for test of $(\alpha, \beta, \rho) = (\alpha, 0, 1)$
Discretionary	Equation (18.4)	147.790	−0.2319	0.1895	1.6662	
		(41.350)	(0.0660)	(0.1060)	(0.4690)	6.34
	Equation (18.5)	6.100	—	—	0.1120	
		(1.757)	—	—	(0.1100)	
Trend Follower	Equation (18.4)	91.602	−0.1690	0.1420	0.8580	
		(31.958)	(0.0610)	(0.1160)	(0.3350)	3.82
	Equation (18.5)	5.033	—	—	0.0530	
		(3.147)	—	—	(0.1150)	
Financial	Equation (18.4)	50.749	−0.1420	0.2120	0.5890	
		(18.449)	(0.0540)	(0.1170)	(0.2410)	3.43
	Equation (18.5)	3.430	—	—	0.1270	
		(1.979)	—	—	(0.1160)	
Diversified	Equation (18.4)	86.360	−0.3620	0.2070	0.9040	
		(20.243)	(0.0870)	(0.1150)	(0.2200)	8.69*
	Equation (18.5)	2.758	—	—	0.0220	
		(1.205)	—	—	(0.1160)	

TABLE 18.3 *(continued)*

Zurich CTA Trading Advisor Subindex		α	β	ρ-1	λ_1	F-statistic for test of $(\alpha, \beta, \rho) = (\alpha, 0, 1)$
Currency	Equation (18.4)	31.6000	–0.161	0.088	0.247	
		(11.2540)	(0.059)	(0.111)	(0.091)	3.76
	Equation (18.5)	1.2250	—	—	0.018	
		(0.5520)	—	—	(0.112)	
European	Equation (18.4)	17.9540	–0.164	0.066	0.087	
		(6.4550)	(0.060)	(0.121)	(0.031)	3.90
	Equation (18.5)	0.4730	—	—	–0.020	
		(0.1777)	—	—	(0.121)	
Systematic	Equation (18.4)	19.2490	–0.166	0.122	0.162	
		(6.8070)	(0.062)	(0.120)	(0.064)	3.64
	Equation (18.5)	0.9520	—	—	0.025	
		(0.4780)	—	—	(0.118)	
Stock Index	Equation (18.4)	6.5060	–0.065	–0.005	0.004	
		(4.1210)	(0.041)	(0.011)	(0.015)	1.26
	Equation (18.5)	0.0890	—	—	–0.036	
		(0.3480)	—	—	(0.110)	

*Significant at the 5 percent level.

Values in parentheses are standard errors of parameter estimates. Critical values for the F-test with $n = 75$ are 6.61 at the 5 percent level and 9.02 at the 1 percent level, from Dickey and Fuller (1981), Table VI.

of random walk behavior in all CTA subindices except for diversified, whose *F*-statistic of 8.69 attains significance at the 5 percent level. It is therefore possible that a trend representation exists for this series. None of the *F*-statistics for the other series are large enough to attain significance. Thus, all classes are better represented by equation 18.5 except diversified, for which equation 18.4 is the model of choice.

Large estimated values of the drift parameter coupled with small standard errors (usually defined as less than one-half of the drift parameter in absolute value) would suggest that a drift could be present in the series. Table 18.3 thus provides evidence of positive drift ($\alpha > 0$) in the discretionary, diversified, currency, and European classes. Only the stock index class appears to behave as a pure random walk.

CONCLUSION

The nonstationarity observed in most CTA subindices implies that portfolio managers wishing to include CTAs within a traditional stock and bond portfolio cannot be assured that their NAVs will be mean reverting. Yet evidence of positive drift in some of the CTA subindices under consideration leaves open the possibility that these NAVs will contain increasing trends. Portfolio managers wishing to obtain reliable predictions of CTA percent changes in NAVs therefore must be careful when using historical data to design future trading strategies. CTAs assume both long and short market positions, and realize profits when there are persistent trends in markets and when those trends can be identified early enough. Thus, the performance of CTAs depends not only on price movements, but also on the managers' ability to identify them.

One possible explanation for random walk behavior during the examination period is due to the fact that traditional CTAs make large profits during extreme market movements, themselves random events. Their correlations may be more accurate and stable if they are used as a hedge against short volatility exposure. The discretionary, currency, and European traders trade in periods of high liquidity, which has been the case since 1995. We found that only one class, diversified, did not behave as a random walk, likely since trends in a diversified portfolio are stable, although they may not produce sufficient profits to satisfy the expectations of all investors. Due to their very low or negative correlation to stock markets, CTAs are usually less affected by severe market shocks, such as those caused by the Asian crisis of 1997 and the collapse of the Russian currency in August 1998. By allocating assets into CTAs whose returns are not pure random walks, portfolio managers can, in times of increased volatility, add value to traditional stock, bond, and currency portfolios by providing returns that are more readily predictable. Inclusion of CTAs therefore will provide portfolios with immunization against extreme stock market movements.

This study has attempted to characterize some of the time series properties of CTA classes. Using subindices does not provide information on any particular CTA, only on the overall behavior of CTAs within each classification. Thus, our results are especially useful for investors wishing to allocate holdings into all CTAs within a particular class—in that case the subindex would represent an adequate measure of monthly performance. However, investors wishing to invest in a small number of CTAs would likely benefit from an analysis similar to this one but that targets individual CTAs. Further investigation into the returns of CTAs is warranted, as increased volatility in stock markets is likely to spur additional interest in these alternative investments on the part of investors, academics, and practitioners.

CHAPTER 19

CTA Strategies for Returns-Enhancing Diversification

David Kuo Chuen Lee, Francis Koh, and Kok Fai Phoon

In this chapter, we analyze the risk and performance characteristics of different strategies involving the trading of commodity futures, financial futures, and options on futures employed by CTAs. Differing from previous studies, we employ full and split samples to examine the correlations, and compute risk and performance measures for various CTA strategies. We rank the returns of the S&P 500 and MSCI Global Indices from the worst to the best months, and partition the sample into 10 deciles. For each decile, we compute the relationship between the CTA indices and the equity indices and compare their risk and return characteristics. We find that CTA strategies have higher Sharpe and Sortino ratios compared to other asset classes for the entire sample period under study. Further, unlike hedge funds, the correlation coefficients between CTA and equity portfolios for the first decile (worst performance of the equity indices) are mostly negative. The volatility (measured by downside deviation) of CTA strategies is lower compared to equity indices. And, for the up-market months, CTA strategies are associated with high Sortino ratios.

Our results are consistent with previous findings that returns from CTA strategies are less correlated with equity market indices during down markets than hedge fund strategies. One possible explanation is that CTAs, unlike hedge funds, are exposed to lower liquidity risk in down markets and therefore do not suffer any severe "liquidity" squeeze. Our findings suggest that the negative correlations of CTAs with equity indices during periods of equity downturns can provide an effective hedge against catastrophic event risks. Although hedge funds may provide diversification, they have positive correlation with equity indices in down markets, especially when extreme events occur. Hence, our findings suggest that adding CTA investments to an equity portfolio can improve the risk-return profile of a portfolio. Such strategies not only provide the usual portfolio diversification effects, but, given the negative correlation in down markets, the CTAs are returns-enhancing diversifiers.

INTRODUCTION

In recent years, there has been a marked change in the asset allocation strategy in institutional investors, especially endowment funds. In 2002 and 2003, it was reported that many university endowment funds allocated, on average, about 5 percent and 7 percent, respectively, of their total investable funds to alternative investments. Recently some endowments have increased their allocations to alternative investments significantly, to a figure as high as 40 percent of their assets under management (Lee 2003). In particular, Vanderbilt University (2002) has used alternatives since the 1970s and allocates just under half of its $2 billion endowment to them, including nearly 30 percent in hedging and arbitrage strategies. The endowment has returned 8 percent per annum over the past five years and 15 percent per annum over the past nine years (Vanderbilt University Endowment Review, "2002 Financial Report," 2003).

Alternative investments include hedge funds, private equity, and venture capital as well as commodity pools, also referred to as commodity trading advisors (CTAs). In the current low-interest environment compounded by somewhat bearish equity market sentiments, investors have been flocking to alternative investments to enhance their returns as well as to protect their investments. Institutional investors also have increased their demand for alternative investments in the search for absolute positive returns (Till 2004).

Private equity and venture capital, in the main, provide "direct" investment opportunities for the astute investor. Conversely, alternative investments like hedge funds and CTAs add value "indirectly" through the use of a wide range of trading strategies, techniques, and instruments. In this chapter, we focus on the risk and returns performance of CTAs.

LITERATURE REVIEW

A number of earlier researchers have analyzed CTAs, including Elton, Gruber, and Renzler (1987), who concluded that CTAs offer neither an attractive alternative to bonds and stocks nor a profitable addition to a portfolio of bond and stocks. Brorsen and Irwin (1985) and Murphy (1986), however, concluded that commodity funds produce favorable and appropriate investment returns.

Schneeweis, Spurgin, and Potter (1996) found that a portfolio comprised of equal investment in a managed future index outperformed a protective put strategy consisting of the Standard & Poor's (S&P) 500 index and a simulated at-the-money put. They concluded that managed futures may offer some of the hedging properties of a put option at a lower cost.[1]

[1]Schneeweis and Spurgin (1998b) used a dollar-weighted index of CTAs published by Managed Account Reports (MAR).

Schneeweis and Spurgin (1998b) further presented evidence that hedge funds and managed futures may improve the risk-return profiles of equity, fixed income, as well as traditional alternative investments such as risky debt. Their findings were based on correlation analysis between the underlying factors of:

- Hedge fund indices from Hedge Fund Research and Evaluation Associates Capital Management (EACM)
- CTA indices (from MarHedge, Barclay Trading, and EACM)
- S&P 500 and MSCI World indices for equities
- Salomon Brothers Government Bond and World Government Bond indices for fixed income securities

Kat (2002) studied the possible role of managed futures in portfolios of stocks, bonds, and hedge funds. He found that managed futures appear to be more effective diversifiers than hedge funds. He found that adding managed futures to a portfolio of stocks and bonds will reduce a portfolio's standard deviation much more and quicker than hedge funds will, and without the undesirable side effects on skewness and kurtosis.

For the period 1994 to 2001, Liang (2003) found that although CTAs on a stand-alone basis underperformed hedge funds, returns from CTAs were negatively correlated with other instruments, making CTAs suitable for hedging against downside risks.

Although the performance and risk characteristics of alternative investments as stand-alone investments are interesting and informative, analysis of the contribution of CTAs to a portfolio of traditional investments would be instructive and functionally useful. Finance theory has espoused the concept that the ability to diversify allows for a more efficient return-risk tradeoff. In the mean-variance framework, widely attributed to Markowitz (1952), an existing portfolio becomes more diversified upon the addition of a new asset with a relatively lower correlation.

In this chapter, we attempt to differentiate three categories of asset diversifiers:

1. Returns-protection diversifiers have relatively high correlations in both the up and down markets with a generic asset class (such as the S&P 500 Index).
2. Returns-enhancing diversifiers possess correlations with the same generic asset class in an up market but are relatively less correlated in a down market.
3. "Ineffective" diversifiers are assets that do not add value, even though they may possess significant correlation coefficients with the generic asset class.

To illustrate, a hedge fund strategy that has a negative correlation coefficient in an up-market regime and positive correlation coefficient in a down-market regime provides diversification with no incremental returns. We classify this in the third category, that is, as an ineffective diversifier. Indeed, a strategy with such a characteristic will have the opposite effect of a good diversifier as it weakens the returns on an uptrend and exaggerates the negative returns of the portfolio.

We will show that CTAs are differentiated from hedge funds and are returns-enhancing diversifiers.

CTAs, HEDGE FUNDS, AND FUND OF FUNDS

There are many similarities between CTAs and hedge funds and hedge fund of funds, including the management and incentive fee structures, high initial investment requirements, and the use of leverage and derivatives. However, significant differences also exist. For example, hedge funds engage a variety of dynamic trading strategies using different financial instruments in different markets. CTAs, however, mainly use technical trading strategies in commodity and financial futures markets. The use of different markets and instruments give rise to distinct differences in risk and returns profiles.

On the regulatory side, CTAs must register with the Commodity Futures Trading Commission (CFTC); hedge funds and fund of funds are largely exempt from government regulations. The CFTC is a federal regulatory body established by the Commodity Exchange Act in 1974. It supervises a self-regulatory organization called the National Futures Association and has exclusive jurisdiction over all U.S. commodity futures trading, futures exchanges, futures commission merchants, and their agents, floor brokers, floor traders, commodity trading advisors, commodity pool operators, leverage transaction merchants, and any associated persons of any of the foregoing. CTAs are subject to higher standard of compliance, including disclosure reporting, record keeping, and accounting rules. These requirements are not required of hedge funds (which are not registered with CFTC). Many CTAs may have been losing their assets and customers to hedge funds in recent years partly due to restrictive regulations by the CFTC. As a consequence, some CTAs have started emulating hedge funds, using similar trading strategies and instruments and getting more involved in equities. If this trend continues, the distinction between hedge funds and CTAs may become blurred.

On the subject of returns, Liang (2003) and other past studies found that the correlations among the returns of hedge funds employing different styles are high. But the correlations between the returns from different CTA strategies and hedge fund styles are almost zero or negative. This correlation structure points to a need to distinguish CTAs from hedge funds (as well as funds of funds) in academic research.

TABLE 19.1 Comparison between CTAs and Hedge Funds

	CTAs	Hedge Fund/Hedge Fund of Funds
Risk-adjusted returns	Lower on a stand-alone basis.[a]	Hedge fund are highest followed by hedge fund of funds.
Explanation by factors	CTA returns are explained by option trading factors.	Hedge fund returns cannot be explained by option trading factors.
Attrition rate	Generally higher attrition rate. Relatively lower attrition rates in down markets.[b]	Generally lower attrition rates. Down-market conditions have greater impact on attrition rates.
Correlation structure	Low or negative correlation with other instruments.	Highly correlated with each other with other during down markets.

Source: Bing Liang, "On the Performance of Alternative Investments: CTAs, Hedge Funds, and Funds-of-Funds," Case Western Reserve University, Working Paper, 2003, Cleveland, OH.

[a]Liang used Sharpe ratios after adjusting for autocorrelation in returns. He explained that the difference may be due to the fee structure as well as the risks and autocorrelation structure.

[b]Up and down markets are defined according to the S&P 500 index returns. Up markets are periods when the monthly S&P 500 index returns are positive; down markets are defined as periods when the index returns are negative.

The work of Liang (2003) analyzing CTAs and hedge funds separately also provided several interesting results. Table 19.1 summarizes the results.

DATA AND METHODOLOGY

The S&P 500, MSCI Global, Lehman U.S. Aggregate, and Lehman Global data for the period January 1980 until March 2003 were used in this study. We call these data sources as the benchmark group. With the exception of Lehman Global, which starts from January 1990, we have 279 observations for each series. There are only 159 observations for the Lehman Global Index. For the same period, we used returns data over differing periods of four CTA indices from MarHedge: Universe, Universe Equally-Weighted (EW), Future Funds Index, and Future Funds Equally Weighted (EW). We also conducted analysis on subindices from MarHedge covering six strategies: Currency-Sub, Diversified-Sub, Discretionary-Sub, Stock Index Sub, Systematic-Sub, and Trend Follower.

The data were subsequently ranked according to the monthly performance of the two equity indices, the S&P 500 and the MSCI Global. The worst-returns month was ranked first followed by the second worst. The CTAs indices then are matched in that same order. The ranked sample was then divided into deciles. As we are interested only in a two-asset class situation, we would observe the corresponding S&P 500 and CTAs returns accordingly and calculate the linear correlation coefficient for each decile. For example, analyzing the S&P 500 and Universe indices, we would compute the correlation coefficient for each decile between the two strategies.[2]

FINDINGS AND OBSERVATIONS

Table 19.2 presents the summary statistics and risk-adjusted returns. We reported the standard summary statistics associated with the first four moments for the whole period—mean, standard deviation, skewness, excess kurtosis (in excess of the normal distribution)—and the "down-side deviation" defined as the volatility of downside deviation below a minimum acceptable return of zero, the Sharpe and Sortino ratios, and the matrix of correlations between the different CTA strategies with the stock and bond indices. There are a number of interesting observations.

Most of the CTA strategies have correlations with the equity indices that are close to zero or negative. However, it is interesting to note that the Discretionary Sub Index in Table 19.2 has a negative correlation with the S&P 500 but a high positive correlation with the MSCI Global.

Most historical returns of the various CTA strategies (with the exception of Stock Index Sub) are higher than the benchmark group. Correspondingly, the standard deviations are mostly higher than the benchmark group (but comparable with equity indices with an absolute difference in the order of less than 7 percent).

All CTA strategies have skewness greater than 1 (with the exception of the Stock Index Sub Index strategy, which has negative skewness). Further, all CTA strategies have positive excess kurtosis (between 0.77 and 18.61).

[2]We split the sample into deciles to study the relationships of the subsamples using the Pearson correlation coefficient. It is well known that the correlation is much higher for hedge funds among themselves and with equity benchmarks during crisis than in normal times. It is also known that the better-performing hedge funds have higher correlations with equity indices. We acknowledge that there are other methods, such as Copula-based methods, that will give a more complete picture of the associations among several assets.

TABLE 19.2 Summary Statistics and Risk-Adjusted Measures for CTA Indices, S&P 500, MSCI Global, Lehman Global, and Lehman U.S. Aggregate (Various Sample Periods)

Universe Index								
	Sample Size	Mean	Std. Dev.	DD by MAR[a]	Skewness	Kurtosis	Sharpe	Sortino
Universe Index	279	1.19%	4.76%	4.91%	1.19	3.44	0.75	2.81
S&P 500	279	0.85%	4.52%	4.60%	–0.59	2.16	0.50	2.01
MSCI Global	279	0.72%	4.31%	4.37%	–0.51	1.11	0.42	1.78
Lehman Global	159	0.63%	1.44%	1.57%	0.19	–0.09	1.27	4.99
Lehman US Agg	279	0.11%	1.78%	1.78%	0.60	5.23	–0.03	0.73

Correlation	Universe Index	S&P 500	MSCI Global	Lehman Global	Lehman US Agg
Universe Index	1				
S&P 500	–0.03	1			
MSCI Global	–0.05	0.84	1		
Lehman Global	0.23	0.10	0.20	1	
Lehman US Agg	0.06	0.23	0.20	0.73	1

Universe Index EW								
	Sample Size	Mean	Std. Dev.	DD by MAR	Skewness	Kurtosis	Sharpe	Sortino
Universe EW	279	1.42%	5.19%	5.38%	1.62	4.81	0.85	3.11
S&P 500	279	0.85%	4.52%	4.60%	–0.59	2.16	0.50	2.01
MSCI Global	279	0.72%	4.31%	4.37%	–0.51	1.11	0.42	1.78
Lehman Global	159	0.63%	1.44%	1.57%	0.19	–0.09	1.27	4.99
Lehman US Agg	279	0.11%	1.78%	1.78%	0.60	5.23	–0.03	0.73

TABLE 19.2 *(continued)*

Universe Index EW *(continued)*

Correlation	Universe EW	S&P 500	MSCI Global	Lehman Global	Lehman US Agg
Universe EW	1				
S&P 500	–0.11	1			
MSCI Global	–0.13	0.84	1		
Global	0.20	0.10	0.20	1	
Lehman US Agg	0.10	0.23	0.20	0.73	1

Currency Subindex

	Sample Size	Mean	Std. Dev.	DD by MAR	Skewness	Kurtosis	Sharpe	Sortino
Currency Sub	159	0.81%	3.55%	3.64%	1.53	4.72	0.64	2.58
S&P 500	159	0.65%	4.37%	4.41%	–0.44	0.45	0.35	1.55
MSCI Global	159	0.27%	4.34%	4.33%	–0.39	0.25	0.04	0.49
Lehman Global	159	0.63%	1.44%	1.57%	0.19	–0.09	1.27	4.99
Lehman US Agg	159	0.09%	1.08%	1.08%	–0.27	0.05	–0.13	0.93

Correlation	Currency Sub	S&P 500	MSCI Global	Lehman Global	Lehman US Agg
Currency Sub	1				
S&P 500	0.03	1			
MSCI Global	0.03	0.86	1		
Lehman Global	0.09	0.10	0.20	1	
Lehman US Agg	0.10	0.18	0.14	0.73	1

TABLE 19.2 *(continued)*

Diversified Sub Index

	Sample Size	Mean	Std. Dev.	DD by MAR	Skewness	Kurtosis	Sharpe	Sortino
Diversified Sub	195	0.97%	4.06%	4.17%	1.28	4.45	0.69	2.68
S&P 500	195	0.75%	4.61%	4.68%	−0.83	2.76	0.41	1.71
MSCI Global	195	0.48%	4.45%	4.48%	−0.53	1.18	0.21	1.04
Lehman Global	159	0.63%	1.44%	1.57%	0.19	−0.09	1.27	4.99
Lehman US Agg	195	0.06%	1.18%	1.18%	−0.24	0.03	−0.21	0.54

Correlation	Diversified Sub	S&P 500	MSCI Global	Lehman Global	Lehman US Agg
Diversified Sub	1				
S&P 500	−0.02	1			
MSCI Global	−0.03	0.84	1		
Lehman Global	0.23	0.10	0.20	1	
Lehman US Agg	0.18	0.14	0.05	0.73	1

Discretionary Sub Index

	Sample Size	Mean	Std. Dev.	DD by MAR	Skewness	Kurtosis	Sharpe	Sortino
Discretionary Sub	195	1.44%	3.23%	3.54%	3.28	18.61	1.48	5.10
S&P 500	195	0.75%	4.61%	4.68%	−0.83	2.76	0.41	1.71
MSCI Global	195	0.48%	4.45%	4.48%	−0.53	1.18	0.21	1.04
Lehman Global	159	0.63%	1.44%	1.57%	0.19	−0.09	1.27	4.99
Lehman US Agg	195	0.06%	1.18%	1.18%	−0.24	0.03	−0.21	0.54

TABLE 19.2 *(continued)*

Discretionary Sub Index *(continued)*

Correlation	Discretionary Sub	S&P 500	MSCI Global	Lehman Global	Lehman US Agg
Discretionary Sub	1.00				
S&P 500	–0.17	1.00			
MSCI Global	0.84	–0.13	1.00		
Lehman Global	0.10	0.08	0.20	1.00	
Lehman US Agg	0.14	0.22	0.05	0.73	1.00

Stock Index Sub Index

	Sample Size	Mean	Std. Dev.	DD by MAR	Skewness	Kurtosis	Sharpe	Sortino
Stock Index Sub	111	0.31%	3.00%	3.02%	–0.44	1.09	0.17	1.07
S&P 500	111	0.65%	4.63%	4.68%	–0.55	0.19	0.32	1.43
MSCI Global	111	0.29%	4.25%	4.47%	–0.56	0.35	0.06	0.55
Lehman Global	111	0.52%	1.41%	1.50%	0.30	0.21	0.99	4.22
Lehman US Agg	111	0.05%	1.09%	1.09%	–0.21	0.18	–0.27	0.44

Correlation	Stock Index Sub	S&P 500	MSCI Global	Lehman Global	Lehman US Agg
Stock Index Sub	1.00				
S&P 500	–0.11	1.00			
MSCI Global	–0.11	0.94	1.00		
Lehman Global	–0.04	–0.01	0.02	1.00	
Lehman US Agg	–0.04	0.04	–0.04	0.68	1.00

TABLE 19.2 *(continued)*

Systematic Subindex

	Sample Size	Mean	Std. Dev.	DD by MAR	Skewness	Kurtosis	Sharpe	Sortino
Systematic Sub	135	0.63%	3.16%	3.22%	0.37	0.77	0.51	2.21
S&P 500	135	0.62%	4.27%	4.31%	–0.56	–0.65	0.34	1.51
MSCI Global	135	0.33%	4.06%	4.07%	–0.56	0.43	0.11	0.74
Lehman Global	135	0.55%	1.39%	1.49%	0.19	0.08	1.08	4.49
Lehman US Agg	135	0.06%	1.07%	1.07%	–0.26	0.10	–0.23	0.59

Correlation	Systematic Sub	S&P 500	MSCI Global	Lehman Global	Lehman US Agg
Systematic Sub	1.00				
S&P 500	–0.11	1.00			
MSCI Global	–0.06	0.90	1.00		
Lehman Global	0.31	0.00	0.08	1.00	
Lehman US Agg	0.31	0.06	0.01	0.71	1.00

Trend Follower

	Sample Size	Mean	Std. Dev.	DD by MAR	Skewness	Kurtosis	Sharpe	Sortino
Trend Follower	243	1.27%	6.41%	6.54%	1.05	2.42	0.55	2.09
S&P 500	243	0.84%	4.48%	4.56%	–0.74	2.59	0.50	2.04
MSCI Global	243	0.74%	4.31%	4.37%	–0.51	1.31	0.44	1.85
Lehman Global	159	0.63%	1.44%	1.57%	0.19	–0.09	1.25	4.91
Lehman US Agg	243	0.11%	1.33%	1.33%	–0.16	0.42	–0.07	0.89

TABLE 19.2 *(continued)*

Trend Follower *(continued)*

Correlation	Trend Follower	S&P 500	MSCI Global	Lehman Global	Lehman US Agg
Trend Follower	1.00				
S&P 500	–0.04	1.00			
MSCI Global	–0.07	0.83	1.00		
Lehman Global	0.24	0.10	0.20	1.00	
Lehman US Agg	0.17	0.21	0.16	0.73	1.00

Futures Fund Index

	Sample Size	Mean	Std. Dev.	DD by MAR	Skewness	Kurtosis	Sharpe	Sortino
Futures Fund	279	0.93%	4.43%	4.54%	0.78	2.39	0.63	2.47
S&P 500	279	0.85%	4.52%	4.60%	–0.59	2.16	0.50	2.01
MSCI Global	279	0.72%	4.31%	4.37%	–0.51	1.11	0.42	1.78
Lehman Global	159	0.63%	1.44%	1.57%	0.19	–0.09	1.27	4.99
Lehman US Agg	279	0.11%	1.78%	1.78%	0.60	5.23	–0.03	0.73

Correlation	Futures Fund	S&P 500	MSCI Global	Lehman Global	Lehman US Agg
Futures Fund	1.00				
S&P 500	–0.01	1.00			
MSCI Global	–0.01	0.84	1.00		
Lehman Global	–0.18	0.10	0.20	1.00	
Lehman US Agg	0.06	0.23	0.20	0.73	1.00

TABLE 19.2 *(continued)*

Futures Fund EW								
	Sample Size	Mean	Std. Dev.	DD by MAR	Skewness	Kurtosis	Sharpe	Sortino
Futures Fund EW	279	0.93%	4.73%	4.82%	1.10	2.93	0.54	2.14
S&P 500	279	0.85%	4.52%	4.60%	–0.59	2.16	0.50	2.01
MSCI Global	279	0.72%	4.31%	4.37%	–0.51	1.11	0.42	1.78
Lehman Global	159	0.63%	1.44%	1.57%	0.19	–0.09	1.27	4.99
Lehman US Agg	279	0.11%	1.78%	1.78%	0.60	5.23	–0.03	0.73

Correlation	Futures Fund EW	S&P 500	MSCI Global	Lehman Global	Lehman US Agg
Futures Fund EW	1.00				
S&P 500	–0.01	1.00			
MSCI Global	–0.03	0.84	1.00		
Lehman Global	0.24	0.10	0.20	1.00	
Lehman US Agg	0.07	0.23	0.20	0.73	1.00

[a]DD by MAR measures the volatility of monthly returns below the minimal acceptable return (MAR) as established by the investor (in our case, the MAR is taken as 0 percent).

The Sharpe and Sortino ratios in most cases were higher for the full sample period, suggesting that the return per unit risk is almost always higher than the benchmark group.

In Table 19.3, we take a closer look at the correlation coefficients at different deciles. The ranking of the deciles is in accordance to the performance of S&P 500 or MSCI Global. In other words, what we are attempting to do is to see how correlated the strategies are with S&P at different times, the up markets (bullish period) and the down markets (bearish period) and the times in between. We also have computed the numbers for the up period as well as the down period.

ANALYSIS OF THE FINDINGS

Our results show that all the CTA Indices and subindices generally have negative correlation coefficients for the first decile with the S&P 500 Index. This means that these CTA strategies have negative association with the S&P 500 during the worst periods of the down markets. During the periods that the S&P 500 was doing extremely badly, the CTA strategies were doing much better. In other words, these CTA strategies enhanced portfolio returns during the worst periods of the down market (when the S&P was experiencing negative returns). Thus, inclusion of CTA strategies in equity portfolios would not only reduce portfolio volatility (as good diversifiers) but would also enhance the portfolio returns when times are "bad."

The results are almost similar with MSCI Global. However, 3 out of 10 strategies exhibited positive correlation coefficients. The highest correlation coefficient was only 0.2, indicating that these 3 strategies were still very good diversifiers.

Our results are consistent with previous findings that returns from CTA strategies are less correlated with equity market indices during down markets than hedge fund strategies. One possible explanation is that CTAs, unlike hedge funds, are exposed to lower liquidity risk in down markets and therefore do not suffer any severe "liquidity" squeeze.

Table 19.4 presents the deciles analysis and points to the usefulness of the Futures Fund Index Strategy as a returns enhancing diversifier. For the first decile of both the S&P 500 and MSCI Global indices, the returns of the Futures Fund Index were both positive. This means that portfolio returns would be enhanced in the "bad" period if a Futures Fund Index was included.

We examine the relative advantage of including different percentages of the CTA Futures Index in an equity portfolio (using the MSCI Global) in Table 19.5. The results suggest that several combinations will provide positive absolute returns. For example, a combination of 60/40 of CTA Futures Index/MSCI Global had the highest return, of 10.22 percent. However, this combination did not provide the least number of negative returns. If one

TABLE 19.3 Sample Correlation Coefficients for CTA Indices with S&P and MSCI Global

	Correlation with S&P									
	Universe Index	Universe Index EW	Currency Subindex	Diversified Subindex	Discretionary Subindex	Stock Index Subindex	Systematic Subindex	Trend Follower	Futures Fund Index	Futures Fund EW
1st Decile	−0.21	−0.21	−0.05	−0.03	0.27	−0.30	−0.50	−0.17	−0.15	−0.15
2nd Decile	−0.12	−0.25	−0.04	0.11	−0.01	−0.27	0.39	0.10	−0.14	−0.14
3rd Decile	0.22	0.23	−0.01	0.25	−0.34	−0.57	0.16	0.18	0.02	0.18
4th Decile	−0.34	−0.32	0.35	−0.31	0.03	−0.35	0.02	−0.06	−0.31	−0.37
5th Decile	−0.22	−0.15	−0.52	−0.54	−0.15	−0.35	−0.48	−0.41	−0.21	−0.29
6th Decile	−0.23	−0.23	0.07	−0.17	0.20	−0.36	0.29	−0.24	−0.26	−0.25
7th Decile	−0.20	0.07	−0.02	−0.19	−0.31	−0.33	0.33	−0.21	−0.13	−0.25
8th Decile	−0.27	0.02	0.20	−0.20	0.25	0.35	0.41	−0.32	−0.21	−0.26
9th Decile	−0.08	−0.14	0.14	−0.18	0.18	−0.24	0.21	−0.41	−0.14	−0.14
10th Decile	−0.02	0.04	0.60	0.40	−0.48	0.33	−0.19	0.08	0.02	0.00
Down Half	−0.14	−0.26	0.26	−0.19	−0.51	−0.11	−0.18	−0.15	−0.10	−0.12
Up Half	0.10	0.11	0.08	0.12	0.06	0.02	−0.07	0.12	0.13	0.12
Overall	−0.03	−0.11	0.03	−0.02	−0.17	−0.11	−0.11	−0.04	0.01	−0.01

TABLE 19.3 *(continued)*

	Correlation with MSCI Global									
	Universe Index	Universe Index EW	Currency Subindex	Diversified Subindex	Discretionary Subindex	Stock Index Subindex	Systematic Subindex	Trend Follower	Futures Fund Index	Futures Fund EW
1st Decile	−0.23	−0.54	0.14	−0.09	−0.67	−0.51	0.20	−0.28	−0.13	0.15
2nd Decile	0.11	0.20	0.45	−0.05	0.40	−0.28	−0.07	0.06	0.10	−0.44
3rd Decile	−0.08	−0.17	−0.39	−0.29	−0.43	−0.54	0.10	0.15	0.00	0.60
4th Decile	−0.01	0.02	−0.01	0.31	0.20	−0.33	0.20	0.17	0.13	0.10
5th Decile	−0.34	−0.30	−0.10	−0.02	−0.28	0.31	0.40	−0.31	−0.34	−0.21
6th Decile	0.20	0.13	−0.04	0.18	0.03	0.00	−0.19	0.15	0.21	0.38
7th Decile	−0.09	−0.04	0.01	−0.02	0.20	0.24	−0.07	−0.25	−0.01	−0.05
8th Decile	0.31	0.30	0.13	0.30	−0.06	0.44	−0.36	0.25	0.31	0.51
9th Decile	0.39	0.30	−0.04	0.15	−0.10	−0.37	−0.19	−0.05	0.38	−0.37
10th Decile	0.25	0.15	0.32	0.28	0.37	−0.06	−0.44	0.08	0.26	−0.54
Down Half	−0.18	−0.23	0.04	−0.14	−0.26	−0.06	−0.30	−0.23	−0.20	−0.18
Up Half	0.10	0.12	0.02	−0.01	0.10	0.02	−0.26	0.07	0.13	0.12
Overall	−0.05	−0.13	0.03	−0.03	0.84	−0.11	−0.06	−0.07	−0.01	−0.03

TABLE 19.4 Summary Statistics, Correlation Coefficients, and Risk-Adjusted Measures for Futures Fund Index with S&P and MSCI Global

		0–10%		10–20%		20–30%		30–40%		40–50%	
		Futures Fund Index	S&P 500	Futures Fund Index	S&P 500	Futures Fund Index	S&P 500	Futures Fund Index	S&P 500	Futures Fund Index	S&P 500
Futures Fund Index vs. S&P 500	Sample Size	28	28	28	28	28	28	28	28	27	27
	Mean	2.08%	–7.74%	–0.43%	–3.32%	0.54%	–1.84%	1.90%	–0.59%	0.57%	0.63%
	Std. Dev.	3.69%	3.53%	3.58%	0.64%	5.46%	0.39%	4.43%	0.34%	3.09%	0.29%
	DD by MAR	4.26%	8.63%	3.60%	3.44%	5.49%	1.92%	4.84%	0.69%	3.15%	0.70%
	Skewness	–1.44	–2.70	–0.83	–0.63	0.96	0.12	1.07	0.17	0.58	–0.49
	Kurtosis	3.53	9.00	1.57	–0.67	3.70	–0.99	0.70	–0.86	–0.17	–0.90
	Sharpe	2.00	–5.22	–0.59	–15.76	0.18	–15.82	1.47	–7.13	0.47	6.30
	Sortino	6.35	–7.22	–1.60	–9.69	0.89	–10.44	4.97	–9.95	2.08	11.11
	Correlation		–0.15		–0.14		0.02		–0.31		–0.21

TABLE 19.4 *(continued)*

		50–60%		60–70%		70–80%		80–90%		90–100%	
		Futures Fund Index	S&P 500	Futures Fund Index	S&P 500	Futures Fund Index	S&P 500	Futures Fund Index	S&P 500	Futures Fund Index	S&P 500
Futures	Sample Size	28	28	28	28	28	28	28	28	28	28
Fund	Mean	0.13%	1.48%	0.72%	2.57%	0.29%	3.79%	1.75%	5.20%	2.29%	8.27%
Index	Std. Dev.	3.78%	0.30%	3.01%	0.41%	4.37%	0.25%	5.61%	0.57%	5.93%	1.88%
vs. S&P 500	DD by MAR	3.79%	1.54%	3.10%	2.64%	4.38%	3.87%	5.89%	5.32%	6.37%	8.63%
	Skewness	0.03	0.00	0.71	0.49	0.62	−0.05	1.71	−0.16	0.43	1.05
	Kurtosis	0.41	−1.34	−0.10	−0.88	0.77	−1.21	4.18	−1.30	−0.49	0.26
	Sharpe	−0.06	17.10	0.67	24.23	0.06	63.18	1.01	41.48	1.33	24.23
	Sortino	0.18	12.54	2.73	13.43	0.56	14.55	3.58	15.71	4.51	18.43
	Correlation		−0.26		−0.13		−0.21		−0.14		0.02

TABLE 19.4 *(continued)*

		0–10%		10–20%		20–30%		30–40%		40–50%	
		Futures Fund Index	MSCI Global	Futures Fund Index	MSCI Global	Futures Fund Index	MSCI Global	Futures Fund Index	MSCI Global	Futures Fund Index	MSCI Global
Futures	Sample Size	28	28	28	28	28	28	28	28	27	27
Fund	Mean	2.44%	−7.57%	1.67%	−3.36%	−0.38%	−1.86%	0.31%	−0.58%	0.50%	0.43%
Index	Std. Dev.	2.86%	2.94%	5.41%	0.67%	3.67%	0.29%	4.77%	0.36%	4.23%	0.29%
vs. MSCI	DD by MAR	3.79%	8.25%	5.67%	3.49%	3.69%	1.92%	4.78%	0.69%	4.26%	0.52%
Global	Skewness	−0.12	−1.66	0.92	−0.54	−0.43	−0.06	1.03	−0.47	−0.25	−0.30
	Kurtosis	−0.33	3.01	2.89	−0.95	0.06	−0.61	3.10	−0.79	0.97	−1.37
	Sharpe	3.17	−6.17	0.99	−15.24	−0.53	−21.49	0.06	−6.71	0.24	3.67
	Sortino	8.69	−7.44	3.53	−9.66	−1.42	−10.53	0.52	−9.79	1.18	9.99
	Correlation		−0.13		0.10		0.00		0.13		-0.34

TABLE 19.4 *(continued)*

		50–60%		60–70%		70–80%		80–90%		90–100%	
		Futures Fund Index	MSCI Global	Futures Fund Index	MSCI Global	Futures Fund Index	MSCI Global	Futures Fund Index	MSCI Global	Futures Fund Index	MSCI Global
Futures	Sample Size	28	28	28	28	28	28	28	28	28	28
Fund	Mean	1.18%	1.51%	0.41%	2.42%	−0.29%	3.57%	2.77%	4.94%	1.25%	7.71%
Index	Std. Dev.	4.15%	0.30%	3.88%	0.32%	3.31%	0.43%	5.15%	0.44%	5.56%	1.68%
vs.	DD by										
MSCI	MAR	4.32%	1.57%	3.90%	2.49%	3.33%	3.66%	5.88%	5.04%	5.71%	8.02%
Global	Skewness	0.63	−0.52	0.64	−0.30	−0.48	0.12	1.61	0.47	0.93	0.82
	Kurtosis	0.82	−1.25	2.07	−1.32	0.18	−1.45	4.08	−1.16	0.44	−0.34
	Sharpe	0.87	17.23	0.19	28.80	−0.49	34.47	1.98	50.82	0.65	24.41
	Sortino	3.24	12.56	1.05	13.37	−1.23	14.29	6.28	15.51	2.47	17.87
	Correlation		0.21		−0.01		0.31		0.38		0.26

TABLE 19.5 Combining Futures and Equity Indices in Different Proportions

	0–10%	10–20%	20–30%	30–40%	40–50%	50–60%	60–70%	70–80%	80–90%	90–100%	
Combination	Returns	Returns	Returns	Returns	Returns	Returns	Returns	Returns	Returns	Returns	Portfolio Returns
0/100	–7.57%	–3.36%	–1.86%	–0.58%	0.43%	1.51%	2.42%	3.57%	4.94%	7.71%	7.19%
10/90	–6.57%	–2.86%	–1.71%	–0.49%	0.43%	1.48%	2.22%	3.18%	4.72%	7.06%	7.45%
20/80	–5.57%	–2.36%	–1.56%	–0.40%	0.44%	1.44%	2.02%	2.79%	4.50%	6.41%	7.72%
30/70	–4.57%	–1.85%	–1.42%	–0.31%	0.45%	1.41%	1.82%	2.41%	4.29%	5.77%	7.98%
40/60	–3.57%	–1.35%	–1.27%	–0.22%	0.45%	1.38%	1.62%	2.02%	4.07%	5.12%	8.25%
50/50	–2.57%	–0.85%	–1.12%	–0.14%	0.46%	1.34%	1.42%	1.64%	3.85%	4.48%	8.51%
60/40	–3.08%	–1.02%	–1.34%	–0.16%	0.55%	1.61%	1.70%	1.96%	4.62%	5.37%	10.22%
70/30	–0.57%	0.16%	–0.83%	0.04%	0.47%	1.28%	1.01%	0.87%	3.42%	3.18%	9.04%
80/20	0.43%	0.66%	–0.68%	0.13%	0.48%	1.25%	0.81%	0.48%	3.20%	2.54%	9.31%
90/10	1.44%	1.16%	–0.53%	0.22%	0.49%	1.21%	0.61%	0.09%	2.99%	1.89%	9.58%
100/0	2.44%	1.67%	–0.38%	0.31%	0.50%	1.18%	0.41%	–0.29%	2.77%	1.25%	9.84%

were to look for the least number of negative periods, then the combination of 90/10 would almost ensure that there would only be a 1 in 10 chance of negative returns.

The results illustrate a useful idea: If we are concerned about event risk, we may wish to define our objective function as one that has the least number of negative returns during the investment horizon, with the constraint that the correlation at first decile should be the lowest. This could be a useful framework to carry out constrained optimization of portfolio returns.

CONCLUSION

Our results indicate that the risk-adjusted returns as measured by Sharpe and Sortino ratios are always higher in CTA strategies than in most traditional asset classes for the entire sample period under study. Unlike hedge funds, the correlation coefficients of the CTAs with the equity markets are negative during bad times (worst performance period of the equity markets). Yet the volatility (measured by downside deviation) of CTA strategies is lower compared to equity indices. For the up-market months, CTA strategies are associated with high Sortino ratios.

The negative correlations of CTAs with equity indices during periods of marked downturns of equity markets indicate that CTAs can provide an effective hedge against catastrophic event risks. While hedge funds also provide diversification, they have positive correlation with equity indices in down markets, especially when extreme events occur. Hence our findings suggest that adding more tightly regulated CTA strategies to an equity portfolio can improve its overall risk-return profile. Such strategies not only provide the usual portfolio diversification effects, but, given the negative correlation in down markets, CTAs are returns-enhancing diversifiers. Although our findings present strong reasons to use CTAs, their use may not be without a cost. Liang (2003) found that attrition rates are higher for CTAs when compared with hedge fund and hedge fund of funds. However, the reasons why CTAs are return-enhancing diversifiers deserve further investigation. The level of liquidity risk borne may be an important difference between hedge funds and CTAs.

CHAPTER 20

Incorporating CTAs into the Asset Allocation Process: A Mean-Modified Value at Risk Framework

Maher Kooli

Value at risk has become a heavily used risk management tool, and an important approach for setting capital requirements for banks. In this study, we examine the effect of including a CTA in a traditional portfolio. Using a mean-modified value at risk framework, we examine the case of a Canadian pension fund and compute the optimal portfolio by minimizing the modified value at risk at a given confidence level.

INTRODUCTION

For the individual or the institutional investor who is simultaneously performance-oriented and risk-conscious, the key question is how best to achieve a higher overall rate of return with acceptable risk. The answer may be a diversified investment portfolio with some portion of the total assets invested in alternative investments. According to a survey by Nakakubo (2002), the alternative investment market reached \$550 to \$600 billion at the end of 2001. Pension funds also are increasing the proportion of alternative investments in their asset allocation.

For many institutional investors, alternative investments are viewed largely as private, illiquid, alternative investments that include venture capital, leveraged buyout, distressed securities, private equity, private debt, oil and gas programs, and timber or farmland. However, other alternative investment vehicles, such as hedge funds and commodity trading advisors (CTAs), also have observed a dramatic increase in investment and often provide access to investment not easily available from traditional stock and bond investment. For instance, the Managed Accounts Reports (MAR) cites an increase in managed futures[1] from less than $1 billion in 1980 to almost $35 billion in 1999; hedge fund investment is now estimated to be over $300 billion. Further, Lintner (1983) uses the composite performance of 15 trading advisors and show that the return/risk ratio of a portfolio of trading advisors (or futures funds) is higher than a well-diversified stock/bond portfolio. Furthermore, he finds a low correlation between the returns of trading advisors and those of stocks, bonds, or a combined stock/bond portfolio. Lintner examines the 1979 to 1982 period. Schneeweis and Spurgin (1997) show that various CTA and hedge fund, energy-based investment provide risk and return opportunities not available from a wide range of traditional commodity investments or real estate investments. The Chicago Mercantile Exchange (1999) showed that for the 1980 to 1998 period, managed futures investments (as measured by the Barclay CTA Index) had a compound annual return of 15.8 percent. That compares very favorably with the 17.7 percent return that common stocks had during the same period, one of the strongest stock markets in U.S. history. Further, it exceeded the 11.8 percent return on bonds. Moreover, during a similar period (1980 to 1997), analysis shows that a portfolio that comprised some managed futures had similar profitability with far less risk. Liang (2003) finds that CTAs are good hedging instruments for hedge funds, fund of funds, and equity markets when the others are not well hedged. This is especially true in down markets. Schneeweis and Georgiev (2002), in examining the benefits of managed funds, show that CTAs reduce portfolio volatility risk, enhance portfolio returns in economic environments in which traditional stock and bond investment media offer limited opportunities, and participate in a wide variety of new financial products and markets not available in traditional investor products. However, they note that for managed futures to grow as an investment alternative, individuals need to increase their knowledge and comfort level regarding the use of managed futures in their investment portfolios. For instance, there is still some confusion about the performance of CTAs as supply has expanded. In this study we first analyze the risk and return benefits of CTAs, as an alternative investment, using a more precise measure of risk. Then, we show how CTAs can be integrated into existing investment strategies and how to determine the optimal proportion of assets to invest in such products.

[1]The term "managed futures" describes an industry made up of professional money managers known as commodity trading advisors. These trading advisors manage client assets on a discretionary basis using global futures markets as an investment medium.

MEAN-MODIFIED VALUE AT RISK FRAMEWORK

Investment decisions are made to achieve an optimal risk/return trade-off from the available opportunities. To meet this objective, the portfolio manager has to identify the set of assets that are the most efficient, in the sense of providing the lowest level of risk for a desired level of expected return, and then to select one combination that is consistent with the risk aversion of the investor. Mean-variance analysis has been increasingly applied to asset allocation and is now the standard formulation of the investment decision problem. Although the principle of identifying portfolios with the required risk and return characteristics is clear, the proper definition of risk is vague. Risk may be defined differently according to the sensibility and the objectives of the portfolio manager. One manager might define risk as the probability of underperformance relative to some benchmark level of return, while another may be more sensitive to the overall magnitude of a loss. In a mean-variance framework, risk is defined in terms of the possible variation of expected portfolio returns. The focus on standard deviation as the appropriate measure for risk implies that investors weigh the probability of negative returns equally against positive returns. However, it is highly unlikely that the perception of investors to downside risk faced on investments is the same as the perception to the upward potential. Thus, investors needed a more precise measure of downside risk.

With the value at risk (VaR) approach, it is possible to measure the amount of portfolio wealth that can be lost over a given period of time with a certain probability. VaR has become a widely used risk management tool. The Basel Accord of 1988, for example, requires commercial banks to compute VaR in setting their minimum capital requirements (see Jorion 2001). One of the main advantages of VaR is that it works across different asset classes such as stocks and bonds. Further, VaR often is used as an ex-post measure to evaluate the current exposure to market risk and determine whether this exposure should be reduced.

Our objective consists in drawing the efficient frontiers based on the VaR framework. We also use the Cornish-Fisher (1937) expansion to adjust the traditional VaR with the skewness and kurtosis of the return distribution, which often deviates from normality.[2] We call the VaR with the Cornish-Fisher expansion modified VaR. Favre and Galeano (2002b) show that risk measured only with volatility will be lower than risk measured

[2]Mina and Ulmer (1999) provide four methods—Johnson transformations, Cornish-Fisher expansion, Fourier method, partial Monte-Carlo—to compute the VaR for nonnormally distributed assets.

with volatility, skewness, and kurtosis. Thus, results with modified VaR will be less biased. For details on obtaining the normal VaR, the Cornish-Fisher expansion to VaR, and other VaR methods, see Christoffersen (2003).

CHARACTERISTICS OF CTA

Before we engage in a detailed analysis of the risk-return properties of the CTA, a word of caution is necessary: Unlike traditional asset classes (bonds and equity), where performance data and benchmarks are readily and reliably available, the infrastructure and reliability of performance data for alternative investments, in general, and CTAs, in particular, are still rather underdeveloped. In this chapter, the CTA Qualified Universe index[3] (CTA QU) is used to give an overall picture of CTA, as it is more representative of the performance of trading advisors as a whole and cannot be criticized as having selection bias.

The sample portfolio is made up of CTA, Canadian, U.S., and international equities as well as domestic bonds. Canadian equities are represented by the Standard & Poor's (S&P)/Toronto Stock Exchange index, the CTA by the CTA QU Index (from CISDM database), the U.S. equities asset by the S&P 500 Index, the international equities asset by the Morgan Stanley Capital Index for Europe, Asia, and the Far East (MSCI EAFE), and the bonds by the Scotia McLeod universe bond index. We use monthly data from January 1990 to February 2003.

Within the assets considered (see Table 20.1), the CTA index is less risky than the S&P 500, the S&P/TSX, and the MSCI EAFE indices. In addition, CTA QU index possesses a higher Sharpe ratio than equity indices, indicating that CTAs offer superior risk-adjusted returns. These estimates may understate true risk, so monthly modified Sharpe ratios (using VaR instead of standard deviation) is also presented and confirms the advantage of the CTA QU index. Using VaR and modified VaR to measure risk, the CTAs are still less risky than equity indices. For instance, a one percent VaR of −5.3 percent for CTA QU index means that there is a 1 percent chance that the loss will be greater that 5.3 percent next month (or a 99 percent chance that it will be less than 5.3 percent).

Besides very attractive risk adjusted return characteristics, one of the most important features of CTAs is their favorable correlation structure to traditional assets classes (see Table 20.2). By including CTAs in their portfolios, traditional asset managers are given the opportunity to produce more consistent returns with lower levels of risk in their global portfolio by

[3]See www.cisdm.org for data and description of CTA Qualified Universe Index.

TABLE 20.1 Characteristics of CTA and Traditional Asset Classes, January 1990 to February 2003

Assets	Annual Mean	Annual Volatility	Skewness	Excess Kurtosis
CTA QU Index	11.8%	10.2%	0.7	2.2
SCM Bond Index	9.8%	5.5%	–0.2	0.7
S&P/TSX Index	7.3%	15.7%	–0.7	2.3
S&P 500 Index	11.1%	15.2%	–0.5	0.6
MSCI EAFE Index	1.9%	16.4%	–0.5	0.8

Assets	Monthly Normal VaR	Monthly Modified VaR	Monthly Sharpe Ratio	Modified Sharp Ratio
CTA QU Index	–5.9%	–5.3%	0.18	0.10
SCM Bond Index	–2.9%	–3.4%	0.23	0.11
S&P/TSX Index	–9.9%	–13.9%	0.04	0.01
S&P 500 Index	–9.3%	–11.2%	0.11	0.04
MSCI EAFE Index	–10.8%	–13.1%	–0.05	–0.02

means of diversification. CTA QU index has negative correlation to equity markets (–0.19 correlation to MSCI EAFE, –0.13 correlation to the S&P 500, and –0.12 correlation to the TSX/S&P). Furthermore, CTAs demonstrate remarkably low correlation with the bond market (0.20). Thus, including CTAs in a diversified asset portfolio may provide additional diversification benefits.

TABLE 20.2 Correlations Across CTA and Traditional Asset Classes, January 1990 to February 2003

	CTA QU Index	SCM	S&P/ TSX	S&P 500	MSCI EAFE
CTA QU Index	1				
SCM Bond Index	0.20	1			
S&P/TSX	–0.12	0.32	1		
S&P 500	–0.13	0.26	0.75	1	
MSCI EAFE	–0.19	0.20	0.66	0.70	1

INCORPORATING CTA TO THE ASSET ALLOCATION PROCESS

In this section, we show the results obtained by applying the mean-VaR framework explained previously. We compute the efficient frontier and the optimal portfolio allocation for a Canadian pension fund assuming that the portfolio manager has a VaR limit, that is, the manager does not want to lose more than a specified amount each month, with a specified probability (typically 1 or 5 percent).

The individual asset classes can vary within specific limits. As a result, a relatively conservative asset allocation was chosen to match the allocations of conservative investors, pension funds, and institutions. The weightings of individual asset classes are then changed within the permitted margins to minimize the normal VaR (see Table 20.3). This first step permits us to examine the effect of including a CTA in a traditional portfolio. In the second step, modified VaR values are used to measure risk more precisely.

Table 20.4 shows that CTAs take the place of U.S equities. Once the weights of the tangent portfolios are obtained, we compute the monthly returns that each portfolio would have yielded from January 1990 to February 2003. Based on these monthly returns, we compute the average return over the period and the modified VaR. We obtain the results shown in Table 20.5, which shows that while the average return of the portfolio with 10 percent CTA is less than the one with 0 percent CTA, the level of risk, measured with the modified VaR, is decreased by adding CTA. The modified Sharpe ratio is also improved by adding CTA investments in the traditional portfolio.

TABLE 20.3 Upper and Lower Limits for Individual Asset Classes

Asset Class	Minimum	Maximum
Commodity trading advisors	0%	10%
Canadian equities	10%	40%
U.S. equities	0%	30%
International equities	0%	30%
Canadian bonds	25%	50%

TABLE 20.4 Portfolio Weights from Mean-VaR Optimization

Asset Class	No CTA Available	CTA Investment Limit of 10%
CTA QU Index	0%	10%
MSCI EAFE	6%	8%
S&P 500	29%	17%
SCM Bond Index	50%	50%
S&P/TSX	15%	15%
Total	100%	100%

Further, Figure 20.1 shows the degree to which the sample portfolio with a CTA portion of maximum 10 percent is represented too positively if we do not take into account the skewness and kurtosis of the return distributions—in other words, if we do not use modified VaR. It is assumed that the investor is seeking an annual return of 7.2 percent with this sample portfolio. Our calculation using the Cornish-Fisher expansion shows that the investor will underestimate the risk by 14.28 percent if he or she is looking to achieve this return with normal VaR.

The crucial question for an investor is whether including CTAs as an alternative investment makes sense for his or her portfolio. To assess this, we use both normal and modified VaR with traditional and nontraditional portfolios (with CTA).

The arrows in Figure 20.2 show the shift in efficiency lines or, rather, the positive effect on including CTA QU index in a traditional portfolio. Figure 20.3 shows the added value of CTAs if skewness and kurtosis are taken into account (by using modified VaR as a risk measurement). The two

TABLE 20.5 Average Return, Modified VaR, and Modified Sharpe Ratio

	Average Return	Modified VaR	Modified Sharpe Ratio
Portfolio with 0% CTA	0.593%	5.93%	0.100
Portfolio with 10% CTA	0.581%	4.56%	0.128

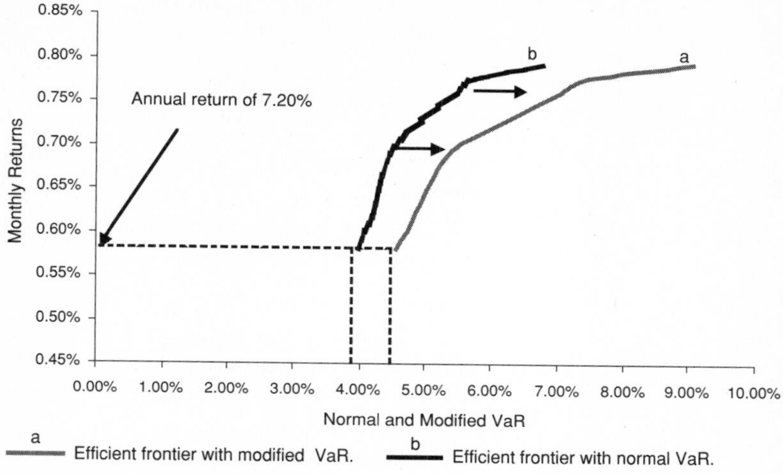

FIGURE 20.1 Pension Fund Portfolio with 10% CTA

figures show the classic picture, as can be seen in a mean-variance diagram. It is obvious that including CTAs with high negative skewness and kurtosis values in a portfolio does bring a benefit in the sense of better risk-adjusted returns.

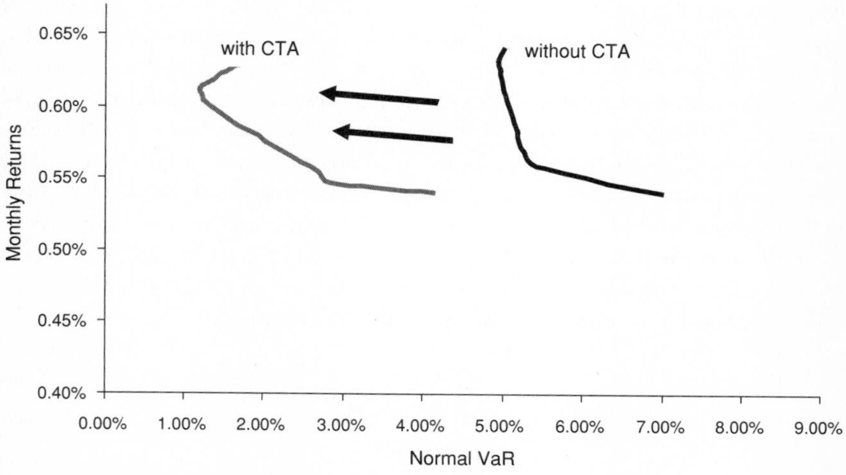

FIGURE 20.2 Pension Fund Portfolio with and without 10% CTA

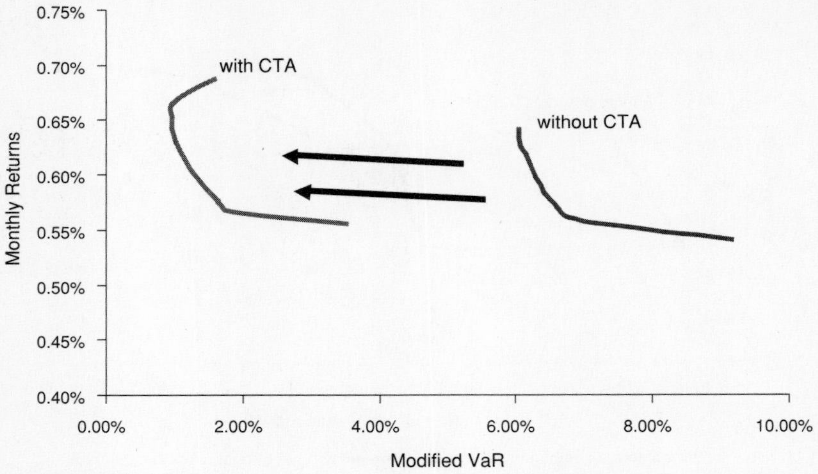

FIGURE 20.3 Pension Fund Portfolio with and without 10% CTA

CONCLUSION

Nowadays it is clear that a traditional strategy that divides investments into asset classes is no longer sufficient. The results of this study provide important information to the investment community about the benefits of CTAs. We show that an efficiently allocated portfolio consisting of CTAs and traditional assets should provide a better reward/risk ratio than an investment in traditional assets. We showed, as did Favre and Galeano (2002), that it is possible to use modified VaR risk measure to build a portfolio composed of traditional and alternative assets and that has the lowest probability of losing more than the modified VaR at a defined confidence level. However, investors must be very cautious in CTA selection. There are various CTAs with different characteristics and strategies. These differences need to be a major consideration, perhaps even more important than the decision of whether to invest in the asset class itself. Finally, analysis of alternative methods of measuring risk for alternative investments, in general, and CTA and hedge funds, in particular, is, of course, required.

CHAPTER 21

ARMA Modeling of CTA Returns

Vassilios N. Karavas and L. Joe Moffitt

In this chapter, we extend previous attempts to model hedge fund returns using ARMA models to the case of CTAs. We show that for the period 1996 to 2003, the return series of the largest CTAs are stationary and that ARMA models in certain cases provide adequate representation of the return series. Comparing to the hedge fund case, we see that a higher order of ARMA model usually is required. We also test for structural changes in the return processes, and we fit similar models for the period 2000 to 2003. Results appear to be no drastically different from those reported in previous studies for hedge funds.

INTRODUCTION

The period 1996 to 2003 offered a number of surprises to investors, with the excellent performance of the equity market during the first four years of the period and the subsequent drawdown for three consecutive years until 2003, when the long-expected economic recovery finally appeared. Commodity trading advisors (CTAs) did not suffer many years of losses, and definitely not at the magnitude of the equity markets' losses. The CTA indices showed that all years (included in this study) were profitable for the CTAs with the exception of 1999, when small losses were reported. CTAs offered investors a safe harbor for the years during which control was lost in the equity markets. In the next section we show pieces of historical evidence that CTAs were more stable over time, from a performance point of view, not only when compared to equity markets but also when compared to hedge funds.

Over the past few years, a large number of hedge fund managers were dragged toward an increased equity exposure, which in several cases

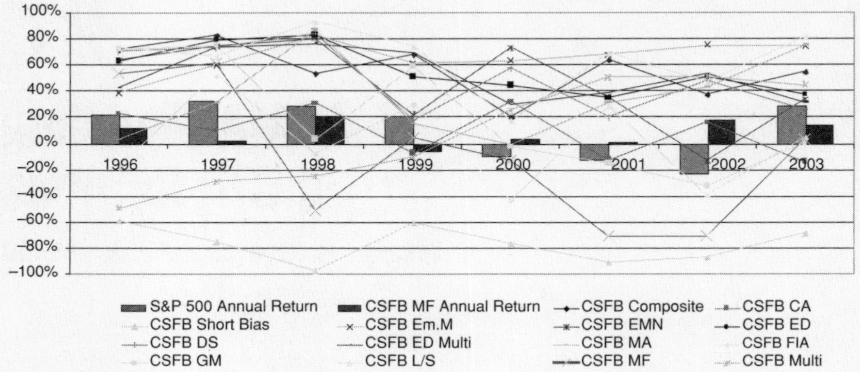

FIGURE 21.1 CTA and Hedge Fund Strategies Correlations with S&P 500

appeared to be rather catalytic for their existence, as the expected economic recovery, after the tech boom, did not arrive until 2003. In Figures 21.1 to 21.3, it is obvious that CTAs (as proxied by Credit Suisse First Boston Managed Futures Index [CSFB MF]) have strongly resisted the downward trend in equity markets. At the same time they have offered positive returns except in 1999, when they suffered mild losses. Figure 21.1 shows the annual correlation of each of the hedge fund strategies and CTAs relative to S&P 500. It also shows how the changes in the correlation with the S&P

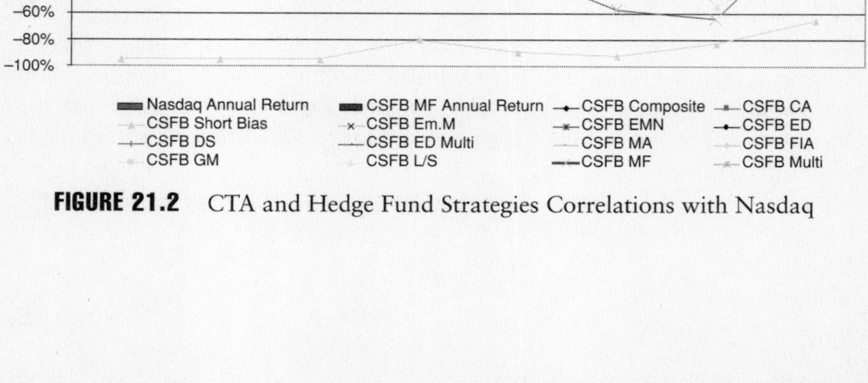

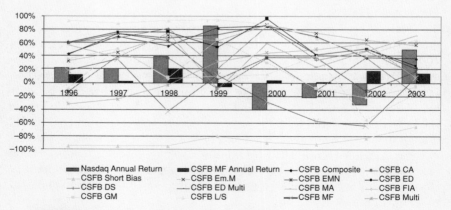

FIGURE 21.2 CTA and Hedge Fund Strategies Correlations with Nasdaq

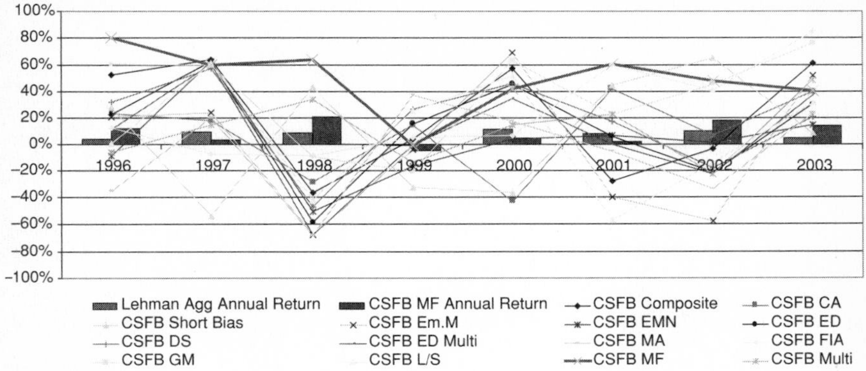

FIGURE 21.3 CTA and Hedge Fund Strategies Correlations with Lehman Aggregate

have affected the annual returns of the CSFB MF. Figures 21.2 and 21.3 show the corresponding results for Nasdaq and Lehman Aggregate Bond Index respectively.

These historical performance comparative results indicate that CTAs are an investment vehicle worth exploring and can offer unique risk/return characteristics in a stock/bond portfolio as well as in a stock/bond hedge funds portfolio. A number of studies have explored the benefits of managed futures (CISDM 2002), so we limit the analysis of managed futures to showing the importance of modeling their return series.

In the next section we examine whether CTAs generate stationary return time series, and we attempt to fit auto-regressive moving average (ARMA) models.

METHODOLOGY

We test for second-order (weak) stationarity in our return time series $\{y_t\}_{t=1}^{\infty}$. In other words, we test whether its first and second moments and its autocorrelations are invariant in time. For comparison purposes, we carry out all the tests that appeared in Gregoriou and Rouah (2003a) for hedge funds, among others. However, we examine a more complete set of CTAs that satisfy certain track record and assets under management requirements, as we have included all the CTAs that report their performance in the database from the Center for International Securities and Derivatives Markets (CISDM). We also extend the analysis to the manager's excess returns as a proxy for determining stationarity of manager's alpha. We use the Augmented Dickey-Fuller

(ADF) test to test for the presence of a unit root in the series. In our examples, intercept and time trend have been taken into account.

$$\Delta y_t = \mu + \lambda t + (\gamma - 1)y_{t-1} + \sum_{i=1}^{N} \varphi_i \Delta y_{t-i} + \varepsilon_t \tag{21.1}$$

After we test for stationarity, we model the return series using ARMA(p,q) processes of different orders using correlograms for each series as a guide. Finally we perform stability tests using the Chow test to investigate possible structural changes in the parameters of the specified ARMA processes.

DATA

For this study we have chosen the 10 largest CTAs from the CISDM database that have complete data series (monthly) for the period from January 1996 to December 2003. Their average assets under management were over $100 million during the fourth quarter of 2003. For comparison purposes, we required that the return series are complete, and we wanted to examine CTAs with relatively long historical track records and that are of significant size (based on the most recent information available). The effects of length of track record as well as fund size have been extensively examined by Schneeweis, Kazemi, and Karavas (2003a, b) for hedge funds. Although similar analysis for CTAs, to the best of our knowledge, is not available, we anticipate that the benefits of larger hedge funds with long track records apply to CTAs, too. Briefly, a long track record provides evidence of manager performance under different market conditions, while high assets under management indicate that the strategy followed can be replicable at larger scale. The latter is important especially for CTAs because of the impact on prices due to trade of high volumes of specific futures; managers with low assets under management impact the prices to a lesser extent.

For the calculation of the excess returns used in the tests, we calculated the excess CTA monthly return from the CISDM Equally Weighted Trading Advisor Qualified Universe Index (CISDM CTA). The CISDM CTA Index is the median return of all CTAs and commodity pool operators (CPOs) reporting to the CISDM CTA database. At the end of 2003, there existed approximately 600 CTAs and CPOs each having approximately an equal share in the database.

The CTA returns, as well the returns of the CSFB/Tremont and CISDM indices, used in this analysis have not been adjusted to eliminate biases inherent in them. A description of potential biases in the indices, some of which apply to the databases as well, can be found in Karavas and Siokos (2004).

The following tables provide descriptive statistics for the data set used in the simulations as well as for the corresponding excess returns. As we see in Table 21.1, CTAs offer a wide range of performance characteristics. It is noteworthy to see that the risk-adjusted return as proxied by the information ratio varies significantly relative to the information ratio of the CISDM CTA index. This means that across the 10 largest CTAs in existence for at least eight years, the majority of them offer returns that are not justified for the amount of risk they undertake (see Table 21.2). Information ratios in bold denote values below the information ratio of the CISDM CTA index.

RESULTS

The ADF tests showed that for all CTAs included in this study, the error terms were white noise; thus all series were stationary. With the exception of one CTA (#3), we could reject the null hypothesis of unit root for all CTAs at 99 percent confidence level (#3: at 90 percent). All the ADF tests were run for four lags; the results are shown in Table 21.3. Similar tests were performed on CTAs' excess returns and are shown in Table 21.4. The results using CTA returns were consistent with those in Gregoriou and Rouah (2003a) for hedge funds. Those authors did not examine excess returns, however, this study shows that the added alpha relative to the strategy (as proxied by the CISDM CTA index) for the 10 largest funds is indeed stationary.

Using the correlograms, we determined that in several cases the autocorrelations did not fade after the first lag, so more lags needed to be included in the models. As we see in Table 21.3, the CTA returns studied carry the effect of previous months return levels. The table shows the different orders of ARMA models that have been utilized to better represent the corresponding return series. In certain cases (CTA: 2, 5, 10) the representation is adequate, evidenced by relatively high R^2 values and significant coefficients. For CTA #9, although there is a relatively high R^2, the MA process is noninvertible. For CTA #3, although we have not rejected the existence of unit root at 95 percent, we have used an ARMA (2,2) model with a low R^2. We note that CTAs #2 and #3 are the only ones that are low negatively correlated with the CTA Index.

Table 21.4 presents similar results to Table 21.3 using excess returns. The benefit of studying CTAs' excess returns is it allows us to see whether and how individual CTAs outperform the strategy to which they belong. It is rather useful when managers of specific strategies are evaluated for inclu-

TABLE 21.1 Statistics for the 10 Largest CTAs, January 1996 to December 2003

	Annualized Return	Annualized Rate of Deviation	Information Standard Ratio[a]	Monthly Min Return	Monthly Max Return	% of Profitable Months	% of Non-profitable Months	Correlation with CISDM CTA	AUM[b] in millions (USD) Q3-03
CTA1	17.04%	14.47%	1.18	−9.62%	12.22%	65%	35%	0.81	$4,523
CTA2	5.92%	5.98%	**0.99**	−5.50%	9.65%	68%	32%	−0.12	$2,103
CTA3	15.73%	14.77%	1.07	−11.97%	9.44%	63%	38%	−0.11	$1,463
CTA4	8.60%	6.00%	1.43	−2.29%	10.39%	69%	31%	0.05	$1,385
CTA5	12.79%	10.32%	1.24	−4.49%	9.48%	58%	42%	0.54	$1.192
CTA6	16.58%	12.58%	1.32	−7.95%	16.50%	58%	42%	0.78	$1,134
CTA7	15.35%	13.84%	1.11	−10.33%	9.54%	60%	40%	0.83	$ 950
CTA8	11.20%	14.42%	**0.78**	−9.68%	11.01%	56%	44%	0.79	$ 890
CTA9	20.87%	15.53%	1.34	−6.99%	14.36%	61%	39%	0.75	$ 839
CTA10	11.22%	15.11%	**0.74**	−8.03%	12.23%	55%	45%	0.52	$ 821
CISDM	9.60%	9.26%	1.04	−4.45%	7.80%	59%	41%	1.00	

[a]CTA information ratios that are lower than the CISDM CTA index information ratio are in bold.
[b]Assets under management.

TABLE 21.2 Statistics for the Excess Returns of the 10 Largest CTAs, January 1996 to December 2003

	Annualized Excess Return	Annualized Standard Deviation	Monthly Min Return	Monthly Max Return	% of Months with Positive Excess Return	% of Months with Negative Excess Return
CTA1	7.07%	8.90%	–5.42%	8.25%	60%	40%
CTA2	–4.26%	11.60%	–8.71%	11.28%	49%	51%
CTA3	4.58%	18.30%	–12.73%	11.08%	59%	41%
CTA4	–1.73%	10.79%	–9.26%	7.81%	50%	50%
CTA5	2.59%	9.43%	–5.59%	6.86%	60%	40%
CTA6	6.46%	7.83%	–4.04%	9.29%	57%	43%
CTA7	5.51%	8.01%	–5.96%	5.96%	55%	45%
CTA8	1.66%	9.10%	–6.96%	6.43%	52%	48%
CTA9	10.59%	10.54%	–4.59%	10.98%	59%	41%
CTA10	1.34%	13.01%	–12.43%	12.21%	48%	52%

sion in portfolios of CTAs (CPOs) or in portfolio of mixed strategies and the objective is to maximize alpha.

Table 21.2 shows that CTA #2 has underperformed the CISDM CTA Index, but Table 21.4 shows its series (excess returns) appears to be stationary. Excess returns of CTA #9 and #10 are adequately represented by the ARMA models shown in Table 21.4, as evidenced by high R^2 and significant coefficients. Both CTAs have outperformed the CISDM CTA Index, but they were the most volatile of the 10 CTAs and the index.

We then performed a stability test on the ARMA model parameters to investigate possible structural changes. For this purpose we utilized the Chow test before and after January 2000. The justification for this breakpoint is that 1999 was a very profitable year for the equity indices; CTAs did not perform as well afterward.

Chow test statistics appear in Table 21.3. The *F*-statistics for three CTAs are relatively high, indicating structural changes. For CTA #9, we did not test for structural changes as the MA process was noninvertible, and the model did not fit better even for the period 2000 to 2003.

For the three CTAs with relatively high *F*-statistics, we fitted the corresponding ARMA models for the period 2000 to 2003. As shown in Table 21.5,

TABLE 21.3 CTA Returns: ARMA Models

	ADF Tests	μ	AR(1) $\alpha1$	AR(2) $\alpha2$	AR(3) $\alpha3$	AR(4) $\alpha4$	MA(1) $\beta1$	MA(2) $\beta2$	MA(3) $\beta3$	R^2	Chow *F*-Stat *p*-value
CTA1	−5.6629	0.0144	−0.4447	−0.8778			0.4511	0.9799		0.04	1.49
CTA1: *p*-value		0.0006	0.0000	0.0000			0.0000	0.0000			0.20
CTA2	−5.6161	0.0015	−0.5618	−0.5106	0.7482		0.6638	−0.6249	−0.9581	0.31	1.40
CTA2: *p*-value		0.2288	0.0000	0.0000	0.0000		0.0000	0.0000	0.0000		0.22
CTA3	−3.4275	0.0141	1.1231	−0.7910			−1.1684	0.9799		0.06	2.25
CTA3: *p*-value		0.0055	0.0000	0.0000			0.0000	0.0000			0.06
CTA4	−5.7926	0.0065	−0.8322	−0.1493			−0.8378			0.03	3.95
CTA4: *p*-value		0.0000	0.0000	0.1632			0.0000				0.01
CTA5	−4.9350	0.0096	−0.4473	−0.9215			0.5598	1.0430	0.1529	0.15	0.23
CTA5: *p*-value		0.0034	−0.0000	−0.0000			0.0000	0.0000	0.0000		0.97
CTA6	−4.9529	0.0138	−0.9249				0.9801			0.01	1.95
CTA6: p-value		0.0005	0.0000				0.0000				0.13
CTA7	−4.7019	0.0111	−0.8566				0.9740			0.03	0.53
CTA7: p-value		0.0000	0.0000				0.0000				0.66
CTA8	−5.4682	0.0097	0.9402	−0.1479			−0.9814			0.06	2.21
CTA8: p-value		0.0000	0.0000	0.1546			0.0000				0.07
CTA9	−5.1140	0.0160	−0.8977				−1.1274			0.20	
CTA9: p-value		0.0003	0.0000				0.0000				
CTA10	−4.5596	0.0098	−1.5509	−1.3294	−0.5811	−0.2769	1.3508	0.9344		0.15	0.34
CTA10: p-value		0.0006	0.0000	0.0000	0.0022	0.0039	0.0000	0.0000			0.93

All ADF tests are at 99 percent confidence level. CTA3 rejects hypothesis of unit root at 90 percent.

TABLE 21.4 CTA Excess Returns: ARMA Models

	ADF Tests	μ	AR(1) $\alpha 1$	AR(2) $\alpha 2$	AR(3) $\alpha 3$	AR(4) $\alpha 4$	MA(1) $\beta 1$	MA(2) $\beta 2$	MA(3) $\beta 3$	MA(4) $\beta 4$	R^2
CTA Exc1	–4.7461	0.0059	–0.7203				0.7109				0.01
CTA Exc1: *p*-value		0.0259	0.0191				0.0262				
CTA Exc2	–5.3094	–0.0043	–0.7132				–0.8592				0.07
CTA Exc2: *p*-value		0.0178	0.0000				0.0000				
CTA Exc3	–4.3574	0.0051	–0.5293	–0.7877			0.5947	0.9800			0.12
CTA Exc3: *p*-value		0.3588	0.0000	0.0000			0.0000	0.0000			
CTA Exc4	–5.3569	–0.0012	–0.3677	–0.8945			–0.4187	0.9617			0.03
CTA Exc4: *p*-value		0.7033	0.0000	0.0000			0.0000	0.0000			
CTA Exc5	–4.1900	0.0025	1.0716	–0.7539			–1.2220	0.9638			0.07
CTA Exc5: *p*-value		0.3855	0.0000	0.0000			0.0000	0.0000			
CTA Exc6	–4.2616	0.0046	–0.5997	–0.4724	–0.7067		0.5722	0.5721	0.9661		0.11
CTA Exc6: *p*-value		0.0473	0.0000	0.0000	0.0000		0.0000	0.0000	0.0000		
CTA Exc7	–4.8709	0.0051	–0.7890	–0.5644			–0.8271	0.6983			0.01
CTA Exc7: *p*-value		0.0572	0.0039	0.0376			0.0009	0.0053			
CTA Exc8	–5.1742	0.0014	–0.4560				0.5768				0.00
CTA Exc8: *p*-value		0.6276	0.1771				0.0706				
CTA Exc9	**–3.9901**	0.0100	0.5498	0.9293	0.1356	–0.6643	–0.4929	– 1.0160	–0.4115	0.9248	0.16
CTA Exc9: *p*-value		0.0000	0.0000	0.0000	0.2974	0.0000	0.0000	0.0000	0.0000	0.0000	
CTA Exc10	–6.7692	0.0016	0.7768	–0.5202			–1.1091	0.3889			0.20
CTA Exc10: *p*-value		0.2435	0.0000	0.0004			0.0000	0.0300			

All ADF tests are at 99 percent confidence level. CTA9 rejects hypothesis of unit root at 95 percent.

TABLE 21.5 CTA Returns, 2000 to 2003: ARMA Models

	μ	AR(1) $\alpha 1$	AR(2) $\alpha 2$	MA(1) $\alpha 1$	MA(2) $\alpha 2$	R^2
CTA3	0.0123	−0.8042	−0.6546	0.9994	0.9800	0.16
CTA3: *p*-value	0.0895	0.0000	0.0000	0.0000	0.0000	
CTA4	0.0050	−0.5734	0.0956	0.8731		0.04
CTA4: *p*-value	0.0288	0.0126	0.5748	0.0000		
CTA8	0.0120	−0.7018	−0.1482	0.9529		0.09
CTA8: *p*-value	0.0831	0.0000	0.3521	0.0000		

there is a significant improvement for CTA #3 and #8 (evidenced by the increased R^2). For CTA #4, ARMA (1,1) (results not shown) appear to better model the return series during 2000 to 2003 than the ARMA (2,1) model utilized for 1996 to 2003 and 2000 to 2003.

CONCLUSION

In this study, we investigated the return series behavior of the 10 largest CTAs in the CISDM database and utilized a number of ARMA models. Results showed that the series are in general stationary (using ADF tests), as are the excess returns of the same CTAs relative to the CISDM CTA Index. ARMA models for the largest CTAs tended to be of higher orders than those in the case of hedge funds (Gregoriou and Rouah 2003b). In spite of the significant parameters in most cases, very few of these CTA models were accompanied by substantial R^2. Unfortunately, this implies that the models have little forecasting power. A few indicated possible structural changes, evidenced by Chow tests. For two CTAs the same models offered a better representation for the period after the breakpoint (January 2000), while for the third CTA a different ARMA model appears to offer better results.

CHAPTER 22

Risk-Adjusted Returns of CTAs: Using the Modified Sharpe Ratio

Robert Christopherson and Greg N. Gregoriou

Many institutional investors use the traditional Sharpe ratio to examine the risk-adjusted performance of CTAs. However, this could pose problems due to the nonnormal returns of this alternative asset class. A modified VaR and modified Sharpe ratio solves the problem and can provide a superior tool for correctly measuring risk-adjusted performance. Here we rank 30 CTAs according to the Sharpe and modified Sharpe ratio and find that larger CTAs possess high modified Sharpe ratios.

INTRODUCTION

The assessment of portfolio performance is fundamental for both investors and funds managers, as well as commodity trading advisors (CTAs). Traditional portfolio measures are of limited value when applied to CTAs. For instance, applying the traditional Sharpe ratio will overstate the excess reward per unit of risk as measure of performance, with risk represented by the variance (standard deviation) because of the nonnormal returns of CTAs.

The mean-variance approach to the portfolio selection problem developed by Markowitz (1952) has been criticized often due to its utilization of variance as a measure of risk exposure when examining the nonnormal returns of CTAs. The value at risk (VaR) measure for financial risk has become accepted as a better measure for investment firms, large banks, and pension funds. As a result of the recurring frequency of down markets since the collapse of Long-Term Capital Management (LTCM) in August 1998, VaR has played a paramount role as a risk management tool and is considered a mainstream technique to estimate a CTA's exposure to market risk.

With the large acceptance of VaR and, specifically, the modified VaR as a relevant risk management tool, a more suitable portfolio performance measure for CTAs can be formulated in term of the modified Sharpe ratio.[1]

Using the traditional Sharpe ratio to rank CTAs will underestimate the tail risk and overestimate performance. Distributions that are highly skewed will experience greater-than-average risk underestimation. The greater the distribution is from normal, the greater is the risk underestimation.

In this chapter we rank 30 CTAs according to the Sharpe ratio and modified Sharpe ratio. Our results indicate that the modified Sharpe ratio is more accurate when examining nonnormal returns. Nonnormality of returns is present in the majority of CTA subtype classifications.

LITERATURE REVIEW

Many CTAs produce statistical reports that include the traditional Sharpe ratio, which can be misleading because funds will look better in terms of risk-adjusted returns. The drawback of using a traditional Sharpe ratio is that it does not distinguish between upside and downside risk.

VaR has emerged in the finance literature as a ubiquitous measure of risk. However, its simple version presents some limitations. Methods to measure VaR such as, the Delta-Normal method described in Jorion (2000), are simple and easy to apply. However, the formula has a drawback since the assumption of normality of the distributions is violated due to the use of short-selling and derivatives strategies such as futures contracts frequently used by CTAs.

Several methods have been proposed recently to correctly assess the VaR for nonnormal returns (Rockafellar and Uryasev 2001). Using a conditional VaR for general loss distributions, Agarwal and Naik (2004) con-

[1]The standard VaR, which assumes normality and uses the traditional standard deviation measure, looks only at the tails of the distribution of the extreme events. This is common when examining mutual funds, but when applying this technique to funds of hedge funds, difficulty arises because of the nonnormality of returns (Favre and Galeano 2002a, b). The modified VaR takes into consideration the mean, standard deviation, skewness, and kurtosis to correctly evaluate the risk-adjusted returns of funds of hedge funds. Computing the risk of a traditional investment portfolio consisting of 50 percent stocks and 50 percent bonds with the traditional standard deviation measure could underestimate the risk in excess of 35 percent (Favre and Singer 2002).

struct a mean conditional VaR demonstrating that mean-variance analysis underestimates tail risk. Favre and Galeano (2002b) also have developed a technique to properly assess funds with nonnormal distributions. They demonstrate that the modified VaR (MVaR) does considerably improve the accuracy of the traditional VaR. The difference between the modified VaR and the traditional VaR is that the latter only considers the mean and standard deviation, while the former takes into account higher moments such as skewness and kurtosis.

The modified VaR allows one to calculate a modified Sharpe ratio, which is more suitable for CTAs. For example, when two portfolios have the same mean and standard deviation, they still may be quite different due to their extreme loss potential. If a traditional portfolio of stocks and bonds was equally split, using the standard deviation as opposed to modified VaR to calculate risk-adjusted performance could underestimate the risk by more than 35 percent (Favre and Galeano 2002b).

DATA AND METHODOLOGY

The data set consists of 164 CTAs who reported monthly performance figures, net of all fees, to the Barclay Trading Group database. The data spans the period January 1997 to November 31, 2003, for a total of 83 months. We selected this period because of the extreme market event of August 1998 (Long-Term Captial Management collapse) as well as the September 11, 2001, attacks. From this we extracted and ranked the top 10, middle 10, and bottom 10 funds according to ending assets under management. We use this comparison to see if there exist any differences between groups in terms of the Sharpe and modified Sharpe ratio. We use the Extreme metrics software available on the www.alternativesoft.com web site to compute the results using a 99 percent VaR probability, and we assume that we are able to borrow at a risk-free rate of 0 percent.

The difference between the traditional and modified Sharpe ratio is that, in the latter, the standard deviation is replaced by the modified VaR in the denominator. The traditional Sharpe ratio, generally defined as the excess return per unit of standard deviation, is represented by this equation:

$$\text{Sharpe Ratio} = \frac{R_p - R_F}{\sigma} \qquad (22.1)$$

where R_P = return of the portfolio
R_F = risk-free rate and
σ = standard deviation of the portfolio

A modified Sharpe ratio can be defined in terms of modified VaR:

$$\text{Modified Sharpe Ratio} = \frac{R_p - R_F}{\text{MVaR}} \tag{22.2}$$

The derivation of the formula for the modified VaR is beyond the scope of this chapter. Readers are guided to Favre and Galeano (2002b) and Christoffersen (2003) for a more detailed explanation.

EMPIRICAL RESULTS

Descriptive Statistics

Table 22.1 displays monthly statistics on CTAs during the examination period, including mean return, standard deviation, skewness, excess kurtosis, and compounded returns.

The average of the compounded returns and mean monthly returns is greatest in the top group (Panel A) and the lowest in the bottom group, as expected. In addition, we find that negative skewness is more pronounced in the bottom group, yielding more negative extreme returns, whereas the middle group (Panel B) has the greatest positive skewness. A likely explanation is that the middle-size CTA may better control skewness during down markets and will have on average fewer negative monthly returns. Large CTAs may have a harder time getting in and out of investment positions.

The bottom group (Panel C) has the highest volatility (standard deviation 32.56 percent) and lowest compounded returns (18.29 percent), likely attributable to CTAs taking on more risk to achieve greater returns.

Performance Discussion

Table 22.2 presents market risk and performance results. First, observe that the top group (Panel A) has, in absolute value, the lowest normal and modified VaR (i.e., is less exposed to extreme market losses). Furthermore, the bottom group (Panel C) has in absolute value the highest normal and modified VaR, implying that CTAs with small assets under management are more susceptible to extreme losses. This is not surprising, because they have the lowest monthly average returns, as seen in Table 22.1.

Concerning performance, the bottom group has the lowest traditional modified and modified Sharpe ratios. It appears that large CTAs do a better job of controlling risk-adjusted performance than can small CTAs. Comparing the results of the traditional and the modified Sharpe ratios, we find that the traditional Sharpe ratio is higher, confirming that tail risk is underestimated when using the traditional Sharpe ratio.

TABLE 22.1 Descriptive Statistics

Fund Name	Assets (Ending Millions $)	Average Annualized Return (%)	Average Annualized Std. Dev. (%)	Skewness	Excess Kurtosis	Compounded Return (%)
Panel A: Subsample 1: Top 10 CTAs						
Bridgewater Associates	6,831.00	11.88	9.75	−0.10	−0.60	119.38
Campbell & Co., Inc.	5,026.00	14.16	13.70	−0.40	0.10	148.53
Vega Asset Management (USA) LLC	2,054.68	9.21	4.60	−1.50	5.00	87.28
Grossman Asset Management	1,866.00	15.64	15.28	−0.10	−0.30	170.81
UBS O'Connor	1,558.00	8.31	8.54	0.30	0.70	73.02
Crabel Capital Management, LLC	1,511.00	7.74	6.31	1.10	3.70	68.29
FX Concepts, Inc.	1,480.00	10.79	15.26	0.30	−0.10	94.63
Grinham Managed Funds Pty., Ltd.	1,280.00	11.69	10.01	0.50	−0.10	116.34
Rotella Capital Management Inc.	1,227.95	11.63	12.19	0.30	0.30	112.10
Sunrise Capital Partners	1,080.96	13.77	13.75	0.90	0.50	142.03
Average	**2,391.62**	**11.48**	**10.94**	**0.13**	**0.92**	**113.24**
Panel B: Subsample 2: Middle 10 CTAs						
Compucom Finance, Inc.	53.00	9.90	22.18	0.50	0.50	68.12
Marathon Capital Growth Ptnrs., LLC	50.10	13.73	14.78	0.00	1.30	139.11
DynexCorp Ltd.	50.00	7.47	12.17	0.10	−0.70	59.25
ARA Portfolio Management Company	47.70	7.05	17.24	−0.10	0.90	47.08

TABLE 22.1 *(continued)*

Fund Name	Assets (Ending Millions $)	Average Annualized Return (%)	Average Annualized Std. Dev. (%)	Skewness	Excess Kurtosis	Compounded Return (%)
Panel B: Subsample 2: Middle 10 CTAs *(continued)*						
Blenheim Capital Mgmt., LLC	46.50	21.66	37.22	–0.10	–0.20	181.17
Quality Capital Management, Ltd.	46.00	13.06	16.34	0.20	–0.40	124.74
Sangamon Trading, Inc.	46.00	9.06	7.30	1.80	6.70	83.40
Willowbridge Associates, Inc.	45.80	14.38	42.44	0.90	4.80	48.89
Clarke Capital Management, Inc.	43.20	16.19	17.41	0.60	0.90	175.78
Millburn Ridgefield Corporation	42.94	5.91	17.47	1.00	0.70	36.04
Average	**47.12**	**11.84**	**20.46**	**0.49**	**1.45**	**96.36**
Panel C: Subsample 3: Bottom 10 CTAs						
Muirlands Capital Management LLC	0.40	16.10	24.11	0.20	-0.70	149.13
Minogue Investment Co.	0.40	9.27	41.88	1.70	8.30	8.10
Shawbridge Asset Mgmt. Corp.	0.22	15.66	33.88	1.00	3.00	102.94
International Trading Advisors, B.V.B.A.	0.20	–6.33	12.22	–1.10	8.10	–38.83
Be Free Investments, Inc.	0.20	14.95	20.49	–1.50	5.70	140.79
Lawless Commodities, Inc.	0.10	–11.10	43.02	–1.70	7.80	–77.22
District Capital Management	0.10	13.80	34.68	–0.50	1.20	67.73
Venture I	0.10	–1.42	21.19	–2.50	11.80	–22.91
Marek D. Chelkowski	0.10	–15.91	78.29	–0.30	0.50	–95.98
Robert C. Franzen	0.10	–8.94	15.79	–2.00	4.70	–50.81
Average	**0.19**	**2.61**	**32.56**	**–0.67**	**5.04**	**18.29**

TABLE 22.2 Performance Results

Fund Name	Normal VaR (%)	Modified VaR (%)	Normal Sharpe Ratio	Modified Sharpe Ratio
Panel A: Subsample 1: Top 10 CTAs				
Bridgewater Associates	−6.42	−6.28	0.09	0.10
Campbell & Co., Inc.	−8.17	−9.13	0.13	0.12
Vega Asset Management (USA) LLC	−1.33	−2.64	0.60	0.30
Grossman Asset Management	−8.99	−8.94	0.11	0.11
UBS O'Connor	−3.91	−3.75	0.25	0.26
Crabel Capital Management, LLC	−2.85	−2.33	0.24	0.29
FX Concepts, Inc.	−9.22	−8.09	0.10	0.11
Grinham Managed Funds Pty., Ltd.	−5.66	−4.23	0.16	0.22
Rotella Capital Management Inc.	−7.33	−6.54	0.12	0.14
Sunrise Capital Partners	−8.08	−4.89	0.11	0.18
Average	**−6.20**	**−5.68**	**0.19**	**0.18**
Panel B: Subsample 2: Middle 10 CTAs				
Compucom Finance, Inc.	−11.07	−12.66	−0.03	−0.03
Marathon Capital Growth Ptnrs., LLC	−10.69	−9.36	0.11	0.10
DynexCorp Ltd.	−6.83	−7.60	0.01	0.02
ARA Portfolio Management Company	−12.24	−10.98	0.06	0.05
Blenheim Capital Mgmt, LLC	−21.76	−21.49	0.08	0.08
Quality Capital Management, Ltd.	−8.81	−9.85	0.11	0.13
Sangamon Trading, Inc.	−2.19	−4.01	0.23	0.12
Willowbridge Associates, Inc.	−3.54	−32.94	0.03	0.02
Clarke Capital Management, Inc.	−8.32	−9.94	0.12	0.10
Millburn Ridgefield Corporation	−7.21	−12.67	0.07	0.04
Average	**−9.27**	**−13.15**	**0.08**	**0.06**

TABLE 22.2 *(continued)*

Fund Name	Normal Var (%)	Modified Var (%)	Normal Sharpe Ratio	Modified Sharpe Ratio
Panel C: Subsample 3: Bottom 10 CTAs				
Muirlands Capital Management LLC	−13.90	−15.98	0.03	0.03
Minogue Investment Co.	−24.62	−29.99	−0.01	−0.01
Shawbridge Asset Mgmt. Corp.	−18.66	−22.18	0.03	0.04
International Trading Advisors, B.V.B.A.	−21.31	−10.86	−0.01	−0.00
Be Free Investments, Inc.	−24.37	−14.15	0.06	0.03
Lawless Commodities, Inc.	−52.03	−29.80	−0.11	−0.06
District Capital Management	−29.99	−24.05	0.02	0.02
Venture I	−26.46	−13.79	−0.06	−0.03
Marek D. Chelkowski	−44.79	−40.25	−0.10	−0.09
Robert C. Franzen	−11.90	−8.34	−0.09	−0.06
Average	**−26.80**	**−20.94**	**−0.02**	**-0.01**

CONCLUSION

It is of critical importance to understand that complications will arise when a traditional measure of risk-adjusted performance, such as the Sharpe ratio, is used on the nonnormal returns of CTAs. Institutional investors must use the modified Sharpe ratio to measure the risk-adjusted returns correctly. The modified VaR is better in the presence of extreme returns because the normal VaR considers only the first two moments of a distribution, namely mean and standard deviation. The modified VaR, however, takes into consideration the third and fourth moments of a distribution, skewness and kurtosis. Using both the modified Sharpe and modified VaR will enable investors to more accurately assess CTA performance. In many cases, if the modified Sharpe ratio is used to examine normally distributed assets, they will be ranked in the same exact order as if the traditional Sharpe ratio was used. This occurs because the modified VaR converges to the classical VaR if skewness equals zero and excess kurtosis equals zero.

The statistics presented can be applied to all CTA classifications displaying nonnormal returns. We believe many institutional investors wanting to add CTAs to traditional stock and bond portfolios must request additional and more appropriate statistics, such as the modified Sharpe ratio, to analyze the returns of CTAs.

CHAPTER 23

Time Diversification: The Case of Managed Futures

François-Serge Lhabitant and Andrew Green

There is a long-standing debate in the financial literature as to whether stocks are more risky over the long term than over the short term. In this chapter, we use an approach based on historical data and analyze the ex-post performance of managed futures over different time periods. We observe that in terms of capital preservation, managed futures seem less risky over the long term than over the short term. However, this superiority is at risk as soon as the benchmark return increases. This fact, combined with the correlation properties of managed futures with traditional asset classes, tends to promote their use as portfolio diversifiers rather than as stand-alone investments.

INTRODUCTION

Adam and Eve, as originally created, were biologically capable of living forever. Unfortunately, eating the forbidden fruit forced them to realize that aging also could mean a process of decay that leads finally to death. Several expressions—*vita brevis* (life is short), *sic transit gloria mundi* (thus passes away the glory of the world), *carpe diem* (seize the day), *tempus fugit* (time flies)—remind us of time's inevitability as well as men's foolish attempts to transcend it or, at least, find an antidote to it.

To our knowledge, the only field where the passage of time actually may provide growth rather than decay is the investment arena, particularly when one takes into account the power of compounding. The latter simply means earning interest on interest, a principle that Einstein used to describe as being the "most powerful force in the universe" and the "ninth wonder of the world." Its consequences are straightforward: The longer you stay invested and reinvest your earnings, the faster your money will grow. The key is therefore to be patient and let time do the work for you.

The power of compounding is universally recognized. Another important theory linked to the passage of time in portfolios is called time diversification. It is well entrenched in the practices of asset management, but raises a healthy dose of skepticism from some in the academic community. Simply stated, it claims that investing for a longer time horizon decreases the risk of an investment. As all experienced investors know, the market is a roller-coaster ride when looked at from a day-to-day perspective. An asset that moves up by 2 percent one day may well drop 5 percent the following day. However, over the long run, the common belief is that markets should tend to move in an upward direction, simply because their returns must include a risk premium to convince risk-averse investors that they should participate. This wisdom advises investors to take a long-term view of the markets and not focus too much on short-term gyrations. With this outlook, the chances are better that investors' portfolios ultimately will increase in value. It follows from this argument that the longer an investor's time horizon is, the more money he or she should place in riskier investments—assuming, of course, that taking more risk implies obtaining a higher risk premium, or rate of return.

Time diversification as a hedge against risk has been widely applied in equity markets and retirement fund planning. However, we have not yet found any research devoted to the validity of time diversification for alternative investments, and more specifically to commodity trading advisors (CTAs). This is rather surprising, as CTAs are well known for their diversification benefits from a portfolio standpoint—what some people call space diversification. With practically a zero correlation to stocks, one of the most attractive features of CTAs is their ability to add diversification to an investment portfolio. As an illustration, a study published by the Chicago Board of Trade (2002) concluded that "portfolios with as much as 20 percent of assets in managed futures yielded up to 50 percent more than a portfolio of stocks and bonds alone." But how long should one wait to observe these benefits? And, ideally, should CTAs be part of portfolios for a long time period or a short one?

In this chapter, we explore the effects of time diversification on portfolios of CTAs. Rather than construct an argument based on financial tools or theoretical concepts, we choose to look at the historical data. We are interested in two questions:

1. How does the terminal value of a CTA's portfolio evolve as the holding period increases?
2. How does the value of a CTA's portfolio evolve within a given holding period when the length of the latter increases?

In the next section we briefly introduce CTAs and their key features. Then we review the various arguments for time diversification as presented for the equity markets. Next we describe the methodology and discuss the major findings. In the last section we draw conclusions and open the way for further research.

COMMODITY TRADING ADVISORS

Commodity trading advisors, also known as managed futures or trading advisors, are individuals or organizations that trade derivative instruments such as futures, forward contracts, and options on behalf of their clients. Investors have been using the services of CTAs for more than 30 years. They started their activities in the late 1970s with the regulatory separation between the brokerage and investment management functions of the futures business. Their group expanded significantly in the early 1980s with the proliferation of nontraditional commodity futures contracts. As their name implies, initially they started trading in commodity markets, but have since evolved to trade in all the markets. Today, contrarily to hedge funds, most of them are regulated. They are federally licensed by the Commodity Futures Trading Commission (CFTC) and periodically audited by the National Futures Association (NFA) in the United States. They are supervised by the Provincial Securities Commission in Canada and by the Autorité des Marchés Financiers in France.

CTAs may use a broad spectrum of different trading strategies. However, their primary investment style is systematic trend following. That is, they use computer programs to perform some sort of technical analysis (moving averages, breakouts of price ranges, etc.), identify trends in a set of markets, and generate buy and sell signals accordingly. These signals then are executed on an automated basis to create a portfolio that strives to be positioned in the direction of any trend that is in place.

Most CTAs follow a disciplined and systematic approach by prioritizing capital preservation, controlling potential losses, and protecting potential gains. The risk they initially take for each trade is usually small, but the size of positions may increase progressively if the detected trends are stable and verified. However, in adverse or volatile markets, automated stops are executed to limit losses.

The basic trend-following programs are relatively simple. One example is an envelope breakout system. If a market is trading sideways in a fairly narrow range, the program might suggest no position. A breakout on the upside or the downside could trigger an entry. Another example is based on the crossing of different moving averages. For instance, if a rising short-term moving average crosses a long-term moving average, this constitutes a buy signal. Inversely, if a declining short-term moving average crosses a long-term moving average, this constitutes a sell signal. Of course, the large trend-following advisors, such as Dunn Capital Management, John W. Henry & Co., and Campbell, simultaneously use multiple models that employ different strategies for entering and exiting trends in markets, often using short, intermediate, and long time frames.

Trend following typically generates strong returns in times when the markets are trending (upward or downward), and will lose money at the end of a trend or during sideways markets. This is precisely where risk management should step in to try to limit the losses. Good trend followers have to inure many small losses. They also may have more losing trades than winning ones, but the average size of the winners is typically two or more times the average of losing trades. To reduce their overall risk, most CTAs also diversify themselves by using their programs to make investment decisions simultaneously across several markets, such as stocks, bonds, foreign exchange, interest rate, commodities, energy, agricultural and tropical products, and precious metals. If they lose money in one market, they hope to make money in another. Over some longer periods of time, say one year or more, a good trend follower should net 10 percent to 20 percent on a broadly diversified program.

TIME DIVERSIFICATION

The conventional wisdom in the professional investment community is that classic one-period diversification (space diversification) across risky securities such as equities handles the static risk of investing and that time diversification handles the intertemporal dynamic aspects of that risk.

The advocates of time diversification point out that fluctuations in security returns tend to cancel out through time, thus more risk is diversified away over longer holding periods. As a consequence, apparently risky securities such as stocks are potentially less risky than previously thought if held for long time periods yet their average returns are superior to low-risk securities such as treasury bills. Empirically, it can be observed that

- The distribution of annualized returns converges as the horizon increases. If returns are independent from one year to the next, the standard deviation of annualized returns diminishes with time while the expectation of annualized returns remains constant.
- The probability of incurring a loss (shortfall probability) declines as the length of the holding period increases. If we determine the likelihood of a negative return by measuring the difference in standard deviation

units between a 0 percent return and the expected return, we see that as the length of the holding period lengthens, the probability of facing a negative return decreases very rapidly.

Those who challenge the time diversification argument, most notably Bodie (1995), Merton (1969), and Samuelson (1969, 1971, 1972, 1979, 1994), contend that the choice of risk measurement used by time diversification advocates is erroneous. They believe that what is important to an investor is not the probability of a loss or the annualized variance of a portfolio but rather how large the potential shortfall might be and how an investor might avoid it. They argue that in using the probability of shortfall, no distinction is made between a loss of 20 percent and a loss of 99 percent in an investment. While it may be less likely, a loss of 99 percent is obviously more painful to the investor, should it actually occur. Although it is true that annualized dispersion of returns converges toward the expected return with the passage of time, the dispersion of terminal wealth diverges from the expected terminal wealth as the investment horizon expands. So losses can be very large in spite of their low probability of occurrence. As investors should be concerned with terminal wealth, not change in wealth over time, and although one is less likely to lose money after a long duration, the magnitude of the loss, if it does occur, increases with duration. So, from a utility of terminal wealth point of view, the reduction in the possibility of loss is just offset by the larger possible size of loss.

Bodie (1995) makes this point quite dramatically by illustrating that the premium for insuring against a shortfall in performance of stocks versus bonds is actually an increasing function of the time horizon over which the insurance is in force instead of a decreasing one, which would be expected with declining risk.[1] Insurance premiums are a particularly appealing measure because they represent the economic cost of neutralizing undesirable returns. However, Bodie's argument is circular, as the same observation applies to the premiums for insuring against a shortfall in performance of bonds versus stocks.

Kritzman (1994) provides a comprehensive review of the time diversification debate and illustrates the delicate balance that exists between one's assumptions and the conclusions that necessarily derive from those assumptions. However, more recently, Merrill and Thorley (1996) reignited the debate by noting that "the differences between practitioners and theo-

[1]Samuelson (1971, 1972, 1979) addressed a similar fallacy involving the virtues of investing to maximize the geometric mean return as the "dominating" strategy for investors with long horizons.

rists . . . are often rooted in semantic issues about risk" (p. 15). In addition, the two camps do not really focus on the same problem. Time diversification advocates are concerned with the impact of increasing the time horizon for a buy and hold strategy, while their opponents are looking at a dynamic investment problem in which a given time horizon is chopped up into several periods. Hence, their divergent opinions are not really surprising.

In our view, CTAs provide a more interesting testing field for the theory of time diversification than equities. The reason is that the majority of them are trend followers and that in the long run, trends are likely to emerge (upward or downward). CTAs should then be able to capture these trends and extract profits from them as long as they last. However, in the presence of trend reversals or trendless markets, their performance is likely to decrease. Remember that trend followers do not know that a trend is over until the market has reversed somewhat, so they actually give back a portion of their accumulated profits, which leads to sizable drawdowns. Their performance, of course, is cyclical or mean reverting because it depends on suitable market environments for the trading strategy. This is particularity interesting when one remembers that Samuelson (1991), Kritzman (1994), and Reichenstein and Dorsett (1995) have shown that the time diversification principle can be justified only if there is mean reversion in the returns.

EMPIRICAL TEST

For the purposes of this exercise, we use the Credit Suisse First Boston Tremont Managed Futures Index to represent the universe of CTAs. This index is asset-weighted and includes 29 of the world's largest audited managed futures funds (see Table 23.1).

The index is only intended as a rough approximation of how a fund of CTAs would behave in reality. Funds of CTAs typically include a substantially smaller number of managers than those represented in the index, and would seek to implement some kind of selection strategy from among the different managers/programs. In addition, the smallest CTAs tend to have an average return significantly larger than the average return of the largest CTAs. Thus, by focusing on larger funds, we may unwittingly cause a downward bias in returns by eliminating some of the small high-return funds.

Table 23.2 summarizes the performance of the CSFB Tremont Managed Futures Index for the period January 1994 to December 2003. CTAs appear to be positioned close to bonds in terms of returns (7.07 percent versus 6.79 percent per annum), but with a much higher volatility (12.84 percent versus 6.76 percent per annum). Their performance is far below that of stocks (11.07 percent per annum), but stocks also have a much higher

TABLE 23.1 Commodity Trading Advisors Included in the CSFB-Tremont Managed Futures Index

Aspect Diversified Fund (USD) Ltd.
AXA Futures
Campbell Global Assets Fund
Chesapeake Select LLC
D.QUANT Fund/Ramsey Futures Trading
Dexia Systemat (Euro)
Eckhardt Futures LP
Epsilon Futures (Euro)
Epsilon USD
FTC Futures Fund SICAV
Graham Global Investment Fund (Div 2XL Portfolio)
Graham Global Investment Fund (Div Portfolio)
Graham Global Investment Fund (Fed Policy)
Graham Global Investment Fund (Prop Matrix Portfolio)
Hasenbichler Commodities AG
JWH Global Strategies
Legacy Futures Fund LP
Liberty Global Fund LP
Millburn International (Cayman) Ltd.—Diversified
MLM Index Fund Leveraged (Class B)
Nestor Partners
Quadriga
Rivoli International Fund (Euro)
Rotella Polaris Fund
Roy G. Niederhoffer Fund (Ireland) Plc
SMN Diversified Futures Fund (Euro)
Sunrise Fund
Systeia Futures Fund (Euro)
Systeia Futures Ltd. (USD)

volatility (17.29 percent per annum). On average, the index experienced 56 percent of positive months, with a better absolute performance in positive months (+2.95 percent) than in negative months (–2.30 percent). Stocks have a higher ratio of positive months (63 percent), but they lose the advantage by having on average a much worse performance during negative months (–3.91 percent).

Although they do not seem to be very good stand-alone investments, CTAs are likely to be good portfolio assets. This is evidenced by their low correlation with stocks (–0.23) and bonds (0.35). As evidenced in Figure 23.1, when the stock market has declined through all of the negative months, the CSFB Tremont Managed Futures Index has generated an attractive performance.

Interestingly enough, there is, in a sense, positive correlation when the stock market is up and, in effect, negative correlation when the stock market is down. This is particularly visible on the drawdown diagram, which considers losing periods only (see Figure 23.2).

The worst periods for futures markets coincide with winning periods for equity markets, and vice versa. Once again, this illustrates the dangers of using a linear correlation coefficient to measure nonlinear relationships. Contrarily to the majority of hedge fund strategies, the histogram of

TABLE 23.2 Statistics of the CSFB-Tremont Managed Futures Index

	CSFB/Tremont Managed Futures Index	S&P 500	SSB World Gvt. Bond Index
Return (% p.a.)	7.07	11.07	6.79
Volatility (% p.a.)	12.84	17.29	6.76
Skewness	0.03	–0.60	0.47
Kurtosis	0.58	0.29	0.37
Normality (Bera Jarque test, 95%)	Yes	Yes	Yes
Correlation		–0.23	0.35
% of positive months	56	63	58
Best month performance (%)	9.95	9.78	5.94
Avg. of positive months returns (%)	2.95	3.81	1.79
Upside capture (%)		26	–64
% of negative months	44	37	43
Worst month performance (%)	–9.35	–14.46	–3.44
Avg. of negative months returns (%)	–2.30	–3.91	–1.09
Downside capture (%)		–22	315
Max. drawdown (%)	–17.74	–44.73	–7.94
VaR (1M, 99%)	–8.37	–10.54	–3.26

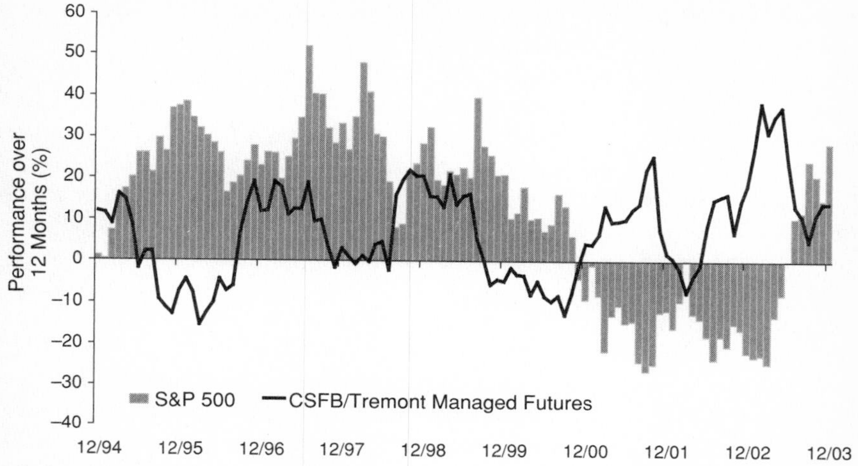

FIGURE 23.1 Rolling 12-Month Performance of the CSFB-Tremont Managed Futures Index Compared to the S&P 500

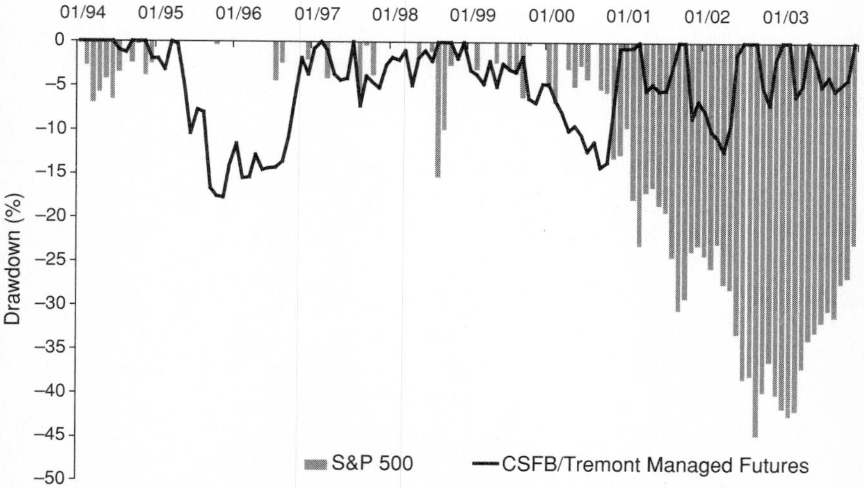

FIGURE 23.2 Maximum Drawdown of the CSFB-Tremont Managed Futures Index Compared to the S&P 500

monthly returns displays no fat tails compared to a normal distribution, and no clear asymmetry (see Figure 23.3).

As mentioned, a large number of CTAs capitalize on market trends, that typically are associated with an increase in volatility. Hence, an environment that may be difficult for traditional strategies, particularly in the presence of down trends, actually presents an ideal trading environment for CTAs. In a sense, they follow long-volatility strategies, whereas most traditional strategies and hedge fund strategies are termed "short volatility" and view an increase of volatility as a risk factor. This qualifies them as interesting portfolio diversifiers to yield better risk-adjusted returns, over the long run . . . or maybe the short run.

To test the impact of the holding period on the performance of CTAs, we first use overlapping blocks of *N* consecutive months, where *N* varies from 1 to 120. Because we have 120 returns in our historical data set, we obtain 120 possible blocks of one month and only one block of 120 months. For each block, we calculate the return obtained at the end of the considered period. Figure 23.4 shows the evolution of this terminal annualized return of the CSFB Tremont Managed Futures Index as a function of the block size.

Figure 23.5 shows the evolution of the annualized volatility of this return as a function of the block size. Both figures tend to confirm that the

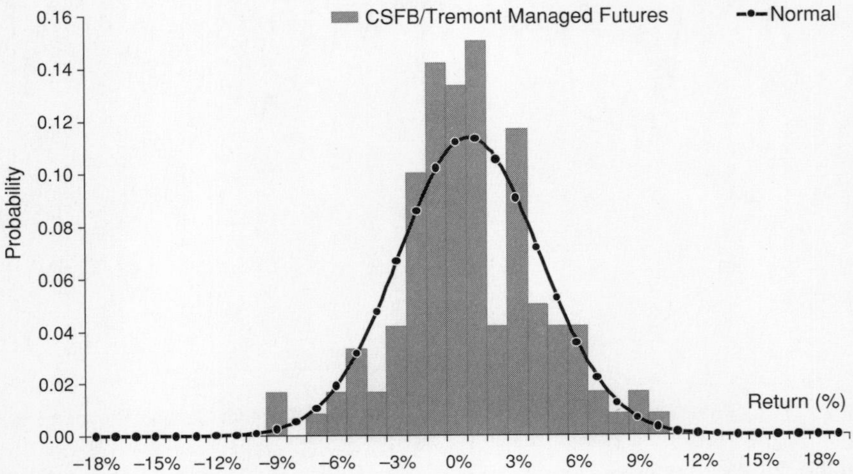

FIGURE 23.3 Distribution of the CSFB-Tremont Managed Futures Index Monthly Returns

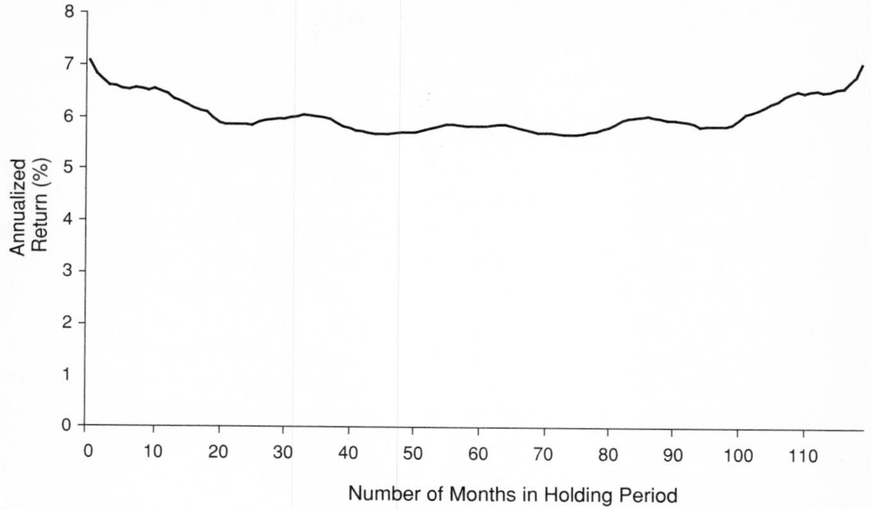

FIGURE 23.4 Annualized Holding Period Return Expressed as Function of the Number of Months in the Holding Period

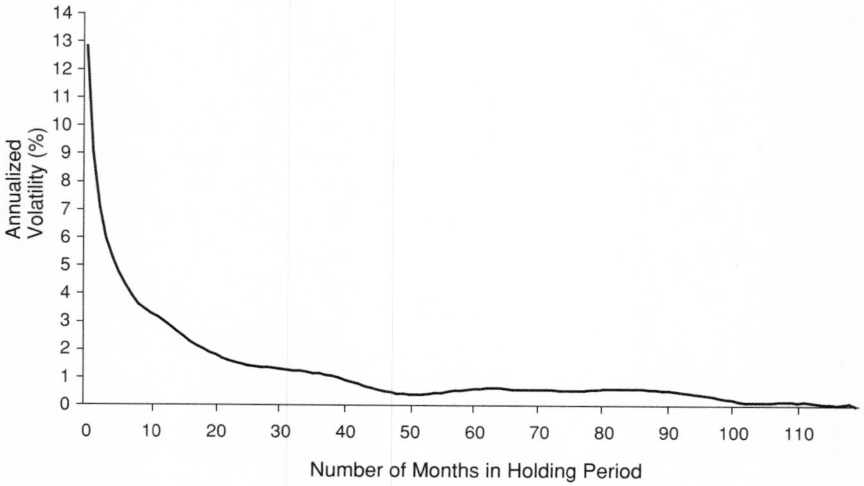

FIGURE 23.5 Annualized Volatility of the Holding Period Return Expressed as a Function of the Number of Months in the Holding Period

longer the investor's holding period, the smaller the standard deviation of the annualized rate of return on the managed futures portfolio, while the return itself remains relatively stable. These results are so convincing that one is left with the impression that over a very long time horizon, investing with CTAs is a sure thing.[2]

However, there does not necessarily exist genuine diversification in this situation. Although the basic argument that the standard deviations of annualized returns decrease as the time horizon increases is true, it is also misleading. In fact, it may fatally miss the point, because for an investor concerned with the value of the portfolio at the end of a period of time, it is the total return that matters, not the annualized return. And because of the effects of compounding, the standard deviation of the total return actually increases with time horizon. Thus, if we use the standard deviation of returns as the traditional measure of uncertainty over the time period in question, uncertainty increases with time. However, in the case of managed futures, some additional elements should be considered.

We all agree that investors should care about the amount of wealth at the end of the period, and more particularly about the severity of a potential shortfall. We therefore need to consider both the severity of a shortfall and its likelihood to conclude anything. Figure 23.6 shows the evolution of the worst historical holding period return of the CSFB Tremont Managed Futures Index as a function of the length of the holding period. This provides a new and interesting perspective. We clearly see that the worst-case holding period return is initially negative (–9.35 percent) and tends to worsen as the holding period lengthens. However, it stabilizes after a few months of holding and starts decreasing in intensity. After 45 months of holding, the shortfall probability is nil, and the worst-case holding period return is positive. This tends to confirm the fact that even in the worst case, managed futures are less risky in the long run than in the short run.

Of course, one may argue that the preserving the initial capital is not a very aggressive target, particularly over the long run. What happens if we have a target rate of return of, say, 3 percent or 5 percent a year? Figure 23.7 provides the answer. The shortfall is the amount by which target goals fail to be achieved. Clearly, the cyclical nature of managed futures penalizes them in the long run when compared to safe investments. Note that we are

[2]One could object that our observation periods are strongly overlapping, so that the resulting rollover returns have a high degree of correlation, which results in a serious estimation bias. To assess statistical significance would require independent returns based on nonoverlapping periods. The existing horizon of experience, however, is too short to obtain enough data of these kinds.

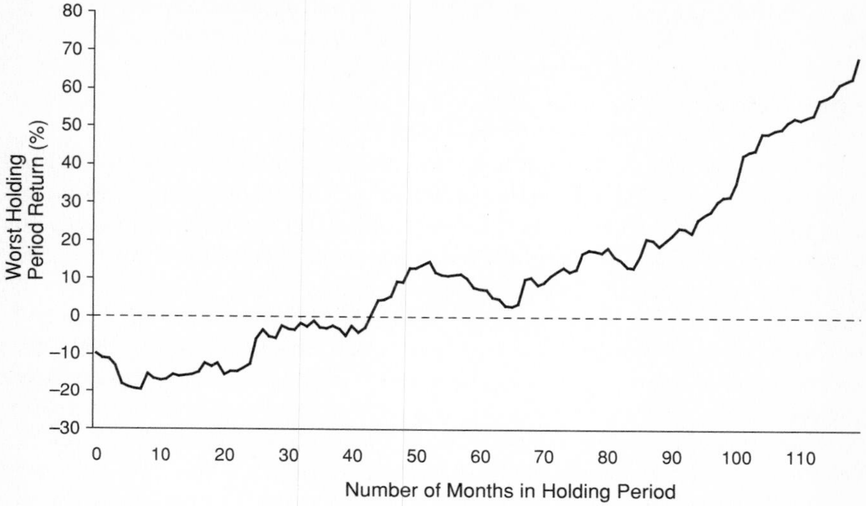

FIGURE 23.6 Worst-Case Holding Period Return Expressed as a Function of the Number of Months in the Holding Period

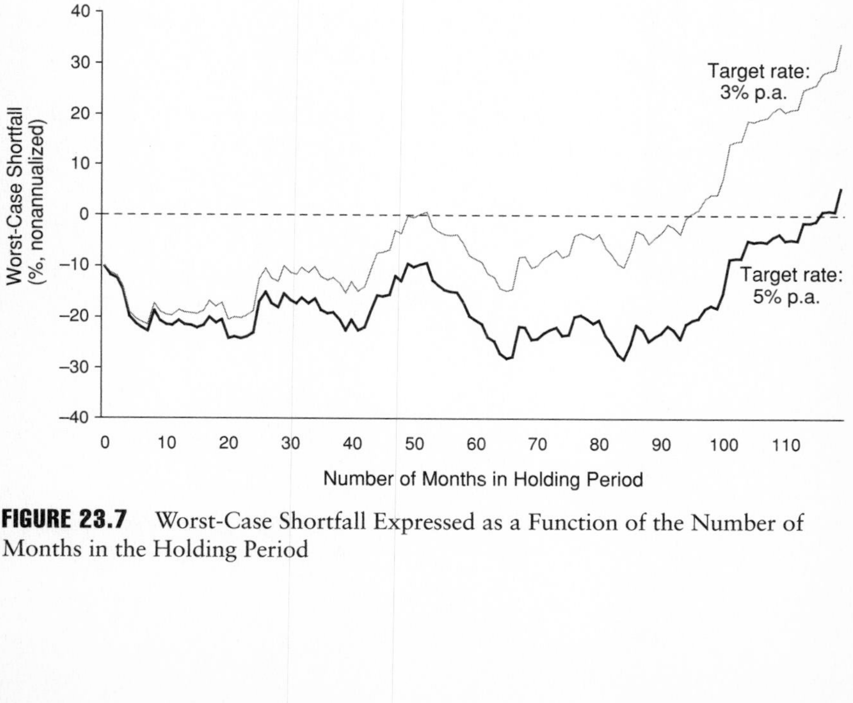

FIGURE 23.7 Worst-Case Shortfall Expressed as a Function of the Number of Months in the Holding Period

only looking at the worst case here, but this is what matters from a risk management perspective.

CONCLUSION

The impact of the time horizon on the risk of stock investments is still a subject of intense and controversial debate within the academic and investment communities. Although it is true under the assumption of normally distributed returns that the volatility increases with the square root of time, the standard deviation of mean returns decreases with longer time intervals. Whether this can be interpreted as stocks being less risky over the long term is still an issue. In this chapter, we use an approach based on historical data and analyze the worst case ex-post performance of managed futures over different time periods. Our results tend to suggest that a diversified portfolio of managed futures is a relatively safe investment over the long run, but remains risky from a shortfall perspective as soon as the minimum required return increases above zero.

References

Ackermann, C., R. McEnally, and D. Ravenscraft. (1999) "The Performance of Hedge Funds: Risk, Return and Incentives." *Journal of Finance*, Vol. 54, No. 3, pp. 833–874.

Adler, N., L. Friedman, and Z. S. Stern. (2002) "Review of Ranking Methods in the Data Envelopment Analysis Context." *European Journal of Operational Research*, Vol. 140, No. 2, pp. 249–265.

Agarwal, V., and N. Y. Naik. (March 2002). "Characterizing Systematic Risk of Hedge Funds with Buy-and-Hold and Option-Based Strategies." Working Paper, London Business School, U.K.

Agarwal, V., and N. Y. Naik. (2004) "Risks and Portoflio Decisions Involving Hedge Funds." *Review of Financial Studies*, Vol. 17, No. 1, pp. 63–98.

Ali, A. I., and L. M. Seiford. (1990) "Tnslation Invariance in Data Envelopment Analysis," *Operations Research Letters*, Vol. 9, No. 6, pp. 403–405.

Ali, P. U. (2000) "Unbundling Credit Risk: The Nature and Regulation of Credit Derivatives." *Journal of Banking and Finance Law and Practice*, Vol. 11, No. 2, pp. 73–92.

Ali, P. U. (2002) "Individual Share Futures in Australia." *Company and Securities Law Journal*, Vol. 20, No. 4, pp. 232–235.

Ali, P. U., G. Stapledon, and M. Gold. (2003) *Corporate Governance and Investment Fiduciaries*. Rozelle, New South Wales: Lawbook Company.

Amenc, N., and L. Martellini. (2003) "The Brave New World of Hedge Fund Indices." Working Paper (February), Edhec Risk and Asset Management Research Centre, Lille, France.

Amenc, N., L. Martellini, and M. Vaissié. (2003) "Benefits and Risks of Alternative Investment Strategies." *Journal of Asset Management*, Vol. 4, No. 2, pp. 96–118.

Amin, G. S., and H. M. Kat. (2001) "Hedge Fund Performance 1990–2000: Do the 'Money Machines' Really Add Value?" Working Paper (December), ISMA Centre, University of Reading, U.K.

Amin, G. S., and H. M. Kat. (2002) "Diversification and Yield Enhancement with Hedge Funds." *Journal of Alternative Investments,* Vol. 5, No. 3, pp. 50–58.

Amin, G. S., and H. M. Kat. (2003a) "Hedge Fund Performance 1990–2000: Do the Money Machines Really Add Value?" *Journal of Financial and Quantitative Analysis*, Vol. 38, No. 2, pp. 251–274.

Amin, G. S., and H. M. Kat. (2003b) "Stocks, Bonds and Hedge Funds: Not a Free Lunch!" *Journal of Portfolio Management*, Vol. 29, No. 4, pp. 113–120.

Ang, J. S., and J. C. Chau. (1979) "Composite Measures for the Evaluation of Investment Performance." *Journal of Financial and Quantitative Analysis*, Vol. 54, No. 2, pp. 361–384.

Anjilvel, S., B. Boudreau, M. Urias, and M. Peskin. (2000) "Why Hedge Funds Make Sense." Quantitative Strategies, Internal Publication, Morgan Stanley Dean Witter, New York.

Anson, M. (2000) "Selecting a Hedge Fund Manager." *Journal of Wealth Management*, Vol. 3, No. 3, pp. 45–52.

Anson, M. (2001) "Performance Presentation Standards: Which Rules Apply When?" *Financial Analysts Journal*, Vol. 57, No. 2, pp. 53–60.

Anson, M. (2002a) *The Handbook of Alternative Assets*. New York: John Wiley & Sons.

Anson, M. (2002b) "Asymmetric Trading Strategies and Symmetrical Performance Measures: A Cautionary Example." *Journal of Alternative Investments*, Vol. 5, No. 1, pp. 81–85.

Anson, M., and H. Ho. (2003) "Short Volatility Strategies: Identification, Measurement, and Risk Management." *Journal of Investment Management*, Vol. 1, No. 2, pp. 30–43.

Arnott, R. (2003) "What Risk Matters? A Call for Papers," *Financial Analysts Journal*, Vol. 59, No. 3, pp. 6–8.

Asness C., R. Krail, and J. Liew. (2001) "Do Hedge Funds Hedge?" *Journal of Portfolio Management*, Vol. 28, No. 1, pp. 6–19.

Australian Prudential Regulation Authority. (2003, March 5) "APRA Alerts Super Industry to the Drawbacks of Hedge Funds," Media Release No. 03-25.

Australian Securities and Investments Commission (2003a, April 16) "Managed Discretionary Account Services PPP." IR 03-11.

Australian Securities and Investments Commission (2003b) "Managed Discretionary Account Services." *ASIC Policy Proposal* April, pp. 13–14.

Australian Securities and Investments Commission. (1998a) "Managed Investments: Compliance Plans." Policy Statement 132.

Australian Securities and Investments Commission. (1998b) "Investor Directed Portfolio Services," Policy Statement 134.

Australian Securities and Investments Commission. (2001) "Disclosure: Product Disclosure Statement (and Other Disclosure Obligations)." Policy Statement 168.

Australian Securities and Investments Commission (ASIC). (2003) "Managed Discretionary Account Services." *ASIC Policy Proposal.*

Banker, R. D., A. Charnes, and W. W. Cooper. (1984) "Some Models for Estimating Technical and Scale Inefficiencies in Data Envelopment Analysis." *Management Science*, Vol. 30, No. 9, pp. 1078–1092.

Barclay Managed Funds Report. (2001) "Top 20 CTA Performers Past Five Years." First Quarter Vol. 6, New York, NY.

Barr, R., L. Seiford, and T. Siems. (1994) "Forecasting Bank Fail-ure: A Non-Parametric Frontier Estimation Approach." *Researches Economiques de Louvain, Belgium*, Vol. 60, No. 4, pp. 417–429.

Basso, A., and S. Funari. (2001) "A Data Envelopment Analysis Approach to Measure the Mutual Fund Performance," *European Journal of Operational Research*, Vol. 135, No. 3, pp. 477–492.

Baxt, R., A. Black, and P. Hanrahan. (2003) *Securities and Financial Services Law*. Sydney: LexisNexis Butterworths.

Bello, Z. Y., and V. Janjigian. (1997) "A Reexamination of the Market-Timing and Security-Selection Performance of Mutual Funds." *Financial Analysts Journal*, Vol. 53, No. 5, pp. 24–30

Bessembinder, H., and P. Seguin. (1993) "Price Volatility, Trading Volume, and Market Depth: Evidence from Future Markets." *Journal of Financial and Quantitative Analysis*, Vol. 28, No. 1, pp. 21–39.

Billingsley, R., and D. M. Chance. (1996) "Benefit and Limitations of Diversification among Commodity Trading Advisors." *Journal of Portfolio Management*, Vol. 23, No. 1, pp. 65–80.

Bodie, Z. (1995) "On the Risk of Stocks in the Long Run." *Financial Analysts Journal*, Vol. 51, No. 3, pp. 18–22.

Bowlin, W. F. (1998) "Measuring Performance: An Introduction to Data Envelopment Analysis (DEA)." *Journal of Cost Analysis*, Vol. 3, pp. 3–28.

Brinson, G., B. D. Singer, and G. L. Beebower. (1991) "Determinants of Portfolio Performance II: An Update." *Financial Analysts Journal*, Vol. 47, No. 3, pp. 40–48.

Brooks, C., and H. M. Kat. (2001) "The Statistical Properties of Hedge Fund Index Returns and Their Implications for Investors." Working Paper (November). ISMA Center, University of Reading, Reading, U.K.

Brooks, C., and H. M. Kat. (2002) "The Statistical Properties of Hedge Fund Returns and Their Implications for Investors." *Journal of Alternative Investments*, Vol. 5, No. 2, pp. 26–44.

Brorsen, B. W. (1998) "Performance Persistence for Managed Futures." Working Paper (March), Oklahoma State University, OK.

Brorsen, B. W. and S. H. Irwin. (1985) "Examination of Commodity Fund Performance." *Review of Futures Markets*, Vol. 4, No. 1, pp. 84–94.

Brorsen, B. W., and S. H. Irwin. (1987) "Futures Funds and Price Volatility." *Review of Futures Markets*, Vol. 6, No. 2, pp. 118–135.

Brorsen, B. W., and J. P. Townsend. (2002) "Performance Persistence for Managed Futures." *Journal of Alternative Investments*, Vol. 4, No. 4, pp. 57–61.

Brown, S. J., and W. N. Goetzmann. (1995) "Performance Persistence." *Journal of Finance*, Vol. 50, No. 2, pp. 679–698.

Brown, S. J., W. N. Goetzmann, and J. Park. (1998) "Hedge Funds and the Asian Currency Crisis of 1997." Working Paper 6427, National Bureau of Economic Research, Washington, D. C.

Brown S. J., W. N. Goetzmann, and J. Park. (2001) "Careers and Survival: Competition and Risk in the Hedge Fund and CTA Industry." *Journal of Finance*, Vol. 56, No. 5, pp. 1869–1886.

Burghart, G., R. Duncan, and L. Liu. (2003 September) "Understanding Drawdowns." Internal Publication, *Carr Futures*, Chicago, IL.

Busse, J., and N. Bollen. (2001) "On the Timing Ability of Mutual Fund Managers." *Journal of Finance*, Vol. 56, No. 3, pp. 1075–1094.

Campbell, J. Y., A. W. Lo, and A. C. MacKinlay. (1997) *The Econometrics of Financial Markets*. Princeton, NJ: Princeton University Press.

Capocci, D., A. Corhay, and G. Hübner. (2003) "Hedge Fund Performance and Persistence in Bull and Bear Markets." Working Paper, Ecole d'Administration des Affaires, University of Liège.

Capocci, D., and G. Hübner. (2004) "An Analysis of Hedge Fund Performance." *Journal of Empirical Finance*, Vol. 11, No. 1, pp. 55–89.

Carhart, M. M. (1997) "On Persistence in Mutual Fund Performance." *Journal of Finance*, Vol. 52, No. 1 pp. 57–82.

Carroll, C., and K. C. J. Wei. (1988) "Risk, Return, and Equilibrium: An Extension." *Journal of Business*, Vol. 61, No. 4, pp. 485–499.

Center for International Securities and Derivatives Markets (CISDM). (2002) 2nd Annual Chicago Research Conference, May 22.

Cerrahoglu, B., and D. Pancholi. (2003) "The Benefits of Managed Futures." CISDM Working Paper, Isenberg School of Management, University of Massachusetts, Amherst, MA.

Chance, D. M. (1994) *Managed Futures and Their Role in Investment Portfolios*. Charlottesville, VA: the Research Foundation of the Institute of Chartered Financial Analysts.

Chang, E. C., M. J. Pinegar, and B. Schachter. (1997) "Interday Variations in Volume, Variance, and Participation of Large Speculators." *Journal of Banking and Finance*, Vol. 21, No. 6, pp. 797–910.

Charnes, A., W. W. Cooper, and E. Rhodes. (1978) "Measuring the Efficiency of Decision Making Units." *European Journal of Operational Research*, Vol. 2, No. 6, pp. 29–44.

Charnes, A., W. W. Cooper, and E. Rhodes. (1981) "Evaluating Program and Managerial Efficiency: An Application of Data Envelopment Analysis to Program Follow Through." *Management Science*, Vol. 27, No. 6, pp. 668–697.

Chen, N., R. Roll, and S. Ross. (1986) "Economic Forces and the Stock Market." *Journal of Business*, Vol. 59, No. 3, pp. 386–403.

Chicago Board of Trade. (2002) Managed Futures: Portfolio Diversification Opportunities, 2002 Edition. Chicago, IL: CBOT.

Chicago Mercantile Exchange. (1999) "Question and Answer Report: Managed Futures Accounts." Report No. M584/10M/1299. www.cve.com.

Christoffersen, P. (2003) *Elements of Financial Risk Management*. San Diego, CA: Academic Press.

Chung, S. Y. (1999) "Portfolio Risk Measurement: A Review of Value at Risk." *Journal of Alternative Investments*, Vol. 2, No. 1, pp. 34–42.

Clark, P. K. (1973) "A Subordinated Stochastic Process Model with Finite Variance for Speculative Prices." *Econometrica*, Vol. 41, No. 1, pp. 135–155.

Clayton, U. (2003) *A Guide to the Law of Securitisation in Australia*. Sydney, Australia: Clayton Company.

Cooley, P. L., R. L. Roenfeldt, and N. K. Modani. (1977) "Interdependence of Market Risk Measures." *Journal of Business*, Vol. 50, No. 3, pp. 356–363.

Cootner, P. (1967) "Speculation and Hedging." *Food Research Institute Studies*, Supplement 7, pp. 64–105.

Cornish, E., and R. Fisher. (1937) "Moments and Cumulants in the Specification of Distributions." *Review of the International Statistical Institute*, Vol. 5, pp. 307–320.

Corporations Act (2001) (Commonwealth). Federal Parliament of the Commonwealth of Australia.

Corporations Regulations (2001) (Commonwealth). Governor-General of the Commonwealth of Australia.

Daglioglu, A., and B. Gupta. (2003a, March) "The Benefits of Hedge Funds." CISDM Working Paper, Isenberg School of Management, University of Massachusetts, Amherst, MA.

Daglioglu, A., and B. Gupta. (2003b) "The Interdependence of Hedge Fund Risk Measures." Center for International Securities and Derivatives Markets Annual Conference.

Dale, C., and J. Zryen. (1996, May) "Non-Commercial Trading in the Energy Futures Market." *Petroleum Marketing Monthly*, pp. 13–24.

De Long, J. B., A. Schleifer, L. H. Summers, and R. J. Waldman. (1990) "Noise Trader Risk in Financial Markets." *Journal of Political Economy*, Vol. 98, No. 4, pp. 703–738.

Dickey, D., and W. Fuller. (1981) "The Likelihood Ratio Statistics for Autoregressive Time Series with a Unit Root." *Econometrica*, Vol. 49, No. 4, pp.1057–1072.

Diz, F. (1996) "How Do CTAs Return Distribution Characteristics Affect Their Likelihood of Survival?" Working Paper, Syracuse University, NY.

Diz, F. (1999) "CTA Survivor and Nonsurvivor: An Analysis of Relative Performance." *Journal of Alternative Investments*, Vol. 2, No. 1, pp. 57–71.

Diz, F. (2003) "Commodity Trading Advisors' Leverage and Reported Margin to Equity Ratios." *Journal of Futures Markets*, Vol. 23, No. 10, pp. 1003–1017.

Diz, F., and R. Shukla. (2003) "Incentive Compensation in the Mutual Fund, Hedge Fund and Managed Futures Industries." Working Paper, Whitman School of Management, Syracuse University, Syracuse, NY.

Doig, A. (2003) "Take Futures Out of Your Hands." *Charting*, No. 2, 78–82.

Doyle, J., and R. Green. (1994) "Efficiency and Cross Efficiency in DEA: Derivations, Meanings and the Uses." *Journal of the Operational Research Society*, Vol. 45, No. 5, pp. 567–578.

Dybvig, P. H. (1988a) "Inefficient Dynamic Portfolio Strategies or How to Throw Away a Million Dollars in the Stock Market." *Review of Financial Studies*, Vol. 1, No. 1, pp. 67–88.

Dybvig, P. H. (1988b) "Distributional Analysis of Portfolio Choice." *Journal of Business*, Vol. 6, No. 3, pp. 369–393.

Ederington, L. H. (1995) "Mean-Variance as an Approximation to Expected Utility Maximization: Semi Ex-Ante Results." In Mark Hirschey and M. Wayne Marr, eds., *Advances in Financial Economics*, Vol. 1, pp. 81–98 Greenwich, CT: JAI Press Inc.

Ederington, L. H., and J. H. Lee (2002) "Who Trades Futures and How? Evidence from the Heating Oil Futures Market." *Journal of Business*, Vol. 75, No. 2, pp. 353–373.

Edwards, F. R. (1999) "Hedge Funds and the Collapse of Long-Term Capital Management." *Journal of Economic Perspectives*, Vol. 13, No. 2, pp. 189–210.

Edwards, F. R., and M. O. Caglayan. (2001) "Hedge Fund and Commodity Fund Investment Styles in Bull and Bear Markets." *Journal of Portfolio Management*, Vol. 27, No. 4, pp. 97–108.

Edwards, F. R., and J. Liew. (1999) "Hedge Funds versus Managed Futures as Asset Classes." *Journal of Derivatives*, Vol. 6, No. 4, pp. 45–64.

Edwards, F. R., and A. C. Ma. (1988) "Commodity Fund Performance: Is the Information Contained in Fund Prospectuses Useful?" *Journal of Futures Markets*, Vol. 8, No. 5, pp. 589–616.

Edwards, F. R., and J. M. Park. (1996) "Do Managed Futures Make Good Investments?" *Journal of Futures Markets*, Vol. 16, No. 5, pp. 475–517.

Eichengreen, B., and D. Mathieson. (1998) "Hedge Funds and Financial Markets: Implications for Policy." In B. Eichengreen and D. Mathieson, eds., *Hedge Funds and Financial Market Dynamics*, pp. 2–26. Washington, DC: International Monetary Fund.

Elton, E. J., M. J. Gruber, and J. C. Rentzler. (1987) "Professionally Managed, Publicly Traded Commodity Funds." *Journal of Business*, Vol. 60, No. 2, pp. 177–199.

Elton, E. J., M. J. Gruber, and J. C. Rentzler. (1989) "New Public Offerings, Informations and Investor Rationality: The Case of Publicly Offered Commodity Funds." *Journal of Business*, Vol. 62, No. 1, pp. 1–15.

Elton, E. J., M. J. Gruber, and J. C. Rentzler. (1990) "The Performance of Publicly Offered Commodity Funds." *Financial Analysts Journal*, Vol. 46, No. 4, pp. 23–30.

Erb, C., C. Harvey, and T. Viskanta. (1994) "Forecasting International Equity Correlations." *Financial Analysts Journal*, Vol. 50, No. 6, pp. 32–45.

Faff, R. W., and T. A. Hallahan. (2001) "Induced Persistence or Reversals in Fund Performance? The Effect of Survivorship Bias." *Applied Financial Economics*, Vol. 11, No. 2, pp. 119–126.

Fama, E. F., and K. R. French. (1993) "Common Risk Factors in the Returns on Stocks and Bonds." *Journal of Financial Economics*, Vol. 33, No. 1, pp. 3–56.

Fama, E. F., and J. MacBeth. (1973) "Risk, Return, and Equilibrium: Empirical Tests." *Journal of Political Economy*, Vol. 81, No. 3, pp. 607–636.

Fang, H., and T.-Y. Lai. (1997) "Co-Kurtosis and Asset Pricing, *Financial Review*, Vol. 32, No. 2, pp. 293–307.

Farrell, M. J. (1957) "The Measurement of Productive Efficiency." *Journal of the Operational and Research Society*, Series A, Vol. 120, No. 3, pp. 253–281.

Favre, L., and J.-A. Galeano. (2002a) "An Analysis of Hedge Fund Performance Using Loess Fit Regression." *Journal of Alternative Investments*, Vol. 4, No. 4, pp. 8–24.

Favre, L., and J.-A. Galeano. (2002b) "Mean-Modified Value-at-Risk Optimization with Hedge Funds." *Journal of Alternative Investments*, Vol. 5, No. 2, pp. 21–25.

Favre, L., and A. Singer. (2002) "The Difficulties in Measuring the Benefits of Hedge Funds." *Journal of Alternative Investments*, Vol. 5, No. 1, pp. 31–42.

Ferson, W. E., and R. W. Schadt. (1996) "Measuring Fund Strategy and Performance in Changing Economic Conditions." *Journal of Finance*, Vol. 51, No. 2, pp. 425–461.

Financial Crimes Enforcement Network. (2002) "Anti-Money Laundering Programs for Unregistered Investment Companies." *Federal Register*, Vol. 67, No. 187 (September 26), pp. 60622–60623.

Financial Services Authority. (2003) "Hedge Funds and the FSA: Feedback Statement on DP16." (March), pp. 18–19.

Fishburn, P. (1977) "Mean-Risk Analysis with Risk Associated with Below Market Returns." *American Economic Review*, Vol. 67, No. 2, pp. 116–126.

French, K., and R. Roll. (1986) "Stock Return Variances." *Journal of Financial Economics*, Vol. 17, No. 1, pp. 5–26.

Friedman, M. (1953) *Essays in Positive Economics*, pp. 157–203. Chicago: University of Chicago Press.

Fung, W., and D. A. Hsieh. (1997a) "Empirical Characteristics of Dynamic Trading Strategies: The Case of Hedge Funds." *Review of Financial Studies*, Vol. 10, No. 2, pp. 275–302.

Fung, W., and D. A. Hsieh. (1997b) "Survivorship Bias and Investment Style in the Returns of CTAs: The Information Content of Performance Track Records." *Journal of Portfolio Management*, Vol. 24, No. 1, pp. 30–41.

Fung, W., and D. A. Hsieh (2000a) "Measuring the Market Impact of Hedge Funds." *Journal of Empirical Finance*, Vol. 7, No. 1, pp. 1–36.

Fung, W., and D. A. Hsieh. (2000b) "Performance Characteristics of Hedge Funds and Commodity Funds: Natural versus Spurious Biases." *Journal of Financial and Quantitative Analysis*, Vol. 35, No. 3, pp. 291–307.

Fung, W., and D. A. Hsieh. (2001a) "Asset-based Hedge Fund Styles and Portfolio Diversification." Working Paper, Duke University, NC.

Fung, W., and D. A. Hsieh. (2001b) "The Risk in Hedge Fund Strategies: Theory and Evidence from Trend Followers." *Review of Financial Studies*, Vol. 14, No. 2, pp. 313–341.

Fung, W., and D. A. Hsieh. (2002a) "Hedge-Fund Benchmarks: Information Content and Biases." *Financial Analysts Journal*, Vol. 58, No. 1, pp. 22–34.

Fung, W., and D. A. Hsieh (2002b) "The Risk in Fixed Income Hedge Fund Styles." *Journal of Fixed Income*, Vol. 12, No. 2, pp. 6–27.

Fung, W., and D. A. Hsieh. (2003) "Hedge Fund Benchmarks: A Risk Based Approach." Working Paper, Duke University, NC.

Georgiev, G. (2001) "Benefits of Commodity Investments." *Journal of Alternative Investments*, Vol. 4, No. 1, pp. 40–48.

Global Advisors. (2003) "The Case for Commodities," London, U.K.

Glosten, L. R., and R. Jagannathan. (1994) "A Contingent Claim Approach to Performance Evaluation." *Journal of Empirical Finance*, Vol. 1, No. 2, pp. 133–160.

Goetzmann, W. N., J. Ingersoll Jr., and S. A. Ross. (1997) "High Water Marks." Working Paper, Yale School of Management, New Haven, CT.

Golany, B., and Y. A. Roll. (1994) "Incorporating Standards via Data Envelopment Analysis." In A. Charnes, W. W. Cooper, A. Y. Levin, and L. Seiford, eds., *Data Envelopment Analysis: Theory, Methodology and Applications*. New York: Kluwer Academic Publications, pp. 313–328.

Goldman Sachs International and Russell Investment Group. (2003) Report on Alternative Investing by Tax-Exempt Organizations. A Survey of Organizations in North America, Europe, Australia, and Japan. New York, NY.

Golec, J. H. (1993) "The Effects of Incentive Compensation Contracts on the Risk and Return Performance of Commodity Trading Advisors." *Management Science*, Vol. 39, No. 11, pp. 1396–1406.

Gordon, D. (2003) "Risk by Any Other Name." *Journal of Alternative Investments*, Vol. 6, No. 2, pp. 83–86.

Greene, W. H. (2000) *Econometric Analysis*, Fourth Edition. Englewood-Cliffs, NJ: Prentice Hall.

Gregoriou, G. N. (2003a) "Performance Appraisal of Funds of Hedge Funds Using Data Envelopment Analysis." *Journal of Wealth Management*, Vol. 5, No. 4, pp. 88–95.

Gregoriou, G. N. (2003b) "Performance Evaluation of Funds of Hedge Funds Using Conditional Alphas and Betas." *Derivatives Use, Trading & Regulation*, Vol. 8, No. 4, pp. 324–344.

Gregoriou, G. N., and F. Rouah. (2002) "Large versus Small Hedge Funds: Does Size Affect Performance?" *Journal of Alternative Investments*, Vol. 5, No. 3, pp. 75–77.

Gregoriou, G. N., and F. Rouah. (2003a) "Random Walk Behavior of CTA Returns." *Journal of Alternative Investments*, Vol. 6, No. 2, pp. 51–56.

Gregoriou, G. N., and F. Rouah. (2003b) "ARMA Modelling of Hedge Fund Returns." Working Paper, University of Quebec, Montreal/McGill University.

Grinold, R. C., and R. N. Kahn. (1992) "Information Analysis." *Journal of Portfolio Management*, Vol. 15, No. 3, pp. 30–37.

Grinold, R. C., and R. N. Kahn. (1995) *Active Portfolio Management*. Chicago: Irwin.

Grossman, S. J. (1987) "A Note on the Elton, Gruber, and Rentzler's: Professionally Managed Publicly Traded Commodity Funds." Working Paper, Princeton University, Princeton, NJ.

Gujarati, D. N. (1995) *Basic Econometrics*. New York: McGraw-Hill.

Gupta, B., B. Cerrahoglu, and A. Daglioglu. (2003) "Evaluating Hedge Fund Performance: Traditional versus Conditional Approaches." *Journal of Alternative Investments*, Vol. 6, No. 3, pp. 7–24

Hamilton, J. D. (1994) *Time Series Analysis*. Princeton, NJ: Princeton University Press.

Hartzmark, M. L. (1987) "Returns to Individual Traders of Futures: Aggregate Results." *Journal of Political Economy*, Vol. 95, No. 6, pp. 1292–1306.

Haug, A. A. (1993a) "Residual Based Tests for Cointegration: A Monte Carlo Study of Size Distortions." *Economics Letters*, Vol. 41, No. 4, pp. 345–351.

Haug, A. A. (1993b) "Tests for Cointegration A Monte Carlo Comparison," *Journal of Econometrics*, Vol. 71, No. 1, pp. 89–115.

Henriksson, R. D., and R. C. Merton. (1981) "On Market Timing and Investment Performance II. Statistical Procedures for Evaluating Forecasting Skills." Journal of Business, Vol. 54, No. 4, pp. 513–533.

Holt, B. R. (1999) *Hedge Funds, Commodity Trading Advisors, and Commodity Pool Operators: The Effects of Their Futures Trading Volume on Market Volatility*. MS thesis, Department of Agricultural and Consumer Economics, University of Illinois, Urbana-Champaign, IL.

Horgan, S. (2003) *Horgan's Law of Financial Services*. Rozelle, New South Wales: Lawbook Company.

Hübner, G. (2003) "The Generalized Treynor Ratio." Working Paper, Ecole d'Administration des Affaires, University of Liège.

Hwang, S., and P. L. V. Pereira. (2003) "Small Sample Properties of GARCH Estimates and Persistence." Finance Lab Working Paper, Ibmec Business School, São Paulo, Brazil.

Irwin, S. H., and B. W. Brorsen. (1985) "Public Futures Funds." *Journal of Futures Markets*, Vol. 5, No. 3, pp. 463–485.

Irwin, S. H., and S. Yoshimaru. (1999) "Managed Futures, Positive Feedback Trading, and Futures Price Volatility." *Journal of Futures Markets*, Vol. 19, No. 7, pp. 759–776.

Irwin, S., T. Krukemeyer, and C. Zulauf. (1992) "Are Public Commodity Pools a Good Investment?" In C. C. Peters, ed., *Managed Futures: Performance Evaluation and Analysis of Commodity Funds, Pools, and Account*. Chicago: Probus Publishing Company, pp. 405–433.

Irwin, S., C. R. Zulauf, and B. Ward. (1994) "The Predictability of Managed Futures Returns." *Journal of Derivatives*, Vol. 2, No. 2, pp. 20–27.

Jaeger, R. A. (2003) *All About Hedge Funds—The Easy Way to Get Started*. New York: McGraw-Hill.

Jarque, C. M., and A. K. Bera. (1987) "A Test for Normality of Observations and Regression Residuals." *International Statistical Review*, Vol. 55, No. 2, pp. 163–172.

Jensen, G. R., R. R. Johnson, and J. M. Mercer. (2000) "Efficient Use of Commodity Futures in Diversified Portfolios." *Journal of Futures Markets*, Vol. 20, No. 5, pp. 489–506.

Jensen, M. C. (1968) "The Performance of Mutual Funds in the Period 1945–1964." *Journal of Finance*, Vol. 23, No. 2, pp. 389–416.

Jorgensen, R. B. (2003) *Individually Managed Accounts: An Investor's Guide*. New York: John Wiley & Sons.

Jorion, P. (2001). *Value at Risk: The New Benchmark for Managing Financial Risk*, Second Edition. New York: McGraw-Hill.

Karavas, V. N., and S. Siokos (2003) "The Hedge Fund Indices Universe," In G. N. Gregoriou, V. N. Karavas, and F. Rouah, eds., *Hedge Funds: Strategies, Risk Assessment, and Returns*. Frederick, MD: Beard Books.

Karpoff, J. (1987) "The Relation Between Price Changes and Trading Volume: A Survey." *Journal of Financial and Quantitative Analysis*, Vol. 22, No. 1, pp. 109–126.

Kat, H. M. (2002) "Managed Futures and Hedge Funds: A Match Made in Heaven." Working Paper, Cass Business School, City University, London, U.K.

Kat, H. M. (2003) "Taking the Sting Out of Hedge Funds." *Journal of Wealth Management*, Vol. 6, No. 3, pp. 67–76.

Kat, H. M. (2004) "In Search of the Optimal Fund of Hedge Funds." *Journal of Wealth Management*, Vol. 6, No. 4, pp. 43–51.

Kat, H. M., and F. Menexe. (2002) "Persistence in Hedge Fund Performance: The True Value of a Track Record." Working Paper, University of Reading, ISMA Centre, Reading, U.K.

Kat, H. M., and J. Miffre. (2002) "Performance Evaluation and Conditioning Information: The Case of Hedge Funds." Working Paper, The Alternative Investment Research Centre, Cass Business School, City University, London, U.K.

Kazemi, H. (1996) "The Stability of Variance and Return Forecasts: A Monte Carlo Simulation." CISDM Working Paper, Isenberg School of Management, University of Massachusetts, Amherst, MA.

Kazemi, H., and T. Schneeweis. (2003) "Conditional Performance of Hedge Funds." CISDM Working Paper, CISDM, Isenberg School of Management, University of Massachusetts, Amherst, MA.

Keating, C., and W. Shadwick. (2002) "A Universal Performance Measure." *Journal of Performance Measurement*, Vol. 6, No. 3, pp. 59–84.

Kennedy, P. (1998) *A Guide to Econometrics*. Cambridge, MA: MIT Press, 1998.

Kodres, L. (1994) "The Existence and Impact of Destabilizing Positive Feedback Traders: Evidence from the S&P 500 Index Futures Market." Working Paper, Board of Governors of the Federal Reserve System, Washington, DC.

Kodres, L., and M. Pritsker. (1996) "Directionally-Similar Position Taking and Herding by Large Futures Markets Participants." In *Risk Measurement and Systematic Risk: Proceedings of a Joint Central Bank Research Conference*, Board of Governors of the Federal Reserve, pp. 221–272.

Kon, S. J., and F. C. Jen. (1978) "Estimation of Time-Varying Systematic Risk and Performance for Mutual Fund Portfolios: An Application of Switching Regression." *Journal of Finance*, Vol. 33, No. 2, pp. 457–475.

Kon, S. J., and F. C. Jen. (1979) "The Investment Performance of Mutual Funds: An Empirical Investigation of Timing, Selectivity, and Market Efficiency." *Journal of Business*, Vol. 52, No. 2, pp. 263–289.

Kothari, S. P., and J. Warner. (2001) "Evaluating Mutual Fund Performance." *Journal of Finance*, Vol. 56, No. 5, pp. 1985–2010.

Kritzman, M. (1994) "What Practitioners Need to Know About Time Diversification." *Financial Analysts Journal*, Vol. 50, No. 1, pp. 14–18.

Kunkel R. A, M. C. Ehrhardt, and G. A. Kuhlemeyer. (1999) "Dividends and Market Efficiency: A Multi-index Arbitrage Investment Strategy. Managerial Finance, Vol. 25, No. 6, pp. 21–34.

Lee, D. K. C. (2003) "Asset Allocation and Absolute Return Strategy: Part 1." *Asia Financial Planning Journal*, Vol. 5, No. 1, pp. 21–24.

Leuthold, R., P. Garcia, and R. Lu. (1994) "The Returns and Forecasting Ability of Large Traders in the Frozen Pork Bellies Futures Market." *Journal of Business*, Vol. 67, No. 3, pp. 459–473.

Liang, B. (2003) "On the Performance of Alternative Investments: CTAs, Hedge Funds, and Funds-of-Funds." Working Paper, Case Western Reserve University, Cleveland, Ohio.

Lintner, J. (1965) "Security Prices, Risk, and Minimal Gains from Diversification." *Journal of Finance*, Vol. 20, No. 4, pp. 587–615.

Lintner, J. V. (1983) "The Potential Role of Managed Commodity-Financial Futures Accounts (and/or Funds) in Portfolios of Stocks and Bonds" Annual Conference of Financial Analysts Federation.

Lo, A. (2001) "Risk Management for Hedge Funds." *Financial Analysts Journal*, Vol. 57, No. 6, pp. 16–33.

Longin F., and B. Solnik. (1995) "Is the Correlation in International Equity Returns Constant?" *Journal of International Money and Finance*, Vol. 14, No. 1, pp. 3–26.

MacKinnon, J. G. (1991) "Critical Values for Cointegration Tests in Long-Run Econometric Relationships." In R. F. Engle and C. W. J. Granger, eds., *Long-Run Economic Relationships: Readings in Cointegration*. New York: Oxford University Press, pp. 216–276.

Managed Account Reports. (2003) "2002: Managed Futures Showed Its Strengths." Internal Publication, Issue 287, New York, NY.

Markowitz, H. (1952) "Portfolio Selection." *Journal of Finance*, Vol. 7, No. 1, pp. 77–91.

Markowitz, H. (1991) *Portfolio Selection: Efficient Diversification of Investments*. London: Blackwell Publishers.

Marmer, H. S., and F. K. L. Ng. (1993) "Mean-Semivariance Analysis of Option-Based Strategies: A Total Asset Mix Perspective." *Financial Analysts Journal*, Vol. 49, No. 3, pp. 47–54.

Martin, G. A., and R. Spurgin. (1998) "Skewness in Asset Returns: Does It Matter?" *Journal of Alternative Investments*, Vol. 1, No. 2, pp. 66–75.

Martin, L., and T. van Zijl. (2003) "Capital Gains Tax and the Capital Asset Pricing Model." *Accounting and Finance*, Vol. 43, No. 2, pp. 187–210.

McCarthy, D. F. (1995) "Consistency of Relative Commodity Trading Advisor Performance." Unpublished thesis, University College Dublin, Ireland.

McCarthy, D., T. Schneeweis, and R. Spurgin. (1996) "Investment Through CTAs: An Alternative Managed Futures Investment." *Journal of Derivatives*, Vol. 3, No. 4, pp. 36–47.

McCarthy, D., T. Schneeweis, and R. Spurgin. (1997) "Informational Content in Historical CTA Performance." *Journal of Futures Markets*, Vol. 17, No.3, pp. 317–339

McMullen, P., and R. Strong. (1997) "Selection of Mutual Funds Using Data Envelopment Analysis." *Journal of Business and Economic Studies*, Vol. 4, No. 1, pp. 1–14.

Merriken, H. E. (1994) "Analytical Approaches to Limit Downside Risk: Semivariance and the Need for Liquidity." *Journal of Investing*, Vol. 3, No. 3, pp. 65-72.

Merril C., and S. Thorley. (1996) "Time Diversification: Perspectives from Option Pricing Theory." *Financial Analysts Journal*, Vol. 52, No. 3, pp. 13–19.

Merton, R. C. (1969) "Lifetime Portfolio Selection: The Continuous Time Case." *Review of Economics and Statistics*, Vol. 51, No. 3, pp. 247–257.

Merton, R. C. (1981) "On Market Timing and Investment Performance: I. An Equilibrium Theory of Value for Market Forecasts." *Journal of Business*, Vol. 54, No. 3, pp. 363–406.

Miller, R. G. (1966) *Simultaneous Statistical Inference*. New York: McGraw-Hill.

Mina, J., and A. Ulmer. (1999) "Delta-Gamma Four Ways." New York: RiskMetrics Group, Working Paper.

Miron, J. (1996) *The Economics of Seasonal Cycles*. Cambridge, MA: MIT Press.

Mitev, T. (1998) "Classification of Commodity Trading Advisors Using Maximum Likelihood Factor Analysis." *Journal of Alternative Investments*, Vol. 1, No. 2, pp. 40–46.

Morey, M. R., and R. C. Morey. (1999) "Mutual Fund Performance Appraisals: A Multi-Horizon Perspective with Endogenous Benchmarking." *Omega*, Vol. 27, No. 2, pp. 241–258.

Mossin, J. (1966) "Equilibrium in a Capital Asset Market." *Econometrica*, Vol. 34, No. 4, pp. 768–783.

Murphy, J. A. (1986) "Futures Fund Performance: A Test of the Effectiveness of Technical Analysis." *Journal of Futures Markets*, Vol. 6, No. 2, pp. 175–185.

Nakakubo, F. (2002, October 22) "Introduction to Alternative Investment Strategies—Risks Lurking Behind the Hedge Fund Boom." NLI Research Institute, Japan. www.nli-research.co.jp.

National Association of Securities Dealers. (2003) "NASD Reminds Members of Obligations When Selling Hedge Funds." *Informational*, No. 30–07 (February), pp. 1, 4.

Okunev, J., and D. White. (2002) "Smooth Returns and Hedge Fund Risk Factors." *Working Paper*, University of New South Wales, School of Banking and Finance, Kensigton, New South Wales.

Oral, M., O. Ketani, and P. Lang. (1991) "A Methodology for Collective Evaluation and Selection of Industrial R&D Projects." *Management Science*, Vol. 7, No. 37, pp. 871–883.

Parkinson, M. (1980) "The Extreme Value Method for Estimating the Variance of the Rate of Return." *Journal of Business*, Vol. 53, No. 1, pp. 417–432.

Patel, N. (2002, July) "It's All in the Technique." *Risk*, No. 49.

Pindyck, R. S., and D. L. Rubinfeld. (1998) *Econometric Models and Economic Forecasts*. New York: McGraw-Hill.

Pool Commodity Trading Service. Daily Market Commentary. (1999, July 29) Internal Report, Winnipeg, Manitoba.

Posthuma, N., and P. Van der Sluis. (2003) "A Reality Check on Hedge Fund Returns." Working Paper, ABP Investments, Amsterdam, Holland.

Prakash, A. J., and R. M. Bear. (1986) "A Simplifying Performance Measure Recognizing Skewness." *Financial Review*, Vol. 21, No. 1, pp. 135–144.

Rahl, L. (2002, December 10) "Hedge Fund Transparency: Unraveling the Complex and Controversial Debate." Capital Market Risk Advisors, RiskInvest 2002 Conference Presentation, Boston, MA.

Reback, R. (1975) "Risk and Return in CBOE and AMEX Option Trading." *Financial Analyst Journal*, Vol. 31, No. 4, pp. 42–52.

Refco Daily Grain Commentary. (2000, May 2). Report, Chicago, Illinois.

Reichenstein, W., and D. Dorsett. (1995) "Time Diversification Revisited." Research Foundation of The Institute of Chartered Financial Analysts, Charlottesville, VA.

Richter, F. G.-C., and B. W. Brorsen. (2000) "Estimating Fees for Managed Futures: A Continuous-Time Model with a Knockout Feature." *Applied Mathematical Finance*, Vol. 7, No. 2, pp. 115–125.

Rockafellar, R. T., and S. Uryasev. (2001) "Conditional Value-at-Risk for General Loss Distributions." Research Report, ISE Department, University of Florida, Gainesville, FL.

Ross, M. (1999, September 20) "CBOT, IFB Trade Observations." *Farm Week*, Bloomington, Illinois, pp. 1–3.

Ross, S. (1976) "The Arbitrage Theory of Capital Asset Pricing." *Journal of Economic Theory*, Vol. 13, No. 2, pp. 341–360.

Salomon Smith Barney Daily Grain Commentary. (2000, May 2) Report, New York, NY.

Samuelson, P. (1994) "The Long Term Case for Equities and How It Can Be Oversold." *Journal of Portfolio Management*, Vol. 21, No. 1, pp. 15–24.

Samuelson, P. A. (1969) "Lifetime Portfolio Selection by Dynamic Stochastic Programming." *Review of Economics and Statistics*, Vol. 51, No. 3, pp. 239–246

Samuelson, P.A. (1971) "The 'Fallacy' of Maximizing the Geometric Mean in Long Sequences of Investing or Gambling." *Proceedings of the National Academy of Sciences*, Vol. 68, No. 10, pp. 2493–2496.

Samuelson, P. A. (1972) "Mathematics of Speculative Price." In R. H. Day and S. M. Robinson, eds., *Mathematical Topics in Economic Theory and Computation*, Philadelphia, PA: Society for Industrial and Applied Mathematics. Reprinted in *SIAM Review*, (January 1973), Vol. 15, pp. 1–42.

Samuelson, P. A. (1979) "Why We Should Not Make Mean Log of Wealth Big Though Years to Act Are Long." *Journal of Banking and Finance*, Vol. 3, No. 4, pp. 305–307.

Satyanarayan, S., and P. Varangis. (1994) "An Efficient Frontier for International Portfolios with Commodity Assets." Policy Research Working Paper 1266, The World Bank, Washington, DC.

Schneeweis, T., U. Savayana, and D. McCarthy. (1991) "Alternative Commodity Trading Vehicles: A Performance Analysis." *Journal of Futures Markets*, Vol. 11, No. 4, pp. 475–490.

Schneeweis, T., R. Spurgin, and M. Potter. (1997) "Managed Futures and Hedge Fund Investment for Downside Equity Risk Management." In Carl C. Peters and Ben Warwick, eds., *The Handbook of Managed Futures: Performance, Evaluation and Analysis*. New York: McGraw Hill, pp. 77–98.

Schneeweis, T. (1996) *The Benefits of Managed Futures*. European Managed Futures Association, London.

Schneeweis, T., and G. Georgiev. (2002) "The Benefits of Managed Futures." CISDM Working Paper, University of Massachusetts, Amherst, MA.

Schneeweis, T., V. Karavas, and G. Georgiev. (2003) "Alternative Investment in the Institutional Portfolio." *Journal of Alternative Investments*, Vol. 3, No. 3, pp. 11–26.

Schneeweis, T., H. Kazemi, and V. N. Karavas. (2003a, April) "Fund Size and Performance in Hedge Funds." CISDM Working Paper, Isenberg School of Management, University of Massachusetts, Amherst, MA.

Schneeweis, T., H. Kazemi, and V. N. Karavas. (2003b, April) "Manager Track Record and Performance in Hedge Funds." CISDM, Working Paper, Isenberg School of Management, University of Massachusetts, Amherst, MA.

Schneeweis, T., and R. Spurgin. (1997) "Managed Futures, Hedge Funds and Mutual Fund Return Estimation: A Multifactor Approach." CISDM Working Paper, Isenberg School of Management, University of Massachusetts, Amherst, MA.

Schneeweis, T., and R. Spurgin. (1998a) "Multifactor Analysis of Hedge Funds, Managed Futures, and Mutual Fund Return and Risk Characteristics." *Journal of Alternative Investments*, Vol. 1, No. 1, pp. 1–24.

Schneeweis, T., and R. Spurgin. (1998b) "Quantitative Analysis of Hedge Funds and Managed Futures: Returns and Risk Characteristics." CISDM Working Paper, Isenberg School of Management, University of Massachusetts, Amherst, MA.

Schneeweis, T., R. Spurgin, and G. Georgiev. (2001) "Benchmarking Commodity Trading Advisor Performance with a Passive Futures-Based Index." CISDM Working Paper, Isenberg School of Management, University of Massachusetts, Amherst, MA.

Schneeweis, T., R. Spurgin, and D. McCarthy. (1996) "Survivor Bias in Commodity Trading Advisors Performance." *Journal of Futures Markets*, Vol. 16, No. 7, pp. 757–772.

Schneeweis, T., R. Spurgin, and M. Potter. (1996) "Managed Futures and Hedge Fund Investment for Downside Equity Risk Management." *Derivatives Quarterly*, Vol. 3, No. 4, pp. 36–47.

Schwager, J. D. (1996) *Managed Trading: The Myths and Truths*. New York: John Wiley & Sons Inc.

Securities and Exchange Commission. (2003, September) "Implications of Growth of Hedge Funds."

Sedzro, K., and D. Sardano. (2000) "Mutual Fund Performance Evaluation Using Data Envelopment Analysis." In S. B. Dahiya, ed., *The Current State of Business Disciplines*, Rohtak, India: Spellbound Publications, Vol. 3, pp. 1125–1144.

Seigel, L. B. (2003) *Benchmarks and Investment Management*. Monograph. Charlottesville, VA: AIMR Publications.

Sengupta, J. K. (1989) *Efficiency Analysis by Production Frontiers: The Nonparametric Approach*. Boston: Kluwer Academic Publishers.

Sexton, T. R., R. H. Silkman, and A. Hogan. (1986) "Data Envelopment Analysis: Critique and Extensions." In R. H. Silkman, ed., *Measuring Efficiency and Assessment of Data Envelopment Analysis*. San Francisco: Jossey-Bass Publishers, pp. 73–105.

Shanken, J. (1992) "On the Estimation of Beta-Pricing Models." *Review of Financial Studies*, Vol. 5, No. 1, pp. 1–33.

Sharpe, W. F. (1964) "Capital Asset Prices: A Theory of Market Equilibrium Under Conditions of Risk." *Journal of Finance*, Vol. 19, No. 3, pp. 425–442.

Sharpe, W. F. (1966) "Mutual Fund Performance." *Journal of Business*, Vol. 39, No. 1, pp. 19–138.

Sharpe, W. F. (1992) "Asset Allocation: Management Style and Performance Measurement." *Journal of Portfolio Management*, Vol. 18, No. 2, pp. 7–19.

Sinquefield, R. (1996) "Where Are the Gains from International Diversification?" *Financial Analysts Journal*, Vol. 52, No. 1, pp. 8–14.

Sirri, E. R., and P. Tufano. (1998) "Costly Search and Mutual Fund Flows." *Journal of Finance*, Vol. 53, No. 5, pp. 1589–1622.

Sortino, F. A., and L. N. Price. (1994) "Performance Measurement in a Downside Risk Framework." *Journal of Investing*, Vol. 3, No. 3, pp. 59–64.

Sortino, F. A., and R. van der Meer. (1991) "Downside Risk." *Journal of Portfolio Management*, Vol. 17, No. 4, pp. 37–42.

Stephens, A., and D. Proffitt. (1991) "Performance Measurement When Return Distributions Are Nonsymmetric." *Quarterly Journal of Business and Economics*, Vol. 30, No. 1, pp. 23–39.

Strongin, S., and M. Petsch. (1996, April 24) "Managing Risk in Hostile Markets." Goldman Sachs Commodities Research, New York.

Sydney Futures Exchange Corporation. (2002) *2002 Annual Report*.

Sydney Futures Exchange Corporation. (2003a) 2003 *Half-Year Financial Report*.

Sydney Futures Exchange Corporation. (2003b, June 25) "Full Participant Compliance Manual," pp. 32–33.

Tavakoli, J. M. (2003) *Collateralized Debt Obligations and Structured Finance.* New York: John Wiley & Sons.

Thanassoulis, E., A. Boussofiane, and R. G. Dyson. (1995) "Exploring Output Quality Targets in the Provisions of Perinatal Care in England Using Data Envelopment Analysis." *European Journal of Operational Research*, Vol. 80, No. 3, pp. 588–607.

Till, H. (2000) "Passive Strategies in the Commodity Futures Markets." *Derivatives Quarterly*, Vol. 17, No. 1, pp. 49–54.

Till, H. (2001) "Taking Full Advantage of the Statistical Properties of Commodity Investments." *Journal of Alternative Investments*, Vol. 4, No. 1, pp. 63–66.

Till, H. (2002, September) "Risk Management Lessons in Leveraged Commodity Futures Trading." *Commodities Now*, pp. 84–87.

Till, H. (2004) "Risk Measurement of Investments in the Satellite Ring of a Core-Satellite Portfolio: Traditional versus Alternative Approaches." *Singapore Economic Review*, Vol. 49, No. 1, pp. 1–26.

Tomek, W. G., and H. H. Peterson. (2001) "Risk Management in Agricultural Markets: A Review." *Journal of Futures Markets*, Vol. 21, No. 1, pp. 953–985.

Treynor, J. L. (1965) "How to Rate Management of Investment Funds." *Harvard Business Review*, Vol. 41, No. 1, pp. 63–75.

Treynor, J. L., and K. K. Mazuy. (1966) "Can Mutual Fund Managers Outguess the Market?" *Harvard Business Review*, Vol. 44, No. 4, pp. 131–136.

Trzcinka, C. (1998, September 29) Congressional Testimony, Subcommittee Investigating Fees and Price Competition in the Mutual Fund Market, Washington, DC.

Vaissié, M. (2004, in press) "Are All Hedge Fund Indices Created Equal?" *Alternative Investment Quarterly*.

Vanderbilt University. (2002) Vanderbilt University Endowment Review, 2002 Edition. Nashville, TN: Vanderbilt University Press.

Vassiloglou, M., and D. Giokas. (1990) "A Study of Relative Efficiency of Bank Branches: An Application of Data Envelopment Analysis." *Journal of Operations Research Society*, Vol. 41, No. 7, pp. 591–597.

Weiner, R. J. (2002) "Sheep in Wolves Clothing? Speculators and Price Volatility in Petroleum Futures." *Quarterly Review of Economics and Finance*, Vol. 42, No. 2, pp. 391–400.

Weisman, A. (2002) "Dangerous Attractions: Informationless Investing and Hedge Fund Performance Measurement Bias." *Journal of Portfolio Management*, Vol. 28, No. 4, pp. 80–91.

Wider, J., and Scanlan, K. (2003) "Hedge Funds: The Regulatory Landscape at a Crossroads." *Journal of Investment Compliance*, Vol. 4, No. 1, pp.7–12.

Wiggins, J. G. (1991) "Empirical Tests of the Bias and Efficiency of the Extreme-Value Variance Estimator for Common Stock." *Journal of Business,* Vol. 64, No. 3, pp. 417–432.

Wilkens, K., and J. Zhu. (2001) "Portfolio Evaluation and Benchmark Selection: A Mathematical Programming Approach." *Journal of Alternative Investments,* Vol. 4, No.1, pp. 9–20.

Wilkens, K., and J. Zhu. (2004) "Classifying Hedge Funds Using Data Envelopment Analysis." In G. N. Gregoriou, V. N. Karavas, and F. Rouah, eds. *Hedge Funds: Strategies, Risk Assessment and Returns.* Frederick, MD: Beard Books, pp. 161–175.

Worthington, R. L. (2001) *Alternative Investments and the Semi-affluent Investor.* Research Report, Undiscovered Managers, Dallas, TX.

Zheng, L. (1999) "Is Money Smart? A Study of Mutual Fund Investor's Fund Selection Ability," *Journal of Finance*, Vol. 54, No. 3, pp. 901–933.

Zhu, J. (2003) *Quantitation Models for Performance Evaluation and Benchmarking.* Norwell, MA: Kluwer Academic Publishers.

Index

Absolute return strategy, managed futures as, 184
ADF test, *see* Augmented Dickey-Fuller test
Administrative fee, 40–44
Agriculture portfolios, 206–209
Alpha, 82–83, 124, 125
Alternative investments:
  allocation of, 11–15
  downside risk protection with, *see* Downside return protection
Anti-money laundering provisions, 241
APRA (Australian Prudential Regulation Authority), 260
ARMA models, *see* Auto-regressive moving average models
Asian currency crisis, 107, 108, 126, 127
Asset class(es), 7
  allocation of, 358–366
  comparison of risk with, 361, 362
  equity markets as, 221
  managed futures as, 6
  upper/lower limits for, 363
Asset diversifiers, 338
Augmented Dickey-Fuller (ADF) test, 326, 328, 329, 331, 369–370
Australian Prudential Regulation Authority (APRA), 260
Australian regulatory model, 259–273
  for collateralized synthetic obligations, 265–266
  and definition of fiduciary futures products, 264
  and fiduciary futures products as financial products, 269–270
  and fiduciary futures products in Australia, 261–264
  and futures market in Australia, 262–263
  for individually managed futures accounts, 266–267, 270–272
  for managed futures funds, 264–265
  and registration of fiduciary futures products, 267–269
Auto-regressive moving average (ARMA) models, 367–376

Backfilling bias, 19
Barclay Commodity Trading Index, 185–187, 189–191, 193, 195–196
Barclay CTA Index, 19, 107–113, 115, 117, 119–121, 127, 308–309
Barclay Currency Traders Index, 107, 108, 110–113, 115, 117, 119, 122
Barclay Discretionary Traders Index, 107, 108, 110–113, 115, 117, 119–123, 127
Barclay Diversified Traders Index, 107, 108, 110–113, 115, 117, 119–121, 127, 185, 187, 190, 191, 194, 197
Barclay Financial and Metal Traders Index, 107–109, 111–113, 115, 117, 119–121, 127
Barclay Systematic Traders Index, 107–109, 112–113, 115, 117, 119–121, 127, 185, 187, 188, 190, 191, 194, 197
Barclay Trading Group, Ltd., 51
Barclay Trading Group database, 51–77
Bear markets, 107–108
Benchmarking, 82–84. *See also* Performance (of CTAs)
  in contingent claim approach, 294
  DEA vs., 129
  Edhec CTA Global Index for, 21–29
  selection of index for, 19
Beta-squared coefficient, 86–87
Bias, 18–19, 26, 56–58

Bonds, 7
Bull markets, 107–108

Capital asset pricing model (CAPM), 83, 84*n*9, 85, 189
CFTC, *see* Commodity Futures Trading Commission
Chase Physical Commodity Index (CPCI), 229
CISDM Equally Weighted Trading Advisor Qualified Universe Index (CISDM CTA), 370–374
Coffee market, 155–160, 163–165, 169–181
Collateralized synthetic obligations (CSOs), 265–266
Combination-term CTAs, 80*n*1
Commission, CTA, 40–44
Commodity futures, 7, 229–231. *See also* Design of commodity futures trading program
Commodity Futures Trading Commission (CFTC), 154–155, 240–241, 260*n*1, 260*n*2, 339, 387
Commodity trading advisors (CTAs), xxv. *See also* Managed futures; *specific topics*
  backfilling bias for hedge funds vs., 19
  benefits of, xxv
  characteristics of, 361–362
  comparison of hedge funds, fund of funds and, 339–340
  compensation of, 248–258
  countertrend, 80
  in CSFB/Tremont Managed Futures Index, 391
  data providers for, 51
  discretionary, 80, 242–243
  efficiency of, in portfolio context, 24–26
  framework for assessing, *see* Three-dimensional framework
  hedge funds vs., xxv, 1
  and increased price volatility, *see* Market volatility
  index heterogeneity for, 19–21
  key performance drivers of, 26–29
  major index providers for, 208–209
  methodologies employed by, 242–244
  quantitative description of, 308–312
  strategies for, *see* Strategies, CTA
  styles of, 80, 287–288
  survivorship bias for hedge funds vs., 19
  systematic, 80, 243–244, 387
  technical vs. fundamental analysis by, 242
  trend-following, 7, 80, 244
Compensation of CTAs, 248–258
  Barclay Trading Group data on, 251–253
  performance and, 253–257
  and performance persistence, 40–44
  structure of, 249–251
Contingent claim-based performance evaluation, 296–297
Contingent claim performance approach, 294–306
  efficiency gain/loss measure in, 297–299
  moment-based efficiency measure in, 295–297
  results of, 300–305
  TradeView market data in, 300
Corn market, 155–160, 163–165, 169–181
Cotton market, 155–160, 163–165, 169–181
Countertrend CTAs, 80
CPCI (Chase Physical Commodity Index), 229
Credit Suisse First Boston (CSFB)Tremont Managed Futures Index, 308–309, 390–397
Crises, market, 107, 108
Cross-efficiency model (DEA), 131, 135–145
Crude oil market, 155–160, 163–165, 169–181
CSFB/Tremont Index, *see* Credit Suisse First Boston Tremont Managed Futures Index
CSOs, *see* Collateralized synthetic obligations

CTAs, *see* Commodity trading advisors
CTA Global Index, 58–74, 119–121
CTA Qualified Universe index (CTA QU), 361, 362, 364
Currency portfolios, 209–212

Daniel B. Stark & Co. database, 8
Data envelopment analysis (DEA), 79–104
background of, 95–97
Barclay Trading Group/Burlington Hall Asset Management data for, 137–138
bases for performance evaluation in, 87
CISDM Alternative Investment Database data for, 87–95
cross-efficiency model, 135–138
efficiency score in, 80, 81, 132–133
empirical results of, 138–146
performance evaluation criteria in, 80
power of, 131–132
results of, 98–104
and risk measures in performance evaluation, 82–87
risk-minimizing design of, 81
simple efficiency model, 133–135, 138
in study of CTA performance, 97–98
Tobit regression model in, 98
DD (downside deviation), 86
Decile classification:
and correlation coefficients for performance, 349–351
and dissolution frequencies, 74–77
and performance of funds, 67–74
Decision-making units (DMUs), performance of, 95–97
Design of commodity futures trading program, 277–293
leverage level, 287–289
and overall portfolio design, 289–292
portfolio construction, 282–284
risk management, 284–287
trade construction, 281–282
trade discovery, 277–281
Deutsche mark market, 155–160, 163–165, 169–181
Discretion, performance persistence and, 40–44
Discretionary CTAs, 80, 242–243
Dissolution frequencies, 74–77
Distributed performance evaluation, 295–296
Diversification:
for CTA portfolio, 289, 290, 292
for equities portfolio, 289, 290
equity, 221
for hedge fund portfolio, 291, 292
and interdependence of risk measures, 212–214
for risk management, 244
space, 388
strategies for, *see* Strategies for diversification
time, 385–398. *See also* Three-dimensional framework
Diversifiers, asset, 338–338
DJ-AIGCI, *see* Dow-Jones/AIG Commodity Index
DMUs, *see* Decision-making units, performance of
Dollars under management, 40–44
Dow-Jones/AIG Commodity Index (DJ-AIGCI), 229–231
Down markets, CTAs in, xxv, 1
Downside deviation (DD), 86
Downside return protection, 220–232
commodity futures for, 229–231
with CTAs vs. hedge funds, 50
description of, 221–224
hedge funds for, 224–226
managed futures for, 226–229

Edhec CTA Global Index, 19, 21–29
Efficiency gain/loss measure, 297–299
Efficiency score (DEA), 80, 81, 98–104, 132–133
Efficient frontier (DEA), 131, 132
Emerging CTAs, 81
Equity markets, 220–221
Excess replicating return (ERR), 300–302
Extreme events, performance during, 126–127, 137, 152

Feedback trading strategies, 153
Feedback trading tests, 168, 172–179
Fiduciary futures products (Australia), 261–270
50/50 investors, 9–10, 12–14, 16
Financial futures, 7
Financial portfolios, 212, 215–216
Fundamental analysis, 242
Fund of funds, 339–340
Fund size, 87
Futures. *See also* Managed futures
  availability of information on, 238
  coffee market, 155–160, 163–165, 169–181
  corn market, 155–160, 163–165, 169–181
  cotton market, 155–160, 163–165, 169–181
  crude oil market, 155–160, 163–165, 169–181
  deutsche mark market, 155–160, 163–165, 169–181
  eurodollar market, 155–160, 163–165, 169–181
  exchange-based nature of, 238–239
  gold market, 155–160, 163–165, 169–181
  live hogs market, 155–160, 163–165, 169–181
  natural gas market, 155–160, 163–165, 169–181
  soybeans market, 155–160, 163–165, 169–181
  S&P 500, 155–160, 163–165, 169–181
  traded by CTAs, 7
  Treasury bonds market, 155–160, 163–165, 169–181

Generalized Treynor Ratio (GTR), 124, 125
Goldman Sachs Commodity Index (GSCI), 229, 289
Gold market, 155–160, 163–165, 169–181
GSCI, *see* Goldman Sachs Commodity Index
GTR, *see* Generalized Treynor Ratio

Hedge funds:
  in alternatives allocation, 11–15
  backfilling bias for CTAs vs., 19
  comparison of CTAs, fund of funds and, 339–340
  CTAs vs., xxv, 1
  downside return protection for, 224–226
  elimination of negative skewness from, 15–16
  estimating returns on, 18–19
  investment style and portfolio returns with, 9–10
  large, market volatility and, *see* Market volatility
  managed futures as subset of, 80
  managed futures combined with, 11
  risk and dependence characteristics of, 5–6
  short-volatility strategies for, 198
  survivorship bias for CTAs vs., 19
  Tremont TASS database for, 7
Hedgers, 241
Herding behavior, 152–153

IMAs, *see* Individually managed accounts
Incentive fees, 40–44, 249–251
Indices. *See also specific indices*
  biases in, 19
  comparative performance of, 21–24
  correlation between, 18–19
  heterogeneity of, 19–21
  portfolio of, 21
Individually managed accounts (IMAs), 242, 261, 266–267, 270–272
Ineffective diversifiers, 338
Information Ratio (IR), 124, 125
Interbank, 40–44
Interdependence of risk measures, 203–219
  for agriculture portfolios, 206–209
  CISDM data for, 206
  for diversified portfolios, 212–214
  empirical results of, 206
  for financial portfolios, 212, 215–216
  methodology for study of, 205–206

review of literature on, 203–205
for stock portfolios, 212, 217–219
Investing in managed futures, 235–247
and hedgers vs. speculators, 241
methods of investing, 6–7
minimum investment requirements, 7
portfolio structure for, 241–242
regulatory issues with, 240–241
for risk management, 244–245
timing considerations for, 245–247
IR, *see* Information Ratio

Lehman Aggregate Bond Index, 369
Lehman Global Bond Index, 21–29
Lehman Global Index, 340, 342–348
Lehman Global Treasury Index, 24–26
Lehman High Yield Index, 24–26
Lehman Investment Grade Index, 24–26
Lehman U.S. Aggregate Index, 340, 342–348
Lehman U.S. Treasury Index, 27–29
Leverage, 245
Leverage level step (trading program), 287–289
Live hogs market, 155–160, 163–165, 169–181
Long-term CTAs, 80*n*1, 245
Long volatility strategies, 183–202
demonstration of, 185–188
fitting regression line, 189–191
mimicking portfolios of strategies, 192–195
risk management using, 198–201
and value at risk, 195–198
Losses, investing with CTAs after, 45–47

Macroportfolio hedging, 286–287
Managed Account Reports, 51
Managed futures. *See also* Commodity trading advisors; *specific topics*
advantages of, 237–238
in alternatives allocation, 11–15
and asset allocation, 24–26
as asset class, 6
for downside return protection, 226–229
growth of, 235, 236
hedge funds combined with, 11
index heterogeneity of, 19
industry review, 184–185
investing in, 235–247
investment style and portfolio returns with, 9–10
mutual funds vs., 239
performance measures for, 79–80
performance persistence of, *see* Performance persistence
and portfolio performance, 237
recent performance of, 235, 236
return data for, 8
riskiness of, 385
skewness reduction with, 15–16
as subset of hedge funds, 80
trend-following nature of, 7
ways to invest in, 6–7
Managed futures funds (Australia), 261, 264–265
Managed money accounts (MMA), 155. *See also* Market volatility
Management fees, 249–251
Manager of managers (MOM), 7
Margin, 40–44
MarHedge CTA indices, 240
Market conditions (1990-2003), 105–128
constructing empirically valid models of, 118–123
data and sample period, 107–113
during extreme events, 126–127
measurement of performance, 124–127
multifactor model of, 111, 114–115
multi-moment model of, 116–118
return-generating processes, 111
subperiods of, 107
Market crises, 107, 108
Market volatility, 151–182
data on, 154–156
and descriptive analysis of trading behavior, 156–161
empirical studies related to, 152–154
positive feedback trading tests, 168, 172–179
profitability tests, 175, 180–181
variance ratio tests, 166–171

Market volatility *continued*
  and volume–market volatility relationship, 164–181
  and volume–price volatility relationship, 161–164
Markowitz, Harry, xxv
MAR (minimal accepted return), 86
Mean-modified value at risk framework, 358–366
Mean-variance sufficiency, 85–87
Medium-term CTAs, 80*n*1
Merger arbitrage, 198–201
Mimicking portfolios, 192–195
Minimal accepted return (MAR), 86
MLMI, *see* Mount Lucas Management Index
MLM index, *see* Mount Lucas Management Index
MMA (managed money accounts), 155
Modern portfolio theory, xxv
Modified Sharpe ratio, 279, 377–384
Modified value at risk, 22–23, 360–361, 379. *See also* Mean-modified value at risk framework
Moment-based efficiency measure, 295–297
MOM (manager of managers), 7
Monte Carlo simulation, 35–37, 195, 196
Mount Lucas Management Index (MLMI), 7, 8*n*1, 8*n*2, 84,185, 187, 188, 190, 191, 195, 198, 229–230
MSCI EAFE Index, 362, 364
MSCI Global, 340–355
Multifactor model, 111, 114–115
Multi-moment model, 116–118
Mutual funds, managed futures vs., 239

NASD, *see* National Association of Securities Dealers
Nasdaq, 368
National Association of Securities Dealers (NASD), 259–260
National Futures Association (NFA), 240, 387
Natural gas market, 155–160, 163–165, 169–181
Net asset values (NAVs), 326–328
NFA, *see* National Futures Association
Noise factor, 152
Non-U.S. markets, performance persistence and, 40–44

Omega ratio, 23–24
Open interest, 156–157, 238
Options, 40–44

Performance (of CTAs):
  Barclay Trading Group data study, 51–77
  comparative overview of indices, 21–24
  contingent claim approach to, 294–306
  CTA Global Index as methodology for analyzing, 58–74
  DEA evaluation of, *see* Data envelopment analysis
  debate on measuring/evaluating, 130
  and dissolution frequency, 74–77
  Edhec CTA Global Index for benchmarking, 19, 21–29
  effect of compensation on, 248–258
  key drivers of, 26–29
  low predictability of, 47
  measures of, 79–80
  persistence of, *see* Performance persistence
  previous studies on, 49–50
  risk measures and evaluation of, 82–87
  and survivorship bias, 56–58
  from 1990 to 2003, *see* Market conditions (1990-2003)
Performance persistence, 31–48
  Barclay Trading Group data study, 51–77
  and characteristics of CTAs, 40–44
  of CTA Global Index, 67–74
  global results for, 67–69
  and historical performance, 37–40
  importance of using large amount of data for analyzing, 47
  and investing after recent losses, 45–47
  LaPorte Asset Allocation data on, 32–33

literature review for, 49–50
Monte Carlo simulation of, 35–37
and regressions of returns against lagged returns, 44–45
regression test for, 33–35
strategies analysis of, 71–74
subperiod analysis of, 69–71
Portfolios:
benefits of CTAs in, xxv
CTAs and optimization of, 315–324
downside risk in, 222–224
futures trading program in, 289–292
managed futures and performance of, 237
mimicking, 192–195
replicating, 297–299
single investor vs. group, 241–242
three-dimensional assessment of, *see* Three-dimensional framework
time diversification of, 385–398
Portfolio construction step (trading program), 282–284
Positive feedback trading tests, 168, 172–179
Price volatility, 153, 161–164
Private commodity pools, 241, 242
Profitability tests, 175, 180–181
Public commodity funds, 241, 242

Random walk behavior, 50, 326–335
Regulatory issues, 240–241
Replicating portfolios, 297–299
Returns:
with alternative investments, 11–13
on hedge fund indices, 18–19
and portfolio mix, 83
random walk behavior of, 326–335
risk-adjusted, 377–384
from 1990 to 2003, *see* Market conditions (1990-2003)
Returns-enhancing diversifiers, 338
Returns-protection diversifiers, 338
Risk:
for comparative indices, 22–23
CTA characteristics and level of, 43–44
downside, 221–224
interdependence of measures for, 203–219
mean-modified value at risk framework, 358–366
performance evaluation and measures of, 82–87
time diversification as hedge against, 385–398
time-varying, 84–85
Risk-adjusted returns, 377–384
Risk factor exposures:
biases and measurement of, 26
with Edhec CTA Global Index, 26–29
and heterogeneity of indices, 19–21
Risk management:
with commodity futures, 229–231
diversification for, 244
downside, 220–232
with hedge funds, 224–226
leverage for, 245
long volatility strategies for, 198–201
with managed futures, 226–229
managed futures for, 14
stop losses for, 244–245
Risk management step (trading program), 284–287
Rolling windows, 311, 313–315
Russell 3000 Index, 111–113, 117, 119
Russian debt crisis, 107, 108, 126, 127

Salomon Brothers Government Bond index, 7
SCM Bond Index, 362, 364
Securities and Exchange Commission (SEC), 260
Semivariance, 85–86
September 11 terrorist attacks, 107, 108, 126, 127
SFE, *see* Sydney Futures Exchange
Sharpe ratio, 21, 54*n*3, 82, 85–86, 341, 377. *See also* Modified Sharpe ratio
Short-term CTAs, 80*n*1, 245
Simple efficiency model (DEA), 131, 133–135, 138–145
Skill-based investing, 221
Sortino ratio, 21, 22, 85–86, 341
Soybeans market, 155–160, 163–165, 169–181

Space diversification, 388
Speculators, 241
Standard & Poor's (S&P) 500 Growth Index, 24–26
Standard & Poor's (S&P) 500 Index, 7, 19, 21–29, 155–160, 163–165, 169–181, 340–355, 362, 364, 368
Standard & Poor's (S&P) 500 Small Cap Index, 24–26
Standard & Poor's (S&P) TSX Index, 362, 364
Standard & Poor's (S&P) 500 Value Index, 24–26
Stark 300 index, 8–9
Stock portfolios, interdependence of risk measures for, 212, 217–219
Stocks, 7
Stop losses, 244–245
Strategies, CTA, 88, 90. *See also* Long volatility strategies
  benchmarks for, 83
  correlation among, 54–56
  by decile classification, 71–74
  descriptive statistics on, 53–54
  grouping of, 52–62
  number of CTAs using, 91
  subperiod performance of, 61–65
  trend following in, 183
Strategies for diversification, 336–357
  analysis of findings, 349, 352–357
  and CTAs/hedge funds/fund of funds comparison, 339–340
  findings and observations, 341–351
  literature review of, 337–338
  methodology for, 340
  sources of data for, 340
Styles, CTA, 80, 88, 90, 101, 242–244
Survivorship bias, 19, 56–58
Sydney Futures Exchange (SFE), 261, 262, 270–271
Systematic CTAs, 80, 243–244, 387
TASS Management, 51
Technical analysis, 242
Terrorist crisis, 107, 108, 126, 127
33/66 investors, 9–10, 12–13, 15, 16
Three-dimensional framework, 307–325
  and CSFB/Tremont vs. Barclay Group indices, 308–309
  and portfolio optimization with CTAs, 315–324
  quantitative description of CTAs, 308–312
  rolling windows technique in, 311, 313–315
Time diversification, 385–398. *See also* Three-dimensional framework
Time in existence, performance persistence and, 40–44
Time-varying risk, 84–85
Timing of trades, 245–247
Tobit regressions, 98, 103
Trade construction step (trading program), 281–282
Trade discovery step (trading program), 277–281
Treasury bonds market, 155–160, 163–165, 169–181
Tremont TASS, 7
Trend-following CTAs, 7, 80, 183–184, 244, 287–288
Treynor ratio, 82

Value at Risk (VaR), 358
  mean-modified value at risk framework, 358–366
  measuring, 378–379
  for mimicking portfolios, 195
  modified, 379
Variance ratios, 166–171
Volatility, *see* Long volatility strategies; Market volatility